Christmas 1992
lots of love from
Anthony Moira
Anna and John

# THE HAPPY ISLES OF OCEANIA

PAUL THEROUX

# THE HAPPY ISLES OF OCEANIA

PADDLING THE PACIFIC

HAMISH HAMILTON · LONDON

HAMISH HAMILTON LTD
Published by the Penguin Group
Penguin Books Ltd, 27 Wrights Lane, London W8 5TZ, England
Penguin Books USA Inc., 375 Hudson Street, New York, New York 10014, USA
Penguin Books Australia Ltd, Ringwood, Victoria, Australia
Penguin Books Canada Ltd, 10 Alcorn Avenue, Toronto, Ontario, Canada M4V 3B2
Penguin Books (NZ) Ltd, 182 190 Wairau Road, Auckland 10, New Zealand

Penguin Books Ltd, Registered Offices: Harmondsworth, Middlesex, England

First published in Great Britain by Hamish Hamilton Ltd 1992
10 9 8 7 6 5 4 3 2 1

Copyright © Cape Cod Scriveners Co., 1992

The moral right of the author has been asserted

Filmset in 11/13 pt Baskerville

Printed in Great Britain by Clays Ltd, St Ives plc

A CIP catalogue record for this book is available from the British Library

ISBN 0-241-13184-7

*To Mee Ling Loo and Sheila Donnelly*

God bless the thoughtful islands
　　Where never warrants come;
God bless the just Republics
　　That give a man a home . . .

– Rudyard Kipling, *The Broken Men*


　　　Come, my friends,
'Tis not too late to seek a newer world.
Push off, and sitting well in order smite
The sounding furrows; for my purpose holds
To sail beyond the sunset, and the baths
Of all the western stars, until I die.
It may be that the gulfs will wash us down:
It may be we shall touch the Happy Isles . . .

　　　　　　　　　– Tennyson, *Ulysses*

# *Contents*

# PART ONE
# MEGANESIA

# I

## New Zealand: The Land of the Long White Cloud

There was no good word in English for this hopeless farewell. My wife and I separated on a winter day in London and we were both miserable, because it seemed as though our marriage was over. We both thought: *What now?* It was the most sorrowful of goodbyes. I could not imagine life without her. I tried to console myself by saying, *This is like going on a journey*, because a journey can be either your death or your transformation, though on this one I imagined that I would just keep living a half-life.

From habit, when I was alone, I slept only on the left side of the bed, and so I felt lonelier when I woke up with a big space beside me. At last I felt so woeful that I went to my doctor.

"Your blood pressure is fine," she said, "but I don't like the look of that."

She touched a discoloration on my arm. She used the misleadingly sonorous name "melanoma" to describe it. I heard melanoma and I thought of Melanesia, The Black Islands. Eventually she gouged out the black spot and put in four stitches and said she would let me know if this piece of my arm, this biopsy the size of an hors-d'œuvre, was serious. "I mean, if it's a carcinoma."

Why did all these horrors have pretty names?

Needing to be reassured by the familiar sights and sounds of the place where I was born, I went to Boston, but I felt too defeated to stay. And home is sometimes so sad. One day a message came from Melbourne: *Are you free for a book promotional tour in New Zealand and Australia?* I thought, *Any excuse.* So I continued on my journey, carrying a tent, a sleeping-bag and collapsible kayak. I headed west, by plane, to Chicago, San Francisco and Honolulu where, to cheer myself up, I took the big bandage off my stitched arm and put on yellow Garfield the Cat bandaids.

I went farther away, deeper into the Pacific, thinking: Planes are like seven-league boots. I could be in New Zealand or Easter Island tomorrow. And yet the Pacific was vast. It had half the world's free water; it was one third of the earth's surface.

More than an ocean, the Pacific was like a universe, and a chart of it looked like a portrait of the night sky. This enormous ocean was like the whole of heaven, an inversion of earth and air, so that the Pacific seemed like outer space, an immensity of emptiness, dotted with misshapen islands that twinkled like stars, archipelagos like star clusters, and wasn't Polynesia a sort of galaxy?

"I've been all over the Pacific," the man next to me said. He was from California. His name was Hap. "Bora-Bora. Moora-Moora. Tora-Tora. Fuji."

"Fiji," his wife said.

"And Haiti," he told me.

"Tahiti," his wife said, correcting him again.

"Oh God," he said. "Johnston Island."

"What was that like?"

This sinister little island, with the Stars and Stripes flying over it, is 800 miles west of Honolulu, and was formerly a launching site for H-bombs. More recently, nuclear waste was stored there, along with nerve gas and stacks of hydrogen bombs. A recent accident had left one end of Johnston Island radioactive. Few Americans have heard of it. The anti-nuclear New Zealanders can tell you where it is and why it terrifies them.

"Who said I got off the plane?" Hap said.

"We're members of the Century Club," his wife said. "You can only join if you've been to a hundred countries."

"What does 'been to' mean? Pass through the airport? Spend a night? Get diarrhea there?"

"Guess he's not a member!" Hap said, joyously.

*Tourists don't know where they've been*, I thought. *Travellers don't know where they're going.*

Then it was dawn, but it was the day after tomorrow, a narrow band of ochreous light like sunrise in the stratosphere. In this part of the Pacific, at the 180th meridian of longitude, the world's day begins. When the plane arrived in Auckland, New Zealand, it was like touching down on a distant star.

"What's that?" It was the inspector: Immigration and Ethnic Affairs, poking my big canvas bags.

"A boat," I said. "Collapsible."

"What's wrong with your arm? Hope it's not contagious."

*It might be cancer*, I wanted to say, to wipe the smile off his face.

"Welcome to Na Zillun," he said quietly.

It was nine in the morning. I had an interview at ten ("Is your novel based on real people?"), and another at eleven ("What does your wife think of your so-called novel?"), and at noon I was asked, "What do you think of Na Zillun?"

"I have been in New Zealand three hours," I said.

"Go on."

Provoked, I said, "This is a wonderful country – or would you call it an archipelago? Most New Zealanders seem to wear old shapeless hats. You see a lot of beards and kneesocks. And sweaters. You also see an awful lot of war memorials."

I was led into a ballroom where I gave a luncheon speech. It was the first meal I had eaten in thirteen hours, but I had to sing for my supper. They wanted autobiography; I gave them Chinese politics.

A person in the audience said, "Are you working on a book at the moment?"

"No, but I'd like to write something about the Pacific," I said. "Maybe the migrations. The way the people went from island to island taking their whole culture with them, until they found a happy island, and spread it all out, like a picnic that would last until the end of the world."

Saying it aloud made it seem like a promise, something I ought to do. I needed a friend. There was always the possibility of friendship in travel. It was an odd place for such an observation, yet in *The Secret Agent* Joseph Conrad wrote, "But does not Alfred Wallace relate in his famous book on the Malay Archipelago how, amongst the Aru Islanders, he discovered in an old and naked savage with a sooty skin a peculiar resemblance to a dear friend at home?"

The great naturalist Wallace had been looking for specimens of the bird of paradise on the Aru islands, which are off the southwestern coast of New Guinea. He had written about "one funny old man, who bore a ludicrous resemblance to a friend of mine at home . . ."

That was not very surprising. The oddest part was that it had only happened once in the entire book. It happened repeatedly to me. In Africa, in India, in South America, in China and Tibet, I had constantly run into indigenous people who rang bells like mad and reminded me of old schoolfriends at the Roberts Junior High, and Medford High, of Peace Corps buddies. People who bore a resemblance to members of my own family popped up from time to time.

Suddenly I wanted to see the extreme green isles of Oceania, unmodern, sunny, and slow, with trees to sit under and bluey-green lagoons to paddle in. My soul hurt, my heart was damaged, I was lonely. I did not want to see another big city. I wanted to be purified by water and wilderness. The Maori people, who had come to New Zealand via the Cook Islands from Tahiti about a thousand years ago, called the Pacific Moana-Nui-o-Kiva, "The Great Ocean of the Blue Sky." And the image of the night before came to me again, of the Pacific as a universe, and the islands like stars in all that space.

Auckland has the largest Polynesian population of any city in the world – fully half the people are dusky islanders, and looking at them you might think: They all come from Fatland. Many of them were organized into street gangs with names like the Mongrel Mob and the Black Power Gang, the Tongan Crypt Gang, the United Island Gang, and the Sons of Samoa. Where were the women? The ones I saw were pot-bellied men, some of them so fat they had an odd twisting walk, like penguins waddling down a plank. Their skin had gone gray in the chilly New Zealand climate. Their swollen cheeks gave them squinty gimlet eyes. It was hard to imagine any of them paddling a canoe. Roughly ten percent of them, the Maoris, had arrived from Tahiti via the Cook Islands about a thousand years ago, and named these islands Aotearoa, "The Land of the Long White Cloud."

Plenty of them are nice as pie, people said, but lots of them are rapists. Everyone had an opinion about them: You should see the thighs on some of them, people said. You should see their tattoos. Your Maori just doesn't want to work, they said. And they're not really full-blooded. The half-castes, the quarter-castes – they're the troublemakers. Your Tongan is a decent chap, but your Samoan can be a terror when he's the worse for drink. If you see a Samoan full of grog just turn around and walk the other way. Your Fijian? Let's face it, they're cannibals, simple as that, and your Indian is a terribly hard-working person – work like dogs, most of these Hindus. Your Mohammedan is another story. They're randy wee buggers – I hate to say it. But while we're on the subject, a lot of these island women are root rats. They bang like a dunny door. Your Rotoruan, your Nuiean, your Cook Islander – oh it's a mixed bag, no question about it. Some of them are doing very nicely, thank you, drive flash cars, own tidy houses and land. But you just go to one of their bloody wee islands and try to buy a block of land and see what happens. They'll laugh in your face.

Islanders were religious, islanders were gamblers and drinkers, islanders were devoted to their families, islanders were dole scroungers, islanders fought among themselves, islanders were economic refugees, islanders were villains. They towed your car away at night and the next day called you up and demanded money to return it. They practiced extortion, protection rackets, mugging and racial violence in this pastoral republic – seventy million sheep farting in the glorious meadows.

But these days the gang violence of islanders had been pushed off the front page by the news that the prime minister, David Lange, had just left his wife and run off with his speech-writer, Miss Margaret Pope. *Lange's Mother Denounces Him*, the headlines said. *Claims She Regrets The Day He Was Born* . . . Mr Lange's wife Naomi was screeching on radio and television, demanding her rights and trying to get even. In what seemed the direst threat of all she said that she intended to publish a book of her own poems.

The papers were full of separation and divorce, the whole world was splitting up. The sheep-shearers were on strike. They wanted $46 for shearing a hundred sheep.

Carrying my collapsible kayak, I went to Wellington, where a television interviewer gloated to me that old Mrs Lange had been on his very program saying that her son should never have been born, and why had he run off with this scarlet woman, and marriage was supposed to be sacred. Did I have any views on that?

No, I said, I was just passing through.

Another man I met said, "This Lange. He's got some Maori blood in him."

It wasn't true but it was supposed to explain why he had ditched his wife.

I sat in my hotel room reading *The Sexual Life of Savages*, by Bronislaw Malinowski. When I ordered room service, the man in the hotel kitchen snapped at me, "Did you order this yesterday?"

I said no, but why?

He said, "We need one day's advance notice on room-service orders."

What a bungaloid place, I thought. It is bungalows and more bungalows and little fragile chalets in Wellington and none of them is higher than the trees around it, so that at a distance all you saw was roofs, mostly tin roofs painted browny-red. The rest was bare hills and a wind so strong it seemed to have shape and substance. The wind scoured the streets and whipped the dark waters of the harbor.

I read Malinowski. I tried to imagine the Trobriand Islands. I noticed that most stores in Wellington sold camping equipment, and I bought some more. I sat in my hotel room with my collapsible kayak feeling morbid. I also worried about David Lange. What if I ended up with cancer and a divorce? I was now using Betty Boop bandages. One night, with nothing better to do, I did my arm – took off the Betty Boop bandage and cut and tweezed out the stitches with my Disposable Suture Removal Kit.

Among the Trobriand Islanders, Malinowski said, *The formalities of divorce are as simple as those by which marriage is contracted. The woman leaves her husband's house with all her personal belongings, and moves to her mother's hut, or to that of her nearest maternal kinswoman. There she remains, awaiting the course of events, and in the meantime enjoying full sexual freedom.*

The next day I went to Christchurch, on the South Island. It looked prim and moribund, like the sort of South London suburb I had mocked in England on Sunday outings with the kids, driving through on the way to Brighton thinking: This is the English death, the indescribable boredom that makes you desperate to leave. Life is elsewhere, I thought in Christchurch, but in this purgatory I began reliving my past. I saw frightful bungalows and dusty hedges and twitching curtains, and at last in front of the California Fried Chicken Family Restaurant on Papanui Road in the district of Merivale I saw a family of four, Dad, Mum, and the two boys, eating happily in the glarey light and joking with each other, and at the sight of this happy family I burst into tears.

Still, nearly everyone I met asked me, "What do you think of Na Zillun?"

"It's wonderful," I said.

They always shrugged and denied it. New Zealanders, smug and self-congratulatory about David Lange's non-nuclear policy, seemed to me the hardest people in the world to compliment. There was something Calvinist in this refusal to accept praise, but it was so persistent it was almost as though in their stubborn humility they were fishing for compliments.

If you spoke about their well-maintained cities they said they were actually very disorderly. Tell them their mountains are high and snowy and they retorted that yours were higher and snowier. "New Zealanders are fitness fanatics," I said to a man. "That's a myth," he said. "We're very unhealthy as a nation. We're poofs." If I said New Zealand seemed prosperous they claimed it was dying on its feet. Mention the multiracial aspect of the North Island and they said, "We hev ithnic unrist. There'll be a blow-up any munnit."

"But it's much better than Australia, I hear."

"Bitter by a long chalk. Your Aussie's an enemal."

Secretly, I said to myself: Everyone's wearing old ill-fitting clothes and sensible shoes. They carried string bags. They shopped in places with names like Clark's General Drapers and Edwin Mouldey Ironmongery. It was the indoor suburban culture of the seaside suburbs of 1950s England, Bexhill-on-the-Pacific, with strangely colored plates (*Souvenir of Cheddar Gorge*) on the mantelpiece and plump armchairs and an electric fire where there used to be a hearth. The older people were dull and decent, the younger ones trying hopelessly to be stylish, and the students – Kiwis to the tips of their pinfeathers – aggressively scruffy and gauche. Here and there you saw a Maori, often working a cash-register. They were supposed to be clubby and faintly menacing, but they were all smiles and inhabited big solid bodies; they were the only people in New Zealand who looked right at home.

I went to Dunedin, which was cold and frugal, with its shabby streets and mock-Gothic university, and talked to the students.

"They're very shy," I was told.

Really? They seemed to me ignorant, assertive and dirty. It felt like the end of the world, and when I looked at a map this seemed true: we were only about twenty degrees north of the Antarctic Circle – leave the southern tip of New Zealand and the next upright mammal you are likely to see is an emperor penguin.

Back in Christchurch, I sat in my hotel room, staring at my feet. I watched a New Zealand version of *This Is Your Life*, paying tribute to a middle-aged Maori singer, and when the man wept openly at seeing his family traipse into the studio, I became so depressed I drank most of the mini-bar. The hotel was in the tudor style, with fake beams and mullioned windows. I was consoled by my luggage, the boat I had carried with me but not yet paddled.

What was the Pacific Ocean like? I rented a bicycle and rode it about five miles to Sumner Bay, where surfers were lazing like seals and the cold blackish breakers were much too big for me to penetrate them with my boat. There was another harbor – Lyttelton, over the hill. I cycled a steep circling road and after an hour came to another surfy harbor, but it wasn't Lyttelton – it was Taylor's Mistake.

In 1863 Captain Taylor thought this was Lyttelton after a round-the-world voyage, and ran aground, losing his ship. It was my mistake too. I cycled back up the Port Hills and over another range of hills to Lyttelton Harbor, which was lovely and long, a safe anchorage, with Chinese shops and pretty houses. There was a short-cut back to Christchurch, a tunnel under the hills, but bicycles weren't allowed in it. Procrastinating in the town, I passed a bloody sanitary towel, where someone had thrown it on the street, and I thought: Because of that disgusting thing I will never come here again.

Pushing and pedalling I made it back over the hills to Christchurch, tired after my forty-mile cycle ride and frustrated by not having found anywhere in the nearby Pacific to paddle my boat.

I called my wife and told her what an awful time I was having. We both cried. She was miserable, she said. I said, So was I!

"But it's better that we stay apart," she said.

Then she begged me to stop calling her.

She said I was like a torturer, calling her out of the blue and making her feel like a prisoner being given a cup of tea by a quixotic jailer. But all I could think of was myself tearfully pedalling the wonky bicycle, all alone, in the wind, up the steep hills at the edge of Christchurch.

And I probably had cancer. In the seedy tudor-style hotel I looked up from *The Sexual Life of Savages* and saw that the people in the next room had gone, and left the door ajar, and a new set of people were sitting in the same chairs and laughing, having displaced them. Life was like that! The tide came in and went out. People died and others took their place, not even knowing the others' names. They sat in your chairs, they slept in your bed. And you were probably lost somewhere in the Pacific – gone and forgotten. *I wonder where this thing came from?* someone said, scribbling at your beautiful desk.

The next day, Sunday, still feeling morbid and stunned by the sunny emptiness and indifference and the almost indescribable boredom of sitting alone in front of a fan heater in Merivale, in a transported culture of houses named "Oakleigh" in suburbs called Ponsonby, that looked second-hand and small and seedy, ill-suited and mediocre – the most terrible aspect of which was that the New Zealanders themselves did not seem to know what was happening to them in their decline – there stole upon me the sort of misery that induces people in crummy hotel rooms to make sure the cap is on the toothpaste and the faucet is turned off, and then they kill themselves, trying not to make too much of a mess.

*Get me out of here*, I thought. And I headed for the wilderness.

# 2

## New Zealand: Sloshing through the South Island

As long as there is wilderness there is hope. I went southwest from Christchurch to Queenstown, at the edge of the waterworld of Fiordland. Even today it is one of the world's last real wildernesses. But a thousand years ago, before the arrival of any humans, it was like the world before the Fall.

Then, there were no predators except falcons, hawks and eagles – no other meat-eaters. There were no browsing mammals, no land mammals at all, apart from two species of small bat. Everything grew and flourished, and the weather came up from the Roaring Forties, watering this corner of New Zealand with twenty-five feet of rain a year. It is still one of the wettest places in the world.

It was once so safe here that the birds lost their sense of danger, and without enemies some stopped flying – among them, the flightless New Zealand goose and the Fiordland crested penguin, now extinct. Others evolved into enormous and complacent specimens, like the spoiled and overfed children I had seen in Auckland – the giant rail, more than a yard tall, or the feathered long-necked moa, a distant relative of the emu and the ostrich and Big Bird, which grew to be ten feet tall.

In that old paradise the trees grew abundantly and the moss was two feet deep – a perfect seedbed for new trees. The creatures lived on roots and insects, and not on each other. The foliage grew without being cut or grazed. Fiordland, which had been created by glaciers, was the Peaceable Kingdom.

After the Maori arrived, probably in the tenth century, from the Cook Islands in tropical Polynesia, with the dog (*kuri*) and the rat (*kiore*) they kept for food, they made forays into Fiordland from the north. They had a great love for decorative feathers, and in their quest for them, and for food, they hunted many birds to extinction. The Maori dogs and rats preyed on the ground-dwelling birds. For the first time since its emergence from the Ice Age, Fiordland's natural balance was disturbed. The arrival of these predators produced the ecological equivalent of Original Sin.

There were always treasure-seekers in Fiordland – Maoris looking for feather and greenstone, *pakehes* (whites) looking for gold – but such people were transients. Fiordland never had any permanent settlement, only camps and way stations and the temporary colonies of sealers and whalers at the edge of the sea. People came and went. Fiordland remained uninhabited – a true primeval forest.

But the humans who passed through left many of their animals behind. They introduced various species either for sport or food, or in the mistaken belief that one animal would stabilize another. The pattern is repeated all over the Pacific – there are wild goats gobbling up Tahiti, and wild horses chewing the Marquesas to shreds, wild pigs in the Solomons, and sneaky egg-eating mongooses, presented to the islands by missionaries, all over Hawaii. The rabbits and wild dogs in Australia did so much damage that a vermin-proof fence was put up across New South Wales that is longer than the Great Wall of China.

The foreign animals brought a subtle chaos to Fiordland. When the rabbits went wild, the stoats and weasels were introduced to keep them in check, but instead they ate birds and bird eggs and the rabbits increased. Every other non-native creature was similarly destructive. The New Zealanders I met hated these foreign animals even more than the islanders, but they hated them for the same reasons – because of their indecent fertility and their breeding habits and their excessive greed, eating everything in sight.

The greatest threat to vegetation was the red deer. Deer breed quickly and can go anywhere. Helicopters flying over almost inaccessible hanging valleys could spot three or four hundred deer in the steepest places. The Norway rats that came to New Zealand on ships have multiplied and reduced the native bird population. There are American elk in Fiordland, the only herd in the Southern Hemisphere.

"They're a nuisance," Terry Pellet told me. He was the District Conservator of Fiordland. "There are so many exotic species that thrive here and harm the local flora and fauna – possums, chamois, and hares."

And the Germans, he said, were terrible about paying hut fees.

What is native and what is alien is a Pacific conundrum. In New Zealand all strangers were suspect, whether they were animal or vegetable. You can shoot a red deer any day in Fiordland and it is always open season on elk. Foreign trees are regarded as unsightly weeds, whether they are Douglas fir, silver birch, or spruce, and no growing things are hated more than the rampant gorse and broom planted by sentimental and homesick Scots.

Nearly all the people I met said they wanted to reclaim their hills and make them bald and bright again, ridding them of these alien plants and animals, to bring about the resurgence of the flightless birds, vegetarians and insectivores, and to preserve the long valleys of native conifers and beeches. There have been some pleasant surprises. One guileless, ground-dwelling bird, the plump beaky takahe, which the Maoris hunted, was thought to be extinct. In 1948 some takahes were found in a remote region of Fiordland. Although protected, the bird faces an uncertain future.

Old habits of contentment, curiosity, and trust – the legacy of paradise – remain among the many bird species in Fiordland. Anyone taking a walk through the rain forests will be followed by the South Island robin, the fantail, the tomtit, and the tiny rifleman, New Zealand's smallest bird. These birds seem absolutely without fear and will flutter and light a few feet away, pecking at insects the hiker has disturbed. The kea, or mountain parrot, is so confident it becomes an intruder, squawking its own name and poking into your knapsack.

So, in magnificent Fiordland, far from the dreary frugality of Christchurch and its suburbs, the birds were unafraid and all the water was drinkable; the birdwatcher didn't need binoculars and the hiker had no use for a canteen.

I cheered up and decided to go for a one-week hike over the mountains and through the rain forest. I would paddle my kayak somewhere else.

The best-known long-distance walk in Fiordland is the Milford Track, but it is now a victim of marketing success, and "the finest walk in the world" is simply tourist board hyperbole. It has become crowded and intensely regulated, and as a result rather hackneyed.

The Routeburn Track was my choice, because – unlike the Milford, which is essentially a valley walk with one high climb – it rises to well above the scrub line and stays there, circling the heights, offering vistas of the whole northeast corner of Fiordland. I decided to combine the Routeburn with the Greenstone Valley Walk, so that I would have a whole week of it and so that I could enter and leave Fiordland the way people have done for centuries, on foot.

There is an intense but simple thrill in setting off in the morning on a mountain trail knowing that everything you need is on your back. It is a confidence in having left all inessentials behind, and of entering a world of natural beauty which has not been violated, where money has no value, and possessions are a deadweight. The person with the fewest possessions is the freest: Thoreau was right.

Even my recently gloomy mood had lifted. I felt a lightness of spirit, and the feeling was so profound it had a physical dimension – I felt stronger and that eased my load. From the age of nine or ten, when I first began hiking, I have associated camping with personal freedom. My pleasure has intensified over the years as equipment has improved and become more manageable and efficient. When I was very young, camping equipment was just another name for "war surplus." Everything was canvas. It was made for the Second World War and Korea. It was dusty, mildewed and very heavy. I struggled with my pup tent. My sleeping-bag was filled with cotton and kapok and weighed fifteen pounds. Now all the stuff is light and colorful and almost stylish.

And hikers are no longer middle-aged Boy Scouts. A violinist, a factory worker, an aspiring actor, a photographer, a food writer, a student, and a grumpy little man with an East European accent made up our Routeburn hiking party. We were, I suppose, representative. Some dropped by the wayside; the photographer stayed on at one hut to take pictures, and the man who kept interrupting discussions with, "Hah! You sink so! You must be choking!" at last went home, and when we finished only three of us pushed on to the Greenstone. Isidore, the violinist, cursed the water and mud and apologized for being a slow walker, but he was better at other pursuits – he was concert-master of the New Zealand Symphony Orchestra, and he had a knack for beating me at Scrabble during the long nights at the trackside shelters.

We started walking up a muddy track at the north end of Lake Wakitipu in sight of deer and majestic stags.

"I find it hard to view these creatures as pests," I said. "Vermin is not the first thing that comes to mind when you see the monarch of the glen."

"Vermin!" Isidore said, mockingly. He had the northern Michigan habit of talking with his teeth clamped together. He soon stumblingly fell behind.

He caught up at lunch, while we ate beside a stream (which we drank from). We were bitten by sand flies there and we set off again. After a horizontal stretch across Routeburn Flats, among the tawny blowing tussocks, we climbed steeply on a track that took us through gnarled and ancient beeches to Routeburn Falls. This was a succession of cataracts which cascaded over black rocks on about six levels of bouldery terraces.

From this level, it was possible to see clearly how the glaciers carved Fiordland, creating the characteristic U-shaped valleys, whose sheer walls gave them the illusion of even greater height. The dragging and abrasive glaciers smoothed the valleys' walls, but here the ice had been about five thousand feet thick, and so the tops of the mountains were jagged and sharp where the glacier didn't reach.

That night we stayed in a hut. A hut on the Routeburn Track I discovered is essentially a small drafty shelter erected over a Scrabble board. At the Falls hut that night we talked as the rain began to patter on the roof.

"How did the Maori withstand this cold?" Isidore asked, massaging life back into his sensitive violinist's fingers.

James Hayward, the aspiring actor, did not have the most accurate explanations, but they were always memorable.

"The Maori kept warm by catching keas," he said, referring to the mountain parrots. "They hollowed out the birds and strapped them to their feet and used them for slippers."

"I sink you are choking," came a voice. "Hah!"

James merely smiled.

"You're talking crap, Jim," someone said. "They've found Maori sandals on the trails."

"You see a lot of interesting things on the trails," James said. "I once saw a man on the Routeburn in a bowler hat, a pin-striped suit, a tightly rolled umbrella, and all his camping gear in a briefcase."

He had had to raise his voice, for the wind and the rain had increased. It kept up all night, falling fast and turning to sleet and making a great commotion, with constant smashing sounds, pushing at the side of the hut and slapping the windows.

I played Scrabble with Pam, the student. She said that she beat most of her friends.

"You won't beat me," I said. "Words are my business."

She was a big strong girl. She had the heaviest rucksack in the group.

"If you beat me, I'll carry your pack over the Harris Saddle tomorrow."

She beat me easily, but in the morning I felt sure that I would be spared the effort of carrying her pack. The rain was still driving down hard. Visibility was poor. Between swirling cloud and glissades of sleet, I could see that the storm had left deep new snow on the summit of Momus and other nearby mountains. From every mountainside, cataracts had erupted, milky-white, spurting down the steep rock faces.

"Let's go walkabout," James said.

The narrow footpath near the hut coursed with water and I had wet feet before I had gone ten yards. We tramped up the path in the snowy rain and wind, marveling at how the Routeburn Falls was now about twice the torrent it had been the day before. We climbed for an hour to a hilltop lake that lay in a rocky bowl, a body of water known here, and in Scotland, as a "tarn." ("Burn" is also Scottish, for that matter, meaning "stream.") The storm crashed into the tarn for a while, but even as we watched, it lessened and soon ceased altogether. Within fifteen minutes the sun came out and blazed powerfully – brighter than any sunlight I had ever seen.

The photographer, Ian, said, "This sunlight is three-quarters of a stop brighter than anywhere else on earth I've taken pictures."

It seems that the greenhouse effect can be measured with a light-meter.

In this dazzling light, Pam helped me strap on her fifty-pound pack and we climbed upward. Lake Harris, a few miles up the trail, was greeny-blue and enclosed by cliffs. Then we were above it, tramping through alpine scrub and the blowing spear grass they called spaniard. Staggering under the weight of Pam's pack, I tottered towards Harris Saddle (4,200 feet), which stands as a glorious gateway to Fiordland. Beyond it is the deep Hollyford Valley, which winds to the sea, and high on its far side the lovely Darran Mountains, with glaciers still slipping from their heights and new snow whipping from their ridges.

The Harris Saddle was worth the long climb for the sight of the panorama of summits to the west, a succession of mile-high mountains – Christina, Sabre, Gifford, Te Wera, and Madeline. I could not imagine mountains packed more tightly than this – a whole ocean of whitened peaks, like an arctic sea.

Apart from the wind whispering in the stunted scrub, there was silence here. At this height, among powerful mountains, I felt that I had left mean and vulgar things far behind, and entered a world without pettiness. Its counterpart, and a feeling it closely resembles, is that soaring sense of well-being inspired by a Gothic cathedral – not a nineteenth-century New Zealand imitation, of which there were many, but a real one.

Walking along the ridge of the Harris Saddle, I had a clear recollection of the London I had left, of various events that people talked about: a steamy affair between a literary editor and one of her younger assistants; of a famous widow, an obnoxious Ann Hathaway type, who gave parties – drinkers jammed in a room full of smoke – that people boasted of attending. I saw people – writers – talking on television programs, and partygoers smoking, and snatching drinks from a waitress's tray, and shrieking at each other, and talking about the literary editor and her younger lover, and then they all went home drunk.

From this path blowing with wild flowers and loose snow these far-off people seemed tiny and rather pathetic in their need for witnesses.

"Bullshit!" I yelled into the wind, startling Isidore until he discerned that I was smiling.

I needed to come here to understand that, and I felt I would never go back.

Walking these New Zealand mountains stimulated my memory. My need for this strange landscape was profound. Travel, which is nearly always seen as an attempt to escape from the ego, is in my opinion the opposite. Nothing induces concentration or inspires memory like an alien landscape or a foreign culture. It is simply not possible (as romantics think) to lose yourself in an exotic place. Much more likely is an experience of intense nostalgia, a harking back to an earlier stage in your life, or seeing clearly a serious mistake. But this does not happen to the exclusion of the exotic present. What makes the whole experience vivid, and sometimes thrilling, is the juxtaposition of the present and the past – London seen from the heights of Harris Saddle.

Leaving the others behind I started the long traverse across the high Hollyford Face – three hours at a high altitude without shelter, exposed to the wind but also exposed to the beauty of the ranges – the forest, the snow, and a glimpse of the Tasman Sea. It was more than three thousand feet straight down, from the path on these cliffs to the Hollyford River on the valley floor. The track was rocky and deceptive, and it was bordered with alpine plants – daisies, snowberries and white gentians.

Ocean Peak was above us as I moved slowly across the rock face. It was not very late, but these mountains are so high the sun drops behind them in the afternoon, and without it I was very cold. The southerly wind was blowing from Antarctica. As the day darkened I came to a bluff, and beneath me in a new valley was a green lake. I was at such a high altitude that it took me another hour to descend the zigzag path.

Deeper in the valley I was among ancient trees; and that last half-hour, before darkness fell, was like a walk through an enchanted forest, the trees literally as old as the hills, grotesquely twisted and very damp and pungent. A forest that is more than a thousand years old, and that has never been touched or interfered with, has a ghostly look, of layer upon layer of living things, and the whole forest clinging together – roots and trunks and branches mingled with moss and rocks, and everything above ground hung with tufts of lichen called "old man's beard."

It was so dark and damp here the moss grew on all sides of the trunks – the sunlight hardly struck them. The moss softened them, making them into huge, tired, misshapen monsters with great spongy arms. Everything was padded and wrapped because of the dampness, and the boughs were blackish green; the forest floor was deep in ferns, and every protruding rock was upholstered in velvety moss. Here and there was a chuckle of water running among the roots and ferns. I was followed by friendly robins.

It was all visibly alive and wonderful, and in places had a subterranean gleam of wetness. It was like a forest in a fairy story, the pretty and perfect wilderness of sprites and fairies, which is the child's version of paradise – a lovely Disneyish glade where birds eat out of your hand and you know you will come to no harm.

I began to feel hopeful again about my life. Maybe I didn't have cancer after all.

It was cold that night – freezing, in fact. I woke in Mackenzie Hut to frosty bushes and icy grass and whitened ferns. There was lacework everywhere, and the sound of a far-off waterfall that was like the howl of city traffic.

There were keas screaming overhead as I spent that day hiking – for the fun of it – to the head of Lake Mackenzie. The paradise shelducks objected to my invading their territory, and they gave their two-toned complaint – the male duck honking, the female squawking. I continued up the valley, boulder-hopping much of the way along a dry creek bed. It was steep, most of the boulders were four or five feet thick, so it was slow going. I sheltered by a rock the size of a garage to eat my lunch. The wind rose, the clouds grew lumpier and crowded the sky. The day darkened and turned cold.

I climbed onward, and the higher I got the freer I felt – it was that same sense of liberation I had felt on Harris Saddle, remembering the trivialities of London. At the highest point of the valley face, an uplifted platform just under Fraser Col, the clouds bulged and snow began to fall. I was in a large quarry-like place littered with boulders the size of the bungalows in Wellington, in a gusting wind. I decided not to linger. The commonest emergency in these parts is not a fall or a broken limb but rather an attack of hypothermia. I descended quickly, moving from rock to rock, to whip up my blood and warm myself, and I arrived back at the hut exhausted after what was to have been a rest day.

That night was typical of a stop at a trail hut. Over dinner we discussed murder, race relations, AIDS, nuclear testing, the greenhouse effect, Third World economies, the Maori claim to New Zealand, and Martin Luther King Day.

The Czech, whom I thought of as the Bouncing Czech – he had emigrated from Prague to become a businessman somewhere in California – said, "I never celebrate Martin Luther King Day at my plant. I make my men work."

"How long have you lived in America?" I asked.

"Since sixty-eight."

"Do you know anything about the civil rights movement in the United States?"

"I know about my business," he said. That was true – he spent a great deal of time boasting about how he had made it big in America.

"But you're doing it in a free country," I said. "When you left Czechoslovakia you could have gone anywhere, but you chose America. Don't you think you have an obligation to know something about American history?"

"As far as I am concerned, Martin Luther King is not significant."

"That's an ignorant opinion," I said.

Isidore said, "Does anyone want to play Scrabble?"

The hut was small. I was angry. I went outside and fumed, and through the heavy mist an owl hooted, "More pork!"

I woke early and left the hut quickly the next morning, so that I wouldn't have to talk to the Czech. He was a rapid walker and what is known in camping circles as an equipment freak: very expensive multicolored gear.

It was raining softly as I set off, and roosting on a branch above the path ahead was a New Zealand pigeon. It was like no other pigeon in the world, fat as a football, and so clumsy you wonder how it stayed aloft; it does so with a loud thrashing of wings. In the past, the Maori who walked this way snared these *kereru* and ate them. They needed them to sustain themselves in their search for the godly greenstone, a nephritic jade hard enough to use for knives and axes and lovely enough for jewelry. They dug this rare stone all over the Routeburn Track. On that same stretch, from Mackenzie to Lake Howden, I heard a bellbird. This remarkable mimicking bird trills and then growls and grates before bursting into song. It was much admired by the Maori. At the birth of a son they cooked a bellbird in a sacred oven in a ritual of sacrifice meant to insure that the child had fluency and a fine voice.

The light rain in the morning increased to a soaking drizzle, turning the last mile on the Routeburn Track into a muddy creek. I passed under Earland Falls, which splashes 300 feet down – the water coursing onto the rocky path. There was water and mist and noise everywhere, and it involved a sort of baptism in order to proceed. Farther down the track the woods offered some protection from the rain, and yet we arrived at Howden Hut drenched. That is normal for Fiordland. Photography cannot do justice to rain, and so most photographs of Fiordland depict a sunny wilderness. But that sunshine is exceptional. At Lake Howden, for example, there are roughly two hundred rain days a year, producing twenty-five feet of rain.

It was still raining in the afternoon, and yet I was looking forward to three more days walking, down the Greenstone Valley to Lake Wakitipu. It was the sort of rain that makes local enthusiasts start their explanations with *if only* –

"If only it weren't so misty you'd be able to see wonderful –"

Wonderful peaks, lakes, forests, cliffs, waterfalls, ridges, saddles, and ravines. They were all obscured by the rain. But the wonderful woods with their mossy grottoes were enough. This was a famous valley, one that had been pushed open when a glacier split off from the Hollyford Valley and flowed southeast about thirty miles to Lake Wakitipu. It was another Maori route to the greenstone deposits at the top of the lake. Its presence so near the rivers and lake confirmed them in their belief that the stone was a petrified fish. Greenstone had both spiritual and material significance and was cherished because it was so difficult to obtain.

Isidore still struggled along, humming Brahms. The Czech evaporated – we never saw him again – and we were joined by two New Zealanders, a courting couple, who were terrific walkers and who tripped and pushed each other, threw blobs of mud, splashed each other in the icy streams, wrestled at lunch in the tussocky meadows – kiwi courtship. And there was an elderly lawyer and his wife, from somewhere in Oregon.

Seeing the mixed bunkroom at one of the Greenstone huts, the man said, "Oh, I get it. It's bisexual!"

Not exactly, but we knew what he meant.

The Greenstone was a walk down a river valley – no snow and sleet here. After breakfast we set off together but since everyone walked at a different pace we ended up walking alone, meeting at a rest spot for scroggin (nuts and raisins) and then onward through the forest for lunch – on the Greenstone it was always a picnic by a drinkable river – and finally slogging throughout most of the afternoon toward one of the riverside huts. As the river widened to a mile or two it became louder and frothier, and the soaked graywacke stone that lay in it made it greener.

Cataracts poured from the mountains above the trail, but they were so high and the wind so strong that they were blown aside, like vaporizing bridal veils – a gauze of mist that vanished before it reached the valley floor. We were followed by birds and watched by deer and hawks and falcons. The weather was too changeable and the prevailing westerlies too strong to assure one completely rainy – or sunny – day. Clouds were always in rapid motion in the sky and being torn apart by the Livingstone Mountains at the edge of Fiordland – for we had now left the park proper and were making our way through Wakitipu State Forest to the lake.

The silver beeches of the high altitudes gave way to the thicker, taller red beeches of the valley and the slender and strange young lancewood trees with their downward-slanting leaves at the margin of the valley floor. We walked across the sluices of long-ago rockslides and through a forest of whitened trunks of trees killed by a recent fire, and by a deep gorge and a rock (called a *roche moutonnée*) too stubborn for the glacier to budge, and through cool mossy woods, and knee-deep in a freezing creek – the courting couple shrieking and kicking water at each other – always followed by birds.

At the last swing bridge that trembled like an Inca walkway near the mouth of the Greenstone, where the Caples Valley converged to form an amphitheater of mountainsides, the foliage was of a European and transplanted kind – tall poplars in autumnal gold, standing like titanic ears of corn, and dark Douglas fir, and the startling red leaves of copper beeches – the trees the New Zealanders call foreign weeds and would like to destroy, root and branch.

I was sorry to reach the end of the trail, because there is something purifying about walking through a wilderness. To see a land in the state in which it has existed since it rose from the waters and let slip its ice, a land untouched, unchanged, its only alteration a footpath so narrow your elbows are forever brushing against ferns and old boughs, is greatly reassuring to the spirit.

Bush-bashing on these tracks had stimulated my imagination, and the vast landscape had a way of putting human effort into perspective. The smaller one feels on the earth, dwarfed by mountains and assailed by weather, the more respectful one has to be – and unless we are very arrogant, the less likely we are to poison or destroy it. In the Pacific the interlopers were doing the most damage – bringing nuclear waste to Johnston Island, digging a gigantic copper mine at Panguna in the North Solomons, stringing out miles of drift nets to trap and kill every living creature that came near its ligatures, testing nuclear devices at Moruroa Atoll in the Tuomotus.

But this too was Polynesia – this rain forest, these Southern Alps. *Te Tapu Nui*, the Maori called their mountains. "The Peaks of Intense Sacredness."

# 3

## Waffling in White Australia

Australia, the gigantic Pacific island of Meganesia, is an underdeveloped country that is bewildered and at times terrified by its own emptiness. People shout as though to keep their spirits up. *G'day! How's your rotten form! Good on yer!*

As on every other Oceanic island, most of its people live at its shores and beaches, so its edge is bricked and bungaloid, the rest an insect-haunted wilderness of croaking wind and red desert.

And the whole place is fly-blown. "It seems an unfortunate habit of Australians to speak through their teeth as if they came from the fly country," a Sydney judge remarked about fifty years ago, and he went on, "afraid to open their mouths for fear of flies." People there blink at the flies and turn their backs to the desert, showing total native imbuggerance, and say *Go and have a roll!* or *Who gives a stuff?* – in snarly voices. And maybe Australians talk a lot louder because they are so far away from the rest of the world. How else will anyone hear?

The Australian Book of Etiquette is a very slim volume, but its outrageous Book of Rudeness is a hefty tome. Being offensive in a matey way gets people's attention, and Down Under you often make friends by being intensely rude in the right tone of voice. Australian English (one of Australia's glories and its greatest art-form) is a language of familiarity. *Goodoh! How yer doin' mate, all right? How's your belly where the pig bit yer?* Understanding the concept of mate-ship is the key to success in Australia; and mockery is the assertive warmth of mate-ship.

Australians are noted for the savage endearments in their mockery, and as for self-criticism, no one is more mocking of Australia than the Australians themselves.

"This is the arse of the world," I heard an Australian say on television. He was from Melbourne, which some Australians call "Smellburn." He was commenting on the Bicentenary, the anniversary of the ignominious arrival of the first convicts at Botany Bay. "Look at us on the map," he went on. "The country resembles a bum. And, look" – he was pointing to its contours – "two sagging bum-cheeks!"

I brought my collapsible boat to the coast of Western Australia, which is a state the size of Mexico, a place which that man would have termed the left buttock. This was Perth, and you never saw such wind.

"We're on the edge of the earth," a woman said to me in the nearby harbor town of Fremantle. "And guess which other writer was here?" she said. "D. H. Lawrence. For two weeks."

"Australia is outside everything," D. H. Lawrence said in *Kangaroo*, the novel he wrote while he breezed through Australia in 1922. It took him less time to write this book than I took to read it, because it is practically unreadable. He started writing the thing, anatomizing and fictionalizing Australia, about ten days after he got to the country and he finished it less than a month later. Five weeks to write a 400-page novel. Lawrence is flat-footed in this book, but never mind! You have to admire his speed. And now and then he surpasses himself, describing a plopping wave or a jellyfish.

My idea was that my trip, beginning as a publicity tour on which I would be speaking – or more properly, waffling on – about my own work, would end as a trek in the wilderness. Perth was the first of the five Australian cities I had agreed to visit, to give lectures at literary lunches and submit to interviews. For me, it was total immersion from the first, because Australia is a country of readers and viewers, among the best informed and most outward-looking people in the world, and with the most predatory journalists in the business – they rejoice in being "journos" and hacks in a place that is saturated in newspapers, magazines, radio and television. Australia is full of news media but generates very little national news; so the media are hungry, they retail the world's news and culture and any newcomer – author, actress, politician, fellow hack – is pounced upon. Anyone is fair game – anyone from beyond the Great Barrier Reef.

And it was total immersion for another reason: Australians have the American habit of greeting most outsiders as though they are potential immigrants. They reserve some of their most picturesque mockery for such people, referring to Jewish refugees as "refujews," Italians as "dingbats," "eyetoes," "spiggoties," and "spagies." New Zealanders are "pig islanders," and the English are "poms," "pommies," or "pongos." They seem to have invented the word "chink" for Chinese – they were certainly the first to use it, in 1879, twenty-two years before it was recorded in America; but they also refer to Chinese as "canaries," "dinks," and "chow-chows." Americans are universally "yanks" or "yank wogs," and the English are occasionally "pom wogs." This distinguishes them from the real McCoy, known in Australia as "wog wogs." This is not to be taken as abuse, but rather as an obscure but none the less genially Australian form of hospitality.

Here I was among the "sandgropers" – the term the rest of the country uses to describe Western Australians – in Perth, a big brand-new boom city surrounded by empty bush, tall buildings in the middle of nowhere, with the scale and optimism and much of the brightness of a place like Portland, Oregon. It was a good place to start a life in, which was what a lot of the people I met seemed to be doing – they had come from South Africa, from Europe, even from America.

Australia is the only country in the world I have visited where Americans in large numbers have made serious efforts to put down roots. Thirty years ago, when the so-called White Australia Policy was in full swing, they – and other nationalities – set sail because it was a country of white exclusionists; and any number of pale jug-eared boofheads were eager to become migros and have their passage paid by a desperate government grateful for white workers. Now they go for the opposite reason, because Australia seems politically even-handed and has become, racially, a free-for-all. Many Americans there said to me, "I consider myself an Australian." Not once in eighteen years of living in Britain did I ever hear a transplanted American say, "I consider myself British."

I traipsed around Fremantle harbor, right next door to Perth, wondering whether I should launch my collapsible kayak. But the wind blasting off the Indian Ocean was much too strong for me. Out past the surf zone the strangely shaped sheep-carrier ships toppled in the heavy swell. They were like floating ten-storey buildings, and packed closely into open wire cages were thousands of live sheep, off to the Persian Gulf to be slaughtered by the *halal* method – throat-slashed, facing Mecca. It is a fact that most of the mutton in Arabia comes from Meganesia. Australia supplies the jumbucks for stews; and the majority of New Zealand lambs end up on shish-kebab skewers in Iran and Iraq.

My books made a sea voyage to Australia, and two editions had just arrived, a novel and a travel book. I was beginning my Australian tour by publicizing both of them. And so I did the rounds of interviews.

"What's your opinion of the Chinese people?" a woman journalist in Perth asked me on behalf of her magazine, and I reminded her that this was not an easy question, as there were one billion Chinese people.

"How long does it take to write a book?" was another question I pondered over until I realized that I did not have the answer.

The supplementary question to this was, "Do you respect the main character in your novel?"

That puzzled me. Was this a sample of the sort of question I could expect in the rest of Australia? I said yes, I respected all the characters in my books, and I thought: *Even you, digger, if ever you become a character.*

But there were questions I could easily answer.

"What's the main difference between a novel and a travel book?" a man asked me over lunch in Fremantle, holding a tape recorder under my chin.

It seemed to me an easy matter to be a journalist in this part of Australia. For example, one day I was wakened from a nap in Fremantle (I had been having a nightmare about suffering from cancer), and hurried to a Perth newspaper, an easy-to-remember tabloid called the *Daily Mail*, for it had made itself famous by printing a big beefcake picture each day, entitled "Your Daily Male."

I was asked to wait for ten or fifteen minutes, and then I was escorted to a cubicle where an eighteen-year-old boy was sitting at a tidy desk. One feature of this cubicle interested me: there were little snipped-out pictures of Elvis Presley taped to his blotter, his noticeboard, his calendar, and even on the dial of his telephone.

"Been in Perth long?"

No, I said. I had just flown at great expense and enormous personal inconvenience from America via New Zealand to join him at his desk here in a big building off the Mitchell Freeway, on the outskirts of Perth, Western Australia. He made no comment on this, didn't even make a note on his clean pad; so I asked him about the Elvis pictures.

He smiled – glad that I had asked. He said, "I just fell for him."

He turned his gaze onto the snipped-out and yellowing pictures of the doomed American singer. In the long silence that ensued I wondered whether I should ask another question. Then the boy looked at me, as though remembering where he was.

"Well, where shall we begin?" he said smoothly.

It was not a rhetorical question, so I said, "Have you read anything I've written?"

"No," he said with hearty confidence – it was as though he was boasting.

"Perhaps you saw the movie of *The Mosquito Coast?*"

"Oh, yes. I liked that." And he doodled on the pad.

"Now you can read the book!" I said, and felt I had made a breakthrough.

"No. I'll never read that book. Because I really liked the movie. I mean, I liked it too much. What if I read the book and didn't like it?"

I was staring at him, but he had leaned over urgently to divulge a confidence.

"Then the movie would be spoiled for me," he said, and tapped his pad. "It's too much of a risk."

"Too much of a risk. I see."

We got nowhere. Perhaps there was nowhere to get? I turned the conversation to Elvis, and we chatted about him.

The young man saw me to the door and asked me the only literary question of the interview.

"How do you get your characters? You just think them up?"

"Sometimes I think them up," I said. "And sometimes they appear before my eyes."

"Good on yer!"

These clumsy encounters sometimes left me feeling alienated and depressed. That night I was the guest speaker at a literary dinner at the Fremantle Town Hall, a lovely gilded building – like many in this beautifully preserved harbor town – put up to celebrate Queen Victoria's Jubilee in 1896. I felt wobbly with sleeplessness and I began to worry that I would burst into tears if anyone mentioned my wife.

Almost the first thing anyone asked me at the Town Hall was, "So you didn't come with your wife!"

I went to the men's room and sighed and almost sobbed, and then I washed my face and joined the others at the head table. I thought, *I am the shakiest person in this entire room and I'm the one who has to get up and speak.*

The woman on my left said, "Roald Dahl was here last month with his wife."

I went quiet. The meal was served. Four hundred and fifty people, all talking at once, and drinking, and having a wonderful time. Looking at them and hearing their laughter I lost my appetite.

The woman on my right said that she worked in a bookstore and that I was one of her favorite authors. She said, "You should write some short stories!"

Was this another Australian leg-pull? I said, "I've written some."

"Why don't you publish them?"

Australians are famous for being familiarly sarcastic in this obvious way, but in my solemnity I became very literal.

"I did."

"I mean publish them in a book."

"I've published four collections. About eighty stories."

The woman on my left said that she had lived in Perth for about fifteen years.

"It seems very nice," I said. "Fremantle is very pretty, and Perth reminds me of an American city in the Pacific Northwest. All this clean air."

"I hate it," she said. "This is like another planet. The people in Perth are so strange. I can't describe it. I felt happier in Africa, among Africans."

The next sound I heard was a man clearing his throat loudly into a microphone, and enthusiastically introducing me.

I did not have a prepared speech. I made some remarks about traveling in general and I spoke anecdotally about China, which was the subject of one of the books I was supposed to be promoting. This sort of speechifying is an awkward business. You feel you are being scrutinized, like someone looking for work. You feel that you are standing here talking your head off so that at the end of it they will say, *He seems an awful nice bloke, Fred. Let's buy his book.*

As I stood there, speaking, I noticed a large man lurch out of his chair at a table at the back of the hall. He still had a glass in his hand, but he put it down as he staggered forward. He was well over six feet tall and very heavy – fat as a poddy, as he himself might have put it. He wore a long overcoat, and there was anger in the way he moved towards me – for that indeed was his direction. The hall was so spacious that it was quite a while before anyone else saw him. I watched him advancing upon me, as I spoke about the death penalty in China. And now a woman, much smaller than he, took hold of his arm and tried to restrain him. The way he tipped her over and dragged her told me that he was an engine of determination.

Was he going to throw up? Was he going to shout? Perhaps he was going to attack me?

I faltered and stopped speaking when he broke free of the woman and stood menacing me before all the diners. He thrust his fingers at me, making obscene gestures and gargling, while the woman – surely an embarrassed companion? – heaved herself at his coat.

"You're a wanker, mate!" he said. "You're a fucking wanker!"

There were hisses of distress and clucks of disapproval from the uneasy audience. Yet no one rose to eject him. Only that tiny tenacious woman was doing anything – now she was dragging him sideways, as he fought to shake his fat fingers at me.

By this time I had abandoned any pretense of continuing my talk, and I simply waited for him to rush forward and bash me and throttle me in front of the Fremantle Literary Dinner. I prayed that the woman tugging at him would be strengthened. My prayer was answered, as she pulled the huge brute to the door. Then he was gone. But not for long. A moment later, like the corpse that springs alive to scare you in the horror movie, he lurched powerfully through the door and shouted, "You fucking wanker!" And he was dragged away once again.

"People like that call the Chinese 'chinks' and say they have awful manners," I improvised nervously. I mumbled some more and then I abandoned the effort.

*He was just drunk*, people said later. *Probably hates books. His missus made him come to the dinner. Probably thought you were boring. Couldn't take any more of it.*

One recent migrant explained to me, *They're pretty frank, the Aussies. They don't mind telling you to fuck off if they don't like you. I mean, they'll just look at you and say, "Get stuffed" – right to your face.*

Another said, *I had my eye on that big bloke. I was watching him. Hey, I could have handled him. I've done martial arts.*

I did not dare to confess that I had been afraid, and that I had fully expected him to attack me. His being drunk didn't seem like much of an explanation in a country where most of the men seemed drunk most of the time.

I heard even odder things, as I sat at a table and signed copies of my books. It is impossible to anticipate the oblique and nervous utterances of readers jostling. *I thought you were taller*, they say. *I thought you were younger. When did you shave off your beard?* or *My husband and I are going to India next month – can you recommend an inexpensive hotel in Darjeeling?* or *You should use a word processor,* or *You're my mother's favorite author – will you come to her birthday party? It's Tuesday.*

A scowling woman, with the face of an emu, stared me down at Fremantle Town Hall and shook a copy of my book at me.

"I've never read anything by you," she said. "This better be good."

Another peered at me pityingly and said, "Why do you hate Australians?"

And while more people filed past, with books for a signature, or with *non sequiturs*, a man stood just behind me and breathed into my ear, "You're pissed off, aren't you? Admit it – go on. You hate doing this. You hate these people. You're pissed off."

I turned to him and said, "Friend, this is my living."

When I was done I walked the windy streets of Fremantle, and it did seem to me a very precarious place, half a town on a little surfy strand, between the ocean and the desert. White Australia.

"Where are the Aboriginals?" I asked any number of people in the days that followed.

Most of them shrugged, some of them jerked a thumb in the direction of the outback.

"In Woop Woop," one said, explaining that it was the generic name for the uttermost place in Australia.

After that, whenever anyone asked me where I really wanted to go in Australia, I said, "Woop Woop."

But first I had to finish visiting these cities. I went to Melbourne by plane, two thousand miles away, across the great Australian emptiness, where Australians say nothing at all lives.

*They call this the Paris end of Collins Street*, someone said to me in Melbourne. Many people told me how European-looking it was: the brownstone churches, the venerable railway stations and the marshaling yard and the trams and the soot.

But no, I didn't think so. It was more spacious, much younger, and had more the aspect of a city in the American Mid-West. European cities have a damaged and repaired look. Melbourne's most American feature was that it was obviously a city that had never been bombed.

My various encounters in Perth had given me pause, just as though I had been stung. I became wary. And after that, my overriding feeling, facing a large seated crowd of people in Australia, any gathering at all, or dealing with these people in banks or restaurants or on street corners or in taxis – buying something or just passing the time of day – my feeling, as I say, or to be more precise, my fear, was that they were not being polite to me but simply restraining themselves. Nothing personal. They just wanted to hit me.

Australians (it seemed to me) were people who appeared to be at ease when in fact they were simply controling their emotions, and being on good behavior, because the slightest relaxation of this stiffened vigilance would have them howling. They were like people who had only recently been domesticated, like youths in their late teens sitting among adults, rather upright and formal and wooden, because as soon as they loosen their grip or have one beer too many they slip into leering familiarity and all hell breaks loose. What you took to be good manners was simply the forced, self-conscious behavior of someone holding on. Much of the time they had the exaggerated and unconvincing manners of drunks pretending to be sober.

A friend of mine had emigrated in the sixties to Monash ("The Farm" – it was a country of fond nicknames), a university near Melbourne. He told me, "Australians are aggressive and envious, but they'll end up liking you."

In Melbourne I saw my first Aboriginal. He was at a street corner, pushing the button at a crosswalk, waiting for the *Walk* sign to click on before he could venture across. I watched him from a little distance and wondered why I found this solitary man so strange. It was not his smooth face or matted hair, his lopsided posture or broken shoes. It was the very fact of his being there on the curb. Because there were no cars on the street. Because it was his country. Because this nomad was seeking permission to walk.

"They hate the Abos, really hate them," a newish immigrant from the north of England said to me. "The things they say amaze me – the hate, I mean. Me, I don't care one way or the other. Sometimes I look at them and feel really sorry for them, though –"

People talked about them; and I looked for them; but they seemed not to exist. They were less than shadows. They were lost in the crowd, and those Aboriginals who had become city-dwellers lived in locations that were given a wide berth by everyone else.

My question, "Are there many Aboriginals here?" was usually answered by an Australian saying, "Too bloody many." But where were they?

Meanwhile, I was the one who was supposed to be answering the questions.

"With all this traveling of yours doesn't your wife miss you?"

*My wife and I are calling it quits.*

"Yes, I think she does," I said.

"You go to such strange places, how do you stay so healthy?"

*As a matter of fact, I might have cancer.*

"I never drink the water," I said.

"Don't you ever get diarrhea in these countries?"

*Constantly.*

"No. Usually constipation," I said.

"You're so cheerful. But your books are so depressing at times."

*Exactly. Because I feel alienated and depressed. Particularly now.*

"Are you planning to write a book about Australia?"

*Yes.*

"What do I know about Australia?" I said.

Melbourne, settled and social, looked especially prosperous in bad weather, its buildings darkened by rain and its streets shining with the reflections of busy crowds. There, as elsewhere, the papers were full of harsh self-analysis. The Australian image abroad is one of swaggering confidence and contented good humor, but in Australia itself there is nagging self-criticism, a constant theme of *What's wrong with us?* The visitor is frequently asked for a frank assessment of the country. If you praise it they jeer and call you a poof or a gussie (their language abounds with abusive expressions for gays: quince, queen, spurge, pood, sonk, and Are you Arthur or Martha? are just a few). What most Australians seem to want in the way of a response is something funny and familiar, such as *You bloody diggers are rough as pig's breakfast, but that's what I like.*

I did my lunchtime spiel for 500 people in Melbourne's Regent Ballroom, as they tucked into their meal of lamb and potatoes. I wondered whether a crowd this size would have turned up in an American city to hear me stammer. This was an odd crowd, my Australian readers, ranging from very elderly fiction buffs and railway enthusiasts, who invited me to tea, or to trips on train junkets, to furtive youths with tobacco-stained fingers and tattoos, who leaned over, reeking of dope, and proffering dog-eared paperbacks. Two of these younger readers were musicians, who handed me an invitation to their concert that night.

*Dan Loneway and the Fellow Travellers, debut gig and record launch at Dan's Hashish Centre – serving the best Nepalese Hash and Ganja – Wed. Free.*

"I love to see young people reading," someone said, as Dan Loneway packed his books into his Balinese shoulder-bag and glided out on a cloud of smoke.

"I seem to have a very wide spectrum of readers in this country," I said.

When it came time to head for Sydney there was an airline pilots' strike, and no planes were flying.

"This strike is shocking," a man said to me. "This place is ridiculous. We're going down the gurgler."

"You're the great railway traveler," a reader told me. "You should have taken the Indian-Pacific from Perth to Melbourne across the Nullabor Plain. This is your chance to take the train to Sydney."

I had two objections. One, I had vowed that I would not board a train in the Pacific. Two, I was in a hurry to begin my real trip, going walkabout in Woop Woop and paddling beyond. I was still reading Malinowski's *The Sexual Life of Savages* and was playing with the idea of going to New Guinea after Australia.

But I kept careful notes on the people who interviewed me, and I asked them questions, too. I had the idea of writing a little portrait about everyone who was writing about me. Theroux has a rather strange taste in leisurewear, an English interviewer, in a stained tie and a checked shirt and a rumpled sweater, had written, filling me with an urge to have the last word. I wondered what these frank Aussies would say about me and my clothes. Several of them had asked what these two canvas bags in my room were, and when I said, "A boat," they simply made ambiguous noises that put me on my guard. Perhaps this publicity-tour prologue was also part of my trip?

When I finally decided to take the train I was warned against it and urged to take another instead – "a lovely old atmospheric train." Well, I didn't say so, but they are frequently the worst ones. I didn't want atmosphere, I wanted a train with privacy and comfort, and when I boarded this sleeper I was happier than I had been since arriving in Australia.

This train had the sort of dining car that had just about disappeared in the rest of the First World: tables, chairs, clinking cutlery, and servers hurrying back and forth with platters of food on tin trays. The menu of the day was tomato soup followed by grilled flounder and two vegetables, and stodgy pudding for afters. No one ever ate this satisfyingly on an airplane. My waitress was Lydia, a small brisk woman with a pencil jammed into her hair, who had recently arrived in Australia from Poland, but was already using Aussie vowels and converted the simple word *now* into a triphthong. She intended to stay for ever, she said.

And at the next table a man was offering a bag of candy to his son and saying, "Want some jolly boins?"

Mark Twain took this train in 1896, on his lecture tour through Australia. He remarked on the good berths and the bad coffee (he suggested improving it by adding sheep-dip). He spent much of his trip staring out of the window, trying to get a glimpse of a kangaroo or an Aboriginal. At about the same time, Dame Nellie ("Sing 'em muck") Melba was a frequent traveler on this line, going back and forth for concert engagements. She took her last trip, too, as she was carried in her coffin on this train from Sydney to Melbourne.

It had always been a busy line. Before the promotion of Canberra to the nation's capital, Melbourne was the administrative center, and I was told by older Australian civil servants that a great deal of government business was transacted on these railway carriages. One man told me that just a few years ago prostitutes worked these coaches, turning tricks in the sleeping-cars – the whole train heaved with bag-swinging chippies, while their look-out men – called gigs and cockatoos – warned them of the approach of the train conductors.

So I went head-first, horizontally, 500 miles in my swaying berth, through Euroa, Benalla, Wangaratta and Wodonga, and across Father Millawah, the Murray River, to Wagga Wagga, Junee, Cootamundra, Yass, Goulburn and Mittagong. Towards dawn I lifted my windowshade and looked at the bush – the stringybarks and the blue gums and the mulga trees at the edge of pebbly yellow gullies. The land was stony and eroded, and when the train slowed down, the bungalows began, and the first large settlements and suburbs – Campbelltown with its jammed level-crossing and inevitably a sign saying *Trusses*, and then Liverpool, Lidcomb, Homebush, and finally, Sydney.

"Mr Theroux, I am your butler."

This was the Presidential Suite of the Regent, thirty-eight floors above the Sydney Opera House, facing east to the mouth of the magnificent harbor and beyond to the Tasman Sea. My butler was an upright man, with a hint of Oz in his middle-European accent, and he wore a white bow tie, a white bib-like dickey, a black tailcoat and striped trousers. He had delivered me my luggage and was holding my collapsible boat, a bag in each hand.

"May I unpack your bags and put your things away?"

My camping clothes for Woop Woop, my kayaking shorts and T-shirts, my sleeping-bag, my water bag, my tent, my cookstove and pots, my two-part paddle, first-aid kit, compass, bilge pump, insect repellent, and assorted tools.

"Shall I start with these?"

He heaved my kayak bags over to the closet, and began fumbling with the knots on the drawstrings.

I said, "That's not necessary."

He straightened himself and said politely, "I am at your service. If there is anything you need, just ring eight."

There was a bottle of Dom Perignon in an ice bucket with a pleasant note from the general manager. In the living-room – I had four rooms altogether – there were baskets of fruit and more flowers. There was a drinks trolly, with bottles of scotch, bourbon, port, vodka, sherry, gin, each wearing an identifying silver necklace. A bowl of candy, another of nuts. And the best touch of all, a powerful telescope.

I trained the telescope onto Sydney Harbor, conning east to the Pacific. It was the most beautiful harbor I had ever seen in my life, long and wide, spangled with sunshine, and filled with coves and bays. I focused on the little white tiles on the Opera House roof, and farther to Port Jackson and the ferries and sailboats and the mansions and tower blocks on the cliffs of the gorgeous bays, the breakers smashing against the low black headland at the harbor mouth at North Head. Down below me at Circular Quay, where the ferries docked, commuters mingled with guitarists and conjurers, and an Aboriginal sat with his knees together on a bench on Sydney Cove, nearer the Harbor Bridge. I toyed with the frivolous idea of writing a detailed profile of Sydney and its people by sitting here in this penthouse drinking champagne and looking at the city through this telescope.

The butler came and went, taking away laundry to be done, bringing me food and faxes, and rehearsing his Jeeves role for the benefit of the reporters.

"I was in this room once before," a woman said, "to do Lord Lichfield."

And there were the standard questions: "Doesn't your wife miss you?" one said, and another, "I'd like to ask you about the novel you wrote about yourself—"

I spoke at the literary luncheon, another ballroom, another meal, another head table, but in spite of all the good-will, I wished with all my heart that I could simply sit there and eat and listen to someone else. By that time I had read enough of Lawrence's *Kangaroo* to discuss its presumptions about Australia, but the only questions people asked me were about the railway trains.

"I look like you," a man said afterward at the book-signing.

I said, "Do you?"

He was middle height and rather Latin-looking, with a beaky nose, scraped-down hair and tinted glasses, and he frowned at me.

"I very seldom read books," he went on, "but about fifteen years ago when I looked at your picture on your book jacket and realized that I resembled you I bought the book. As a result I have read every one of your books. And I still look like you, don't you think so?"

I said, "You're much better looking."

He said, "May I take you to lunch?"

I had other plans, I said, but that was the first of many invitations, often scribbled on a card, or in a note that was pressed into my hand –

   – *Come to dinner . . .*
   – *My wife and I would like to have you round for drinks . . .*
   – *If you're at a loose end please call me . . .*
   – *I'd like to show you Sydney . . .*
   – *May I interview you this weekend? It might be fun . . .*
   – *You are the funniest man I've ever read. Please don't waste your comic gift.*
    *Write a book about Australia . . .*

They were eagerly, spontaneously hospitable. But I kept to myself. I bought more camping equipment. I went to concerts and an opera, *The Pearl Fishers*, at the Opera House; and I drank champagne and searched the city through my telescope. *You're the funniest man . . .* Now and then I thought about my life, about cancer and divorce, and became maudlin.

The room was my refuge. Of course, my first experience of such luxury – isn't everyone's? – was to wallow in it and wolf it all, gobble the fruit and the chocolate mints, drink the champagne, unwrap the soap, smell the flowers, take long bubble baths with the cobalt-colored bath crystals. But after a day or so, I became abstemious. I woke early and ordered porridge and green tea and a grapefruit. I spent the day doing publicity ("How long does it take to write a book?") and when I returned to the security of this penthouse I read Malinowski and studied maps of the Trobriands. I annotated travel guides to the Solomon Islands, and Tonga and Vanuatu. How odd, I thought, to be reading about the vast and dangerous estuarine crocodiles of Guadalcanal and North Queensland, and the orgiastic yam harvest in Kiriwina, as I sat here in the Lord Lichfield suite sipping champagne.

One night I was at my telescope when the phone rang. "It's a call from London," the operator said.

I said hello but there was no greeting or salutation from the other end.

"I just got your medical report." It was a familiar voice, distorted by distance and emotion. "You don't have cancer."

"Thank God for that."

The contours of the harbor and every object in it collapsed before my squinting eye and the odd liquefied light of my tears.

A button came off my shirt, and I sewed it on myself, rather liking the thought of such a mundane chore amid all this luxury. At eight the maids came to turn down the bed. They placed a bottle of cognac and a snifter and a bottle of mineral water on the bedside table. I drank the water. I read until I fell asleep, and I woke, exhausted by my dreams.

With breakfast, the butler brought me messages on a silver salver.

– *If you're at a loose end, please call . . .*
– *May I take you hacking? My horse-farm is not far . . .*
– *My husband urged me to get in touch with you . . .*

But I was happy with my telescope, and never went nearer any of these people. One day I went out, past the swimming-pool and the five-star restaurant, and rented a beach chair at Bondi Beach, and I ate fish and chips among the surfers hanging five on the screamers and greenies and watched by lounging surf bunnies baking their bare tits before the startled gaze of Japanese tourists, who gave a convincing demonstration of never having seen such tits before, crowding out of their pausing tour bus, and madly snapping pictures of them with all the concentration they would have given photographing prize jumbo melons. Elsewhere on the beach, there were weightlifters and big hairy men and sufferers from melanoma. Bondi, something of a cliché in Australia, is a lovely beach. The people who go there praise it and defend it; the ones who stay away claim that it is unsafe and dirty, and that if the undertow doesn't yank you under for ever, you'll gag on the raw sewage.

I was happy to return to my luxury suite in this penthouse with my camping equipment. But deeper than the sense of isolation I felt in all this luxury was a feeling of vulnerability, verging on paranoia, every time I left it. I couldn't wait to get back to the paintings, the sofas, the champagne and the cool fruit, and my boat. I liked this comfort and quiet solitude. Sluttish comfort is one of the most corrupting things of all, and it easily becomes a dependency, even an addiction. At first I had wanted to share it; and then I saw it as my refuge and wished to keep it for myself; finally, I regarded it as a necessity, and I dreaded losing it. After even a short experience of luxury, anything less is like punishment.

Obviously it was time to leave.

In Brisbane, a celebrated trial, "The Vampire Murderers," had riveted the city's attention. "Vampire" was not newspaper hyperbole. Witnesses in Brissie testified on oath that three youthful lesbians who spent their evenings sucking blood from each other's arms had grown tired of this tame domesticity and gone out, abducted a man and killed him by stabbing him in the back. His throat had been slashed and one of the women had drunk his blood. "I have fed on him," one of the women said – she was grossly fat and had piggy cheeks and a crewcut and was eventually convicted of the crime.

The riverside city was large and sunny, but my impression was of a great sadness in this sunshine and heat. Or was it me? The interviewers were more aggressive and blunter.

"I wonder about all these crazy people you meet," one reporter said. "They seem a little improbable."

"More improbable than that book that just appeared here, called *Australian Thinkers*?" I said. "More improbable than your monthly magazine, *Australian Gourmet*? More improbable than your vampires?"

He squinted at me as though I had unmercifully bowled him a googly. It was odd. They could be so thin-skinned. The very mention of a funny name like Wagga Wagga could make them cross.

A note of archness had crept into some women's questions.

"In what ways are you different from the main character in your novel?"

"He is a sexual athlete," I said.

"And how do you know you're not?" the woman said, tossing her hair.

Several of them asked me, "What does your wife think of your book?"

Exercising restraint, I asked, "Is that a literary question?"

My throat ached from all this talk. My eyeballs felt swollen and boiled. The interviewers went on twitting me. I sat in empty studios that smelled of musty rugs, broadcasting my opinions to Hobart, Tasmania. My roomboy called me "Mr Thorax." When I confided to a journalist that I had no intention of writing a book about Australia, but only wanted to go walkabout in Woop Woop, and paddle my collapsible boat in North Queensland, she said, "If the sharks don't get you, the crocodiles will."

Everyone in a jeering, mocking, we-know-better way warned me of the dangers in the outback – of the snakes and lizards, of the biting flies, of the heat and the blinding sun and the thorns and the terrible roads. The coast was much worse, they said: there were sea-snakes, and sharks, there were sea-wasps, poisonous box-jellyfish, venomous stonefish, and seagoing crocodiles fourteen feet long. They warned me of the plants and the wildlife.

There is a great fear of natural things in Australia. But no one mentions the drunks, who are everywhere and are a great deal more dangerous.

There were many croc stories in Cairns, my last city in white Australia, but there were even more drunks, and drunks gave me the most persistent and colorful warnings.

"You have to carry a gun and shoot their nose off," one man said. "Bullets won't penetrate their thick skin."

"If you see one, *shout* at it," another said.

"Once they submerge you you're dead," yet another said. "They can't swallow you. They come up under you and whack you with their tail, and then they hold you under in their jaws and drown you. When your body begins to rot they eat you."

The more people warned me, the more determined I was to set off – first into the fly-blown outback I remembered from Patrick White's *Voss*, and the Nic Roeg movie *Walkabout*, and then up to North Queensland, beyond Cooktown, to a part of the coast that was nearer New Guinea than Sydney, a part of the map which no one had written about.

For some people Cairns was the outback. It was not, but it was on the very edge, and it was a pleasant place. It seemed to me an overgrown town on a muddy estuary. It had become prosperous because of its wonderful weather and its boat charters to the Great Barrier Reef for scuba divers and snorkelers. Most of its signs were bilingual, English and Japanese. It had the greatest concentration of shops selling T-shirts and opals of any I saw in Australia.

From the publicity point of view, this was my last stand. I was interviewed by seventeen-year-old Sandra from the *Cairns Post*. She was nervous, she said she had not read anything I had written, she was serving what she called her cadet-ship at the paper, she said, "I've never interviewed anyone before." She was stumped for questions, so we talked about her family. She said she loved her parents, her new baby sister, her house in Cairns, her bedroom with her posters and her records. She said, "I'd hate to go to Brisbane to work. Then I'd have to leave home." I decided not to disillusion her with stories of my traveling. Later, I gave what I felt was a spirited talk at another literary lunch, and when I described how the Chinese government frequently sentenced thieves, arsonists and racketeers to death an older woman in the front row grinned and burst into applause.

Queensland is known for its conservative views and its gun-owning rednecks. Politically, it resembles a state in the American Deep South, and with these attitudes it even produces similar crops – tobacco, sugar cane, cotton, bananas, mangoes. The farther north you go in Queensland the tougher the views. And in Cairns, as in the South before Martin Luther King, there are somber gatherings of benighted-looking blacks –

odd, soft, misshapen folks, with soft pretty eyes and long lashes. Even the fattest of them have skinny shanks and all of them look bowlegged. None looks alike and they shamble around in town clothes and the dusty slouch hats locally known as Cunnamulla cartwheels, the broad-brimmed diggers' delight.

From a distance Aboriginals were a menacing smudge at the road-side; but up close they seemed oblique and fearful or else very shy, and their clothes seldom seemed right for their odd shapes – they were either rail-thin or very fat, and many were barefoot. None of them ever came to my lectures. They were never at the literary lunches. They never entered the bookstores – not even the bookstores that featured Aboriginal literature. They never interviewed me. I saw them, but they never returned my gaze. It was as though they did not exist. Some were not locals at all, but rather Thursday Islanders from the Torres Strait.

"More like your blokes," a man in Cairns told me, meaning that these smooth-faced Thursday Islanders were like black Americans, and when I asked why he claimed this was so, he said, "Well, they're further down the tree, aren't they?"

I had been traveling in white Australia. I wanted to see more of the country, if for no other reason than to look deeper into the lives of the Aboriginals. Now that I was done with this waffling I could go walkabout.

# 4

## *Walkabout in Woop Woop*

Ask white Australians what "walkabout" means and they will tell you it is an Aboriginal's furious fugue, shambling off the job or out of the shelter of the humpy, and heading into the outback. It is a sudden departure, a bout of madness almost – after which the Aboriginal chases his tail. But is that so?

Back in Sydney, I looked for an Aboriginal to ask. "Don't call them Abos," people cautioned me – not that I ever called them that – but privately they muttered a dozen or more different names for them, of which "boong," "bing," and "murky" were just a few. Yet those Australians who were bigoted were completely impartial: "a boong with boots on" was a Japanese and "a yank boong" was a black American.

Searching for Aboriginals in Australia was a bit like bird-watching. Birds are everywhere, but only real birders see them clearly. Without warning, bird experts lean slightly forward, then stiffen and whisper, "Yellow-vented bulbul," and you see nothing but fluttering leaves. In a similar spirit, making a point of it, developing a knack, I began to spot Aboriginals. They were so often camouflaged by gum trees or splotches of shadow. They were frequently motionless, usually in the shade, often in city parks, nearly always under trees. There were many.

"So poor," as the saying went, "they were licking paint off the fence."

Perhaps they were visible to everyone, but if so, Australians never pointed them out. I began to think that Aboriginals were only visible to those people who were looking for them. I kept track of my sightings, like a birder.

Mark Twain was in Australia for more than a month in 1895 and regretted the fact that he never saw either a kangaroo or an Aboriginal.

"We saw birds, but not a kangaroo," Twain wrote, in one of the Australian chapters of his round-the-world tour, *Following the Equator*, "not an emu, not an ornithorhyncus, not a lecturer, not a native. Indeed, the land seemed quite destitute of game. But I have misused the word native. In Australia it is applied to Australian-born whites only. I should have said that we saw no Aboriginals – no 'blackfellows.' And to this day I have never seen one."

"I would walk thirty miles to see a stuffed one," he sighs towards the end of his Australian tour.

It seemed to me that the people and the problem were unavoidable. There was a tidy Aboriginal settlement in La Perouse, at Botany Bay, near Sydney's airport. I walked through it one wet afternoon with a man from Sydney who had told me about it, and we looked at the hundred or so prefab houses – down Elaroo Avenue, up Adina, across to Goolagong Place. There were very few people outside and, seeing us, some Aboriginals who were gathered around their motorcycles mounted the machines and roared away, scowling into the wind.

"They're strange people," Tony said. He was Italian – first-generation Australian. He was small, the sort of man Australians describe as being so short he had to stand on his head to get his foot into a stirrup. He didn't hate Aboriginals, he said, but he pitied them – and he didn't understand them. "They never fix anything. If they break something it stays broken. If they knock a tooth out they don't bother to replace it."

Certainly there was a dark fatalism about many of the Aboriginals I met; sometimes it made them seem sad, at other times it made them seem indestructible.

"There's no trouble here," Tony said. "It's not like Redfern, where there are pitched battles with the police."

Many of the Aboriginals in the Sydney district of Redfern were notoriously scruffy. "Rough as guts," said the white Australians – these could be last month's immigrant Turks, or last year's Sicilians, or the pompous people who snobbishly boasted about their convict ancestry – and they went on to generalize about Aboriginals on the basis of these rather derelict urban specimens. The Aboriginals aroused pity or disgust, they provoked feelings of violence or mockery. They were joked about, especially by schoolchildren.

    *Q.* Why are the garbage bins in Redfern made of glass?
    *A.* So that the Abos can window-shop.
    *Q.* What do you call an Abo with a stick through his bum?
    *A.* A choc wedge (fudgicle).
    *Q.* What do you call an Abo in a limo?
    *A.* A thief.

Everyone had an opinion and no one had a solution.

I tried to reach Patrick White, Australia's greatest living writer, who was a vocal advocate of Aboriginal rights. He had created a memorable portrait of an Aboriginal, Alf Dubbo, in his novel *Riders in the Chariot* – Alf's walkabout, his vast vivid paintings, his confusion, his culture shock, his drinking, his martyrdom. What about the word "walkabout" as a sudden departure, I wanted to ask him; indeed, what about *Walkabout*, the classic film by Nicolas Roeg, which – with Mr White's novels – had been my only previous experience of Australia? I was having trouble with the meaning of the word and wished to leave white Australia for the distant outback that it summed up in the name Woop Woop. I felt that Patrick White could help me. In his advancing and opinionated old age he had been pronouncing on most subjects.

"I can't meet Paul Theroux. I am too ill to meet celebrities," the Nobel Prize winner said, from his home in a Sydney suburb.

He died two days later – speaking of sudden departures – and the Australian obituarists went to work on him. Nothing made national traits more emphatic than a victory in an international sport or the death of a prominent citizen. In this case, the obituarists kicked Patrick White's corpse from Maggoty Gully to Cootamundra. There was almost no evidence that any of these people had actually read the man's novels. The vindictive philistines on Rupert Murdoch's national paper *The Australian* put a portrait of Patrick White's old enemy, A. D. Hope, on the front page instead of a picture of the man himself, and in any number of other papers White was depicted as a meddlesome old poofter.*

Never mind his novels, what about the dreadful things he had said about Australia? True, he had been characteristically crisp.

"After I returned to this country," Mr White had written, "one of the most familiar sounds was the heavy plop-plop of Australian bullshit."

In a public lecture he had called Bob Hawke, the prime minister, "one of the greatest bull artists ever," and said he had a hairstyle like a cockatoo. He had been cruel about the British Royal Family – "Queen

---

*From the Sydney *Daily Telegraph Mirror*, 21 February 1991: "A magistrate has outraged police by ruling that it is acceptable to describe them as 'f— poofters.' . . . On Tuesday, magistrate Pat O'Shane dismissed a charge of offensive language against Geoffrey Allan Langham, 43. Sitting at Lismore on the State's north coast, Ms O'Shane said the words 'f— poofters' were not as upsetting as the term 'collateral damage,' used by military officials to describe human casualties. In the past three months, the NSW magistrates have ruled it acceptable to call police 'pigs' and to use the word 'shit' in public."

Betty" and "The Royal Goons." He had ridiculed Dame Joan Sutherland.

But on the day the Nobel laureate was cooling quietly in his coffin in Centennial Park, La Stupenda was being draped with paper streamers, the sort you fling at ships. They were strung out from all tiers of the Sydney Opera House, and her vast preponderant bulk could have been mistaken for an ocean liner as, after her final bow in Meyerbeer's religious farrago, "The Huge Nuts" (as I heard it jocosely called), she said she was proud to be an Australian, sang "There's No Place Like Home," announced that she would never sing again, and flew back to her mansion in Switzerland. It was all walkabouts that week.

Reminding myself of the details in the movie, I used *Walkabout* to guide me around the city, and beyond it to the outback, because that is precisely the direction of the movie's plot.

No one I met in Australia or elsewhere who had seen *Walkabout* had forgotten the film's power or denied that they had been enchanted by it. After being released in 1969, it soon vanished, and had never been re-released. It was not available on video anywhere in the world. It was never shown on television. It languished, the victim of Hollywood in-fighting, in some obscure and spiteful limbo of litigation.

Yet it still existed as a notable conversation piece in the "Did-you-ever-see?" oral tradition among movie buffs, and it endures that way, because it has a simple tellable story. Those who have seen *Walkabout* always speak of their favorite scenes – the opening, a salt-white tower block in Sydney with its swimming-pool smack against the harbor; the frenzied picnic in the outback where the father tries and fails to kill his two children; the father's sudden suicide against a burning VW; the desperate kids faced with an immensity of desert; the girl (Jenny Agutter, aged sixteen) peeling off her school uniform; the shot of an ant made gigantic in front of tiny distant kids – and every other creature in the outback crossing their path – snakes, lizards, birds, beetles, kangaroos, koalas, camels; the discovery of water under the quondong tree, after which the ordeal turns into a procession into paradise, as they all swim naked together in the pools of sunlit oases; the close call with the rural ockers; the wrecked house and its curios; the lovestruck Aboriginal's dance, ending in his suicide; the madman in the dainty apron in the ghost town howling at the children "Don't touch that!" – and no rescue, no concrete ending, only a return to the tower block (it seems to be years later) on a note of regret.

And that is the film, really, almost all except the spell it cast on me. In a seemingly modest way it encompassed the whole of Australia – nearly all its variations of landscape, its incomparable light, its drunks and desperadoes, all its bugs – from its most beautiful city to its hot red center. A work of art, and especially a film or a novel, with a strong sense of place is a summing-up, fixing a landscape once and for all in the imagination.

The director, Nicolas Roeg, was an adventurer who relished the difficulties and improvisations of film-making on location. His was a triumph over mud, dust, rain, heat, impassable roads and deserters from the crew.

"A few went apeshit in the night and started smashing things," he had told me. "They couldn't take the isolation. One of the toughest sparks [electricians] deserted. The grip freaked out. The cook went crazy one night, and crept off and sat on a chair near the airstrip. This was in the outback. He flew off without speaking. It was his fear of all that empty space."

The movie seemed to me to contain the essential Australia, even its bizarre and rowdy humor – most notably in the scene in an abandoned mining town, miles from anywhere, where a loony man, hanging on, stands in a ruined building wearing an apron and ironing a pair of pants.

"It doesn't have Ayers Rock in it," Roeg said. "Everyone expected that it would. I was determined to make a film in the Australian outback that didn't show Ayers Rock. But it has everything else."

And it was the first feature film in which an Aboriginal played a starring role. David Gulpilil had had no training as an actor – had probably never seen a film in his life. He had been about fifteen years old, a dancer on his Aboriginal reserve somewhere in the north, in Arnhemland.

I wanted to look at Aboriginal Australia. Going on the trail of *Walkabout*, in Woop Woop – the remote outback – meant going walkabout in the Aboriginal sense of the word – setting off in search of old visions and sacred sites.

The Botanic Gardens in Sydney were easy enough to find, and it is possible to sit under the spreading tree where the little boy hurries towards Woolloomooloo Bay after school in one of the early sequences. But his home on the harbor, the tower block with the swimming-pool, was harder for me to locate. I knew it lay next to the water, and there is a glimpse of Sydney Harbor Bridge in the distance, but there are no other landmarks.

Thinking the tower block might be at the far edge of the harbor, I took the Manly Ferry and on the way scrutinized the shoreline: south side going out, north side on the return. Any visitor to Sydney would be well advised to take the Manly Ferry soon after arriving in the city, just to get the lie of the land. It is a long inexpensive ferry ride that takes in the entire length of the harbor, from Sydney's Circular Quay to distant Manly – an Edwardian township by the sea, with teashops and palm trees, its back turned to the harbor, and facing the breakers of a beautiful bay.

Manly's smug and tidy little houses have names like "Camelot" and "Woodside." The town was named by an early settler who regarded the local Aborigines as fine specimens of manhood. But no Aborigines are found there today. Manlyness in the municipal sense is the epitome of the Australian good life: a snug bungalow of warm bricks by the sea, with a privet hedge and a palm.

Here and there on Manly beach were delicate dying jellyfish, small and blue, and so thin, so bright, so finely shaped, fluttering on the sand, they reminded me of little hanks of Chinese silk. Beyond them, some boys were surfing the waves, which was appropriate, because the first surfing – body surfing – was done here at Manly around 1890 by an islander from the New Hebrides. (It was not until 1915 that surfboards were introduced to Australia, when the technique was demonstrated by the great Hawaiian surfer and Olympic swimmer, Duke Kahanamoku.)

Manlyites who commuted from here to their jobs in the city had the best of both worlds, but the despairing father in *Walkabout* was obviously not one of them. I walked from one end of Manly to the other and could not locate the white tower block. Nor was it apparent on any of the bays on the harbor.

"You're looking for a needle in a haystack," a woman on a bench said to me one day as I searched nearer the city, among the bobbing sailboats.

And she explained. In the twenty years since the film was made Sydney had become extremely prosperous – there were plenty of stylish tower blocks now, there were lots of swimming-pools by the sea. It might have been torn down, she said. That is another aspect of a movie with a strong sense of place: it is an era in history, it is the past.

I was told by Grahame Jennings, a Sydney movie producer who had helped *Walkabout* get made, that the tower block was out by Yarmouth Point, past Rushcutters Bay.

My taxi-driver was Cambodian, six years in Australia, where he had arrived as a political refugee ("I would have gone anywhere except China"), but less than a year behind the wheel. He had struggled to pass his driving test. And his knowledge of Sydney's streets was shaky. He agreed that he was somewhat handicapped as a cabbie. Australian passengers often berated him.

"They say 'You fucking stupid.' But I smile at them. I don't care. This is a nice country."

I roamed the harborside back streets, I detoured up Yarranabee Road and saw a familiar tower block – the one from the movie, with improvements; and beneath it, at the water's edge, the greeny-blue swimming-pool. I congratulated myself on this little piece of detection, but I was also thinking how lucky all these people were who lived around Sydney Harbor. Because of the jigs and jags of its contours it is one of the most extensive pieces of real estate in the world.

The taxi-driver who plucked me from Rushcutters Bay was an economic refugee from Pakistan. We talked about Islam, about the similar stories in the Old Testament and the Koran – Joseph (Yusof), Jonah (Yunis).

"This is the first time I have ever spoken of religion with one of my passengers," he said – he was pleased.

But this was merely ice-breaking on my part. I came to the point. Had he heard of Salman Rushdie?

In his monotonously sing-song Pakistani accent, he said, "Salman Rushdie must be punished with death."

"I don't agree with you," I said. I leaned forward, nearer his hairy ears. "And no one in this nice law-abiding country agrees with you."

"Rushdie is a bad man – devil, I should say."

"And you know why people in Australia don't agree with you?" He was still muttering, but what I said next shut him up. "Because they're not fanatics."

The man's bony hands tightened on the steering wheel, and when I got out of his taxi he gave me the evil eye.

"*Walkabout* was quietly released," Grahame Jennings told me. "I collected the reviews. Of the thirty-odd I saw from around the world, four were negative. Three of those negative reviews were written by Australian critics."

"Why Australians?" I asked.

"Tall poppy syndrome."

Anyone who spends even a little time in the country hears this odd phrase, which means simply that people who succeed in Australia – or who distinguish themselves in any way – can expect to be savagely attacked by envious fellow Australians. It is also used as a verb: to be "tall-poppied" means to be cut down to size. That was the reason that Patrick White, in spite of his Nobel Prize – or perhaps because of it – was spoken of as an insignificant and nagging old gussie. This merciless national trait is regarded as the chief reason for gifted Australians emigrating to countries where they are – or so they say – properly appreciated.

"'What right does this foreigner have to come and make a film about Australia?' was one criticism."

"That's ridiculous."

"'Too many contradictions about the geography in the film,' was another. 'You can't get to the outback by driving from Sydney –'"

But you can. You might be the desperate alcoholic father leaving Yarranabee Road with his kids, intending to shoot them, or you might be a visitor to Sydney with a rental car, yearning for the open spaces. In either case, you head up George Street and keep driving, first following signs for Parramatta. In this sprawl of sunburned bungalows, each one with its own lizards and its own dead hedges and its own peculiar-smelling lantana (but this bush usually smelled of cats); the discount stores and bad hotels and bottle shops and used-car lots with tacky flapping banners, through Emu Plains and Blacktown – almost until the road rises into the first wooded slopes of the Blue Mountains – you begin to understand the disgusted snarl with which people in Sydney always utter the phrase *the Western Suburbs*.

Ascending the escarpment that winds towards Katoomba, I was in a different landscape – mountainous, cool, green, with ravines and canyons, the gum trees having given over to pines. After these heights, it is a long slow descent to Lithgow, and not many miles farther on I felt I was truly in sunset country. Here, near Wallerawang on the Great Western Highway, less than two hours from Sydney, the proof of it: a big brown kangaroo, lying dead by the side of the road.

Dubbo, where Alf the Aboriginal in *Riders in the Chariot* could have come from, is two or three hours more, and Bourke four or five. But out there in the west of New South Wales – Bourke in one direction, Wilcannia in the other – you will have achieved your simple goal of driving from Sydney to the outback in a long day.

"Back o' Bourke" is an Australian expression for any out-of-the-way place, and there are dozens more – perhaps more euphemisms in Australia for remoteness (outback, wayback, back o' sunset, behind death o'day, Woop Woop, and so forth) than in any other language; but this is obviously because there is more remoteness in Australia than in most other countries – more empty space. These words are like little lonely cries of being lost, speaking of a solitude that is like exile on this huge island.

Somewhere before Dubbo I was distracted by bewitching names on the map and found myself detouring to places like Wattle Flat or Oberon or Budgee Budgee (turn right at Mudgee), just to look at the small round hills, the frisky sheep and the gum trees. It is hard to imagine anywhere on earth so pretty and peaceful as these hamlets in Australia's hinterland, green and cool in springtime September.

I was halfway to Woop Woop. I continued the rest of the way, to Alice Springs in the dead red center of the island of Australia, leaving my collapsible kayak behind in Sydney with my butler, who still believed the two big bags contained clothes.

I have usually yawned at travelers who describe landscapes from the window of a plane passing overhead, but the Australian landscape is well suited to such treatment, the bird's-eye view.

After the hills and square patches and pockets of farmland just west of Sydney, the greeny-yellow crops vanish, the rivers and lakes turn white and great gray ribbons appear and fade like enormous drips and spills of a red so red that they seem like bloodstains a hundred miles long. This is the beginning of the Simpson Desert, and there is so much of it that it takes hours to cross it flying in a jet at 500 miles an hour, and even at that you are only halfway over the country. With every passing minute the colors change from gray to mauve to pink and to a bleached bone-white that is chalky enough to pass for the Chinese color of death. No road, no water, no life, not even names on the map. I remembered Bruce Chatwin in 1983 stabbing his finger excitedly onto the map of the outback, thrilled by its emptiness, and saying to me, "Nothing there! Nothing there! Nothing there! I want to go there!"

(Later that year, Chatwin sent me a postcard from the outback: *All going well down-under . . . Have become interested in a very extreme situation – of Spanish monks in an Aboriginal mission, and am about to start sketching an outline. Anyway the crisis of "shall-never-write-another-line" sort is now over. As always, Bruce.*)

The Australian surface is stubbly, the gravelly texture a wilderness of boulders and wind. Then there is the so-called Dingo Fence, or vermin-proof fence, put up by the Wild Dog Destruction Board to keep the dingoes out. This structure is such a serious effort it is longer (they say) than the Great Wall of China, and much more secure, and more clearly visible from the moon.

Farther on, below the flight path the land is scooped out and whitened. It is drizzling with sand – vast streaks of it. It becomes a rucked-up and striped horse blanket, a thousand square miles of wool. And soon after there are ridges of red hills and black patches of trees and the gouges of dry creeks, literally billabongs (dead creeks).

And it occurs to me that this is not like another planet but like the bottom of the sea after an ocean has drained away. It is Oceania after someone has pulled the plug. And sure enough a few days later I was hiking in the cliffs of those same mountains, in the MacDonnell Range, and found small broken fossils in the red rock – "nautiloids," the distant cousins of squid deposited here when this was an inland sea.

Alice Springs is here in the middle of these red ranges, a jumbled little one-storey town, which is a railhead and a road junction and the conflu-ence of three rivers – billabongs once again, because there is not a drop of water in them, only hot sand and tilted gum trees and Aborigines squatting in family groups in the splotches of shade. The Todd River is the widest, and the driest. Like many Australian rivers – few of them contained water – it looked like a bad road, but wider than others I had seen. It is said that if you've seen the Todd River flow three times you can consider yourself a local.

I walked around town, noting the meeting-places of Aborigines and generally chatting.

"I'm not a racist – I just hate Abos."

This neat and commonly uttered absurdity was put to me by a woman on my first day in Alice Springs. When I said that I had come to the town to meet some Aborigines she began seething. It is probably worth putting down what she said, because so many people I met said the same things, and only the tone of voice varied – ranging from sorrowful to apoplectic. Hers was outraged.

"They drink – they're always drunk and hanging around town. They're slobs, they're stupid. Their clothes are in rags – and they have money too! They're always fighting, and sometimes they're really danger-ous."

I always smiled ruefully at this rant, because it was a true description of so many white Australians I had seen. I could never keep a straight face when I heard one of these leathery diggers turn sententious over the drinking habits of Aboriginals, for whom they themselves were the alcoholic role models.

"There was a blackfella, worked for Kerry's father as a stockman outside Adelaide. He went walkabout. He comes back after aideen months and says, 'Where's my job?'"

The speaker, Trevor Something, was barefoot, twisting his greasy hat, a tattooed and ranting ringer, snatching at his three boisterous kids, and snarling at Kerry. He had a stubbie of Castlemaine Four X in his fist.

I wanted to laugh, because he was another one, a white Australian imputing slovenly habits to Aboriginals and then behaving in precisely the same way, except the white Australian always did it wearing a hat — a Sewell's Sweat-Free Felt for preference, and in certain seasons in a brown, ankle-length Driazabone raincoat.

"We're not racists any more," Trevor said. "They're the racists!"

It was true that Trevor was a ringer, an ocker — a redneck — but I had heard the same twanging sentiments more prettily phrased from the mouths of accomplished and well-educated people in Sydney and Melbourne, and a well-bred woman from Perth had said to me, "All Abos are liars."

When I encouraged Trevor to reminisce, he said, "We used to come up here to Alice Springs and get into fights with the blackfellas. Mind you, there are some first-class blackfellas. Some of the nicest blokes you'd ever want to meet."

"They've got some funny ideas, though," his wife Kerry said. "We just come up from Ayers Rock. Blackfella we met said he wouldn't set foot on it. It would be like climbing over a pregnant woman's belly. He says to me, 'That rock is the pregnancy of the earth — swelling up, see.' Yairs, but there were plenty of drunken blackfellas all around Ayers Rock, and they didn't look too bothered."

"Maybe they had gone walkabout?" I asked.

"Yeh. They disappear," Trevor said. "They go mental."

The notion was that the Aboriginal lost his grip and in a severely manic mood whirled out of sight, endlessly perambulating the outback.

The Aboriginals I met denied this, and they were unanimous in agreeing on the meaning of "walkabout."

"It means walking," Roy Curtis said. Roy was an Aboriginal of the Walbiri people in Yuendumu, 400 dusty kilometers to the northwest.

It is in that simple sense of walking that the word is used in, for example, Psalm 23 in Aboriginal pidgin: *Big Name makum camp alonga grass, takum blackfella walkabout longa, no frightem no more hurry watta.* ("He maketh me to lie down in green pastures: He leadeth me beside the still waters.")

Big soft pot-belly, skinny legs, long eyelashes, whispering Roy Curtis was a part-time painter of dot pictures, waiting under gum trees in Alice Springs for compensation from the idiot who cracked up his car.

"It means going home," he said, and sounded as though he yearned to do that very thing.

"The word has a specific meaning," Darryl Pearce, director of the Institute of Aboriginal Development, told me. "It is when a person leaves to go to the outback on ceremonial business or family business, to visit sacred sites, to be with people of his own nation."

I had left my car and walked across a wide dry riverbed in Alice Springs to reach Darryl's office. This river, a tributary of the Todd, was crammed with cast-off beer cans and wine jugs from Aboriginal drinkers, and here and there against its banks, under the gum trees, were little abandoned camps, tattered blankets and a litter of torn paper.

Two Aboriginals were sitting impassively under a gum tree like people cast in bronze, a man and woman holding hands. I talked to the man, who was named Eric, about a scheme to dam one of the rivers. It was one of the explosive Aboriginal issues in Alice Springs at the moment; if the scheme went ahead it would mean that an Aboriginal sacred site would be under water.

"How would you like it if Westminster Abbey were destroyed?" some people argued, fumbling about for an analogy.

They were often greeted with a reply something like, "That site's about as sacred as a fly's arse."

There were sacred sites all over town. One was a fenced-off rock protruding, like a small fallen asteroid, from a parking lot of a pub that had borrowed its name: The Dog Rock Inn.

What was more important – I asked these two people sitting on the bank of the dry river – saving the town from flooding, or preserving the sacred site?

Eric said, "Preserving the site, I reckon."

Then I walked on to the Institute and heard a fierce version of this view from Darryl.

As for the word "walkabout," Darryl said he understood the concept well, because he himself was an Aboriginal. He could have fooled me. He was pasty-faced, freckled, somewhat stocky, with brownish hair cut short. I would have guessed Irish. He looked like any number of the drinkers and shopkeepers and taxi-drivers who denounced Aboriginals as boongs and layabouts.

"The expression 'part-Aboriginal' is bullshit," Darryl said. "Either you are an Aboriginal or you aren't. It's not a question of color but of identity. We are all colors."

His mother had been a full-blooded Aboriginal, one parent a Mudbara from the Barkly Tablelands, the other an Aranda from near Alice Springs.

"People ask us why we're angry," he said.

I had not asked him that. Angry was not a word I associated with any Aboriginals I had met, who had seemed to me more waif-like and bewildered.

"We've been in Australia for forty thousand years, and what good has that done us? Before 1960 it was illegal for a white Australian to marry an Aborigine. We had no status. Until 1964 it was illegal for an Aboriginal to buy or drink alcohol – and anyone supplying an Aboriginal with alcohol could be jailed. We weren't even citizens of Australia until 1967."

"If Aboriginals weren't citizens, what were they?"

"We were wards of the state. The state had total power over us," Darryl said. "The 1967 Referendum gave us citizenship. Wouldn't it have made more sense to ask us whether we wanted to be citizens? Yet no one asked us."

"Isn't it better to be a full citizen than a ward of the state?"

"We don't want to be either one. Something was taken away from us in '67. It was the blackest day in our history."

Before I could ask him another question – and I wanted to, because I did not understand his reasons for seeing the citizenship issue as sinister – he went on, "We pay for things we don't use. Lots of things are offered to us, but what good are they? We're entitled to so many services that mean nothing to us. We don't access the mainstream. It doesn't matter whether roads and schools and hospitals are built for us if we don't want them."

I said, "Then what do you want?"

"Our aim is to control our own future," he said. "We want to make our own decisions."

In a word, Aborigines had no power. Keeping the Aborigines powerless, he said, was the hidden reason behind many government policies.

"Look at the Aboriginal languages – what do you know about them?"

I said I had been to the Central Land Council in Alice Springs, because so many of the Aboriginal issues related to land questions. I had asked an official there about Aboriginal languages. How many were there in the Northern Territory – his own area?

"Umpteen," he said. Then, "Maybe two hundred and fifty?"

In fact he had no idea. I subsequently learned that when the first colonists arrived in Australia two hundred years ago, there were 500 different Aboriginal languages in use. Only a fraction of these are still spoken.

"Aboriginal languages are not taught in Australian schools," Darryl said. "Why not? Because it would empower us. We would have to be taken seriously. It's ridiculous. An Australian student can choose between French, German, Italian, Greek – even Japanese, for God's sake! – but not any Aboriginal language."

This powerlessness he saw as the condition of many other native peoples – Maoris, Fijians, Inuits, black South Africans. But Maori was taught in New Zealand schools (and, ironically, the highest marks in it had been attained by white Kiwis); ethnic Fijians had recently taken control of their islands – with illegal force and the imposition of martial law; and as for black South Africans, Nelson Mandela was very shortly to be visiting Australia on his round-the-world tour after his release from a South African prison, and Darryl was going to meet him with an Aboriginal delegation.

"Indigenous peoples all over the world get shit land that can't be farmed." Darryl was saying. "And then someone discovers minerals on it and the government wants it back."

"I've heard Australians say that in the course of time assimilation will occur and –"

"Assimilation is a hated word. We don't want to assimilate. Why should we?"

It seemed to me that Darryl himself – Irish-looking Darryl – was already assimilated. But I said, "I don't know the arguments. But do you really want apartheid – separate development?"

"This whole country is our land," Darryl said. "White people need permits to go on our land. Now they're saying that we'll need special permits to come into town. And it's all our land!"

The lack of water in Alice Springs was no deterrent to the annual Henley-on-Todd Regatta, which is held in the dry riverbed. When I heard that it was happening I headed for it, in a walkabout way – you couldn't miss it: I followed the roar of the crowd and the plumes of dust rising like smoke from the gum trees.

The events were in full swing: "Eights;" "Yachts" – bottomless boats carried by running men; "Oxford Tubs" – six people carrying a bathtub with someone sitting in it; "Sand Shoveling" – a relay race to fill a 44-gallon drum with sand; and men racing each other lugging sacks of wet sand.

The announcer was yelling himself hoarse, but there was no cheering. The large audience – thousands, it seemed, looking like jackaroos and jillaroos and the sort of cattle rustlers known locally as poddy-dodgers and cattle duffers – stood in the blinding sunlight and dust, wearing sweaty T-shirts and wide-brimmed hats and rubber flipflops, drinking beer. Like many another outback event – the Birdsville Races, the rodeo in distant Laura – the Henley-on-Todd was merely another excuse to get plastered in the most good-humored way.

"This place is a dump," a photographer friend confided to me in Alice Springs. He was doing a photographic essay about Australia, and the stress was beginning to become apparent. "Birdsville is a madhouse. I hate the cities. I get depressed in the suburbs. I can't win. To me, Australia is one big beer can."

By mid-afternoon the spectators at the Henley-on-Todd were so drunk they hardly seemed to notice who was competing and they paid no attention to the skinny biting flies that are a plague in the outback. These flies are pestilential but much too small to show up on photographs of Australia. If they did, prospective tourists might think twice about going.

From where I stood, in the sand in the middle of the Todd River bed, I could see dark clusters of Aborigines under the distant trees. They were no more than insubstantial shadows. Two of these shadows were Michael and Mary, an Aboriginal husband and wife. I introduced myself to them that day and met them again a few days later in town. They told me that when they were in town they slept under the gum trees. Today they were standing mute and barefoot not far from the Dreamtime Art Gallery. They were covered in buzzing flies and looked quite lost. Michael had a rolled-up painting under his arm. They were both drunk but reasonably coherent. I looked at the painting.

"It's a kangaroo," Michael said. "I painted it."

"Do you paint, Mary?"

"I help with the dots," she said.

It was almost all dots, an amorphous pattern – perhaps a kangaroo but one that had been squashed by a truckie with a 'roo bar on the road to Tennant Creek. Michael said he would sell me the painting for $200.

He turned towards the art gallery and said, "They know me in there."

He took me inside. The gallery owner was a white Australian woman in a bright dress, sorting Aboriginal drawings in a folder.

Michael approached her. He said shyly, "You have my painting?"

"I think we sold it," she said.

"It was there," Michael said, pointing to a space on the gallery wall.

His wife in her torn dress stood on the sidewalk, staring through the plate glass and somewhat unsteady on her feet, sort of teetering.

The gallery was full of paintings in a similar *pointilliste* style, dots on canvas, some showing identifiable creatures – kangaroos, lizards, crocs – and other paintings depicted the collapsing geometry of Aboriginal designs, which occasionally had the look of those dotty eye charts that are used in tests for color-blindness.

I said, "You understand these pictures?"

Michael nodded. He blinked. The flies had followed him into the gallery. Some flies hurried around his head and others rested on his shoulders.

I pointed to a painting showing two crescents and a blob. "What's that?"

"People sitting in a circle."

I pointed to one showing just a blob, dots of two colors.

"An egg."

"That's a goog?" I said, trying out a Australian word. Chooks laid googs.

"Yah."

"What's this?" I said, in front of a large canvas covered in squiggles.

"Water. Rain."

"And that?" It looked like an irregular horizon of dots.

"A snake."

Michael said he bought canvas and paint here in Alice Springs and took them back to his house in the reserve near Hermannsburg where he did the paintings. Many of the canvases in the gallery were priced in the thousands.

"How much do you get for your paintings?"

"Not much," he said. "But enough."

I wanted to go to a reserve. I had been told that I would need an official permit to enter an Aboriginal reserve, but in the event I simply drove into Amungoona, a reserve outside Alice Springs, and asked the man in charge – Ray Satour, formerly a bulldozer-driver, now a headman – if I could look around.

"Sure thing, mate," he said. He said I should pay special attention to the tennis-courts, the swimming-pool, the gymnasium and all the new houses.

Why had he said that so proudly? Amungoona Aboriginal Reserve was fenced and ramshackle and looked like a cross between a free-range chicken farm and a minimum security prison. It was very dirty. The tennis-courts were derelict, there was no water in the swimming-pool, the gym was a wreck and so were the houses. This was all something of a conundrum to me.

I thought: Perhaps rather than build swimming-pools, the authorities should plant more gum trees for Aboriginals to sit under. There was surely something amiss when almost no white person spoke an Aboriginal language, and this in a country where a good two-thirds of the place names had Aboriginal roots. It made for alienation and hard feelings.

My intention was to go to Palm Valley, which was part of Michael and Mary's Aboriginal reserve, beyond Hermannsburg, about a four-hour drive west from Alice Springs.

"I wouldn't go if I were you," the clerk at the car rental agency told me.

A half a dozen times I was told this same thing, about other places. Some of my informants were Americans. There seemed to me many Americans in Alice Springs – they said they loved it there and wanted to stay as long as possible. They were the dependants, wives mostly, of the American soldiers who worked at the Joint Defense Facility at Pine Gap – a satellite tracking station or perhaps a nuclear missile base: it was secret, so no one knew.

"Whites aren't welcome in Palm Valley."

I could not determine whether these warnings were sound. I felt that much of it was just talk. After all, I had simply waltzed into the reserve at Amungoona – my being polite and respectful had worked. And I had made a point of saying that I was not an Australian.

Being a foreigner helped me in so many ways. But it sometimes provoked Australians to give advice. I kept noticing how Australians – the most urbanized people in the world – were full of warnings, full of anxieties about the sun and the sea and the creepy-crawlies and what they call "bities," snakes, spiders, box-jellyfish, crocodiles, kangaroos bursting through your windshield, wild pigs eating your lunch. It is apparently a fact that the Australian desert contains more species of reptile (250 – many of them venomous) than any other desert in the world, and it has been proven scientifically that the Australian inland taipan is the most poisonous snake on earth – its bite will kill you in seconds. But none of this ought seriously to deter anyone from confronting the outback on foot, or even on all fours.

I was doing this very thing, perambulating on my hands and knees, at Glen Helen Gorge, 130 kilometers from Alice Springs, climbing the red cliffs, looking for the shy black-footed rock wallaby. Beneath this magnificent ridge of crumbly russet sandstone was the Finke River – one of the few rivers in the outback that actually had some water in it – and there was a large cold pool of black water at the gorge itself. I climbed to the top of the hill, a hot two-hour trek up a fissure in the cliffs, and wandered around and then lost my way – couldn't find the return fissure, only a sheer drop to the valley floor. But just when it seemed to me that *Walkabout* was turning into *Picnic at Hanging Rock* I saw a way down and followed it.

There were Australians swimming at the pool at Glen Helen. They were shrieking at their kids, they were munching sandwiches, they were drinking beer, they were sitting under trees with their white legs thrust out, and they had hiked up their T-shirts to cool their bellies. The T-shirts said, *Freddy Krueger*, and *These Here are Strange Times* and *I Climbed Ayers Rock*. It was all families. They were having a wonderful time.

These white Australians were doing – perhaps a bit more boisterously – what Aboriginals had always done there. Because there was always water at Glen Helen it had been a meeting place for the Aranda people, who wandered throughout the central and western MacDonnell Ranges. This waterhole was known as Yapalpe, the home of the Giant Watersnake of Aboriginal myth, and over there where Estelle Digby was putting sunblock on her nose (and there was something about the gummy white sunblock that looked like Aboriginal body paint) the first shapeless Dreamtime beings emerged.

The pool at Ormiston Gorge was even prettier – shadier, more secluded, with pure white tree trunks looking stark against the cracked and branched red rock. It looked as serene as Eden, even under the bluest sky. And here too kids were yelling and adults snoozing and a few old women with scowling emu-like faces, totally unfazed, were kicking through the loose gravel. They happened to be white, but they could easily have been Aboriginals. It just so happened that Aboriginals chose to gather at other waterholes – the large dark pool at Emily Gap, east of Alice Springs, was one. There I saw Aboriginals swimming or snoozing or dandling their babies, doing what they had done for tens of thousands of years, but now wearing shorts and T-shirts.

It is perhaps over-simple to suggest that white Australians are Aboriginals in different T-shirts, but they are nearer to that than they would ever admit, even though they are rather trapped and blinded by the lower-middle-class English suburban culture they still cling to. After all, a bungalow is just another kind of humpy.

About twenty or thirty miles northwest of Alice Springs on the road to Tanami, I stopped the car to look at a lizard squatting by the roadside, and heard the wind plucking at the thorn bushes and moaning in the telephone lines. And then I realized that some cattle behind a fence were looking up, with rapt expressions. It was the music I had on the cassette player, Kiri Te Kanawa, singing *I know that my Redeemer liveth*. I played it louder, and the cattle crowded closer, listening to that glorious voice.

I got out of the car and walked up the road. It was a typical outback road, with dust and corrugations, hardly distinguishable from a riverbed except that it was straighter.

A tin sign was nailed to a tree:

> *This plaque in memory of Jonathan Smith*
> *who if he hadn't jumped the fence in Darwin*
> *would have been able to do kaig. 13-8-88.*

I had no idea what it meant, but I was sure that Jonathan Smith had been an Aboriginal, and this was one of those gnomic expressions of Aboriginal grief.

Going walkabout myself had led me here, looking hard at some of Australia's empty places, and I realized it was not just a dramatically beautiful land but a unique one, full of wild creatures which were just as strange as its people – its skinks and snakes and adders and wasps. Some I saw a few feet off on a track of red dust, others squashed in the middle of the road to Tennant Creek, and many were the subject of horror stories.

Some of the ugliest creatures were harmless, such as the thorny lizard, a horrible-looking but innocent spiny and scaly harlequin. Yet the eastern brown snake – second most toxic in the world – was an unprepossessing reptile. There was Spencer's goanna, with its baggy yellow belly and black tongue, the gidgee skink, a spiny lizard with a fat prickly tail, and the shingle-back lizard that was so flat it looked as though it had been mashed by a car even when it was fully alive. The frilled-neck lizard looked like a lizard's version of Bozo the Clown, and the desert death adder tricked its prey with its grub-like tail. And if you went down the road slowly you might see, watching by the roadside, the military dragon, a patient creature that squatted on the shoulder of the road, scoffing up insects that had been smashed by oncoming cars. As for the carpet python, which hunted at night, it had heat receptors in its head and a whip-like response that allowed it to catch a bat blindfolded.

Aborigines had learned to live with these creatures. Some they caught and skinned and ate raw, others they chucked into a fire and left them until they were black and bursting like sausages, and then they stuffed them into their mouths. They were not frightened of snakes. They believed they were related to snakes – to kangaroos, to the whole earth; and they did not see the point where the earth began and their lives ended. It was all part of a continuum, a natural process, in which with the blessings of the gods they whirled around with the rocks and stones and trees.

They coped well with the inland taipan and the death adder. It was the white Australian who presented problems.

"Very little has been done to give [Aborigines] a sense of security in the country we invaded," Patrick White wrote on Australia Day in 1988, the year of the Australian Bicentenary. "In spite of a lot of last-minute face-saving claptrap from the Prime Minister – one of the greatest bull artists ever – Aborigines may not be shot and poisoned as they were in the early days of colonization, but there are subtler ways of disposing of them. They can be induced to take their own lives by the psychic torments they undergo in police cells. It's usually put down to drugs or drink – and some of them are on these – they learned it from the whites. In a town like Walgett, prestigious white characters can be seen reeling about the streets on important occasions. In my boyhood when I used to go there to my uncle's sheep station on the Barwon, and he drove me in his buggy past the shanties on the outskirts of town, he said, 'There's nothing you can do for these people.'"

The statistics for Aboriginal suicides in jail are terrifying, because a jail cell is an Aboriginal's idea of hell on earth, and waking up sober after being hauled in for drunkenness – or for possession (being found with alcohol within a hundred yards of a bottle shop) – the realization of being penned in is such a nightmare to a nomadic soul that many hang themselves in these hot little holding cells before guilt or innocence can ever be determined. Yet drinking was not the main reason for younger Aboriginals entering the criminal justice system. They were usually arrested for petty nuisances – for breaches of "good order," or for property offenses, burglary and vehicle theft. But seldom for traffic violations or shoplifting, offenses in Australia which were monopolized by whites. In the normal way, Aborigines did not kill themselves, though you would have expected them to be hanging themselves left and right from gum trees on the basis of the jail suicides – somehow deducing that they had a propensity for it. But no, it was the result of their having been taken captive.

There was no question that Aboriginal drunks had become a problem. But were they more of a problem than white drunks? With the possible exception of Finns in winter, I had never in my life seen so many people, black and white, dedicated to intoxication as I did in Australia. And it was not socially disapproved of, not any more than football rambunctious-ness, nor obscene rugby songs, nor the peculiarly insulting manner that in Australia was taken to be a form of mateyness – "mate-ship" being the concept that helped Australia operate. In Australia generally a non-drinker was regarded as a much greater irritation, not to say a threat, than a shouting puking drunk.

So why in a drinking and drunken land were Aboriginals blamed for being drunks? Perhaps it was their cheerlessness. All the Australian boredom and desperation was evident in Aboriginal drinking. They didn't sing when they were drunk, they didn't dance or become matey. They simply hurled up their supper and fell down and became comatose in a pool of their vomit. There was a furious singlemindedness about it all, and it was not unusual to see Aborigines under the gum trees getting through a four-liter box of Coolabah Moselle in a morning, and when money was short it was time for a "white lady" – methylated spirits and milk. All I had was anecdotal evidence, but statistics were available, and they were surprising. An authoritative report (by Pamela Lyon, for Tangentyere Council, June 1990) on alcohol abuse by all racial groups in Alice Springs stated that Aborigines drank less than whites but were more affected by it, suffered more physical disability and died earlier as a result.

I was told that David Gulpilil might have a thing or two to say on the subject of Aboriginal drinking. As the first Aboriginal movie star, he might also have views on fame and fortune. I had wondered about his life since that movie. He had apparently been given rather a raw deal by the makers of the movie *Crocodile Dundee*, his only other movie effort.

"He's gone walkabout," a woman in Sydney told me. That word again. Then I was told that he had been sighted in Darwin, and in Alice Springs. Everyone knew him.

"I saw him the other day walking down the street," someone else told me in Sydney. "A tall skinny bloke. Couldn't mistake him. He's such a beautiful dancer."

I was given a telephone number for him – the phone was in a reserve up north. I called but there was no answer. I tried a number of times, and then I was told that it was a public call-box, somewhere on the reserve in Arnhemland, another Woop Woop place. I had seen call-boxes like that – dusty, vandalized stalls, scratched with dates and nicknames and obscenities, baking in the sun, the phone almost too hot to hold. I never spoke to him – no one picked up the phone. Is it any wonder? But I kept imagining the phone ringing on a wooden post in Woop Woop, under a cloudless sky – ringing, ringing – and a tall black figure in the distance, not deaf, just not listening to the thing, and walking away.

# 5

## *North of the Never-Never*

I picked up my collapsible kayak, flew north almost two thousand miles to Cairns, kept going by road to Port Douglas, caught a boat to Cooktown – which is spitting distance from New Guinea – set up the kayak and started paddling the thing offshore, near the mouth of the Endeavour River, fishing for mackerel with a handline – bliss. But for nearly everyone in Australia this area is regarded as Crocodilopolis.

The wind was strong, a gusty twenty-five knots from the southeast, the sort that whips your hat off and stretches a flag straight out and lifts a sea into a short stiff chop with breaking waves. Everyone had warned me of sharks and man-eating crocodiles; no one had mentioned this wind. That seemed to me the proof that they didn't know what they were talking about.

All the way from Port Douglas to Cooktown the hovercraft, *Quicksilver*, had been buffeted. Port Douglas was a newly Nipponized resort, with golf courses and spruced-up shopping malls. Japanese tourists in silly hats flew here from Tokyo to buy designer merchandise and to hit golf balls. They said it was cheaper to do this than to join a Japanese golf club. I was happy to board the big boat and take off, but I was surprised by the way the white foam was blown alongside by the wicked wind.

"It's always like this," one of the deckhands had said. "It's the worst place for wind. Going up to Cooktown, eh? It's bloody awful there."

The headlands and bays that Captain Cook named were a record of the emotions in his progress up the coast – Weary Bay, Cape Tribulation, Hope Island. The hills are arid and scrubby, the headlands rocky and scoured smooth by the wind. This same wind had blown Cook's ship, the *Endeavour*, onto a reef just here in June 1770, and then he had limped to shore to patch the boat. He slid up the river, watched from the bushes by the Aboriginals of the area who called the river *Wahalumbaal*, which meant "You will be missed," a word of farewell, for these Aboriginals paddled canoes out of this place.

"People up in Cooktown get crazed by the wind," the deckhand said. "One bloke couldn't take any more of it. Started screaming about the wind – raving, actually. Went mental. Climbed onto the roof of his house and started firing his shotgun into the wind."

Windy conditions are the very worst for a paddler – much worse and more wearying than high waves or a big swell. But I was so impatient to be paddling, so glad to have a chance to do so, that I spent most of the day fighting the wind. I caught no fish.

"You're bloody lucky you didn't get a fish!" a man shouted at me when I got to shore. "Some of the mackerel here are a hundred and eighty pounds. They'd sink your little boat in short order. Some of those buggers are as big as me!"

He was very fat and had (as they said in Cooktown) a face like a gumnut. His T-shirt advertised a brand of beer, and he was smacking his lips. He clearly loved telling me how I had almost lost my life to a giant fish.

"I was more worried about the wind," I said.

"Never stops," he said.

I was about to ask him how many calm days they had at this time of year, and whether I should wait for the wind to slacken. I knew there had to be flat days, but if I asked him this he would have laughed and mocked me for being a bloody yank and a tourist.

There were mangroves at the bank just below the town, and there I left my boat, tying it bow and stern so that the tide wouldn't take it away. I had spent my first night at a hotel in Cooktown, but I had wanted to make camp, so I pitched my tent on the far bank of the Endeavour River, which was just bush and dunes, and wild pigs. And as for the river, everyone said – of course – that it was full of crocs. A fourteen-footer had just been trapped and sent to the croc farm at Cairns where it was called George and photographed by tourists.

Cooktown, the classic dust-and-bungalow settlement of the Never-Never, or distant outback, was one main street and not much more. It resembled an African town out of the 1950s, complete with barefoot beaten-looking blacks, and those who were not downright lugubrious were roaring drunk in one or other of the town's many pubs. It was pay-day for the Aboriginals – they got money every week, like a welfare check, but it was also compensation for the use, by miners and exploiters, of their reservation or their traditional lands and stomping grounds. Just up the coast the Japanese had started a silica industry, turning the Aborigines' sand into Japanese sake bottles, and paying for the privilege.

"It's drip-feed money," a drinker at the Sovereign Hotel bar told me. He was a local electrician, self-sufficient and somewhat a loner, like many men I had met in outback towns. "It's intravenous money. They just sit on their arses and they get it."

Cooktown was full of wild white men – fuller than any Woop Woop I had seen in the whole of Australia – and they were not just dirty and drunken, but sunburned and pugnacious as well, with filthy bare feet and torn T-shirts. Locally they were known as "ferals," they too were on the dole, and they poked their sunburned noses and whiskery faces into mine and warned me of the Aborigines in Cooktown, as they warned me of the sharks and the crocs and the poisonous box-jellies.

"There seem to be a lot of bars in this town."

"Not that many, mate," the man said. "But every place has three bars inside it. There's the animal bar, the regular bar and the snobs bar."

"What's this?" We were at the Sovereign.

"This is the regular bar. Around back – that's the animal bar. The ringers, the ockers, the ferals and the Abos."

He didn't like the ferals much but he resented the Aborigines even more.

"They're paid for being black. They get drip-feed money and two-percent loans. They borrow money and buy fancy trucks and jeeps. And maybe they forget about the loan. If they default they still keep the vehicle, and their organization comes in and pays it off."

He was drinking slowly and eyeing two Thursday Islanders playing billiards – they were bald beefy Melanesians with the look of boxers, and they were watched by some rather gaunt and drunken Aborigines who were waiting for their turn at the table.

"They're demoralized," he said. "Why work if people are paying you not to?"

He asked me where I was living in town.

"I'm camping on the other side of the river."

"Got a gun, mate?"

"No."

"You should have one. Everyone who camps out here needs a gun of some kind." He thought a moment, "There's pigs, crocs, all kinds of things."

If he had been like the others – warning me away from the bush, trying to frighten me with tales of giant fish and mammoth crocs, I would have dismissed this. But he was a different sort – encouraging me but suggesting that I go armed. He recommended a gun dealer on the main street, Charlotte Street.

Padlocked and fortified against thieves with iron grids – standard protection for a rural gun dealer – the shop was dusty and temporary-looking, with most of its merchandise in cardboard cartons. The man inside was middle-aged – a tough man with graying hair and a sensitive and watchful gaze.

"New in town?" he said.

"Yes," I said and told him where I was camping and that I was planning to kayak up the coast.

"I have just the rifle for you," he said.

It was no more than the black plastic stock of a rifle, but nesting inside (you pulled off the shoulder-rest to find them) were the barrel, the action and a magazine. It was easy to assemble – screw on the barrel, clap the action on underneath and secure it with a wingnut, shove in the eight-shot magazine. Not only waterproof and foolproof, it was also semi-automatic: one pull of the bolt and then you could fire as fast as you pulled the trigger.

"It floats, too."

"But do I really need it?"

"Ever see a feral pig? The wild ones? They have big tusks and they root around the beach looking for oysters." He smiled at me. "I've seen 200-pound pigs. Terrible tempers. What would you do if one of those came at you?"

I bought the rifle and thought: 200-pound pigs, 180-pound mackerel, 14-foot seagoing crocodiles, man-eating sharks. Some camping trip this was going to be.

"I'd like to try out this rifle," I said.

"No problem."

We drove just outside Cooktown to a little quarry that served as a rifle range. On the way he told me about himself – his name was Fred Hardy and he had come to Cooktown because he liked the open spaces. He was not a native-born Australian. He said he made a point of never using the word "mate." He ran several businesses and, as he was able to repair most machines and do electrical work, his skills were in demand. Cooktown was a place where motors were always breaking down and spare parts were in short supply. Any welder or mechanic could find work here. It was the frontier in many senses, a new start for some people, and escape for others, a fortune for a few of those prospecting for gold in the outback.

A hundred and twenty years ago, there had been a real gold rush, and Cooktown had swelled almost to the size of a city, with 30,000 people – half of them Chinese prospectors wearing pigtails. This being Australia, a Chinatown sprang up by the river. The town was famous for having 163 brothels and 94 bars. Goldseekers traipsed over Aboriginal land to get to the Palmer River goldfields and to look for areas with more gold; there were pitched battles between prospectors and Aborigines (who were suspected of being cannibals). Not far away was the settlement of Battle Camp, the name a reminder of a well-known slaughter of Aborigines by white goldminers. Some great fortunes were made from gold in just a few years. Then the gold ran out and Cooktown reverted to being a little spot with a tiny population, at the far edge of the Never-Never.

"But it's funny," Fred Hardy said. "A fellow came in the other day and asked me to fix his cradle. Know what a cradle is? For sluicing gold. And his was huge. He's got a bloody great gold operation going on somewhere in the bush – no one knows where – and for all I know he's got bags of gold, too. I fixed his cradle. I didn't ask any questions. You learn not to ask where the gold prospecting is going on. Showing too much interest could be fatal."

We riddled a half a dozen targets with bullets, and when the sun went down and the light was too poor to shoot by, we packed up our guns.

Fred said, "Want to see a bit of the outback tomorrow? I have a few errands to run. You could come with me."

I said I would, and the following morning I left my camp and paddled across the river to town once again to meet him. He said that because of the rutted road we would have to weigh down his pick-up truck to keep it from jouncing. We loaded it with fourteen sacks of cement – about half a ton – and set off.

In the yellowy bush of thin gum trees and pale dry soil just ten minutes out of Cooktown Fred peered at the wheeltracks in the straight flat road ahead and said, "It's all like this – for hundreds of miles. This is what we'll see all day. This is Australian bush."

*Then why not turn back?* I wanted to say. I hated the narrow track and the way the pick-up slewed in the ruts, and whenever another truck passed us we were overwhelmed with choking dust. There was no shade here – the trees were too thin, the leaves too small. Sunlight slashed through the woods.

Several hours passed. He asked what I did for a living. In a rare burst of candor, I told him I was a writer. Normally, this admission makes the listener self-conscious; it strikes people mute or else makes them talkative – non-stop questions, unedited monologues about unforgettable trips or colorful characters. When they don't know you are a writer most people tell much better stories and converse more naturally. Fred was unfazed. He had read three of my books, and we talked about them, but he was as eager to tell me about Australia as I was to listen – and this was a guided tour of one of its strangest corners.

We went through Battle Camp and at the Normandy River we had lunch – he had brought a picnic basket – and had target practice: shooting the bolts off an old boiler that had become mired at the river's edge. He was a crack shot with his ·38. He described a trip he dreamed of taking down this river in a croc-proof boat of his own design. He had actually seen crocodiles here; he was not afraid of them, though he said that on any trip down this river you would have to take them into account. He told the sort of sensible, rational croc stories that I liked to hear. His point was always: Be careful of crocodiles but don't let them dominate your life.

"I have a greater problem with sharks," I said.

"I don't know much about them around here," Fred said.

"Peter Benchley told me to be careful of sharks on the Queensland coast," I said. "When the author of *Jaws* tells you something about sharks, you listen and take heed."

"I suppose it's a bit like you telling someone about railway trains," Fred said.

More miles into this dry yellow bush took us to Laura, a small cattle station deep in the Never-Never, which contained one pub and several houses, and rumors of Aboriginal cave paintings. It was too small to be a town, too small for a village – "station" was about right. It was a proper Australian word, meaning a farm with the status of village; it was larger than a "property" or a "run." Laura was very tiny in the silence and the heat. There was no breeze; the only movement was that of the flies.

Lakeland Downs was farther on. Each station had a gas pump and a pub. Soon we were on the main road north to Cape York. Max, a peanut farmer whose crop had failed, was directing traffic on a construction site on this empty and dead straight Cape York road. He was terribly sunburned. He said, "There's a car about every fifteen minutes."

Fred gave him a cold beer.

A kangaroo, pumping its legs, dashed in front of us, moving fast through the trees on a gravelly back road. I marveled at its speed. Fred just shrugged and said there were millions of kangaroos around. Paradoxically, kangaroos are listed under the United States Endangered Species Act, as a threatened species, but in Australia they are not protected. In fact, the Australian government encourages the slaughter of kangaroos, and in 1991 sanctioned the killing of 4,208,800 kangaroos to be made into dog collars, stuffed toys, sports shoes and whips. In the shops selling tourist curios in most of Australia you can buy a little leather purse made from a kangaroo's scrotum. Down the road, we saw magpie geese. We saw vultures. Towards the end of the afternoon we saw big pale turkey-like birds pecking in a field, browsing among the corn shucks.

"Bustards. Endangered species," Fred said. "They taste fantastic."

"You eat them?"

"'Don't shoot them!' people say." Fred derided the thought and mimicked again in a nasal nagging voice. "'They mate for life! The poor mate will grieve!'" And then he smiled. "But I have the perfect answer to that."

"You do?" I said, because he was staring knowingly at me.

"Yup. Shoot 'em both."

At sundown, after this long dusty day of sunshine and buzzing flies, we found a bar back in Cooktown.

"Can I tell you something – and promise you won't take it the wrong way?"

It was an awkward moment – I could see that Fred Hardy was a man not given to exchanging confidences – but I said, "No problem."

'You're the only person in the world that I envy," he said.

I then realized how little I had told him of my life.

"See those ringers?" he said, abruptly changing the subject. He indicated a table near the back of the bar.

There were four people sitting together – two heavily tattooed men who were bearded and barefoot, wearing dirty shorts and torn T-shirts, and two Aboriginal woman. The women, in faded shapeless dresses, had scraggly hair and big soft faces; they sat with cans of beer resting on their skinny thighs.

"Gin jockeys." Fred said.

And he explained it was the local expression for a white Australian who lived with an Aboriginal woman, a so-called "gin." All Aborigines got a weekly check and so the relationship, which might very well have been a fulfillment of true love, was regarded by most white onlookers as easy money for the man in question.

*Think I'll go round back and bang a boong*, Fred once heard a drunken man say in a bush bar. In the outback Aboriginal women were often abducted for sexual purposes. "Gin burglar" was another term. They looked for what they called "creamies" or "halfies," preferably a *lubra*, a girl.

"Tell you something, Paul," Fred said. "Some of those Abo women are all right. They buy guns from me and shoot pigeons – they like four-tens or twelve-gauge shotguns. They're good shots. The men couldn't care less. The women shoot, the men drink."

There were six or seven drunken Aborigines at other tables, swigging beer together, and they looked miserable – red-eyed, skinny, and very dirty, with matted hair. It was almost frightening the way an Aboriginal's bones were so obvious, and some of them looked like skeletons wrapped in crushed velvet, like zombies, or like their own horrific water monsters, the bunyips.

"They own a lot of guns," Fred said, "but they don't shoot each other. Matter of fact, they have a low crime rate. They drink and fight – the ones that come to town. I can't blame them. I've been in a fair few fights myself. By the way, I've been meaning to write a letter to someone in Hollywood. Why is it that fights in movies last so long? You see these blokes punching each other back and forth for ten or fifteen minutes." He thought a moment and then said, "Ever been in a fight?"

"A fist-fight? No," I said.

"I've been in lots of them and they were all settled with the first punch. *Bang*, right in the face, *splat*, and it's all over. Never more than one punch. I'm not saying I'm tough or anything – all the fights I've seen have been settled with one punch. What are you grinning at?"

"At the idea of you punching one of these ringers in the face."

"I did that very thing not very long ago – a man made a remark about my wife. I gave it to him in the face and that was that. See, I have a problem. I suffer from a medical condition known as a very short fuse."

"Would you say these Aborigines are pugnacious?"

"One or two. But there are plenty of quiet respectable blacks in Hopevale, on the reserve, across the river," Fred Hardy said. "Listen, did you know you're camped on their land?"

I had not immediately realized how much land these Hopevale Aborigines possessed, but it turned out that everything north of the Endeavour River was theirs, a large notch of North Queensland. This included the little place I had hacked out for myself, which I called Windy Camp. After what Fred had told me about my trespassing I had an urge to go farther up the coast – it had been my original intention in any case – so that I would be smack in the middle of the Aboriginal reserve.

It took me three trips to town to carry enough food and drinking water for another week on the coast. The heavily loaded kayak sat well in the ocean, stabilized by all the food jammed fore and aft in waterproof bags. The weather that day was similar to that on all the other days I had been on the coast – sunny, temperature in the low eighties, south-easterly winds twenty-something, gusting to thirty. Beyond the harbor mouth there were waves breaking all over the sea, a short breaking chop, as the wind whistled around Anchor Point, Cooktown's headland.

The stiff wind annoyed me, but I was determined to stay afloat, and on this coastal run I could go ashore at any time and make camp, write something, listen to the radio. Or eat a meal – I vastly preferred my own cooking to the Australian tucker I had found in hotels and restaurants – flyswisher stew, fried barramundi, snorkers and googs, roast chook; bewitching names for uneatable meals. I had never in my life felt more portable or self-sufficient. I had shelter, food, water, medical supplies and a seaworthy boat. No one was waiting for me at either end.

There were three- to four-foot breaking waves all over the ocean, as far as I could see. I set off for the headland I could see, Saunders Point – a high hill and at the foot of it foaming surf. It was clumsy paddling in a beam wind, the waves breaking against the side and twisting the boat. But it was well known that both crocodiles and sharks avoided such suds – it was much too exhausting for them – so at least I didn't have to worry about being eaten.

My problem lay in trying to stay upright in the kayak with the wind and waves beating against me on one side. Being heavily loaded was a help – the kayak moved slowly but smoothly; and just the thought of leaving Cooktown, the last settlement of any size in Queensland, lifted my spirits. Most people I had met in Australia regarded Cooktown as the limit, the real bush, the Land of Wait, the Never-Never – few had actually been there. Now I was going beyond it, and going north of the Never-Never was like going off the limit of the known world.

I paddled in this beam wind until early afternoon when the gusts became more frequent, and then taking a compass reading, I was caught broadside by a boomer that turned the boat. Before I could recover – I was bracing myself with the paddle – another wave sent me surfing towards shore. I struggled to balance on the wave and shot down, picking up speed. To my right were the spiky rocks of the headland, but just ahead, on shore, there was sand beneath the breaking waves. Nearer the beach, I managed to slow myself and turn, and I went into shore backward – doing a backshoot, a surfer would say – and beached the boat without a wet exit.

It was too surfy at that moment to re-enter the ocean and go around the headland – anyway, what was the hurry? I dragged the boat through the shallow water, found a sheltered spot to sit and rest in and beached the boat, tying it to an enormous log. I walked to Saunders Point and climbed high enough to see where the good camping places were – and I also saw a beachcomber's shack (or was it an Aboriginal's humpy?) which I decided to avoid. Walking on I came to a cluster of logs, a sort of picnic site, with a fire smoldering at the center of it. This was obviously where the Aboriginal fishermen cooked their food. The fact that the fire was still smoking unsettled me – it seemed to indicate that whoever had lit it would be back fairly soon and might object to my presence.

There were rusted cans near the fire – food cans, beer cans – and bits of plastic. Looking closer I saw that on every yard of this stretch of beach there were bottles and fragments of plastic debris: sandals, torn nets, lengths of line. There were cast-off aerosol cans, rubber tires, hunks of cork and wedges of styrofoam. The plastic net-floats were inevitable, but what of all the plastic bottles, the beer cans, the empty oil drums? They had obviously been chucked off boats sailing the Coral Sea, they had been blown from the islands of Vanuatu and New Caledonia, and the trade winds had swept them to this shore. There was an enormous and ugly tidewrack of this indestructible stuff that gave this long windward coast a look like the rim of a junkyard.

It was too depressing to camp within sight of the junk, so I walked down the beach, found a good camping place behind a dune and set up my tent. It was so hot, and I was so tired from the effort of paddling in the high wind, that I crept inside and napped for an hour. Afterwards, I removed all my gear from the boat and got organized: hung up my water bag, set out my stove, unpacked my sleeping-bag and let it swell and loft, sorted my food and hung that out of the way of foraging pigs.

There were pig tracks and lizard tracks all over the sand beneath the trees. In the cool of the later afternoon, I assembled my rifle, filled my pockets with bullets and looked around. Fred had assured me that I would meet an enraged pig. At least I had protection from that ignominious end – not that I relished killing an animal. I had owned a gun of some kind since the age of ten, but I had not shot any living thing since my early teens and I hated anyone who killed animals for sport. I regarded this rifle as a form of self-defense and recreation. I practiced on a tin can and then walked on, listening for the snuffling of pigs.

This is perhaps the place to say that in a year and a half of traveling in the Pacific I did not kill any animal and only ate a few – I remained a fish-eating vegetarian except on the rare occasions when it would have been an unforgivable insult to refuse to eat meat ("We killed this pig in your honor, Mister Paul"). Why should any animal have to die in order for me to make my trip?

Beyond the coastal fringe of trees there was a huge stinking swamp, and this I guessed – from the tracks and the situation – was where the wild pigs lived. Overhead and in the trees were birds of all kinds – fish eagles and kites, plovers and whimbrels and curlews, and nameless whistlers and twitterers.

At sundown I made couscous and had it with beans and tuna, and a pot of green tea. I regretted that I had no beer, but beer cans were heavy. As I ate I listened to the radio – and when darkness fell and the night grew buggy I got into my tent and, by the light of my overbright flashlight, read *The Sexual Life of Savages*. After that I listened to the BBC World Service in the darkness: news of the other world, all of it sounding inconsequential.

The wind blew all night and it reached me even in this depression behind the barrier dunes. My tent flapped, and the boughs above me, which were all thin pines, swished and howled. The wind affected everything here, living and dead. It washed junk and driftwood onto the beach, it whipped up the sea and made it beat the rocks into spikes, it piled the sand into dunes, and it made those trees grow at an unnatural angle – all of them leaning away from the wind.

Dreaming hopelessly, I slept until dawn, when certain birds – I never found out their name – began their wolf-whistles.

The strong wind made cooking difficult – no matter where I placed my stove the wind reached it and blew the gas jet sideways. I peeled an orange and ate it and eventually the water boiled for my noodles and a pot of green tea, a nutritious breakfast vouched for by farmers all over China.

While I was eating, sitting crosslegged on the dune, my tent rose up like a kite and blew into the boughs of a small pine tree. I intended to look for a new place to camp that day so I packed and stowed the tent with the rest of my gear, hung it from a tree, and set off with my rifle. I saw pig tracks, but no human footprints. In the shadows of the trees at the edge of the denser woods I sometimes heard a giggle or a loud squawk, but I never saw the birds that produced these sounds.

Beyond Saunders Point was a steep hill – Mount Saunders – and dotted on its slopes were giant boulders. But after I climbed halfway up I saw that these boulders were in fact ant-hills, seven to ten feet high. There was no path; I scrambled from one rain gully to the next, and in a shallow one a dark snake crossed my path, taking quite a while to do so. I tried to calculate its length, as I watched it slowly sliding through the depths of the tussocky hill grass. I am not afraid of snakes but I cannot rid myself of the African notion that it is very bad luck for a snake to cross your path once you have begun a journey. Caving in to this superstition I changed direction and almost immediately stumbled upon an Aboriginal's humpy hidden in some bushes in the saddle of the hill, out of the wind.

"Hello," I called out, startling myself with my own voice. All around me were bees and butterflies. I looked closely at the humpy. (This small windowless shelter made of sticks and rubbish is also known by other names – a *mia mia*, a *wurley*, or a *gunyah*.)

There was no one home.

From here I had a wonderful view of Indian Head farther on and the long crescent of white sandy beach beneath it. One of the greatest features of Australia were these tropical beaches all the way north of Never-Never – miles of lovely sand and surf, and no one swimming anywhere near them. There are many large empty countries in the world, but few are as lovely or as habitable, or in a certain sense, as happy, as Australia.

The beaches were nameless, because people so seldom used them. Anyway, this was all Aboriginal territory. If they had a name for it they had not divulged it to the cartographers. The mountains and headlands had all been named by Captain Cook, two hundred-odd years ago: he had only been able to pick out the higher ground from his ship.

Back at my camp I carried my gear to the kayak and went farther along the coast, looking for a less windy spot. I struggled to get free of the surf zone but I saw – with dismay – that there were breaking waves all the way to the horizon: a wide foaming sea. Nearer shore I dragged the kayak along and, just ahead, was a four-foot shark – the sort of sand shark that turns up every now and then on Cape Cod beaches. I splashed my paddle and he took off: no need to spear the poor creature.

I had lunch on a sandy shelf on the steep back side of a dune: no wind at all, but because it was so still the dune was very hot and rather smelly and it was teeming with mosquitoes.

Kicking along the beach, pondering where to camp that night, I saw a figure in the distance coming towards me. When he came nearer, I saw it was a small grubby man, moving slowly, looking down: beachcombing. His shirt was torn, his trousers rolled to the knees. Every so often he picked up something, examined it, then either put it into his satchel or chucked it away. A dejected-looking dog trotted beside him.

I said hello. We talked about the wind. He was eyeing my boat.

"Collapsible," I said.

He said, "Want some home-brewed beer?"

One of the warnings I had received in Cairns was: "Don't trust anyone who's very friendly. A mate of mine did. He ended up with broken bones." At the time I had put it down as just another strange Australian warning, in a class with the fat man shouting: "Those mackerel are bigger than me!"

But this beachcomber was small and weedy.

"Lead the way," I said.

He blundered straight up to the dune and through a dense thicket, going a very circuitous route.

"There's no proper path," he said.

We walked on, bush-bashing.

"I don't want to make a path."

The pine boughs were snapping in my face and even the dog looked confused.

"Then everyone visits," the beachcomber said. "Especially official-dom."

He had a rather formal way of speaking, and I thought I caught a whisper of London in the way he swallowed the "L" and said, *Offishoodum*.

Finally we came to his camp. It was a patch of disorder in the bowl between two dunes. At the center was a pallet, with the dimensions of a queen-sized bed, with a tattered canvas canopy suspended over it by guy ropes. This sleeping place was surrounded by immense clutter, but what looked like junk and debris at first glance was, if you looked closer, a collection of glass bottles and containers arranged by size and shape – stacks of them, and ones in long rows set up against the sand banks, cups and tubs nested together. There were also net floats – the large plastic balls that broke free from the wicked, turtle-strangling, dolphin-killing drift-nets of the Japanese. A rusted wood stove had been set up next to the bed – I could see how this beachcomber might recline and cook at the same time – the beachcomber's economy of effort.

"This is what I call home," he said.

There were blackened bones, animals' bones, on top of the stove's grille. To the side of the stove a heap of magazines – the *Reader's Digest* dominating the heap; and on a log, looking prim, a large pink plastic radio.

The man fossicked among the bottles and drew one out, while the dog yapped at me. I hated being barefoot here; I had thought that the camp was nearer the shore. But it was quite a distance from it, obviously to avoid the scrutiny of officialdom.

"Try this," the beachcomber said, and jerked the cap of the bottle.

I said, "Oddly enough, I'm not thirsty."

He took a swig. "Not bad." He took another, and wiped his mouth. "I made this batch last week." He swigged again. There was froth on his lips. "Thing is, the bottles have been exploding."

I distinctly heard him say *bottoos*.

"You're English," I said.

"From Kent," he said. He licked the froth from his lips. "Which is near London." He took another swig. "I was born in Gravesend. It costs six dollars to make about forty bottles of this beer. You just use a tin of this" – he indicated an empty can – "and a few pounds of sugar."

He became very intent on finishing the bottle of beer. He drank the rest of it in sips, neatly, staring between sips at the mouth of the bottle.

"And now you live here?"

"That's right," he said, and glanced around at the clutter. "In actual fact, I'm constructing a raft. That's why I have those pipes and those plastic balls. That's all my flotation, see."

Any purpose or design of those balls and pipes had been hidden by all the clutter.

"What will you do with the raft?"

"I'm aiming to build this raft and sail it in a northerly direction," he said with a certain precision.

"How much more northerly can you get than where we are now?"

"Around Cape York."

Good God, I thought. "Through the Torres Strait?"

One of the worst currents in the world – twelve turbulent knots of ocean rushing like white water squeezed between New Guinea and Australia.

"Yes. Through there."

"Any particular reason?"

He was smiling. His hair was wild. He was unshaven.

"That way I can go to Darwin."

"On a raft across the Gulf of Carpentaria."

"And the Arafura Sea. Yes." He had finished the beer. He put the bottle neatly away with the empties and said, "I'm not in any hurry. I've sailed rafts before. Down the Cabrera River in Colombia. I spent six months in South America. That was about eight years ago. Lots of adventure. Some dangers, too."

"Dangerous Indians?"

"No. I traveled with the Indians. In the South American bush you can't do anything without Indians." He seemed a little tipsy now. He struggled towards the bottles, rearranging them. "Kept a diary. I always said I should write a book about it."

Somehow, even standing barefoot in his beachcomber's camp on the shore of an Aboriginal reserve in North Queensland, it did not seem so odd that he should express this writing ambition. After all, I had the same ambition, and I was barefoot and whiskery too.

"Why don't you write a book about your South American trip?"

"I would," he said, "if I was in a hospital."

He was scratching his dog behind the ears as he spoke, and looking into the middle distance.

"In a hospital, with two broken legs. Then I'd do it," he said. He reflected on this a moment. "But I probably wouldn't want to do it if I had two broken legs."

"You seem to have plenty to drink here," I said. "What do you do for food?"

"Fish. Plenty of fish in these waters. I've got a crab pot. That's what I do with these bones." He poked the blackened bones on the stove. "Put them in the pot. Crabs love them. Also onions."

A bag of onions hung from the limb of a tree.

"Onions will keep for months."

We both looked at his bag of onions.

"Also 'roo meat," he said. "Plenty of that around. Here – have some."

He handed me a brown strip of meat that had the look of leather, exactly the shape and size of the tongue of an old shoe.

"That there is smoke-dried. Done it meself. Lasts for a long time. Years, actually." He became reflective again. "I found some 'roo meat under a box once. Forgot I had it. Two years old, it was."

"What did you do with it?" I said, trying to egg him on.

"Ate it."

"Two-year-old kangaroo meat?"

"Smoke-dried. It was delicious. Wonderful in soups."

"You make soup here?"

"All the time," he said. "Lovely stuff."

"Do the Aborigines mind you camping on their reserve?" I asked.

"They don't make a fuss. The ones in town are a bit rough. But the Abos here are good people. They're losing their old ways, though. They caught a big turtle the other week down where your boat is. They took some of the meat and left the rest to the wild pigs. Years ago they would have eaten the whole thing."

That was very much a beachcomber's point of view, the obsession with other people's wastefulness.

I told him I was camping myself, but that I was looking for a place out of the wind.

"Have you tried Leprosy Creek?"

"No. But I kind of like the name," I said.

He gave me directions to the inlet. I paddled there and at a little bend in the creek, I found a good spot – no wind and quite sheltered and there I pitched my tent and spent the night. My only moment of anxiety came in the dawn, when I heard big feet crashing through the leaves. I grabbed my rifle as the noise came nearer – very loud now. I peered out of the tent flap and saw two wild turkeys – brush turkeys, with bald heads and yellow wattles, sleek black feathers, handsome, strutting past my tent.

"You can eat them, you know," the beachcomber said, when I saw him at the shore the next morning. He had just checked his crab pot: nothing inside. "You pluck the turkey and put it into a pot with a brick. You put some water in and boil the whole thing, until you can shove a fork through the brick. Then you throw the turkey away and eat the brick."

He did not smile.

"That's very funny," I said. "What is your name?"

"You can call me Tony," he said.

I was sure that Tony was not his name. He was, in spite of his apparent friendliness, deeply suspicious of strangers, and from time to time he lapsed into silence, self-conscious because of my persistent questions.

He was very interested in my gear – my well-made tent and boat: he examined the stitching and the fittings. He looked closely at my pots and my stove, the water bag I had bought in Sydney.

He said, "That's just what I need for my trip around Cape York on my raft."

I said, "Where do you get your water?"

There was no drinking water anywhere to be found on this sunbaked coast; the pools of water I had found were brackish.

"I go to Cooktown in my canoe when the wind drops," he said. He made a face. "But the Cooktown water is no good. They put fluoride in it."

It was completely in character for this beachcomber to be very fussy and complain about the quality of water in the town. Most tramps I had met in my life believed there was something profoundly unclean about towns and cities, and many of the homeless men I had run across in London – the ones who slept on the common land outside London in camps very similar to Tony's here in Queensland – many of them had spoken with disgust about the beetles and the filth in the charitable wards and dorms. The grubby beachcomber invariably believes he is living the cleanest life possible on earth, and personal hygiene is always a popular topic with tramps who invariably boast of their fastidiousness.

I said, "Aboriginals aren't very popular in Cooktown."

"That's because Australians are racists, aren't they?" Tony said. "If it wasn't the Abos it'd be the Italians or the Yugoslavians. They need someone to hate."

This lucid statement from a barefoot wild-haired man with a dog in his arms, standing in torn pants in the wilds of Queensland.

"There's some towns in Australia, like Katherine" – in the Northern Territory – "where whites and blacks actually fight all the time. But Cooktown is mainly a peaceful place. I get my beer ingredients there. When the road gets bituminized it will all change."

"Tony, it seems you're well set-up here."

"I reckon I am," he said, looking pleased. "I've got all the necessaries."

"See any crocs?"

"Only little buggers. There are pigs around but they don't bother me."

"Mosquitoes?"

I had mosquito net on my tent. Tony slept in the open air.

"When the wind drops there's mozzies. But the wind don't usually drop." He hesitated a little – it was a sign that my questions were making him anxious.

"Catch you later," he said – the Australianism that means: This conversation is at an end. And he appeared to be heading back to his camp.

"Aren't you going for a walk today?"

He was carrying his beachcombing satchel. His shoes were inside, with his water bottle, his hat, and something to eat wrapped in paper. He never went out on the beach without his survival kit, and it gave him a look that was at once shabby and respectable.

He said he had been on a walk but that he had turned back. "The beach was getting a little crowded."

I looked down five miles of beach on the great sweep of bay and saw no one.

"I saw someone else on the beach. Beside you."

This was too much for him. He went back to his camp, and I fished from my boat. I caught nothing but it was a good excuse to bob in the ocean all afternoon. At one point I thought I saw some Aborigines fishing in the surf about a mile farther up the beach – perhaps they were the people Tony had seen? – but when I paddled towards them they vanished.

At dusk I made my dinner to the sound of pigeons' wings – they were making for the trees to settle for the night. There was wind in the upper branches, but it was quiet down below in my camp. Just before I crawled into my tent I saw, clinging to the fly, a large brown spider, about two or three inches long. I flicked it away ("You got some of the most poisonous spiders in the world here, mate. One bite and you're dead as a mutton chop") and zipped myself in for my nightly ritual: drinking tea, writing my notes, and after lights out, radio programs from distant lands. This sound of bad news was mingled with the frog croaks from Leprosy Creek.

Dawn was sudden and hot in the still air of Leprosy Creek, the sun striking my tent the second it rose over the mangroves on the distant bank. The sunlight turned the surface of the creek into a blinding sheet of tinfoil. And with this heat and light the birds in the mangrove boughs over my head giggled and whistled. These trees had wet twisted root systems that held the sand bank together, and the murky pools beneath them teemed with mosquitoes. This was a tidal creek and at high tide I was at the creek's edge. I could not leave my tent without spraying myself with insect repellent. Still, I was happier here at Leprosy Creek than I had been in any Australian city, and I preferred camping in these lumpy dunes to sitting in the Sydney Opera House.

After breakfast (more noodles, green tea, a Queensland banana) I paddled out of the inlet and up the coast. The great sweep of beach was empty all the way to the point, and I paddled along under a sunny sky, thinking how lucky I was to be here, and laughing when I remembered Tony the beachcomber praising the taste of two-year-old kangaroo meat and saying, when asked if there were any crocodiles around, *only littoo buggers.*

Some supine humans a mile up the beach turned out to be Aboriginals, reclining against a log, kicking their heels – an elderly black man, a full-blooded woman and a boy of about six. The small boy was combing nits out of the woman's hair. He did it with solemn attention, searching the hair, fingering it, and pinching the nits and lice in his nails, while the woman sat slightly turned away from me. The old Aboriginal man simply sat looking at the sea.

From their patch of shade on the beach, they watched me come ashore. I dragged my boat onto the sand and said hello, and asked them – only making conversation – whether it was all right for me to camp on their reserve.

"No worries, mate," the old man said. His accent was pure Australian, with more strine in it than almost any of the people, natives and immigrants, whom I had heard abusing Aborigines. "You can do it. Now, your boat – we don't call that a dinghy. That's not a dinghy."

"What would you call it?"

"It's a *wongka*."

This was the first time I heard this term for canoe: I was pleased to get it from an Australian Aboriginal. Later, I was to hear it, or a variation of it, again and again, throughout the Pacific. It is one of the proofs that the Pacific was populated from South-East Asia and not (as Thor Heyerdahl claimed) from South America. In *Canoes of Oceania* – the three-volume authority on the subject, published in the 1930s – the authors provide extensive detail in describing canoe terms; they write, "The *wangka* or *waka* term is ... widely distributed over the whole Malayo-Polynesia area ... It is found in Indonesia, the Philippines, Micronesia, Melanesia, Polynesia ..."

I said, "You speak the language."

"I do speak it," the old man said. He was completely toothless.

He was wearing blue jeans and a shirt. He was eighty-two (though looked much younger) and his name was Ernie Bowen. The woman – wearing a torn dress – was his wife Gladys. She was thirty years his junior, but she was toothless as well. The boy was their grandson,

Shawn, and he wore blue shorts. He remain intently combing and picking through the woman's loose hair.

"What language is that?"

"Guugu Yimidirrh."

He had to say it five times before I could hear the words clearly enough to write them down. The word "Guugu" sounded like "Koko." He explained that the expression meant simply "Our Word" or "Our Language " and it was the name for the people who lived here in the area north of the Annan River and south of the Jennie, beyond the headland of Cape Flattery.

Meeting the three folks was a stroke of luck for me, because these people are historically unique in Australia. The Guugu Yimidirrh were the ones whom Captain Cook referred to on 16 June 1770 when in his crippled and leaking ship he wrote tersely in his ship's log, *Some people were seen ashore today.*

Captain Cook found them very timid. At first, with the sense of apprehension resembling that of Robinson Crusoe in precisely the same circumstances, he noted, "their footmarks upon the sand below the high tide mark prov'd they had very lately been here." Soon he encountered them in the flesh but they were not interested in his presents of cloth or nails or paper. They were delighted when he gave them a fish, which they regarded as a symbolic gift. They worshipped fish, they painted pictures of it on the walls of their caves – they were great painters of their other totems: turtles, demons, naked people, dugongs.

"They were clean limn'd, active and nimble," Cook wrote. "Cloathes they had none."

A misunderstanding over some turtles provoked some musket fire from Cook's men, then peace-making. And they told Cook some of their words. Fifty words were taken down in Cook's detailed log, and in this way it was the first Aboriginal language to assume written form.

"What is this?" one of Cook's men had said, showing an animal he had shot that morning as it had jumped past the camp.

"*Gangurru,*" an Aboriginal informed him, and a Guugu Yimidirrh word became known to the world. They were particular in their nomenclature. It happened to be a big brown animal that was shown. They had eleven words for the different varieties of kangaroo and wallaby, from the small swamp wallaby *bibal*, to the *galbaala*, the large red kangaroo.

They were hunters and fishermen. They had weapons, they made dugout canoes. They had lived in this area for thousands of years. They did not practice circumcision or tooth extraction. Their great fear was of *Yigi*, an evil spirit which went about at night. For this reason they seldom went out after dark.

They had no word for love. For the Guugu Yimidirrh friendship was everything, the strongest bond in the world. Marriage was regarded as a bond of friendship, not love. This surprised the missionaries, who thumped them over the head with the Christian Bible and turned many of them into Lutherans. Yet even the missionaries could not change the language, and the expression "I love Jesus" they rendered as "Jesus is my best friend."

Cook was deeply impressed by these people. And even though he had just come from Tahiti, islands of "dissolute sensuality," he was startled by the Aborigines' utter nakedness: "They go quite naked both men and women without any Cloathing whatever, even the women do not so much as cover their privities." Joseph Banks, the botanist on the *Endeavour*, reflected that the Aborigines were like people before the Fall – peaceable, well-fed, nomadic, naked: "Thus live these I had almost said happy people, content with little nay almost nothing."

After repairing his ship, a process that took six weeks at the riverside, Captain Cook set sail, the Guugu Yimidirrh watching him, and he took up his log again.

"From what I have said of the natives of New Holland they may appear to be some of the most wretched people on Earth," he wrote. "But in reality they are far happier than we Europeans, being wholly unacquainted not only with the superfluous, but with the necessary Conveniences so much sought after in Europe; they are happy in not knowing the use of them. They live in Tranquility. The Earth and the Sea of their own accord furnish them with all things necessary in life . . ."

A hundred years passed. Then gold was found on their land. They were slaughtered for being cannibals. They fought back but when their numbers were reduced they dispersed. It was assumed that they would die out. They fled to the north shore of the river, and to the coast where I was camped: "Swampy stony country that no white man would want."

One day in the 1880s, in the town of Oberfalz in Bavaria, a Lutheran pastor read a German edition of *Cook's Travels*. The Guugu Yimidirrh people were described ("clean limn'd . . . Cloathes they had none"). This pastor, Johann Flierl – his name and mission were eventually known to every Aboriginal in the area – received God's summons to seek out "a totally untouched heathen people." The fate of the Guugu Yimidirrh was sealed, and it was *wahalumbaal* to their customs and habits.

German missionaries descended upon these innocent people and this stony Cape Bedford coast. Fifty-one hymns were translated into Guugu Yimidirrh. Luther's *Catechism* went into the language. And a missionary named Pastor Poland started on the New Testament, but before he got to Luke the catastrophic 1907 cyclone hit the coast, leveling the mission and scattering the pages of the translation.

The Guugu Yimidirrh people prayed. Nothing happened. Then in the 1930s a great shortage in China of sea-slugs — so-called sea-cucumber and bêche-de-mer — and trochus shells gave the people something to provide for the outer world. The Cape Bedford Aborigines revived and, in a small way, prospered.

When the war came, and Japanese planes flew over the heads of the Guugu Yimidirrh people, they were evacuated, and their German missionaries were interned as possible Nazi spies.

In 1942, Ernie Bowen was in that evacuation to Rockhampton — so he told me. Born on Cape Bedford in 1907, the year of the great storm, he had spent most of his early life fishing and diving. Diving was his real trade, for the trochus shells — the source of all the buttons on fine clothes until the plastic industry rendered them unnecessary.

I asked Ernie to tell me about the evacuation which uprooted nearly six hundred Aborigines from this place.

"See, Lutheran is a German religion," Ernie said. "And the war was on, mate. Some of your mob was here, too. Yanks. They was all over. They thought we might spy for the Germans — there were real German missionaries here."

"What was the trip to Rockhampton like?"

It was a distance of some fifteen hundred miles, for people who had never left their traditional land.

"Terrible, mate. One day and one night on a ship. No food. People crying — didn't know where they were going." He stopped speaking and looked at the sea. He had an old man's clouded eyes. "After the war we came here — not to Cape Bedford but to Hopevale Mission."

"Where is that?"

"Just inside."

He explained that this legacy of Johann Flierl was an Aboriginal settlement of a hundred or so houses at the end of a dirt track in the reserve.

"May I pay the place a visit?"

"You're welcome, mate," he said, and looked closely at me. "Where is your swag?"

"My swag is behind that point," I said, showing him. "Do you own some land around here?"

"I don't own anything except these clothes and a vehicle. If the white man wanted to walk in and take the reserve he could do it, like he did in Cape Flattery."

"But you're being paid some money by the Japanese who are mining up there, aren't you?"

"Yes."

"Is it enough money?"

"Yes."

Gladys looked up from the busy hands of her grandson – he had tangled her hair and he held the skeins of it in his little fingers. She said, "The government is on our side. The white people were much worse before."

"In what way?"

"They were very rough."

Ernie glanced down the coast and said, "It's all hooligans in Cooktown. Some of those Aboriginal boys drink too much."

I told them I had seen a humpy on the slopes of Mount Saunders.

"Must be a fisherman," Ernie said.

"You call it a humpy?"

"No. We do call that a *bayan*."

"See many crocs around here, Mr Bowen?"

"Lots of crocs in Leper Creek."

"That's where my swag is," I said. "I was told the crocs there are little buggers."

"There's some big buggers too."

"Is it Leper Creek or Leprosy Creek?"

"Leper Creek. Because long ago there were some lepers there, with the disease."

"Do the crocs bother you?"

"The salt-water ones we call *kanarrh* and they grow very big. They took some people here – they usually take women. Don't know why, mate. Maybe because they're weak."

I said, "Or maybe because the women are doing the laundry in the creek."

"Maybe," he said. "If there's four or five people swimming the croc won't take anyone, but when they get out of the water the croc will take the last one."

"What would you do if you saw a croc when you were swimming, Mr Bowen?"

"If I saw a croc, heh, I wouldn't swim."

Gladys said, "Sit with us. You can sit here." And she patted the end of the big log.

I sat with them and said, "Do you speak English when you're with your people?"

"No," Ernie said. "We do speak Guugu Yimidirrh, mate."

"That's good."

"Yes. It is good to have a language. Now listen. I can say" – he spoke some words quickly, a muttered rumbling that sounded like *worrojool gangaral* – "and you wouldn't know."

As he had spoken, Gladys jerked her head out of her grandson's hands, and blinked hard, and looked away.

"What wouldn't I know?"

"I said, 'Kill that white man,'" Ernie said, looking pleased, "and, see, you didn't know what I said."

He had a twinkle in his eye.

"It is good to have a language," he said.

Gladys still looked pained.

"American Negroes, what language they do speak?"

"English."

"They don't have their own language?"

"No."

"What a shame. It's only right that they should have one. What language people do speak in America?"

"English mostly."

This perplexed him a little. He said, "In Germany the white people speak German."

I said, "Mr Bowen, are you a Lutheran?"

"Yes, mate."

"Still diving?"

"I left that years ago."

"Did you kill turtles and dugong?"

"So many times."

"How do you kill a dugong?"

"Spear it with a harpoon, turn it up and hold it against the boat and drown it. Oil is good for your aches and pains. Good meat, too."

I later found out that the Guugu Yimidirrh are among the last people in Australia still allowed to hunt the endangered sea-cows, the dugong, and the endangered green sea turtle.

We talked a while longer, and I asked for directions to the Hopevale settlement. I would have no problem visiting, I felt, if I knew someone there; and Ernie and Gladys said that I could come any time.

"I'll drop in some time," I said.

"That's good, mate."

"I think I'll get back to my swag," I said.

But Ernie was not listening to me. He was staring in the direction of the point, where there was a single palm tree.

He said, "That palm. Never seen that palm before."

I met another beachcomber the next day. He said hello, then thought better of it and ducked into the woods. This was another mile up the beach. I later learned that he had a sailboat moored out of sight, in a tidal creek. These people, beachcombers and Aborigines, were miles apart, but even so they seemed to think they were too close. Tony certainly believed that. I saw Tony over the next few days, and I had the idea that he coveted some of my equipment for his voyage around Cape York.

I encouraged Tony to visit my camp. I wanted to know more about his beachcombing. I began to see a kind of luxury in his life that would be very hard to buy – it was not just comfort but privacy. I was interested in his periods of activity, his plans, his days of total idleness; his total self-absorption, and in his pleasures.

There was something deeply respectable and orderly about him. There was his satchel, containing his day's essentials – shoes, hat, food, water. He always wore a shirt and trousers, though buttons were missing from his shirt, and his trousers were torn in half a dozen places. He never went anywhere without his dog, which was a tiny mutt with a hoarse and timid bark.

I asked him one day whether the dog had a name.

"No," Tony said. "Well, he's so small" – as though his size did not justify having a name. He went on, "Sometimes I say 'chop chop' meaning hurry up. Maybe that could be his name."

The dog loved him, needed to be picked up and hugged. I was especially interested in the idea of Tony's trying to survive in this difficult place, and needing to find food for a dog, but when I mentioned it to him he simply shrugged.

Tony's routines and opinions, and the way he ran his life, suggested respectability. He could not bear the proximity of other people, and I knew from his reactions to my questions that he had a real aversion to anyone discovering where or how he lived. He was entirely self-sufficient, contemptuous and selfish. The fact that he was a beachcomber did not mean that he was an exile. He had a place in the world, which was wherever he happened to be. Beachcombing, though, was his pre-occupation: he needed bottles for his beer-brewing, floats and cast-up line for his raft, driftwood for his stove. The rest of the time he went after fish, oysters and crabs. He was proud of his soup-making and his bread-making. He was often very busy, involved in the process of survival – and he managed this without spending any money at all – but he also had immense leisure.

He said to me one morning, "I drank eight or twelve bottles last night, listening to the radio. I slept late. Had a bit of a hangover. Then I put out my crab pot. Now I'm going for a walk."

This was his whole life on the hot windy coast of Cape Bedford, and it amazed me, because it combined the most rigid discipline with an utter disregard for time.

And sometimes I seriously wondered: *Am I like him?*

The night before I left my camp, I asked him whether he had been back to London.

"Oh, yes, I went back once. About ten years ago. Didn't have no money, so I got a job in the post office, the central one, in West One." He smiled. "It was all Indians and Jamaicans. Blacks from the West Indies on my right, Hindus from India on my left. I couldn't understand a word they said, and they were always jabbering. I said to myself, 'What's this country coming to?'"

He was in his early fifties, small and rather slender, scorched by the sun that always burned in a cloudless sky.

"That's why I couldn't see any point in staying."

I was tying my boat to the mangrove roots so that the tide wouldn't take it away.

"And I'm not even a racist," he said, in a complaining way.

I aimed to set off for the Aboriginal mission, and I wanted to lighten my load, so I gave him some food I would not need and my spare water jug that held two and a half gallons.

"I'll use it on my raft," he said, "when I go north."

"I wish you luck."

"I'm not bothered," he said, and then in a casual way he summed up what I took to be his guiding philosophy, "What I find is that you can do almost anything or go almost anywhere, if you're not in a hurry."

After so many warnings about crocodiles, I was determined to see one. I had read the pamphlet, *Living with Wildlife: Crocodiles*, published by the Queensland National Parks and Wildlife Service, and that seemed to contain sensible advice: "Avoid murky water . . . Don't trail arms and legs from boats . . . Pitch camp at least 50m from the water's edge [that was inconvenient; I took the risk] . . . Don't leave food scraps around your camp . . . Be careful during the breeding season, October through April . . . Never feed crocodiles . . . Never approach them: crocodiles have been known to charge boats and canoes . . . Be particularly wary of any large crocodile floating high in the water or with its tail arched out of the water. This is often a sign that the animal is likely to be aggressive . . ."

If I had a nightmare it was based on that last warning, with the image of a large bobbing croc, his tail erect and arched, coming at me like a monster scorpion.

I paddled up Leprosy Creek to where it became narrow, and almost a mile from the creek's mouth, I saw two small crocs at rest at the edge of a sandbank, their bug eyes and their snouts just above the surface. Maybe their mother would get crazed and attack me!

I looked around, but of course I saw nothing.

"You will never see the croc that eats you," a man in Cooktown told me. This sounded true. "You'll never hear it. You'll never know what hit you. You see nothing. They are simply not there. And in the next second you'll be in its mouth. They have this incredible capacity for sudden movement. And of course, they don't eat you. They twist you underwater and hold you there until you drown. Then they hide your corpse in the mud, and when your flesh is rotten and falling off your bones, they'll devour it."

I paddled back to the creek mouth and in the Cape Bedford direction to the point. At least now, if someone asked me if I had seen any crocs, I could say casually, *A couple*.

The Hopevale Mission was some miles inland. I started walking through the pig and lizard tracks, found a path, and after a while came to a road. I was picked up by a man in a fairly new four-wheel-drive vehicle – many of the Aborigines in Hopevale seemed to own them.

He was a fat cheery man named Paul Gibson. "G'day – where you headed?" He was coffee-colored, frizzy-haired, and wore a trimmed beard. He was extroverted in a way that I had not seen in any of the Aborigines I had met. I asked him his business.

"I'm a disc jockey."

"Is there a radio station here on the reserve?"

"Everyone listens to it."

"What's the most popular music on your show?"

"Country music. Aborigines love country music."

"Willie Nelson? Dolly Parton? Loretta Lynn? That kind of thing?"

"Too right, mate."

So we discussed country music until we came to the settlement.

No one was quite sure just how many Aborigines lived here. Some people said six hundred, other people said seven hundred. They lived in houses that ranged from *gunyahs* or glorified humpys to large well-maintained brick-fronted bungalows, with planted trees and vegetable gardens and fences. The last thing I ever thought I would see in an Aboriginal reserve was a fence. But these were Lutheran Aborigines.

It was a flat place of wide streets and low dwellings, all sun-struck and dry, with the look of a camp that was evolving into a village. It had that company town sense of order: the stores on the main street hadn't sprung up – they had been imposed, according to a designer's scheme. The store, the post office, the community center, the gas station – someone had put them here. Some Aborigines were working on the roads, and some were leaning on their shovels. But the work was slowly being accomplished, and there was no question but that the curbs and sewers and roads were superior to those in Cooktown.

I lurked at the community center. I had now been among Aborigines long enough to see that they carried silence with them. They didn't shout, they chatted softly when they chatted at all, they moved keeping themselves very straight, loping quietly along on big flat feet. When I said hello they didn't speak to me but only nodded.

On the bulletin board a large notice read *Pig Dogs For Sale See Steve Lee*. Pig dogs were ferocious hounds that went after pigs in the bush.

Another notice read, *Could Owners of the Horses which is wondering about the Community please collect them by next week and put them in your paddocks. If you cannot do that, well your horse will be trucked away and sold.*

One of the notices concerned the Aborigines' weekly payments: *Those people who has missed out on wages will not be paid by cheque until next week's wages.* "Wages" was a euphemism for their share of the money paid to the community by the mining company, and the implication of the notice was that some of them were too lazy to pick it up on the appointed day.

*Anyone wanting their dogs to be shot*, another notice ran, *please see Goombra Jacko.*

Half a dozen surnames dominated in the community – Flinders, Gibson, Deemal, Woibo, Cobus and Bowen. The place was full of Bowens, but I could not find Ernie or Gladys.

"Probably off fishun," Lynton Woibo said.

This was in the store that was run by the mission, and it was more thoroughly stocked than any food store in Cooktown. The only thing missing was alcohol – the reserve was dry. That was the primary reason for any of the Aboriginals going to Cooktown: to buy liquor. I was surprised that the Aboriginal store had such expensive and fancy food – duck-liver pâté, Sara Lee Black Forest Gâteau, frozen quiche lorraine, Birdseye Chinese Vegetables, and Papa Giuseppi's Microwave Pizza. And, in a reserve that had tillable soil and irrigation, canned vegetables. I kept trying to imagine the spear-throwing, dugong-drowning Aborigines I had seen in the bush, coming back from an unsuccessful expedition and flinging a Papa Giuseppi's Pizza into the microwave.

Microwaves were on sale in the dry-goods store, along with toasters, video machines, radios and axes. The butcher shop was well stocked and also expensive (rib fillet at twelve dollars a pound).

This settlement, as Ernie Bowen had told me, was started after the war, when the Aborigines had been taken back from Rockhampton. The history was recorded on a plaque at Pioneer Hall, but it was a short history – three lines, about its beginnings in 1949 and *In Memory of Our Pioneers*, with a column of the familiar surnames.

There was no single color, or face, or racial type in the community. They were all colors, from the deepest, purplest black to plain pinkish white.

Barry Liddie was a great deal paler and more civilized than most of the white Australians I had met elsewhere, yet he had several Aboriginal grandparents. His house at the edge of the settlement was low and rambling and rather littered, with a clutter of dead and rusted machinery all over the garden and the porch. He was sitting on his veranda. He had locked himself out of the house. Instead of looking for his wife, he simply sat down. She'd be home later to let him in.

He was stocky, with reddish hair, and handsome in a beefy way. He came from the hot far northern town of Coen in the deepest outback. After marrying Lynette Deemal, who had been born right here at the mission, they had come here to live. He fished. She worked at the council offices. Besides this house they owned a boat and two large four-wheel-drive vehicles.

To kill time waiting on the veranda for his wife's key, Barry had a few beers. I declined the beer – too early: it was about eleven in the morning.

"It's never too early," he said, but he drank furtively, hiding the bottle with his hand. The place was supposed to be dry.

When Lynette arrived and let him in he disappeared, and Lynette told me about their twenty-three-year-old daughter, whose name was Sacheen – pronounced "Sha-heen." I asked if that was a Guugu Yimi-dirrh name.

"No. Don't you remember that Indian girl who collected the Academy Award for Marlon Brando? She was called Sacheen. The name just stuck in my mind, and when we had a daughter I knew that was what I wanted to call her."

"Does she go to school here?" I asked.

"No. She's at school in Cairns. I think she's better off there than in the reserve," Lynette said. She was articulate and poised; it was hard to tell what proportion Aboriginal she was. She had the features and the complexion of a Tamil, from south India. "Sacheen is studying hard. She might do hairdressing later on, or business."

"Would you like to see her get involved in the life of the reserve?"

"I don't want to influence her. I want her to do whatever she wants to do. I'd like her to stand on her own two feet."

It was an admirable sentiment, because here on the reserve, where every Aboriginal was a landlord, money was free: no one ever had to work. I remarked on what a quiet place Hopevale seemed.

"It's noisy here on Fridays, when the people get their money," Lynette said. "Then all the drunks are out."

I said I had to get back to the coast – to my boat. Barry helped me find a lift, and when I left him I shook his hand. He took my hand without gripping it, one of the strangest handshakes I have ever experienced – stranger even than that of the most tepid non-handshaking Englishman.

I mentioned to an Australian that I found it odd that Barry claimed to be an Aboriginal. He was white, after all.

"How can you tell he's really an Aboriginal?"

"Did you shake his hand?"

"Yes."

"Did it feel like a dead fish?"

"Yes."

"That's the proof. They don't shake hands."

This was back in Cooktown. I had not had a shave or a hot bath for a week. As an experiment I walked into the so-called animal bar to see whether I would blend in. My disguise worked: no one took a second look at me.

"Quiet tonight," I said to the young man next to me.

He was not quite as grubby as I was, but he was barefoot.

"Wait till check day," he said. "The Abos'll all be in here. They love fire water. They get their money and then go on the piss."

"Is it dangerous?"

"They're not too violent," he said. "No knives. Nothing like that. They might use the broken end of a glass stubbie. Yeah, some of the younger footballers are tough, but most of the Abos just drink and fall down."

Then he started the old refrain: government money, land royalties, free cash, land rights, two-percent housing loans. "And what have I got?"

It seemed to me that he had a very great deal if he lived in this lovely climate on the dole and could sit on his ass drinking beer throughout the night, chatting to the pretty barmaid, seemingly without a care in the world. But I said nothing.

"Ever heard of this bloke," he said, becoming warmly vindictive, "down in Melbourne who's trying to prove that the first people in Australia weren't the Abos?"

"Never heard of him," I said. "But if the Aborigines weren't the first people here, who were?"

"That's just it. According to this bloke, it was the Jews."

"The Jews were here first?"

"Right," he said, and he was triumphant. "And if he proves it, then these Abos are up the creek."

I said, "Then Jews will be collecting money from the mining companies. They will control the sacred sites. And they will be getting two-percent loans."

His eyes became very small. He swallowed some beer. He saw my point.

"Yeah. Rather have the bloody Abos."

He had been counting on disinheriting the Aborigines, but this conclusion made him thoughtful. He was glassy-eyed anyway, but his eyes grew glassier. After a while, realizing that I had not moved or spoken, he piped up again.

"Have I seen you in town before?"

"Probably not. I'm camping up the coast, Cape Bedford way."

"Place is full of Abos. And bloody crocs."

I smiled harmlessly, conveying the thought *That's obvious!*

"You seen any crocs?" And he put his whiskery face closer to my whiskery face.

"A couple," I said casually. "What do you call them – estuarine crocodiles?"

"A couple! Good on yer!"

# PART TWO
# MELANESIA

# 6

## *Buoyant in the Peaceful Trobriands*

I was nearer to the mangrove coast of Papua New Guinea, when I was up among the Aborigines and beachcombers of Cape Bedford, than I was to Brisbane or any other Australian city of any size. And now that I knew I wanted to see the Islands of Love, described in graphic detail in Malinowski's *The Sexual Life of Savages*, couldn't I simply get in my collapsible kayak and paddle there from here?

A map of the Torres Strait, the passage between Australia and New Guinea, made the trip seem pretty straightforward. I would paddle to Cape York, camping on the way, and then I would go island-hopping across the strait – no island involved much more than a twenty-mile, or one-day, crossing: from Thursday Island, to Moa Island, and from one rock to another, heading for the New Guinean depot of Daru Island near the mouth of the Fly River; across that estuary and up the coast, where there were little stations and muddy harbors to Port Moresby – a couple of weeks. If you're not in a hurry you can go anywhere, as the man said. Then I would figure out how to get to the Trobriands.

Maps, especially simple ones, can offer very hospitable and kindly portraits of a place. Maps of the Torres Strait cannot depict the powerful current rushing between the islands, the strong wind, the numerous reefs, the few real refuges in case of trouble, the absence of freshwater sources, the miserable insect-ridden mangrove coast of the far side, and – in the vast muddy estuary of the Fly River – the crocs. I did not get my information from townies; I asked old black Thursday Islanders, and fishermen, and boatmen in Cooktown who had cruised and worked in the Torres Strait. They didn't tell me scare-stories, they told me what they had seen. And they didn't try to discourage me. Don't go alone, they said, and they told me to allow a month or six weeks for the trip. And on no account was I to spend a night among the savage and desperate (so they said) mud men in the unfriendly stilt-villages of the Fly.

I collapsed my boat and took a plane from Cairns to Papua New

Guinea. It was a little over an hour's flight to the capital, Port Moresby, one of the most violent and decrepit towns on the face of the planet. Dusty and falling apart, it had been thoroughly vandalized before it could ever be finished, and so it looked like an enormous building site, slums and flimsy bungalows scattered across a number of ugly hills. It was full of ragged bearded blacks, New Guinea highlanders, most of whom bore an exact facial resemblance to the distinguished jazz pianist, Thelonious Monk.

"*Wonem dispela?*" asked the New Guinea customs officer, a wild-haired woman in a filthy dress, at the terminal. She began pinching my canvas sacks.

This was incidentally the first time New Guinea Pidgin rang against my ear. "Neo-Melanesian," as it is known by linguists, is one of the fascinations of the Western Pacific: ". . . many commentators err in thinking of Pidgin as static baby-talk . . . This is quite wrong . . . Pidgin is both complex and precise." That is the opinion (*ting*) of a distinguished (*gat nem*) teacher (*tisa*) who has given this language (*tok*) a great deal of thought (*tumas tingktingk*) – according to Captain J. J. Murphy in his *Buk Bilong Tok Pisin*.

Later, speaking it – saying the days of the week, for example – I felt that I had talked my way onto the pages of *Finnegans Wake*, where Joyce writes the days as *moanday, tearsday, waitsday, thumpsday, frightday, shatterday*. In Pidgin, they are *mande, tunde, trinde, fonde, fraide, sarere, sande*.

"This fellow is a boat," I said.

"*Yu tinka dispela bot? How long dispela bot blong yu?*"

"Four years, approximately."

"*You taking dispela away wit' you when you lusim hia?*"

"I imagine so."

"*Wonem dispela bek?*" Now she was gesturing to the lunchbag I had intended to throw away.

"Trash," I said.

"*Samting-nating,*" she said, using a precise Neo-Melanesian expression, as she looked inside. "You pas."

She made a chalk mark on my canvas sacks.

I said, "I'm looking for the plane to the Trobriands."

Hearing me, one of her colleagues said, "*Balus I laik go nau.*"

"Does that mean the plane is leaving?"

"*Yesa.*"

In fact it was leaving in fifteen minutes from the domestic terminal, a shed up the road reeking of fruit peel and urine. I was forcibly helped by a dwarfish highlander in a wool hat. His teeth were black, his feet and his hands were huge, and he was wearing one of the dirtiest shirts I had ever seen. We struggled with my boat and my camping equipment.

"*Yu kam olsem wonem?*" he asked. He was grinning. He was sweating. He himself was from Mount Hagen, he said. "*Yu kam we? Yu go we? We yu stap long?*"

"I'm just visiting," I said.

"*Wat dispela bikpela kago?*"

"It's a boat."

"*Kago bilong yu, putim long hap, klostu long dua.*" And he dropped my bags near the door.

"Where's the plane?"

"*Balus i bagarap.*"

"It's buggered up?" I said.

The man smiled, he pulled off his wool hat and wiped the sweat from his face, and he then demanded oysters. But the word for oysters in Pidgin was also the word for money. I handed some over and he saluted me.

The Twin Otter wasn't buggered up, it was only out of gas, and the Australian pilot was saying to a bearded highlander, "I can't go to Losuia without fuel now, can I?"

The Men's Room (*Haus Pek Pek*) outside the terminal was almost too disgusting to use. A prominent warning was in two languages: *Do Not Misuse the Toilet/No Ken Bagarupim Haus Pek Pek*.

In the end, I was the only passenger on the little plane to the Trobriands.

After an hour of high clouds and blue ocean the green islands shimmered into view. They were in the middle of nowhere: it was another experience of the Pacific being like the night sky, like outer space, and of island-hopping in that ocean being something like interplanetary travel. In the Solomon Sea below, there were about a dozen islands big and small; and they could not have been flatter. Only a few feet above sea-level, without a single hump or mound, they appeared to be floating, like a thin layer of green weed rippling upon the sea. At the center of each of the larger islands was a bright boggy swamp, and I could see the tall coconut palms lining the dirt tracks, their long shadows stretching across the low bush. The pattern of each village was the same, just as Malinowski described – the lovely huts ranged around the stately carved and painted yam house. A great deal was obvious from the air: no cars, no paved roads, no power lines, no billboards, no tin roofs, no motor-boats. The promise of this simplicity thrilled me.

The airstrip was a grassy swathe that resembled the fairway at a public golf course – rather trampled and untended. The terminal was a shed slightly smaller than a one-car garage. Two battered vehicles were parked near it, and about two hundred brown people were ranged around it. They wore shorts, and the sarongs they called *lap-laps*; some wore flowers behind their ears, or coronets of white wilted frangipani blossoms. About half a dozen carried carvings – walking sticks, salad bowls, war clubs, statuettes; the rest simply gaped as the plane taxied to a stop. This was one of the group activities of Kiriwina – the main Trobriand island – watching the Moresby plane land and take off.

On the evidence of this crowd, there was no Trobriand face: these people had few features in common. The people ranged from black, smooth-skinned Nat King Cole Melanesian to light-skinned straighter-haired Polynesian types who would not have looked out of place in a hula competition in Waikiki. And every racial graduation and hair-type in between. Here and there was a woman with sun-scorched hair, almost blonde; and there were a handful of redheads, who looked as though they had overdone it with the henna treatment. It was a very odd assortment of people – there was even a scattering of albinos – and much odder for representing the population of a relatively small island in the middle of the ocean.

I was approached by a fat little Trobriand woman. The pencil bristling from her frizzy hair gave the appearance of being stuck into her skull.

"You can get in," she said, and motioned to a rusted pick-up truck.

She worked at the lodge, a tumbledown seaside inn, which was the only place to stay on the island – or in the entire archipelago, for that matter. It was assumed that any visitor who got off the plane was headed for the lodge. I had planned to get a lift to the shore, and camp there, but this arrangement suited me even better.

"What is in all this luggage?"

"A boat."

She shrugged, sighed, and made a face. On the way she sat clutching the steering wheel and glowering at the rubbly track ahead, hardly speaking. After a while I coaxed from her the information that her name was Amy and that she had spent some time in Australia. I put her sulkiness down to the fact that she had probably been treated rather badly there – or in the same offhand way as she was treating me.

"Is there any sort of administration center on this island – a town, or a market?"

"We just went through it," she said.

I had not seen anything but palm trees and wooden sheds.

"Is there anyone else at your lodge?"

"Some *dim-dims*," she said, using the local word for white person. "Australians."

They were seven expatriates who had flown from a town on the north coast of New Guinea on a private plane for a weekend of heavy drinking and horsing around. They had with them – it seemed to be their only luggage – a number of cases of beer. It was mid-afternoon and they were already drunk, in the state of clumsy geniality that I had come to recognize from my stay in Cooktown.

They were sunburned and glassy-eyed, all of them fleshy, and they were as friendly as they knew how to be. They became hearty, seeing me and sizing me up, and one handed me a beer, for drunks love companions and hate sober witnesses. I shook hands with the fattest one.

"G'day. I'm Mango. That's Fingers. That's Big Bird – he owns the plane. That's Booboo. That's Ali –"

It was all nicknames. We had another beer and sat on the veranda, watching the tide drain out of the flats of the lagoon.

"Fingers saw a croc here just a minute ago."

"Unless it was a fucken *meri* out swimming."

*Meri* was Pidgin for woman.

"I had three national *meris* last night."

"Fingers is a fucken animal."

Fingers was freckled and had close-together eyes, and the odd set of his jaw – his underbite – gave him a moronic expression when he smiled.

"They're all looking for white husbands," Booboo said.

"Do you find them madly attractive?" I asked.

"Some of them are pretty and others are ugly as hell," Mango said. "But they all fuck."

This was one of their topics of conversation, but in their telling they were always passive, the women always the aggressors: *So I hear this fucken noise at the window and I look out and it's a* meri *lifting up her* lap-lap –

Other topics were the laziness of highlanders, the high crime rate, particularly destructive car crashes, good meals, the horror of Port Moresby, and the good fun of heavy drinking. They were loud and jolly and fairly harmless. They said as much.

"We're all going troppo."

"What are the symptoms?" I asked.

"The first one is that you don't want to go home," Fingers said. "You go a bit round the twist, see."

"And the national *meris* look bloody marvelous," Booboo said.

"And you sit in places like this with a stubbie in your hand," Mango said.

Big Bird stood up and walked to the veranda rail. "That's a croc," he said. "That's definitely a croc."

A low log-like shape darker than the water around it trembled in the muddy lagoon and then sank, leaving subtle ripples.

"Ugly bugger," Mango said, staring at the widening ripples.

"That one was eight foot at least," Ali said.

"Ten is more like it," Booboo said.

They discussed the length of the croc, and it kept growing, until Amy appeared on the veranda and sulkily announced dinner.

We were served by two bare-breasted girls in grass skirts, who managed to look demure, even as Fingers was blatantly leering. The girls were small – Trobrianders were small of stature anyway, but these could not have been older than thirteen or fourteen. Their grass skirts were short and dense, and fitted them like dancers' tutus. Malinowski remarked on how the grass skirt "is very becoming to fine young women, and gives to small slender girls a graceful, elfish appearance."

"Elfish" was just about perfect. And the shell anklets and bracelets and necklaces they wore made pretty wind-chime chuckles as they walked. No one spoke – there were only sighs and murmurs of concentration from the Australian men – as the girls glided near the table, padding around it on bare feet.

The food was unappetizing and uneatable – fatty meat and boiled white tubers, served with hunks of Spam.

"What do you think of this food?" I asked.

"It's crap," Mango said, stuffing Spam into his mouth.

There was dancing afterwards, by the bare-breasted waitresses and some drummers who had been hauled in from the road. A crowd of people always gathered there under the lights; they crouched and chattered. The rest of the island seemed to be in darkness but people habitually sat outside the lodge at night because it had a generator and a few electric lights.

When the music was over, and the Australians stumbled outside to look for women, and after Amy had firmly put me in my place ("We don't have coat-hangers"), and I found out where I could get food and supplies for tomorrow, I went to bed, vowing to paddle away in the morning.

"*Waga,*" I heard them say. "*Waga. Waga,*" as the kayak took shape. A crowd of about fifty men and boys were squatting at the edge of the lagoon watching me assemble it. Most of them were gaping, some were mocking me, some fooling with the kayak pieces, and two or three were in my way, competing to help me put the thing together.

After that, whenever I put the kayak together, or took it apart, a crowd of males gathered (the women had better things to do) to watch me, or to fool. On this sort of occasion – a hot humid day on a muddy Trobriand foreshore, picking my way among the broken coral, and hearing the laughter of the islanders and their certain mockery ("what is the *dim-dim* doing now?"), I was often reminded of how Malinowski, the most sympathetic of anthropologists, would spend a day among these laughing people and then go back to his tent and scribble vindictively in his private diary.

"The natives still irritate me, particularly Ginger, whom I would willingly beat to death," he wrote. "I understand all the German and Belgian colonial atrocities." Or: "Unpleasant clash with Ginger . . . I was enraged and punched him in the jaw once or twice." Or: "I am in a world of lies here." Or worse. Publicly he called them "the Argonauts of the Western Pacific," but in his diary he had his own private name for the Trobrianders. "The niggers were noisy . . . General aversion to niggers . . ."

The entries could have come from the intimate journals of Mistah Kurtz in his hut at the Heart of Darkness, but no, they are those of the founder of the modern discipline of social anthropology, the man who had made it a highly literate, observational science. There was a general outcry when Malinowski's private diaries were posthumously published in 1966, but they were harmless enough – just trivia, ranting, loneliness, insecurity and self-pity. What is clear in them is that what he hated most – what all travelers hate – was not being taken seriously.

They teased him and they teased me. It is irritating, but so what? The Trobriand children are rambunctious; they are seldom scolded. No children I had ever come across lived a less repressed existence. The youngest played all day, and on the moonlit nights they all went frolicking – I was often to hear kids' laughter at midnight. Yet they do what they are expected to – work in the gardens and pick coconuts and go on fishing expeditions. There are schools, but though half the village children never see a classroom, they are skilled in the arts of the island and have an intimate knowledge of their own stories and traditions. This attitude of self-possession, which seemed like arrogance – the teasing of *dim-dims* – had kept the Trobriand culture intact and was perhaps the key to their survival.

And after I pulled the pieces out of my two bags and assembled the kayak, I stowed my food and the rest of my gear, and – as they watched, still muttering and laughing – I simply pushed off and paddled away. This was on the east coast of Kiriwina, near the village of Wawela. On my chart I saw a break in the reef marked "Boat Passage" – and I paddled to it. A strong riptide was moving through it and waves were breaking just outside it, so I stayed inside the lagoon and paddled south along the reef in pretty, greeny-blue water, across shelves of brightly colored coral.

I paddled about five miles south, until the lagoon narrowed, squeezing me into a small neck of water between the reefs and the beach. I looked onshore and saw a crowd of people, seemingly camped – but there were no huts or shelters of any kind. I thought perhaps they were killing time, waiting for a boat to Kitava Island which lay about five miles in the sea beyond the reef.

Seeing me, several men began waving and whistling, gesturing for me to come over. Having nothing better to do, and wishing to add a little coastal detail to my rather stark fifty-year-old chart, I paddled towards them.

A green sea turtle lay on its back on the sand near the men, gasping and feebly working its flippers. From time to time, whenever the turtle tried to turn itself over, a man would kick it.

The men who had called me over did not speak English, but another fellow, named Sam, spoke English fluently. Pidgin would have been of little use. It is regarded as pig-English in the Trobriands and is spoken self-consciously and with great reluctance. Sam had learned English in Port Moresby, where he had worked in a bank. But he hated the city and when he had earned enough money returned to his Trobriand village, Daiagilla.

"It is in the north of this island, near Kaibola, but not on the beach," he said. "That is our problem. We have trouble fishing there. So many people, and all of them fishing."

The solution was to come here, fifteen miles away, and establish a temporary fishing camp, which was what this group of thirty-three men and boys comprised. They wore ragged bathing suits. One was feeble-minded. One was deaf and dumb. They lived in complete harmony. They had made an arrangement with the village that owned this beach, and they fished day and night, using spears and nets, until they had enough fish to bring back.

"Why is this village willing to help you?"

They said that the local village was given some of the catch, and in return they brought vegetables and drinking water to the fishermen.

"There is no trouble," Sam said. "We don't fight. We want to live in peace."

They had been there for four days, and when they weren't fishing they were processing the large (eight- and ten-pounders) coral trout, smoke-drying them on a sort of rickety table erected over a smoldering fire. Fish hung from lines that stretched from palm trunk to palm trunk.

"We catch more at night," Sam said, and showed me the long waterproof flashlights they used for night-fishing. He showed me a wooden spear with a rusty barbed point. "And these harpoons are good, too. This is a good place for fishing. But we don't come here much. This is only the second time this year."

"What do you eat the rest of the time – yams?"

"Yam is for feasts. It is special. We don't eat it when we are in our huts, but when we are together at a feast we eat it. We eat other vegetables. Taro. Sweet potato. Pumpkin tops."

"I don't see any women here," I said.

"The women don't fish. They are home tending the gardens, looking after the little children, and preparing for us to return." He glanced at the struggling turtle and gave it another kick. "When we return there will be a great feast. We will eat most of the fish. We have to eat it – there is no way to keep it."

I said, "Have you ever heard of Malinowski?"

"I have heard of him," Sam said, and he laughed. "'The Islands of Love.' I have never read his books, but someone told me about him when I was in Moresby."

"What did they say?"

"He came here. Maybe he came during the Yam Festival. So he thought we were like that all the year. I think he generalized about us."

"Tell me about the Yam Festival," I said. Malinowski had compared it to a bacchanalia and had given graphic examples of sexual license.

"The Yam Festival" – Sam smiled and looked at the others, who were picking through my boat, examining my own fishing spear, knotting and unknotting my nylon lines. "It is in June and July. The women do silly things. And the men do silly things. And I also do silly things. It is a funny festival."

They invited me to stay at their camp. It was only mid-afternoon, but the day was hotter than I had expected, and when they brought out a big smoked fish, steaming on a palm leaf, I ate with them and abandoned any plans to go farther south that day. They expressed an interest in my food. I was happy to give them a loaf of my bread, which they passed around, and some fruit and cookies.

I often had this frustrating experience of handing out goodies. I would take a whole box of cookies or a giant chocolate bar and I would see it subdivided and wolfed down so quickly it was as though I had given them nothing at all. They always shared the food, they never fought over it, and yet food – especially cookies – seemed to vaporize in their eager hands. This stuff was a frivolous and insubstantial present anyway. I had brought spear points and spear rubbers and fish-hooks to give as gifts.

That night around the fire, Sam asked me the questions the others relayed to him – where was I from? What was my name? Was I married? Did I have children? How had I heard about the Trobriands?

I answered the best way I could, and I told them about Malinowski.

Sam said, "I don't want to read his books. Why should I?"

"You seem to be happy people," I said. "But what if you had a chance to improve your lives. What would you do?"

He thought a long time, and he consulted the others before he answered. Then he said, "If only we had a vehicle. It is so expensive for us to come here on the government truck" – two or three trucks passed for public transport on Kiriwina, and there were no vehicles at all, nor any roads, on the other islands. Though this seemed to me a delightful situation, Sam disagreed. "But we will never have the money. We get some money by selling carvings and selling food at the market. It is so little."

I told him that I thought the virtue of the Trobriands was that it did not have a money economy. He said, Yes, but there were some items you just couldn't barter for – school fees, canned meat, good clothes, and the sort of vehicle his village craved but would never have.

In the darkness beyond the camp fire, the younger men and boys fussed with spears and flashlights. Sam had once or twice referred to the chief. It turned out that he was with them, a toothless, betel-chewing man in a torn T-shirt, named Goody, or perhaps Gudi.

"He owns the land of our village," Sam said.

Because of the steady wind there were no mosquitoes, so I dug out my sleeping-bag and found a patch of sand to sleep on. It was a night of their muttering and splashing, and when the wind shifted I got a face full of wood-smoke. In the morning I could see clearly what a mess the camp was, a great litter of smashed coconuts, fishbones, crab shells, smoking fires, reeking fish and the same gasping, dying turtle.

Through Sam, Gudi said, "Let me paddle your boat."

The shoreline was all coral and I was afraid he would puncture it, so I said, "Not today. Maybe when I come back for the Yam Festival."

Towards the bottom of Kiriwina Island, at Gilibwa, there was another boat passage which I paddled through to cut over to the swampier, western side. Here there was no wind inshore, but the water was shallow, and in some places I had to get out and drag the boat along by its bow line. I sloshed along in rubber reef-shoes because of the stonefish and the sea-urchins and the sharp coral, but listening to Mozart on my headphones and feeling safe among these hospitable people, I found the whole trip around the south end of the happy island of Kiriwina extremely pleasant.

The lodge was empty except for a sunburned French couple in green army fatigues who complained that the fan in their room didn't work.

I restocked with food and water and prepared to head west out of Losuia on about an eight-mile paddle to the next island, Kaileuna, which I intended to circumnavigate.

"A woman was taken by a croc near Boli Point," Bill, the Australian manager of the lodge, told me just before I left.

I would be passing Boli Point in a few hours.

"When are you planning to be back?" he asked.

"Tuesday afternoon."

"If you're not here then we'll come looking for you," he said in a neighborly way. "One other thing. Don't camp at random. Get permission from the village nearest the beach. They might charge a few *kina*, but not more than that. The person who does all the talking is usually the least trustworthy. It could cost you a lot if you're not careful. Don't go along with them if they say, 'Never mind – we'll settle it tomorrow' because by tomorrow you could be in deep shit. They could charge you a hundred and you'd have to pay."

Just before I got into my boat the sky grew black and rain came down, such a heavy downpour that I was prevented from leaving for another hour. The men and boys laughed when they saw me dripping in my wet clothes and fussing around my boat – the sudden storm had dumped an inch of water in the bottom. They stopped laughing and came closer, seeing me working my bilge pump – just a simple handpump, but quicker and more effective than the wooden scoops they carved to bail out their canoes.

"You give this to me," one of the men said.

"Sorry," I said, and stored it.

He fooled for his friends. "The *dim-dim* no give to me!"

"Because you laughed at me," I said.

Steam was rising from the lagoon, and the air was heavy and humid, all the big trees on shore drizzling, as I set off across the flats of Losuia Bay, picking my way among the muddy chunks of coral. Fish were jumping, and birds squawking, and kids screaming and splashing at the bank.

There was little wind at first, but I was fighting an incoming tide. I left the shallow area and paddled to the main channel of dark blue water, deep enough to take the trading-boats that crossed Milne Bay with supplies from the New Guinea mainland port of Alotau.

Approaching Boli Point I thought of Bill's croc and kept about a mile offshore in a freshening wind and three-foot waves. I could see the muddy inlet where the crocodiles were reputed to be. There is a certain stagnancy and opaqueness to crocodile-inhabited water, a sheltered quality to the vegetation, stillness and stinky shadows. I could well believe there were crocodiles in this smelly estuary.

Beyond the point I saw Kaileuna Island, flat and deep green, about two miles away, across a stretch of open water. I paddled across to the far point, Mamamada, which was a chunk of spiky coral and a narrow beach. By then it was early afternoon – lunchtime – and as I ate I congratulated myself on having reached one of the smaller islands in the group. There were no villages here that I could see, though I had seen some huts farther up the eastern shore. I decided to avoid them, to paddle along the south side of the island.

I came to a white sandy beach, protected by a pair of jutting cliffs. There were green parrots in the trees, a big eagle overhead, and terns strafing the lagoon. There were no human footprints, only lizard tracks, and it looked like a perfect camping place, but while I was sizing it up a dugout canoe went past, two bare-breasted women paddling it, and they called out, sort of yodeling at me. So now my presence was known. I got back into my boat and paddled in the direction they were headed. Soon I saw a plume of smoke about a mile away and the light outline of some roofs of huts lining the beach. The village was not marked on my chart.

I first came to a little thatched pavilion at the end of a pier, and I nearly beached my boat there. It was a good thing I didn't, because this was the toilet for the women of the village – the men's was on the beach at the other side of the village. As I paddled parallel to the shore a group of boys began following me, running along the beach, whooping and hollering. I waved back at them.

By the time I got to the village's main beach a large number of people had gathered to watch me drag my kayak onto the sand – jeering boys, frightened infants, boys in *lap-laps* and bathing shorts, topless women, muttering men – some of the older men were holding lime-gourds and sucking betel juice from sticks.

"As soon as an interesting stranger arrives," Malinowski wrote of a typical reception in the Trobriands, "half the village assembles around him, talking loudly and making remarks about him, frequently uncomplimentary, and altogether assuming a tone of jocular familiarity."

This was the general impression I had of my arrival, but what drew my attention most was the good health of the villagers, in particular their good teeth.

"Does anybody speak English?" I asked.

"Everybody speaks English here," a man said.

An older man came towards me and shook my hand. He said that he was the chief, and asked where I was from, and what kind of a boat was this?

I told him and explained that I was paddling around the islands and that I had found a camping place about a mile away. Could I have his permission to camp there?

"Why don't you stay here in the village?" a man standing beside him said. "The missionary will show you a place."

"Where is the missionary?"

I expected to see a *dim-dim* in a black frock, but instead I was greeted by a Trobriander in a T-shirt and bathing-suit.

"I am the missionary," he said.

He said his name was John. He was a tall brown skinny man with frizzy gingery hair and, close up, I saw that his skin was reddish. He was holding a small naked child, and for some reason the child was clutching a long carving knife and slashing the air with it and snorting through his snotty nose.

Some small children trooped after us, as John led me through the village. The rest of the villagers had gone back to their chores – seven or eight of the men were building a large sailing canoe, some women were tending smoky fires, and a soccer game resumed nearer the edge of the clearing.

Toddlers, seeing me from their mother's arms or from where they were playing on straw mats, howled and pissed in fear. To torment them further, people picked the kids up and pretended to hand them over to me, and the more the kids screamed at the sight of the *dim-dim* the louder people laughed.

John said that he was from Alotau and that God had sent him here to Kaisiga – which was the name of this village. This was a very fortuitous choice on the part of the Almighty because it so happened that John's wife, Esther, was from the next village, Bulakwa, just along the coast. John and Esther had two children – the snotty one in his arms, and another one torturing a cat under the ladder to their hut: Cleopas and Waisodi. Esther was heavily pregnant and she sat in an open-sided shelf by the sea cutting vegetables.

"I would like to have a little girl," Esther said. "What is your wife's name?"

Whenever my marriage was mentioned, even in the most casual way, I grew sad and felt silent. At first I pretended I had not heard, but Esther persisted and eventually I gave her the information she wanted.

"I like that name," Esther said, placing her hands on her belly. "If we have a girl we will call her Anne."

Meanwhile, John was telling me about his conversion.

"I was blind. I spent many years as a blind man," he said. "Then I became a Seventh-day Adventist and I learned to see. Paul, would you like to learn how to see, like your namesake on the road to Damascus?"

So they were Seventh-day Adventists: that obviously explained their good teeth. They did not smoke or drink, the younger ones did not chew betel. No pig-eating.

"Do you want to convert me?"

"Yes. I do."

"I'll have to think it over, John. It's a pretty big decision in any person's life."

"That is true," he said, and then looked doubtful. But his mind was on other matters. "The trouble with camping here is that the small children will bother you. They are very curious and troublesome."

"Why don't we tell them not to be curious and troublesome?"

'They will just laugh at us."

Another man confirmed this. "Yes," he said. "They just come and go as they wish, the small boys."

"What time do they go to bed?"

"Whenever they like," the man said. "At eleven or twelve, or even later."

"And the other problem for you," John said, "is that I will beat the drum early in the morning to call people to the morning service. So don't put your tent close to the drum."

"What do you call early?"

"Maybe six o'clock."

"I think I'll put my tent way over there," I said.

I went back for my kayak and dragged it through the shallows of the lagoon to the edge of the village and when I unloaded it a crowd gathered – forty-seven people, big and small, I counted as I started to set up my tent. The little kids were touching everything – feeling the tent cloth, the kayak skin, twisting the ropes and stakes, most of them hindering me and getting underfoot in their attempts to help me. The naked, dusty munchkins rather fearlessly fingered my gear, and yelped and grabbed and passed various items to their parents for inspection.

"They are impressed with your tent," John said.

I shot out the shock-corded poles and, as they clicked together into their nine-foot length, there was applause and laughter. The people sat down around me, awaiting more. I hung up my water bag on a tree, turned the kayak over so that the kids wouldn't get in, and then, distracted by all the people, took a walk down the beach. When I returned at dusk the villagers had gone away. I crawled into my tent, took three swigs of sherry from my bottle, so as not to demoralize the Adventists, and started cooking my dinner.

Before leaving Losuia I had bought some kerosene for my camp stove. I got the stove going and boiled some water and made tea and then noodles, which I had with beans and canned mackerel.

While I was eating, John came over, still holding his snotty child.

"They think you are strange," he said. "But I told them you are not strange."

"I appreciate that, John."

"They have never seen anyone eat alone, but I told them that Westerners do it all the time. When you arrive in a place you make your own food."

"Very true, John," I said. "Have a cookie."

He took a handful and we wandered back together in the fading light, to the thatched pavilion they called a *bwayma* by the sea, and I passed out cookies to the others there and we sat and talked while the kids still chattered and splashed at the edge of the lagoon.

"What do these kids do until midnight?"

"They play. They sing. They tell stories," he said. "No one tells the children to go to bed."

It was supper time, a bright fire blazing in front of each hut, the woman poking it and cooking, her husband sitting on the porch of the hut eating.

"We share everything here," John said. "If the men catch fish, every family will get some. We have the same garden. We cook for each other. Whatever someone has, he shares."

Five of us were sitting in the breezy pavilion, eating the last of the cookies. John wanted to tell me about the Seventh-day Adventists, but I headed him off asking him about the Yam Festival.

"The Yam Festival is very un-Christian," John said, and the others smirked at me. "The girls and the women just rush at you. They grab at you anywhere" – and he gestured at his groin and frowned.

The others shrieked with laughter.

"It is not funny," John said, sadly.

"It is unusual," I said.

"It is worse than unusual," John said. "The women can hold you down. There might be seven or eight of them. They hold you and one of them sits on your face and laughs at you and she presses her waist against you."

"Presses her *waist*?"

"Her thing," John said.

"Her *wila*," someone said, and there was more laughter.

"I get it," I said.

"There is much fornication, and even rape," John said, with great solemnity. "Yes, I tell you, five or six girls can rape a man. They take a man and they sit on him, and they touch him and when his –"

"*Kwila!*" someone said.

"Yes, when his *kwila* gets hard the lucky one sits on it. What do you think of that?"

Everyone looked in my direction. I was smiling. I said, "Honestly, it sounds like traditional fun."

The men began to laugh at John, and I thought, *Tennyson, anyone?*

> *I will take some island woman, she shall rear my dusky race.*
> *Iron-jointed, supple-sinewed, they shall dive and they shall run,*
> *Catch the wild goat by the hair, and hurl their lances in the sun;*
> *Whistle back the parrot's call, and leap the rainbows of the brooks,*
> *Not with blinded eyesight poring over miserable books.*

The men were poking John and demanding that he speak up.

John said, "The Bible says that your body is the temple of God."

"It does say that," one man said, and was jeered at by the others.

"But God is love," I said. "And the Yam Festival is love, isn't it?"

"Yes! Yes!" the men and boys were chanting at their missionary, who was looking miserable.

He said, "Adultery can break up a marriage."

"Do the marriages of these people get broken up by this Yam Festival fornication?"

"No," John said, frankly. "For two months the husband goes this way, the wife goes that way. Then after the Yam Festival is over they come back together and all is the same as before."

"So there is no problem," I said.

"But the body is the temple of God," John nagged despairingly. "And there are worse things."

"I would love to hear them."

"The *mwaki-mwaki*. Tapioca dance," someone said. "It is shameful."

"And tug-of-war," John said. "They challenge the other villages. Boys from this village challenge the girls from that village. The girls from here tug-of-war against the boys from there. They are half-dressed. Only bottoms. They pull the vines, and whichever side wins chases the other, and when they catch them they fornicate on the grass, just like that."

"Then what happens?"

"Then they put their pants on and have another tug-of-war."

"That really sounds like fun," I said.

Everyone laughed except John, who left the pavilion and went to his hut. He returned a moment later with a copy of an Adventist magazine, *The Voice*, which he urged me to read. Then he said he wanted to tell me how it happened that he came here to Kaisiga village.

"This village was all United Church once. But one morning the people saw that a very big whale had come to the beach and was just lying there at the edge of the sand. The chief of the village had a dream. In the dream a voice told him about the whale. 'Because you asked for food,' the voice said. They got ropes and they pulled it out to sea. But the next day it came back. The chief had another dream. This time the voice said, 'Not physical food but spiritual food.' So instead of pulling the whale to sea, they took it and buried it on the next beach. The chief had a dream and he was told the meaning of the whale. 'You are asking to be fed another religion.' So they left the United Church and they invited the Adventists and I was sent from Poppondetta to lead them."

It was now dark over half the sea, though a pinky seashell light still lingered where the sun had set, making looming shadows of the high humpbacked islands on the horizon, Fergusson and Normanby and

Goodenough, in the distant southwest. Part of the lagoon was a great pink lake, and the more shadowy ocean close by sloshed against the edge of the village.

"How do you say 'good-night'?"

"*Bwoyna bogie*," John said.

"*Bwoyna bogie*," I said, and left them and crawled into my tent.

And most of the night, under the brilliant half moon that lighted the starry sky and the jungle treetops and the high clouds breezing across it and made silhouettes of the coconut palms, the children sang and laughed, by the surge of the sloshing lagoon.

The banging of the drum came early – it was a steel oil-drum and made a hell of a noise and went on for ages, because the drummer was another village kid, having fun. It was five-thirty in the morning – first light. Then I heard whispering and laughter and padding feet on the hard tramped earth of the village, and then the creaking planks of the church floor, and then the sweet harmony of children's voices singing,

*Weespa a frayer in da morning,*
*Weespa a frayer at noon.*
*Weespa a frayer in da evening*
*So keep your heart in tune.*

*Jesus may come in da morning,*
*Jesus may come at noon,*
*Jesus may come in da evening*
*So keep your heart in tune.*

And then I heard part of John's sermon as he read some verses from the Bible and began explicating it, saying, "Now that is not alcoholic wine. It is pure wine. It is, let us say, something like grape juice –'

I was up, making green tea, when the people from the morning service left the tin-roofed building that served as the church – it was nearly all children, and some women, and a few of the hecklers from last night at the seaside pavilion.

Seeing John, I said, "You were up early."

"Six-thirty, every morning," he said.

I said, "You mean five-thirty."

"Was it?" he said. "Well, we don't have a watch in the village. But that's a nice watch."

As he was looking at mine and seemed to be on the verge of breaking the Eighth Commandment, I thought how wonderful it was to have so little idea of the right time.

"What is this you are making?"

"Green tea."

"We don't drink tea," John said. "Or coffee. The body is the temple of God."

He was speaking as a Seventh-day Adventist, but it seemed odd to be making a virtue out of something that was untraditional on these islands anyway.

I drank some tea and almost choked. John took this as a sign from God, but I realized that I had accidentally filled my water bag with brackish water in Losuia. I was angry at myself for having lugged three gallons of undrinkable water in my kayak.

He invited me for breakfast. The mashed taro cooked in coconut milk and the bananas led us to a discussion of the pleasures of vegetarianism.

"Also we don't eat pigs or bats. Or Tulip," John said.

Tulip was not his pet chicken but rather a brand name, generic for any fatty pork in a can.

"Or coneys," John said.

"Did you say *coneys*? Rabbits? Are there any rabbits here?"

"No," John said.

"Which book of the Bible talks about food?"

"Leviticus. Chapter eleven," he said. "Also something in Deuteronomy."

He showed me his Bible and, reading the chapter in Leviticus, I concluded that it was like an environmentalist's charter and probably had done more to protect endangered species than all the nature charities put together.

"I can see you are interested," John said, sensing my imminent conversion.

While I was sitting there, eight or ten older boys came over, one with a *lei* of frangipani blossoms they called a *katububula*. The boy, whose name was Wilson, said, "The old man asked, 'Why didn't you give him flowers yesterday?' But we said, 'We didn't see him coming.'"

"Are you through with that?" a boy named Zechariah asked me, seeing that I had put my plate aside – I had eaten half of the stodgy mixture.

"I'm done," I said.

He snatched up the plate and ate what I had left. Then he smiled and said. "*Sena bwoyna!* That was very good."

They asked me what I was doing. I said I was on vacation and that I was just paddling around the islands. This to them seemed a perfectly natural way of passing the time. A man named Micah said, "But do not paddle to Tuma Island."

"Why not?"

"It is where the dead people go."

I found it on my map, a slender island, about five miles long to the northwest, and questioning them further I learned that it was a haunted place where no living person went because it was where the dangerous spirits of the dead resided. In Malinowski's description it was the Trobrianders' heaven, a place of eternal youth and perpetual copulation – an erotic paradise, if you were a *khosa*, a spirit. Even the Seventh-Day Adventists of Kaisiga village did not deny this, though they said that the *khosas* flitted around tormenting and tricking living people.

I put Tuma high on my list of destinations of places to paddle.

One of the boys was the son of the master canoe-builder, Meia. I was taken to where they were working on the large outrigger canoe I had seen when I arrived. This labor had occupied them for almost a year, they said. I sketched a picture of it, so that I could remember the names of all the parts – the splashboard and prow were beautifully carved and painted, and clusters of little cowrie shells had been strung along the gunwales. They had given it a name, which translated as "Sailing with the Wind."

"Will you take this fishing?"

"No," the old man Meia said through an interpreter. "This is for playing."

It was to be used in the *kula* expeditions, as the men from Kaisiga sailed from island to island giving and receiving the elaborate arm-shells (*mwali*) and necklaces (*soulava*) that were involved in this enigmatic game. It was outwardly a ceremony of exchange, with people taking shell ornaments from island to island and passing them along to friends (the *kula* partners), who, in turn, took ornaments to other islands. The so-called *Kula* Ring was partly social and partly magical, a game that has been played in the Milne Bay area for thousands of years, as the players – all of them expert sailors – traveled among the islands. The arm-shells went counterclockwise around the islands, the necklaces clockwise, and they were valuable because of their history, and their power deepened as they passed from person to person over the years. That supernatural power in Polynesia was known as *mana* – it was soul and strength. Each object (there are hundreds in circulation at any one time) has its own name and pedigree and personality. It is not owned by anyone. It would be unthinkable to sell any of these shell artifacts.

Joining the *kula* voyages was not for all Trobrianders. I had the impression that only a minority of the islanders were actually *kula* people, and that they were brought into the small circle of *kula* society by friends and relatives, the way one might be asked to join a bowling club in another culture – the comradeship was the important thing, and – this being the Trobes – women were also included.

All this I learned from Meia, the master canoe-builder. The seagoing canoe, the *masawa*, was essential to the *kula* expedition, since the islands were so far-flung.

As he spoke to me, Meia was mixing betel with lime in his little pot and sucking red globs of it off a stick. He was one of the few people in Kaisiga who was addicted to this stuff, a mild intoxicant.

"What is that?" I asked.

"Beer," he said, and smiled his toothless lime-rotted smile.

It was impossible to tell how old Meia was, but I could estimate his age. He remembered helping American soldiers carry boxes of food and ammunition after their amphibious landings in the Trobriands. (General MacArthur had thought the grass airstrip on Kiriwina might be useful in the Allied air war against the Japanese.) That was in June 1943. If Meia has been fourteen then, he was sixty-one now. His toothlessness and his skinny withered face and cloudy eyes made him look a great deal older than that.

No one I met in the Trobriands knew his or her exact age, and many could not even guess at it. A birthday, or year, was simply not recorded or remembered. Little breastless girls said, "Feefteen!" and big buxom ones said, "Seex!" "I am one hundred years old," a schoolboy told me in his teasing way, but when I promised him some candy if he told me his true age he could not do it. Speaking of their parents they would say, "Forty – or maybe fifty – or something."

I explained what a birthday was to Zechariah, who was in his early twenties.

"It is an interesting idea," he said. "But I don't know. My father and mother don't remember when I was born."

I had not planned to stay long at Kaisiga, but once my tent was pitched and I had ceased to be an oddity I decided to stay. Kaisiga was a good place to set off from to visit the rest of the villages on this fairly large island; and it was a good place to return to in the evening. There was drinking water here, the village was clean and orderly, the villagers were hospitable – they didn't importune, they didn't borrow, they didn't steal, and after a few days they didn't stare. Most of all they were gentle and peace-loving. That was what impressed me most, the peacefulness of the place. I decided to stay longer.

My food supplies were gone, but by a happy accident I discovered that I had an appetite for their food. Their staples were steamed or boiled taro roots and sweet potatoes and yams, and the greens they called "pumpkin tops," and a spinachy green they referred to as *ibica*.

They cooked with coconut milk – shredding the coconut meat and squelching it with fresh water. Now and then they had fish, smoked or steamed. Bananas and guavas were plentiful. For religious reasons they never had meat. They never fried anything, they used no salt or spices. It was a nearly perfect diet – in fact, it closely approximated the no-fat, high-energy diet that had been advocated in America and turned into a best-selling book by Nathan Pritikin.

"Obesity is extremely rare, and in its more pronounced forms is called a disease," Malinowski had written seventy years ago on the Trobriands. This was still true. One Saturday when there was nothing to do in the village – no one could cook or work on the sabbath – I persuaded a small group of villagers to come on a nature walk with me so that I could learn some of the island's names for these creatures (most of them proscribed in Leviticus – herons, snakes, lizards, turtles). I quizzed them on the topic of obesity, and with real emotion Lyndon (Leendon) said, "It is horrible."

The rest of them agreed. It was almost unknown in the Trobriands for anyone to be *napopoma* (pot-bellied), they said, and a fatty was in their view as unerotic as an elderly person, a cripple, a leper or an albino.

The Saturday sabbath in Kaisiga was a day for eating cold yams and clammy greens; for sitting around and talking; for sleeping, while the younger villagers sang and prayed or listened to Pastor John's biblical texts – he called them "Memory gems." However distant and solitary I felt all week in this little eventless village on this little humid island, I felt even more so on a Saturday. It made me jumpy and watchful. But by my second Saturday I had learned to glide along, and when John asked me to speak I decided to give a vegetarian sermon. I read from the Book of Daniel, of how Daniel had refused to defile himself with Nebuchadnezzar's meat and wine and how he had grown healthy and wise insisting on his diet of lentils and water.

John felt that I was ripe for conversion, and whenever we were together he preached the Adventist message. One day I expressed an interest in seeing the communal gardens, which were a mile or so in the interior of the island. We trekked in on a path that was partly mud and partly coral, and in the jungle the air was still and humid. I tried to leap from one tree root to another over the black shiny millipedes, and the mud, as I was stung by no-see-ums and mosquitoes – here and there was an eight-inch spider clinging to a web the size of a wagon-wheel, bits of the web smeared on my face and I was hot and thirsty and gasping and my feet hurt from my stumbling on the coral – and all this time John was sermonizing.

"Jesus said, 'No man can serve two masters: for either he will hate the one, and love the other, or else he will hold to the one and despise the other. You cannot serve God and mammon.' Now what does that mean when Almighty God says that? It means –"

And perspiring and stung and covered with mud, I staggered onward, batting the spiders away, and each time I brushed past a tree trunk the ants leapt from the bark to my skin and began biting me.

"Wide is the gate and broad is the way that leadeth to destruction," John was saying.

The gardens, when we reached them after an hour of bush-bashing, were rubbly and helter-skelter, the yams, the sweet potatoes, the taro, the paw-paws thriving among chunks of coral and tree roots on uneven ground.

"I tell them not to waste food," John said, standing on a coral boulder. "There are people in this world who are starving to death!"

I saw a chicken scratching in the garden. I said, "Do you eat chickens?"

He frowned at me. "The body is the temple of God."

This was his text for the return trip.

"The yam harvest is terrible," he said, clucking. "Everyone commits fornication."

"In the village?"

"Yes, they do it right in the village."

"Can you see them?"

"Yes, they do it while people's eyes are on them!" he said, batting branches. "Yes, you can see them going up and down! Oh, it is ter-rible."

"I don't even like to think about it," I said, and I clucked in disapproval as he gave me more details.

At night the church services were held in the dark – there were no working lanterns in Kaisiga; the flashlights were used only for fishing. In the early evening I went to my tent and drank sherry and wrote my notes, and heard the children singing *Weespa a frayer in da morning*. I knew the service was ending when they sang,

> *Lord keep us safe dis night,*
> *Secure from all our fees*
> *May ainjoos guard us while we sleep*
> *Till morning light appees.*
> *Amen!*

And then they left the church and hurried into the dark, where they ran and played and sang, giggling and fumbling and sometimes – in spite of all their apparent piety – raising hell, and often singing,

> *London Bridge is palling down,*
> *Palling down, palling down,*
> *My pair lady!*

The best beach on the island was on the western side, in an uninhabited cove, a two-hour paddle from Kaisiga. It was a white crescent of sandy beach with clear water and shady trees. On some days I brought my lunch here and swam and watched the parrots and fish eagles.

But that was only part of it. The rest, and in a way, the most blissful, was sitting in the pavilion on the Kaisiga shore, among a dozen softly chatting villagers, as the sun went down and the cool breeze wafted from the lagoon. We drank the sweet water from green coconuts.

When you come back bring us chocolate, they said. Bring us spear rubbers, bring us spear points and fish-hooks and fishing-line. Bring us T-shirts. Bring me a lantern, Micah said. Bring me baby clothes, Esther said. Bring me a watch, John said.

And on those nights we talked in whispers about ghosts. So many ghosts in the Trobriands! It was the reason people lived in huts that had no windows – they barricaded themselves in at night, even as their children were out playing. They told me about the *khosa*, the spirits of the dead. "They come and trick us!" About the *mulukwausi*, the invisible flying witches who perched in the trees and on the hut roofs and then swept to the ground and penetrated people's bodies, and lived in their hearts and lungs, killing them that way. Or the *bwaga'u*. No, they are not ghosts, they whispered: they are real men who kill at night. The *bwaga'u* were sorcerers.

"Give me an example," I said.

This was on one of those moony nights at the pavilion by the lagoon when the bliss of the South Seas dream was palpable – the breeze on my face, the sound of the sea, the aroma of blossoms, the last squawks of the birds settling in the branches for the night.

"Two years ago," Lyndon said, "there were two small children in the village who were thought to be evil. They were causing bad things to happen. That's what people said."

The breeze ruffled the thatch on the pavilion roof, and I could hear the low breathing of the villagers.

"So what happened to the children?"

"They were killed."

"How?"

"Poisoned."

"By whom?"

"A *bwaga'u*. Someone in our village."

"Do you know who?"

No one replied. There was darkness and silence. *Someone in our village.* A sorcerer. But it was a very small village.

# 7

# Aground in the Troubled Trobriands

"We cannot take the short cut. I saw some naked girls this morning on that road," Simon said, smiling – but there was a tremble of anxiety on his purplish lips.

This was my second visit to the Trobes – I had just been dropped at the airstrip by the Moresby plane and Simon, barefoot and toothless, had met me at the airstrip in his rusty pick-up truck. Simon disproved Malinowski's observation, "They give at first approach not so much the impression of wild savages as of smug and self-satisfied bourgeois."

The surprise to me was that Simon was smiling at all. At the road-side a little earlier an elderly Indian priest wearing a straw hat and shorts had asked him for a ride. Simon said, "You Catholic mission?" and when the priest nodded, Simon said, "No, no, no!" and gunned the engine. The mission was next to his village. "They are bad people," he explained to me. "They are troubling my village."

My collapsible kayak was in the back with all my camping gear, and a large bundle of presents – the T-shirts, the lantern, the spear points and fish-hooks, and all the rest of the stuff the people from Kaisiga had asked me to bring.

"I saw the girls doing the *mwaki-mwaki*," and he giggled at the thought of it. He had dusty hair and a brown scarred face. "Wearing short skirts." That meant the brief, bristly grass skirts. "They lifted their skirts up. They show their arse and private parts."

"What will happen if we go there?"

"They will rape us."

"How can they rape us if we just lie there? It's physically impossible."

"They will" – and now he smiled his red-toothed betel-juice smile – "sit on our faces."

"Does that frighten you?"

"Very much."

"They wouldn't attack a *dim-dim* like me."

"Yes. One was attacked some years ago. And Dennis" – Dennis was the local Member of Parliament, but a *dim-dim* – "they chased Dennis last year."

"The Yam Festival isn't supposed to start until next week," I said.

"It started today," Simon said. "This is the first day of yam harvest."

*Perfect*, I thought.

The Trobrianders who hung around the lodge, or who worked there – it was never clear who was who – greeted me in a friendly way and helped me carry my gear. "This is your boat, Mr Paul!" In places where the passage of time is unimportant, where there are no deadlines, where there is little sense of urgency – Pacific islands, the landlocked countries of Africa, the clearings in the South American jungle – people seem to have excellent memories. And they seldom remark on how long it has been since your last visit. You are welcomed, not effusively but warmly. You are fed. It is as though you had never left.

"Anything new?" I asked them.

"No," they said.

The food at the lodge was much worse than before. I sat down to the first course, which was a dish holding one orange segment, a small withered carrot, some brown discs of banana and a cold gray cut-open hot dog.

"The cook is on strike," Gertrude said. She was skinny and wizened, though she was no more than thirty-five. In a place where the average life-expectancy was forty-something – because of malaria, TB and bacterial infections – Gertrude was regarded as (and looked) rather old.

I asked her to bring me fish, yams and sweet potato, and if they didn't have it in the kitchen, I said, why not get it at the village next door? She brought it, and then sat with me while I ate, and we talked about the yam harvest. Just that morning some girls had accosted a man as they were leaving the gardens with some yams. The yams were special, magical; the carrying was always done by women, and in this matrilineal society the women had power.

"They took him on the ground," Gertrude said. "They scratched him on his arms."

"Girls or women?"

"Just the girls. Not the women. The girls are young. They can do as they like. They are public property. But even some women wear short skirts at this time of year. Their husbands cannot do anything about it."

"Do you wear a short skirt sometimes?"

"If I want to!" she said, and laughed hard. "What do they do in America?"

"Men and women chase each other all year, not just at harvest time. But it's not so much fun. Also they pay the women sometimes."

"They pay here, in some villages. Five *kina*. Or two *kina*, if the man doesn't have a job."

I loved that.

"They call it the 'Two Kina Bush.' You pay the money and do it in the trees."

The wind had blown all night and it was still blowing hard in the morning, which would make for rough paddling conditions. It was cooler than on my previous visit, with scattered clouds. But I wanted to set off, so I carried my gear to the shore and – as men and boys wandered over to watch ("*Waga*," they muttered) – started assembling my boat. Nine of the men carried bunches of betel nuts. They were from the island of Munawata, which lay a few miles to the west of Kaileuna. They sat and watched and spat blood-red betel juice, and they laughed each time they saw me stumble or heard me curse, as I put the boat together.

Two Chinese men joined them. They said they were from Malaysia and I guessed they were here in the Trobriands to buy some bêche-de-mer, the sea-slugs the Chinese regard as a delicacy and call sea-cucumbers. Local divers found the best of these creatures in deep water, and got about fifteen cents apiece from island traders, who processed them. The fat squishy sausages were smoke-dried and turned into hard little dicks, then bagged into forty-pound sacks and exported – with carvings, sea-slugs were one of the few Trobriand exports. (Trochus shells for buttons and pretty butterflies – sold to lepidopterists – were others.) Selling sea-slugs was the only thing to do with them. Most Trobrianders laughed at the thought of anyone eating them, though when there was not much food available some people ate them.

Mr Lim and Mr Choo watched me loading my boat.

"You are going out in that little boat alone?" Mr Lim asked.

"Yes."

"That's adventurous," he said.

"If you say so."

"But you don't look adventurous," he said. "You look like a professor."

"Thank you, Mr Lim."

Mr Choo said, "I am adventurous."

"Good for you," I said.

"But I wouldn't go alone. It is dangerous to go alone."

Mr Lim was scowling at the group of men from Munawata.

"But the Aborigines seem friendly," he said.

Andrew, a dark sturdy fisherman who worked at the lodge, was talking to the men. When they spoke to him, he laughed, and said, "They told me, 'Tell the *dim-dim* to be careful.'"

"Why do they say that?"

"Because the water is very rough around Kaileuna," Andrew said. "That's why they are here. They are waiting for the weather to improve."

It might have given me pause, but I knew their canoes well enough now. They were well built but did not have much freeboard and in a heavy sea they shipped water. They could go anywhere, even in fairly poor sea conditions, but there was often a lot of bailing to be done, with their wooden scoops. My boat could go anywhere, in almost any weather: that was the great virtue of a kayak.

But I had never paddled this boat so heavily laden. Besides my food and my gear, I had bundles of presents, and some of the presents – the fifty T-shirts and the fishing tackle, for example – I had crammed into a big canvas sack about the size of a mail-bag and tied to the stern deck of my boat, where it sat like a carcass.

The weight thrust the boat into the water and all this wetted surface gave it stability. But it was harder to paddle and, beyond the clay-colored channel and the weedy shallows and the crocodile nostrils poking up at Boli Point, where the open water began there was a strong wind blowing and four-foot breaking waves.

And the high lump of cargo lashed to the boat caught the wind and I was turned like a weathervane. I seriously wondered whether I should go back, or camp on this western side of Kiriwina Island and wait for better weather. As I pondered this – Kaileuna Island lay in the distance – the wind was still spinning my boat sideways, and waves were breaking across the bow deck, and I realized that in my indecision I had been blown quite far from shore.

So I kept at it. If you are stuck in chop and wind, kayakers say, just stay upright and paddle through it. I had the entire day ahead of me, there was no hurry, all I had to do now was plow on to Kaileuna. The breaking waves were the worst of it, and every now and then I was drenched – being slapped in the face by a cold frothy wave inspired a nervous dread in me, the feeling (as the water ran down my neck) that there was worse to come.

I headed for the nearest part of Kaileuna, which was a point of land, so that I could shelter and have a drink before pushing on along the coast to Kaisiga. It took me three hours to reach this rocky nose, but before I had time to celebrate my little achievement with a swig of water, two boys appeared on the beach, carrying spears – straight shafts with home-made rusty points.

"We will not hurt you," one said. He was wearing a pair of goggles that gave him the popeyed appearance of a villain.

But that in itself was a kind of warning. I took out my own spear – a long fiberglass one with a wicked-looking trident on the business end.

"Want to see my spear?"

They admired it, looking suitably respectful. "Where are you going?"

I said, "To Kaisiga."

"We do not like those people," said the boy with the goggles. "We are from Giwa."

I said, "Are the girls in Giwa raping the men this week?"

"On the mainland the girls rape men. Not here."

"Mainland" meant Kiriwina. This larger island was always called "the mainland." And the real mainland they called New Guinea.

"Come to Giwa," they said, as I paddled away. "We will show you our village."

It was another hour or so to Kaisiga and, in a stretch of water where there were normally lots of fishing canoes, little dugouts and larger outriggers, there were no boats at all, only a sea of rough water. And there were no people on the beach, only the sweeping wind and the thrashing of thatch and the loose panels of the woven huts.

I was spotted – first by some children, then by some men sheltering behind a hut – and they helped me ashore, Micah, and Josiah, and Lyndon, who called himself Leendon.

Josiah said, "You came from the station?" – meaning Losuia – "In this wind? Eh! Eh!"

I could see that they were pleased. They themselves had planned to go fishing today, but instead stayed ashore because of the stormy weather. They were flattered that I had come all this way in the wind and the waves to see them – and, more than that, risked getting wet in order to bring them T-shirts and fishing tackle.

John was at the garden, but Esther was at her hut. She was sitting crosslegged, suckling her infant.

"This is Anne," she said. "As I told you. We named her after your wife."

"It's a nice name," I said.

It was simply impossible for me to explain to her, or anyone on these happy islands, the derangement in my life.

I gave Esther the pressure lamp I had brought her from Moresby, and then I unloaded my boat. As I was setting up my tent, the wind rose, gusting madly and lashing the coconut palms. Meanwhile, about ten children were kicking a football nearby – every so often the ball would bash into my tent. I waved the kids away, but they just laughed at me – they were fearless. And when the rain started they kept kicking the ball and screeching, as they ran and splashed.

The frenzied kids, and the rain and wind, exhausted me. I went into my tent and made notes about my morning paddle in the high wind, while sipping the sherry that I hid from these prohibitionists. Every so often the children booted the ball into the side of my tent, but they laughed when I told them to play somewhere else. Finally I dozed off.

The gong woke me. I heard the kids hurrying in the pattering rain, and then,

> *Weespa a frayer in da morning*
> *Weespa a frayer at noon . . .*

The sweetness of their voices was undeniable, but in it was a note of mockery. They no longer sounded innocent to me. These prayer rituals were no more than momentary pauses in their relentless teasing, and indeed seemed to make their teasing worse.

Pastor John had come back from the gardens in order to conduct this evening service. I met him amid the blowing trees a little later and told him that I had brought the things they had asked for – the watch, the lantern, the T-shirts, the fishing tackle.

A number of villagers gathered in the wind and drizzle to watch me unpack the bundle of T-shirts which I had collected from friends to bring here. I let them choose the ones they wanted, and they immediately put them on – *Boston Celtics, Hard Rock Café, Me and My Girl, Punahou School, Great Wall Hotel Beijing, Dream Girls, Braves*, and so forth. They took them without ceremony. Though there was gratitude in the way they accepted them it was wordless thanks, yet it was so muted and perfunctory it seemed to verge on disappointment.

I gave Leendon some fish-hooks. He smiled at me. "But where is the line. What good are hooks without line?"

Zechariah thanked me for the spear point. He said, "Now I need a spear rubber" – meaning the tube of surgical rubber they fastened to the shaft of the spear to give it propulsion.

"You can borrow Micah's," I said. I had given Micah a length of rubber.

But Zechariah had seen that I had several more – ones I had planned to use for trading in other villages.

"I want my own rubber," he said.

"Did you get me extra batteries for my watch?" John asked.

"This shirt does not fit me," Derrick said, exchanging a *Braves* T-shirt for one that said *A Day in the Life of Canada*.

In a society that operated on a principle of continuous gift-giving, what I had done was merely to perform a ritual, fulfilling an obligation, which was why they felt free to nag me. And when I showed myself completely indifferent to their nagging, they changed the subject.

"There is a feast at Sinaketa tomorrow," Leendon said. "I am sailing there. You could come with us."

"What if the weather is bad?"

"I am a good sailor," Leendon said, and laughed. "I am big-pela, strong-pela. Ha!"

"I might paddle in my boat," I said.

The wind blew so hard that night it lifted the fly of my tent and soaked the mosquito net. And the pelting of raindrops and the sound of the wind in the trees woke me and made me anxious. Hearing the waves loudly hitting the beach I poked my head out of the tent, but in the blackness I saw nothing. So I switched on my flashlight and disturbed a dusky crab twice the size of my hand clawing at my tent flap.

I made green tea with my little stove, and had this for breakfast with Esther's rice, and pumpkin tops boiled in coconut milk. The wind was still blowing hard and I could see that the whole lagoon was frothy with chop and breaking waves. Was this a day for sailing or paddling anywhere?

Leendon said, "We are going. Come with us."

This man had once told me: *We sail out, and if it gets dark, we find an island and stay there for the night. There are islands everywhere in this sea, and there is always an empty island at night*. So I trusted him.

The whole village turned out to launch Leendon's outrigger canoe into the surf. I carried my binoculars and my compass. There were nine of us on board, including just one woman who crouched at the bow. I sat on the gunwale of the canoe and the seven men were occupied as crew members, two adjusting lines and trimming the rigging, two using the steering paddles jammed between braces, one on the main sheet, one standing at the bow and yelling about the heading, and Leendon alternately grunting orders and bailing the canoe. It would have been hard to sail this twenty-foot canoe with fewer than seven men. We began to ship water as soon as we left shore and, when we burst over the reef, sea water streamed in. Most of it came through the uncaulked seam in the longitudinal planks that had been added to give the vessel greater height and volume. No one seemed worried by this, least of all Leendon, who bailed with an old wooden scoop they called a *yatura*.

We had a lateen sail made of thick blue plastic sheeting and we sailed with the wind striking us on our outrigger side, which lifted the platform towards the body of the boat and almost submerged the seam of the plank on the opposite, down-tilted side. We could not sail very close to the wind, and at the beginning everything seemed very chaotic to me; but after a while I saw that each person on board had a specific role to play and in this rough sea was very attentive to his task.

The canoe was slow to respond to any trimming, even slower to turn, and was sluggish in the waves. We were all soon soaked to the skin as soon as we were past the reef.

"Leendon, does this canoe have a name?"

He said the name, *Toiyokwai*. "It means, 'Too Big-Headed.' You say, 'Do this,' 'Do that' but the person don't listen. They got their own way. You can't tell them a thing."

*Pompous, Arrogant, Over-Confident.* "I know the type."

"But why are we heading out to sea?"

"It is better in this wind."

We looked back at the disappearing islands, where another canoe was struggling against a lighter wind.

"We're going to beat him," I said.

They laughed, and clearly it was what they intended, and they continually fine-tuned the paddles they used variously as leeboards and rudders.

"Look at him," Micah said.

The other canoe rocked and slewed in the wind, and half a mile of choppy water lay between us. We were heading southeast towards the sea-arm of Kiriwina, to the coastal village of Sinaketa.

Micah spoke in Kiriwina to the other canoe, a voice of casual contempt and glee, which made the others laugh.

"What did he say?"

"Micah say, 'Go fuck your mother.' 'Go fuck your sister.'" And I must have frowned, because he added, "We are just joking him."

The wind was now tearing at our sail and straining the ancient-looking lines.

I said, "This is what we call a steep and confused sea."

"The current is running *this* way, and the wind is blowing *that* way," Leendon said, enunciating an immutable law of the sea. "That is why there are waves."

"Does the village have a motor-boat?" I asked.

"Yes, a dinghy, but the motor is buggered," one of the oarsmen said. "And there are problems."

Leendon changed the subject. We talked about crocodiles. They had no fear of them. *They used to come to the village to eat the dogs*, one of them said. And another put in, *You see them at low tide at Boli Point looking for something to eat.* Leendon said, *One* dim-dim *shot a big crocodile that had killed a small girl. They cut it open and found her bones and the earring from her ear.*

We were now way past Kaileuna and almost out of sight of the main island, all the lines tightened and the various sticks and braces in the canoe creaking. Leendon kept up a running commentary on the adjustments, while at the same time answering my questions about marriage in the Trobriands. Not marrying was unthinkable, he implied. ("The Trobriander has no full status in social life until he is married," Malinowski had said.) There was a partner for everyone. Wasn't that true of America?

"Some people never marry," I said. "I know a man who is fifty-something. He was supposed to marry a woman but at the last moment she changed her mind. He found another. Just before they were to be married she met another man. A third one dropped him – *bwoyna bogie*, bye-bye, and she was gone. A fourth one agreed to marry him but they argued one day and she went away and sent his ring back in a little parcel."

"He is very sad," Leendon said.

"He says he hates women now."

"He has no wife. No kids. That is terrible. What does he do all day?"

"He writes things."

"He is wasting time. He should come here. We will find him a wife."

I said, "A fourteen-year-old girl in a grass skirt with flowers in her hair?"

"Maybe fifteen," Leendon said.

The rest of the way to Sinaketa they told me what I should bring them the next time I came (waterproof watch, a tent like mine, a water bag like mine, more fishing tackle) and we trolled for fish, using fragments of a plastic bag for bait.

"I ran out of plastic last month when I was out fishing," Micah said. "I just cut my shirt and used little rags for bait. I caught many fish."

At Sinaketa we beached the canoe and went ashore, where the feast was in progress. Our little canoe party found the large number of decorated and dancing people rather overwhelming, and we stayed together. Leendon pointed out Pulayasi, the Paramount Chief of the Trobriands, from the powerful Tabalu clan, who lived in Omarakana with a number of wives. Sir Michael Somare, the former New Guinean prime minister, was seated under an awning. And a man as black and as hip as any American rapper was a Melanesian nutritionist from New Ireland in the Bismarck Archipelago.

Frowning, bare-breasted girls in straw tutus danced in a sort of conga line, egged on by sweating drummers. Some of the girls wore *kula* artifacts – jangling arm-shells and necklaces. They were followed by boys with talcum on their faces – strange white masks – who did the *mwaki-mwaki*, the so-called "tapioca dance." This was an explicitly sexual, buttock-slapping, bump and grind, with lots of shouted grunts, and it made the audience scream with approval.

The dancers wove their way among tall towers made of branches and containing yams which had been provided for the guests of honor. There were flags and flowers, and here and there were hairy black pigs tied up and whimpering as they struggled against their knots.

I fell into conversation with a man named James from Sinaketa, and asked him about burial customs.

"There isn't much burial here," he said. "The people die and their bones are put into clay pots and hidden."

Now I saw that Leendon had led Micah and the others to the little shelters that had been erected for the occasion. On long tables there were heaps of rice and boiled yams and bananas, and the sailors from Kaisiga were snatching handfuls of it and stuffing their mouths.

"But on Kitava," James was saying, "they take the dead man and butcher him while the widow is lying underneath the body. The blood spatters her clothes. She wears the clothes for three days while the village cleans her husband's bones. The bones end up in a clay pot."

This village was wilder and so much more festive than any I had seen elsewhere that I pestered Leendon on the way back for an explanation. And it became clear to me that this main island, where there were a few schools and the only vehicles, was also the most traditional island. It was the Paramount Chief's island, it was where the strongest clans and the wealthiest villages were located. This was where the yam harvest rituals were strictly observed, and although there were missions here the missionaries had little influence.

Normally, traditions were strongest the farther I had been from the center of things; but in the Trobriands, the hinterland, the outer islands, the little atolls regarded the big island as a throwback, full of primitives. That was why the villagers from Kaisiga were so eager to leave the big royal island of Kiriwina. Anything could happen to you there.

I had a vivid demonstration of that a few days later. Oppressed by the solitude of the village – everyone was working in the hot, mosquito-infested gardens – I had paddled to a swampy mangrove island called Baimapu to go bird-watching. The wind had died, and the morning was lovely and peaceful, and the sea a mirror of limpid light all the way to the horizon, all pinky-blue pastels. Red and black parrots were chasing each other through the trees, and the herons and other fish-eaters were wading in the shallows.

The water here was shallow and muddy, but a channel ran around the island. I tried to stay in this deeper water, away from the shadowy mudflats where there could have been crocs and where paddling was difficult – in places the water was only a few inches deep.

Ahead I saw seven or eight boys sloshing through the shallows, occasionally chucking spears into the water in front of them, going for fish. Seeing me, they changed direction and came near.

"Where you come from, *dim-dim*?" one said. He was a boy of thirteen or so, and his long spear – he wagged it at me – had a rusty point.

He was challenging me and being intentionally rude, so I said, "Don't call me *dim-dim*. I come from America."

Another said, "Give me PK" – the brand name was a generic term for chewing-gum.

The others pestered me for gum, and then some of them began fingering the boat.

"We want to ride in your *waga*."

One tried to sit on the stern, another pressed his spear point against the fabric of the boat.

"Don't touch it," I said sharply. "Get away from it."

By this time I had drifted out beyond the edge of the channel and was wedged in the shallows. The boys surrounded me, lifting their spears. They wore ragged shorts and their legs were muddy and there were smears of mud all over their bodies.

Shaking his spear at me, one of the smaller boys began running back and forth, shrieking, "I keel you! I keel you!"

As he jabbed the spear at me he made a hideous face, scowling and sticking his tongue out.

I dipped my paddle blade but my boat was stuck in the mud and I could not move it. I tried not to show my nervousness. In a tone of forced calm I said, "Don't be silly."

But seeing that I couldn't move, the others took up the chant, "Keel the *dim-dim*! Keel the *dim-dim*! Keel heem!"

The smaller boy came close to me and shook his spear and hissed at me, "Run you life, *dim-dim*."

"Keel heem!"

All this time I was smiling my rigid smile and speaking slowly and trying to move myself off the mudbank with my paddle. I did not want to get out of the boat, nor did I wish to show my alarm.

It was a nightmare – the shrieking youngsters, the way they pranced and plopped in the water threatening me, their fierce dirty faces, their hideously dangerous spears. I was seated, they were standing. And of course I was stranded – they saw that I was helpless. I could not understand whether it was merely a macabre game or genuinely hostile. But I decided not to antagonize them – only to ignore them and get myself out of there.

Turning my back on them, I dislodged the boat. It moved slowly, but still they pranced and chanted ("Run you life!"), and cried out, "Look at me!" – they wanted me to see their threatening spears. I deliberately kept my back turned to them and disguising my effort (I was sure that if they saw that I was nervous they would pursue me) kept my boat sliding away from them. I went on talking monotonously to myself in an unconcerned way, "There is no reason for you to be shaking those ridiculous spears at me . . ."

"Look!" One of them was holding a small, dead, discolored stingray – a despised fish in the Trobriands, eaten only in the poorer inland villages. "Eat it, *dim-dim*!"

They ran in front of me, so that I could see them with their spears, but I tried to appear calm, and I paddled past them. They threw the stingray at me and kept yelling, working themselves into a fury – horrible boys, with rusty spears and dirty faces.

In deeper water I dipped the paddle and took hard strokes. The boys followed me for a while – I was holding my breath, I had a sense that one of them would fling his spear at me – but I sprinted away and I did not stop paddling until I saw that they were astern, at a safe distance.

They had threatened me because I had been alone and had not given them any gift, and because they outnumbered me. I had left my fishing spear at the village. If I had shaken my own spear at them, or on the other hand if I had been a total wimp, they might have been much more hostile. I was the perfect victim: an outsider. It would not have been hard for them to injure me, even kill me. Just the bacteria on one of those rusty points would have done the job. What had surprised me most was their sudden cruelty.

I paddled to the wharf at Losuia, where a number of canoes were tied up. I was feeling unsteady and simply wanted to get out of my boat and sit down. If the little trade-store was open I would buy myself something to eat.

A fisherman at the wharf said, "You want to tie up your boat?"

I said yes. I had tied it there many times.

"It will cost you thirty *kina*," he said.

What was this? Over thirty dollars, for something that had never cost me a cent. A crowd gathered behind the man.

"In that case, I won't tie up."

"What will you pay?" the self-appointed extortionist asked me.

"Nothing."

The rest of the people stood gaping at me from the wharf, no one saying anything. Again, I felt a sense of threat. Everyone I ran into seemed hostile. As I paddled away someone called out, "Come back! We will help you!" but I was sure they only wanted to torment me, so I kept going, back to my camp at Kaisiga.

Even the people at Kaisiga were acting strangely. One day I paddled to the eastern shore of the island, to Koma village – a spooky inland village full of black snorting pigs – where I swapped a couple of silk scarves for some carvings (a canoe prow, an ebony lime-pot). *Don't go to Koma*, they said afterwards. *The people in Koma are bad.*

The villagers seemed restless and preoccupied. I suggested that we all go fishing in Leendon's canoe.

Zechariah said, "I will go if you let me have your goggles and your spear."

"I'll share them with you," I said.

In the end, twelve of us set off in Leendon's canoe and as soon as we were a mile or so offshore they all stood up in the canoe to look for submerged rocks, where there would be fish. The water was so clear the rocks were visible for some distance, and when we found one – it was actually a cluster of rocks and coral – they all dived in and began thrashing towards the bottom.

The clarity of the water had disguised the depth. I slipped into the water but the others were way below me – thirty feet down, among the twinkling yellow and green tiddlers and the hordes of plump parrot fish. I had never seen people dive so deeply, and they stayed at the bottom, hanging on the rocks with one hand and jabbing with the other. When they needed a breath they kicked to the surface, leaving their spear wedged in the coral; and then they swam down and resumed. I got within about ten or twelve feet of the bottom and then felt pain in my ear drums and had to hover nearer the surface. The others were oblivious to the depth and they stayed down for two or three minutes at a time. They were deadly with the spears, too, for soon after we arrived at the spot they were bringing up fish – parrot fish, reef trout, and a dark surgeon-fish with a poisonous spur near its tail they called a blackfish.

Noticing that the canoe had begun to take on water, I sat in the sunshine, amid the flopping fish, and bailed, scooping with Leendon's *yatura* – and the water was pink from the diluted blood of the speared and wounded fish. We had brought coconuts – to drink, to eat, and as a native skin remedy (the others rubbed crumbled coconut meat over their shoulders and arms for protection and to ease the scorching). From time to time they brought up fish.

When I dived back into the water I saw that the others were ranging all over the broken reef, chasing fish until they cornered them in the cleft of a rock and then jabbing fiercely. I took several deep dives and I was about to take another when I saw – unmistakably – the silvery snout and torpedo body of a shark, drifting downward in the long shafts of sunlight that penetrated the deep water, towards some of the swimming spear-carriers.

It was the smooth wickedly smirking shark of scare stories, huge and hungry-looking, surveying the naked swimmers with a kind of monstrous patience. The dark cigar-shape of our canoe was just above me. With the fewest strokes ("sharks know when you're scared") I made for the canoe and in one motion shot out of the water and tumbled into it, among the frantic fish.

Wiping fish-slime from my arms and hands, I tried to see beneath the water. The breeze rippling the surface was like a curtain being drawn across it, and nothing was clear to me.

Leendon was the first to surface. He snatched the canoe and took a great gasping breath. Then Derrick and Zechariah did the same, and others followed, clinging to the boat.

"Did you see the shark?"

Leendon said, "There were three sharks. The big one and two behind him. They were swimming to Zechariah, but he was on the rocks and he did not see them. So I shouted to him."

I could just see Leendon's howling twenty-five feet under water.

"I turned around and they were near me," Zechariah said. He was smiling.

I said, "Were you frightened?"

"No. I shout at them. 'Hoop! Hoop! Hoop!' That scared them away. They are stupid fish."

"Why didn't you swim away?"

"If they see you are scared they eat you."

"Leendon," I said. "Aren't you scared of sharks?"

He laughed at me and said, "No!"

"Do you know anyone who was bitten by one?"

"No one."

"But you can kill sharks."

Now he looked indignant.

"No. I am a Seventh-day Adventist."

And he referred me to Leviticus 11, where fish without scales are proscribed as an abomination.

We continued to dive, though I stayed close to the canoe. I was certain that the fish blood I had bailed out had attracted the sharks, and I was not comforted by the serenity of the others. I was afraid. And I disgraced myself again when, seeing a yellow sea-snake moving sinuously through the water above me, I hurried into the canoe.

Leendon had seen me. "Why you fearing?"

I said, "Big-pela snake. Long pela. Yellow pela."

"They not hurt you," Derrick said. "We play with them."

Later, looking for better fishing grounds, more tumbled coral rocks, we saw what could have been a coconut bobbing about thirty yards away.

"Turtle," Leendon said.

"It is a big one. We can chase it," Micah said.

"Do you eat them?"

Leendon said, "No. We are SDA. But the old men in the village eat them. They have a good taste."

It was a green sea turtle, with a shell the size of a manhole cover. We went after it, but it slipped away.

"It is better to catch them at night, when they are sleeping under the reef," Leendon said.

We were sitting crosslegged on the platform of poles that had been lashed across the outrigger of his canoe – a comfortable spot that could accommodate eight or nine people. He was watching the others count the fish. *Porty-pive*, someone said – ps and fs were interchangeable in the Kiriwina language.

"The current is too strong," Leendon said, signalling to the others to prepare the rigging for the return trip. "That is why we get pew pish."

Forty-five was quite a few – it was sixty pounds, or more, of fish. But the whole village had to be fed – that was his point. They would need twice that amount of fish to be able to smoke them and keep them for tomorrow.

On the way back we ate bananas and drank coconut water, and they eviscerated one coconut and rubbed the crumbled meat on their skin to ease their sunburn.

Out of the blue, Leendon said ruefully, "I am sorry we did not catch that turtle."

When we got near to shore the fishermen threw the fish out of the canoe into the water and the children splashed around snatching them up and washing them. Then they carried them to the village where another group of children had made a windbreak and erected a grill over a fire. There were twenty children involved in grilling the fish, many of them the boys and girls I had thought of as the village brats. When it came time for a village chore to be done, everyone lent a hand, even the brats.

The women, who had been awaiting the return of the fishing party, were steaming yams, bananas and sweet potatoes by the underground-oven method that is used all over the Pacific, from New Guinea, where it is called *mumu*, to Hawaii, where it is known as *imu*. The Trobriand word, which is almost certainly cognate with these, is *kumkumla*.

I tried to get the fishermen talking about the *kula* expedition after we had sat with our food – we were all in a long row on the ground, eating off palm leaves. Leendon was the most serious *kula* man in the village, but he was reluctant to talk about the arm-shells and necklaces he had in his hut. Finally he said, "I don't want to show Faul my *bagi*. He will want to buy all of them."

I persuaded him to show me the best necklace, which was a long beautiful string of tiny polished shells and then I said, "I don't want to buy it. It is not nice enough. In fact it is very ugly. It is nogut, samting-nating."

"He say it samting-nating! Ha!"

They all laughed. Heavy sarcasm was just the sort of clumsy teasing that they loved.

John was revolving his sister-in-law's six-month-old daughter Primrose over a smoldering coconut shell as he listened to all the banter. There were so many words in Pidgin for worthless things. ("It is *bullseet* . . . It is *rabis . . . Namba-ten . . .*").

They also found Pidgin as funny as I did, and because they seldom used it in the Trobriands the effect was always comic. And speaking Pidgin I could often ask questions that were awkward in plain English.

Dog-eaters always interested me, so I used this little feast as an occasion for asking, "*Yu-pela kai-kai dok?*" – *Do you people eat dogs?*

"*SDA-pela no kai-kai dok,*" Leendon said.

"*Yu traiem kai-kai dok – nambawan, moa beta,*" I said, patting my stomach.

John was smiling, still rotating the naked infant in the smoke. "*Alotau people traiem dok tumas. Tu, kai-kai pusi.*"

The Kaisiga women stared at him and the men began to shriek with laughter.

"Why are we speaking Pidgin?" I said. "Let's talk normal English. We are all normal English speakers, aren't we?"

"I am the most normal," Leendon said, and everyone laughed.

But I was looking at John. "Let me get this straight. You say that people in Alotau eat pussycats?"

"Some of the people," he said. "But not our own dogs and cats. We get other ones from the bush or running in the roads, and we cook them just like any other meat. Yes, sometimes it is sad, because a dog is man's best friend. But they taste good."

"Are dogs and cats mentioned in Leviticus?"

"No," John said, still dipping the infant into the smoke. "And not in Deuteronomy."

"What are you doing with that baby?"

He lifted the coconut shell and showed me a smoldering object beneath it, the size of a walnut.

"You see this grasshopper's egg?" he said, indicating the smoky walnut. *Grasshopper's egg?* "We burn it and when the smoke comes through the coconut shell we let the baby smell it. It is so the baby will walk straight."

"Do you believe that?"

"Yes. I have seen it."

I had found him monotonously biblical – his lengthy way of saying grace was so sententious it set my teeth on edge; so, seeing this Christian islander espousing magic and superstition, I encouraged him.

I had promised myself that I would paddle to the tiny islands at the edge of the Trobriand group. I could not interest anyone in Kaisiga in coming with me – visiting another village or another island involved a complex ritual of gift-giving and they couldn't be bothered. It was easier for me to show up, shoot the breeze and placate them with some sticks of tobacco or fish-hooks: a *dim-dim* was hardly human in any case.

It took a day to paddle to and from the island of Munawata. The sailors at Munawata remembered me from the days of bad weather when I had paddled off and they had stayed on shore. Their lovely island had only their village on it, and when I praised its beauty they said, "But we have no water."

The penalty of living on this island paradise, with sandy beaches and fertile soil, was that whenever they needed freshwater they had to get into their canoes and sail over a mile to Labi Island, where there was a spring. And when there was a northwest wind blowing they couldn't get there at all. This might last for days.

"Then we eat green coconuts and try to save rainwater and wait for the wind to change."

On Munawata there were traditional bachelor houses, in which young boys lived and where they brought their girlfriends. The girls might stay with them for weeks, though they always had their meals with their parents – a very civilized arrangement, I felt. The boys on Munawata wore flowers in their hair and the teenaged girls and women were bare-breasted and had deeply rouged cheeks. The girls were assertively sexual in their manner and the way they dressed because the yam harvest was in progress.

It was so strange to paddle from that village of free love back to Kaileuna where the pious folk in Kaisiga laughed at these old ways and clung to their new-found Adventist beliefs. But even they were rooted enough in Trobriand culture not to find a trip to the forbidden and haunted island of Tuma too spooky for words. No one would go with me, and they urged me not to go – the island was full of voices and shadows, the ghosts of everyone who had ever died in the Trobriands lurked in Tuma, and if I spent the night there I would get no sleep. I paddled there – it was another lovely island, empty and overgrown because of its reputation – but in the event I did not camp there. I camped back at Kaisiga and then kept going the next day to the main island of Kiriwina. On the way a motor-boat came alongside – a German anthropologist, Dr Wulf Schievelhövel, and his son Fridjtof. Wulf said he had recognized my collapsible kayak as German.

"I have never seen anyone paddling a kayak here before," he said.

We tied our boats together and shared a Pepsi he brought from his cooler and talked about the Trobrianders. He had been studying them for twenty years. They had an almost perfect diet, he said; they had no heart disease or coronary problems at all. Their blood pressure went down as they grew older, and yet he confirmed what I had heard, that they didn't live long: their life expectancy was less than forty, because of the high risk of bacterial infections.

"But so little has changed here, it is as though these people have walked straight off the pages of Malinowski," he said.

He urged me to see more of the main island and to visit Omarakhana, the village of the Paramount Chief. Then he snapped my picture – I had found it inconvenient to carry a camera – and we continued on our separate ways, he to his village on Kaileuna, I to Kiriwina, in the blinding afternoon sunshine.

The heart of the Trobriands, its chieftainship and culture, is Omarakhana. "Ever since we came out of the caves," Trobrianders say, "our chief has lived here." They never said that their ancestors might have migrated from other islands; indeed, they firmly do not believe it. Long ago, their people emerged from the caves of coral rock near Kaibola at the top of the island and they divided into separate clans. One of the most respected is the Tabalu, clan of the present Paramount Chief, Pulayasi, who had been chief for about three years.

Because of the danger of rape – and rape wasn't a joke; it was exactly what it was anywhere, a violent assault, a humiliation – I went in a truck with a friendly villager named Matthew. On the way he told me that this chief was better than the last one. Traditionally the Paramount Chief controls the weather. The previous chief, always in a foul mood, gave them miserable weather – too much rain, too much sun, and then days of wind.

"If I say, 'Please make it rain, chief,' will he do it?"

"If he want, he do it."

It seemed wonderful to live in a place where you could actually blame someone you knew for the weather.

The royal village was muddy and humid, in the center of the island, far from the sea breeze, two miles or more from its beach, at the end of a bad road and an overgrown path. It was nowhere near as tidy or pleasant as the villages I had seen on the outer islands. It seemed neglected and rather haunted, with shabby huts and bad thatching and ramshackle pavilions. Pigs rooted and snorted near the huts, and the snotty-faced children and the scruffy dogs fought one another for scraps. The chief's hut was one of the flimsiest looking, but Matthew said that he had several, because he was still acquiring wives – he had three at the moment.

A balding man in torn shorts and a dirty T-shirt lettered *Coca-Cola Fun Run 1988* came out of the hut, and spat. He was smoking acrid Trobriand tobacco in a rolled-up tube of newspaper. He was barefoot. He approached me and smiled a stained betel-juice smile and beckoned to a boy who hurried towards him and set up a rickety beach chair in one of the wall-less moldering pavilions. And then he sat and the frayed blue plastic webbing creaked. This was Paramount Chief Pulayasi.

I sat at his feet – it would have been unthinkable for me to sit at the chief's height and look him straight in the eye – and introduced myself as a traveler and a grateful guest on the Trobriands. I then gave him twenty dollars' worthy of sticky black tobacco.

And the chief, who knew no English, mumbled something to one of his courtiers.

"The chief wishes to know how did you hear about the Trobriands."

"I read some books about the Trobriands, by a famous *dim-dim* named Malinowski."

"He lived in this village," the man said. His name was Joseph Daniel and he wore a pair of torn brown trousers. "The people could not pronounce his name, so they called him *Tolibwoga*, which means 'Master of Stories' or 'Historian' – something like that. He was always telling old stories."

Hearing the name, the chief smiled and puffed his newspaper cheroot. I asked where Malinowski lived.

"Over there, where you see the string and the clothes."

"Near that clothesline?"

"Yes. He lived near Chief To'uluwa. That man was Chief Pulayasi's mother's grandfather."

In this matrilineal society all titles and lands passed through the mother's line, and a woman's brother was closer to her children than their father, who was hardly even regarded as a blood-relation (but there was no question about the link of the uncle to his sister's kids).

"Do they tell stories about Tolibwoga?"

"No. But the chief knows some stories."

"Did Tolibwoga travel to other islands?" I asked, and my question and the reply were translated.

"He never traveled, because they could not guarantee his safety. At that time there were quarrels on the other islands. The people were fighting. Tolibwoga stayed here."

I pretended to write this in my notebook. What I wrote was: *Fun Run T-shirt, beach chair, shaven-headed women, spider webs on all houses, pigs and dogs, neglected houses in need of repair.*

The chief mumbled to Joseph, who said, "The chief wants to know if you have any questions for him. He wants to help. You are welcome to ask all questions."

I asked a few harmless questions and then decided to risk the one that had been nagging at me.

"Is it true that Chief Pulayasi has magic that lets him control the weather?"

When this was translated, the chief chuckled condescendingly and mumbled and puffed his burned tube of newspaper and plucked at his filthy T-shirt.

"Yes, he can control it."

"He has magic?"

"Yes."

"Did someone give him this magic when he became chief?" I asked. I had been told that the chief had advisers who were sorcerers, who could bring about a person's death. If Chief Pulayasi raged, "Who will rid me of this turbulent priest?" the clergyman was as good as dead.

Joseph said, "No. The chief has had his magic for many years. He was doing the weather even before he became chief."

And Pulayasi smiled. He had chubby cheeks. He was one of the rare plump men I had seen in the Trobriands. It was the confident smile of someone who can arrange it so that you will be rained on if you ask too many obnoxious questions.

He was happy to talk about his wives – his courtiers were smoothing the way for a young girl to be sent from each of the major clans in the Trobriands, and he would probably end up with a dozen wives, like his predecessor. The brothers of those women would all work for the chief, tending their own gardens and bringing him the harvest. Yes, it was hard work and it was a job for life, but it was also useful to be able to remind people that your brother-in-law was the Paramount Chief.

"How long have there been chiefs here?"

"Since we came out of the caves."

That answer reminded me of a question I had been meaning to ask. Had the Trobrianders of long ago sailed off in their canoes to live in other islands in the Pacific?

"Yes. In Fiji," one man said. His name was Patimo Tokurupai and he spoke English well. "We know that because of the facial resemblance. Some Fijians visited us and they said, 'Our ancestors came from here.'"

I was getting stiff sitting crosslegged on a loose plank, so I asked whether I could see the chief's yam house. Only the Paramount Chief can decorate his yam house in an elaborate manner, and this was festooned with shells, pictures of birds and fish, and was surmounted by a strange head – the only head I ever saw carved in the Trobes – at the apex of the roof, a black and white glowering face that looked like that of Mr Punch.

On my way out, I asked one of the men from Omarakhana why the village seemed so neglected. He told me that it had been deliberately neglected – no one was allowed to repair the huts or cut the grass, because one of the chief's brothers had died. The widow shaved her head and each day she smeared her face with mud and ashes – I caught a glimpse of her kneeling in the mud, and she looked corpse-like herself. After this five-month period of mourning was over they would repaint and rebuild the village and restore it to its former glory. In the meantime, it looked hideous.

It was stifling there, and so I was glad to leave a few days later for Kaisiga. But this time, even after I had paddled for four hours, I was given only a perfunctory welcome by Leendon and the others. They were in no mood for joking in Pidgin, or sitting in the *bwayma* by the sea and chatting. This was uncharacteristic, but I could see that the villagers were preoccupied. They made rather a point of asking me to buy things for them (duct tape, rope, plastic sheeting, another lantern, spear points, knives, fishing-line) and then seemed to suggest that I ought to be on my way.

They did not ask me to stay, which was the classic villagers' way of telling me to go.

They were laconic, thoughtful, apprehensive. I was struck by this wholly different mood, and especially by their eagerness for me to leave. I had not planned to stay long in any case – I would be flying out the day after tomorrow – but I regretted the muted goodbye. Perhaps it was not muted. It was deep emotion, a mood of bewilderment and sadness when words are no use at all, the sort of silent summing-up that is a final farewell. I now knew that sort of farewell.

I paddled away thinking how I had once seen these islands as idyllic. I had been wrong. An island of traditional culture cannot be idyllic. It is, instead, completely itself: riddled with magic, superstition, myths, dangers, rivalries, and its old routines. You had to take it as you found it. The key to its survival was that it laughed at outsiders and kept them at arm's length. And although it seemed strange that they thought of themselves as human and me as subhuman, a *dim-dim*, I could now see the utter impossibility of my ever understanding the place. On this second visit I had felt an undercurrent of violence – and it was not only because I had been threatened. It was something in the air – a vibration, the cries of certain birds, the way the wind whipped the trees, the stifling darkness of some jungle paths and the sudden noisy jostling in the leaves that shocked me and left me breathless.

"What was that?" I would ask.

"A leezard."

A 200-hundred pound lizard?

"Maybe a wild pig."

But sometimes even they seemed worried.

Two days after I left Kaisiga, on the night before I was to take the plane to the Solomons, I ran into an Australian shopkeeper in Losuia. He said, "Did you hear about the battle? Koma village marched on Kaisiga. There was quite a fight, I understand. They've sent boats to take some of the people to hospital. About thirty people were injured and some of them are in very bad shape."

Before catching the plane out, I mailed a letter to John at Kaisiga, asking for details, and eventually his reply, in neat mission-school handwriting, caught up with me:

*SDA Mission Kaisiga, Trobriand Islands PNG*

*Dear Paul,*

*You've asked about the fight between Koma and Kaisiga. Well, the fight was about a dingy that belongs to Kaisiga Community. After an agreement that has been made by the 2 villages, Koma people began to run the dingy for 2 weeks. After the 2 weeks were over they (Koma) refused to return the dingy to the Kaisiga people and planned to hold it back for a year. Therefore the Kaisiga men went to Koma beach on Monday night and pulled it back to Kaisiga – the dingy.*

*Early on Tuesday morning, all the Koma men, with Giwa and Lebola, came to fight us, on Kaisiga beach about ¼ mile away from the village. They were blowing a shell very loud. They came with bush knives, short sticks, iron rods, and even a few diving spears. The fight began at about 6:30am and lasted until 11:30. I went to stop the fight, but I could not. After the fight finished, the police from Losuia came for investigation. We all went for court. The court fine for Kaisiga was K1920. The fine for Koma was 7 months imprisonment, for all people about 30 in all, including the women who brought food to the fighting ground.*

*There were some men from Kaisiga who were injured, people like Micah, Lyndon, Peter and others. Two men from Koma who were seriously injured were flown to Alotau Public Hospital. After a week one died. When the Koma men return from prison there will be a big party* [a feast to reconcile the warring villages.]

*Please Paul I need a new watch, because the old one is no more in use. My Mrs needs a wrist watch. Also when you are shopping at Port Moresby when coming, please could you buy us about 3 bolts with flowers on. Nothing much to say, so better pen off from here. May God richly bless you.*

And then his scribbled indecipherable signature, an English name rendered in a twitchy Trobriand hand.

But that bloody battle was not the whole story. I kept remembering my happy days and nights on these islands, and they became emblematic of the Pacific. It was in the Trobriands that I had realized that the Pacific was a universe, not a simple ocean.

I especially recalled how one day sailing back to an island we were delayed, and night fell. There were stars everywhere, above us, and reflected in the sea along with the sparkle of phosphorescence streaming from the bow wave. When I poked an oar in the ocean and stirred it, the sea glittered with twinkling sea-life. We sped onward. There were no lights on shore. It was as though we were in an old rickety rocket ship.

It was an image that afterwards often came to me when I was traveling in the Pacific, that this ocean was as vast as outer space, and being on this boat was like shooting from one star to another, the archipelagoes like galaxies, and the islands like isolated stars in an empty immensity of watery darkness, and this sailing was like going slowly from star to star, in vitreous night.

# 8

## *The Solomons: Down and Dirty in Guadalcanal*

The great canoe route of migration, which was my itinerary, cut through the mountainous islands and coral atolls of Milne Bay and headed east to the Solomons. I wished to follow this old oceanic thoroughfare. The nearest Solomon islands to me were just off the eastern tip of New Guinea – the so-called North Solomons, which were, confusingly, a province of Papua New Guinea. I had the idea of paddling there, and then onward to the vast archipelago – 992 islands and atolls – that is the Republic of the Solomons, named by a fanciful Spaniard, four hundred years ago, after King Solomon.*

Before I was able to do this, I met Takaku, an islander, who confirmed the rumor that the North Solomons had seceded from New Guinea and that his fellow islanders, under siege, had taken up arms. These guerrilla fighters called themselves "Rambos," and generally modeled themselves and their hit-and-run killings after the ugly bulgy little palooka they had seen in videos.

Takaku frightened me. It was not just his great size but his anger, and his threatening T-shirt depicting a Solomon Islander Rambo celebrating his freedom, rather prematurely I felt, dancing wildly with a machine-gun.

"*Dim-dims* say I look like Idi Amin," Takaku said.

I was another *dim-dim* who agreed. He had two blazing bloodshot eyes in a rich rubbery face of astonishing blackness. His teeth were sharp, his gums were the color of tar. His belly was vast, and his enormous feet had crushed the life out of his rubber sandals. He was the sort of man teasing Trobrianders (who thought of themselves as white) called *Tabwaubwau* – "Blackie."

Takaku said he believed that the New Guinean province of North

---

*The captain, Álvaro de Mendaña, had sailed from Peru, inspired by Inca stories that islands of gold lay 600 leagues to the west. This seemed to me a brilliant way for the Incas to rid themselves of another conquistador.

Solomons, its rich copper deposits exploited by foreign interests, ought to be a sovereign state. Having recently declared themselves independent, the local people had killed some foreign-born miners to show they were serious, and driven the rest back to Australia. The armed rebellion was led by one Francis Ona, a nationalist, who was seen by the islanders as a visionary, and by the miners as an opportunist and a rabble-rouser. A nationalist is nearly always a pest.

"Ona is a great environmentalist," Takaku told me. "He wants to give the land back to the people. You see, our land was raped by the minority interests in Panguna."

Panguna was the capital of the main island, Bougainville.

"You mean the local people don't want money from the mining firms?"

"No. If we show my people gold and silver they will say, 'What is this? It is just metal. We don't want it. We want taro and cassava. Why are they digging up our land and sending it overseas?'"

This was not a time to remind him that most New Guineans, even Trobrianders, needed money occasionally to buy necessities (fish-hooks, rope, cloth, pots) and occasional luxuries. They had put me in my place by telling me so. For one thing they preferred the taste of Japanese canned mackerel to any fresh fish they caught themselves. But the territorial problem was, at the moment, a stand-off. The North Solomon secession had become a military issue.

"Is it true that the government of New Guinea has blockaded Bougainville?"

"Yes, but it will have no effect," Takaku said. "People say to them, 'You will have no energy or lights.' But my people say, 'Can you keep the sun from rising? Can you prevent the rain from falling?' They give very poetic answers. It is a wonderful poetic language. It is not an Austronesian language."

"Will this new republic have a new name?"

"Francis Ona wanted to call it 'The Sacred Land' but so many languages are spoken there he thought it was better to call it Bougainville."

"Does it seem to you to be a sacred land?"

"Yes. We don't need radios and cars and money. My people say, 'We will drive our cars until we run out of petrol and then we will push them into the sea to make homes for fishes. We have canoes, we have food, we will dance and sing.'"

But Takaku had a complaint. He said that he had been trying to rally support for the new republic and had not made any progress.

"I went to the New Zealand High Commissioner in Moresby and asked, 'Why don't you recognize us?' He said, 'If we do, we will be the laughing-stock of the world.' But why don't they?"

I said, "Because they don't need you. If you don't reopen the copper or gold mines, and if you don't buy anything from overseas, why would anyone want to recognize you? What's in it for them?"

"We want to protect our land," he said.

"But the more solitary you are the more vulnerable you will be."

"It doesn't matter. We will be weak. But we will have our own country. We don't want foreigners. You see what happened in Fiji – the Indians tried to take over. But they will be kicked out."

We talked for a while more, and as I became firmer in my resolve not to go to this rebellious province of New Guinea – I had no wish to risk death among these quarreling islanders – Takaku told me of his Melanesian uniqueness and how proud he was not to be a Polynesian.

The North Solomons were not happy islands. It did seem to me strange that this little group of islands belonged to New Guinea and not to the Republic of the Solomons, the hundreds of islands just south of it, with whom they shared both language and culture. But that was just another anomaly of history.

Taking my collapsible boat, I bypassed Panguna, and flew with it to Honiara, the capital of the Solomons, the harbor city at the edge of the island of Guadalcanal. The name was Arabic, from *Wadi el Ganar*, which was the name of the home town of its first European discoverer, the Spanish explorer Mendaña.

*A definite sense that the world is elsewhere*, I wrote in my notebook in Honiara.

My first impression was of a place so ramshackle, so poor, so scary, so unexpectedly filthy, that I began to understand the theory behind culture shock – something I had never truly experienced in its paralyzing and malignant form. The idea that this miserable-looking town could be regarded as a capital city seemed laughable.

And I also wrote, *Why would anyone come here?*

It was not only hideous, it was expensive. Nearly all the food in Honiara's stores was imported – from Australia, New Zealand, Japan and America. It is often possible to gauge the prosperity of a place by looking at the central market. Honiara's central market was pathetic – a few old women selling little piles of blackened bananas and wilted leaves and some tiny fly-blown fish.

"If I were a king, the worst punishment I could inflict on my enemies would be to banish them to the Solomons," Jack London wrote in his Pacific travel book, *The Cruise of the Snark*. He added, "On second thoughts, king or no king, I don't think I'd have the heart to do it."

The Solomons and Melanesia in general frightened and inspired London much more than the Klondike had done. The Solomons were synonymous with horror, in his view; the most savage islands in the Pacific.

You consider that a moment, and then you want to see more.

I walked farther, past the wrecked and vandalized buildings, and the gangs of teenagers in dirty T-shirts. Honiara had the decrepit and resentful look of Haiti, or one of the plundered coastal towns of West Africa. There were a few hundred yards of wide paved road before it gave out and became a broken road, full of pot-holes. Even the trees were shabby. The ships tied up at the quayside, or moored in the harbor, were rusty hulks. Most of the shops were owned by Chinese and contained identical merchandise: cloth, soap, shoes, tin pots, lard, matches, and the Ma Ling range of canned goods – luncheon meat, chicken-feet, lychees in syrup, corned beef, goose meat in gravy. A Japanese store advertised its offer of big money for endangered species, and urged islanders to bring in turtle shells, giant clams, and rare birds. Before I had gone fifty yards an islander sidled up to me and showed me a necklace made of about three hundred teeth – they were dolphins' teeth, pretty little pearly ones, and he urged me to count them, because such necklaces, representing the slaughter of perhaps twenty dolphins, were sold at so much a tooth.

I walked to the harbor. A little wooden fishing-boat was grandly named *PT-109* in homage to the boat that had been torpedoed under John Kennedy near an island not far from here. The wicked-looking spikes and rusty guts of Second World War wreckage – abandoned landing-craft and the hulks of larger vessels – poked up from the water, posing severe hazards. Garbage and raw sewage sloshed against the shore, and what I had first taken to be a beach toy was the gray corpse of a pig, swollen in death and bobbing on the dirty water and seemingly on the point of bursting. Watching that dead pig impassively were three fat Melanesian boys in torn shorts sharing a bag of Cheez Doodles.

The Solomon Islanders in Honiara were among the scariest-looking people I had ever seen in my life – wild hair, huge feet, ripped and ragged clothes, tattoos on their foreheads, ornamental scars all over their faces, wearing broken sunglasses. They loped along in large groups, or else idled near the stores that played American rap music and looked for all the world like rappers themselves.

That, as I say, was my first impression of Honiara. Yet as time passed and I shopped for expedition food and asked directions and bought maps and generally hung around, this impression softened. The town had been a village that the war had turned into a capital; it had only existed since the war, less than fifty years. Knowing this, I did not regard the place with less horror, but I came to realize that these wild-looking people were friendly and approachable.

*Gude apinun, mistah, yu stap gut?*

Yes, they spoke Pidgin here.

*Ples bilong yu we? Wanem nem bilong yu? Mi laikim America tumas. Yu savvy Michael Jackson himpela sing-sing?*

As for crime, I decided to talk to someone who might know about it. This was Officer Saro of the Honiara Police. His Christian name was Marcelline – the name had been suggested to his parents by a French priest in Malaita, the Western Province. Malaita was a traditional place, Saro said. Some men still wore bones in their nose. Some villages attacked any outsider who came near. Some villages worshipped sharks – his did, as a matter of fact.

"But Honiara is a safe place," he said. "Guadalcanal is quite safe. Just petty crimes – mostly drinking and fighting. Some driving offenses. Maybe one murder in two or three years, caused by drinking. That's about all."

We were drinking beer under the trees at the edge of Honiara's stinking harbor, looking out upon the channel called The Slot, and Iron Bottom Sound, which got its name from the great number of ships – sixty-odd – that were sunk in the battle of Guadalcanal, a six-month ordeal that ended in an American victory in February 1943. It had been one of the crucial Pacific battles in the Second World War. The Japanese headquarters had been at Tulaghi, across Iron Bottom Sound, at the northern side of the Sealark Channel – The Slot. This battle was perhaps the turning point in the war, at the great cost of 30,000 lives.

Marcelline Saro had discovered that people elsewhere knew the name Guadalcanal. He had been an amateur boxer and then became a coach on the Solomon Islands Olympic boxing team.

"I went with them to the Los Angeles Olympics," he said. "I liked Disneyland the best. People asked me if I was from Africa. I said no, but when I told them I was from Guadalcanal everyone recognized the word. Because of the war."

"Did they know where Guadalcanal is?"

"No," he said, but he did not mind that.

He had also gone to the Seoul Olympics.

"What impressed you in Korea?"

"I realized how lucky I am to speak English. They don't speak it at all there."

His own children, he had five of them, learned English at school. He and his wife spoke their own language – she was from Malaita – and he also spoke Solomon Pidgin to his kids.

When he had saved enough money he would take the whole family back to Malaita and have a farm. He disliked cities, he said. He could never have lived in Los Angeles or Seoul. If he had the chance of going to another country he would travel to the countryside and see how the farmers lived.

"My island is traditional," he said. "We have no electricity. It is dark at night."

And, he implied, the missionaries had lost their grip. At that point I asked him about traditions and he told me about the shark worship.

"We respect the shark, that is why we worship it," he said. "And that is why we never eat the shark. We believe it will save us and protect us – the shark has magic –"

In the same spirit, the ancient Russians of the steppes venerated the fierce brown bear and called it *medved* – "honey wizard."

"Every year," Saro said, "we have the sacrifice ceremony of the roasted piglet. No woman may come near the altar, ever. The shark-caller summons the shark – he stands at the edge of the sea and calls the fish. When he sees it swimming towards him, he throws the piglet to it. And the shark eats it, and then protects us."

Saro saw his friend William Fagi walking along the sea-front and called him over, to share another beer with us. William was a cook in the Happy Café in Honiara, and he had just knocked off work. He too was from Malaita – another part of the island, but just as traditional as Saro's village. Both men used the Pidgin word *kastom* to describe how traditional the places were. They believed in *kastom*.

Fagi said, "In our *kastom* we worship the eagle. Eagles deliver messages – they are strong. No one may kill or eat the eagle."

It was nearing sunset and at that time of day, as so often seemed to happen in this part of the Pacific, the wind dropped and the horizon in the new light of early evening became lumpy and irregular with the pronounced shapes of islands which the haze of day had obscured.

Seated comfortably under the trees, we could see the Florida Islands, the two Nggelas, big and small, across the channel and in the northwest the simple hump of a volcano rising from the sea. This was Savo Island.

"That is an active volcano," Saro said. "I have never been there but they say that the volcano erupts now and then. There is a scrub duck that lives there and lays eggs in the sand. It is a strange place, but I think the people are friendly."

As he spoke I began to calculate how long it would take me to paddle there if I started here, went along the coast, and then struck out across the channel – twenty-odd miles.

Meanwhile, Fagi must still have been ruminating on his village in Malaita, and the creatures worshiped there, because he said, "A certain snake is also important to us, especially when we travel. It is the *baeko* – black with white spots. This snake can save you and bring you back alive."

"Tell me about it," I said, because – traveling – I often felt the lingering anxiety that I was doomed.

Traveling would kill me, I felt. I had always had the idea, and still do, that my particular exit would be made via an appointment in Samarra: I would go a great distance and endure enormous discomfort and trouble and expense in order to meet my death. If I chose to sit at home and eat and drink in the bosom of my family it would never happen – I'd live to be a hundred. But of course I would head for the hinterland, and pretty soon there would be some portion of a foreign field that would be forever Medford, Mass. And I imagined that this overseas death would be a silly mistake, like that of the monk and mystic Thomas Merton at last leaving Gethsemane, his monastery in Kentucky, after thirty secure years, and popping up in Singapore in 1970 (while I was there) and accidentally electrocuting himself on the frayed wires of a fan in Bangkok a week later. All that way, all that trouble and fuss, just to yank a faulty light-switch in a crummy hotel.

I wanted to hear about this snake which might save me that fate.

"Before we go on a trip," Fagi said, "we go to the *baeko*'s hole and put our hand in and touch all the snakes. Then we reach for the fattest one and hold it."

"This is a poisonous snake?"

"Oh, yes, very poisonous. And when we hold it we take a good hold and squeeze it."

Later I found out that this *baeko* snake is the venomous and fanged *Loveridgelaps elapoides*, one of the deadliest snakes in the Solomons. This might have been the Malaita way of breaking the appointment in Samarra, but I found it unlikely that I would ever get on my knees and stick my hand deep into a black hole and grasp one of these creatures by the waist.

I asked Saro and Fagi where they thought the Solomon Islanders had originated from. Had they come from Australia?

Fagi said, "No, not from Australia. We are nothing like the Aborigines. They have rounded noses and wide faces and soft hair. They are more like Indians, from India."

"Sometimes I see people from Israel and the Middle East and I think – 'They are like me,'" Saro said. "But if you ask me who in the world looks like us and has our *kastom* I would say Ethiopians."

"Is there any connection at all between the Solomon Islands and Ethiopia?" I asked, and I thought, Yes, there is a certain resemblance.

"I will tell you a story," he said. "There was an Ethiopian on a certain ship. He was there illegally –"

"A stowaway," I said.

"Indeed. And when they found him after some days at sea they wanted to send him ashore. They said, 'Who are you? Where do you come from?' And the Ethiopian looked straight at them and said, 'I am from the Solomon Islands.'"

Fagi said, "I have heard this story myself."

"The ship continued onward and when it arrived in Honiara the man was put off. We took him into custody in the police station. He spoke perfect English. He looked exactly like us, and he lived here for over a year. While he was here, no one ever questioned him or asked him where he came from. The people looking at him believed he was from the Solomons. He wanted to stay longer, but his government was notified and he was sent back to Ethiopia."

It was now dark, and the channel was silvery-black, like a sea of ink. The islands we had been looking at for the past hour, while we had been drinking, had vanished, blackened, and become part of that depthless night.

"Savo's gone," I said.

"They have no lights," Fagi said. "They have no electricity, no roads, no telephone. Only those funny scrub ducks they call megapodes."

It sounded a wonderful place.

"Megapode means 'big foot,'" I said.

"I think you are a teacher," Fagi said.

"Do I need permission to go to that island?"

"Yes. It is a good idea. You must ask permission to go to such places. But you always get it. And I know the man you should see."

It was the Minister of Housing, one Allen Kemakeza, whose home village was on Savo Island. I did not imagine that a government cabinet minister would see me at short notice to discuss the possibility of my paddling to an obscure island for the purposes of my camping and examining the nesting habits of the big-foot bird. But as this was the Solomons I gave it a shot the very next day, calling his office the first thing.

"He is not here," his secretary said.

"When do you expect him?"

"He usually comes to the office at nine. But you could call him at home."

It was eight-thirty in the morning, and I was a perfect stranger – nevertheless, she did not hesitate to give me the minister's home telephone number, so that I could ask him to do me a favor. From my point of view, this seemed a happy way of running these islands.

I called the minister's house and asked if I could see him.

He said, "I have a little problem here, but I will be at my office in an hour. Meet me there and we can talk."

He had no idea who I was or what I wanted, yet at a moment's notice he was prepared to meet me.

The new six-storey Ministry of Housing, in which Mr Kemakeza's office was located, was the most obvious building in Honiara – it was four storeys higher than any other building in town, and contained the country's only elevator. Barefoot youths in T-shirts and sunglasses sneaked in and went for joyrides on the elevator, leaving timid graffiti behind on the walls as a testimony that they had been there.

This building was so inappropriate it had to have been a result of foreign aid – one of those self-serving boondoggles in which a Western country gives money in the form of a contract to one of its own builders to put up an expensive structure no one really needs. It was dungeon dark inside this strange building – strange, because in spite of its newness doors were broken, locks hung loose, doors were off their hinges, floors unswept, and all the signs were scribbled on pieces of paper and taped to walls. Few lights were working. Most of the offices were empty. It was clearly a building no one had gotten used to, but it was being broken in – neglected and vandalized in a way that would make it seem habitable to a resident of Honiara.

I followed a scribbled sign and its arrow to an office that was bare except for a Melanesian boy sitting in a chair. He had golden skin and fuzzy blonde hair, worn in an Afro the dimensions of a basketball.

"I have an appointment to see the minister," I said.

"Dis way," he said.

Allen Kemakeza was in an office that was equally bare of furniture. He was seated at a desk, initialing tattered file folders. Stocky, about forty or so, he wore an old faded shirt and shorts. Later he told me that he had been a policeman for about twelve years, and that he had risen in the ranks of the People's Rights Party. But he still had the look of a policeman – tough, skeptical, ironic, physical, resentful, suspicious, not particularly talkative but very attentive; the sort of man who looks as though he has survived a few fights. He had a cop's hard gaze.

I introduced myself, told him where I was from, that I had been traveling around the Pacific and that I was interested in going to Savo, preferably by paddling my collapsible boat, to look at the egg fields of the megapode birds.

"Are you a teacher?"

"Do a little teaching, do a little writing," I said, smiling fatuously and trying to sound like a harmless pedagogue.

"What made you start traveling around the Pacific?"

"My wife and I separated, and it seemed a good way of, um," – I thought fast – "*no getum bikpela bagarap in hia*," and I tapped my skull.

"*Mi savvy tumas*," he said. "I can make arrangements for you on Savo." Then he fidgeted and hesitated, and finally said, "What do you know about this Iraq business?"

"Only what I hear on the radio. I listen every day – to Radio Australia, the Voice of America or the BBC, whichever comes in clearest."

This was at the time President Bush had given Saddam Hussein an ultimatum for withdrawing Iraqi troops from Kuwait; the multinational force was in place, and the deadline was a few weeks away. It was that period when everyone speculated about what might happen in a shooting war – when people said that casualties on both sides could run in the tens of thousands, that Israel would be attacked, that a nuclear device might be detonated by the Iraqis, and so forth. In fact, no one had any idea at all what would happen in the event of a war, and so anything was possible, even Doomsday.

"You think there will be a war?"

"I have no idea. I hope not."

He pushed his file folders aside. He said, "It will be terrible. Already we are noticing the effects of the trouble in the Middle East. The price of fuel in Honiara has skyrocketed."

There were very few motor vehicles in town, and just a handful of trucks and buses on Guadalcanal, but the overloaded boats and rusty ferries that ran among the islands needed fuel. Even the short trip to Tulaghi in a little boat with an outboard motor cost the equivalent of about five American dollars, which represented a week's pay for a Solomon Islander.

"If there is a war, do you think it will lead to World War Three?"

"No. Because the Soviets wouldn't be able to afford it. They seem to be on our side, or at least neutral, because they need economic assistance from the US and Europe."

"They are poor now."

"Everyone is poor except the Japanese."

"But why are they the only rich ones?"

"Because it is a one-race, one-language, one-family island of desperate overachievers who have a fascist belief in their own racial superiority," I said, and I could see that I had struck a chord, because Mr Kemakeza clasped his hands and smiled. "These little people have a palpitating need to dominate the world and will do anything at all to sell their stuff. In the nineteen-seventies when the rest of the world refused to trade with South Africa because the whites there were treating Africans like scum the Japanese were so eager to do business they had themselves reclassified as white and made billions. They eat whales, they strew drift-nets all over the Pacific, and they accept no immigrants. They are frugal, too – the largest money-savers in the world, which means they have the richest banks. Everyone on earth owes them money."

"They are doing business here."

"*Bikpela no lilik?*"

"*Bikpela pis bilong tins,*" he said. "Fish cannery. I am also Minister of Taxation, and I have been dealing with a complaint from this Japanese company here, Solomon Taiyo, fish business. They heard that I was giving a tax concession to a Canadian company. They said, 'Why don't you give us a tax concession?' I pointed out to them that they had a tax concession twenty years ago, when they started. It is an incentive to new businesses. They said, 'But we have been losing money for twenty years.'"

"What do they do with their canned fish?"

"Some they sell locally and some they export."

"How can they have lost money all this time and still be in business?"

"I don't know. But they say so. It is a joint venture, with the Solomons government."

"So you haven't been earning any money from it?"

"It is hard to say. Their book-keeping methods are complicated. For example it is all done in Japan. We never see their records."

"Fish in Japan is expensive, and everyone eats it. I should say that they have been making a fortune. They are using you – probably cheating you. Why don't you consider the fact that they need you much more than you need them?"

It seemed to me grotesque but typical that the wrinkleproof executives in this Japanese company were taking advantage of this poor barefoot country, robbing them of one of their few valuable commodities and staple foods, fish.

The minister said, "Solomon Islanders are too kind." He looked out the window at the patched and broken roofs of Honiara. "But when we lose patience – then, you will see."

"What will I see?"

"We will ask questions."

"Don't ask questions. Threaten them, close them down, freeze their assets," I said. "Or why not demand that they allow you to send a delegation to Japan to start a business there?"

I could just imagine the welcome they would get in Japan, these black bushy-haired Solomon Islanders, with bones in their noses and the raised welts and scars of x's cut into their foreheads and cheeks. Even an unscarred minister like Kemakeza would be treated as though he was subhuman and offered shiny trinkets in return for his country's natural resources of timber and fish. And what laughs of derision would greet the islander's request to start a business in Nippon: *Mi laik opim kwiktaim kampani bilong bisnis.*

"Why do you let them manipulate you? You're a government minister. You deal with taxes. This is your country. Summon the book-keepers and accountants to your office and *mekim long pinga long* – point that out."

He was smiling broadly now. "Yes, yes."

With a flourish, he wrote a letter and folded it and slipped it into an envelope marked *On Her Majesty's Service.*

"When you go to Savo, give this to my brother. His name is Nathaniel Mapopoza."

On the way to the elevator he told me that, as a policeman, he had gone to England, to Bradford in the north to take a course in police tactics. He had liked England, he said.

"You can walk at night. Go to a pub. Go to a disco. The people are friendly. In New York it was the same. I was safe."

"So you liked New York?"

"Yes. But New Guinea is wuss," he said, slipping mildly into Pidgin. "There it is more dangerous. Why is it more, Mr Paul?"

I told him why I thought Port Moresby was dangerous — too many homeless people from the highlands, no common ground, no shared culture; and he inquired further, listening carefully to my answers.

At last he released me, saying, "Go to Savo. Stay as long as you like. I hope I will see you again, and we can talk."

"I have to buy some food now to take with me."

He then uttered a strange sentence: "There are many eggs in Savo."

# 9

## The Solomons: In the Egg Fields of Savo Island

A large group of gaunt and hollow-eyed Solomon Islanders watched me set up my boat under the palm trees at Honiara. Untypically for Melanesians, they made no move to help me. It was hard to tell whether they were pirates or castaways – they could have been either. At times like this, laboring under the unfriendly gaze of pitiless islanders, I seriously wondered whether my solitary island-hopping was such a great idea. But I knew that if I were home I would be cursing the traffic and wishing I were here, on a sunny day under the palms, preparing to launch myself across the open water.

I left my boat in the care of a sympathetic-looking old man, and set out to buy a week's provisions in town – the standard items. Afterwards, seeing that I still had spare room, I bought a few extras – two six-packs of beer and some five-pound tins of Australian cookies labeled "Conversation Biscuits."

Outside one of the stores a ragged boy was showing some passers-by a bird squashed into a narrow basket and so I joined the curious group. The bird was green and red, the size of a small thrush, and cheeping miserably.

I said, "Where did you catch this bird?"

The boy did not understand.

I said, *"Dispela pisin where you gettim?"*

*"Inna boos."* In the bush.

*"Wanem nem bilong dispela pisin?"*

*"Dispela 'laru.'"*

A lorikeet, one of the twenty-one species found in and around the Solomons.

*"Is gutpela pisin?"*

*"Ya, dispela numbawan. Dispela pisin savvy toktok, savvy sing-sing. Everyting numbawan."*

But trapped in the basket it certainly was not talking or singing now.

I was torn between interfering, buying the bird and liberating it (as I had once done to an edible owl in China), and simply observing the daily life of a Solomon Island poacher – seeing what would happen. Within a few minutes a Melanesian man wearing bangles and earplugs stepped forward and thrust the equivalent of nine American dollars into the poacher's hand and carried the protesting lorikeet away.

Back at the shore, the group of fifteen bedraggled men with wild hair, wearing only shorts, still stared at me with hollow eyes but now they were on the deck of a battered sailboat anchored just off the beach.

"They are from the weather coast," an islander named James told me. That explained their piratical faces: they had a weatherbeaten, windward look.

I was glad to be heading off the lee shore, in a calm sea, with plenty of time to paddle to Savo. James came from Savo himself, from the village of Monagho, where he urged me to stay. But I told him that I was going to Kemakeza's district. I told him I would visit him.

"That is the north of the island, where the eggs are."

Another gnomic utterance.

"Is there a strong current out there?"

"Not bad."

"Any sharks?"

"During the war, when all those boats were sunk, there were *planti tumas sak*, because of the bodies," James said. "And for years *planti moa*. But these days not many."

Rather than head straight out from Honiara, paddling across fourteen miles of open water, I kept near to the coast, using an excellent nautical chart showing the whole of the Sealark Channel. I paddled west about twelve miles to the village of Visale at Cape Esperance, where I had a rest on the beach, and then struck out north for a six-mile crossing. I was always somewhat wary of these channels, because of the current, or a sudden change in weather, so I paddled hard for an hour and did not ease up until I was near the island.

Savo, which from Honiara had seemed like a small hump in the ocean, was on closer inspection a mountain in the sea, a gently rounded volcano, with green slopes. The southern end was rocky, but I could see palms and white beaches along its eastern side. I chose to paddle along it because I was tired, and I knew that I could safely go ashore at any point.

The villages were small, set just inland, and I was reassured by the pretty huts. People who wove huts out of split bamboo and thatched them and lashed them as carefully as these Savo islanders had done, had to be hospitable traditionalists. If I had seen tin roofs and cinder blocks, the sort of sheds with swinging doors and padlocks that aid agencies often built for such people – in the innocent belief they were doing them a favor – I would have been very worried. I regarded such dwellings and such violated villages as unpredictable, full of nuisances. Villagers living under tin roofs stenciled *A gift from the people of the United States of America*, and eating food aid, regarded people like me as a soft touch. I was all for foreign aid, but there was a certain type of aid that undermined people and made them dangerous.

In Savo there was no apparent sign that any village had been penetrated by the West. And just offshore men and boys fished from dugout canoes. Seeing a settlement on a great sandy beach, I paddled to one of these canoes.

"*Wanem nem bilong dispela ples?*" I asked a fisherman, pointing to the huts.

"*Dispela Pokilo,*" he said.

"*Balola village i stap we?*"

He waved his hand to the west and said, "*Klostu liklik. Go stret.*"

He was right. Balola was very near, but when I landed and dragged my kayak up the sand I was surprised by its air of desertion. No one watched me come ashore, no children shrieked at me, no dogs barked at me, no women were dumping trash on the beach, nor were any men fishing in the low surf. I passed from the early evening light of the beach to the cool crepuscular darkness of the small village that lay damply beneath the dense foliage of trees. Some chickens hurried and clucked on the path, but it was only after walking from one end of the village to the other that I found a person – a man named Aaron, who had bushy sidewhiskers and a gammy leg.

"*Hello. Yu savvy tok Inglis?*"

"*Pisin,*" he said.

"*Plis yu nap halpim?*" I asked and showed the letter the minister had given me. "*Mi laik toktok Nathaniel Mapopoza. Mi givim dispela pas.*"

"*Yumi go,*" he said. "*Mapo i stap long ples*" – and he pointed down the muddy path.

"*Emi longwe o nogat?*" I asked, because if it was far I was much happier simply waiting here.

"*Klostu liklik,*" he said, setting off, and I followed.

It was a forty-five-minute walk along a narrow path; it was the only thoroughfare, and it circled the island. I could see at once that it was an island without a road, or a motor vehicle, or electricity. We passed through six or seven small villages and in each one Aaron called out in the local language that he was taking me to see Mapo.

Mapopoza was seated under a pawpaw tree, chewing betel and stuffing his mouth with lime, at a village called Bonala. The village presented an odd spectacle. About a hundred people were milling around whispering and examining great stacks of bananas, baskets of potatoes and more coconuts than I had ever seen piled in one place. And three fat pigs, whickering and squealing, because their feet were tightly bound.

"Feegs," Aaron said, attempting English. He gave me to understand that a wedding was about to take place, but that this was the fixing of the bride price. No money was involved; there was little money on this island.

I handed my letter to Mapo. He shrugged – did not meet my gaze – and looked away. He was bit dazed from the betel nut, but that was not the only reason for his obliqueness. It soon became clear to me that he could not read, but it was not odd that his brother should write him a detailed letter. Mapo simply handed the thing to a boy nearby, who clawed it open, and as people gathered round, the boy read the letter in a superior way, as though he was rather stuck on himself for being so literate.

I stood there with salt in my eyes and my arm-muscles screaming from the long kayak trip.

My name was mentioned – *Mistah Foll* – and the listeners turned to me and stared. And then, *Amerika*.

Mapo was vague. Not only was he illiterate, he did not speak English. But none of this mattered. I only needed his blessing, I didn't need his hospitality. What I wanted most was his permission to put up my tent, my *haus sel*, in Balola village.

So I said, *"Plis, mi laik putim haus sel long Balola na stap long?"*

*"Orait,"* he said. *"Mi kam bai."*

He gestured, showing me that he was being detained. I could see he had a role to play in this betrothal, but still he urged me to sit down and sip some coconut water from a freshly hacked nut. He said nothing. He had a crooked smile. A few feet away the tied-up pigs were quivering with thirst and suffocation. To amuse themselves, some village boys went near and began kicking the poor creatures.

Women with streaks of white paint on their cheeks wandered around muttering – part of the betrothal, I guessed – and others were talking and spitting betel juice and slurping lime. I noticed another group of people crowding into an open-fronted hut, and asked Aaron what was going on. He didn't know, but he asked a Bonala man who spoke directly to me.

"There is a man from Africa in there."

"Africa?"

It was a bit like Saro's story of the Ethiopian stowaway who had claimed to be a Solomon Islander. But who could this man be, and what was he doing? I thought he might be a preacher or a healer, granting an audience to these villagers.

I sidled up to the hut, wondering how I might introduce myself, and came face to face with a sturdy fellow who greeted me, "Hey, man."

This was Bilal Mohammed, an American Peace Corps Volunteer from Brooklyn, New York, shaven-headed, and very black from the Solomon sun, wearing a jolly T-shirt and baggy Bermuda shorts.

He was a teacher on another island, Makira, but as he was on vacation he had come here to Savo in a motor-launch to visit some friends. He asked me whether I knew anything about the stand-off in the Gulf.

"Just sabre-rattling so far," I said.

"I've got a bet with a guy in Honiara that there won't be a war," he said. "Because no one is that stupid."

"It looks bad," I said, and yet I had no idea where I would place my bet. It was a period of great uncertainty. "There are more than two hundred thousand troops in Saudi Arabia, waiting for the word."

Bilal said, "People think they are making plans, but they don't realize that God has his own plan, and we can't outwit God."

It was spoken with true Islamic fatalism and a rueful smile. We shook hands, and both of us said that we hoped it would all end peacefully. Then he went back into the hut and I walked three miles back to Balola village with Aaron and put up my tent in the dusk, at the edge of the beach.

Before I had finished making camp, a fat man in a dirty *lap-lap* stepped out of the bush − clearly a busybody − and told me that I would be much happier camping near his hut. Before I could react, he was scooping up my gear and helping me move.

"I am president of Savo," he said in a lordly way.

I had been in Melanesia long enough to know that even if this were true it did not mean a great deal. As it turned out, his being president did not mean much more than that his T-shirt was slightly less dirty than other people's.

This man was Kemakeza's other brother, but they were not on speaking terms − nor was he on speaking terms with Mapo, who he quickly told me was an ignorant villager. His name was Ataban Tonezepo – there were no common surnames here – and he was well-spoken. He said he thought Pidgin was a silly language.

"But it is useful," I said, "because people speak it."

"That is a very wise observation," he said, and I suspected on the basis of this obsequious turn of phrase that he might turn out to be a royal pain.

When we had settled on a place where I might put my tent – it was a freestanding Moss tent, we just swung it fully pitched, twenty feet along the beach – Ataban said, "I am former premier of Central Province, but I lost at the last election. So here I am, back in Balola."

"But your duties as president must keep you busy."

"That is very true."

In the growing darkness people had begun to gather, trying to help me. There were now twenty-eight of them – I counted as I set out my gear, hanging my food from trees, so that the rats wouldn't get it. As we were facing north, there was no dramatic sunset, only a diminishing glow on the water, and the shapes of the distant islands of Nggela, Isabel and Russell.

"We used to sail there," Ataban said.

"You might be sailing there again, if the fuel prices rise."

"That is very true."

The twenty-eight men and boys sat down and watched me start my kerosene stove and eat my hurried supper of beans and mackerel and fresh bread from the bakery in Honiara. I gave Ataban a beer and some "Conversation Biscuits" to the others. And when I had finished eating, Ataban demanded that four of the boys take my pots to be washed.

"Do you think there will be World War Three after January?" Ataban asked.

"Frankly, no."

"We think it will come here. Everyone is worried."

"Believe me, you are safe here," I said.

"World War Two came here," he said. "Right here. To this island."

"*Yupela bigpela, strongpela*," I said. "*Yupela nogat pret*" – you guys aren't afraid – "*Yupela kilim i dai.*"

They laughed at me, and then Ataban sent everyone away and told them to let me sleep in peace.

"In the morning you can't go down to the beach," he said. "The women will be using it. Doing shit there – right there. And the men will be over there, doing shit."

The village beach was the toilet in the Solomons; it was where people shat. Even in simple grubby New Guinea people said *Mi go haus pek pek*, and looked for the privy or the thunderjug. In the Trobriands they had a pavilion on a pier, with a long drop into the sea; and there was a word for toilet in Kiriwina. But in the Solomons things were different. *Mi go nambis* – "I'm going to the beach," in Pidgin – meant one thing only, a BM by the sea. It never meant swimming – that was *waswas*, and anyway only little kiddies did that, frolicking in the excrement and the fruit peels – for the beach was also the village dump, littered with rusty cans and plastic bottles.

It was extraordinary how the islanders fouled their beaches, always expecting the tide to purify it twice a day. But I preferred to camp on the beach. The fact that it was generally regarded as a toilet made it emptier – no intruders – and I disliked the mosquitoes, the human gabbling and the cockcrows in the damp shadowy villages.

The beach was also a graveyard. One of the keenest nineteenth-century observers of the Melanesians was R. H. Codrington, a missionary-turned-anthropologist, who wrote, "In Savo . . . common men are thrown into the sea, and only great men buried." Codrington also remarked on the fact that the people of Savo were renowned in Melanesia as poisoners.

That night while I lay in my tent writing notes, under my swinging flashlight, I heard children just outside whispering. After I switched the flashlight off they went away.

For hours after that I heard them singing and strumming, making their way around the village from hut to hut, like carolers at Christmas.

Large crabs gathered against my tent at five in the morning and their scratching woke me – the rising sun gave them distinct silhouettes. Remembering what Ataban had said about the women *doing shit* I stayed in the tent and listened to my short-wave radio for the Gulf update. The Voice of America, which sounds like a local radio station, had hardly altered its programming schedule to take account of the crisis – it still ran its trivial music and frivolous features, interspersing them with little bursts of solemn news, delivered by credulous-sounding journalists. Radio Australia and the BBC had actually changed their whole news format – they reported news, scoops, rumours and in-depth pieces, and in the mounting suspense gave a plausible commentary on the crisis.

Yet I listened to it all feeling that I was a million miles away, on another planet, lost in the galaxy of Oceania.

After the news I crawled out and shooed the crabs away, made tea and noodles and sat listening to music and looking at the sea until Mapo came by, to ask me the news. It was hardly past five-thirty in the morning.

"*Sapos ol bigpela kaontri pait,*" he said, "*mi tingting ol kam na pait long Solomons.*"

Which in fact was everyone's fear: if the superpowers went to war they would eventually fight in the Solomons. This lurking fear was evident in the questions of nearly everyone I spoke to in that period, and for some it was an absolute terror – the complete disruption of their way of life and a brutal disorder imposed upon them.

They had not felt liberated by World War Two; they felt as though a succession of cyclones had passed through their islands – first the Japanese one, the invasion, the take-over, the occupation; then the allied bombing, the fire-fights, the battle of Guadalcanal, and the destruction of villages, the sinking of scores of ships, the deaths, the arrival of the sharks to feed on the bodies.

The aftermath – the post-war chaos – had been just as bad. American troops attempting to disentangle themselves from the islands and demobilize had been nearly as disruptive. During the war, there was little fishing, and very little farming was done – three years' crops were lost. With no harvests the islanders had become dependent upon the foreign soldiers, and had developed a dreary taste for canned food, in particular for the corned beef and pork luncheon meat that persists to this day.

I gave him my now standard reassurance in Pidgin: if the war started it would not come here. For emphasis, I said it was *Tru tumas.*

Mapo smiled. He did not believe me.

He said, "*Yu laik lukim megapode pisin?*"

Savo was not an island that was short of strange features – it had an active steaming volcano, it had hot springs, it apparently had a president – but the megapode birds were the strangest of all.

The local word for the birds was *ngero*; in Pidgin they were called *skraeb dak*; ornithologists called them "mound-builders;" but most people on Savo, when speaking to strangers, called them by their scientifically correct name, megapodes, from their family, *Megapodidae*. It was a fairly rare variety of big-footed bird, of which twelve species were known from Indonesia to Vanuatu. Its distinguishing habit was that it relied entirely on environmental heat to incubate its eggs. The bird laid its eggs in sand that was always warm because of its nearness to the volcano. The megapode had the most precocious hatchlings of any bird – the birds did not sit on the eggs, they did not feed or tend their young. After they had dug a deep hole in this unnaturally warm sand, they laid the egg, covered the hole and flew off.

Three weeks later the bird hatched, dug itself out of the hole and, fully fledged in a matter of minutes, started running. Within hours of its birth the baby bird had learned to fly, and – if it had managed to elude the pariah dogs and the bush pigs – it made for the trees.

But relatively few of the eggs ever hatched. Mapo told me in Pidgin that they were disinterred by egg-diggers later in the morning. We walked through the bush, parallel to the beach, for about half a mile and down a narrow path to a stretch of fenced-off beach where, in the dawn light, I could see hundreds of squawking, strutting moorhen-like birds digging holes or kicking sand with feet the size and shape of salad tongs.

Mapo sat on a rock in the shade and smoked a cigarette, while I crept forward on my belly and watched, fascinated, relieved that I did not have a camera. The sight was unphotographable – the birds were too deep in the holes, a camera could not do justice to the noise, and clearly the birds were skittish – they would have run from a photographer. All you heard were squawks, and all you saw were bunches of sand being flung out of the holes. Now and then a nervous bird would emerge from a hole, fill it hurriedly, and flap away, like a startled coot.

In the rising heat of early morning – even in the palmy shade I was perspiring heavily – I watched for almost an hour, and by the time I was about to leave many of the birds had finished burying their eggs and flown.

I wondered whether they ate the birds, and so on the way back to the village I asked, "*Yupela kaikai megapode pisin?*"

Mapo said, "*Sapos dok i gat long tit, mipela kaikai.*"

If a dog gets it in its teeth, we eat it.

But it was forbidden to kill the bird, he said, and he said rather obscurely that once *tambu* ceremonies were held in which the bird was worshipped.

Mapo took me to his house and introduced me to his wife, Rebecca, who served us each a megapode egg omelette with rice. And he showed me an egg from his kitchen. It was an extraordinary size – the thing was large – about four inches by two, larger than any duck egg I had ever seen, and heavy.

People on Savo really depended on the eggs, he said. They collected them, they ate them, they sold them in Honiara for a Solomon dollar apiece. I began interrogating him, as best I could in Pidgin, about the history of the island, the worship of the birds, the mythology of the eggs. He answered in a halting way.

But then he said that I would have to ask someone else – and he said shyly – it was a try at English, it was not imperfect Pidgin – "I no have education. No school." And he smiled sadly. "Now I too old to go school."

One of his children was nearby, and Mapo swept the little boy onto his lap and pushed his half-eaten megapode omelette aside.

"*Dispela pikanin savvy toktok Inglis!*"

Because of the megapode eggs this half of the island was prosperous and well fed. The eggs were greatly in demand on Guadalcanal. The opposite side of the island was well-off, too – it had a reef and plenty of fish. The whole of Savo was rich in fruit trees – oranges, lemons, guavas. There were betel-nut trees and *ngali* nuts (which were similar to macadamias) and coconuts. But gardening was basic – cassava, taro, beans – fairly easy crops. The result of this abundance was that life was undemanding, a little sweeping, a little weeding. The villages were very quiet and had little of the harum-scarum that I had grown used to in the Trobriands. Most of the time Savo slumbered.

What terrors would the Japanese have had in store for these happy indolent folk if they had won the war? At the very least there would have been a golf course here, and someone like Mapo would have been a caddy, and Rebecca would have had a job in the kitchen of the golf club, rustling up megapode omelettes for the hungry Sons of Nippon.

In the first few days I camped on Savo the stillness and inactivity were profoundly apparent, and there was even something lugubrious about it, as though the place were haunted.

I paddled south to Mbonala, a village in a little bay, where children were splashing, and boys were spear-fishing, and women were washing clothes. The men of the village sat under trees, chewing betel nut. A screeching crowd gathered on shore as I asked directions to Monagho. Savo on my chart was a yellow disk, showing topographical lines and a few elevations. Whenever I spoke to someone I added detail, and filled in the blanks, noting the names of villages, and bays, and streams.

The village of Monagho turned out to greet me. It was – like Balola and Mbonala – a village of topless women, many of them smoking briar pipes. Soon James joined them – he had been thatching the roof of his house. He introduced me to his family. His pretty sister Mary, who was about sixteen, wore a necklace of dolphin's teeth. James said he was looking for a husband for her.

"*You marit pinis?*" he asked me – but the fact that he spoke in Pidgin meant that he really did not expect an answer.

"It's a long story," I said.

He showed me his house, which was large and well-built like most of the houses and huts on Savo – thickly woven palm leaves on a strong frame of poles, with an ingeniously woven roof that was both waterproof and graceful. While I sat talking with his family he borrowed my kayak and amused the village, as he paddled up and down the shore.

I paddled three miles farther to Kaonggele, the village which had the right of way to the volcano, and when I came ashore I was helped by twelve boys, who put my kayak on the village canoe rack. I told them I wanted to see the volcano.

"You will have to pay that old man," one boy said. "He is our chief."

He was sitting on a log under a tree, listening to an early model transistor radio the size of a Kleenex box. It was bruised and dirty and patched with tape, but a buzzy voice was murmuring in the speaker.

The old man's name was Marcel Devo – this was another Catholic village: St Theresa's Church was on the bluff just above it – and he said he thought he was seventy-seven. He did not speak Pidgin or English, only Savosavo.

"Ask him if he remembers the war," I said to one of the boys.

"I was already married when the war started," he said, and the boy translated.

"What do you remember?"

"Everything," he said, in a croaky voice. "I helped carry the American food and equipment. I worked hard. You see this road?" He gestured to a rutted path that sloped from the beach. "The Americans built it. It was the only road we had in Savo."

"Did you see fighting during the war?"

"There was fighting everywhere." And he raised his red eyes to me. "Smoke and fire. And loud noises. Ships all over the water."

Putting his radio down he nearly dropped it. He was very feeble, but I had reminded him of the nightmarish years of the war.

"It was terrible" – the boy was still translating – "Some bodies washed ashore and others were eaten by sharks. We were frightened. We did not know what to do."

"What were you listening to on your radio?"

"The news," he said. "The war will start in Iraq and it will come here. Either the Iraq people will come first and then the Americans will drive them away, or else the Americans will come and the Iraq people will fight them here."

"Tell him I don't think that will happen," I said.

When he heard this he muttered to the boy, who said, "You are wrong."

Normally the chief was paid five Solomon dollars by anyone who wanted to use Kaonggele's path to hike up to the volcano, but the old man said I did not have to pay.

"I saw you paddling your canoe here, so you can go for nothing."

Eight of the boys came with me – they had nothing else to do, they said. It took an hour up to the rim of the crater where I looked down and saw the gray steam blowing out of the cracks down below. That to me was a less impressive spectacle than the hot springs here and there on the upward path – little boiling pools, where people gathered to cook their food. I hung around one group which was simultaneously steaming cassava and sweet potatoes and ears of corn – the vegetables were thickly wrapped in leaves. A man offered me an ear of corn, which I ate, and looking for a place to fling the cob after I had finished I stepped into a puddle of sulfurous water and scalded my foot.

Cooking on free hot water on the slopes of a volcano! These people had everything! Birds flew in and gave them hundreds of huge eggs a day, and all they had to do was carry them up the hill and boil them. They had nuts and oranges and lemons and breadfruit and papaya – the trees required no care at all. Their pigs looked after themselves, so did their chickens.

It seemed an almost unimaginably pleasant life.

"Do you have missionaries here?"

"No. But a priest comes once a month for mass."

They showed me the church. It was wooden, and rather roughly put together, and big and musty and empty.

"What about mosquitoes?"

"They don't trouble us."

But they troubled me. The only aspect of this island I did not like was its pestilential insects – fleas and midges and mosquitoes, and most of all its skinny biting flies that never left me alone, in spite of my insect repellent.

I gave the boys some chocolate cookies and made a point of saving three or four for the chief, Marcel Devo. In return they climbed the coconut palms and hacked open some nuts. I drank a whole one and filled my water bottle with the sweet water from the others.

A few days later I paddled back to Kaonggele, but instead of a somnolent village I found boys and men engaged in furious activity on the beach, setting out piles of yams and bananas on palm leaves. One boy, whom I recognized from my previous visit, was hacking a dead pig to pieces with a bloody machete.

"What is this all about?" I asked.

"For peace," the boy said and smiled knowingly.

"Do you mean there was trouble here?"

"There is peace now," a furtive man said.

"This man Phillip make trouble," the boy with a machete said.

Phillip, the furtive fellow, was skinny, about thirty years old. He had a pinched and rather anxious face, and did not look at all like a troublemaker. He squirmed and said, "Sha-sha-sha," trying to shut the boy up.

"That is Phillip's pig," another boy said teasingly, and laughed.

"There was fighting," the first boy said.

"Did you fight?"

"No. Ask Phillip."

Phillip was sorely embarrassed. He said in a low voice, "I made the trouble with that other village. I made a fight. So I do this to stop the trouble."

This feast was a *zokule*, a peacemaking meal. Phillip had quarrelled with a man from a neighbouring village, and caused bad feeling. To bring peace he had offered his pig and the others had provided vegetables. When the food was all set out the offended village would walk down the beach and eat it and in that way, having shared this food and especially Phillip's pig, would be placated.

That day and other days, when I encountered men or boys in canoes – not outriggers, but the slender dugouts they used for fishing and playing – they challenged me to races, and I beat them. Their canoes were sleek enough but their paddles were single-bladed and rather heavy and hard to handle. I had a carbon-fiber double-bladed paddle – the usual for kayaking. When I loaned it to any of them, and I used that person's paddle, I always lost. So I encouraged them to use my paddle and tried to convince them to carve long double-bladed paddles for themselves, using this design.

They usually said they would try. They were certainly open to suggestions. Ataban's schoolgirl sister Agnes, who was a plump and mature fourteen, had a large fresh set of scars on her cheek – a circle radiating wiggly lines.

"Dis da sun," she explained.

Yes, a radiant sun, carved into her cheek.

"Is that a custom here on Savo?"

"No. On Malaita. It is not our custom. I asked the Malaita people to do it to me. They came here to dance. One month ago."

"Did it hurt?" I asked.

"Yes. Very much. They did it with a fork and a knife. Afterwards they put salt water on it."

I thought, *How strange*. Because another group of people in the Solomons had a tradition of scarring their faces, this Savo schoolgirl had offered hers, and had her cheek painfully knifed open with an obnoxious disfigurement she would carry on her face for the rest of her life.

"You like it?" she asked.

I told her what she wanted to hear.

The nights were so starry they lit the island even before the moon had risen. The children played and sang until midnight. I thought they were bratty, but one day they brought me a chair and I felt ashamed of myself. I could actually sit comfortably under a palm tree, writing or reading, while they swatted flies. I usually waited until the shore was empty of people and I went *nambis*, feeling like an utter fool, so exposed. You squatted at the tidemark, facing inland.

Except for the insects, and the occasional snake, life for me on Savo was idyllic. But I soon realized that I was caught between the feuding of two brothers – Ataban, the fat former politician, who spoke English well if a bit pompously; and Mapopoza, the skinny illiterate who did little except stuff his mouth with betel and lime. Both men were capable of being jolly. But of course, Mapo, who had no pretensions, who had never left the village, had the most power.

Ataban, however, controlled the egg fields – actually owned a quarter mile of beach where the eggs were laid. It was strange that these wild birds were in a sense privately controlled. This was an almost inexhaustible source of wealth, and it was obvious that he was rather resented for it – but what could anyone do? He charged the diggers five eggs a day in order to go on digging for more eggs. On successive days I met Ataban in the egg fields, and what I had thought to be easily-won food turned out to be hot, dirty, tiring work.

So as not to risk breaking the eggs, the men began digging with a small flat piece of wood, but after they had dug about eighteen inches they lay on their bellies and used their bare hands. The volcanic sand was heavy and the men labored in the full sun, sometimes digging to three or four feet before they came upon the egg. It amazed me to think of the bird digging that deep, laying the egg and then pushing all the sand back in with its scratching feet. All morning, in the egg fields of Savo, there was the curious spectacle of men stuck in holes, chucking sand out, and all you saw were their sweaty kicking legs smeared with sand grains.

A young man named Walter told me he was saving up his eggs. He had eighty-five at the moment. He wanted to take a hundred eggs to market in Honiara. It would cost him twenty-four Solomon dollars for the round trip on the motor-boat, and a few dollars to hire a table at the market. His profit for fourteen days of laborious egg-digging would be less than thirty American dollars.

Peter from the village of Alialia presented a strange sight. He had been to London in the 1970s on a parliamentary delegation. He had met the British foreign secretary and the Queen, and had worn a borrowed suit, and here he was lying on his belly in his Foster's Beer T-shirt, sand in his springy hair, his arms filthy, his face gleaming with sweat, scrabbling in the sand with his bare hands, searching for a megapode egg.

The egg fields were sort of a men's club – women were not allowed to dig or even to set foot in the place. The diggers joshed each other and gassed with me, while Ataban sat plumply in the shade of a tree, accepting his tribute of five eggs from each man – he collected between twenty and a hundred eggs a day in his cloth bag. When he had three hundred or so – a week's accumulation – he sent his son to Honiara to sell them at the market.

"Everyone wants them," Ataban said.

One day I said, "Do you have the same number of megapode birds as years ago?"

"No. We have less."

It was predictable enough. "So why don't you give the eggs a chance to hatch? That way you'd end up with more birds and more eggs."

"The young people would never accept it, although that was done in olden times, when the bird was worshiped with sacrifices."

That day he showed me the grave of the man who was the last person to carry out sacrifices. The man, Kigata, had died in 1965. The usual sacrifice was the burning of a pig to ashes in a tabu-grove on the cliff behind the village. But Ataban explained a sort of Manichaean idea that the bird was also associated with a certain snake, its "devil" or spirit.

On the way back to the village, I said, "What month do you harvest the yams?"

"Usually in June."

"You have plenty of food that month. Why not forbid the digging of eggs then? Set June aside for hatching. A few weeks later you'd have megapodes hatching all over the place, and you'd have more eggs."

"That is a very wise observation," Ataban said.

It was hard to tell whether he was satirizing me.

"I will put that idea to the council," he said. "We will make it a bylaw."

It was in the egg fields, in the breather between eggs, that they became very chatty. They asked about the price of oil in other countries, about the power of the Soviet Union and Japan, about the greenhouse effect (this question raised by a very old man who said, "A man in Honiara told me −"), the cost of living elsewhere, and how much you would have to pay for a house in various countries. Invariably the talk in the egg fields turned to the stand-off in the Gulf, and after Ataban demanded my assurance that in the event of a war the Americans would win ("No problem," I said. "But men will die"), he began teasing me.

"Put away your guns!" he said. "Put away bombs and planes and bullets. Fight with your hands. We Melanesians can beat you − with our hands!"

"*Rabis. Bullseet,*" I said, and the others tittered. "That is all *nambaten.* You wouldn't have a chance. We are *bigpela, strongpela.*"

"No! We are Melanesian!" Ataban said. "We are warriors, and we have magic."

"Ya, ya," the men said, and began jeering at me.

"Where was your Melanesian magic in 1942?" I asked.

"Oh, dear," Ataban said in a squeaky voice. "We no have no magic at that time. We just ran into the bush and let the Americans fight the Japanese. Ha-ha."

After that particular discussion a twenty-year-old named Edward sidled up to me and said, "But Rambo is very strong. He can fight without guns."

Rambo is one of the folk-heroes of the Solomons − indeed, his fame pervades Oceania. Anyone hastily condemning this credulity as simple savagery must recall the utterance of the American President Ronald Reagan in which he mentioned how he had seen a Rambo movie at the White House, and how the witless brute in this worthless movie had inspired him.

Over dinner at his hut one night (megapode eggs, the Spam they called "Ma Ling," and *kumara*, sweet potatoes), Mapo asked me, "*Mi laik lukim* Rambo *video tumas. Yu lukim* Commando? *Nambawan man long* Commando."

"*Yu lukim video long ples Balola?*"

"*Ya. Mi kros. Dispela generator bagarap.*"

The one generator on the island had no use except as a source of energy to show videos here.

Pidgin was in fact rarely spoken on Savo, except to outsiders. The island language, called Savosavo, was said by linguists to be Papuan – not Melanesian at all. Ataban denied this, but there were many Polynesian-sounding words in the language. For example, the Savosavo word for "island" was *molumolu*, undoubtedly a cognate with Polynesian forms (*motu* in Tahiti, *moku* in Hawaiian, and so forth).

"Where did Savo people originally come from?" I asked Ataban.

Before he could answer, Peter the egg-digger said, "Asia."

"I don't think so," Ataban said. "We believe that we were always here. That we came from a bird or a snake. The bird – maybe it was a frigate bird – laid an egg, and a woman came out. That is what I think."

"What about the people on other islands? What about those people who live on Ontong Java?"

They were Polynesians on this small atoll in the north of the Solomon group.

"Maybe they sailed there," Ataban said. "But we came from birds and sharks and snakes."

And, he explained, after death they turned back into sharks. It was a belief on Savo that sharks were the ghosts of dead people. For this reason sharks were often spoken to and given food.

There was no fear of sharks in the Solomons, but then there was no fear of sharks anywhere I went in the Pacific. This was not so strange. It is a statistical fact that only twenty-five people a year are killed by sharks. Many more people are killed by pigs.

Most of the time, paddling around Savo, I wore earphones and listened to my Walkman, the same tape – because I only had one at the time – which was of Puccini and Verdi arias sung by Kiri Te Kanawa: *Vissi d'arte* from *Tosca*, *O mio babbino caro* from *Gianni Schicchi*, *Un bel di, vedremo* from *Butterfly*, *Fors'è lui* from *La Traviata*, and others. It is almost imposs-ible to describe the peculiar poignancy of being close to a small, lovely island, passing under the high cliffs surmounted by slender palms, the strange lumpy hills and calderas created by the vulcanism of the fairly recent past (the explorer Mendaña saw Savo in eruption in 1568), the surf whitening the rocky beaches, and the children with sunburned hair running from the bamboo huts and playing in the waves, all of them – the people, their huts, their canoes, their little gardens, the women gaping up at me from their washing – dwarfed by the active volcano just behind them, as I listened to the rich soprano voice singing *Quel'amor* with piercing sweetness as I paddled on.

Or, more appropriately, *Se come voi*, the aria of the pretty flowers – because the flowers were visible from where I paddled. If I were as pretty as they, then I could always stay close to my love, and would say "Don't forget me" –

> *Se come voi piccina io fossi,*
> *O vaghi fior, sempre sempre*
> *Vicina potrei stare al mio amor . . .*

Under the pink and purple sky of early evening, paddling in a sea the color of rose-water, while the cockatoos flashed from tree to tree and the frigate birds soared, I felt lucky. I had found this island by chance, and it seemed to me that if the people were not interfered with by tourists or bureaucrats, the island would remain intact and the people would be able to manage well on their own. It daunted me to think of the permanence of that strange simple life, but it must have been a fruitful life or else the people would not have been so generous and unsuspicious.

When I perceived this place as sad, as I sometimes did, listening to those arias and watching this green island revolve past my boat, I realized that the sadness was mine. I had brought it here. It was part of my mood in the day. It affected my dreams, which were of gray chaotic London and steep stairs leading to thick locked doors – no doors here, no locks, no stairs even – and dreams of delay and missed appointments, almost meeting my wife and then bamboozled by a sudden orgy of naked people on a street corner or a bolted back door, and arriving and whimpering *Too late*, and waking up in a sweat, hearing the sloshing surf and remembering I was in Savo, in the Solomon Islands, alone in a tent on the beach.

I paddled because it was a way of being alone. I paddled because I liked listening to music. I paddled because the water was too filthy for swimming in. I also paddled to give the day a shape, because I usually wrote my notes in the morning, exerted myself in the afternoon – only eight or ten miles, but in that equatorial heat the sun shone from a cloudless sky. I paddled because it was often the only way of getting from one place to another.

If Mapo was not with me at sunset, Ataban (who hated him) stopped by for a chat. One day he asked whether I thought it was odd that he should regard his brother as an enemy. I said I found it much more understandable that he should dislike or pity his brother than feel that way towards a vague acquaintance.

"In a way, you can only really dislike a member of your family or someone you know well," I said. "But I think Mapo is a good fellow."

"That is because you do not know him," Ataban said. "Ha!"

He usually greeted me with, "You had a good pandle?"

"A very good paddle."

"You like to pandle," he said. "And I am so busy!"

"You mean busy sleeping under a tree while people bring you megapode eggs?"

He took this mockery well, and even seemed to regard it as a gesture of friendliness. "No. I am a poor Melanesian. I have to work. I am not lazy like you Americans. I have to feed my feegs."

Then he would sit down and talk until it was dark. Usually I pestered him to show me the tabu-groves, where the megapode birds were worshiped, but he said it was too *tambu*, and that it would be very bad for me to go there. After a week, I stopped asking him.

"Tomorrow I will show you the place where we sacrifice to the megapode birds," he said one night. "And I will tell you the story of the bird and the devil."

"Tell me now, Ataban."

He made a face. "It is too long. And my feegs are waiting."

"*Yu go we tude?*" Mapo asked me the next day. "*Yu wokabaot Kwila? Yu laik samting, yu laik kaikai?*"

It was a charade, but so as not to make the brothers' feud any worse I said I was simply going for a walk and did not need any food.

Ataban met me at the edge of the village and introduced me to an old man – he said he was seventy-four – who had brought him some eggs. Whenever I met someone that old I asked them about the war. The man had lived on Savo his whole life. He said that nothing had changed, and the only interruption had been the war. Ataban acted as translator.

"The Japanese came here. One Japanese man said, 'We are powerful and we are staying here – in Tulaghi. We will never leave. Go to your fields. Pick coconuts, make copra, grow bananas. Cultivate vegetables. Go fishing. We will buy everything you have to sell.'"

"Did they mention the Americans?"

"They said, 'The Americans are very strong. They will come and try to fight. But we will beat them.' We were frightened of them."

"But why?" I said. "The Japanese are little bowlegged people who can't see without glasses. They are smaller than you. Why were you afraid?"

The old man laughed and spoke again, and Ataban translated. "It's true, they looked strange to us. But some were tall. And they had guns. A little while later the Americans came and it was all different. There was fighting. Many people died. I was afraid. And I still think about it."

"But this was a long time ago."

"No! It was recent. It was just a little while ago. I was already married and had children," the old man said.

After the old man left us, Ataban changed his mind and said that it wasn't such a good idea for him to take me to the place of sacrifice, because it was too *tambu*. But I urged him and when he still seemed reluctant, I asked him why.

"Because I believe in *kastom*. I am not a Christian. This place is *tambu*."

"I won't step on it. I won't touch it. I won't even go near. I just want to look."

"That's better," he said. "Look at a distance."

We set off on a steep overgrown path and immediately saw a brown snake, the thickness of a garden hose – a four-footer – and, according to my handbook, *Reptiles of the Solomon Islands*, probably a venomous land snake of the genus *Salomonelaps* (it flattened itself when provoked, and hissed, and made a chewing movement with its jaws; "The toxicity of its venom is unknown but could be regarded as potentially dangerous to humans . . .").

Farther on, there was a big clumsy crashing in the bush, and I had a glimpse of a creature I took to be a dog.

"No. It is a lizard," Ataban said.

A lizard as big as a cocker spaniel? The reptile handbook suggested monitor lizard.

How different it was just a half a mile inland from the breezy beach! Here it was still and hot and steamy, and the air stank of wet and rotten leaves. There was a spider on every bough, and even in the daytime the air was thick with mosquitoes. Merely by grazing a tree trunk with your elbow you picked up a mass of biting ants. We had not gone fifty yards when the ants had worked their way to my neck.

Fat Ataban walked ahead, slapping his arms.

We came to a rectangle of stones.

"This is the grave of the man who first welcomed the birds to Savo," Ataban said. "He was on the hill. The bird came and wanted to stay. But the devil – the snake – would not allow it. Then the bird laid an egg. The man ate the egg and said, 'This is good.' So the bird was allowed to stay, as long as it promised to go on laying the eggs."

We walked farther; all the while Ataban was muttering in a complaining way, "This is *tambu*," and waving his arms.

"No trees may be cut here," he said. "No ropes" – he meant vines – "may be cut."

And because the bush had never been cut, and was seldom visited, it was vast and green and dark – very dense and tall. The megapodes were squawking like chickens in the tree branches. This was their haunt.

A large black spider hung in a web just in front of the tabu-grove. The spider's body was about the size of a silver dollar and the legs were each about three inches long. Passing it, Ataban punched the web.

"Did you see the spider?"

"Yes. It will not hurt you."

We did not go very far into the grove. There was no path, for one thing. The whole place was overgrown, and the trees were thick – their trunks averaging about two feet in diameter. It was so strange to see such old trees on a small island: normally they would have been cut for firewood or for houses. The bamboos which grew everywhere here in dense clusters, were deep green and fat, the thickness of a drainpipe.

Ataban was nervous. He said, "It is just there. And I tell you it is very *tambu*. Look at it, but do not go near."

I saw a pile of boulders.

"That is where they burn the feegs to ashes in the sacrifice."

"I can't see very well. There are too many trees."

"We believe that if anyone cuts down a tree here he will get sick. He will probably die."

The word *tambu* – taboo – had a definite meaning in this creepy place. The sunlight hardly penetrated the trees, and because there was no path we had to push the bamboos aside in order to move – and the whole place hummed with insects and the *kuk kuk kuk* of the roosting megapodes. And as we moved slowly through the grove a pig blundered out of the sacred place and Ataban kicked at the startled creature and yelled "*Yu *gettim bek!"* – as though the only proper way to address a pig was in Pidgin.

We crashed through the bush a bit more, he showed me another sacred hill, and I asked, "Why don't you have ceremonies these days?"

"If a person carries out a sacrifice and burns a pig to ashes he can't go to church. But I could do it, because I believe in *kastom*."

When I pressed him, saying that the megapodes were in danger of not being respected, and might fly away for ever, he said that an old woman came once a year and sacrificed a pig to the birds.

Back on the path, badly bitten, after two hours of that tangle of spiders and vines – we were both drenched from the wet leaves and the heat – Ataban said protestingly, "I tell you I have shown many people the megapode fields, but I have never taken anyone to the *tambu* place. You are the first one, ever."

I told him that I appreciated the trouble he had taken.

"Now you will go back to your camp and write about it in your notebook."

"How do you know?"

"I see you sitting and writing all the time."

I thought I was alone on the beach, but I should have known better. There is no privacy in a village.

"Don't be silly, Ataban. I can keep a secret. Of course I'm not going to write this down."

But as soon as he was out of sight it was exactly what I did.

I stayed on Savo longer than I intended, and after I ran out of food I simply ate yams and megapode eggs, which were the yolkiest eggs I had ever seen. One day James came by in his motor-boat and after a little bargaining – I gave him my fish spear and a full tank of gas – we went fifteen miles across The Slot to Nggela, to look at Tulaghi. The town had been captured by the Japanese in January 1942. It was retaken by the Americans in August, and because of its deep harbor, this was the headquarters for the invasion of Guadalcanal. There were rock walls at the harbor entrance. Once they had been painted with American war cries, on the instructions of Admiral "Bull" Halsey.

"... we steamed into Tulaghi Harbor," an American sailor wrote, remembering his first sight of the place in 1944. "There were great tall bluffs, palisades towering out of the sea on both sides of the entrance, and there painted on the bare rock in letters that were maybe a hundred and fifty feet high was a message. The top line read *KILL ... KILL ...*

*KILL*, second line, *KILL MORE JAPS*, third line signed, *HALSEY*. We all cheered, because we were all trained killers, parts of a powerful killing machine. But later, it made me think about the ways we had been settling differences with the Japanese."

Now the town of Tulaghi was even more deserted and derelict than it had been in the war – beer cans everywhere, paper blowing, broken bottles, empty houses.

As we walked around, James told me stories of his days on a Japanese long-line tuna boat, earning forty dollars a month. The boat brought the fish directly to Japan, where in Yokohama, James had fallen in with American blacks, who asked him whether he was from the States. "They didn't know where the Solomon Islands is. But they took me to bars and bought me beer." He found Japan expensive. He swapped cuts of tuna with bartenders for bottles of whisky. Japan bewildered him. "It is all Japanese people. There was no one like me there."

Eventually I loaded my boat and said goodbye to the people at Balola. I gave the men fish-hooks and the women some silk scarves. It was a perfunctory goodbye. Only the children came to the beach, and when I saw Rebecca hurrying towards the beach I greeted her, but she didn't look up. She chucked a basket full of garbage into the water and walked away.

Back in Honiara, I visited Bloody Ridge, where thousands of men died in 1942. I paddled up the gray-green Lungga River for five miles, but it was a much more noxious sewer than the sea, because it ran more slowly, and wherever I looked there was trash, or shit, or dead animals. The people looked wild, yet they were unfailingly courteous, and everyone I greeted said hello.

The town was dreadful. I wanted to get out of it, but not leave the Solomons. And remembering how I had circled the green volcano in my boat, paddling slowly, and listening to Puccini, I had a strong desire to return to Savo.

The night before I left Guadalcanal I fell into conversation with a Solomon Islander named Kipply and told him I was off to Vanuatu.

"You will enjoy it. They are like us there," he said, and I felt better.

# 10

# Vanuatu: Cannibals and Missionaries

I soon found myself in White Grass village on the island of Tanna, in Vanuatu (formerly the New Hebrides), living in a three-roomed bamboo hut with four burly, bearded New Zealanders. They murmured all night and sometimes yelped, sounding as though they had hit on an idea.

When Glen, the battiest one, confided to me that the impending Gulf War might be Armageddon, and that all over the world silicon chips were being inserted under people's skin – "the Mark of the Beast, see, foretold in the Book of Revelation" – I suspected that they were born-again Christians, come to save Tanna, an island with a past rich in cannibalism. I was right, they read their Bibles by the light of a kerosene lantern – we had no electricity – and when it rained the hut leaked. But there was nowhere else for me to stay.

The fundamentalists loved the rain and regarded the dark clouds with dull slow smiles of approval.

"Behold!" said Douglas cheerfully one rainy morning. Douglas was nearly as batty as Glen. He had a suppurating sore on his leg that he bathed in sea-water every day, not realizing – though I told him – that he was only adding to the infection. "He's putting obstacles for us!"

Now they were all outside the bamboo hut, getting drenched, but agreeing like mad.

"Who's putting obstacles?"

"The Devil," Douglas said.

"Why would the Devil do that to you today?" I asked.

"Because we're walking to north Tanna to preach," Douglas said. "It's an all-day hike. Very tough bush. He doesn't want us to preach."

Later that morning, Glen hurried back to the bamboo hut. He was soaking wet, his face was muddy, his hair was plastered against his scalp, his hands were greasy. He told me delightedly that their Jeep had broken down on their way to the path.

"Obstacles!" he cried.

The rain, the breakdown, the native hostility, my indifference, the

Devil's obstacles – it all seemed a testimony to the sanctity of their mission. And I was sure that Tanna's long anthropophagous history, its people-eating, was another factor – rumors of cannibalism are like catnip to missionaries, who are never happier than when bringing the Bible to savages. Missionaries and cannibals make perfect couples.

Just the swiftest glance down the library shelf devoted to the New Hebrides had to be enough to convince any evangelist that these happy islanders were in need of the Christian message. A partial chronology included *Missionary Life Among the Cannibals* (1882), *The Cannibal Islands* (1917), *Cannibalism Conquered* (1900), *Two Cannibal Archipelagoes* (1900 – the Solomons included), *Cannibals Won for Christ* (1920), *Cannibal-land* (1922), *L'Archipel de Tabous* (1926), *Living Among Cannibals* (1930), *Backwash of Empire* (1931), *Backwaters of the Savage South Seas* (1933), *The Conquest of Cannibal Tanna* (1934), *Savage Civilization* (1936), Paton's *Thirty Years With South Seas Cannibals* and Evelyn Cheesman's *Camping Adventures on Cannibal Islands*.

I had found circumstantial evidence for cannibalism – the liking in Vanuatu (and it had been the case in the Solomons too) for Spam. It was a theory of mine that former cannibals of Oceania now feasted on Spam because Spam came the nearest to approximating the porky taste of human flesh. "Long pig," as they called a cooked human being in much of Melanesia. It was a fact that the people-eaters of the Pacific had all evolved, or perhaps degenerated, into Spam-eaters. And in the absence of Spam they settled for corned beef, which also had a corpsy flavor.

But cannibalism was less interesting to me than cargo cults. Most of all I wanted to visit Tanna because I had heard that a cargo cult, the Jon Frum Movement, flourished on the island. The villagers in this movement worshiped an obscure, perhaps mythical, American named Jon Frum who was supposed to have come to Tanna in the 1930s. He appeared from nowhere and promised the people an earthly paradise. All they had to do was reject Christian missionaries and go back to their old ways. This they did with enthusiasm – booting out the Presbyterians. Jon Frum had not so far returned. The Jon Frum villages displayed a wooden red cross, trying to lure him – and his cargo of free goods – to the island. This iconography of the cross was not Christian, but rather derived from the war, from the era of free food and Red Cross vehicles.

The believers sat in hot little box-like structures and prayed to Jon Frum. Some had visions of the strange American. They sang Jon Frum ditties in Bislama, the local Pidgin.

I mentioned this to the God-bothering New Zealanders.

"Obstacles!" they cried.

I had come here from Port Vila, on the island of Efate, because I had found Port Vila too tame and touristy. It was a pretty town built against a hill, and its harbor was deep. Cruise ships from Australia anchored and then went on to Noumea, and other sunny islands, which retailed baskets and T-shirts and shiny shell necklaces and five-dollar bottles of Perrier. The shops in Vila were full of goods, the place was clean and tidy and had at least a dozen comfortable hotels, two or three of them luxurious. They held pig roasts. Their guests went snorkeling in the lagoon. Islanders serenaded them at night, strumming ukuleles and singing *"Good Night, Irene"* in Bislama.

I was convinced that the town was profoundly civilized when I saw multiple copies of my books displayed in the Port Vila Public Library. In addition the islanders were pleasant and not at all rapacious.

Tipping was discouraged in Vila, and throughout Vanuatu. This was usually the case in countries where most of the tourists were Meganesians – New Zealanders and Australians. Living far from Europe, they had had to be self-sufficient. No tipping was the rule in Meganesia. They had learned frugality and were eager to teach it.

"It's a bit of luck that you're here, Paul," a Vanuatu soldier named Vanua Bani said to me. "You will be safe from the Gulf War."

"Very true," I said. Then we talked about the possibility of war.

"I don't think there should be a war," he said, "because too many people would die."

"Would you fight, if Vanuatu were in the multinational force?"

He was evasive, and then said, "I would fight for my own country, but I would not let myself get killed for another country."

He was not in uniform. He wore a T-shirt that said, *Vanuatu – Ten Years of Peace and Prosperity – 1980–1990*.

"Did you fight the British?"

"Oh, no," he said. "We wouldn't do that. We like the British."

But it had been a circuitous route to independence. After a free-for-all by French and British land-grabbers in the nineteenth century, both countries agreed to joint responsibility and they turned the islands into a condominium government. The local wags called the condominium "the pandemonium." It wobbled along largely because, in the words of an English settler named Fletcher, "these poor beggars have more manners and more virtues than their masters."

The settler–missionary structure was altered by the Second World War, when the New Hebrides was a base for US troops fighting in the Solomons and elsewhere in the Coral Sea. But afterwards life resumed and the islands reverted to fishing, timber-cutting, and mining (manganese mostly). In the late 1960s and early 1970s decolonization began in a series of conferences, but the sides (British, French, islander) were too self-interested to find common grounds for agreement.

Two leaders emerged in the 1970s – Jimmy Stevens, a charismatic figure with a Moses beard and an Old Testament manner, who called himself Moses; and Father Walter Lini, a Presbyterian – a shrewd, English-speaking, conservative, missionary product. Lini had a broad base of support. Stevens's followers were mostly on his home island, the large island of Espíritu Santo, with its French planters, opportunists, bush folk, upstarts, and eager secessionists. Stevens also had the support of a meddling right-wing American organization, dedicated to eradicating communism, called the Phoenix Foundation. Stevens's threats to make Santo independent worried the electorate on the other islands and after several national elections Lini was elected prime minister. At Independence, Stevens led an unsuccessful armed rebellion which became world news as "the Coconut War" for a few days in 1980, until the bearded one was jailed.

After ten years, Lini was still prime minister and Jimmy Stevens was still in jail.

Vanua Bani assured me that Father Walter, as he called him, was very popular and much loved.

He confirmed that the Jon Frum Movement was flourishing on Tanna, and he also said that if I was going there I ought to make a point of seeing Chief Tom Namake, who knew a bit about it.

I packed my boat and left the tourists – Gloria and Bunt ("the blacks here are ever so sweet – not like ours") and their kids Darrell and Shane, from Adelaide – the cruise passengers, the snorkelers, the Women's Conference on Nuclear Policy in the Pacific (moved from New Guinea because the women's safety could not be guaranteed in Port Moresby), and I took a small plane to Tanna.

Chief Tom happened to be elsewhere on the island, and while I waited for him I had the New Zealand born-again Christians to contend with. It so happened that camping was not allowed on this part of the island, and the bamboo hut was the best I could find.

Whenever they were not having a prayer meeting or a preach-o-rama in a village, the born-agains lay in wait for me and ambushed me. It was not hard. The driving rain made it impossible for me to go very far. At first I was more or less supine and let them preach, but I retired to a corner with the Bible and found passages that I asked them to explain. For example, Matthew 10:34–38, in which Jesus says combatively, "I will set son against father, daughter against mother . . ."

They said I needed faith. I needed to be born again, and they flipped pages until they came to John 3:3 ("Unless a man be born again –").

I noticed that they were indiscriminate and passionate carnivores. At breakfast they made greasy bacon sandwiches, at lunch they fried sausages, and on some days they spooned tuna fish straight from the tin. My experience among the Seventh-day Adventists of the Trobriands stood me in good stead here.

"The Bible says you shouldn't eat that meat," I said.

Their smiles were torpid and condescending, but they went on munching.

Glen said to the others, "Paul's got spirit. But he needs the holy spirit. He needs Jesus."

"Leviticus. Chapter eleven. Also Deuteronomy. It's all forbidden – pork, fish without scales, all of it."

"There have been directives about that," Douglas said vaguely.

"He needs the name of Jesus," Glen said.

I said, "You told me that you believed in the strict word of the Bible. What about all that stuff you told me about the Flood?"

The previous night Douglas had asserted that the Flood had covered the earth. They had found evidence of it in Australia, for example. He believed in Adam and Eve, and in Noah's Ark. He believed that Mrs Lot had been turned into a pillar of salt. Why didn't he believe in the prohibitions of Leviticus?

I nagged them for a while, because it was raining and I had nothing better to do. Later that day I read them parts of the Book of Daniel, which had wonderful arguments for vegetarianism: Daniel refused Nebuchadnezzar's meaty feast, and insisted on eating his usual diet of lentils, which gave him a rosy complexion and helped make him a healthy magician.

"Don't you think you could learn something from that, Glen?"

"You need Jesus," Glen said, tucking bacon into his mouth.

"There is nothing in the Bible that says that Jesus ate meat," I said, and wondered if that were so. They did not dispute it. I liked talking to them on this subject of vegetarianism while their mouths were stuffed with bacon sandwiches.

"Don't get so intellectual about it," Brian said.

Brian worried me. He had a loud shouting laugh that was like a warning. He could be rather sulky, too. Brian was the hairiest one, the most bearded, the leader. I was wary of him most of all because whenever he told me how he had found Jesus it was accompanied by stories of how he had been a violent and wicked sinner. *I did terrible things*, he said, and gave me a hard look, and I took this as a warning that he would do terrible things to me if I didn't listen to him. I had a feeling terrible things had happened to Mrs Brian, back in Auckland. *I defiled the name of Jesus – I wouldn't even tell you half the things I did. I was horrible.*

And he sometimes still looked horrible when we sat at the wobbly table, with his enormous Bible between us. In the margins were his notes, written in ballpoint. Handwriting – just its contours – can look violent. I found his blue scribble alarmingly slow-witted and threatening.

Still the rain came down.

Brian insisted (and the others closed ranks behind him) that nothing on earth was older than four thousand years. Not dinosaurs, trilobites, Chinese tombs.

"Carbon dating has been totally disproved."

"You're saying that Tyrannosaurus Rex was running around less than four thousand years ago?"

"It certainly couldn't have been more than four thousand years ago, because the world hadn't been created," Brian said. He pretended to smile in triumph but if you looked at his teeth and his eyes you knew that he wanted to bite you.

Glen then told me about the silicon chips.

"And the Mark of God will appear on the foreheads of those who are saved," Douglas said.

"But obviously not on mine, is that what you're saying?"

I did not push these paranoiacs too far. The trouble with such Christians was not their faith in God but their hearty, adversarial belief in the Devil. It seemed to me that it could be a fatal mistake for me to dispute too strenuously with them. There were no doors on this bamboo hut. I heard the men murmuring at night. *I did terrible things.* They were completely convinced that the Devil himself was at large, roaming to and fro, around White Grass village, perhaps in their very hut, trying to confound them. They might get it into their heads that I was the incarnation of the Anti-Christ and drive a bamboo stake through my heart.

They were "God-swankers" – one of the paradigmatic types that Elias Canetti describes in his strange book *Earwitness*: "The God-swanker never has to ask himself what is correct, he looks it up in the Book of Books. There he finds everything he needs . . . Whatever he plans to do, God will endorse it."

Because of the storms we had each night, the villagers were spared our night-time disputations. In times of high wind and rain everyone in the village ran into a specially constructed hut – rounded and very tightly woven – and there they huddled, one on top of the other, until the storm passed. There was no room in their emergency hut for the shouting, praying New Zealanders.

The Melanesian people of Tanna were small scowling knob-headed blacks with short legs and big dusty feet, and some of them were the nakedest I saw in the whole Pacific, the women in tattered grass skirts, the men and boys in "penis purses" (in the words of a Tanna man). These little pubic bunches of grass were about the size and shape of whisk brooms and were worn over their dicks. This bunch of grass, secured by a vine, a belt or a piece of string, was a male's entire wardrobe. The Bislama word for this item was *namba*, literally "number." In Vanuatu one group of people were known as the Big Nambas and another as the Small Nambas.

Most of these grass-skirted and namba-wearing folks were happy heathens living in *kastom* villages in the muddy interior of the island. Whether or not they were cultists in the Jon Frum Movement was something I hoped to establish, and so I went by Jeep to one of the *kastom* villages to find out.

It was raining in Yakel village, and it looked as though it had been raining for two thousand years – the huts were soaked, the thatch was soggy, the sky was black, the air was chilly, the ground was a quagmire, and the naked people were huddled – men under one tree, women under another – hugging themselves to keep warm. Rain ran down their backs and dripped from their bums. The women had hoisted their grass skirts around their necks, wearing them for warmth, like cloaks; the men squatted so close to the ground, their nambas drooped into puddles. It was a village of runny noses. In the persistent drizzle it was a gloomy little glimpse of the Neolithic Age, complete with muddy buttocks.

The men smoked bitter-smelling tobacco and passed coconut shells of kava back and forth, and when they smiled at me – which they did often: they were extremely friendly – they showed me black stumps of teeth.

"Yu savvy Jon Frum here?"

They grinned and waved me away. "No Jon Frum."

It was strictly a *kastom* village – no Christians, no politics, no Jon Frum – and there were many such villages on the island, though this was the only one which allowed contact with outsiders. The other *kastom* villages, deeper in the interior, were fierce and xenophobic, and – I had the impression – nakeder, though a namba made you nearly as naked as it was possible to be. In Yakel, a namba was called a *kawhirr* in their language, which was Nahwal. The language had never been written down and was one of the few languages in the entire world into which the Bible had never been translated.

At the center of the crouching group was the chief, a tiny skinny man with a bushy grizzled beard and clouded eyes and tufts of yellow-white hair over his ears. He was entirely toothless. I took him to be about seventy. I asked him in Pidgin how many Christmases he had had which was the standard way of asking someone's age – but he said he had no idea, and added that his Pidgin was none too good.

His name was Chief Johnson Kahuwya. He hadn't a clue as to where the Johnson came from. He was spokesman and leader. He led the dances. He directed the planting of the gardens. He gave advice. He was the father of the village.

Using a man from a nearby village as my interpreter, I asked the chief how long he had allowed outsiders to come to his village.

"Since 1983. That was when we first saw white people."

"What did you think of them?"

"We decided not to chase them away," the chief said.

*The Melanesians did not have any organization larger than a village, nor did they have any conception of themselves as branches of a major race,* Austin Coates writes in *Islands of the South,* a book about the attitudes and movements of Pacific populations. *When a Melanesian encountered someone not of his group, though he denoted a likeness, he did not think, "It is a man." The word "man" applied solely to his own group, or tribe. Between his own tribe and others he made an enlarged distinction, much as he would between a pig, a bird or a fish, or between himself and any of these animals. The concept of mankind was absent.*

This was also an explanation for the Trobrianders' belief that they were human and that *dim-dims* were not. A non-Trobriander was of a different species.

"What about Christian missionaries?" I asked the chief.

"We have no missionaries here."

"But did Christian missionaries come here?"

"Yes. Long ago. They came." He was puffing a cigarette – tobacco rolled in a withered leaf. The rain kept dousing it. "They held a service. We watched them. They were talking and singing."

"Were you impressed – did it seem a wonderful thing to do?"

"No. We watched them. That was all."

"What did they tell you?"

The chief laughed, remembering, and then he imitated the missionaries talking, " 'After we go, you do this – what we have been doing?' "

"Did you do it?"

"No."

Now the other men laughed and slapped their wet goose-pimpled arms.

"Why not?"

The chief said, "We are not Christians."

Nor were they Muslims, nor Hindus, nor Buddhists, nor Jews. They were totally traditional and wished to remain so. I had never met such confident animists in my life – neither in Africa, nor South America, nor Asia. They had no interest whatsoever in changing their way of life. I found the whole set-up heartening, muddy buttocks and all.

"We are *kastom* people," the chief went on.

"But the missionaries might come again," I said, thinking of the four New Zealanders over at White Grass.

"It is okay for them to worship as they want," the chief said. "But we have different ways. We go our own *kastom* way."

"Do you pray sometimes?"

"Yes. We pray for food."

"How do you do that?"

"We sing for harvests," the chief said.

All this time the snotty-nosed boys laughed among themselves and the dripping men murmured and passed the kava. And I crouched with them, making notes. I was wetter than they, and more uncomfortable, because I was wearing clothes and I was soaked. Their nakedness made complete sense.

"Where did your ancestors come from long ago?" I asked. "Did they travel from another island?"

"No. They came from this island."

"Maybe you came from birds and snakes?" I asked, thinking of what the Solomon Islanders had told me of themselves.

"No. We are people. We have always been men."

In Melanesia, creation stories were always intensely local. The tribal name usually meant "man." The people of the tribe had either always been there or else had emerged from the land – from live creatures or from trees. Melanesians never said they had arrived from another island, and they never made reference to boats or the sea-journeys when telling creation stories.

The rain with its crackling drops swept through the towering trees and dense bush around us and coursed through the sodden hillside. The grass huts were so wet they looked as though they were in a state of collapse – heavy and toppling.

"You live far from the sea. Do you ever go fishing?"

"Yes. There are *kastom* villages near the sea. They let us fish."

"How do you return the favor? Do you give them some of the fish you catch?"

"No. But we give them our trees for wood, and sometimes we make canoes for them."

"Do you go to other *kastom* villages in the bush?"

"We do," the chief said, still sucking on the cigarette. "For weddings and circumcisions."

A wedding was a straightforward feast, he said, but a circumcision was rather more complicated. He told me about it. It took place when a boy was four or five, and it began first as a great feast – many pigs being killed. There would be a dozen or so boys involved. After the snipping – a sharp knife was used – the boys were sent into the bush for two months. They could not be seen by any woman. They could not touch food with their hands – they used a certain designated leaf, scrunched up, to eat with, scooping the food. They were not allowed to touch their hair, or pick out lice, and if they wanted to scratch their head they had to use a twig. Men were appointed to cook for them. After the two months were up, when the cut had healed, they went back to the village wearing a namba they had made.

I asked the chief, "What food do you like to eat?"

"Taro. Yam. Leaves. Pigs."

"If you get money, what do you buy in the trade-store?"

"A knife or an axe. Or rice. Or corned beef."

"How many wives are you allowed to have?"

"In the past, two or three. Now we have one, usually."

"Have you ever left this island of Tanna?"

"Yes. During the war. I helped to build the airfield at Vila."

It was now called Bauer Field, named after the valiant Lt-Col. Harold Bauer, a fighter pilot in the US Marine Corps who, in 1942, battling against great odds, downed eleven Japanese planes and was eventually killed in Guadalcanal. Posthumously, Bauer was awarded the Medal of Honor, and a brass plaque at the airport recorded his courage and his deeds. Bauer Field was presently being enlarged and improved by a Japanese–Vanuatu joint venture, to accommodate Japanese planes and tourists, and I was very curious to know what the Japanese construction company would do with the plaque when the airport was complete. Would they hide it; would they lose it; or would they hang it in the new terminal to enlighten future generations – and the visiting Japanese – of Bauer's war effort? Time would tell.

"Did you wear a namba when you were building the airport?"

"No. I wore a *kaliko*."

"Why not wear a namba?"

"I wanted to. But the American said, 'Don't wear this thing.'"

Although the rain had not let up, they took me – the chief leading the way – on a tour of the village, which was nestled against the hillside in tall grass that was shoulder height. Cross-faced men squatted under the drooping eaves. Naked women knelt in smoky huts. The children shrieked at me, their faces smeared with snot. Everyone in the village had filthy muddy legs. They showed me the large round hut they hid in when the weather was very bad: they had spent the previous night in it, all of them piled in, nearly eighty of them.

Later, under a dripping banyan, they did a loud stamping dance, pounding their big flat feet hard into the mud, slowly at first, then quickening their pace, and each time they brought their feet down they yelped and their nambas flopped up and down. The mud dried on their buttocks, giving them brighter smears on their bum cheeks, like perverse war-paint. They skipped in a circle, and shouted hoarsely – egged on by the chief – and clapped, and stamped again, heavily, a thumping that seemed to make the forest tremble and shook droplets from the boughs.

They were not much bigger than pygmies, and they were blacker and more naked. They had terrible teeth – stumps and canines broken into fangs. They looked like cannibals. Indeed, they had been, although on Tanna cannibalism was a privilege usually reserved for chiefs, nobles, and dignitaries.

Once, in Christie's auction rooms in London, I had seen a large and horrific painting titled "Cannibal Feast on the Island of Tanna, New Hebrides," by Charles Gordon Frazer, a widely traveled English landscape artist. It had been worked up in 1891 from a sketch he had made of a jungle scene he had actually stumbled upon on Tanna in the

1880s. It has been claimed that Frazer was the only white man ever to witness a cannibal ceremony. He recorded the scene faithfully in his celebrated painting, which showed two victims being brought into a shadowy jungle clearing – just like this – on poles; the gloating villagers (there are almost a hundred figures in this enormous canvas), the muscled, tufty-haired warriors, the women preparing the cooking fires.

"The bodies of the two victims, slung on poles, are painted in a masterly style," an English critic wrote when it was first exhibited, "the one being evidently dead, the other in stupor approaching death in its growing muscular relaxation." Another critic, Australian, described Frazer's painting as a "walkabout by a load of washed-out niggers."

Put on the defensive by alarmed and nit-picking gallery-goers, Frazer explained in an essay why he had chosen to paint the cannibal feast. "It was not from any desire for sensation," he wrote, "but from the fact of having by accident witnessed a scene of superstition so ancient, a custom that must soon become extinct all over the world before the great march of civilization, that I considered it my duty to illustrate this dark and terrible phase in the history of man . . ."

He was certainly telling the truth about having been an eye-witness – it was obvious in the painting's shocking details; and now, on Tanna, I knew that Frazer had been on the island, sketching in the gloomy light of this dense forest. It seems that Frazer's jungle clearing was farther east, at Yanekahi, near Tanna's volcano – and near Port Resolution, where Captain Cook landed in 1774.

Frazer also wrote, "If it were not for their superstitious rites [by which he meant cannibalism], these black people are no more cruel than the white men. If a boat lands and treats the natives brutally it is not unnatural that the next white man who lands will be revenged upon." And he went on, "There is much that is beautiful in these black savages . . ."

I left Yakel and went a hundred years or so across the island, to White Grass. Chief Tom Namake had returned from his trip to the bush. He had a fat sweaty face and a big belly. He spoke quickly – so quickly he sounded as though he was being evasive. He wore a dirty T-shirt that said *Holy Commando*, with the motif of an archer, and motto from Isaiah 49:2, *He made me into a polished arrow.*

He was not only a Christian, he said he also believed in the spirit world, and Jon Frum and *kastom*. He believed in magic stones and magic dances. He believed that all the people on Tanna Island had sprung from the twigs of two bewitched trees. His strongest belief was in traditional magic. But the T-shirt seemed the appropriate thing to wear around the New Zealanders. "Everyone must be allowed to do as he wishes, even them," he said of the Kiwis. At that moment they were preaching nearby. And they were planning some late-night prayer-meetings in the village. It struck me that they held their services at very odd times of day, favoring night-time.

"I have just come from Yakel," I said.

"What do you think?"

I hesitated and then said, "Were those people cannibals at one time?"

"Oh, yes," Chief Tom said, and seemed pleased to be disclosing it. "Many people were cannibals. But cannibalism on Tanna stopped about a hundred years ago. It was mostly over land disputes that they killed and ate each other. The Big Nambas were the last people to be cannibals."

"What about *kastom* people like the ones in Yakel. Are there people like that elsewhere in Vanuatu?"

"In Santo and Malekula you will find them. If they see you they will chase you around. What are you writing?"

"Nothing," I said. But I had been scribbling in my tiny notebooks, *Big Nambas chase you around.* I tucked it into my pocket.

"If you promise not to write it down I will tell you something," he said.

"Look, I'm not even holding a pen!"

Chief Tom glanced around and then looked at me with his bloodshot eyes and said, "I think some of those *kastom* people are still cannibals today, but they wouldn't tell you."

Chief Tom's son Peter was reading the Australian weekly magazine which had a lurid cover showing a grinning young woman in a bikini. She had freckles on her shoulders and she looked deeply unreliable.

Peter suddenly snatched up a sharp knife and slashed out a page and stuffed it into his pocket.

Later, I asked him why he had cut the page out of the magazine, and he shyly showed it to me. It was a full-page advertisement, which I read closely:

BODYWISE – *the Female Attractant that makes 9 out of 10 men more attractive to women.*
*With Bodywise Spray you can become a walking magnet to women!!*
*You will be amazed at the results!! Only $39.95!!*

*Comments:*

*"Your product really works!"* – CG, NSW

*"A much younger beautiful lady sitting next to me at a formal dinner whispered that she wanted to make love to me!"* – MF, Pomonia

*"As a professional chauffeur I find my clientele has increased"* – BC, NSW

Peter took the torn page back, and folded it and put it into his pocket. He was smiling.

Then he said in a low voice, "Me want dis."

The following day, Chief Tom said in an accusatory tone, "I saw you writing."

"Just a letter to my mother," I lied.

"That's all right then," he said. "If you promise not to write it down I will tell you a true cannibal story."

"Why can't I write it?"

"You will take my magic if you do! Don't fool with such things! Oh, I don't think I will tell you after all."

"Please," I said. "Look, no pen. No paper."

His expression was untrusting. We were sitting on a bluff above the chop of the wind-blown sea. It was a rocky coast, with rough ledges instead of beaches. There was nowhere here that I had found where I could launch or beach my kayak, and yet I remained hopeful.

Chief Tom squinted into the wind and then stole a glance back at me, as though he expected to find me sneaking out my notebook. He had become suspicious of my writing. Out of boredom I had been doing a great deal of writing at White Grass, describing the New Zealanders, making notes on the Bible for future disputations, noting down the conversation I had had at Yakel village. Chief Tom regarded all writing with alarm, because it was a way of stealing someone's magic. I understood exactly what he meant, and I agreed with him. It was a fact, not a savage superstition. If he told a story, and I wrote it down, the story became mine. I did not have the guts to tell Chief Tom that writing was my business.

Wiping his hands on his *Holy Commando* shirt, he began.

"It was just down the road here, near Imanaka village, about a hundred years ago. A certain European trader came in a ship looking for – what? Some things – food, water, what-not.

"The Tanna people saw him at the beach. They listened to him and said they could help him. They tell him to follow them and still talk to him in a friendly way, and when they get down into the bush they take out bush knives and kill him, then stab him with spears. He is dead.

"They carry him to their village and prepare the fire and the stones for the oven to cook him. And then they take his clothes off. One man feels the arm and says, 'I like this – I eat this!' And another says, 'I want this leg.'

"And another and another, and so on, until they have the whole body divided, except the feet.

"The last man says, 'I want these' – meaning the feet."

Chief Tom smiled and smacked his lips and poked his thick black forefinger into my chest.

"The dead man is wearing canvas shoes!" he cried. "They never seen canvas shoes before! They take the shoes off and say, 'Hey, hey! This must be the best part!' So they throw the body away and keep the shoes. They boil them for a while, then they try to eat them, the canvas shoes!"

I interrupted at this point and said, "I don't understand why they threw the body away."

"Because it is nothing to them, but the feet you can remove – that is special."

"The feet you can remove are the shoes, right?"

"They never see such things before," Chief Tom said. "That is why they boil them. After they take them out of the pot they chew and chew. Cannot even bite the canvas shoes. They try to tear them with their teeth. No good.

"Everyone has a chew.

"'What is this? Cannot eat his feet!'

"They take the shoes to another village and those ones try to eat the canvas shoes, but it is impossible.

"So they dig a big hole and throw in the canvas shoes and cover them. Then they plant a coconut tree on top of it. That tree grew up very tall – and when the storm came in eighty-seven it blew the tree down, so they planted another tree. It is still growing. I can show you the tree tomorrow."

# 11

# *The Oddest Island in Vanuatu*

Looking for the cannibal palm and the burial place of the canvas shoes late on one hot afternoon, I discovered a wonderful thing: Imanaka was a Jon Frum village – there was the red cross, in wood, at the center of the lopsided woven huts. A cargo cult flourished within.

Imanaka, wreathed in smoke from cooking fires, was in the woods, on a stony hillside, behind a broken fence, at the end of a muddy track. It was easy to see how such a hard-up village would take to the idea of deliverance and develop faith in the idea that one day an immense amount of material goods would come their way, courtesy of Jon Frum, only if they believed in him and danced and sang his praises. But it was also an article of faith that Jon Frum villages had to neglect their gardens and throw their money away: when Jon Frum returned he would provide everything.

I had no idea what sort of reception I would get. I was watched from a distance by a group of dusty women, and the first men I met spoke neither English nor Bislama – which was simply a version of Pidgin (the word Bislama being a corruption of *bêche-de-mer* – it had started as a trader's language).

It occurred to me that this visit might be an error of judgment. I was alone. It was obviously a poverty-stricken village. Hungry people can behave unpredictably. Who knows – they might get it into their head to kill me and eat my shoes. Smoke swirled around the village and the smoke alone, the way it straggled this way then that, gave the village a profound look of dereliction.

Men came forward and stared at me. One was clearly a mental case. He giggled in bewilderment. Another had a rag tied around his head. There were six more. They carried sticks and bush knives. Behind them were the women. Every one of them looked very dirty. Still I wondered: *Is this a mistake?*

"*Yupela savvy tok Bishlama?*" I asked, and when they shook their heads and grinned, I asked, "*Yupela savvy toktok? Chief bilong yupela i stap we?*"

One boy stepped forward and said, *"Parlez-vous français, monsieur?"*

*"Je parle un peu,"* I said. What was this, a French-speaking village? *"Les gens en ce village parlent français?"*

He said some of them did and others didn't. The chief didn't, for example. He would be joining us soon, the boy said, but in the meantime perhaps I would like to sit on this log in the shade of this thatched shelter.

I did so, and while we waited he asked me whether I had news of the war in the Gulf. I bumblingly explained what I had heard that morning – that there were diplomatic missions flying back and forth in the hope of averting war.

The chief, whose name was Yobas, shambled over to the shelter. He was old and feeble, carrying a stick that was smooth where his hand gripped it. He wore a torn undershirt and a dirty cloth tied like a sarong, and he had the oppressed and wincing expression of a chief who was probably being blamed by everyone, including his own people, for presiding over such a miserable village.

*"Yu savvy tok Inglis?"*

Incredibly, he nodded: yes, he did.

I greeted him by making an insincere speech saying what a delightful village it was and how happy I was to be in it, and I hoped that this would put all thoughts of killing me out of their minds.

"So this is a Jon Frum village?"

"Yiss. All dis. Jon Frum." And he motioned with his stick.

"The village dances for Jon Frum?"

"We dance here" – it seemed that we were sitting in the open-sided dance hall. "For Jon Frum. Also sing-sing. For Jon Frum."

"Sometimes do you see Jon Frum?"

"Nuh. But the old fella they see him."

"What does Jon Frum look like? Is he black or white?"

"White like you. From America. He is a beeg man – very fat! He strong!"

"What does he wear?"

"He wear clothes. He wear everyting. He wear hat."

I was wearing a baseball hat. I said, "Like this?"

"Nuh. Big hat. Like a missionary."

I took out my notebook and drew a picture of a wide-brimmed hat. He said, Yes, that's the one. And when he spoke the other men and the children crowded around me and jostled for a look at the notebook page.

Later, when I had spoken to more Jon Frum adherents, I discovered that I might have confused the chief with my questions, because he seemed to be describing a Jon Frum emissary who was known as "Tom Navy." This Floridian was a Seabee who had turned up on Tanna in 1945 and briefly had the island at his feet. Another Jon Frum had appeared in 1943 and proclaimed himself "King of America and Tanna" – and an airfield was cleared on the north of the island, so that when his cargo planes arrived they would have a place to land.

I wondered about the prayer houses, in which certain Jon Frum prophets, called "messengers," knelt and had visions of their benefactor. I asked the chief about this.

"Old fella talk to him," he said, "but me no talk."

The crucial question – crucial for the Vanuatu government, at any rate – was the extent to which the Jon Frum Movement displayed American paraphernalia. The most egregious aspect, from the government's point of view, was whether these villages flew the American flag. The notion was that since Jon Frum was an American, the cargo would come from America, and mixed up in this iconography of the red cross and the mysterious vanishing American was the Stars and Stripes. In some villages the American flag was flown often; in others, every February. The Vanuatu government frequently lost patience with the Jon Frum people and actively persecuted them, jailing them or confiscating their American paraphernalia.

I decided to be blunt. "Do you have an American flag?"

Chief Yobas hesitated for a while, but finally made a sheepish face and nodded. I asked him why the flag was necessary.

"During the war he come again and he give an American flag to an old fella."

"Do you raise the flag on a pole?"

This was too much for him. He said, "You go to Sulphur Bay. See Chief Mellis. Isaac One. He tell you everyting."

I pretended not to hear him. I smiled at the men with knives and sticks who hovered around me. It was about five in the afternoon. The sun was just low enough to slant through the thin tree trunks and it seemed to be much hotter at this hour than it had been at noon. I was reminded of how dreary such a village could seem, and this was – dusty and fly-blown and poor, clinging to its belief in Jon Frum – sadder than most I had seen. It was silent, except for the clucking of chickens and the crowing of an occasional rooster.

Gesturing at the thatched shelter in which we sat, I said, "You sing-sing here?"

"Yiss. We sing-sing."

"Please. Sing-sing for me."

The old chief considered this, and then hitched himself forward and in a whispering voice that rustled and hissed like tissue paper he began to sing.

> *Jon Frum*
> *He mus come*
> *Look at old fellas*
> *Give us some big presents*
> *Give us some good tok-tok*

He wheezed and riffed, sounding a good deal like the groaning blues singer he much resembled – John Lee Hooker came to mind – and he continued.

> *Jon Frum*
> *He mus come*
> *Mus stap long kastom*
> *Mus keep kastom*

He looked squarely at me and rolled his head and whispered again,

> *Jon Frum*
> *He mus come.*

When he had finished I fossicked in my knapsack for my gift bag, a plastic sack of fish-hooks and spear points and trinkets and scarves that I gave to people who were hospitable. I had made several rules on my trip. One was that I would not kill or eat any animal. Another was that I would not give anyone money in return for a favor.

Chief Yobas spread his fingers and clutched a slightly used but still radiantly colored Hermès scarf. He touched it to his face.

"Handkerchief," he said.

"They were lying to you," Chief Tom told me that night. "Jon Frum was not fat. He was small, very slight. A small man. This is the truth. If you write this down I will not tell you anything. He could speak all the languages. He saw one man and spoke that man's language. He saw another man and spoke to him in his own language. And so on."

"How do you know this?"

"You promise not to write it? You promise not to steal my magic?"

"I could never steal your magic, chief."

"My grandfather met him and shook his hand. This was my mother's father – he was prominent in the Jon Frum Movement. My father's father was a Presbyterian minister."

We were alone. I no longer disputed over the Bible at night with the evangelists from New Zealand. They had now based themselves among some tenacious heathens at the north of the island. The great number of obstacles they had encountered on the way convinced them that the Devil did not want them to go there; and so, wishing to defy the Prince of Darkness, they had hotfooted it to North Tanna, to preach.

"How did Jon Frum get to Tanna?"

"In a plane. There was no airstrip. He landed his plane in the tops of trees."

"Where was this?"

"At Green Point."

Examining the map, I saw that if I had a lift past this rocky part of the coast, where there was no break in the reef, I could launch my kayak and paddle to Green Point.

I managed this the following day. Peter – Chief Tom's son – gave me a ride in his jeep on the understanding that when I was back in Vila I would send him any information I could find on "Bodywise," the female attractant that made you "a magnet for women."

"Listen, Peter, do you have trouble meeting women?"

"No trouble," he said. "But me want dis."

He regarded the stuff as a sort of magic that would give him power over women. I said I would do what I could.

The wind was discouragingly strong, and the absence of any canoes offshore was the unmistakable sign that it was a bad day for small boats: not even the local fishermen dared to go out. But I found that by staying just inshore, paddling along the cliffs, I was out of the strongest wind and waves. I crept around the black walls of the island, past the blowholes, and found a dark gravelly beach near Green Point, where I went ashore and ate the bananas I had brought for lunch.

I had the absurd thought that I might be seen by a Tanna person and mistaken for Jon Frum, and I was half-fearful and half-eager that my arrival at this significant place might provoke that reaction in an onlooker.

As it turned out, some children fishing there asked me to give them my Walkman. I was listening to Chuck Berry – rock-and-roll here made paddling as pleasurable as opera had in the Solomons. I said to the children, no, I needed it, and so they simply ignored me, and went on fishing.

It was not until I was on the point of leaving (I had been procrastinating, because there was so much paddling ahead of me) that I ran into a man. He asked me the usual questions about my boat. Where did it come from? How much did it cost? How had I brought it here?

The man's name was Esrick – at least that was what it sounded like. He was a teacher at one of the schools on Tanna. He was presently on vacation. He said he neither believed nor disbelieved in Jon Frum.

"I think he was one of our old speerits appearing in the shape of an American white man."

"Why would one of your spirits want to come back and visit you?" I asked.

"Because at that time Presbyterianism was very strong. So he appeared at the right time, because the foreign missionaries had banned kava drinking, magic stones, and dancing. Jon Frum said, 'Destroy what the missionaries gave you. I will give you goods.'"

It was a fortuitous visitation. Just when Protestantism had taken hold of the islanders and the missionaries had begun to write their *Cannibalism Conquered* and *Cannibals Won for Christ* memoirs, the strange little man with piercing eyes had popped up here at Green Point and said: Lose those Bibles. He urged the people to revive the important traditions – kava-drinking, dancing, and the swapping of women for sexual purposes. About three years after Jon Frum's first appearance in 1938, half the island had abandoned Christianity.

"They forsook Christianity," Esrick said. "Because he said he would be back with plenty of goods if they went back to their old ways."

I said, "So when do you think this will happen?"

He laughed at me. "It has already happened! In spirit! Jon Frum's spirit is everywhere. He is in every village."

"But you said you didn't believe in him."

He accused me of being literal-minded, without using that expression.

"You see," Esrick explained, as though speaking to a moron, or one of his schoolkids, "he has come back in the form of development and progress. We have goods now. Go to the shops. Go to Vila. You will see that we have what we want. We have kava. We have dancing. He is back in spirit. He knows he has won!"

Was Jon Frum a friendly American pilot who had brought supplies here and shared them around? And perhaps he had said, *I am John from America*. And then had the war convinced the villagers on Tanna how wealthy America was?

It hardly mattered now. The dogma of the movement seemed to

suggest that Jon Frum was a sort of John the Baptist, preceding the savior, who was a redeemer in the form of cargo – every nice and useful object imaginable. And the important aspect was that it had come to the island directly, without the help of missionaries or interpreters. No money, no tithing was involved; no Ten Commandments, no Heaven or Hell. No priests, nor any imperialism. It was a Second Coming, but it enabled the villagers to rid themselves of missionaries and live their lives as they had before. It seemed to me a wonderfully foxy way of doing exactly as they pleased.

On my way back along the coast, the wind was behind me.

I was still listening to Chuck Berry on my Walkman.

> *Get a house*
> *Get married*
> *Settle down*
> *Write a book!*
> *Too much monkey business!*

I rode the swells, slipping forward on the faces of the waves – and rather breathlessly, too: if I turned over here with the surf breaking on the rocky shore I was out of luck. I was fearful until I was past the shoaly headlands and the biggest breaks, and then something just as bad happened.

I felt a sharp knifing against my fingers, like ten bee-stings, and I saw a gooey, spittle-like substance that had wrapped around my hand dripping like snot from my paddle shaft. Blobs of it hit my arm, stuck to my elbow and stung me there, and when I tried to flick it off it became molten and blistering, hurting me more.

It took me only a short time to work out that it was a cluster of jellyfish tentacles – they were so misshapen and long it was impossible to tell how many. I had picked them up with my paddle blade and they had slipped down the shaft and over my right hand and forearm and elbow, shooting stingers into me. A neurotoxin, marine biologists say; and if a swimmer gets wrapped in one of these creatures it is serious illness, if not certain death.

Probably a Portuguese man-of-war – just my luck, in this wind, on a rocky coast, in a heavy swell off Cannibal Island. My whole arm burned with pain, and I could not flex my fingers. The folk remedy is urine. I clawed my earphones off and pissed into my left hand, and rubbed the burning area. There was a slight momentary relief, but the pain returned.

It was a good thing the wind was at my back. I was able to steer the boat with my good arm. After an hour or more I saw the headland where I had put in, and when I landed I looked for a papaya tree. This is folk remedy Number Two for jellyfish stings. Papaya sap is generally reckoned to be good medicine for much of what ails you in the tropics – the flesh and seeds are good for diarrhea, the leaves contain an enzyme that acts as a meat tenderizer, and the sap is said to ease the pain of stings. I found a tree, I squeezed the sap onto my arms, and again I noticed a slight lessening of pain. But it came back, and it burned for three hours more, and then it was gone.

Hearing that the Kiwi God-botherers had returned to White Grass village, I decided to stay on this southeastern part of the island. Here I ran into a mad Irishman, Breffny McGeough. Breffny was a yachtsman who had come ashore here with his girlfriend; and they were in the process of creating a resort hotel of little bungalows from what had been a rather derelict venture run by a man known as Bungalow Bill.

One day, in a heavy rain, Bungalow Bill had heard a strange noise. Leaving his wife in bed, he had rushed out of his bungalow and listened hard. The sound came nearer and nearer – a rumbling, like a tremendous herd of wild pigs moving through the forest. The sound soon revealed itself to be a wall of water, tumbling down the creek bed towards his bungalow. Bill jumped back and saw the water smack the side of his bungalow and carry it off its foundations and into the bay, where it sank, with Mrs Bill and everything he owned.

"Hell of a way to go," Breffny said. "In bed, in a bungalow, in a bloody gale. Poor old thing probably never knew what hit her."

Breffny had recently given up smoking and drinking. But when the urge was on him he drank kava (which was not the same as beer – quite the opposite), and smoked the sort of local reefer I had seen being passed around by the naked Little Namba people in Yakel village.

I let Breffny play with my kayak and for a small fee he let me sleep in a deserted house, full of dead flies, at the top of a hill nearby, where the only sound in the day was a bird that peeped like a microwave timer, and at night barking dogs in the woods and the odd but unmistakable lolloping and thrashing, in bushy boughs, of fruit bats.

"We eat them," a villager named Carlo told me. "We boil them or throw them on the fire. They taste like birds a bit."

"Tanna kava is the greatest drink in the world," Breffny said a day or so later. "There's of course the two-day kava which puts you out for twenty-four hours – I mean, you're paralytic. Nothing like it. And there's the village stuff. We'll go up there some time, what? Have ourselves a few shells, what?"

And he winked his Irish wink.

"Seen the volcano, have you?" he asked. "It's marvelous, it really is."

Near sundown one day, he arranged a ride across the island for me with a Tanna girl named Pauline who came from a village near the volcano. The volcano was called Yasur in her language (twenty-nine different languages were spoken on this small island), and this meant "God." The winding bumpy road soon came to a strange, poisoned-looking area of smooth bald hills – it was down-wind from the crater, where the prevailing wind flung the hot, sulfurous ashes from the volcano, killing every living thing. In the distance I could hear the volcano grumbling and cructating, the amplified belches like those of a fat man after an enormous meal; and these sounds of digestion were accompanied by distant crepitating rumbles like those of loosened bowels. The expression "bowels of the earth" just about summed it up.

We parked in a lava field up-wind of the stope and walked to the rim of the crater. Here the farting and belching of the thing was explosive – more like cannon fire. It was a far cry from the steaming cone of Savo Island, where grinning villagers harmlessly boiled megapode eggs.

The crater of Yasur the godly volcano was almost a mile wide and half a mile deep, and at times it was like a vision of hell. It was full of smoke and fumes, and at its deepest point, like two malevolent eyes, were a pair of fiery holes, each of them gurgling wickedly and tossing out red gobs of molten lava.

Under me, against the steep side of the crater, about halfway down near a ledge, there was another hole that was hard to see. But roughly every five minutes it gave forth a thunderous explosion that echoed inside the crater's hole and this mighty crack cast forth a shower of lava, all red and orange, that twisted and lighted the entire crater, and then flopped and blackened as it cooled. This eruption added to the plume of ash that continuously rose from the volcano and wandered off, enlarging the blighted area of the island.

Later I heard that there is a theory that Jon Frum lives deep in the maw of the volcano with an army of five thousand men.

There were no other islanders here. I mentioned this to Pauline.

"The local people don't come here," Pauline said. She knew – she had grown up only three miles away in one of these benighted, African-looking villages. "They are afraid. They say that when you die you come here and you remain inside."

So the volcano was God, Heaven and Hell, all at once; like Tuma Island in the Trobriands – the bourne from which no traveler returned.

"Did the people in your village talk about how this volcano started?"

"Yes. They say that two ladies, Sapai and Munga, were making *lap-laps* one day –"

The New Guinea Pidgin word for a sarong was the local Pidgin word for vegetables wrapped in palm leaves.

"– and then an old lady appeared and talked to them. She said she was very cold. Could she sit by their fire, she asked. Sapai and Munga pitied her, so they said yes. The old lady sat near the fire. After a little while she began to make noises. She was growing. She was bigger and bigger. She covered the two ladies and turned into the volcano."

"What was the old lady's name?"

"We do not know," Pauline said.

Meanwhile, the volcano was filled with cannon booms and such diabolical fire and noise that the frightening thing prompted Pauline (perhaps without her realizing it) to ask me whether I knew anything about the situation in the Persian Gulf – did I think a war was going to start?

It was a difficult coast for paddling; the wind was strong, usually blowing twenty-five knots and roughing up the sea. Tanna was just a rock in the middle of the western Pacific. And there were not many places to launch a boat from – Breffny's was one of the good sheltered coves. But I had brought my boat, so I was determined to use it.

One of the advantages of paddling was that I could listen to music as the shoreline unfolded – and the lava sections of this shoreline were full of blow-holes: incoming waves washed under the lava shelf and burst through the hole, making a twenty-foot spout of water. Another advantage was that, in my boat, I did not have to swat flies. Tanna was as fly-blown as the Australian Woop Woop and the Solomons had been. Flies were the curse of villages. Insect repellent did not have a noticeable effect on them. It was a relief to be in a kayak, away from these tiny biting flies.

I was dismayed that no fishing canoes were out – when I saw them upturned on the cliffs of black porous stone.

Encouraged by the sight of some boys paddling small canoes and dawdling in a little bay, I asked them how far out they went. They said they didn't go out far at all.

"Who made these canoes?"

"My father made them," one boy said, speaking English clearly. "He goes out far."

"How far?"

"Sometimes he goes outside" – and he pointed.

He meant outside the reef, in the open sea, the water that has a different name.

Usually I thrashed into the headwind, knowing that if I got tired or if something went wrong, I would have this same wind to bring me back. Often I got to where I wanted only to find that, because of the heavy dumping surf, it was impossible for me to land my boat. On two successive days I tried to get to a place called Imlao, but on reaching the beach had to turn back, not daring to risk a surf landing. The waves were high dumpers, and if I miscalculated my boat would be smashed. Since the only intention I had in landing was to eat and then shove off again, I ate in my boat, and then headed back.

Captain Cook landed here on his first Pacific voyage. The Tanna people defied him, and after one encounter Cook wrote, "One fellow shewed us his backside in such a manner that it was not necessary to have an interpreter to explain his meaning."

One day I saw a man in an outrigger canoe riding the swell about a mile offshore. He was not paddling – he was simply letting the wind take him, and fishing with a hand-line.

I headed towards him and when he looked up I waved. Nearer, I said hello, and asked him whether he wanted a drink of water.

"Me have water," he said. He showed me the corked bottle lying in his dugout. But when I took a drink of mine, I offered him some and he had a swig.

"Where are you from?"

"*Me stap long Tanna.*" Then he hesitated. "My home Futuna."

Futuna is an island east of Tanna, a small rock with not more than three hundred people on its eight square miles of surface. And yet it is a distinguished place, for this tiny spot in the middle of Melanesia is inhabited, like the atoll of Ontong Java in the Solomons, by Polynesian-speaking people. In his book about Pacific migrations, *Islands of the South*, Austin Coates explains that wandering Austronesians avoided large, mountainous islands, preferring smaller and more isolated atolls.

"Such was the people's prestige that these dots on the ocean map became more important than the substantial islands, including New Guinea, which they embraced like a chain of distant sentinels. In the framework of an ocean civilization, these dots were the centers, mountainous islands the periphery."

They had settled on small wild islands that had been considered uninhabitable (because of course the islands had been known to Melanesians). And they regularly conducted family business and contracted marriages between islands a thousand miles away – from Futuna to Ocean Island, from Ontong Java to the Gilberts. There was a good reason for their being fearless on these lone rocks and atolls. They were brilliant navigators, they were great seamen and skillful canoe-builders.

"Never before or since was there an age when people were so at ease in the ocean."

Wishing to talk to this Futunese fisherman I rafted up, tying a line to his outrigger. He did not mind – my rafting up did not hinder his fishing; and what else was there to do, a mile or so from shore on this windy day, except drift and talk?

His name was Lishi. He had some Melanesian features but not so strong as those of the Tanna people. I might have assumed that he was part Polynesian if I had had time to consider the matter, but really the physical aspect was minor compared with the language.

I said, "Do you say *moana* for this?" And I slapped the ocean with my paddle.

"This *tai*," he said. He pointed out to sea, beyond the reef. "That is *moana*."

I said, "What is this?" – indicating my kayak.

"*Wakha*," he said. A version of the Aboriginal word I had heard in Australia, and in the Trobriands and elsewhere.

I said, "You're Polynesian?"

"Yes," he said.

"Where do your people in Futuna come from?"

"From Samoa, I think. Maybe from Tonga."

Quite a different reply from the Tanna people saying, *We come from two magic sticks*, or the Solomon Islanders claiming ancestry from sharks or snakes.

"Is Futuna a nice place?"

"Is small. Few people."

"What is good in Futuna?"

"Good *kaikai*. Good fish. Good wind."

I reached into my waterproof bag and took out my notebook and pen, and while we were blown along, side by side, over the curving blue belly of the swells, and sometimes riding the crest of the breaking waves, I asked him certain words and he told me the Futunese equivalent. Many of them were identical to, or cognate with, the languages spoken in Hawaii and Tahiti.

Often, Oceania seemed not one place but many – a universe of distant islands. But sometimes – like today, with Mr Lishi translating these words for me – it seemed like a small area, with a common language.

Apart from the deep sea being *moana*, and the lagoon being *tai*, big was *nui*, water was *vai*, and hand was *rima*, the same as the word for five. Fish was *ika*, house was *fare*. A Samoan, a Maori, even an Easter Islander from seven thousand miles across the open ocean would have been able to converse with Mr Lishi, here in western Melanesia. Thank you was *fafatai* – the same word in Samoan. I wrote down others, and they too sounded familiar: sun was *ra*, moon was *mrama*, and the numbers one to five were *dasi, rua, toru, fa, rima*. Dugout was *porogu*, probably from pirogue, and hello was *rokomai*. Heaven was *Rangi* exactly as in Tahiti (*lani* in Hawaiian) and woman was *finay*, cognate with the Tahitian *vahine*.

I made notes, marveling at the linguistic similarities, and we drifted. Meanwhile, Mr Lishi caught some fish, but most of them were tiddlers, fewer than six inches long.

He wore a crushed straw hat and tattered shorts. He was wrinkled. His outrigger canoe did not look at all seaworthy. He was a small Futunese fisherman and we seemed to be in the Oceanic version of outer space – beyond time – drifting on this dazzling blue day in the chop some miles off Tanna, the oddest outside-time island in Vanuatu.

That was the setting. That was the mood. I mention this because of what Mr Lishi said next.

"*Yu savvy war long Iraq, long Gulf?*" he asked.

I was startled by the question, but I recovered and said, "No war yet."

But I was wrong. After I got to shore I turned on my radio and heard the Pidgin broadcast – the Bislama news on Vanuatu Radio. This was about noon on 17 January, Tanna time, which was early morning in Iraq. The first attack had come in the early hours of the morning, at roughly the time Mr Lishi, the Futunese fisherman in his outrigger canoe, had asked me the question. It was not telepathy on his part: the matter was on everyone's mind.

"*Fait blong Persian Gulf we i brokaot finis,*" the broadcast began, the announcer jabbering very fast. *"Mo plante pipol oli stap ting se bae hemi savvy lid i go long wan wor bekegen sapos ol bigfela kaontri —"*

The superpowers.

*"— oli no stopem quik taem, hemi holem, wan bigfela kwesten mak i stap se bae who nao i winim fait ia —"*

The fear was that it would turn into a world war, involving the superpowers.

I then tuned my short-wave to Radio Australia, which had a strong signal in the daytime, and I heard that the United States had attacked first by flying 400 missions against sixty targets in Iraq. The newscast spoke of the mood of euphoria surrounding the aerial attack, and even I who had hoped there would be a diplomatic solution felt that same unholy energy, which is the emotion in Louis MacNeice's poem "Brother Fire," in which he describes the blitz in London:

> *O delicate walker, babbler, dialectician Fire,*
> *O enemy and image of ourselves,*
> *Did we not on those mornings after the All Clear,*
> *When you were looting shops in elemental joy*
> *And singing as you swarmed up city block and spire,*
> *Echo your thoughts in ours! "Destroy! Destroy!"*

Five men on the beach saw me listening to the radio. They had heard their own Bislama broadcast. They knew what was happening.

One said, *"Plante pipol heli kilim ded?"*

I said there were no casualty figures yet. There was a major difference between *kilim*, which meant hit, and *kilim ded*, which meant killed.

They were very concerned and they knew a great deal about the lead-up to the fighting — the invasion of Kuwait, the aggression of Saddam Hussein (and they knew his name), and the dangers of Israeli intervention. It impressed me that ragged fishermen in such a remote island on the Pacific should know so much or care so deeply; but of course a war had come this way before, and it had involved everyone, and had caused a convulsion in their lives.

*"Rambo hemi faet nao — Rambo stap long, long Gulf,"* another man said, somewhat lessening my respect for the accuracy of their views.

"Where did you hear that?"

The fellow swore that Radio Vanuatu had disclosed the fact that Rambo had been hurried to the Persian Gulf, to help win the war.

*"I strongpela tumas,"* another said.

"How true."

I saw Breffny McGeough and told him about the aerial bombardment. It was the first he had heard of it. His reaction was characteristic.

"A drop of kava would help."

We went on his motorcycle to a *nagamiel*, a village clearing that was also known as a *yimwayim*, about five miles in the bush. The clearing was surrounded by elephantine banyan trees.

"And this is me friend, the chief," Breffny said, greeting a toothless grubby old man squatting on the damp ground with four other men. Three men stood nearby, chewing.

The chief and the others greeted him as a friend, while Breffny said that I was in for a treat – the real McCoy – some shells of Tanna kava, probably the best in the Pacific. It was certainly the best Breffny himself had tasted, and he had sailed all over Oceania. Fijian kava and Tongan kava were piss compared to this, he confided.

I had brought my little radio to keep up with the news of Brother Fire. I listened as I watched the kava being prepared. It was being done from scratch.

– *Missile installations were attacked and destroyed. B52 bombers flew numerous missions and damaged Iraqi airfields* –

One man was cutting the kava plant, *Piper methysticum*, a dusty little cluster of dry twigs and spindly roots. As he hacked with a bush knife, making a pile of roots, another man scraped and peeled each root, while a third man worked on the half-peeled root with a coconut shell, rubbing off some – but by no means all – of the red dust.

The coconut rubber handed the piece of root to the men who were standing. They opened their mouths. They had black teeth and gummy, coated tongues. They stuffed the woody kava roots into their mouths and with a crunch like chicken bones, they began to chew them.

These chewing men – one in a straw pie-plate hat, another wearing a T-shirt that said *Alaska – The Last Frontier*, the third in a sensationally filthy sarong – walked in circles, chewing seriously, their cheeks bulging.

I heard, *Many eye-witness reports of bombs falling on the Presidential Palace in Baghdad.*

At that moment, one of the men leaned over and spat a big wet wad of masticated wood, the size of a scoop of ice-cream, onto a green leaf that had been spread on the ground, apparently for this purpose.

– *Bombs also fell on Baghdad Airport, destroying runways* –

*Splat* went another blob of kava and spittle, as the man in the T-shirt bent from the waist like a bobbing duck and released it onto the leaf.

*Splat* – more mush hit the leaf: it was like a kid spitting up baby food he hated. That was the consistency of the stuff – a cowpat of Gerber's baby food.

"Bloody marvelous stuff," Breffny was saying, as he sucked on a stinking cigarette. "What's the news, Paul?"

I had the radio to my ear. I said, "Bombing."

*Splat.* Another disgusting cud hit the leaf. It was pale and juicy, and it turned my stomach just to look at it.

Now, with a leaf of three blobs of masticated kava root, the chief went to work. With his dusty fingers he picked up the blobs and placed them onto a small, finely woven square of matting. This he held over a chipped enamel bowl, and while a man poured a few cups of water onto it the chief twisted the mesh, twisted the whole mixture – chewed and pulped kava root, saliva, water, dirt – and forced a trickle of water into the bowl.

"Tanna kava," Breffny said, smiling in anticipation.

The chief filled half a coconut shell for him, and the jaunty Irishman lifted it, and drank, and sighed with pleasure.

He wiped his mouth and said, "In Fiji they pound the roots and stew it. But this – it's all in the chewing, you see."

I was still listening to the bombing, and the chewers were still masticating ostentatiously, and splatting it onto the leaf.

"Now you're sure you won't have a shell?"

He was whispering. It was one of the rules of Tanna kava-ritual that none of the drinkers was to speak loudly.

It was a feeling like novocaine, he said. And he claimed that his whole body was going numb, as we headed back to the shore, in twilight, in an explosive sunset that was appropriate to the first day of war.

The next day I went out paddling again. I brought my radio and listened with my earphones. Israel was hit by eight missiles. Two people were taken to the hospital, with heart failure. Some others were treated for shock. An Israeli woman's kitchen was destroyed. There was general outrage. You could hear it in their complaining voices. Meanwhile, in Iraq and at the borders of Kuwait, the first of 150,000 people began to die: the nameless, faceless enemy.

Paddling in that day, I saw a couple on shore. They stepped into the surf and grabbed my bow-line and helped me beach my boat.

They were from New Zealand, they said. Odd place Tanna, they said, wasn't it? I agreed. We talked about the *kastom* people, the volcano, the Jon Frum cargo cult, the rumors of cannibals, the unbridled attentions of missionaries. But the Solomon Islands, I said, were equally interesting.

"You travel all over," the woman said. "Do you write about your travels?"

I said, yes, I did. Articles. Books. Whatever.

"You must write Paul Theroux-type travel books," she said.

I said, Exactly, and told her why.

Eventually I went back to the island of Efate, another happy isle. I paddled out to Pele Island and Nguna. These were protected waters on the lee side of the island, nothing like the gales of Tanna. Off Nguna I could see Epi Island, and the islands in the Shepherd group. I fantasized about staying and paddling and camping on these happy islands, watching the men make copra and the women doing laundry in streams.

I paddled to an island called Kukula, only a mile or so at the edge of the lagoon. It was idyllic, although there was no fresh water there. And when I landed I stepped into the water and saw a whitish snake, with black bands, floating near the sandy bottom. I poked him with my paddle and the thing recoiled and bit my paddle blade, before it took off.

Some of the smaller islands were uninhabited, but the rest were populous. The people I met were cheerful and friendly. There was no theft, nor any stories of it. The villages were rather empty. The weather was perfect. Business was terrible, people said, but no one seemed seriously to mind.

Most days I had enough of the news. I left my radio on shore. I listened to my Walkman. But Chuck Berry was too cheerful for me. For the hundredth time, among the pretty islands, I paddled slowly and listened to a Puccini aria of hope, how one fine day a white ship would appear on the sea and then sail smartly into harbor, and all would be well –

> *Un bel di, vedremo*
> *Levarsi un fil di fumo sull'estremo*
> *Confin del mare.*
> *E poi la nave appare.*
> *Poi la nave bianca*
> *Entra nel porto . . .*

I ate the local delicacy, coconut crab. At night, when the air waves were louder, I monitored the news. I shared what I knew with the islanders, who always mentioned Rambo. Some people said that after the war was over the American troops would head for Tanna and liberate all the people, in the name of Jon Frum.

When I heard that I was reminded of Tanna – how I had known almost nothing about it before I arrived, and what an odd and pleasant island it had been. I hoped to find another, but that night I had a dream, a rather mournful one, of one of my children writing a story that began, *Long after he died – for weeks, for months – we kept receiving postcards from Dad, because he had traveled so far and to such small and insignificant places.*

# 12

## Fiji: The Divided Island of Viti Levu

At the very frontier of the Black Islands lies Fiji, the edge of Melanesia – so close that some of its tinier islands, Rotuma and the Lau group, for example, overlap Polynesia. In these transitional straddling dots of land, the people are regarded as Polynesian. There is a strong Tongan influence in the Lau culture. They make and sail canoes in the Lau group. They wear crunchy mats around the waist, Tongan-style. They paddle. They fish. They dance. They recall their great sea ventures. In a village on the Lau island of Lakeba they hold an annual ceremony in which sharks are summoned – a "shark-caller" up to his or her neck in the lagoon is circled by a school of sharks, attracted by the person's chanting.

On the Lau islands, you see Mormons. In Oceania, where Mormons regard Micronesians as the sons of Cain, and Melanesians as the dark, scruffy descendants of Ham, the surest sign that you are on a Polynesian island is the sight of Mormons.

The American Mormons who evangelize on these islands can seem rather fearsome and intrusive, like the worst sort of door-to-door insurance salesmen – black tie, white shirt, dark trousers, breast-pocket nameplate (*Elder Udall*), all the answers, clutching copies of the book that the Angel Moroni gave in the form of golden tablets to Joseph Smith in 1827. Smith put "peepstones" on his eyes and a blanket over his head and translated the tablets, dictating the text to Emma, the first of his fifty wives. ("When I see a pretty woman I have to pray," Smith once said.) These prophetic books in the Book of Mormon not only foretold – if belatedly – that Columbus would discover America but also described how American Indians, descendants of the Lost Tribes of Israel, had got it into their heads to sail across the Pacific and settle these islands. It was not a question of Polynesians becoming Mormons. They have, according to the Book of Mormon, been Mormons all along. They simply needed to be reminded of the fact.

Yet the Lau group is one of the pretty little star-clusters in the universe

of Oceania. Melanesian Fiji is another story. Fiji is like the world you
thought you left behind – full of political perversity, racial fear, economic
woes, and Australian tourists looking for inexpensive salad bowls (though
why anyone would think a race of Queequegs, proud of their cannibal
past, might excel at making salad bowls is not only a cultural mystery,
but proof that tourists will believe almost anything as long as they are
comfortable). Fully half the population is ethnic Indian – Muslims,
Parsees, Buddhists – wearing turbans and skull-caps, and Hindus with
big staring red dots on their foreheads. They run shops that sell over-
priced "duty-free" merchandise and native curios, spears, napkin rings,
the salad bowls, and other nameless-looking bits of hacked wood.

"What is this wooden spindle?" I asked an Indian shopkeeper.

"Gannibal imblement, sah."

"Did you say 'cannibal'?"

"And gannibal glub," he went on, showing me a shiny skull-crushing
bat of the sort that had once been used to bash out an enemy's brains
(and then you ate them, so that you would be as intelligent as he was).

He showed me the section on cannibal artifacts from the catalogue of
the Suva Museum. Yes, they somewhat resembled this tourist stuff. And
they proved the truth of the travelers' tales about cannibal Fiji – colorful
accounts such as that of the swashbuckling Irishman, Peter Dillon, who
in the 1820s made a narrow escape from a Fijian cannibal feast but not
before witnessing two of his fellow crew members being baked in ovens
and gobbled up. There is a lurid summary of Fijian cannibal practices in
the usually authoritative eleventh edition (1911) of the *Encyclopaedia
Britannica*: "The Fijians were formerly notorious for cannibalism, which
may have had its origin in religion, but long before the first contact with
Europeans had degenerated into gluttony. The Fijian's chief table luxury
was human flesh, euphemistically called by him 'long pig', and to satisfy
his appetite he would sacrifice even friends and relatives. The Fijians
combined with this a savage and merciless nature. Human sacrifices
were of daily occurrence."

You want to say *Really?* The same entry mentions how many Fijians
are a racial blend of Polynesian and Melanesian, with "the quick intellect
of the fairer, and the savagery and suspicion of the dark." On such
ludicrous assumptions, the Pacific was evaluated and plundered by the
missionary, the trader, and the planter – an unholy trinity who were, it
must be said, often the same person, neatly illustrating one of the central
mysteries of the religion they crammed down these cannibals' throats.

When I inquired about cannibalism, Fijians never denied the

anthropophagy of their ancestors – on the contrary, they talked with lip-smacking enthusiasm, reminding me of Australians reveling in stories of how their distant relatives had been convicts.

"Fahmerly this island was all ferocious gannibals, sah," the Indian said, glancing furtively behind him. "Feezee pipple, sah."

But the reason he looked so nervous, and lowered his voice, was because the Fiji people – most of them, and the government, which was only one man, Lt-Col. Sitiveni Rabuka, known to all as "Steve" – wanted to send them back where their grandparents, and in some cases, great-grandparents, had come from, the Indian subcontinent. (The first Indians arrived in Fiji as indentured laborers to work in the cane fields over a century ago.) In another age, they might have wanted to eat the Indians. Now they wanted to return them – something like disgusted diners sending unappetizing food back to the kitchen.

But it was a mistake to think of the Fijians as angry.

"Just because we're not as intelligent as Indians," Steve said, in a widely quoted observation, "doesn't mean that Indians can take advantage of us."

"We have the land – you have the brains," he said on another occasion, addressing Indians directly. "Why should you be richer just because you've got a bit more brains?"

He was no more subtle when he came to write about the affair in his book, *No Other Way*. In it he described the Indians as "an immigrant race" who "wanted complete control of the government." A *coup d'état* was the only solution "for the survival of the Fijian race. As simple as that."

But wasn't the coup racist? he was asked on a New Zealand news program. He cheerfully admitted that this was so. He said, "It is racist in the sense that it was in favor of one race."

The Indians were equal in numbers to the Fijians, who had only recently begun to worry about their being overwhelmed. And even now the Fijians' spirits were not dampened. They laughed and numbed themselves with kava (they called it *yanggona* here) six days a week and spent the seventh in Methodist chapels – every village had one – singing deeply lugubrious hymns and generally condemning the behavior of the heathenish Muslims, Hindus, Buddhists and Zoroastrians who had, they said, hijacked their country by outbreeding them and voting Melanesians out of office.

Then God spoke to the Fijian, who assembled his God-fearing commandos and led them masked into the Fiji Parliament, and marched the newly elected prime minister and most of his cabinet out at gunpoint.

After this 1987 military coup in which Col. Rabuka took power (he had been alarmed by an election which had produced – in his view – the nightmarish prospect of a multiracial government), he immediately decreed that Sunday was a holy day which had to be observed by everyone – no commerce, no travel, no buses, no cane-cutting, no games, nothing but solemnity and Methodist hymns.

Later he played himself in a starring role in a Fiji government video about the whole business. An early scene went like this:

INT. – RABUKA HOUSE – MORNING:
*A room in the Fijian household of "*STEVE*" RABUKA. MRS RABUKA and little "*SKIP*" RABUKA are seated at the breakfast table, eating a traditional Fijian breakfast of tea and porridge.*
*Enter* STEVE RABUKA *in military uniform.*

SKIP RABUKA. Where are you going, Daddy?
STEVE RABUKA. I am on a mission from God.
MRS RABUKA. What do you mean, husband?
STEVE RABUKA. God has told me to overthrow the government.

This was revenge on the worshipers of Allah and Hanuman the monkey god and gold calves and elephantine Ganapati with his snout and his smile. And for a time this decree gave Sundays in Fijian villages and towns the atmosphere of desertion you associate with cholera epidemics, or nuclear holocausts, or Welsh Sundays.

"Fiji is a Christian country," Rabuka said repeatedly, and he spoke of Fiji's solemn traditions and strict morality – quite funny, really, when you thought how he had come to power by gun-toting commandos, declaring martial law and tossing out an elected government.

Ethnic Fijians had gotten even with the Indians by shouting hymns at them – overwhelmingly fat Fijian women in Mother Hubbards, and enormous, skirt-wearing, bushy-haired Fijian men with Bibles the size of paving stones stood there and bellowed *Come to Jesus* in A-flat at the top of their lungs. This of course terrified the Indians.

I rented a car and put my kayak and camping equipment inside, so that I could drive around the island of Viti Levu ("Big Fiji"), looking for the best place to paddle.

"Do you sell maps?" I asked the Fijian at the car rental agency in Nandi. I had nautical charts of Fiji but no road maps.

"Why you are needing a map?"

"So I'll take the right road."

"You don't need a map. There is only one road."

This was not strictly true, and anyway the idea that I might have needed it for other reasons had not occurred to him.

"You American?" he asked. And then he marveled in a gloating way about the violence in the Gulf War, now in its second week looking more and more like a punitive mission of the most destructive kind. In the Solomons and Vanuatu the fear was that the war would come to their islands. The Fijians would have ridiculed that notion. But they had no political views. Theirs was a simple-minded fascination with the spectacle of it all – the pyrotechnics, planes taking off, bombs dropping, sirens wailing, bloody people trundled in stretchers through smoke and flames. News reports were like Rambo videos, and they seemed to give all Fijians pleasure.

I had a slight problem. I had picked up a fungal infection in Vanuatu – I blamed it on unwashed sheets. It could hardly have been anything else. I was nearly always a model of rectitude. Oceania was full of AIDS posters, and an AIDS poster in Pidgin was an explicit and frightening warning.

"Do you have the name of a doctor?" I asked at my hotel, the Regent, in Nandi.

"What's the problem?" the desk clerk asked – impertinently, I felt.

"Fungal infection," I said. "Nothing serious. It's on my foot."

This was a lie, of course. But I did not have it in me to say *It's on my willy* to a Fijian woman who was a Methodist.

"Athlete's foot. You can get some powder for that at the chemist shop."

The next day was Sunday. *Nothing is more pacific than a Pacific Sunday*, I wrote in my notebook later. I suspected from the first that it was a deliberate Fijian ploy to make the non-Christians feel like heathens and aliens. The attitude was one of *Shut up and let us pray* as the uncompromising Fijians beat the non-Fijians over the head with the Bible.

Nandi was full of doctors' offices, but none were open – and by the way, every one of them had an Indian name on the door.

The very settled, messy and domesticated look of Viti Levu was an effect of the fields of sugar cane, the floppiest and most ragged crop imaginable, and one which becomes floppier as it matures. And when it is harvest-time the cane is shaggy and peeling, yielding a very messy harvest. All over coastal Fiji the trees have been cut down to make room for the crop, and so the slopes were either bare or else they supported ill-assorted pines and scrubby bushes. The roads were also in a state of

decay, some of them falling apart. I had been used to the underdevelop-
ment and jungle of western Melanesia. But this was a heavily populated
and prosperous place that was desperate to attract tourists. Altogether
it was a landscape under stress, and many of the hills looked denuded,
their muscles showing just beneath the grass.

On Queen's Road, the main street of Nandi, were rows of Indian
shops, with signs saying *Prices Slashed* and *Stock Close-Out* and *Sale*. This
was not cynical salesmen's hyperbole. The Indian merchants really
wanted to sell their inventory and emigrate – to Canada, to Australia, to
New Zealand, to wherever they could buy land and start again. There
was a hint of panic in most Indian signs, and though some shopkeepers
professed to be optimistic no one sounded more desperate than an Indian
protesting that things were rosy.

The fact was that under the newly rewritten Fiji constitution –
proposed, but so far unratified – ethnic Fijians would not only be
guaranteed control of the government for ever, but also all the old leases
and land deals would be renegotiated, so that no land would be in non-
Fijian hands. Even the leases were being rejigged – an Indian with a
100-year lease would end up with a twenty-year lease and a Fijian
partner. It made no difference that the Indian had Fijian citizenship.

This seemed laughable but the Fijians were in deadly earnest.

"We see what has happened to our Maori and Hawaiian brothers
elsewhere in the Pacific," ran a letter in the *Fiji Times* while I was there.
"Second-class citizens in their own islands."

"I understand the Indians are experiencing difficulties," I said to
Vishnu Prasad, a Nandi storekeeper airing his guard-dog.

Vishnu went silent, and when I pressed him he giggled in terror.

"I am knowing nothing about politics. Hee! Hee!"

At the time of the coup in 1987, indigenous Fijians rioted in the streets
of Nandi and Suva, attacking Indian shops and looting them. A number
of shops were burned. After a caretaker government was installed, Steve
lost patience again and staged a second coup four months later.

An Indian *yanggona* seller said to me, "This was a happy and good
place before the coup, but they spoiled it."

"But the money has been devalued and business is terrible and the
future looks bleak, so the Fijians are worried, aren't they?"

"No. They are looking backward. This is a return to the chiefly system."

"But who wants the chiefly system?"

"The chiefs," he said.

That dead Sunday I drove east from Nandi to Singatoka, a largely

Indian town, where I was told a doctor's office might be open. This was not the case, but when I asked for a vegetarian restaurant – one of the great attractions of any Hindu town – I was directed to "Go Kool Hot Snax," where I met Subhash, who stuffed a curry puff into his mouth and told me he disliked Fijians.

He had just come from church. Yes, on Sunday. He was an Indian Christian.

"I go to Church of Christ," he said.

He wasn't married, he said, so I asked him whether he would want to marry a Christian or a Hindu.

"When I get married it will be to an Indian or a European – never to a Fijian," he said.

"Why not?"

"Because they have no morals," he said, practically exploding. And then he spoke with the single-minded conviction you hear in the monologues of bigots. "Even the schoolgirls behave like prostitutes, taking men to the beach and sometimes robbing them. Ha! A Fijian wife would commit adultery with other men while you are away. They go with anyone. They don't care. Even though they are Christians they still behave like heathens. I would never marry one. Never!"

The Indians were hardly conservative-looking, though. The girls wore dresses and cut their hair, they had loud liberated-sounding laughter, and they stared at me. Staring at men was something that women in India never did. I was told that marriages between Muslims and Hindus were common, though there were few Fijian–Indian marriages. This was nothing new. A turn-of-the century English writer observed, "The Fijians show no disposition to intermarry with the Indian coolies."

Driving onward from Singatoka, I picked up a hitch-hiker named Akiwila. He was Fijian, a Methodist. Like Subhash, he too had just come from church. He carried his Bible. The Sunday roadsides were crowded with these Bible-carrying men, and I imagined they seemed rather menacing to an unbeliever.

He was black, his head surmounted by a bush of thick kinky hair. He had a snub nose and a heavy jaw – the classic virile mask that was a Melanesian face. He was like many male Fijians I met, a big breezy specimen, all smiles, with a mustache that made him look older, and more serious and somewhat formidable. Yet he was friendly – and respectful rather than shy. He wore the gabardine skirt Fijians call a *sulu*, a white shirt and tie – you were not considered well dressed in Fiji unless you wore that gabardine skirt and a necktie.

Akiwila was on his way to his brother's house for a meal, before the next church service. No, he said, they were not allowed to cook on Sundays, but the food had been prepared yesterday. I tried and failed to imagine a Deity that would be deeply offended by someone's cooking. But of course Methodism in the Pacific was stuck pretty much in the nineteenth century, when fat furious hypocrites from England and American laid down the law – no cooking, no dancing, no games, and two church services on Sunday.

After a little while I said, "Akiwila, what is your opinion of the military coup?"

"It was very good," he said, smoothing the leather cover of his Bible.

"But it was against the Indians, isn't that right?"

"Yes." And he smiled. "You see, they are now almost half the population."

"You have to keep the Indians in their place, is that what you mean?"

"Yes. Very much so."

He went on smiling and nodding his head and tugging his *sulu* modestly over his knees.

After I dropped him, I drove on. I gave a ride to Joe and Helen, two homeward-bound Fijians who worked at a local hotel. They were so pleasant, I was seized with uncharacteristic reticence and did not ask them how much they earned. Of Americans, New Zealanders and Australians, I asked, who were the most obnoxious guests? "They are all nice," Joe said, mildly, and when they got out Helen offered me a dollar for the ride. A mile farther on, I was flagged down by some boys who were also headed home after a Sunday service. They were teenagers – Moses, Yakobi and Kamwela (Fijian for Samuel). They agreed that everything ought to be closed on Sunday, especially Indian shops.

"Sunday is for church," Moses said.

This sanctimonious insistence on de-secularizing Sundays was expressed with the greatest friendliness. The Fijians were calmly assertive, while the Indians either falsely claimed to be unworried or frankly expressed their hysteria. Both sides seemed to be equally bigoted, and each dismally ignorant of the other's culture.

The most sustained vilification of Indians in Fiji was that of James Michener in *Return to Paradise*. It is a rehash of his *Tales of the South Pacific*, and it is superficial and dated and rather poorly written. But his attack on Indians (this was in 1951) has a definite horror-interest:

"It is almost impossible to like the Indians of Fiji. They are suspicious, vengeful, whining, unassimilated, provocative aliens in a land where they have lived for more than seventy years. They hate everything: black natives, white Englishmen, brown Polynesians and friendly Americans. They will not marry with Fijians, whom they despise. They avoid English ways, which they abhor. They cannot be depended upon to support necessary government policies. Above all, they are surly and unpleasant. It is possible for a traveler to spend a week in Fiji without ever seeing an Indian smile."

Now he set his overwhelming dislike of Indians beside his jolly acceptance of Fijians: "It is doubtful if anyone but an Indian can dislike Fijians. They are immense Negroes modified by Polynesian blood. They wear their hair frizzed straight out from the head ... They are one of the happiest peoples on earth and laugh constantly."

These judgments are much too silly to discuss. Michener is just another in the long parade of explorers and travelers and tourists who felt a need to invent the Pacific and to make it a paradise. How misleading it all is. The very name of the Pacific is a misnomer. But I should say that the fact that so much written about the Pacific is inaccurate – indeed, most of it is utter crap – intensifies the pleasure of traveling there and gives it so much unexpectedness.

My visit to the doctor became urgent – I had run out of fungal cream – and so on Monday I hurried back to Singatoka where I chose a doctor at random – Dr S. K. Naidoo, near the market. It was a hot, dusty office, with a calendar showing Hanuman, the monkey god, and advertising an Indian electrical goods shop in Suva.

The receptionist was Fijian. She broke off an animated conversation with a girl who was sitting next to her and asked me why I wanted to see the doctor.

"Infection," I said. "Sore foot."

She leaned over and looked at my feet.

"Which one?"

"Right one," I said, wagging it.

I took a seat and picked up an old tattered Australian *Cosmopolitan* magazine, and became engrossed in a quiz entitled *How Good is your Sex Life?*. The preface said, *Work your way through the four-part questionnaire and you'll learn a great deal about yourself*, but it seemed to me that the further I read the more I learned about the sort of people who made up these titillating quizzes. *Do you find sex boring?* was a question in Part One, and in Part Two, *Rating your partner's sexual skills*, I had to evaluate my partner's "ability to see the funny side and laugh about it" on a scale of one to five, and I thought *Funny side of what?* Part Three asked me whether I had "anxiety about the size and shape of a particular part of my body," and though it didn't specify I thought only of my nose. Part Four was blunt: *Do you ever go to sex orgies?* and *Do you take part in sex photo sessions?* and *Do you make love with other people watching?*

Ha! I could just imagine what these puritanical Fijians would make of this, and how they would whisper about the sexual savagery of Australians in much the same way as Australians whispered about Fijian cannibalism.

"The doctor will see you now."

I entered the next room, pushed a greasy curtain aside, and found myself face to face with Dr Naidoo, a small and rather young Hindu woman in a sari, fingering a clipboard.

"You are having a problem with your foot, Mr Thorax?"

"A slight problem," I said, moistening my mouth. "My main problem is a fungal infection on my, um, genital area."

Dr Naidoo did not blink.

"I caught it – or rather *got* it – in Vanuatu. Strange sheets, I think. It wasn't from sexual contact."

"Though it can be transmitted that way," the doctor said – pedantically, I thought. Hadn't I just told her how I'd got it?

"I'll have to have a look at you," she said. "Step behind the screen, please."

I did so. She joined me. With trembling fingers, I exposed my weepy member, and she crouched and squinted at it. Though she was thoroughly professional – or perhaps that was the reason – we seemed for a split second to be enacting exhibitionistic Position Forty-five ("Admiring the Lingam") from the *Kama Sutra*.

As she prescribed a cure, scribbling on a pad, I asked her where she had gone to medical school. I had asked her the question nervously, simply to fill the silence, but I must have sounded skeptical, because she seemed defensive when she replied, "In Suva. It is a highly respected medical faculty."

Ten dollars for her, two dollars for ointment. Then I bought a tape for my Walkman, the sound-track from *The Big Chill*, which an obliging Indian at the music store copied from a master tape, an act of piracy that did not worry anyone in Fiji (video cassettes were similarly pirated). It was yet another Fijian bargain.

Recession, devaluation, the low sugar and copra prices, Indian fears and tourist anxieties had all combined to make Fiji rather empty and pleasant. That was obvious as in the next few days I explored the island east of Singatoka, working my way towards Suva. Business was terrible. In the competitive atmosphere of Fiji it made traveling rather inexpensive. And Fiji was well set up for travelers. The efficient airport was at Nandi, the busy harbor – said to be the best in the Pacific – was in Suva. There was extensive development in between. What I had seen so far of Viti Levu was uninspiring – muddy beaches, messy crops, too many hotels, too many duty-free shops, ugly villages of huts that looked like pre-fab chicken houses – but I could not complain: the people were friendly and the place was cheap, as well as safe.

I rattled around the bad roads, looking for a camp site on a pretty beach. The beaches were undramatic – the lagoons too shallow, the reefs too surfy for launching a kayak. And there were settlements everywhere.

All the land was spoken for. This was fine in theory but it made camping on this Nandi to Suva stretch impossible. And anyway I did not want to camp within hailing distance of the Golden Sands Motel or the Coral Coast Christian Camp. There was either a house or a village or a hotel on every mile of the southern coast, which was both densely populated with locals and also tourist-ridden – Aussies and New Zealanders, mostly, with sunburned noses, seeming somewhat disappointed by the tameness of this part of Fiji and wearing T-shirts that said *My Job is So Secret Even I Don't Know What I'm Doing* and *It's Not Beer, Mate, This Is Just a Fat Shirt.*

I found a launching place near the town of Nasavu and set up my kayak intending to paddle across the five-mile channel that separated Viti Levu from a largish oyster-shaped island called Beqa (pronounced *Benga*), where there were said to be firewalkers.

No sooner had I cleared the reef than I was battered by a strong wind from the east. I found I was expending most of my energy trying to keep myself upright – the wind was hitting me broadside – and so after less than two miles I abandoned the effort, and with great difficulty (because I had been pushed some distance to the west) I paddled back to my beach.

I was sorry I had missed the firewalkers – and my kayak trip had been an experience of wind and slop. But that night I met a man who said that he had mastered the art of firewalking and that I could do it too. He would teach me how to walk on hot coals.

We were drinking South Pacific Beer in the grim lounge of one of the tacky hotels on the way to Suva. The man, Norman, was American, originally from California, but he had left home to wander in the Pacific. Like me, he had been in the Peace Corps in the 1960s. We talked about that and then I had mentioned how I had been frustrated in my attempt to reach Beqa to see the firewalkers. Forget it, he had said – firewalking is simple.

"What is it, then, mind over matter?"

"No, no, no" – and in his impatience Norman started to get cross. "It's simple physics. You just walk across the hot coals. They're very bad conductors of heat. You don't need thick foot soles or anything like that. You just walk."

"And get charbroiled."

"Bull," Norman said. "You can stand the heat for up to five seconds. Say you're in a twelve-foot firepit. You just walk down it – you don't even have to go fast. You could do it – I guarantee you wouldn't get burned."

"Have you ever done it?"

"Yes. Lots of times."

"Hot coals?"

"Hot coals!" Norman said. "Of course hot coals."

"Done it lately?"

"I did it in" – and he mentioned the name of a village that I could not quite catch. "The guys there almost shat when they saw me."

"And you didn't get burned?"

Norman stared at me, as though this was the dumbest question imaginable.

"But charcoal fires are hot," I said. "You stand next to one and you get burned."

"See, that's the strange thing," Norman said. "Charcoal fires are much hotter when you're standing next to them than when you're walking across them in your bare feet."

"How did you get interested in this?"

"Read an article. 'The Physics of Firewalking' – something like that." He put his face close to mine. "Anyone can do it," he said, and hissed "*You can do it.*"

"Walk on glowing coals in my bare feet?"

"Oh, God, what did I just tell you."

I did not do it, but his certainty made me want to try.

"Suva reminds me of an aunt of mine who drank too much," a

Canadian woman, resident in Fiji, said to me. "She was delightful. But she was prone to stumble. Her clothes were a little askew, and there was always a strap of her slip showing."

Yet seedy, friendly Suva, with wet green mountains behind it, and sloping on twisting lanes of cheek-to-cheek shops down to the sea, was probably the most habitable and busiest harbor city I saw in the South Pacific (Honolulu is in the North Pacific). A settled place, with a look of comfortable monotony, Suva was a city to live in, not to visit. And it was not for tourists – tourists seldom visited anyway, because it rained so often there, and it was more than a three-hour drive across the island from Nandi, and it had no beaches or hotels to speak of. The nearest resort, Pacific Harbor, was thirty miles away. In any case, tourists tended to avoid Suva. The Fiji experience for tourists was a week or so in a resort in the drier part of the island near Nandi where they stayed behind the hedges, sipping drinks, playing tennis, and if they penetrated Melanesia at all it was in small-talk with dusky, smiling room attendants and waiters.

"I like Fiji, because this is one of the few places in the world I've been where the blacks didn't hate me," a woman from Los Angeles told me in a Nandi resort hotel – and it seemed to me one of the silliest summaries of Fiji I had heard.

Suva was an Indian city, not only in its population but in its layout as well – it had compounds, and tenements, and back-alleys, and the hectic atmosphere of a bazaar. There were many benefits of Suva, because it was a city of shopkeepers and rooted families where everyone was local and as urbane as it was possible to be in Oceania. Tourists become lonely and uncomfortable in such places, seeing residents so preoccupied with their own lives – work, school, bills, friends. It was the sort of place where you could buy a screwdriver or a teapot or a roll of duct tape, but you'd never find clothes or a pair of shoes you liked. Suva people themselves ate in the restaurants, which were inexpensive and served good plain food. This was a wonderful change from the mock-coconut-isle Fijian hotels that made inedible attempts at *nouvelle cuisine* such as Carpaccio of Slack-Jawed Sea Bass (thirty-seven dollars and fifty cents) and Goujons of Owlet's Thighs Presented on a Bed of Warm Lettuce (forty-five dollars, subject to availability).

The city had grown up around the harbour of its large bay, and it had prospered through its shipping when Nandi was just a village. Even now Nandi was no more than a scruffy small town – one main street and a market. Suva's market was vast and noisy, teeming with activity, full of vegetables, fish and fruit – and shells. "I can give you a good deal on some shells," an Indian said to me with a desperate wink. The shell and curio business was terrible, but it was interesting to see how Indians, who never drank kava, had more or less cornered the kava market. They did a brisk trade in *yanggona*, selling dusty roots or bags of high-quality powdered root to Fijian men who did little else but squat around a bowl and guzzle it. I bought four pounds of the stuff – roots and powder – because I was told that it would come in handy if I wished to ingratiate myself in a Fijian village. I give you *yanggona*, you let me camp here.

As in Nandi, nearly all the shops in Suva were Indian, displaying panicky-looking hand-painted signs saying *Close-Out Sale!* and *Prices Slashed!* – and though the city had the look and feel of a provincial town in India, looking closer anyone could see that it was a polyglot place. It was a mishmash of Muslims and Hindus, representing most of the larger provinces in the subcontinent. There was a Chinese community in Suva, too, and Australian franchises, and a residue of British commerce.

The sidewalks were crowded with shoppers and strollers – Indians mostly, with a scattering of Fijians. The merchandise in the stores looked rather old and shop-worn, and even the duty-free goods for which Fiji was famous looked a bit old-hat, overrated, old-fashioned. Why order a shipload of new models if you were about to lose your lease and Doomsday was just around the corner? There was such a variety of prices that I didn't buy anything except a map of Ovelau, an offshore island where I hoped to paddle. I went back and forth to Natovi Landing to launch my boat, but I was always facing the teeth of the wind that blew from the east. I decided to suspend paddling for now, and to pursue it when I got to the lee of this island, or to the larger island to the north, Vanua Levu.

In the steamy, humid interludes between the bouts of cold drizzle, Suva looked miserable and friendly. I liked the vegetarian restaurants – where else in carnivorous Oceania would I find others? It could be pleasantly informative to eat in the Hare Krishna vegetarian restaurant on Pratt Street and, over a healthy meal, listen to Indians complaining about the Fijians. I said nothing; I felt they needed each other.

If Fiji had been an Indian island it would have been charmless and frenzied, a hotbed of litigious warring sects, at each other's throats. As a homogenous Fijian island it would have been something like the sleepy Solomons, hospitable but hardly functional. As a multiracial place

(Indians in towns, Fijians in villages) it seemed to work. What surprised me was that the Indians wanted to live there at all, since they had no political future, were frankly hated, were forced to pay lip service to a military government, and had to make do with minimal profits.

"Situation is stagnant," an Indian named Kishore told me in a gloomy voice, and then attempted to bamboozle me into buying an over-priced wristwatch.

Perhaps the hustle-bustle of the packed streets in muddy claustrophobic Suva explained it. This was obviously an easy place for an Indian to live because it was predominantly Indian, a bunched-together place that had a life of its own. It was unlike any other town in Fiji, or the Pacific for that matter. You could imagine someone arriving and seeing all the people and the built-to-last buildings and the busy quays at the harbor and thinking: *There's money to be made here.*

Fijians were in the minority in Suva, and the few that loitered in town shopping or eating kept to themselves. They tended to prefer porky Chinese food over Indian curries. Apart from the market stalls, there were no Fijian restaurants. In my days in Suva – waiting in vain for the weather to break: but it did nothing but drizzle and blow – I noticed that when Fijians dined out they gorged themselves on fatty meat and gravy, with taro or rice. As with other former cannibal islanders – "reformed cannibals" was the missionary phrase – they loved Spam and corned beef.

Their carnivorous appetite alone could have been the reason they were so much out of key with the Indians. It was hard to see what Fijians and Indians had in common, culturally, and though there were moderates in Fiji from every racial group (a moderate coalition had won the election), the loudest people in Fiji were those who exploited the conflict and eagerly exaggerated their differences – the Indians boasting of their ancient culture and complex family structure and their skill at arithmetic, the Fijians smilingly reminding them that they were here first, on this tight little archipelago of cannibals and Christians.

Having just come from wild but coherent islands which had resisted the pressure of colonials and aliens, and where race was not an issue, this Fiji strife was a tiresome novelty. It also tested the patience of all right-thinking New Zealanders who smugly condemned apartheid and championed human rights in South Africa, but hadn't the slightest idea of how to react to this racial conundrum. After a hundred years, the Indians in Fiji – fully half the population – had found themselves a politically oppressed and soon-to-be-disenfranchised people. Yet they were prosperous!

*Go home*, the Fijians said to Indians who knew no other home but Suva.

Other foreigners in Fiji avoided the pickle that Indians had found themselves in by buying islands outright. After they became wealthy, the Banaban people of Ocean Island (little more than a three-mile-wide lump of coral and phosphate in the Gilbert and Ellice group) came to Fiji and bought the island of Rambi, off eastern Vanua Levu, because mining had made their own island uninhabitable. A number of other islands in Fiji are also privately owned. On a whim, Malcolm Forbes bought Lauthala island off Taveuni, and at least six whole islands in the northern Lau group were bought by aliens – one by a Japanese hotel company, another by an Australian export firm, one by an American messiah named Jones, who after colonizing the island with his acolytes began calling himself Baba Da Free John. A number of other islands are owned by obscure millionaires – there are 300 islands and atolls in the Fiji group. Paddling off the north shore of Viti Levu I often landed on a small pretty island only to see a sign saying *Private Island – No Trespassing*. Private islands in Fiji change hands for a million and a half and up.

Here are some Fiji island offerings – "Entire Islands Freehold/Fee Simple" – from a current (1991) real estate brochure called South Pacific Opportunities:

**Tivi Island** – NE of Labasa, Vanua Levu: 204 acres, white sand beaches. US $1,500,000

**Adavaci Island**: 104 acres, superb beach and anchorage, perfect for small exclusive resort or private estate. US $1,500,000

**Savasi Island**: 52-acre plantation, 2 nice residences and related, lovely residential estate or major resort. US $2,000,000

**Kanacea Island** – Near Vanua Balavu: Operating copra plantation, over 3000 acres, suitable for major resort. US $4,500,000

I heard there was a private island, called Mana, in the Mamanuca group – owned by Japanese, so I was told – where if I played my cards right I could visit. "Playing my cards right" simply meant paying a large sum of money to an excitable Fijian who owned a small speed-boat. I would not have dreamed of paddling across those eighteen treacherous miles in a high wind and six-foot waves, though Mike the Fijian was not fazed in his boat, even when we were on the point of being swamped.

Smacking his boat into the steep faces of waves, he denied that the sea was rough.

"What's rough then?"

"Waves more than two meters!" he shouted. "This is a bit less!"

We wallowed in the troughs of waves and then banged forward with such force that fixtures fell off the boat – the binnacle compass hit the deck, and then its bracket, and then the lugbolts from a bench. For an hour and a half, Mike fought the breaking waves, skirted the reefs and shoals, and plowed into the headwind. We arrived at Mana Island soaked to the skin.

I had expected to find a Nipponese outpost, full of little Japanese vacationers in floppy hats snapping pictures of each other. All I saw were sunburned Australians sleeping off their lunch on the beach and playing with their scorched-looking children.

"You should have come this morning," Geoffrey, the general manager, said. "We were full of Japanese. We'll get another batch tomorrow."

There was a weekly plane, he said, Tokyo to Nandi, and then the people were shipped out to the island, where they were dispersed among a hundred little tidy bungalows. There were three or four beaches, some restaurants – one was Japanese – and various sports facilities. Many of the Japanese were honeymoon couples. New Japanese brides, horrified by what marriage entailed, regularly flung themselves out of the windows of Honolulu hotels, but Geoffrey said his honeymooners were no problem and anyway could not harm themselves by jumping out of the windows of his bungalows.

"Is there a language barrier?"

"Not really. I encourage my Fijian staff to learn Japanese," he said. He sent a dozen or so of his workers every few months on a Japanese language course. And in the staffrooms at Mana, as in the equipment sheds and dive-shops of resorts elsewhere in Fiji, there were blackboards, chalked with Japanese phrases and their English (but not Fijian) equivalent: *Konnichiwa* – hello. *Arrigato* – thank you. And so forth.

The Mana Resort was owned by a Japanese company, Nichiman, which had negotiated a ninety-nine-year lease from the island's owners, the Fijians who lived in Aro village at the eastern end of the island. The Fijian village was ramshackle but no worse than any other slap-happy Fijian village of flat-roofed prefab huts. One proviso in the lease was that first preference for jobs had to be given to the villagers living in Aro.

There were no gardens on Mana Island, there was no fresh water, no fishing. The Fijians in the village lived off the money they got from the Japanese tenants. They did a little fishing, but only for their own amusement.

"Do you collect rainwater from roofs?"

"No. We barge it in," Geoffrey said.

Twice a week a water barge made the forty-mile round-trip from Lautoka, the western harbor of Viti Levu, and the water was stored in big ugly tanks.

Solar power was not used. They had, instead, a generator that ran on diesel fuel. That too was barged in from Lautoka. In fact, everything was barged in – food, water, fuel, guests, equipment and the majority of the workers, because most of the people in Aro were unwilling to work at the resort.

It was a strange artificial way of inhabiting the island – totally dependent on barges, boats and the occasional sea-plane. Nothing at all was generated locally, and even the coconut trees were seen as something of a liability.

"One of our guests was hit by a falling coconut," Geoffrey said. "He was hurt really bad. We flew him to Nandi for X-rays. Thank goodness, he was all right in the end. Those coconuts can be lethal."

One day in Fiji a man I knew vaguely said, "Want to meet the Governor-General?"

He meant of New Zealand, but I said yes anyway. The nights could be long and very quiet in Fiji.

A curious aspect of my traveling in Oceania was that I found most people accessible, and I met everyone I wanted to meet. In New Zealand I had wanted to speak to the new Governor-General, the first woman to hold the post, Dame Cath Tizard. She also had the reputation for being enormously shrill and good-hearted. She was notorious for having called one of her political opponents a "fuckwit." And when asked to apologize, she refused, saying that in fact the man was demonstrably a fuckwit. I left New Zealand before I was able to arrange to see her, but she turned up in Fiji when I was there – she had just come from the United States on a junket ("I think you Americans call it a freebie"), where she had been the guest of a company that sold expensive diet food.

We met for dinner at a resort restaurant near Nandi – Dame Cath, my friend Andrew, and Jock and Helen, a husband and wife who had fled Scotland some years ago to set up a fitness program in Auckland. I was struck by Jock's involvement in health matters because he was a heavy smoker and had downed the best part of a bottle of wine not long after we sat down.

"And you say you're a mastermind of fitness programs?" I said.

With a cigarette bouncing in his lips, he said, "What does it matter if you die at the age of sixty, as long as you die with a smile on your face?"

"I want to die with a smile on my face at the age of a hundred and twenty," I said.

"Bloody Americans! Obsessed with extending their lives!"

Still, I pestered him about his smoking, because with all his talk about health he was such a contradiction, not to say hypocrite. At first he denied that smoking was bad for him. He said he was more stressed when he didn't smoke. Then he twisted his face at me and said in a rather pathetic way, "I *have* to smoke. I'm addicted. I can't stop. I've tried everything."

"Americans are always going on about smokers," Dame Cath Tizard said. "But have you seen how fat they are? Some of them are just incredible."

"Fat's as bad for you as smoking," Jock said irritably.

This topic seemed unfortunate since both Jock and Dame Cath were hefty people, but they seemed oblivious of that and indifferent to the anomaly of wolfing down huge helpings of dinner while they talked about fat Americans. Dame Cath paid little attention to Jock and when she did speak it was in a drawling Scottish manner that is a variety of Kiwi speech.

Dame Cath had an odd, coarse way of eating. She scraped food onto her fork, but before she heaved it she nudged more onto the fork with her thumb. And after she ate the forkful she licked her thumb. Once I caught her grinning at me, but she was not grinning. She was trying to dislodge a bit of food that had found its way between her teeth, and still talking to me and grinning, she began picking her teeth. Having freed the food from her teeth, she glanced at it and pushed it into her mouth.

Eating in this manner, she said, "People kept telling me I was going to be chosen Governor-General, but I couldn't believe it, so I just put it out of my mind."

"How does one get to be chosen?"

"Well, that's just it." *Will, thet's jest ut.* "The Queen does the choosing."

Her finger was in her mouth, fishing for bits of trapped lamb sinews.

"When I got the news – in effect, here was the Queen asking me to be Governor-General."

And she slurped the food off her finger, and then began again scraping her plate in the waste-not, want-not manner of a Kiwi who had been through the war.

Jock said, "I know what I'd do!" and raised a glass to the absent Queen of the United Kingdom, Northern Ireland and Overseas Territories and Commonwealths such as New Zealand.

"Yes," I said. "If the Queen asked me to be Governor-General, I would say, 'As Your Highness commands.' "

"It wasn't that simple," she said, obviously wanting to make a meal of her dark night of the soul when she received the Royal Command. "I thought about it for two weeks."

"I'd think about it for about two seconds," Jock said.

"My daughter said, 'Don't be so effing silly, Mum – take it!' "

She smiled, enjoying this chance to tell the story of her ennoblement, and I realized I disliked her politician's vanity and her interminable way of telling this simple story. She was picking her teeth again, and baring them at me.

"I was Mayor of Auckland," she said, somewhat defiantly.

"More Polynesians in Auckland than in any other city in the world," I said.

"And some very sad Indians from Fiji, I'm afraid," she said. "We're getting an awful lot of them. But they're no trouble. I had other problems."

One problem widely reported was that she had been faced with repeated calls for her resignation following a government investigation into a project for an entertainment center in Auckland, in which she had been involved which had quadrupled in cost from $25 million to $106 million. In a threadbare and over-taxed country this was not merely excessive, this was egregious and stupid. The opposition and her critics – many of whom had once been her supporters – were eager to see her humiliated before she took up the post of Governor-General.

"What finally decided you?" I asked, hoping to cut this short.

"After six years of mayor I was really tired of the hassles," she said. "And this way, as Governor-General, I could get my superannuation."

It seemed to me rather a mundane notion that one would agree to such a post simply in order to qualify for a state pension, but then the New Zealanders are a practical people.

At that point, out of the blue and fairly tipsy, Jock said he loved New Zealand for its rugby.

"I hate rugby," Dame Cath said. "I think it is violent and that it inspires violence. That's one of the reasons New Zealand is such a violent place. I'm sure rugby," she went on, though I could not follow her reasoning, "causes a lot of rape."

"I was born in Glesgie," Jock said. "Know how they deal with rapists there? Aw, there was one wee lad raped a girl. They took this lad and kneecapped him. Hammered five-inch spikes through his knees."

He waited for a reaction. I put down my fork. No one said anything.

"He's not raping anyone now, I can tell you," Jock said. "He's in a wheelchair."

"I wonder how those men who did it feel," Dame Cath said, and you knew she thought: Those men were brutalized and remorseful!

"Bloody happy, I think," Jock said.

I said, "Do you think they should introduce kneecapping in New Zealand?"

"Kneecapping is too good for some of these rapists!" Jock said.

Mrs Jock, meanwhile, did not say anything.

The subject of rapists and rugby turned into a discussion about South Africa, which New Zealand had boycotted because of the way the teams were selected. When I introduced the subject of New Zealand playing Fiji in rugby — what about the undemocratic government here? — they winced at me, as though I had farted in church. No one had an answer to this quite simple matter of political oafishness.

"Anti-apartheid people say they're for freedom," Jock said. "I want to watch my rugby, but I'm not allowed to! What about my freedom?"

"It's not a question of freedom," Dame Cath said. "It's a question of justice. Apartheid is an injustice."

"What do you think of the Fiji constitution?" I said.

"It's a proposed constitution," she said. "Who knows what will happen? Did you say you're a writer? What sort of books do you write?"

"All sorts," I said, but already she seemed bored.

"I am reading a marvelous book at the moment," she said. "About John F. Kennedy. It is very naughty — he committed every indiscretion you can name. And with Marilyn Monroe!"

"I hate those books," I said.

"I think it has historical value," she said.

*Oh, sure you do.* It irritated me that this New Zealander, and politician to boot, seemed to be gloating insincerely over a sensational book.

"But of course you have to admit that your interest in this book is almost purely vulgar," I said. "That's the fun of it, right? It's a cheap thrill, isn't that the whole point?"

She began yammering sanctimoniously about politicians not being above the law and so forth.

"But you're a politician," I said. "And you were a human being before you became a politician."

She glared at me and said that politics was her life – well, anyway, until she had been appointed Governor-General. There was something formidable about the way she commanded the table, doing nearly all the talking, being right all the time.

"So you approve of this type of Kennedy book," I said. "How would you like it if someone wrote one about New Zealand politicians? Would you write that sort of book?"

"New Zealand politicians are too bloody boring. They don't even have sex lives."

"Isn't your husband a politician?" I said.

"I left him," she said.

"I read somewhere that David Lange has recently run off with his speech-writer and left his wife. What if someone wrote a book about his libido?"

Dame Cath said, "What do you mean 'libido'? You mean screwing around?"

"So to speak. I mean, you say you approve of this type of book, right? It's a historical document, right? Well, I'm sure you know all sorts of dirt about New Zealand politicians. So would you write a book like this about New Zealand indiscretions?"

"I can't write," she said.

"I am being hypothetical," I said, trying to pin her down. "You are in the know. All sorts of secrets. You love to read books about sexual revelations. All I'm saying is – would you be prepared to spill the beans and write the kind of trashy book you like to read?"

This threw her. She fussed and mumbled, and finally said, "If I thought it would help," blah-blah-blah.

"And what if someone wrote a vicious little portrait of you?"

"Let them," she said.

She seemed in the end rather silly and shallow and unimaginative, as well as bossy, vain and cunning, but principled in a smug and meddling way. And a New Zealander to her fingertips, worthy of the Queen's Honours List.

In a silence after the meal she hitched her skirt and suddenly spoke up.

"I once called a man a fuckwit," she said in her Governor-General's voice, dredging up one of her political victories. "Of course I didn't apologize. He *was* a fuckwit."

# 13

## Fiji: Vanua Levu and the Islets of Bligh Water

In Viti Levu, there was no avoiding the tourists. I kept hoping for something wilder, more remote, a bit emptier, no golfers. Yes, here and there, in an isolated part of the island was a valley of dark green jungle, but really what sort of jungle was it when you went for a hike and after a few hours ran into an Indian family picnicking? They had driven there, all eighteen of them, by car on a back road; they left empty squash bottles and orange rinds and cookie wrappers behind – and sometimes chicken bones. It was a fact that some Hindus, especially in Fiji, hid themselves and secretly gobbled meat, the way teenagers in America sneaked illicit cigarettes.

I heard there was a ferry that sailed from the north coast of Viti Levu, across the twenty-mile-wide channel called Bligh Water, to the much emptier and reputedly rather strange island of Vanua Levu.

"There are no tourists in Vanua Levu," an Indian in Nandi told me. "It is too far and too primitive."

*Perfect.* Taking my collapsible kayak and all my equipment, I went there on another paralytic Fijian Sunday, stopping for a curry in Lautoka and, out of curiosity, attending a Methodist church service in the northeast town of Mba. The church was full, but many in the congregation were coughers and fidgeters, and during the long hectoring sermon – in Fijian – a number of people dozed off. Dealing with the sleepers, a smiling Fijian man in a traditional *sulu* skirt walked up and down the aisle with a long pole, prodding the sleepers and waking them.

In Rakiraki at the top of the island I visited the grave of a nineteenth-century chief of this area – the Province of Ra – Ratu Udre Udre, who had distinguished himself by eating 800 humans. In a hotel nearby a drunken Australian, seeing my boat, accused me of being a CIA agent. This seemed a reasonable presumption, so I did not deny it. That night, even drunker, he sang tunelessly in the hotel bar while Fijians on the veranda sniggered among themselves and sneaked looks at him through the window. The village nearby was full of aggressive and hysterical dogs; they fought all night, and their barking woke the roosters.

In the morning I found the ferry landing, Ellington Pier, a rubbly platform near a sugar mill. In the blue distance was Vanua Levu. A sugar worker told me I would have to buy my ticket in the next town, Vaileka. The ticket-seller said the ferry would be at the pier at noon and that I could take my rental car.

Vaileka, this small town on the north coast of Viti Levu, had a narrow main street and one row of shops. On this hot day the dust on the dry street seemed to blaze. At the shops and the open-air market – no more than twenty fruit-sellers squatting under an enormous fig tree – I bought provisions for a week. It was not a bad place, but it was very small, it had an air of discouragement about it, the rather sleepy atmosphere of an outpost, and in the silence, with so little stirring, it seemed about as out of touch as a town could possibly be. The world was somewhere else.

That was how it seemed to me: another world. Before I left London, I had been in touch with Salman Rushdie – I wrote to him, he phoned me – and I commiserated with him. I considered him a friend; and his confinement pained me – it was like house arrest. I had suggested that he remove himself to a town like this in Mexico or South America or Australia or the Pacific. I had specifically mentioned Fiji. He could be safe, he could be free, he could write in such a place.

"You know Salman Rushie?" I asked several Muslims in this distant place, Vaileka.

"Yes," one said. "He must die."

And the other said, "Rushdie is a devil."

There were pairs of Mormons in Vaileka, too, which was proof that the town was not as Melanesian as it seemed.

Back at the pier I waited for the ferry. Lizards skittered on the pilings. Birds of prey came and went. Fish jumped. There was no ferry at noon. I listened to news of the Gulf War on my short-wave: more bombing missions, no invasion, a great anxiety over the possible use of nerve gas.

An Indian fished from the pier.

I asked him, "Where is the ferry?"

"Him leave ready. Ten clark."

I thought, *Damn*, but when I questioned him further he appeared not to understand English. He also began to clamber among the rotten pilings humming to himself and I thought he might be demented.

Another Indian sauntered by. He had been burned black by the sun. He was whistling through the gap in his teeth. I asked him about the ferry that was supposed to have come at noon. It was now nearly two.

"Fiji time," he said.

This was a frequent response in Fiji – no offense was meant or taken. Most people laughed about lateness or irregular hours. It simply meant: wait.

But then I saw the black smudge on the horizon, which swelled into a top-heavy ferry, its white hull streaming with rust stains. It was a typical Pacific ferry, down to its greasy decks and broken fixtures and its pretty name painted over Chinese characters – Pacific ferries were always cast-offs, second-hand vessels from Hong Kong or Taiwan that someone had managed to sell to a coconut kingdom instead of to a scrapyard.

This one was called the *Princess Ashika*. It docked; six timber trucks heavily laden with logs rolled off it and headed down the dirt road that led away from the pier. I drove on board. I was the only passenger. Within fifteen minutes we were at sea – no time-wasting at all.

The *Princess Ashika* was soon rolling across Bligh Water in a thirty-knot headwind and bright sunshine. With a steady wind like this blowing west across this part of the Pacific it was not hard to see why Captain Bligh had made such good progress on his epic forty-eight-day journey in an open boat, with eighteen of his men, after the mutiny on the *Bounty*. They had been cast adrift by Fletcher Christian off Tonga, and had sailed among these islands, between Viti Levu and Vanua Levu. Captain Bligh was the first European to map this part of Viti Levu. Bligh had sailed onward, through the Coral Sea, past the Queensland coast and Cape York, squeezing through the Torres Strait, and finally reached landfall at Kupang in Timor. It had been a voyage of almost 4000 miles, and his men had been frightened for most of the way – a fear of cannibals, mostly, and amply justified. In fact, just after their longboat passed this point several canoes crewed by fierce Fijians gave chase and kept after them almost until Bligh had cleared the Yasawas, about twenty-odd miles west of here.

Passing this way, Bligh had looked at the islands and described the landscape in his log, remarking on the "cockscomb mountains." It was an accurate image. The mountains were high and green, with gently rounded lobe-like peaks. Clouds gathered around the summits of the old volcanoes inland, but the coast was bright, and even on this north coast of Viti Levu, which was as quiet as the island could be, it was possible to ascertain that Viti Levu had been spoken for. It was not that the island was crowded, but rather that it was settled. It was farmed and deforested. In a word, it was possessed.

I hoped for better in Vanua Levu. This ferry was headed for a small pier at the southwestern tip of the island, Nabouwalu. No one I had spoken to knew anything about Nabouwalu – so I was heartened.

Since I was the only passenger – this ship was used mostly for ferrying timber to Viti Levu – the crew had little to do en route. They sat on the broken benches in an upper-deck lounge watching a video. The movie, ostensibly a costume adventure about a band of pirates looking for treasure in the West Indies, was a thin excuse for showing sex and violence – two rapes, the beating of a woman, lots of cleavage, a simulated act of sodomy (a pirate and a busty, gasping woman in a hiked-up prom gown) and a number of whippings. Dungeons and rats figured in a number of scenes. The Fijian deckhands laughed delightedly at the rapes and were so riveted by the floggings that they almost missed the docking procedure and had to be summoned by the captain.

The sun was setting beneath Coconut Point as we docked. I could take in the whole place in one glance. Nabouwalu was the pier, two shops, some scattered huts and a stony road. Little wonder no one had said anything about it. What was there to say? Driving in the darkness on such a bad road was ill-advised, so I asked a strolling Fijian where I might camp. He directed me to the Rest House. This bungalow was fully occupied – three or four Fijians in residence – but one of them, a strapping fellow in a skirt named Jone Kindia, said that the only really safe place to camp was at his workers' compound. He took me there and he explained on the way that Fijians were funny about their land. They were suspicious of strangers who showed up without an introduction, wishing to camp.

"They wonder how long you are going to stay," Jone said. "Maybe you will want to stay for years. That is what they worry about."

"I just want to stay for a few days," I said.

"But how do they know that?"

"Good point."

The workers' compound was a clearing on a hillside outside Nabouwalu – a few flimsy huts, a wooden bungalow that served as an office, and an unfinished building in which day and night the local Fijians sat around a bowl drinking kava. They did not call it kava, nor even *yanggona*. They called it grog.

"Where is Masi?" Kindia asked a woman in a field.

She mumbled a reply.

"Drinking grog," Kindia translated.

He was sitting around the bowl with Yoakini and they both had the stupefied, slightly stunned and smiling expression of kava-drinkers. Kava-drinkers were never aggressive. They looked numb, like hypothermia victims, or patients who had just been dragged from a dentist's chair. Kava-drinkers were weak and compliant; they whispered; they swayed when they tried to stand straight. Kava was like chloroform. "He's not feeling any pain," was truer when spoken of a kava-drinker than an alcoholic. And because kava deadened the lips and tongue one never heard a harsh word from one of these men.

Yoakini said, "You stay at my *bure*."

"That's all right. I have a tent."

Masi wore a slap-happy smile. He looked at me through heavy-lidded eyes and said, "Do not go to the beach."

Kindia muttered impatiently.

"Never go to the beach," Masi said. He was on his feet and swaying.

"Why not?"

'Alfred Hitchcock is there," Masi said and stopped smiling.

"Did you say Alfred Hitchcock?"

The fellow simply stared at me.

I set up my tent away from the coconut palms and hurriedly ate dinner – it was a starry moonless night. Just before I turned in, Masi came by. He teetered for a moment and then spoke.

"Remember, Alfred is at the beach," he said, and then staggered into the darkness.

Yoakini was a soldier in the Fijian army. "I am about twenty-eight," he said. He described himself as a "sapper" – a military engineer. Carpentry was his specialty. He was very black, with thick hair and a fierce mustache, and he was bulkily built, his body like a fortification. He said he drank grog every night when he was off duty. He showed me where I could get fresh water, where I could take a shower, and where the best latrine was located.

He was shy, but not timid, and though he was quiet, he answered my nosy questions. When he said that he had been in Suva during the coup and the ensuing riots in 1987, I asked whether he found it exciting to be in the thick of a battle on his own island (he was from a village in Viti Levu): the Fijians storming the Indian shops, burning and looting.

"Yes, it was exciting," he said. "It was very exciting."

"Have you traveled overseas?" I asked.

"I was in Lebanon twice."

"Lebanon?"

"In the peace-keeping force. In 1982 and in 1984," he said. "I was in Cairo, in Beirut, and in South Lebanon. I visited Israel, too. It was nice."

"Weren't you afraid to be in a place where there was so much fighting?"

"No. The worst is the weather. Very hot in the day. Very cold at night."

"Did you have grog?"

"They flew in *yanggona* sometimes – the roots. We pounded it and drank it in our tents. Some we saved for Christmas. We had a good Christmas in Lebanon, drinking grog."

"What did you think of the situation there?"

"It is a mess. I don't know the answer. I was a soldier in Sinai. The Arabs asked us for food, the Israelis asked us where are we from? Then they said, 'Where is Fiji?' "

Yoakini laughed at the memory of it – of the ignorance of the Israelis, these embittered and confused civilians living at the edge of the desert. "In Fiji we study geography. We know where all countries are. We know where Israel is."

"Were you doing carpentry in Sinai?"

"No carpentry. In Sinai they gave me a weapon," Yoakini said.

"But isn't it ridiculous that a Fiji Islander should be in the Middle East, risking his life because of a local conflict?"

"Maybe. But the money is good," he said. He told me what he was making. I estimated that he was earning ninety dollars a month.

"Are you willing to risk dying to earn that?"

"I don't know," he said. "Thirty Fijians have been killed there – by single bullets, by accidents, from sickness. It is a mess."

What he did not say – something I discovered later – was that Lt-Col. Steven Rabuka had served twice in the Middle East with the Fiji army, in the same places Yoakini had been posted, in Lebanon and in Sinai.

I asked Yoakini whether he would serve in the Gulf War. He said it depended on whether the Fiji army was involved, and if it was a question of volunteering the money had to be good – though his idea of good was ninety dollars a month. I had heard that the Fijian soldiers had been highly effective in the Second World War – they had the essential military virtues, a legacy of the British colonial past: they were ferocious, loyal, politically disinterested, impervious to bad weather, and would eat anything. They fought when they were ordered to. They were professionals. They soldiered for money. They were the perfect mercenaries – not elite troops and janizaries, but workhorses and warriors.

I gave Yoakini some of the *yanggona* roots that I had brought with me, and he invited me to drink grog with him. Because it was considered rude to refuse I joined him that night around the kava bowl, the *tanoa* – which was about twice the size of a salad bowl and beautifully carved. These bowls were the only accomplished carvings I saw in Fiji.

With my lips going numb and my tongue thickening, I said that what I really wanted was to go paddling.

"But where will you stay?"

"I'll just ask someone in a nearby village."

"It is better you stay here."

When I explained that my boat was collapsible and that I could take it back here to this camp site – something he urged me to do – Yoakini showed me a good place to paddle that was east of the little town, beyond Solevu Point. The water was muddy and shallow near shore, but out at the reef I could make headway. I realized that this was what I had missed on Viti Levu. Though the Fijian resorts were pleasant, there was a fence around each one, and people could stay for weeks and never know Fiji. Even people who had lived in Fiji for a long time told me that they had not been to this island, Vanua Levu. There was nowhere to stay on this western end of the island, they said. There were no restaurants. It was just jungle and scattered villages. The beaches were muddy and thick with mangroves. The people were simple and suspicious. The roads were appalling.

This was music to my ears. And these perceptions of the island proved to be true. But I had a tent, and a stove, and food, and a boat. I even had a car, so I could tote all this stuff around. But I paddled during the day, exploring the large bay and the inlets west of Nabouwalu; at night I went back to my tent and stayed put in Kindia's compound.

Long after night had fallen, and often until quite late, I heard the villagers pounding the *yanggona* root in their big wooden mortars. This thudding was continuous, like the sound of a stirrup pump, and it was always a woman using the pestle. The Fijian method was different from the Vanuatu way. In Fiji they sluiced this pounded root through a piece of cloth and the narcotic drink was squeezed into the kava bowl.

"We don't chew," Masi said.

But I now know that human saliva reacted with the root and made a stronger drink – that was why they called Tanna product "two-day kava": you were stupefied for two days on a few shells of the stuff.

At one time, village girls in Fiji had prepared the root by chewing it and spitting it out. Having a winsome Fijian girl smilingly masticating by my side seemed infinitely preferable to me than a filthy man with black tooth stumps munching and drooling. But as Masi said, *We don't chew*. Non-chewing islands in the Pacific were invariably the islands where the missionaries had exerted the strongest grip, for nothing was more disgusting to a European than drinking someone else's saliva. Missionaries had encouraged the use of mortars and pestles.

I usually dropped off to sleep to the rhythm of *yanggona* being pounded. One night in my tent in that compound I dreamed that I was going home – "home" was the concept I had in my dream, but it was not my house. It was a mansion set amid parkland, very serene as I approached it, but chaotic and filled with people when I stepped inside the ornate front door. There were a number of women in the mansion: all of them at one time had been married to me. And there were many children, all mine. It dawned on me that I had been away a long time, and these wives and children had multiplied in my absence. They were all having a wonderful time, and yet there was great confusion. I wandered outside, to the swimming pool, on which floated chunks of blue ice.

Jone Kindia was the *Roko* or head of the Fijian Affairs Board. This was a glorified name for an agency that spent most of its time settling local disputes. The burden fell upon Jone. He was the dispute-settler. He set off each morning for his office in his starched shirt and his wraparound gabardine skirt and his polished sandals. There were usually a dozen people waiting at the veranda of the wooden bungalow which housed his office, and one by one Jone listened to their tales of woe. On the walls of his office were lithographs of British coronations, a large one of George V, and other portraits of George V and VI. Jone said they dated from before independence, when an Englishman had had this office. Jone had not taken them down. He said he thought they were very pretty, and they took his mind off his wearying job. He said sometimes he spent days or even weeks on just one dispute.

"What sort would that be?"

"Land dispute. They are the worst," he said, smoothing his mustache. "There is no end to them, and I find it very hard to straighten them out."

Fijians were intensely territorial. But of course all the islanders in the Pacific were territorial: land was their birthright, their wealth, and in Melanesia it was the origin of their creation – they had sprung from this soil. *We came out of the caves at Kaibola*, as they said in the Trobriands. They could account for every foot of land, and because it was family land it had been extensively subdivided – that also made it unsaleable, for how could you get all these people to agree to sell? If you made the mistake of camping without permission on an uninhabited island, God help you – because someone owned it, and camping on it meant that you were attempting to claim it. Fijian territoriality was at the heart of their animosity against the Indians. Fijians did not mind being out-numbered – in fact, Fijians had been outnumbered by Indians off and on from as far back as 1946 – what they minded was losing their land to these pagan aliens.

"I own this beach," a Fijian said to me, up the coast at Nasavu. "You go two chains and that is Tumasi's. Three chains and it is Alesi's."

They often used this old English measurement, too. A chain is equal to 100 feet. Ten square chains is an acre.

Jone, Masi and Yoakini became protective of me in a way that puzzled and irritated me. I knew they were trying to prevent mis-understandings, but I felt I could handle myself – hadn't I managed in Vanuatu and the Solomons, reputedly much wilder places?

They always wanted to know exactly where I was headed. I would find a place on the map and say, "I am going to Wailiki."

Jone or one of the others in the compound would then say, "Where will you stay?"

"I'll pitch my tent. I'll ask permission."

They would go silent, or else mumble among themselves.

"It is better you stay here."

"I want to go to Wailiki."

Then they would giggle, and this meant that going to Wailiki was difficult. Loud laughter was the Fijian way of conveying the bad news that something was impossible.

"Someone can go with you."

"I want to go alone. Why does someone have to go with me?"

"To introduce you."

"Can't I introduce myself? I'll give them some *yanggona*." I still had three dusty bunches of the horrible stuff.

"Yes?" they would say, meaning no.

They weren't kidding, and after a while I knew that their anxiety was justified. At three villages I was asked the same insulting question: "You're a businessman?"

The feeling was that I had come to diddle them out of their birthright, when all I really wanted was to pitch my tent and paddle my boat.

I paddled down the coast, and at Sawani, Solevu and other coastal villages, I presented myself to the *Yaganga ni Koro*, "Master of the

Village" (*Yaganga* was also the word they used for Almighty God), who was a sort of chief or headman. I had a message from the *Roko*. This cut little ice. They were not used to seeing travelers here. They had heard about them.

They winced at me. They smiled – this was an expression of disagreement – and they said: It is not nice here. It is not even clean. This is a poor village. You would do better to keep moving and to go somewhere else.

"Can't I put my tent here?"

Their bewilderment seemed to say: Why would you want to do that?

When I camped I did not stay longer than a night. Their suspicion and anxiety made me uneasy – although I should add that they were pleasant people, gentle, unthreatening, helpful to each other.

But an encounter could be an unusual experience. One day after paddling three or four miles I stepped on shore and saw a bushy-haired man and woman. The woman was carrying a dog in her arms like a baby. The man wore a filthy T-shirt lettered with the slogan *Nibble Nobby's Nuts*. He carried a wicked-looking bush knife, a slasher that was about two feet long. They were both very dirty and rather apprehensive.

"Where is Nakawakawa village?" I had found it on my map, but there were no huts in sight.

"Just here," the man said.

"Can I get there on this path?" I asked.

"You want to go there?"

"Yes."

"Yes?"

"If it's all right" – a man carrying a knife like that could make me very circumspect. "Otherwise, I'll just paddle away."

"Yes," he said, which I took to mean: *That is what I advise you to do.*

And then – and this was also typical – the man asked whether he could be my pen-pal.

Farther up the coast I paddled into a little bay where there was a large cathedral-like church, made of wood and gray plaster. A horse cropped grass in the churchyard, and there were school buildings behind the church. But there were no people anywhere. I crept into the church and in the large dusty nave there were no pews, only wall-to-wall mats, and over the altar verses from the gospel in Fijian.

I found two Fijians sitting on the floor of a nearby wooden building. There were chairs in the room, which had the look of an office, but the men were drinking kava. It was unthinkable to engage in kava-drinking while sitting in a chair. You had to sit crosslegged, around the bowl.

"What are you doing?"

"Drinking grog."

They must have started early. It was nine-thirty in the morning and both men had the dazed and somewhat anesthetized expression of kava-drinkers who had knocked back a dozen shells.

"Where is the priest?"

"At the priest's conference in Savusavu."

This was obviously the priest's office – his desk, his papers, his crucifix. It was a good secluded place, perfect for kava-drinking.

"Very nice," I said, watching the bigger of the two men working a coconut shell around the bowl, stirring the opaque muddy liquid. This dishwater color was standard, no better or worse than any other I had seen.

The man filled the shell and offered it to me.

By now I knew the ritual. I sat and clapped a little as he handed me the shell – and drank it down in a gulp – then handed the empty shell back and clapped again. It had a revolting taste. It was lukewarm, and it had the slightly medicinal flavor of mouthwash to which some mud had been added. There was nothing alcoholic in it, though there was a mild afterburn and a hint of liquorice.

With the first shell my lips were numb and my tongue was furry. The second shell deadened my tongue and killed my facial nerves. Successive shells paralyzed my legs, reaching my toes first then numbing my shanks.

"It is a good safe drink," an Indian told me in Nabouwalu. Though Indians themselves didn't touch the stuff. "People just get very sleepy and tired. They are slow. There is never any violence. They are too weak to fight."

No one ever went haywire and beat up his wife after bingeing on *yanggona*. No one ever staggered home from a night around the kava bowl and thrashed his children, or insulted his boss, or got tattooed, or committed rape. The usual effect after a giggly interval was the staggers and then complete paralysis.

These men were at the giggly stage. They answered a few simple questions I had about the church – it was called the Immaculate Conception Church, it had been founded by French priests, and they said it was 120 years old, which seemed unlikely; and then they smiled and passed the shell.

This was the last thing I wanted to do. The kava sapped my energy and made it a chore to paddle. But I did not wish to be offensive, so I sat for a while and asked them about it. They told me about the girls who had once chewed the root and they said that in some places the root was still chewed. But they had little conversation. This was not an activity that induced high spirits. Most men sat around the bowl mumbling. Initially a kava ceremony was an occasion to gossip, but the more people drank the less coherent they became.

These men said they would be there most of the day. They had nothing else to do. When I asked them how much they could drink they said, "Two kilos" – they meant of the pounded root, which was gallons of the muddy liquid.

It was a struggle to paddle onward from there, but I had no choice. I had intended to reach the far side of the bay, where a town showed on the map. The effects of the kava did not wear off until mid-afternoon, and then I made better time, reaching the settlement just before sunset. But the name on the map was misleading – as names so often were on maps of Pacific islands. It was simply a crossroads, and a small store, run by a small grizzled Indian named Munshi.

Munshi said I could camp on his land, a little clearing just inland from the mangroves. He claimed to own it outright. He said his grandfather had bought it – his grandfather had come to Fiji to work on a sugar estate in the 1890s. Munshi had been born in the same house where his father had been born, on the other side of the island at Votua.

He watched me pitch my tent and to make conversation I asked how he was getting on.

"This is a bad place now," Munshi said. "This is no place for Indians. We are suffering."

I found this all depressing – the undercurrent of resentment, the silliness of the tourists, the fact that no one in the world paid the slightest attention to it. It was a lost cause, the kava-drinking Methodists on the one hand and the cliquey puritanical Asians on the other. All they had in common was a love of video cassettes – a shared fondness for *Rambo* and *Die Hard* and *Predator II*. Apart from that, there was no sympathy, much less any intermarriage. Here and there – and sometimes in the wildest, emptiest places of Vanua Levu – was a Chinese shop, its owner looking like a Martian behind the counter, utterly indifferent to it all.

The next day, a hot humid morning, Munshi sold me some Shell-Lite fuel for my stove and explained his predicament. I had asked him what he wanted to do.

"I want to leave. To go anywhere."

"Have you ever been away from here?"

"No," Munshi said. "But my father went to India. He made the *Haj* pilgrimage. I would like to do that."

He was barefoot and dirty. His wife, who never spoke, swept the yard with a twig broom, shifting garbage from one side of the yard to the other. His kids squawked on the porch, and some Fijian boys sat on the steps, one holding a loaf of bread, the other a can of corned beef, listening without understanding.

Munshi said, "Where do you come from?"

"America."

"I would like to go to America."

Munshi handed me my fuel and replaced the bung on his oil drum.

"This is a bad place." He snatched off his greasy skull-cap and scratched his head. "Why you come here?"

"Just looking around."

"You like?"

"Very nice."

He shook his head.

"No," he said.

The Fijian boys on the porch began to eat their breakfast. They knifed open the can of corned beef, tore the loaf of bread into hunks, and took turns scooping smears of corned beef out of the can with the bread hunks. These they stuffed into their mouths, until the can was empty. There was little fresh fish here. People ate canned fish, as they had in New Guinea and the Trobriands – pilchards, mackerel, "tuna flakes."

Munshi had baked the bread. He made it fresh every day, with flour that came on the ferry that he trucked to his kitchen. His shop was the only source of bread on this entire end of the island, for fifty miles or more. All the Fijians ate bread. None of the other shops – the other Indians, the Chinese man – made bread.

I was certain that he would leave – he said his land was for sale, his shop for sale. If he couldn't go to Canada or America he would go to New Zealand. Then there would be no bread. I imagined that his bread would be missed, even if he were not; but the Fijians would learn to do without it. They would eat crackers instead – cream crackers. There was a traditional diet in Fiji, as there was on other islands; but along with this was another kind of food, the sailors' diet which was standard on many Pacific islands and was eaten with relish: ship's biscuit, corned beef, Spam, tinned fish, and for sweets, jars of marmalade and canned plum duff.

No fishing canoes were made or used in Viti Levu nor even in simpler and more traditional Vanua Levu. I never saw anyone fishing beyond the reef. Inshore, they waded up to their thighs and cast small nets. They threw dinky spears. They caught tiny fish. Off the beaten track, there were some thatched huts on Vanua Levu but mostly the roofs were corrugated tin, and the villages tended to be ramshackle – no evidence of weaving, carving, or lashing poles. It was the apotheosis of missionary effort, a great evangelical success. All the people went to church. But they had lost most of their traditional skills. Even their gardens were unimpressive – they only grew enough for themselves, and they still patronized the Indian shops. They needed Munshi more than they realized.

When the tide was out – and it went very far out on this Bua coast – the place seemed even more remote and abandoned, a distant muddy shore. In so many words, Munshi told me he was simply going through the motions; he was waiting for his chance to leave.

I was grateful for his letting me camp on his land. He expected nothing in return. When I offered him *yanggona* he just laughed at me. We were sitting on his veranda. He repeated that this was an awful place. What should he do? Where could he go?

"I am like a prisoner," Munshi said.

This reminded me. "You know Salman Rushdie?"

"I have heard of him."

"What did he do?"

"Bad things."

"Is he a bad man?"

"I think so, yes," Munshi said.

I said, "The Ayatollah wants to have him killed."

"Yes," Munshi said, and smiled, and made a harsh noise as he scraped at his whiskers with his skinny fingers.

"You want to kill him?"

"Maybe not me. But it is better if he die."

I paddled back to Nabouwalu and camped up at Yoakini's and drank grog in the kava circle. When Masi got stiff he began warning me about Alfred Hitchcock. I thought I would load my boat and drive north eighty miles to Labasa, where there was a sugar town and some offshore islands. I asked them what it was like there.

They said, *It is like this.*

I went to bed feeling as though I had just been at the dentist's, my mouth full of novocaine.

It was another hot day in Nabouwalu. I was in the car. My gear was packed – my tent folded, my boat collapsed. I began driving through town and out of the corner of my eye I saw that the ferry was docked at the jetty. An immense timber truck was waiting to drive on board. Another was trundling down the stony road to the pier.

The wind lifted, and an overwhelming stink of rotting vegetation rose from the shore to the west and blew past me. It carried with it muddy beaches and buggy mangroves and decrepit tin-roofed villages. It even carried with it a glimpse of the big bushy-haired man with the wicked cutlass and the T-shirt that said *Nibble Nobby's Nuts*. I looked up and saw the rutted road, and envisioned how bad it would be after fifty or sixty miles – the dust, the pot-holes, the hairpin curves above the sludgy lagoon. *It is like this.*

On a sudden impulse I swerved onto the road, jounced towards the pier, and a Fijian stepped out of the way and waved me on board. Within minutes we were out of there, and then Vanua Levu was astern, just another Fiji island smothered in cloud and haze.

Paddling in the cluster of reefs and islets and remote villages, off Viti Levu, in Bligh Water, I met Ken MacDonald, who was building a hotel for scuba divers on the island of Nananu-i-Ra. He suggested that camping might be misunderstood on the island and said that I could stay at his bungalow while I explored the islands in the area – and I might find an island to camp on later.

MacDonald, who looked as Scottish as his name, surprised me by saying that he was partly Tongan and Samoan. This ancestry was unfortunate, he said. Though nothing specific was mentioned about it, he felt that it had been the reason he had been unable to marry the daughter of the Fijian nobleman Ratu Sir Kamisese Mara. He had romanced the woman for nine years. If he had been part-Fijian, or wholly Scottish or English, he thought he might not have been rejected. This was an insight into the Melanesian social system – and it was true that behind this façade of religion and tourism and sugar cane and the rather decrepit modernism of Fiji, was an inflexible and ancient infrastructure of chiefs – the *ratus*, and real power, where caste and blood mattered.

I wondered what Ken might mean when he warned me that he could be moody, with sudden lapses, and odd humor, unpredictable opinions and slight tetchiness. He seemed very pleasant, if a bit quiet. It was an advantage to me that he was somewhat remote, and preoccupied with the building of his resort. I hated being anyone's house guest. I disliked being shown around, cooked for, and patronized. It suited me that Ken was too busy for this, and I could see that his diving resort, Mokusiga (the word meant goofing off), had been designed to be as unobtrusive as possible on this pretty island. It was taking all his savings and most of his energy to see it through.

His house was crammed with books and cassettes, and the shelves in the kitchen lined with cans of mackerel, the sort I always brought along when I was camping.

"So you eat this stuff too," I said.

"That's for the cats," Ken said.

But he said that there were very few people who went fishing in a serious way. Now it was all vegetables and corned beef and soft drinks; a pretty awful diet.

"Fifteen years ago you saw outrigger canoes," Ken said. "The men went fishing beyond the reef. Now you might see some people with nets, but not much more."

In the evenings after I had returned from paddling we sometimes sat in the darkness, under his trees, slapping mosquitoes and drinking beer.

He said that it seemed to be simply a stand-off between Fijians and Indians. But it was much more complicated than that. There were all shades of political opinion – very right-wing Fijians, very nationalistic parties, like the Taukai. It was during the second coup that this party emerged – significantly, the word *taukai* in Fijian means "landowners" – and Fijians from all classes became members.

"The Taukai burned shops and beat up Indians," Ken said. "And some of the Indians were militants. Arms – all sorts of guns and ammo – were found in some Indian areas. And a boat with arms for Indians tried to slip in here – through the channel. But there were soldiers watching from the hills and they intercepted it."

"Do you think the Indians will leave?"

"Some have already left. The ones that stay are not persecuted. They are just left out," Ken said. And it seemed to me that this was so. "Anyway, they never had a lot of faith in the Fijians."

"For Fijians the feeling is mutual," I said. "So what if the Indians are forced to leave, as they were in Uganda? It was an economic catastrophe for Uganda. If that happens in Fiji, there will be very few shops, poor supply lines, a scarcity of goods and services, a shortage of skilled manpower – teachers and medical people, for example. Then Fiji would be in a very bad way. It will be an island of ghost towns."

Ken said, "Yes, that's a possibility."

He was being realistic, but had no sense of urgency. He was not alone. The general feeling among Fijians and other aliens was that the Indians would stay as long as there was business to be done and money to be made – the idea of profit overrode any political consideration.

Personally, I did not agree. It seemed to me that Fiji had an uncertain future and that there was a great deal of bitterness and resentment. Unless a democratic constitution was enacted there would be trouble – if the Indians stayed they would be bitter and angry, and if they left there would be economic collapse.

Some neighbors of Ken were old soldiers – part-Fijian – who had served during the Second World War, in the Western Pacific. They had be in the struggle to take Bougainville Island, in the north Solomons. Every night they met Ken under the trees, and sat in the darkness, chatting amiably and drinking beer. I asked them about their role in the war.

"You Americans had a small beach-head, about six miles wide, on Bougainville," a man named George told me. "The rest was held by the Japs. We were trying to get them out. I am not boasting but I can say that we were well trained and we were used to the jungle. We knew better than to wear helmets and we knew how to be very quiet."

He was laughing, perhaps wondering whether I would be insulted by what came next.

"I am sorry to say but your American troops weren't used to the jungle. And there was one of these Negro battalions. All black. Very scary."

It seemed unusual that a Fijian soldier would say this. "You were scared by black soldiers?"

"No. Only by soldiers who shoot at every sound they hear. An American said to me, 'We had to chase them and put shoes on them, and then we sent them over here.' They shot at birds. They shot at each other. They never hit anything! And every morning they did the heebie-jeebies. Heebie-jeebies! Up and down!"

He stood up from his canvas chair, mimicked a prancing minstrel and made his friends laugh.

"One American colonel saw us going into the jungle. He said, 'These men will protect you on your way out.'

"I said, 'No sir! I am going the other way! I don't want these men protecting me!'

"We went on patrol. I was with my men, about six of us. Of course we never talked. We stopped to rest at noon and were lying there, no talking, when I heard a loud click – a helmet hitting a rock. We never wore helmets. If you see pictures of soldiers wearing helmets in the Solomons they are untrue – they are posed.

"Hearing this click, I got up slowly and looked through the bushes. And about fifteen feet away, just on the other side of the bushes were some Jap soldiers, resting, like us."

George was still on his feet, showing us how he had moved in that jungle clearing, still gesturing and whispering hoarsely.

"I signalled to my men to fan out – the right and left. Just hand signals, no talking. Then I gave the signal for – you know what enfilade fire is? Sweeping them with bullets? We did that, caught them in a crossfire, you might say. We killed six of them. We wounded more. We followed the trails of blood but those Japs escaped."

"How did you feel at the end of that day?" I asked.

"Lucky. And tired," George said. "We buried their bodies. We were not savages. We gave everyone we killed a decent burial."

It was said that the Fijian soldiers were so tough, and were preceded by their reputation for ferocity, that surrendering Japanese sought out American marines for fear of being used brutally by Fijians.

There were six or eight other islands, small and large, around Nananu-i-Ra. One, Dolphin Island, was privately owned and on the market for a few million. Another private island was a coconut plantation. I was making a sixteen-mile circuit of Nananu-i-Ra, and had my tent and food with me in case the weather suddenly turned foul. Yet it brightened, the clouds dispersed, the wind dropped, and I was paddling on an incandescent mirror, watching the plopping terns and the patient herons and the kite-like motion of the frigate birds.

Although I was well protected, wearing a shirt and a hat and sunglasses, the blinding light on the ocean drove me into the shore of a bay at noon, where I looked for a shady spot to rest, before pushing on in this circumnavigation of the island.

There were two other people on the beach. I said hello. They had just gone snorkeling on the reef and they too had been driven onto the shade of the beach by the blazing sun.

They were the Garstangs, originally from South Africa but now living in Virginia. Michael was a meteorologist, who had been one of the first people to work on the change in the world's weather pattern and the possibility of a greenhouse effect. He had recently been teaching in New Zealand and was about to embark on a weather expedition to Borneo.

Michael said. "People mainly think about Brazil – the rain forest – when they worry about the ozone layer. But there are three hot spots that determine the world's weather. Brazil, Borneo and Congo–Zaire, the middle of Africa. They produce the heat and the force" – and he pushed upward with his fist – "that drive El Niño."

"Is it just Borneo that's the hot spot?"

"No. New Guinea – the whole region. You probably noticed how warm the water was there. That's another factor."

"Does it bother you that everyone claims to be an expert on global warming?"

He smiled and said, "Not really. But accurate data is very hard to obtain. You might have a calculation on warming, but if there is just the slighest amount of cloud cover your calculation can be thrown off by an enormous amount. The fact is that no one really knows the answer."

"Michael has been studying this for years," Mrs Garstang said.

Michael said, "Did you know there is an ozone surplus in the South Atlantic?"

"I was under the impression there was ozone depletion – an ozone hole," I said.

"Yes. Over Antarctica. But I'm talking about the South Atlantic. This ozone surplus has just been discovered and has only recently been studied."

We stood knee-deep in the lagoon talking about the world's weather, and then about the changes in Fiji – he had first seen the island many years before and said that it had deteriorated. And it struck me that the people who knew Fiji best removed themselves to be as far from Nandi and Suva as possible. The Garstangs had begun their life in America at Wood's Hole, when Michael had worked at the Oceanographic Institute, and so we chatted about Cape Cod – places we knew and liked – and we were so engrossed on this sunny day that it was as though we were there, in a little cove, passing the time of day.

At one point Michael said, "The nineties will be a hot decade" – he seemed to mean by it, lots of action – volcanic activity, earthquakes, storms.

In New Zealand, I had noticed how my memory was provoked by travel – I think this is perhaps true of many people – and how remote places could induce in me the most intense reveries of home. This little conversation at the edge of the lagoon cast a spell upon me. I paddled on in this Cape Cod reverie, my mind was in Nantucket Sound, and so I was startled a few minutes later to see naked Fijian boys with water droplets glistening in their hair, clambering on rocks and flinging coconut husks at each other.

Soon I was in open water, being driven by the same stiff wind that had sped Captain Bligh on his way. I found an empty beach at the western tip of the island, and had lunch, cat food – as this Japanese mackerel now seemed to me – and fruit. I had a nap in the shade of a tree and afterwards went snorkeling. About sixty yards offshore there was a ledge and then great black depths of cold water. Parrot fish and tiny fish, brilliant yellow and blue, glittering like jewels, massed along the ledge of coral and crown-of-thorns starfish, nibbling and darting with a thousand other fish.

I drifted and watched the fish, but I did not linger. Now I knew enough about the features of Oceania to recognize a perfect habitat for sharks. Normally when I snorkeled I kept looking behind me for a shark and this day I was especially careful. And I did not press my luck. I soon swam back to my camp on the beach, and when it was cooler I continued around the island.

Just at dusk, in a lovely orangey-pink lagoon off the last point in the island, wavelets lapped against black rocks. Lingering here, before my last push to circle the island, I marveled at the play of light and shadow, the way the water glowed, and I soon realized that two of the waves were a pair of sharks, with spots on their dorsal fins – epaulet sharks. They were mottled and elegant, and I had a sense that they were playing – simply fooling in the water.

I reached for the spear that I kept tied down on the deck of the kayak. The sharks were each about five feet long, and they were side by side in only a few feet of water. How could I miss? Already I could see myself paddling into the bay, and Ken under his tree with a beer would stand up and goggle at me in my kayak, with two plump sharks slung on my thwarts. Fijians would be dumbstruck seeing my prowess with the spear, my fearlessness at facing sharks. I would say to them, *I learned to deal with sharks in the Trobriand Islands.*

I threw the spear as hard as I could at the nearer shark, and it hit the thickest part of the creature's long body just behind its head. Both sharks thrashed and were gone. No damage was done: in my hurry I had not removed the lump of coconut husk I had rammed on the end of my spear-point – I had been afraid that this sharp trident would puncture my boat. I might have given one of the sharks a bad bruise, but nothing worse than that – and when I thought about it I was glad. The sharks had not menaced me or even bothered me. They were apparently enjoying themselves. But in trying to kill them – so impulsively, from a sense of power and domination – I was behaving with the sort of malicious wickedness that we always attribute to sharks.

One island in this north coast group was often on my mind, because it was visible even at night. This was Malake. It was constantly on fire. During the day it smoked – gray and black smoke billowing from the steep sides of its hills – and at night it was lighted with the flames of circling fires, creeping sideways towards the summits. On my map the island was not much more than a mile long and a half a mile wide. The parts of it that were not on fire were already black.

"They're always burning that bloody island," an old-timer said to me. "They got nothing to do, so they set fires."

I wanted to visit the arsonists of Malake. It was ten miles down-wind – too far to reach and get back on one of these very hot days. So I decided to make an expedition of it, and bring water and food and my tent, and a bunch of *yanggona*. I left early one morning, and helped by the wind I moved swiftly along, listening to the old rock-and-roll songs on my *Big Chill* tape.

It had seemed an unpopulated island – its fires had given it a strange character – but nearer I could see a little settlement, where the arsonists lived, and that it had a distinct reef. The tide was ebbing and the coral protruded so near the surface that in places my boat bumped and snagged. Closer still, I could see signs of cultivation – taro patches, papaya trees, cassava plants. But these were small and they were in the isolated parts of the island. The rest had been burned. I could see the blackened grass, the new erosion, the scorched trees, and the newly dead pines with orangey needles.

The settlement faced the north shore of Viti Levu, but what had seemed a busy village of huts was up close no more than a cluster of tin shacks on a littered beach. I paddled behind the island – the northern slope of the mountain and the foothills that were black from the grass fires.

I paddled out to sea, to avoid the sharp coral that I thought might tear the hull of my boat. And, paddling, I began to feel weary. Until then I had felt healthy, but I had caught a cold somewhere – perhaps at my camp site in Vanua Levu, perhaps from that damned kava, where we all drank from the same coconut shell. Anyway, I was sure that I was coming down with a cold – I had a headache, my eyes hurt, my throat was sore, my nose was blocked, and my muscles ached. The best thing, I felt, would be to go ashore and make camp and simply stay there, resting and keeping out of the sun. I had enough food and water for three days.

Looking for deep water on this coral shelf, I heard a chopping sound from shore – like that of someone cutting wood – and so I paddled away, and put in farther down the coast, on a little bay. As I was tying up my boat on a mangrove root five men materialized from the bushes, brandishing the bush knives that looked like pirates' cutlasses. So these were the arsonists of Malake. They had come out of nowhere.

I was about to get into my boat and paddle away when they surrounded me. I felt foolish. If I tried to escape from them they could easily have stopped me – the water was shallow for some distance, I would have had to paddle carefully because of the coral. One swipe of a knife would sink my boat anyway. So I brazened it out. I said hello. I smiled.

They were ragged Fijians, with the jutting cannibal jaw of the rural Fijian, and the sloping forehead, the tiny eyes, the crow-black mustache. They wore torn shorts and T-shirts.

"Where you come from?"

"Nananu-i-Ra – over there."

"No. What country?"

"America."

"America is very rich."

I was unshaven. I felt ill. I had a collapsible boat. I slopped along in soggy reef shoes, wearing a baseball hat.

"You think I'm rich?"

They stared at me. They were among the poorest Fijians I had seen – they were dirty, their clothes were rags, several of them had teeth missing, which is not only a sign of poverty but suggests violence. Most of all I was wary of their rusty cutlasses.

I said, "Look at me. I am not rich. No money."

They were touching my boat, poking their fingers at its canvas and rubber hull. They could have chopped it – and me – to pieces in a few seconds.

"What are you doing with those knives?"

They did not answer.

"Cutting trees?"

They smiled, meaning no.

"Cutting coconuts?"

The stockiest and toughest and dirtiest one of them had done all the talking so far, and I guessed that only he knew English. Pidgin was not spoken here.

This grubby little man said, "You want coconuts?"

I said yes.

"You come."

Two walked in front of me, three walked behind, and once we were off the beach, walking through the dry yellow bush, the breeze was cut off and without a breeze it was very hot and buggy. There was no path, just the semblance of a track, littered with rubbish from the trees, dead boughs and piles of leaves.

I had not wanted to go with them, but somehow I had agreed. I had thought it would seem unfriendly, not to say cowardly, to refuse. And I had been curious – I had a fatal nosiness in places like this. This was in a sense the ultimate Fiji – the offshore island of an offshore island, where nothing grew except vegetables. No sugar cane, no tourists, no cars, no roads, no electricity. Just a heap of grassy hills burned black and still burning, because the people had nothing better to do. Like the Trobrianders, they called the big island that they could see "the Mainland."

These strange, silent, grubby men had a disconcerting habit. Whenever we passed a particularly shapely bush they assaulted it, and hacked it to pieces. Even before we had left the beach one of the men had attacked a mangrove, smashing his cutlasses against the frail branches, whipping at the leaves and the trunk – his nostrils flaring – and finally demolishing the tree, leaving the white slashed bits of it lying in the mud.

He had cut it for the sheer wicked hell of it, just like that, vandalized it, the way kids in big cities snap the trunks of saplings that have recently been planted.

I found that alarming, the suddenness of it, a filthy little man going to town on a tree with his rusty knife. It was nasty-mindedness, and a show of strength, and ill-will. They weren't clearing a path or anything like that – it was just dicking around. But it also reminded me of that moment in the Melville story, *Benito Cereno*, when the mutineers smile and sharpen their knives – and come to think of it, these men looked malevolent enough to have been members of that mutinous crew.

I was dizzy from the heat, and it was odd to be with five other people when I was usually alone. This part of the island was penetrated with a smoky odor and I could see some of the burned hillsides – the burned areas looked much worse up close. The landscape looked devastated. It was as though they were simply destroying their island.

"Why do you burn the trees?"

"Yes, we burn the trees. We burn. We burn." The little man gestured with his knife.

We were well into the island now, walking across the lower slopes of the hills. I thought about turning back – inventing an excuse and taking off. That was when I saw the palms.

"There are the coconuts," I said.

This seemed to confuse them. It was as though they had forgotten why we had come here.

"Who will climb the tree?" I asked.

There was some mumbling.

"That boy will climb."

But the boy was hacking at a stunted tree, whacking its fragile trunk apart. He turned, he looked up, he spoke some words – mumble, mumble – in the sulkiest way.

*I am not climbing that tree for anyone.*

The stocky little man said something more, and the young man mumbled again and hacked the stunted tree with his cutlass.

*If that white man wants a coconut he can climb the tree himself.*

The funny thing was that I actually did want a coconut. I was thirsty, and I still felt faint. But we stood in silence in the heat. I tried to take a deep breath and realized that my lungs were congested. So I had creeping bronchitis. I wheezed and sat down. I hated this. I thought of the time in the Trobriands when I had had a paronychia – infection of my thumbnail – and I had had to boil my thumb twice a day to keep the infection down. And small children would gather round, watching me pump my stove, and fill my pot, and boil my thumb.

I put my head in my hands.

"No. We go."

It was another one, speaking English – a fat man, with teeth missing, slashing with his knife.

I said, "I can't go with you."

"Yes," he insisted.

"No. Because," and now I was thinking hard, "I want to bring you *yanggona*."

They chewed their lips and smiled, recognizing the word.

"And my *yanggona* is at my boat. In my *waga*, see."

I pointed through the yellow bushes towards the shore.

"You give us?"

"Yes. I give you. But first" – and I was smiling in terror, like a hostage promising his ransom – "I have to get it for you."

I kept talking, promising, smiling, trying to sound reasonable – I had an irrational thought that as long as I kept talking they wouldn't kill me. It seemed rude and unsporting to stab someone to death while he was talking to you. Still, I felt uneasy with these men walking behind me, and the idiots kept whacking innocent trees.

I handed over a bunch of *yanggona* wrapped in the *Fiji Times*, and while they clawed it open, I untied my boat. One of them called out, "Come back!"

"I'll be right back!" I said, and climbed into my boat.

*Sure*, I thought. But I still felt rotten. Instead of heading away from the island I paddled towards its western tip, where there was a rocky headland. Near shore I heard someone mumbling, not to me, nor about my approach; it was the monotonous yammering of someone talking to himself – just blabbing aimlessly. I kept going until, on an isolated beach, surrounded by rock, I found the sort of sheltered area that had the look of a camp site that fishing parties probably used. It was secluded, a cubbyhole against a cliff, with part of it open to the sea.

Thinking that hot liquid might be good for my cold, I boiled some water and made green tea and soup. After that I began to perspire. I lay down and went to sleep I was so tired.

When I woke, it was too late to go back. I carefully made a circuit of the perimeter of the little beach. I looked and listened for strangers. There was no one. And I knew no one would come out at night – no one wandered out in the dark here.

I waited until the last moment, sitting, listening carefully, and just before night fell and the mosquitoes swarmed, I pitched my tent and crawled in and slept for nine hours, waking just before dawn to the smell of burning and then I remembered that I was on Malake, island of arsonists. The sleep had restored me. I made more green tea, and had beans and bread for breakfast and set off around the other side of the island, to pass the settlement of Malake village.

I paddled near it, but when I saw the ragged people waving me to shore, and the old men, and the small children, their faces shining with snot, I turned my boat to catch the incoming current that would take me east and away from here.

Farther on, feeling freer, I experienced something that had happened to me in the Trobriands, in the Solomons, in Vanuatu, and again and again in the offshore waters of Fiji. Paddling along, the sound of the paddle or the slosh of the boat would startle the fish, and they would leap from the water and skim across the waves, shimmying upright, balancing on their tails – more than one, often eight or ten fish dancing across my bow as I paddled towards a happy island. It entranced me whenever it happened, because it was comic and unexpected, as though the fish had been bewitched into unfish-like behavior, walking upright on the surface of the water.

But I had not been wrong about feeling unwell. Soon after, I ran a temperature of 103 and the doctor diagnosed pneumonia.

"Bloody Indians, what do they know?" a Fijian said.

I suffered for a few days, and then took antibiotics and simply felt frail and lonely, but after a few weeks I was breathing normally. Oceania was a wonderful place if you were healthy, but it was the worst place on earth if you felt sick.

# PART THREE
# POLYNESIA

# 14

## Tonga: The Royal Island of Tongatapu

A big square-headed Tongan official in a blue skirt with a hem below his chunky knees, after asking me the usual questions about my boat bags, said, "You must pay wharfage."

*Wharfage?* He had to repeat it several times before I understood. And then I jibbed. Wharfage was payment for a boat's use of a wharf, surely, but my boat was in two canvas bags and where was the wharf?

We were standing in a wooden shed at the Fua'amotu Airport on the island of Tongatapu with other burly jostling Tongans, many of them wearing big crunchy mats around their waist to celebrate their arrival home. Some of them carried Desert Storm videos – the war so far – that they had bought in Fiji, from Indians who had pirated footage from CNN television news and then sold for sixty Fijian dollars each.

I told the man that it was a rather small collapsible boat, and I described it.

Ignoring me, he began to fill out a form which was headed *Kingdom of Tonga* and under "Description of goods" he wrote, "1 boat" and under *wharfage* he wrote "*Two pa'anga, fourty cents*". Two dollars. That calmed me. I paid in Fiji dollars, the handiest cash I had.

Then I declared on my printed form that I had no "potable spirits . . . fruit or micro-organisms . . . used bicycles . . . obscene books . . . indecent photographs . . . fireworks . . . noxious, stupefying or tear gas."

What struck me was how sturdy these Tongans were and what a filthy little place this terminal was. That contrast continued to puzzle me in Tonga, the physical power of the people – their big solid bodies, in great contrast to the decrepitude of their flimsy houses and island structures.

"What you are doing in Tonga?"

"Just looking around," I said. "A little paddling."

*I want to see the King*, I almost said. I intended eventually to go to the northern archipelago, called Vava'u, and camp on a desert island – there were many in that group. But what I wanted to do on this island was meet His Majesty, King Taufa'ahau Tupou IV, the King of Tonga.

Salesi and Afu Veikune and their friend, Mrs Vahu, I was told, might be able to help me in my royal audience. Like many Tongans, Afu had spent some years as a house servant for a family in Honolulu. Salesi had been a driver for Budget-Rentacar – his sign read *Your Courteous Driver is Salesi Veikune*. Mrs Vahu had worked for Budget in San Francisco.

Menials and drivers, you would say. But that was in America. In Tonga they had royal connections. Afu, a mediocre cook, scorching eggs and Spam in Honolulu, had been the lady-in-waiting to the famous and much-loved Queen Salote of Tonga, the present King's mother. Afu's father was a *Tui*, a chief, and a considerable landowner. Their son had married a royal cousin. The King had come to the wedding. They were closely acquainted with princes and princesses. The present Queen often visited their house. Never mind that in Hawaii one drove a bus and the other did housework; in Tonga they were highly regarded, they had land, they had power, and they owned more fat black pigs than I had ever seen snorting and oinking in one place.

"Maybe you talk to Mr Mo'ungaloa," Afu said. She did most of the talking. Even after many years in America, Salesi was uncomfortable speaking English. Perhaps that was a result of the occupational hazard of his work. *Do not speak to the driver while the bus is moving*, another of his signs had said.

"Who is Mr Mo'ungaloa?"

"The King's secretary."

"Putt dee no workeen now," Mrs Vahu said. "Dee haveen lanch."

We were traveling at fifteen miles an hour along Taufa'ahau Road, the main thoroughfare of Nuku'alofa ("Abode of Love"). From the airport to the capital we passed twenty-seven Mormon churches – some of the villages had two of them. This was Polynesia for sure. The road was riddled with pot-holes, which accounted for our slow speed. No one drove fast anywhere in Tonga. The roads were appalling. The buildings were grim, too. You would look at this royal capital and probably sum up its stricken look by guessing, *Severe shortages*.

But this was not so. The place was unattended to and beneath notice. Islanders on Tongatapu were personally neat and tidy, though of a dour temperament, and they lived in a state of continuous disorder. Certainly, Nuku'alofa was in greater disrepair than any island capital I had seen since Honiara, back in the Solomons. Not long ago, perhaps at the time of King Tupou's coronation in 1967, this might have seemed a charming place, with its crumbling stucco churches, its wooden shops, its wooden Royal Palace – the only wooden palace on earth. It had lost whatever charm it had had. It seemed simply neglected, but like many neglected backwaters in the world it had the great virtue of very little traffic.

Nuku'alofa had no visible industry. It looked dusty and down-at-heel. Even its singular building the Royal Palace resembled nothing so much as a Christian church, wooden and white, with a bulky steeple and a prospect of the sea – indeed, Christianity came into full flower with the approval of the monarchy. Nothing locally made was for sale in Nuku'alofa except postage stamps. What money it had came from the remittances of Tongans in Meganesia – Auckland in particular – and in America, mainly Hawaii, where Tongans were employed as domestics, gardeners, car-washers and tree-trimmers. Pretty stamps and family remittances were the standbys of other destitute countries in Oceania, such as the Philippines and Samoa, which produced immigrants.

Another source of revenue in Tonga – a bizarre one – has been the sale of Tongan passports. This was the brainchild of a Hong Kong Chinese man, one Mr George Chen, who was asked by the Tongan King for advice on how to raise revenue. "Sell passports," Mr Chen said, knowing that many would be sought after by Hong Kongers who watched with horror the approach of the People's Republic takeover of the colony in 1997. For $10,000, someone who was otherwise stateless could become a Tongan Protected Person (TPP) and carry a Tonga passport, which conferred the freedom to travel to any country in the world except Tonga, where a TPP was forbidden to settle.

When some countries considered these passports invalid, the King was informed and a new model Tongan passport went on sale for $20,000 (or $35,000 for a family of four). This gave the holder Tongan nationality and a right to settle. South Africans and Libyans, as well as hundreds of Hong Kong Chinese, were quick to snap up these passports. Imelda Marcos bought one, and in the process became a Tongan citizen. In the past seven years this has produced $30 million for Tonga as well as a constitutional crisis – angry Tongans demonstrating their opposition to the sale of Tongan nationality, calling for the limitation of the King's powers (because His Majesty approved the whole thing) and demanding to know what happened to the money.

And another source of wealth was the returning Tongans, like Afu and Salesi, who had made a few dollars overseas, and who had come back to retire and sit under the trees and raise pigs.

"That is Queen Salote's grave," Afu said, pointing across a weedy field to what looked like a war memorial surrounded by a large iron fence.

Queen Salote (Tongan for Charlotte) had more or less upstaged Queen Elizabeth at her own coronation in 1953. It rained hard that day. Tongan custom insists that in order to show respect you must demonstrate humility, and you cannot imitate the person you are honoring. At the first sign of rain, Queen Elizabeth's footmen put the hood on her carriage as it rolled towards Westminster Abbey. Hoods were raised on the rest of the carriages in the procession – all but one, that of the Queen of Tonga. She sat, vast and saturated and majestic, her hair streaming with rain, in a carriage that was awash; and from that moment she earned the love and affection of every person in Britain.

Only one person mocked the Queen of what had once been cannibal islands – Noël Coward. Queen Salote sat in the carriage with a tiny retainer. "Who is that person with the Queen of Tonga?" someone asked and Coward quipped, "Her lunch."

"But what shall I tell Mr Mo'ungaloa?"

"Tell him who you are," Afu said. "He wishes to check your background."

"What does he want to find in my background?"

"Nice tings," Mrs Vahu said.

Salesi chuckled in a wheezing way at the thought of this. Did he know something? He was big and slow, and when he uttered a word, he was soft-spoken. He was fat and fifty-eight. As we wobbled through the holes in the road, the car jounced and the mat around his waist made crunching noises, like a cow chewing hay. I found the crunching of his waist mat oddly satisfying. Sometimes it sounded like a cookie being crumbled.

We went to a small red-roofed building in another weedy field. This was outside the high fence of the Royal Palace and was the Secretary's Office. We all entered the building together, and they were like parents on my first day at school. There was an open room with some desks and perhaps ten fat men in skirts sitting and bantering with each other in Tongan. You could almost determine a person's social status from his obesity – these chunky men were all nobles. They also wore layers of fraying mats around their midriff.

Though they hardly knew me, Afu and Salesi and Mrs Vahu energetically testified to my fine character, and at last Mr Mo'ungaloa agreed to see me.

"Yes?"

Mr Mo'ungaloa was a small bespectacled man in a cramped side office. It was an unprepossessing cubicle for the royal secretary, but perhaps no stranger than the outer office with its hooting fatties.

"You wish to see the King?"

"Very much," I said. And I went on to say that about fifteen years before I had met Crown Prince Tupou'toa in London. He was about my age. He had been to the Military Academy at Sandhurst. He played the piano. He had formed his own jazz combo called The Straight Bananas.

"Prince Tupou'toa is now the foreign minister," Mr Mo'ungaloa said. He had winced at my innocent mention of The Straight Bananas.

The prince was unmarried and it was said that he could often be found in one of Nuku'alofa's clubs, an easy task to find him therefore, since there were not more than two clubs. His family was still pestering him for an heir.

A photograph of the prince showed him to be wearing a much larger size uniform than in his London days. There were also photographs of Queen Salote, and old Tongan kings – including the first Christian king, George Tupou I (baptized in 1831), and of the British Royal Family. A framed letter from the President of the All-Japan Karate-Do, stated in English and Japanese that King Taufa'ahau Tupou IV had been created an "Honorary 7th Dan" in Karate. There were other obsequious letters, and a friendly one from Betty herself, the Queen of England, in which she was described as Queen of the Realm and Defender of the Faith, and addressed to His Majesty.

"Sendeth Greeting! Our Good Friend!" this one began, which interested me as a salutation – so this was how one amiable monarch wrote to another. In this letter she was introducing the British High Commissioner, praising his accomplishments, and wishing him well, and she signed off with a formula to the effect that it was 1970 *in the 19th Year of Our Reign* and ended, *Your Good Friend, Elizabeth R.*

Why frame that letter and not all the others she must have sent? But I didn't ask Mr Mo'ungaloa. I was busily trying to impress him with my seriousness.

I wrote books, I said. I was traveling in the Pacific. Had he ever read the *National Geographic Magazine*? I sometimes appeared in those pages. I was very interested in the peoples of Oceania – in their voyages (Mr Mo'ungaloa stifled a yawn), and their arts and crafts. I had once been a university professor. Mr Mo'ungaloa's eyes were glazing over. I had recently been to Fiji, I said, and before that, the Solomons.

"Which university do you teach at?"

"Used to teach," I said. "Oh, several."

"And you are presently working for?"

"I am unemployed at the moment," I said. "I mean, I write for a living, but I don't have a job. One with a salary, that is. This sounds much worse than it actually is."

But I thought: an unemployed middle-aged foreigner in a sun-faded shirt shows up unannounced, claiming to be a writer, and asks to see the King. If I had been the secretary I would have sent me away.

Incredibly, he said that the King would see me. What did I wish to discuss with His Majesty?

"Nuclear policy in the Pacific? Polynesian migration? The future of tourism?"

Mr Mo'ungaloa seemed satisfied.

"The King will talk freely," he said, with confidence, and we settled on a date and time for my royal audience.

After they vouched for me at short notice, saying how well they knew me and what a splendid person I was, it seemed only right that we give some reality to this sudden fiction. I made an effort to know the Veikunes and Mrs Vahu better. They told me that although they had spent many years in the United States they had always intended to return to Tonga.

Afu said, "We came back because Tonga is our home."

They showed me a picture of an Eskimo. He was dark, his cheeks gleamed, he was squinting out of a fur hood, he was wearing a thick parka, and snow and ice was crusted to the fence-post just behind him. Was this Jerry Amlaqachapuk, an Inuit? No it was not.

"This is our son. He lives in Alaska," Afu said. "Ketchikan."

Salesi whispered, "It is very cold there. I no like."

Mrs Vahu, who was only in her middle thirties, and was chubby and very cheerful, had six children, ranging in age from three to fourteen. All the children had been born in the United States, and had American passports, and yet Mrs Vahu had decided to head home.

"I came here because I want my children to know *faka tonga*, the Tonga way. It is more expensive, and very little work. But it is better for them."

They were not unusual in their having returned. It was a proven fact that of all the islanders in the Pacific, Tongans found it hardest to adapt to other cultures – to the work, the stress, the deadlines, the moods and way of life – and a very high proportion returned to Tonga. They told horror stories about New Zealand and Australia and America to their relatives who had wisely stayed on the islands. Tonga was simply Tongans. Tonga had never been colonized or conquered, except in the profoundly ambiguous way that Christian missionaries managed. This involved preaching against evil and nakedness, and solemnly convincing people that they were sinners, their bodies were shameful, and generally encouraging the intense and rather joyous hypocrisy that you find among God-fearing people.

Tongans did not know the world, nor did the world know them. Even their King, one of the last absolute monarchs on earth, was known only as a very fat man − his weight was given whenever his name was mentioned. This made about as much sense as regarding the British queen's small stature as important: "Five foot two inches high Queen Elizabeth," such a sentence might begin. There were few expatriates and hardly any tourists in these islands. The tourists that did visit saw that Nuku'alofa, the royal capital, was a backwater, just a small seedy town, and became visibly depressed. And seldom have I felt more unwelcome at a hotel than when checking into what is regarded as Nuku'alofa's best hotel, the International Dateline. (The smaller grubby places were full.) I carried my own bags, including my boat, although the lobby was thronged by able-bodied Tongan hotel staff. And when I asked for someone to show me to my room, the desk clerk snorted and pointed and said, "Up dey! Too-oh-tree! Turd flo!" as though to an imbecile. When I remarked on this to people who knew the place I was told that Tongans were renowned for their unhelpfulness, unless they knew you, in which case they made you one of the family. Yet one of the family was a condition I had no wish to enter into, here or anywhere.

There was little understanding of − and no interest in − the outer world, apart from the worst of its popular culture, rock music and violent videos (there was as yet no television in Tonga). Tongans regarded non-Tongans with a kind of pity and disdain, as though they were all sinners and suckers, and people who foolishly worked their heads off. Tongans had a reputation for thievery that exceeded even that of the light-fingered Samoans, but only in Tonga did I suffer serious theft − a rather nice pen, my Walkman, my 300-dollar cowboy belt with the silver buckle. Towards each other Tongans seemed to have more complex attitudes − different from anything I had seen so far. Quite early on in my travels in Tonga I found that Tongans regarded each other with a certain amount of envy and suspicion, and these were the only islands in Oceania where I discerned an attitude that I could describe as haughty.

"Honolulu was nice," Afu said. "Good work, good money. Plenty of Tongans there."

That seemed consistent: Tongans could not live or operate in a place where there were no other Tongans.

"But California," Mrs Vahu said, heaving a sigh.

"You didn't like it?" I asked.

"Well, Los Angeles, sorry to say, is full of colored people," Mrs Vahu said. "They just sitteen around. Watcheen you. Hey, you can get scared of them! You see them standeen. So many colored people!"

I guessed that the snobberies, the racial confusion and suspicion I detected in Tonga might have arisen because of the Tongan class system in which there was a king and nobles and an aristocracy at the top and landless peasants at the bottom. And when I inquired, Afu said that there was indeed a strict class system and each class had its own language. Royalty had its own language, and a Tongan fortunate enough to speak to the King had to use an archaic tongue, which was totally dissimilar from the language spoken by all Tongan commoners. In between, the nobles had their own language, which bore no resemblance to either of the other two languages.

"But can you tell a noble people when you see them?"

"We know them," Afu said. "And we also know their children. And when they have girlfriends, and those friends has children, we know who they are."

Afu went on to say that Tonga was full of noble – and in some cases royal – bastards. Some of the Tongan kings had had mistresses who had borne them children, and so there was an illegitimate line, much as there was in Europe, but unlike Europe these secret nobles occasionally became useful. If a nobleman had one child, a daughter, who was rather hopelessly single and there was a danger of the line dying out with her childlessness, one of these royal bastards would be rustled up – everyone would know that though his mother was common his antecedents were regal – and a marriage would be arranged. His children would inherit his father-in-law, the nobleman's title, because this bastard's blood was noble enough – and everyone knew it. This was, after all, a small group of islands, with a total population of less than 100,000. Being noble could be a meal ticket. Among other things it could get you a seat in the King's rubber-stamp Legislative Assembly, half of which was noble and non-elective, chosen by other nobles.

The commoners tended to emigrate or else become Mormons, though this often amounted to the same thing.

"They think if they become Mormons they will go to America," a Tongan told me.

And it was true; many are sent to Salt Lake City to delve deeper into the sanctities of Mormonism. But the Mormons also looked after their flocks in Tonga and they took up a lot of social slack, built clinics and schools, as well as their interminable Latter Day Saints' churches, all of which looked like Dairy Queen franchises.

My audience with the King was still almost a week off, and so I tried to make the most of being in Nuku'alofa. It was the sleepiest, the dustiest, the slowest, and one of the poorest of the Pacific ports. Honiara was uglier, Port Moresby much more dangerous, Papeete tackier, and Apia more sluttish and decrepit, but there was something extraordinary and unmoveable about Tongan torpor – it was both regal and lazy. Some Tongans were friendly, but few were cooperative, and it was maddeningly difficult to make onward plans. Phones didn't work, offices were empty or locked when they should have been open, and in some placcs I was simply waved away – too much trouble, it seemed. It was a society that was used to dealing with beachcombers, who had all the time in the world.

I was trying to make arrangements to travel to Vava'u, a large archipelago about a hundred and seventy miles north of this island Tongatapu. There were fifty islands in the Vava'u group and many of them, I had been assured, were uninhabited. A boat left Nuku'alofa once a week for Vava'u.

"It is better you take plane," Salesi said.

"I want to catch the boat."

"Plane is better."

"I prefer the boat," I said.

"Boats make you seasick," Salesi said.

"I don't think so."

"I get sick every time."

That was a familiar refrain. In Polynesia I rarely met anyone who did not claim to get horribly seasick on a boat, no matter how short the trip. Even on the brief inter-island ferry rides this race of ancient mariners puked their guts out.

Again I was surprised by the Tongans as physical specimens. The girls and women were the most attractive I had seen so far – not just winsome and willing, as Melanesians had been, bare-breasted, with their shrieking laughter and their splayed feet, nudging you in the guts after each wisecrack or snatching with tough hard hands. These Tongans were elegant – it was something in their posture, in their features, many actually looked noble – a prince here, a princess there. Something in their very langor (a nice word for laziness, after all) was sensual. Of course, many were fat and jolly, the big soft women, the chunky web-footed men, each fat Tongan packed with Pacific Brand corned beef, with salt, fat, natural juices and nitrites.

Men and women, old and young, walked slowly and very erect. Each person wore a mat tied around his or her waist, and some of these mats were no larger than a cummerbund, though some were enormous flaking carpets, crunched and wound clumsily around a person's midsection, making them look even fatter, and some of the mats twisted and dragged and frayed against the ground.

None the less, in these days of preparation in Nuku'alofa, I could not remember having seen a people so bereft of enterprise, so slow of speech, so casual in manner, so indifferent to a schedule, so unable or unwilling to anticipate. Being inattentive, they were physically clumsy and had little manual dexterity. They dropped things, they forgot things, they broke promises. They drove slowly – who else in the world did that?

Salesi had a friend, Alipate. He had done Alipate a favor – something connected with land. By way of returning this favor to Salesi, Alipate looked after me for a while. Alipate was a wily bird, and rather unwilling. Sometimes after we agreed to meet, because I needed a ride – which he had offered – he didn't turn up. The concept of face-saving was nearly as important in Tonga as it was in China. I could not mention that he had let me down. I had to pretend to be grateful to him, and Salesi, for a favor neither of them had done me. In fact reneging on the promise had complicated things for me – I had had to get a taxi, not an easy matter in a place where phones seldom worked. I visited the sacred flying foxes of Kolovai – feathery casuarina trees draped with great shitting fruit bats – without Alipate's promised ride.

"We are going to be late," I said one day to Alipate.

We were on our way to the airline office. Since the boat wasn't going this week to Vava'u I would have to fly.

"Yes, but they will be late," Alipate said.

This was *faka tonga*, the Tongan way.

Desperate to involve myself, I took an interest in Tongan graves. These were not the ancient pyramids and terraces and stately mounds that I saw elsewhere in the Pacific, but rather small earth mounds ringed with beer bottles shoved into the dirt. Granny's grave, Mom's grave, little Taviti's grave. Some were in fenced-off plots, under large cloth canopies, with embroidered tapestries flapping in the wind – Jesus, the Last Supper, crosses; and underneath them, rows of Foster's Beer cans, arranged symmetrically; or red banners and bunting; or tinsel –

Christmas decorations were popular on Tongan graves, and Christmas was a long way off. They were everywhere, by the roadside, in cemeteries filled with big flapping banners and the funereal beer bottles, and in the yards of little huts, the grave being an adjunct to the house. Some were strung with tassels, or plastic flowers, or bunches of yellow ribbon; some had bottles as well as beer cans on the periphery; some had wind-chimes. Chinese funerals sometimes looked like this, but in a few days the ribbons were gone and the banners removed. In the case of Tonga the graves were everlastingly decorated.

Here and there was a tiny bungalow on a lawn, with windows, a little dwelling that you might mistake for a dog house. But no, it was a mausoleum – there was a grave inside.

While I was out visiting graves, someone stole my pajama bottoms. I had moved to a different hotel in the meantime but it seemed you were robbed wherever you went. (And isn't hotel-room theft the worst? The thief sees you leave the room and they have all the time in the world to take what they want.) I was fond of the pajama bottoms. The great thing about camping on islands was that you could wear your pajama bottoms all day.

I went to three tailor shops in Nuku'alofa and asked whether they could make me some more pajama bottoms. The women in these shops sat idly, propped against their sewing-machines, not working.

"We are too busy," was the excuse at one shop. At another: "We are making school uniforms." At the third: "Come back in a month."

But I persevered and found a willing woman and her assistant, a boy who in the Tongan way had been raised as a girl – because there were no girls in the family, and a girl was needed. He was known as a *faka leiti* ("like a lady") and he was helpful – responsive, competent. He conferred with his boss, who did not speak English. Yes, he said, they could make two pairs of pajama bottoms in a few days, for twenty dollars.

I decided to suspend judgment on Tonga – I would not generalize from what I saw in Nuku'alofa, and I wrote in my diary: *Tonga is itself.* It had no investors, no immigrants, no history of occupation by foreigners. It had no desire to see strangers. Long-termers were actively discouraged. They did not even issue tourist visas to Fijian Indians (Fiji was only an hour away by jumbo jet) for fear they would stay and contaminate this Christian kingdom with Islam. I wondered whether there was another group of islands in the Pacific that was so much itself – one people, one language, one set of customs, one way.

Or was it changing? Viliami Ongosia, who lived in a lopsided hut outside Nuku'alofa, had once been a Methodist. But recently he had switched his allegiance to the Assembly of God. I asked him why. He said, "Because it has more spirit."

"Methodists drink and Methodists don't do what they say" – hypocrites, he implied, without using the word. These happy-clappy religions were gaining ground, and even the Jimmy Swaggart Ministries had a following in Vanuatu, on the island of Efate. They sold video cassettes of Swaggart himself, the old whore-hopper preaching his head off, and of course they solicited funds.

Viliami, like Salesi, became so seasick that although his mother was from Vava'u and most of his relatives lived there, he never went to the islands – the boat was out of the question, and he couldn't afford the plane fare. He had sailed there once. He said, "I was so seasick I thought I was going to die. I could not hold my head up straight. It was terrible."

I liked hearing stories of Polynesian seasickness. It was like discovering people you had always regarded as cannibals to be vegetarians. In fact, the Tongans had once been nearly as cannibalistic as the Fijians, but unlike the Fijians, who gloried in their cannibal past, the Tongans made nothing of it and seemed to resent any mention of it.

One year, seeking work, Viliami had gone to Fiji. He found no work, though he had gotten on well with the Fijians.

"But the Fijians are Melanesians and you are a noble Polynesian," I said.

He smiled; he knew I was being sarcastic. He said, "I like them. They are good people."

"What about the Indians there?"

"I never talk to them. They just look at me, and I look at them. They know how to save money."

"How?"

"They carry their lunch to work. Just some curry. Never go to restaurants, never spend money."

"Tongans go to restaurants all the time, of course," I said, watching him closely. "Nuku'alofa is full of wonderful restaurants and delicious food."

He shrugged. "But we don't carry our food in a bag." And he explained, "We too lazy to cook at home. We don't care about saving money. But the Indians, they don't eat meat – no pig, no cow, no horse."

Vegetarianism was a way of saving money: it was not only a Tongan point of view. I had heard Fijians say as much. Vegetables were cheap. The expense in any of these island households was the meat supply. In a word, it was the high price of corned beef, imported from New Zealand. But if money was plentiful what these Tongans wanted was to get their teeth into a roast pig.

"And the Indians don't eat dogs," I said.

"Yes. No dog."

"And no fruit bats."

"Yes. No fruit bat." He smiled. "You like fruit bat?"

"Never ate one, Viliami."

"Taste good."

"I'm sure," I said. "In a soup?"

"No. *Umu*." The underground oven had a similar name all over the Pacific.

"What about dogs? You stew them or *umu* them?"

"Always *umu*. I like to eat dogs but I don't like to look at it when they are cutting it. I don't want to see it. But it is all right in the oven. And I like to eat the dog meat."

We were at the seafront, on a beach, watching some young girls swimming. A group of boys were also watching. This being Tonga the girls swam and thrashed into the water with all their clothes on. It was unheard of – because it was sinful – for any girl to wear a bathing-suit. And because wet clothes could be so revealing, the girls wore several layers – two shirts, two soggy skirts, trousers. They shrieked, mimicking suicide, and rolled off the pier, then thrashed and climbed back onto the pier, streaming with water, wearing every article of clothing known to man, and grinning with great big booby faces. It was a wonder they didn't drown.

After a while, Viliami, who had a strong Tongan accent, uttered an incomprehensible sentence.

"Tocks putt not gets."

Perhaps this was Tongan? No, what he meant was, *Dogs but not cats*.

"But does anyone in Tonga eat cats?"

"Plenty people in the bush eating cats. Not in Nuku'alofa, they don't eat," implying the enormous sophistication of not indulging in cat stew, "but in the bush, they do eat them and they say, 'We eat *gets!*'"

The Tongans talked about food a great deal of the time. I was sheltering in a doorway one night during a drenching rain on my way back to my hotel (where, because of the terrible service, I swore I would never eat). In this same doorway was a Tongan named Koli, a man of about thirty.

After a while he said, "Boll, you like Tonga girls?"

"Yes," I said. "Do you like American girls?"

He thought a moment, and then said, "No, I don't like."

The rain fell. The road was flooded. You could not walk – the pot-holes brimmed, the monsoon drain was clogged. The rain had brought darkness to Nuku'alofa.

"Boll."

"Yes?"

"You like Tonga food?"

"Do you mean dogs and cats and horses and fruit bats?"

"Everyting."

"I have not eaten much of that food."

"Boll. You come to my house. You eat Tonga food. My wife cook it."

"Maybe sometime," I said, and thought: Perhaps I have them wrong. Perhaps they are friendly and warm and hospitable. But I had never found them nasty – that wasn't the issue; I had found them unpredictable.

A Tongan Sunday was even deader than a Fijian Sunday. It began at midnight Saturday, when everything shut until Monday morning. At 5am on Sunday the church bells rang, and soon after a dirge-like harmonizing was heard from every Methodist chapel and every Free Wesleyan church. At 10pm that same night the voices were still raised in song, in praise of the Lord. And once during the day. Tongans went to church three times on Sunday, and they roundly condemned anyone who failed to. If you wanted to go snorkeling or swimming you had to make arrangements to do it on an offshore island.

*The Sabbath*, an official government handout stated, *from midnight Saturday until midnight Sunday, is a day of rest in Tonga. The law says it shall be kept holy and no person shall practise his trade or profession, or conduct any commercial undertaking on the Sabbath. Any agreement made or document witnessed on the Sabbath shall be counted null and void of no legal effect. Please do not date your cheques on a Sunday . . .*

No planes land or take off on a Tongan Sunday. No one is allowed to play games or to swim – Tongans are fined or given three months in jail for violating this law.

"Would it be appropriate for me to jog today?" an American asked – rather delicately I felt – at the hotel.

The answer was no: it was sacrilegious. If anyone was observed enjoying themselves on a Sunday there was hell to pay. Yet I never saw any evidence, in Tonga or elsewhere, that the sabbath exertion of three church services, three sermons, umpteen hymns and all those prayers made them better people the rest of the week. They were usually late, unapologetic, envious, abrupt, lazy, mocking, quarrelsome, and peculiarly sadistic to their children. On small islands where there were two different churches, the church members fought.

They claimed to observe the proprieties. It was for example unthinkable (and illegal) in Tonga to be without a shirt in a public place, and their crunchy waist-mats were always neatly tied, and they constantly alluded to their loyalties towards *faka tonga*, the Tongan way. And yet they spat, they swore, they shouted, they razzed outsiders, they threw my change at me in shops, they seemed to consider it an indignity to carry anything for me, and certainly not my heavy bags.

"They often let air out of my tires," the captain of a sailboat told me. A New Zealander who had been in Nuku'alofa for a short time, this man's present means of livelihood was ferrying people back and forth to the outer islands on Sunday. On these islands you could swim undisturbed. But the penalty for this was that he frequently came back to his van and found the tires flat. Who did it?

"Church people," he said.

They were the Tongan equivalent of the *mutawwaain*, the religious police of fanatic Arabia, who throw paint on unveiled women, and who once pushed my brother Peter into a mosque to pray because infidel horoscopes ("the evil work of credulous infidels") appeared in the pages of the newspaper he worked for in Riyadh.

Still waiting for the day of my audience with the King, I went on one of these Sunday day-trips with Big Jim, skinny Dick and their wives. They were from San Clemente, California. Bob was retired from the auto parts business. We talked about the drought in southern California. I said that it was odd that the government did not supply water to every household. Jim said, "That's socialism!"

Why was it that Republicans traveled all over the world, shouting their views, and that it was so seldom that one found oneself listening to a fellow American deploring, say, capital punishment?

Dick was more reasonable. We talked about the Gulf War and skeet shooting.

As for their wives, "They love shelling. They're happy as long as they're shelling," Jim said.

Shelling was what a lot of people did on luxury vacations.

Jim, I discovered, simply liked to be blunt, if not downright crude.

He was fairly stupid and rather prided himself on his vulgarity. Later, he walked by me while I was eating alone, and slapped me on the back, jostling the plate on my lap, and said, "How do you like that mess?"

The only other people on this Sunday jaunt were Steve and Anne. We were talking about Japanese honeymooners in Hawaii, where they had just been, and Anne said, "Just like us."

They wore identical baseball hats that said *Oregon*, though they themselves were from Burbank, California. "They were a gift from a friend," Steve explained. They were a small-sized couple and seemed ill-at-ease – still getting acquainted with each other. Anne was the talker, Steve a self-confessed introvert. They had met at a community choir – they were both singers – on 30 October 1989. By Christmas, Steve had marriage in mind. Anne took a bit longer to decide. It was more or less settled by March of the following year that they would marry. A year of seeing each other, as the expression goes, and they were married two weeks ago – two weddings, one small Saturday nuptial at a Russian Orthodox church (Anne: "I converted. I used to be a Methodist") and a big one, a hundred and fifty-odd people, on Sunday at Steve's Episcopal church. Their community choir had sung at the service. Then early the next morning to Honolulu, two nights at the New Otani Hotel ncar Waikiki and – possibly a mistake, Steve felt – a luau, or Hawaiian party, at Germaine's.

"It was an hour and a half bus ride," he explained in his gentle way. He had a high voice and was a small, sweet-tempered man. "The bus ride was more or less dominated by the other people."

"Who were they?"

"An Australian rugby team," he said, "and they were drunk."

"Good God," I said. And then, as he smiled, perhaps recalling the ordeal of listening to the rugby team's singing, I said, "What line of work are you in, Steve?"

He cleared his throat and adjusted his slightly-too-large baseball hat and said, "I'm a nuclear astrophysicist."

It said as much on his business card: *Stephen E. Kellog – Nuclear Astrophysicist*, a Pasadena address, a Caltech address (his lab) and a little quotation from Walt Whitman that ran, *I believe that a blade of grass is no less than the journeywork of the stars* . . .

"Is that a kind of motto for you?"

"Yes."

I said,

"To see a world in a grain of sand,
And a heaven in a wild flower,
*Hold infinity in the palm of your hand,*
*And eternity in an hour.*

"William Blake. That kind of thing?"

"I believe that, too."

"I speak French," Anne said. "In France I was taken to be a French person. That's how good my French was. I've got a good ear, I guess."

Jim from San Clemente said, "I have trouble with English!"

This was the truth. He said *fillum* for film, for example. He said *nucular* for nuclear.

"What sort of nuclear astrophysics do you do?" I asked Steve. "Stephen Hawking generalizations about the nature of the universe? And by the way, did you hear that Hawking's wife has just left him? Amazing. The guy's a genius, slowly wasting away in a wheelchair, and she ups and leaves."

"Are you married?" Anne said.

"No. I upped and left," I said. "Kind of."

"Hawking is interested in the big questions," Steve said. "I deal with particles. Nuclei. But they contain what human life contains – helium, oxygen –"

"He told me that on our first date," Anne said.

I said, "You do research?"

"Yes." And he frowned. His hat was slightly crooked, his shirt hung out. "Mainly the nucleosynthesizing of tantalum-one-eighty."

I may have seemed a little slow – at least I had no immediate response to this.

"It's the rarest of the stable isotopes," he said.

"Of course."

"We were trying to find out how it was made." He smiled a scientist's smile. "We found out how it wasn't made."

"Tantalum-one-eighty?" I said.

"Yup."

Jim said, "Looks like rain, Dick."

After we reached the island, Atata, which was about eight miles offshore, we went snorkeling. We had lunch. It rained. We looked in the gift shop. Postcards, T-shirts: *Tonga – Paradise in the Pacific.*

"Steve, do you have a necktie I can borrow?" I asked on the way back. "I have to meet the King."

\*

"And you need a suit to see the King," Afu said, the night before my audience. Nor was she much impressed with Steve Kellog's dark Mormon-style tie. She said Salesi had better ones.

"I don't have a suit."

The virtue of traveling in the Pacific is that a suit and tie is never necessary. True, a tie is required in some restaurants but you can always be assured that the food in those places (always served by candlelight) is pretentious, saucey, over-priced, and strictly for honeymooners.

"But you have a lounge jacket."

"I don't have any jacket," I said. It was often ninety in the shade here.

"You try Salesi's jacket," Afu said.

Salesi was a short stout man. I am not a short stout man. The shiny ill-fitting jacket made me looked like a bum. That odd jacket with the neatly knotted tie made me looked like a mentally defective bum.

I tried on the tie and jacket for Afu's inspection. She was dissatisfied but resigned. I was staring at my reflection in a mirror.

"It is the best we can do," she said.

"I look like a Mormon," I said.

They had invited me to their house – "farm" was the word they would have used – for dinner. They had said dinner, but I did not see any food. We spent an hour or more drinking Kool-Aid and going through their son's wedding pictures, all seven albums. It had apparently been a very grand affair – great rolls of finely woven mats, and dead pigs everywhere. I remarked on the pigs.

"You want to see some pigs?" Salesi said.

We went outside. The pigs were active. I counted thirty-three porkers, big and small, under one tree. Some of them resembled the wild pigs I had seen on the Hopevale Aboriginal reserve on the Queensland coast – hairy, snouty, narrow-eared creatures.

"Yes. It is related to the wild pig," Salesi said.

"So what you've got here, really, is a kind of pig farm."

The pigs screeched and snuffled. They butted each other. They trotted from one patch of grass to another. They sucked dirty water out of puddles. They jostled, hoofing it in and out of the shed under the tree.

"Yes. You can say that. I eat them. I sell them."

"Do you kill them yourself?"

"Yes," Salesi said sadly. "But I don't like to. A pig can be your friend."

We were joined by Afu.

"They sleep in that shed?" I asked.

"Sometimes," Salesi said.

"That was our first house," Afu said.

It was a tiny wooden-plank hovel. They kept it, they said, to remind themselves of the days when they had been struggling. They had married against the wishes of their parents; their early married life had been made difficult by this disapproval.

"How did you meet?"

Afu said, "At the palace."

Salesi said, "I just sneak in and want to talk to her."

This was when Afu had been eighteen, the lady-in-waiting to Queen Salote.

"The Queen was very cross when I marry Salesi. She did not know he was visiting me. I just say to her, 'I'm getting marry.' But she had another man picked out for me, with an education. And she had a girl picked for Salesi, a girl with an education –"

I got the idea of Queen Salote as a meddler, an arranger, a manipulator – and Afu confirmed this was so. She was after all an absolute monarch. She made a point of teaching Afu simple household chores – how to clean a room properly, how to dust shelves, how to sew, how to make dresses.

"She didn't think I would be happy," Afu said, and she beamed. "I wish she could see us. I wish she could see that we have been so happy."

Afu told me the Coronation story, how Queen Salote had distinguished herself by showing respect for Queen Elizabeth.

"If someone has an umbrella you stand in the rain, to show respect," Afu said. "If someone is on a chair, you sit on the floor." Then she told me a detail that no one else had mentioned. Apparently there had been another foreign dignitary in the carriage – not "her lunch" but another head of state.

"He was from some country," Afu said. "He don't speak English good. He say, 'Up! Up!' He getting wet. But Queen Salote say no. He very cross!"

At last, quite late, we had dinner – chicken and taro and cassava and a delicious bowl of soupy greens, which were taro leaves cooked with coconut milk, a Samoan speciality called *palusami*. The chicken came from America. Most chicken eaten in the Pacific came from America – from Tyson's Chicken Farm in Arkansas, to be precise. Even on distant islands in the Marquesas, which are among the most remote islands on earth, they were cheaper than the local birds.

Afu was still talking about her years with Queen Salote, how she had traveled with her, how she knew her moods ("She pretended to be cross sometimes, so we would be frightened"). In New Zealand, the local people recognized the Queen and waved to her. Afu had panicked. "Wave at the people, Afu!" Queen Salote had said sharply.

"So I wave," Afu said and put on a goofy, small-girl face and flapped her hand. " 'Hello! Hello!' "

Before I left Afu reminisced about how sorry she was that Queen Salote had not known what a happy marriage they had had. But Queen Salote had not been healthy. She had had diabetes. "She could not eat pigs." Yet she respected their families. Afu's elderly mother was coughing and spitting in a side-room just off the dining-room, where we were eating. And Salesi's father, Afu said, had real power.

"He is a chief. He owns land," Afu said. "He gives land to people, and then he does nothing. He finds a tree. He goes under it. He sleeps."

"People bring him food," Salesi said. "He does nothing."

"Is that good?" I asked.

"That is what I want," Salesi said.

That was what I kept noticing in Tonga, its traditional class system of nobles and commoners, of landlords and peasants. The first Europeans who had ventured into Tonga had remarked on this same stratification, and the way commoners tried hard to please the nobility, and usually failed. The nobility paid little attention. Why should they? Nothing would ever change. Even the Englishman Captain Cook, who knew the niceties and grovelings of the English class system, was astounded by Tongan servility and he remarked on how the commoners stooped to show respect, touching the sole of a chief's foot as the great man ambled past.

And soon it would be my turn.

Early on the morning of my royal audience I walked down to the palace, just to look at the flag. The King's standard was not flying on the flagpole, which meant he was not in the palace. I began to think that the audience was not going to happen.

Some Tongan soldiers were drilling with fake guns near the palace cannons. This was one of the most rag-tag armies in the Pacific – not more than two hundred men. By comparison, Fiji was a superpower – indeed, in the UN peacekeeping force, posted between the Israelis and the Palestinians, the Fijians had proven themselves courageous and resourceful soldiers. It was unimaginable that the Tongan army would be capable of anything even remotely similar.

I asked the drill sergeant about the King's flag. He said, "The King only comes to the palace on business. He lives at Fua'amotu, near the airport."

By the time I had changed into Salesi's jacket and Steve's Mormon tie, and walked back to the palace, the flag had gone up, though it did not fly. The flag drooped heavily on the pole in the windless sticky heat.

Perspiring, I entered the office of the King's secretary and saw my name chalked on a board and after my name, *Author, former university professor*. I was shown to a waiting-room, which was full of red plush chairs and dusty glass cases which contained labeled items and bizarre memorabilia. An old sextant, a rhino beetle encased in plastic, a cane – *The Walking Stick of King Taufa'ahau I (1797–1893)*, five feathers stuck into a crumbly piece of coral, *Worn by Queen Salote at the Coronation of Elizabeth II*, a silver-plated shovel, a black war club labeled *A War Stick*, photographs of bewildered-looking royal personages, and a jumbled heap of dirty shards: *Pottery pieces found at the hospital site of Havelu-loto, 1969*.

That glass case was unlocked. Discovering this, I was seized with a desire to steal an artifact – anything – in revenge for the things that had been stolen from me in Tonga. As I jiggled the door sideways, fully intending to swipe something, I heard footsteps – heavy heels.

"Mr Paul?"

It was an army officer.

"I am the King's aide-de-camp. Call me Joe. How do you pronounce your name?"

I told him.

"Because I have to announce you," he explained.

We walked through the tall grass and the weeds that lay outside the high palace fence and we then squeezed between a pair of gates that were ajar and across through more tall grass, still wet with the morning dew.

The King's new Mercedes was parked in the portico out front. Joe led me past it to a ground-floor room on the right – with a buffet and a heavy refectory table, it had the look of having once been a dining-room. It was strewn with gifts – an inscribed crystal punchbowl, a framed key, a toy Thai temple, a silver-plated telescope, a lamp with a label on it, a ceremonial dagger, a samurai sword, and a large framed photograph of Tonga's many islands, snapped from space, with a long laborious inscription and the signature of Ronald Reagan in ignorant wobbly handwriting.

A throne-like chair stood at the head of the table. Joe showed me to a chair next to it. I was surprised to see that the throne was the same height as my chair, because I had been told that I would be seated lower than the King, out of respect. I sat and practised crouching to look humble.

There came a wheezing and a shuffling from the hallway. It was a bit like being in a well-furnished boarding-house – it even looked and smelled like one, with wooden panels, varnished bannisters and stairs, and armchairs with doilies.

In his black bombazine skirt, thumping along with canes, the King had the distinct appearance of a landlady, the same bossy authority and eccentric dress, his smock-like shirt buttoned to his neck and a great braided mass of cords around his belly. He had an aluminium cane in each fist, and in each breast pocket a pair of glasses, and a gold watch on each wrist – two of everything. But the details of his person were overwhelmed by the King's size.

One day in Suva, a settlement he called "the white folks' town," Mark Twain reached the conclusion that "in Fiji, as in the Sandwich Islands [Hawaii], native kings and chiefs are of much grander size and build than the commoners." And he might have added that it was true of Tonga – where it is still the case.

Whenever Tonga was mentioned, the King's weight figured. The guidebooks gave it importance: *The current king, Taufa'ahau Tupou IV may be the world's most powerful (as well as largest!) reigning monarch* . . . Or: *The King is known world-wide for his ample girth* . . . (*Lonely Planet Guide to Tonga*) . . . Or: *The present monarch is a 1·9 meter, 22-stone* (308 pounds) *giant* . . . (*South Pacific Handbook*). Travel books also gave the King's weight when dealing with Tongan issues, for example, *Cruising in the Friendly Isles: The King of Tonga weighs 375 pounds* . . . Foreign newspapers described it: *The King – who once weighed in at 210 kilograms* (464 pounds) . . . (*South China Morning Post*, 31 March 1991).

His actual weight (and no one seemed to get it right) seemed irrelevant to me. He was vast, he was slow, an enormous shuffling man whose heavy-lidded eyes and whopper jaw gave him the huge frog-like face you sometimes saw on ancient carved Polynesian tikis. A tiki is a statue, but Tiki is also a god – the greatest in Oceania. A suggestion of divinity is attached to the Tongan monarch, as it is to the English one. Tonga was a kingdom of big men, and this man was the biggest of all – you would have known instantly that he was the King. He also had presence. Superficially his bulk made him a bit of a caricature, a sort of island version of Jabba the Hutt from *The Empire Strikes Back*. But his size also gave him a mythic quality. I had never seen anyone so politically powerful who was at the same time so physically overwhelming.

Tongans could seem oddly inert creatures, and they smirked a great deal when you asked them questions; but the King possessed a monumental serenity, and he had a watchfulness about him – an intelligence and sensitivity – that I had not seen in any Tongan. Tongan silence was like the stillness of a lizard – a waiting to snatch at an insect. But the King's silence was not predatory like that. It was like a supreme indifference, as though he was a titanic spectator – impassive, perhaps wise. There was something oriental in his aloofness, in the detachment of his presence, and at times when we were speaking he seemed like a sultan or an emperor, an eastern potentate. Not the effete and inbred monarch of Europe, but a bigger rougher version, the king of cannibals and coconuts, regal in a distinctly physical sense.

He put his big warm hand in mine and when he said "Sit" I heard it, though the sound was deformed by his jaw or his speech defect – and the word stayed in his mouth.

"He is known for his long silences," an Australian expatriate in Nuku'alofa had told me the day before.

I was close enough to see that each of his wristwatches showed the same time.

To prove I was bona fide I had brought the King a book I had written. This I now handed him, telling him so. The King picked it up. His hands were big and plump, each one like a baseball mitt. His fingers were thick, his fingertips blunt – too blunt to assist him in separating pages. The book looked helpless in his hands, but neither could the King peruse it. It was too delicate a task for those fat royal fingers.

I made a short speech, saying how grateful I was that I had been welcomed so warmly in the kingdom.

Perhaps it was the false suggestion of monotony of his froggy eyes, but he seemed very bored by what I was saying. Minutes had passed and the only word I had heard the King utter so far was, "Sit."

"In the 1890s," I went on, "the Hawaiian King Kalakaua had the idea of uniting the Pacific into a large federation of island nations – a great community of likeminded people. It never happened, of course. But does such an idea interest you, Your Majesty?"

And I immediately wondered whether I should have said *Your Highness* instead.

"I have already started," he said, "though it is not the whole Pacific. It is Polynesia."

I had been right about the speech defect – he had rather a slushy way with s's and with consonant clusters. He hardly opened his mouth. His words remained echoey in his mouth and some of them stuck to his tongue. It was a growly voice, exactly that of someone protesting as he swallows his mashed potatoes. Perhaps it was a dented palate? Certainly there was little effort in the voice. It was languid and somewhat imprecise – not an accent but a difficulty enunciating – bobbling the words, and snuffling whole sentences. Each time he spoke I made a desperate effort to translate. Probably the greatest difficulty in his speech was that it had no emotion in it. Emotion was superfluous to royal speech, anyway. He had known the luxury of never having to persuade anyone of anything; he spoke and was obeyed; he was the King.

"The chairman was a minister from the Cook Islands," the King said. ("Minister" had been a real mashed potato.) "But this man was voted out in the last election, so I am taking charge."

"What is the aim of your Polynesia group? Is it political, Your Highness?"

"It is not political. How could it be? The Cook Islands is a republic. Hawaii is a state. French Polynesia is a colony. Tonga is a monarchy. There are too many differences. No, it will be concerned with culture and society. With language and the arts." He took a deep breath. "We will publish a magazine."

"And Melanesia is not a part of it, Your Majesty?"

He was silent. At last, without opening his mouth, he produced the word *no* and it went on rumbling inside his body.

"Yet Ontong Java in the Solomons and Futuna in Vanuatu are inhabited by Polynesia people," I said.

"We will provide some pages for them in the magazine."

The King now seemed thoroughly bored and I thought for a moment that he was going to send me away.

I said, "Your Majesty, will you deal with questions such as nuclear testing?"

"That is a political matter –"

Not only did he not move his mouth, he did not move his head either, nor his body. He simply sat, huge and immovable, like a great lumpish oracle or the sage in a children's story, the wise old giant of the cannibal isles.

"– but nuclear testing in the Pacific is very bad."

There came one of his silences. It is a TV interviewing technique to say nothing after a question is answered; then the interviewee often tries to fill the silence by babbling, and often this is confessional stuff. I decided to wait.

"I have been to Mururoa," the King said after a while. "I saw the holes in the reef. They drilled down and put the bomb inside, and then filled the hole with cement. They had made so many holes they had very little room left on the reef to dig more. So they had started to dig into the bed of the lagoon, which is of course very dangerous."

On the King's face was something like a smile, the sort of mirthful expression that beholds abject stupidity.

"Your Majesty, did you make your opinion known?"

"At the time I had no opinion," the King said.

"What is your opinion now, sir?"

"Nuclear testing must stop in the Pacific," the King said without any feeling, and in the same monotone he went on, "The French must leave. They import everything from France. It is ridiculous. Although it will be hard financially for the people of those islands, they must decolonize French Polynesia."

"Do you mean soon, or all in good time?"

"Soon," the King said. "Soon."

He was staring at me.

"The atom bombs can be tested elsewhere. Testing is needed. And bombs are needed to stop people like Hussein. To frighten him. He is like Hitler."

"Are you saying, Your Majesty, that they should use an atom bomb on Saddam Hussein?"

"They should put a bomb under him," the King said.

"And you trust the French to test their nuclear devices elsewhere in the world?'

"I don't trust the French at all!" he said, and saying so, he roared with laughter. It was so unexpected, that I twitched with surprise.

Intending to exploit his sudden emotion, I said, "The French are usually self-interested, so they are – in foreign policy at any rate – insincere, unprincipled, and unreliable."

"Totally unreliable!" he roared and he laughed again. "I have been rereading the history of the Franco-Prussian War. Do you know how that war started?"

But it was a rhetorical question; he then summarized the events of 120 years ago that led to the outbreak of war, specifically the so-called Ems telegram sent by King William I of Prussia to his chancellor, Otto von Bismarck. After deliberately editing and publishing the telegram so as to offend the French government, Bismarck succeeded in outraging the French, who declared a war that the Germans wanted (and so did Napoleon III of France, to boost his sagging popularity). In the end the Germans won a humiliating victory over the French.

All this, and more, the King of Tonga told me of the Franco-Prussian War.

"So it was on that little detail of the telegram that the French started the war, which they lost," the King said.

"The French make a detail into a principle," I said, "But they are just as likely to make a principle or a murderous event into a detail. Look at the sinking of the *Rainbow Warrior* and the murder of the photographer on board by the French saboteurs in New Zealand. The French government said it was nothing – they regarded it as nothing. Yet if it had happened to them they might have used it as a pretext for a war."

"But New Zealand can't go to war with France," the King said. "There was nothing that New Zealand could do."

"No one went to bat for New Zealand, though," I said. "The British have a rather ambiguous attitude towards the French. They like the food, they feel somewhat intimidated by the French people."

"The English overlook the French weaknesses," the King said, "and so do your people in the United States."

"Since we are generalizing about national characteristics, what about the Japanese, Your Highness?"

"They are building a new terminal for us at the airport."

"Do they mention wanting to buy islands from you?"

"We will never give our land away," the King said. "That is the worst problem in Hawaii – the loss of land. It now belongs to other people, and the Hawaiians have so little left."

Another silence ensured; I simply listened to its drone.

"The Japanese work very hard," the King said. "It is strange – they think they are pure but they are not pure at all. Their culture is derived from the Chinese. Their language is full of foreign words."

He gave me the foreign derivations of *arrigato* and *tempura* and I gave him *kasteru* and *pagoda*.

"Would you like to see Tonga develop into a great tourist destination?"

"Already we receive many tourists –"

Twenty thousand a year – nothing.

"But when the terminal is in place there will be many more." He clasped his hands, making a great meaty pile of fingers on the table. "We will soon have three television stations. And oil. We have oil in Tonga."

"Oil, Your Highness?"

"Yes. I have seen it myself — gushing from the reef. We will soon have someone drilling."

And not a moment too soon: fuel oil was very expensive in Tonga, and also very scarce. But this could not have been much more than a seep hole from an oil pocket under the reef — hardly a commercial proposition.

We returned to the subject of Polynesia, and I asked whether he felt an affinity with other Polynesians.

"I do. The Samoans are very close. My second son is married to a Samoan. And of course we have a common origin. There is a fellow here at our university who is from Sumatra, and he has told me that there is a village in Sumatra where the language is very similar to Tongan."

I said, "The Polynesians have a sense of having come from a distant place. The Fijians are muddled about that. The Melanesians I've met speak of having come from sharks and snakes and birds. Some people say they came out of the ground."

"We have a sense that our ancestors were voyagers and explorers, that is true."

"But of all the Polynesians you are the last absolute monarch, Your Highness."

He laughed his roaring laugh. "I am not an absolute monarch."

"With all respect, Your Highness, surely you are. In what way are you not?"

"I have a," he said and produced a mashed-potato word. It stayed in his mouth, it had no echo, it was a swallowing sound.

"Excuse me, sir?"

He repeated the word three times. The word was *parliament*. But of course the assembly was no more than a rubber stamp, and half of it was appointed by his allies the Tongan nobles.

Soon after this I asked him whether he had committees that were looking into tourism and oil and television.

He said, "I am the committee!" and he laughed very hard.

"We always have a majority!"

Another laugh, and I of course obsequiously joined him.

"No dissenting voices!"

By any account, the King of Tonga is one of the few absolute monarchs in the world.

He asked me – it was his only question to me – whether I had any news of the Gulf War. I told him what I had heard on the BBC that morning.

The King said, "America could use this as a chance to put their resentments aside and make an ally of the Iranians. America needs allies in the Middle East. Iran is not the same country that humiliated America during the hostage crisis. They have a new government – a good one, I think."

"The Israelis tend to dominate our thinking on the Middle East," I said.

"America should be objective. And Israel has a big responsibility to be fair to the Palestinians. The Israelis should leave the occupied territories and stop killing Palestinians. Israel is strong and the Palestinians are weak. They are a problem because Israel has made them a problem."

We talk some more, about his children, about his liking for French food, about his exercise (he cycled up and down the runway at the airport – he was trying to get his weight down). He then lowered his massive head and said, "I have another appointment."

I scrambled to my feet and thanked him, and then Joe was summoned to lead me away across the weedy lawn.

A day or so later, Afu and Salesi killed and roasted a piglet in my honor and the burned creature was hacked apart and distributed to a number of Tongan men sitting under a mango tree. The women were under a different, smaller tree.

There was no beer. I drove with a man named Meti to the next village and bought a case. He said we would share it – that was the Tongan way. But he kept the beer in his car. I had three bottles, he had two, none was offered to the others, and in the end Meti went off with nineteen bottles of my beer.

"Me I don't drink beer," Alipate had said. He was stuffing his mouth with a pig's muscley bum. "I'm a Methodist." And in almost the same breath he said, "You try any Tongan women?"

No, I said, I hadn't.

"I like *palangi* pussy," Alipate said, and rubbed pig fat from his mustache with the back of his fleshy fist.

"What a delicate fellow you are," I said. It annoyed me that this slob should say that to me. "I'll bet *palangi* women are devoted to you."

"I be careful! I got da wife! She cut da neck! She cut da ball!"

This word *palangi*, the euphemism for white person, was interesting. It meant "sky-burster." In the seventeenth century, Tongans and Samoans believed that their islands lay in a great and uncrossable ocean. The long overseas migratory journey was conjectural in Tonga and absent in Samoa, where the local creation myth described how they had risen from a knot of twitching worms in the soil of their islands. So when the first Europeans appeared in this part of western Polynesia – Tasman in 1643, and later Roggeveen and Cook – the only possible way for them to have arrived was from the sky, exploding from the heavens.

It is one of paradoxes of language as living culture that a vulgar man like Alipate used this poetic and allusive expression all the time – there was no other word for white person except "sky-burster." Alipate was a stonemason. He frequently boasted of the money he had made laying bricks in Hawaii. He liked hoisting his shirt and cooling his belly with the night breeze, and talking about women he had had, or money he had made.

"What you talkeen to da King?" he asked me. His T-shirt was hoisted. His brown hairy belly glistened with sweat.

"He told me you're going to have television."

"In his dreams," Alipate said. He translated this into Tongan and everyone laughed. "Da King all the time dreameen."

They mocked the King for a while. They were like a different race of people altogether. Socially they were another species. A little over a hundred years ago such Tongans had been slaves – King George Tupou I had abolished slavery in Tonga. Alipate saw that I had not touched the clutch of pig ribs on my plate and without saying a word he reached over and snatched it, and when he finished chewing it he went on cooling his belly and jeered at the King some more.

# 15

# *Tonga: Alone on the Desert Islands of Vava'u*

In the way tardy and negligent people are often blame-shifting and chronically mendacious, many of the Tongans I met in Nuku'alofa were unreliable, and some outright liars – or, to put it charitably, they meant very little of what they said. This could be tiresome in a hot climate. My solution was to take my boat to a part of Tonga where there were no Tongans.

I resolved that I would find a desert island in the middle of nowhere and live a beachcombing life for a while. My ideal island would have a sandy beach, and coconuts, and jungle, and no people. About fifty islands, remote and empty, fitted this description, and they lay in Tonga's northern archipelago, called the Vava'u group. I knew somehow that there would be fruit bats. There were bats on every Tongan island. It was said that these islands were among the most beautiful in the Pacific, and many of them were desert islands, utterly uninhabited but pristine – dream islands, each one like a little world.

"The trouble is," a Tongan on the small plane to Vava'u told me, "you'll have to find someone to take you out to the islands."

I did not tell him about my boat, that I could assemble it and paddle to any island, and that I had a nautical chart of the whole group, and survival gear.

This man, Aleki, had with him a video cassette of the Gulf War that had been taped four days before the news footage shown in New Zealand. The war was still being fought, but the Tongan interest in this sort of footage was not very different from their interest in *Rambo* videos. Aleki gave me his address and said that if I cared to, I was welcome to come over to his house in Neiafu – Vava'u's main town – and watch the video of American planes raining bombs down on Iraq and Kuwait. This seemed hospitable enough, though I did not take him up on his offer.

Everything about the Vava'u group pleased me – the islands were not far apart, there were plenty of sandy beaches on them, there were stores in Neiafu where I could stock up on food, and although it was windy I could paddle in the lee of a long chain of islands and stay out of trouble. Most of all, the Tongans on the main island in Vava'u seemed friendly. If they had airs the airs were different from those I had had to contend with in Nuku'alofa. This was not a place of nobles and landlords and peasants, but of hard-pressed islanders – apparently one class – who managed by fishing and farming. Most of the Tongans I met in Vava'u said they hated Nuku'alofa – "The fast life, the noise, the always hurry-hurry," one named Siole said, summing up the Vava'u objections to the royal city. Though I hardly recognized this frenzied Nuku'alofa of their description – it seemed to me a place without any events, except for church services and the occasional funeral or coronation – I came to see that, by comparison with Neiafu, which was very nearly fossilized, semi-moribund Nuku'alofa could seem a trifle hectic.

Siole (Tongan for Joel) had a car, a prized possession in Neiafu, where there were never more than two or three in sight – people tramped the dirt roads of the main island confident that they would never be run down. Siole also had gas, and this was amazing, because there had been no fuel at all in Vava'u for almost a week. No one knew when the next shipment would arrive. Everyone blamed the delay on the Gulf War, which was probably not the reason, though the Gulf War was certainly to blame for the high price – about six dollars a gallon, and rising.

In his old car, Siole took me to the market and the stores, so that I could buy provisions.

We passed a fat pig – very fat, perhaps hundreds of pounds.

"What is a pig like that worth, Siole?"

"Six or seven hundred." He meant pa'anga, and this amounted to about five hundred dollars.

"How would you eat it?"

"At a feast. Maybe a funeral," Siole said.

"Only when someone dies you eat it?"

"If someone, say your mother, gets bad sick, you feed your pig a lot of food. Get him fat."

"Because you might need him for your mother's funeral?"

"Right."

I could just imagine a sick Tongan's sense of doom when he or she looked out the hut window and saw the family pig fattened.

"Also your horse."

"To be in the funeral procession?"

"Not the procession but the feast. We eat the horses."

He was driving slowly along the dirt road of the main street – slowly,

to avoid flattening a dog that was sleeping in the patch of shade thrown
down by the leafy bough of a tree.

"What about them – you eat dogs?"

"Yes."

"You eat flying foxes – fruit bats?"

"Yes."

"How do you cook them?"

"Pigs, horses and dogs we put in the *umu* oven. It makes the meat very
soft. But flying foxes we can just barbecue."

It seemed to be a general rule on Pacific islands that there were few, if
any, food taboos. Wherever I went I asked about diet, and except for
the Seventh-day Adventists in Kaisiga Village in the Trobiands, no one
was very fussy. In Oceania you ate every living thing that fitted into
your mouth.

Dogs had been cooked and eaten in the Pacific from the moment the
Pacific was inhabited. The dogs had come in the canoes of the voyagers
from South-East Asia (where they were – and still are – also eaten).
There was no game to be found on the Pacific islands, and so the dog
was prized – for its taste, its food value, its scarcity (pigs greatly
outnumbered dogs). Its fur was used for decoration, its skin was turned
into articles of clothing, its teeth into necklaces and ornaments, its bones
into implements – hooks and needles. On various islands, Hawaii in
particular, dogs were fed with vegetables or *poi* – thus the term "poi-
dog" still current – to sweeten their flesh, and some were breast-fed by
women. Gobbling the left-over sweet potatoes or scraps of greens, snuffling in the undergrowth for an edible root, most of the dogs and cats I
saw on my Pacific travels seemed to be vegetarian.

All the early European explorers in Oceania mentioned dog-eating.
These men had come from societies in which dogs had status as
sympathetic companions with precise personal names – in Claude Lévi-
Strauss's description, "metonymical humans." Invited to feast on dog
meat in eighteenth-century Hawaii – the Sandwich Islands – a scandal-
ized Englishman wrote, "The idea of eating so faithful an animal as a
dog prevented any of us joining in this part of the feast." He added,
"Although to do the meat justice, it really looked very well when
roasted." Some tried eating dogs – Georg Forster, the German scientist
and chronicler who accompanied Captain Cook, said dog meat was
indistinguishable from mutton. On one occasion in the last century a
group of Hawaiian jokesters served up a dog with a pig's head replacing
the head of the mutt, in order to fool the American visitors who happily

devoured the animal. In the Pacific, a dog might be a household pet but never the sort of companion that possessed an implied taboo against its been eaten.

In *Man and the Natural World*, the Oxford historian, Keith Thomas, lists three features that distinguish eighteenth-century pets in England ("privileged species") from other animals; they were encouraged to enter houses and churches; they were given individual personal names; and they were never eaten − "Not for gastronomic reasons . . . it was the social position of the animal as much as its diet which created the prohibition." In 1616, the first Dutchmen to reach the Tuomotus, Le Maire and Schouten, who had earlier named Cape Horn, called one island Honden, because of its dogs, and they noted that the dogs caught and ate fish and were themselves on the menu and did not bark.

None of these early dogs barked. This was also remarked upon by European visitors. Apparently, wild dogs never bark − they howl and whimper, as dingoes in Australia do − but only the domesticated dog goes woof-woof.

Right here in Vava'u, a young English castaway (fifteen years old when he first arrived), William Mariner, was adopted by a Hapaai chief, Finou 'Ulukalala the First, and went native. He lived in Tonga from 1806 until 1810. Much of what we know about early life in Tonga comes from a detailed account of his adventures taken down by a London physician and published in 1820. In this book he remarks on his benefactor, Finou's, love of cooked dog meat, "but he ordered it to be called pork, because women and many men had a degree of abhorrence at this sort of diet. The parts of the dog in most esteem are the neck and hinder quarters. The animal is killed by blows on the head, and cooked in the same manner as a hog."

My new pal Siole agreed that dog meat was delicious. He was a friendly fellow − relaxed, and helpful, and not rapacious. I needed to buy food, and then to find a place to stay the night and launch my boat. We had struck a simple bargain − for ten dollars he would ferry me around the small rambling town. He took me to the Oceanic provisioners − Burns Philip, Morris Hedstrom − and then to the market, where I bought a basket of small pineapples. Because there was no gas in town I bought kerosene for my camp stove. All this took an hour or more, but Siole did not complain, not even when the rude Tongan woman at the hotel said, "Your taxi-driver can carry your bags."

The hard part about arriving in such a place, with little prior information, was that I did not know what the hazards were − the winds, the

reefs, the shoals, the tides, the currents, the unfriendly villages, the bad
beaches, the creatures – if any. Some hazards were obvious – the pounding surf, the frothing chop of a channel that looked like a river in spate;
others might not be apparent until it was too late. I always remembered
those awful boys in the Trobriands who shook spears at me and said,
"Run you life, *dim-dim*!" or the island of arsonists in Fiji. I made a point
of bringing detailed maps and charts. I often had a guidebook. But there
was no substitute for local knowledge.

So I was lucky in meeting Leonati, a sturdy Tongan who was also a
diver and a fisherman. He watched me put my boat together beside the
little pier, under the limestone cliff where my hotel was situated.

"How much water do you draw?"

"A few inches," I said, unrolling my chart.

"Why not go this way?" he said, and put his finger on a tiny break
between two islands on my chart. I would not have seen it had he not
pointed it out.

"I was thinking of going this way out of the harbor," I said, and
showed him my proposed route through the Port of Refuge, named by
Don Francisco Mourelle, the Spanish discoverer of this place in 1781.

Leonati made a face and said, "It's all villages there."

He was the first person I met not just in Tonga but the whole of
Oceania so far who had said anything like that.

"This island is empty," he said, and circled a small island. "And this
one – no people there. This one is small but very beautiful. And this
one" – he tapped another – "paddle there and the wind will take you
back."

Everyone else had said: Make for the villages. I liked Leonati, the
only loner I had come across. He said he sometimes took his own boat
out and camped on those islands.

"Who owns them?"

He shrugged.

"No one will bother you," he said.

It was a hot and steamy morning in the Port of Refuge, and the
yellow light of early dawn slanted through the haze, hanging like smoky
vapor on the water, where thirty sailing yachts lay at anchor, their wet
laundry drooping where their sails should have been. I was stowing gear
in my little boat and swatting mosquitoes that had been vitalized by the
humid heat. The mosquitoes frisked around my ears.

It had rained hard in the night, and when I commented on this to an

American on the pier coiling a line, he said, "Of course," and seemed surprised that I had bothered to mention it. This was after all the hurricane season – and it was also why there were yachts in the harbor. Most of them had come in November and they would remain moored there until April, when the weather moderated. No one sailed the South Pacific in this dangerous weather.

"I used to work on Cape Cod," the man said, when I told him where I was from. "Camp Seascape in Brewster. It was a summer camp for fat girls. I helped run it." He became reflective, as though he had not thought about this for years. "The average weight loss was twenty pounds."

He drifted away, while I finished loading my boat. My heaviest single item was water, because I was not sure whether fresh water would be available on my desert island. I carried it in two- and three-gallon bags, a week's supply, which I stuffed under the bulkheads, with my waterproof bags containing food, my dry clothes, my stove, my pots, my tent. On the deck, in a plastic holder, I had my map of the whole archipelago, and a water bottle, and a compass. Close to hand I had emergency flares.

I had given my life-jacket to the old Kula man, Meia, in the Trobriands. I had swapped my spear in the Solomons. The last of my fishing gear I had handed out in Vanuata. My Walkman had been stolen in Nuku'alofa. I had broken my spare paddle. I was now so worried about having only one canoe paddle that I usually put on a leash, a line running from its shaft to the deck. It was not theft that I feared but rather the thing being blown out of my hands by a strong wind.

Unnoticed, I slipped away from the shore and paddled south along the inside of the harbor, which was walled by high cliffs and surmounted by tall wet trees. Small boys were jumping from the black rocks, swimming in the early morning. About a mile farther on was a narrow break in this jungly wall, just a slice of air, with birds squawking and flitting on the steep green sides, and water so shallow that the bottom of my boat rubbed against the rocks. This was Leonati's suggested short-cut, Ahanga Passage.

Once I was through it I was in the wind and waves, and I saw surf breaking out on the reef and in the distance a chain of islands. I used my map to keep to the deeper parts of this bay, and paddled out far enough so that I could identify the islands. There were islands everywhere – close to me and on the horizon at various distances, and I knew from what Leonati had told me that most of them were uninhabited. Just to keep my bearings I headed for one called Tapana Island.

I chose that island because it was distinctly noted on my chart. There were islands in this archipelago that were not on it. Fafini and Fanua Tapu, shown as insignificant reefs, were a pair of high hefty islands. My chart had been drawn "from a British survey in 1898" – but was it possible that islands could form and grow in just under a hundred years?

The wind was blowing about ten to fifteen knots, brisk and steady enough to whip up the waves and give them frothy peaks. I dug out a line and tied it onto my paddle as a tether, and I put on the secure storm spraydeck, so that I was completely watertight. This was just as well, because I could see in the distance billowy black clouds, and long gray curtains of rain.

The rain crept nearer and was soon on me, and I was paddling among the faint outlines of islands in a heavy downpour.

Leonati had said, "We had a drought until December, but it has been raining ever since –"

It was no fun paddling in the rain, but the worst of it was the possibility of losing my bearings. Now, in the heaviest rain, a solid sheet of slashing water, all the islands were eclipsed. It was as though I were paddling beneath a waterfall, like *The Maid of the Mist* under Niagara. I used my compass to get to Tapana – following the needle until the gray island emerged. There was no shelter, no beach, only cliffs, so I headed through the crackling rain to a nearby island that I could just discern among the flailing drops of rain. This was Lautala, which Leonati had told me was deserted. It was, but there was no beach; I had no way of landing.

Each island in Vava'u is a limestone block that has been pounded into a dangerous and unapproachable shape by the waves and wind, giving them straight sides, spikes and crags, a ten-foot wall of spiky stone around most of its edge. But on some the wave action had pushed sand behind them – I could see beaches at the backs of other islands farther into the archipelago.

I found a little cleft at the side of Lautala where I sheltered, with water dripping from the peak of my hat. And sitting there miserably dripping I was approached by curious birds – brown noddies that looked like dark terns, and big fearless shearwaters.

Trying to spot these birds with my binoculars I looked around, into the rain, and saw two canoes – four men in each – making directly for me, or perhaps for the island: I would soon find out.

The canoes were ten-foot dugouts with outriggers – vessels for paddling rather than sailing – and experts said they were "the only surviving sea craft of indigenous origin in Tonga." I usually made sketches of the dugouts on particular islands – and I noted the islands where canoeing and canoe-making had been abandoned. These Tongan canoes had a feature I had never seen before – the outrigger attachment (securing the outrigger float to the booms extended from the dugout) was U-shaped. I had never seen this before – all other canoe-makers used a V-shaped attachment, or just a pair of lashed struts. It may seem a small thing, but after seeing so many canoes made in much the same way, this difference, and especially such an elegant object, appeared remarkable to me. And Tonga was a place where no one carved with any precision or troubled themselves to make anything substantial in a traditional way.

When the canoes drew up beside me – they too were sheltering from the sudden storm – I said hello and pointed to the well-made fixture. What was its name?

The men laughed. One mumbled something – mockery, I was sure; *fucking palangi*, something like that – and the other men laughed again.

The rain came down. I asked how they had bent the wood into this U-shape. They shrugged, they mumbled again, more laughter.

You think: They don't speak English. But I was sure they did – most people in Tonga did; and Vava'u with its influx of *palangis* in yachts was even more English-speaking than the main island, Tongatapu. Along with the precepts from the Golden Tablets, Mormons also taught volleyball and English to all the islanders they converted.

"Are you fishing?" I asked plainly.

"Yes," one said, and turned his back on me.

This is not necessarily a hostile gesture, but considering that we were sheltering from a heavy rainstorm at the edge of a remote, deserted island in the distant Tongan archipelago of Vava'u – miles from anywhere – it seemed a trifle unfriendly from an inhabitant of the Friendly Isles.

They had no interest whatsoever in me, nor in my reactions to the storm – they did not inquire (islanders sometimes did) as to whether I was okay, or my boat was leaking, or the waves were too high for me. They talked among themselves. They were incurious, indifferent, probably mocking – because I was alone, and a *palangi*, and posed no threat to them. Had I been big and dangerous, or well-connected, they would have groveled and paid fond attention to my butt, exclaiming upon how the sun shone radiantly out of it.

We sat bobbing in the heavy rain, saying nothing to each other, though they muttered obscurely to themselves from time to time. My consolation was that if they posed a threat to me (Tongans had a reputation for violence) I could quite easily outpaddle them – my light kayak was far faster than their clumsy outrigger canoe.

"Up yours," I said to them, smiling, when the rain eased, and I paddled away.

Later I found out that Vava'u was the only place in the Pacific where this lovely outrigger attachment existed and that it was called a *tukituki*.

I headed across a two-mile stretch of water for a crescent-shaped island which, when I came close, turned out to be two distinct islets joined by a spit of sand: Taunga, where there was a village, and Ngau, which was uninhabited. Beyond it, according to my map, was another uninhabited island, named Pau.

As I approached Pau, two fat fruit bats flew erratically overhead, making for the island. And now I could see through the gently falling rain that the island was small, uninhabited, jungly, and had a narrow sandy beach on its protected western side. It was just what I was looking for. It had another pleasant feature – a grove of coconut palms only eight or nine feet tall, with clusters of green coconuts on top, each nut containing the best drink in the world.

I paddled to the beach and pulled my boat above the tide mark, but before I could locate a camp site the rain increased, pouring straight down, the heaviness of its fat stinging drops making it fall vertically. I found a large green leaf and put it on my head, and there I stood, dripping under a dripping tree, watching the black sky, the churning sea, listening to the deafening tattoo of the rain, and feeling miserable.

Two hours passed in this way, very slowly. To add to my discomfort, clouds of mosquitoes, loving this cool rain-sodden thicket, emerged and began to bite me all over. I had insect repellent but it made no sense – and it was ineffective – to spray it on while I was standing in the rain.

The nearby islands had disappeared in the rain and mist. I was on a tiny corner of Pau Island. There was nowhere to walk to: ahead was a wall of jungle, dense with thorn bushes; behind me was the sea. I stood on a strip of land, with that silly leaf on my head, and began to shiver.

To whip up my circulation I took my paddle and cleared the branches and rubbish – and spiders – from the area around me. I awaited a break in the rain, so that I could unpack my boat and put up my tent without getting everything wet.

When the rain eased, I hurriedly set up camp, stuffing the items that needed to be dry (clothes, sleeping-bag, radio) into the tent, and hanging up the food sack and the water bag. Then I took off my wet bathing-suit and T-shirt and got into the tent naked and warmed myself in my sleeping-bag, until the raindrops ceased to patter on my tent.

I had had no lunch. I had planned to eat on the water, but those unfriendly fishermen had prevented me from eating at that halfway point on Lautala Island. I unpacked my stove, intending to light it to boil water for noodles. But my matches were wet, my lighter wouldn't spark. I began to curse out loud – after all, this was my island.

It would be impossible for me to live on this island for a week or more without matches, and I remembered the village I had seen on Taunga. I got into my boat and paddled two miles to that village, which was a pleasant place – about fifteen simple houses at the sloping edge of a pretty cove. Two motor-boats were drawn up to the Taunga beach, giving the place a look of prosperity. But there was no one in sight.

I walked to the nearest house, where, just inside the front door, an enormously fat woman was weaving a mat from pandanus fronds. Her skirt was hiked up and I could see that her vast thighs were gray and dimpled, and hideously bitten, with many open sores on her legs – perhaps from her scratching them. She was a woman of about sixty and her name was Sapeli.

"Is there a store on this island?" I asked, knowing there could not possibly be.

"Nudding," she said.

"Do you have any matches?"

Without a word, and without rising, she reached to a shelf and picked up a matchbox, removed half the matches in it, and handed the box to me.

She called out, "Lini!"

A group of children, led by two pretty girls, emerged from a nearby house.

The oldest girl introduced herself as Lini Faletau.

"Faletau means 'house-something,'" I said.

"House-war," she said. "People fighting in the house."

"A delightful name."

Since I had paddled all the way there I thought I might as well ask permission to camp on Pau, which – being so near by Vava'u standards – was probably their island. Lini said the chief was in Nuku'alofa, but we could ask someone else.

We traipsed into the bush – girls in front, kids in back, me in the middle – and along the path encountered barking dogs which tagged along, howling and snapping at my bare legs.

"Please eat those dogs," I said.

Lini laughed. She was seventeen. Her sister Deso was fourteen but taller, with a long elegant face and a slender body and a guffawing way of laughing – deep in her throat. Deso's looks reminded me that the prettiest women I had ever seen in the Pacific had been here in Tonga; the loveliest, and also the ugliest – fat hairy things with bad skin. And many of the men were hulking and horrible.

After a fifteen-minute walk through the wet grass we came to a house. Like the others it was a simple box, with a porch and a flat roof. A woman inside was weaving a mat – the room was strewn with dead palm leaves. I said hello. The woman looked at me in an uncertain manner.

"Ask her if I can sleep on Pau Island."

This request was conveyed.

"She said yes."

"Who is this woman?"

"She is my wife," Lini said.

Deso gave one of her deep attractive laughs.

"Your mother surely?"

"My mudda."

"Thank her for me, and tell her that I have brought a present for her from the United States."

I gave her a silk scarf. I had given Sapeli one, too. I never entered a village, no matter how suddenly or how small, without bringing a bag of presents – usually these scarves.

Deso began to bawl out one of the little kids. It was a small boy, who began to cry. Tongans could be very fierce with one another – screeching and scolding.

On our walk back to the beach we were joined by an obviously effeminate young man, possibly a *faka leiti*, who demanded a scarf. He asked me my name, and then I asked him his.

"My name is Russell Go-For-Broke."

"Liar!" Deso shouted at him. "Your name is Ofa."

"But I changed it. Because of Cindy Lauper."

I had no idea what he was talking about. He had a lisping voice and a coquettish manner and he asked me to stay a while.

"I'll come back some time," I said. "You have a nice village."

The beachfront and the boundaries of the village were lined with the bleached valves of the giant Tongan clam.

"The Queen of Tonga came here on December second," he said.

The Queen and King had spent Christmas at their house in Neiafu –
the Queen was a native of Vava'u.

"Did the Queen stay long?"

"Two days," Lini said.

This surprised me. They pointed out the house in which she had
stayed. It was a simple place, and it reminded me how Marie-Antoinette
of France had dressed up as a shepherdess and danced with peasants.

"What did you do for her?"

"We danced. We sang."

"Did she enjoy herself?"

'Yes. She went swimming."

The seventy-year-old monarch had swum in this little lagoon.

"Did you see her?"

"We swam with her!"

"What did the Queen's bathing-suit look like?" I asked.

"She wore a Tongan cloth wrapped around her."

"The Queen of England would never swim with English people at the
beach," I said.

"The Queen of Tonga is very kind."

I gave them the last of my silk scarves. They did not take much
interest in them. One knotted hers around a small girl's head.

"I am called Russell Go-For-Broke because I always go for broke."

"But his name is Ofa."

"Shut up." Seeing me launching my boat, he said, "Please come
back. We will give you a present. Maybe a shell."

Lini said, "Bye for now."

Russell said, "Goodbye for now but not forever." He repeated this,
and then he said, "Are you going back to fight for freedom of Kuwait?"

This they found hilarious, and with their laughter ringing in my ears I
went back to my own island and cooked my dinner while it was still
light. But more rain drove me inside and the whole black night was
filled with dripping and blowing.

The rain continued for the next two or three days, sometimes very
heavy and just as often a light drizzle. Before the hard rain fell on me I
could hear it beating noisily on the trees at the southeast of the island,
traveling towards me like a monster in the forest; and then it was on my
head and all over me.

So far there was no sun. That was the down-side of this island life in

Vava'u, and added to it were the mosquitoes, my damp clothes, the impossibility of walking anywhere on this jungly piece of land. On the plus side, the island was mine, the offshore coral was thick and full of fish, I had plenty of food, and radio reception was excellent. Sometimes the rain came down so hard that it drowned my radio. The other inhabitants of the islands were crabs, herons, and a tree full of hanging squeaking fruit bats.

Mealtimes were irregular because of the rain, and this was irksome, because I always tried to keep to a schedule when I was alone, so that my day would seem sensible and structured. *Now it's time to tidy the camp site*, I would say to myself. *Now it's time for tea. In two hours I will begin writing my notes.*

I hated paddling in the rain. It was not easy to cook in the rain. It was no fun to swim in the rain. As there was nowhere to go, I stayed inside the tent during the storms, listening to news of the Gulf War; and at night I lay there scribbling in my notebook, feeling damp and miserable under the dangling flashlight, hoping the next day would be sunny enough to dry all my wet gear.

In that sort of mood, feeling lonely and clammy, I felt a sense of regret that my married life had ended – I missed dull predictable London, my little family, the ordinariness of my old routine. In that isolation, I saw that my life had been broken in half, and I wrote on a damp page, *Travel is very hard alone, but hardest of all when there is no one waiting for you to come back.*

Usually, seeing a scrawled thought like that in black and white I closed my notebook and simply prayed for sunshine, and in the mornings, out of loneliness, I fed the bluey-gray ghost crabs chocolate cookies and pieces of cheese.

When the sun finally came out after three days my mood lifted and I was energized by the light and heat. I harvested a few coconuts – knocked them down by poking them with the blade of my long paddle, and gouged a hole in them and drank the sweet water. In this good weather I dried my clothes and the rest of my gear, and stowed it, and planned a kayak trip to other uninhabited islands in the Vava'u group, and I made a circuit of Pau Island.

Pau was uninhabited but it was not quiet. The bats made a racket, the birds whistled and squawked, the trees rattled and flapped, the fruit bats lolloped in their branches. The reef heron went *kark! kark!* The water lapped at the shore, and on the large exposed reef that lay between Pau and the next island, Fuamotu, there was a constant roar of breaking waves. I could see eight islands from where I sat slurping noodles or eating fish and pineapples; but not a single person was visible – no village, no boat.

After that day of sun it rained in the night, lashing the tent. I had left a cooking pot out in my hurry to get into the tent. There were almost three inches of water in it in the morning, and it had been sitting under a tree.

I usually woke early, at five or so, and listened to Gulf War news on Radio Australia or the BBC. The war euphoria of the first days had worn off and now it seemed as though it would go on for a long time.

That was what Leonati had said in Neiafu: "They say the war will finish fast. But I think it will go on for a long time. They say they did a lot of damage in the first few days. I don't think they did much damage."

My island was as far as it was possible to be from the Middle East, and yet the war was on everyone's mind. And I heard on the radio that on the Pacific island of Kiribati (a corruption of its former name, Gilbert), prisoners had gone on strike, refusing to enter the exercise yard, for fear they would be hit by an Iraqi "scud" missile.

There was more speculation than news – where were the eye-witnesses? – and so I always crawled out of the tent into a hazy dawn wondering what the world was coming to, and rather enjoying the idea that I was so far away, living the life of a beachcomber. The following days were warm, humid, cloudy with sunny periods and a light breeze.

On these good days, in the dazzling light of sunny mornings, I saw many more islands than I had before – they stretched like stepping-stones into the southwest, and I saw that by island-hopping I could get to most of them. None of them were inhabited, all of them had pretty shapes – hump-backed with good-sized hills, some with cliffs, some with saddle ridges, all of them densely wooded with old-growth forest as well as coconut palms.

It was a perfect area for paddling a kayak – perhaps the best in the Pacific. The islands were well defined and visible for some distance. The wind was strong in the afternoon but by setting out and returning early that was avoided or minimized. There was a surfy side and a safe side to each island – the lee shores usually had the beaches – all were secluded, all were lovely. There were no tourists, no signs at all, and no litter – no indication that human beings had ever set foot on these outer islands. It seemed to me that a person could spend weeks or months in Vava'u, making occasional trips to Neiafu, the town, to restock with provisions. It was a world apart, and solitude was available, because Tongans were not terribly interested in outsiders. Tongans did not take people to their bosoms as Melanesians did; Tongans did not pretend to be friendlier than they were.

My only question regarded the currents: I wondered how strong they were between these outlying islands, and if I paddled eight or ten miles to one of those distant places on my chart, would I risk being swept into a strong current?

I paddled back to Taunga to ask a fisherman. All the fishermen were out this lovely day, but I found Lini and she inquired among the women of Taunga. None of them had the slightest idea about the currents. This was not so surprising – women did not paddle or sail in Tonga.

"The beach at the tip of your island is very beautiful," I said.

"Yes. We swim there."

"Do tourists visit you?"

"Sometimes, in boats. A cruise ship came once. There were many people. They loved our village. They admired our houses and the flowers we planted."

"What did the cruise ship look like?"

"I don't remember," Lini said. "But they loved our beach."

"Where did the people come from – what country?"

"I don't know," she said impatiently, as though it was a silly question.

Just like a Tongan: she remembered only what the strangers had said about her village. She had taken no interest at all in the strangers.

"There is no one swimming on the beach today," I said.

"It is so far to go" – it was about a ten-minute walk. She smiled and added, "A man from overseas told the King that he wanted to build a hotel on the beach. A very big hotel, so that tourists will come."

"What did the King say?"

"He could not say anything to the man until he asked us."

"So the King asked the village about building a hotel?"

"Yes."

"What did the village say?"

"We don't want it," she said, and turned away.

"Why not?"

"We don't want those people."

By *those people* she meant strangers.

Tongan snobbery, offensiveness, incivility and rampant xenophobia had kept the great glorious archipelago of Vava'u one of the least spoiled places in the Pacific.

That day and the next I paddled to the west, making a circuit of the deserted islands and keeping close track of the currents. The limestone cliffs of these places, pounded by the sea, were vertical and the texture of the stone like that of monastery walls in England – the same brown-gray color, the same venerable look, like Gothic ruins, as though if you excavated further you would find an abbey or a cloister or the bony relics of medieval saints.

The white beaches on the lee shores were bright in the sun, and hot and beautiful and empty, with greeny-blue lagoons shining below them. On most of the islands there were coconut palms, and birds. These islands were so lovely that it was hard to be alone on them – it was not that I required company, but rather that I wished that someone else had been there to see them: I wanted another witness, someone to share them with. If the place had been miserable I would have coped – during the days of rain I had not been lonely. ("I can endure my own despair,/ But not another's hope.") But the good weather had changed my attitude. I did not feel adventurous or lucky alone under sunny skies; I felt selfish, in all this splendor.

Most people who sail the Pacific know Vava'u – Neiafu is the destination for many of the yachts, the Port of Refuge regarded as one of the best places to pass the hurricane months from November to April. And these yachts plied around some of the Vava'u islands. But it was a place with many reefs and shoals, and most of the islands were off limits except to a shallow-draft boat like mine.

Paddling past Eua'iki Island I heard a great racket of birds, like a chorus of cockatoos, and went ashore. The area was rich in bird life – herons, and egrets, noddies and swallows and terns. But this bird screech was almost deafening.

I beached my boat and climbed the cliff for a better look, and there, massed on the branches of one tall tree high on a bluff, were several hundred fruit bats, hanging and twittering and quarreling and negligently micturating in slashes and squirts. One broke loose, and looking precisely like Bruce Wayne in disguise, and twice as ugly, it flapped in a great circle and then returned to the tree and re-attached itself, hanging upside-down.

The other bats, still hanging, flexed their membranous wings, looking like a black array of windblown and broken bumbershoots.

On my desert island, Pau, I needed to make specific plans, or else I might lose my bearings and begin brooding. So I ate several meals every day. I had a morning and afternoon paddling objective. I always did the dishes and hung them on my tree. I carefully kept my gear dry. I allowed myself a certain amount of fresh water each day, even though I knew I could get more drinking water at Taunga. I had a nap after lunch and usually went snorkeling in my own lagoon. There were lots of plump pretty fish, but I had swapped my fish spear in the Solomons – and just as well: the islander could use the thing to feed himself.

I had a taste of what it was to be a beachcomber on a happy empty island. It was mostly pure idleness, with the invented urgencies of having to carry out various duties. And then one came to believe in these fictions, and so the day was filled. It meant being alone and self-sufficient. It meant I got plenty of sleep and perhaps a bit too much sun and more mosquito bites than I had ever known. It meant keeping close track of my food and eating coconuts whenever possible. Most of all, because I had very little fresh water for washing, it meant a perpetual state of being sticky and salty.

One day I returned to my camp to see a rental sailboat, a thirty-five-footer from the Moorings outfit in Neiafu, anchored in the channel between my island and Ngau. That stretch was a sandbar at low tide. Did this yachtsman know that in an hour or so he would be aground?

I paddled over and saw four adults on deck, two couples – American, from their greeting.

"You're in very shallow water," I said. And I wondered whether my warning was also stimulated by the feeling that I did not want to wake up the next morning and see this boat wilfully trespassing on my lagoon.

"We were just leaving," the man at the wheel said. "This is a lovely spot. You American?"

"Yes. From Cape Cod."

"We spend summers in Osterville."

"Small world."

The two married couples had rented this sailboat a week ago, and were cruising in the Vava'u group. They took vacations every year in interesting places – hiking in Alaska one year, biking somewhere else another. They seemed happy and fulfilled people – their homes were in Georgia – and I was touched by their close friendship.

They asked me to come aboard, but I still had an errand to run. I didn't, but I was self-conscious about being unshaven and grubby and they looked so shipshape in their trim craft.

We talked awhile about Tonga and Tongan traits.

One of the women said, "We walk down the street and no one sees us. The Tongans don't look. Everywhere else, people look."

"You worried about being alone?" one of the men said, when I told him I was camping on a desert island.

"I'm happy."

We exchanged names, and it seemed that my name had reached their households. More than that, one couple had known one of my older brothers at Harvard.

"He was having woman trouble," the woman said. And then she began to describe him in intimate detail.

She tried hard but it was not he. It never was. Whenever someone who was not a member of my family described my brother, no matter how well they knew him – or whether they were praising or blaming – I never recognized this person in their descriptions as Mycroft. They always had him wrong. Does anyone know know your family better than you?

"What's he doing these days?"

"He lives alone with a cat named Rat on the Cape, rearing turkeys," I said. "Now and then he exhibits them. And he dedicates books to his cat."

The sun was setting by the time I paddled back and got my boat into a safe place under the trees. I was wary of being seen – my tent was behind bushes, my boat was hidden; and taking such care to hide myself I remembered Tony the beachcomber on the coast of north Queensland in his secluded camp, refusing to make any sort of path, so as not to arouse what he called "officialdom." This beachcombing experience was making me similarly furtive.

Each evening I had to write my notes and eat my dinner before night fell, or else I would stumble around in the darkness. And that was when the mosquitoes emerged. It would have been an unbearable island without mosquito repellent or netting on my tent; there were masses of them, morning and evening, breeding fast in the rain-swollen pools.

I sat on a log of driftwood writing notes while two gray herons stood in the shallows waiting for the tide to ebb so that they could more easily fish. All along the beach crabs dug holes, bringing up clawfuls of sand. As the tide went down the reef a mile out was exposed and the waves grew louder, sounding like the traffic roar on a highway.

Because of the mosquitoes and the night rain, I spent nearly all the hours of darkness in my tent, writing, drinking green tea, or lying in the dark listening to the nightmarish news. *You worried about being alone?* the yachtie had asked. No, I felt perfectly safe.

And I loved the stars – big beaming planets and small single pinpricks, fat blinking stars and masses of little peepers but also glittering clouds of them – the whole dome of the sky a storm of light over my island.

*One day, about noon, going towards my boat, I was exceedingly surprised with the print of a man's naked foot on the shore, which was very plain to be seen on the sand*, said Robinson Crusoe.

I had an identical experience, except that it was dusk – the tide had ebbed all afternoon, I looked up from my meal and saw footprints everywhere. They led down the beach and into the woods; up to the cliffs, along the shore, across the dunes, all around the camp, desperate little solitary tracks.

There were hundreds, perhaps thousands of footprints, suggesting vast wandering mobs of idle strangers, and what frightened me – what eventually impelled me to break camp soon afterward and head for the nearest inhabited island, where I was assured of a welcome – and what sent a chill through me, was the thought that every single footprint, every urgent little trail, was mine.

So, with this hint of rock fever, I left my little island, and for the first time on my travels there was no one to say goodbye to. I left this secret place silently – this small mute island in the mist, the haunt of pissing bats and watchful herons. I simply slipped away and made off across the reef, going clockwise among the islands, past Euakafa to the big island of Kapa. I saw a wide reef being lashed by waves on the channel so I stuck close to the shore.

Three miles along I saw a stone jetty and a man struggling with a net while another steadied a dinghy.

The net was underwater, and it seemed to be very heavy. The man was having no success in lifting it.

"You have fish in the net?" I asked.

The fisherman groaned and heaved and muttered yes.

I paddled near and hovered, watching. The men seemed to be blundering, one almost swamping his boat, the other tangling himself in his net. At last the man with the net dumped the catch, a mass of sardine-sized fish, into the dinghy. Then they beckoned to me and offered me a bucket of them, the first time in Tonga anyone offered anything to me. When I politely declined the fish, the men lost interest in me.

More men were fishing under the cliffs of Kapa, catching larger fish on hand-lines. When I said hello they returned my greeting but without moving their heads, without expression, just an impassive "Huh."

To keep away from the yachts – I could see half a dozen here and there, bobbing at anchorages – I decided to paddle through a lagoon, which was too shallow for anything bigger than a canoe. The island just to the west of the lagoon was Utungake, where I intended to camp and, near the shore, women – fifty or sixty of them – were standing waist-deep, holding buckets, and gathering – what?

A woman called me over. Like the rest of the women she was fully dressed and completely wet. She was sitting in water to her armpits with four other women, gutting sea creatures – eels or slugs.

"Where is your wife?" she said, by way of salutation.

"Not here," I said. "Where's your husband?"

"I no gat none." This was Enna, and she was very fat, her hair hanging into the lagoon, her fingers smeared with eel guts the color of butterscotch.

"Why not get one?"

"You can hee-hee be hee-hee my husbeen!"

Another named Melly said, "What is your name?"

"Paul."

"Like dis?" She made a sphere with her fat hands. "Ball?"

"Not ball," I said, but she was tittering – they all were – "but Paul. Like Saint Paul."

"Thank you, Meestah Ball."

"What are you doing?"

"Cutting dese," Emma said. "*Lemas.*"

Now I could see that they were sea-slugs, but limper than any I had seen, the shape and color of bulging condoms. The women were gathering them from the bottom of the lagoon – there were thousands of these creatures in the mud – cutting them open, and extracting a long orange organ, sticky and dripping, which they dumped into the plastic bucket.

"You like?" Enna asked.

"We don't have *lemas* in America."

"You eat."

"I no eat," I said.

Enna twirled the raw gooey thing around her finger and sucked it like a noodle into her mouth and said, "Yum!"

Melly did the same. Then Melly picked up a gelatinous eel from the lagoon mud with her knife and held it dripping in my face.

"You afray of dis?"

"No," I said.

"You eat it den."

It was what bratty schoolchildren did to the school wimp, or the new kid. Melly held the long limp creature on the blade of her sharp knife, while I sat in my kayak smiling at her.

"Put it down, Melly," I said.

"You afray," she said, and jerked the knife at me.

I tried not to blink.

"Why you no eat dis?"

"Because I'm not hungry," I said, and thought, *Fatso*.

I paddled farther into the lagoon, going faster than any of these people could walk. Most of the villagers on Utungake struck me as being incredibly stupid and slow, and they seemed to take only a cruel interest in other people. Everyone was digging for slugs. No one looked at me. A woman carried a big water jug through the lagoon. Like everyone else she was wearing all her clothes. They always swam in dresses and skirts and blouses, like Victorians. The boys wore shirts and trousers. But everyone was barefoot, in spite of the coral and the sea-urchins.

I went swimming myself at the head of the lagoon and in the late afternoon got permission from a nearby village to camp on this deserted beach, distributed some silk scarves, and settled down for the night, which was full of lantern light and laughter and barking dogs.

The next morning I paddled back to civilization.

"And yet the sea is a horrible place," Robert Louis Stevenson wrote in 1888 to a friend in London. He had been wandering the Pacific in a chartered schooner, *Casco*, looking for a happy island on which he would spend the last six years of his life. He liked islands. He hated the sea. Sailing the sea was "stupefying to the mind and poisonous to the temper; the sea, the motion, the lack of space, the cruel publicity, the villainous tinned foods, the sailors, the captain, the passengers – but you are amply repaid when you sight an island, and drop anchor in a new world."

Those were my sentiments exactly: sailing the sea was a monotony of doldrums interrupted by windy periods of nightmarish terror. No desert was ever deadlier or more tedious than an ocean. Then – after weeks or months of your thinking *Life is a reach, and then you jibe* – landfall.

I had never loved a boat enough to want to spend a year in it, and the fact is that yachties loved their boats – every cupboard and binnacle. Yachties were also finicky, orderly, conservative and yet haters of authority; they were self-sufficient – capable menders and fixers of things; they could be peevish; they frequently shifted the topic of conversation to Doomsday. They had little in common with landlubbers – was it this that had driven them offshore? And had these people always been so orderly or had yachting, with its limited space, forced them to become such fuss-budgets?

Whatever, I saw them everywhere in Oceania, and they seemed to me truly a breed apart. They were not intrusive. They were great live-and-let-livers. Yachting involved certain complex courtesies. If you didn't bother them they would not presume on you. They wanted mainly to be left alone – that is why they had weighed anchor in the first place. They spent years and years in their boats. They had sold houses and businesses and cars; they had quit jobs and put their life savings into this venture, the all-consuming occupation of being Flying Dutchmen.

In the Port of Refuge of Vava'u were thirty-four yachts, all bobbing at moorings, waiting out the hurricane season. Most had been there for three or four months, some for several years. On good days the yachties ventured out and might spend a night at an anchorage, near one of the islands; but mostly they stayed here, going ashore from time to time, for water at the dock, or food at the Neiafu shops, though generally they hated the shops for being expensive. (Yachties never threw money around – partly out of frugality, but mostly out of a desire to be anonymous: spenders were always noticed.) They bought bananas and coconuts at the market, bread at the bakery, and they checked the post office or the Moorings agency for mail from home.

They did not often call each other by their proper names, but rather referred to the boat.

"*Windrift* is a plumber," a yachtie told me gesturing to the vessel. "*Southern Cross* is a builder. *Sourdough* is a doctor, though you'd never know it – he's a very nice guy. *Gungha* used to be a lawyer and now he's a salmon fisherman during the season up in Alaska – there's money in that. You get all kinds of people, a real cross-section, you know. Of course in the season people fly in and meet their yachts. 'Take the boat to Tonga – we'll meet you.' They cruise a little, then fly home. 'Take the boat to Fiji –'"

We were on the deck at Neiafu, talking about cruising. I had come in with a week's growth of beard, in my salt-flecked kayak, and a group of yachtsmen had taken an interest. Mine was clearly a seaworthy craft, even if it was only a little more than fifteen feet long. Yachties admired anything functional that was well made and compact, because the best yachts were enemies of superfluity.

*Sundog* said, "We try to spend a year in each place."

And he added that he and his family – two little girls – had been cruising the Pacific for the past seven years.

"We had a great time in Tahiti – not Papeete, but Moorea and Tahiti-Iti, the little island just behind Tahiti. That's another world. Very sensual. Then you come here and everyone's going to church."

"We've been cruising since eighty-six," *Glory* said. "This is our second time in Tonga, and I can tell you it's really gone downhill. This used to be the cleanest harbor in the Pacific."

"I studied history and Polynesia navigation," *Dancer* said. "When I came here I discovered that no one knew a damn thing about it."

*Sundog* was still talking about Tahiti: "Your Polynesian doesn't really have a problem with nakedness the way they do here. They're very welcoming – you see all these smiles."

"Now there I have to disagree with you," *Glory* said. "We brought needles and fish-hooks to the Marquesas. We always try to leave a place a little bit better than we found it. That's our way. But they weren't interested. They couldn't care less. They didn't want our needles and fish-hooks."

"The thing is" – this was *Dancer* speaking – "you always judge a place by the last place you were in. We were last in New Zealand. Everyone talks to you in New Zealand. Great people. Great sailors too. It's blowing a Force Ten and you hear some Kiwi on the radio saying calmly, 'We're okay – just out here with the missus' and the fucken Tasman Sea is like hell on earth."

I introduced the topic of Tongans, because I had been wondering whether I had been imagining their xenophobia and bad temper. It is quite easy in travel to project your own mood onto the place you are in; you become isolated and fearful and then find a place malevolent – and it might be Happy Valley!

"Tongans? They're surly," *Sundog* said. "They're unhelpful. They're resentful. They don't care about you."

"They pretend not to see you – don't even look at you, right?" *Dancer* said. "But they're always looking at you sideways. They see everything."

"I blame the church," *Glory* said. "The Free Wesleyans especially – they're always collecting money. They get thousands from these people, but what do these people have? They're tithing like crazy and in hock to the church."

"Tongans are unteachable," *Sundog* said, beginning to rant. "Hey, they just don't want to learn. They're slow, lazy, and a lot of them are real wise-guys."

"Your Fijian is pretty affluent," *Dancer* said. "But if you have business to do in Fiji you always do it with some downtrodden Indian."

"I'm headed for Samoa," I said.

*Glory* said, "Now I wish – I really wish – there was something good I could say about your Samoan. But I can't." *Glory* smiled a gloating smile. "Oh, sure, your Western Samoan has to scratch a little harder, so he might be a worker. But I was in Pago for two years and I thought the people were horrible – they steal, they lie, they're lazy, they hate you, they're takers. We give them seventy-five million and what do we get for it?" He smiled again. "They're violent, too."

"People get involved there, though," *Dancer* said.

"See, a lot of your so-called expatriates are not very bright lights," *Glory* said. "But they shine more brightly in places like that."

"And this," *Gungha* said. He had just stepped onto the dock and was tying up his tender.

"Your Tuomotuan is a delightful person," *Sundog* was saying. "They'll *umu* a dog or a pig and make you feel very welcome."

So it went, our discussion on the dock. They often had such confabs on this neutral ground. But they also visited each other, rowing from yacht to yacht in their little dinghies, paying calls. Sometimes they yelled from rail to rail. But each boat occupied its own specific area of water. There were no close neighbours. When it was windy they battened down.

"It's funny," Mike of *Gungha* said. "You often find in a place like this the very problems you thought you left behind – pollution, bureaucracy, all that."

*Glory* told me how proud he was of his self-reliance. He had left Honolulu a year or so ago with four thousand dollars' worth of stores – canned his own meat and fish, made his own chutney.

"My wife bakes bread once or twice a week. It's fantastic bread. We give it out," he said. "The one thing we have is time."

Who, in the world they had left, could say that?

They also read books, and *Glory*, the most manic, sententious and domineering yachtie in the harbor told me how much he disliked *The Mosquito Coast*.

"I hated the guy in it. I couldn't stand him. You wrote that book? I really didn't like that book at all."

I said, "I'd probably hate your wife's bread."

"My kids think I'm just like the guy in that book," Verne Kirk of *Orion* said. "So I think that book's a masterpiece."

And that was the end of that discussion. The yachties were soon in their dinghies, rowing home; all except Verne.

"I like that book because it's true," Verne said. "People do that. They leave the States, just like he did. You see them here all the time."

He was the archetypical Pacific wanderer, down to his last whisker and eccentricity. He was nearly always barefoot, with a bandanna around his head; he smoked heavily – yachties were frequently heavy smokers, I found – and played Rolling Stones music on his boat. He had spent years tacking back and forth in Oceania. He was in his mid to late fifties – funny, friendly, and crotchety. "Life is a two-edged sword," he often said. His *Orion* was a battered catamaran that he used for charters, taking people out for a day of snorkeling or a week of cruising. But *Orion* was also his home. He had sailed it from Samoa. It contained all his possessions, the most valued of which was his library. He was always quoting – Margaret Mead, Captain Cook, William Mariner, various historians, and me. Freud's *Totem and Tabu* was a great favorite. He showed me his extensively underlined and annotated copy.

"Business is pretty bad here, but the place is nice," Verne said. "It's true that I have few enemies – *palangis*, naturally. Machiavelli says you should judge a man by his enemies. That's all right with me. My enemies are dipshits."

He had spent five years in Samoa and was alone in my experience in putting in a good word for the Samoan people.

"I liked them," Verne said. "American-ness is only skin deep. They're funny and they left me alone. I pretended to be crazy. I guess I am a little crazy. If people think you're whacko they keep their distance."

"People say Samoans are violent," I said.

"Oh, sure, they are. But that didn't bother me," Verne said. "I had a pretty good job there."

"How was the money?"

"Five bucks an hour – chickenfeed. But I lived on my boat. I didn't have any expenses."

Verne said that "for reasons too complicated to go into now" – he often used the expression when speaking of his exploits, and I liked the "now" most of all – he had been a staff engineer at the Department of Public Works in Pago Pago.

Verne confirmed that Vava'u was one of the great yachting destinations. People sailed from Hawaii to Pago and then here. Or they came from Fiji or New Zealand. But where to go from here was a difficult decision from the navigational point of view. If they continued west to Vanatu and Australia they then had to sail north into Micronesia and more northerly still into cold waters in order to pick up the westerlies that would take them back to Hawaii. The alternative was to sail east out of Tonga and go as far east as necessary, beyond the Tuomotus, heading towards Easter Island, in order to pick up the southeast trade winds for the run back to Hawaii.

It all sounded like hell to me. And for most people in the Port of Refuge leaving Vava'u was the last thing on their nautical minds. Verne had been in the harbor for two years and said he was here more or less for the duration. If you asked what that might be like he would reply by saying that life was a two-edged sword.

I told Verne that one of my canvas boat bags was coming apart at the seams, as a result of being thrown around by baggage-handlers. It was the size and texture of a mail bag and I had repaired it with layers of duct tape.

"I know just the man who can fix that," Verne said.

"It has to be done with an industrial sewing-machine," I said.

"Andy on the *Jakaranda* has got an industrial sewing-machine."

The *Jakaranda* was a sleek green schooner at a mooring some distance from the dock. Andy and his companion Sandy had been coming to Tonga since the mid-eighties. Andy said they had become somewhat disenchanted by the Virgin Islands – the selfishness and rapacity of the locals, the numerous yachts. They liked the pace of life in Vava'u, they liked the people, too.

"Where is your home port?" I asked.

Andy said, "This is. *Jakaranda* is our home. We've been living in this boat for the past twelve years."

It was a beautiful boat, made twenty years before in Holland, lying deep in the water because – Andy said – of the stuff they had accumulated: artifacts from around the world, the sewing-machine, a big tiki from the Marquesas. Even so, there was plenty of room to ramble around in.

"I just got a Tongan work permit," Andy said. And he explained that he would be making and mending sails – all kinds of sewing. "In the season this harbor will be full of boats."

I showed him my boat bag.

"I can fix that," he said.

He tore out all the stitches and mended it expertly in fifteen minutes. It was a brilliant stitching job, and his willingness and his skill made it an even greater act of kindness.

We had coffee and chocolate cookies that had been sent to Tonga by Sandy's mother in Pennsylvania. Sandy was mellow, pleasant, good-tempered and, like many yachties, easygoing because she was on her own boat. That was also a yachtie temperament. You spent years and years in a confined space in all sorts of weather and you either coped and developed a cheery positive outlook, or else you headed home.

Andy and Sandy expressed a genuine liking for the Tongans, and echoed other yachties in saying they had no immediate plans.

"In a way, this is the best place to be," Sandy said. "I mean, with the war on. If the worst happens, we could just settle down and plant taro."

As someone who needed space, I marveled at their capacity for living at such close quarters – and the marriages and friendships that prevailed over those conditions seemed to be as solid as it was possible for a human relationship to be, totally interdependent.

I remarked on this Sandy, who said, "This is the way I want to live."

"Going from one strange hotel room to another can be traumatic," Andy said. "But in this boat we can go anywhere and still have our own bed, our own food." He thought a moment. "Our own toilet."

But it also meant years on the water, years making crossings, long periods in terrible harbors, always sleeping in a narrow berth, often banging your head, a whole life in which the world was elsewhere. To live such a life you needed a companion, who was handy and healthy and optimistic and who didn't get seasick, and who was willing to renounce his or her country; and then you went where the wind took you.

You had to live in a certain way in these island harbors. Yachties could not live too intensely among the local people or they would be destroyed. It was the reason for their watchfulness. It was why they only spoke to me after I had been in the area for more than a week. They bobbed offshore, making the odd foray into town. Who in marine history, or in the history of oceanic exploration, ever lived like this? Either they went ashore and conquered, claimed the island, and left; or they stayed ashore, anthropologizing, botanizing, evangelizing, being a complete nuisance to the locals, whom they wished to subvert.

The yachties at their moorings had the equivalent of a gypsy camp at the edge of town, slightly exotic, occasionally insinuating themselves into the life of the place.

"The tourists do as they like – they wear bikinis – but they leave in a few days," one of the yachties told me. "We have to keep to the rules, because we're staying."

They had to acknowledge the fact that they existed there for months or years because of the hospitality of the Tongans. They did not abuse that hospitality. They didn't litter, they wore modest clothes when they were in town, they endured the Tongan sabbath. The yachties' generally compassionate attitude made me look harder at my own opinion of the Tongans.

I told Verne this – that I felt a bit guilty for distrusting them, and that I had found very little hospitality here. Or was I being too harsh on these people?

"People here – they may not be friendly but they leave you alone," Verne said. "It's a two-edged sword."

We were sitting on the dock at the Port of Refuge, among the perfect little islands of Vava'u, each of which was a perfectly rounded piece of land, many of them just like drops of batter on a hot griddle, the ones that cook quickly – simple little places with no people – that was the thrill, the innocence of it, and anyone with a little boat like mine could play Robinson Crusoe here. Each one was just what you imagined a tropical island to be – palms, woods, surf on the bright beach, limpid green lagoons. I was so glad I had come, and felt that I had discovered an island that few others knew, and had found a way of going there and living on it. That was the realization of the South Seas dream – and I had seen how the dream had been deficient. It was not the mosquitoes or the rain. But really I had wished that there had been someone else with me in that pint-sized paradise – a woman.

Meanwhile, Verne was talking about Doomsday, because a moment ago I had asked.

"The Doomsday thing is very common among yacht people," Verne said. "You hear it all the time. 'The world's going to hell,' 'This used to be a great country,' 'This place is awful,' 'The end is nigh.' So they buy a boat and ship out. They come here and talk about it."

He was quiet a moment, and then glanced up and looked across the lovely harbor to the green wall of Pangaimotu.

"This is a fabulous place to sit around, talking about the end of the world."

# 16

## In the Backwaters of Western Samoa

Apia, the squalid harbor town of Western Samoa (but it was also squalid a hundred years ago in the heyday of its most famous resident, Robert Louis Stevenson), seemed to me mournfully rundown, with broken roads and faded and peeling paint on its ill-assorted wooden buildings, and Samoans rather gloatingly rude and light-fingered, quoting the Bible as they picked your pocket. There were hardly any beaches here, too. But no matter how misbegotten and wayward an island in Oceania happened to be, it always had stars in its sky.

On the nights without rain I sprayed myself with insect repellent, and went out to the shore to look at the stars.

Even in Africa I had never seen such a profusion of stars as I saw on these clear nights on Pacific isles – not only big beaming planets and small single pinpricks (plenty of fat blinking stars and masses of little peepers), but also glittering clouds of them – the whole dome of the sky crowded with thick shapes formed from stars, overlaid with more shapes, a brilliant density, like a storm of light over a black depthless sea, made brighter still by twisting auroras composed of tiny star grains – points of light so fine and numerous they seemed like luminous vapor, the entire sky hung with veils of light like dazzling smoke. Even on a moonless night you could read or write by these stars, and they made night in Oceania as vast and dramatic as day.

That was how people had migrated here to Samoa, from Vava'u in Tonga, culturally its nearest neighbor: the old Polynesian voyagers had made complex charts of these stars – star maps – and traveled great distances with them in their canoes, star-gazing and navigating. This was accomplished 1,000 years before the Europeans – Portuguese in this case – ventured out and discovered the Azores 900 miles into the Atlantic. The Polynesians would have guffawed at such timidity, though these days they are a seasick-prone people.

With daybreak the starry enchantment vanished from Apia, and once more it looked rusted and neglected. And it was much starker on

Sundays, a day observed as fanatically in Samoa as in Tonga, for on Sundays the town was deserted. Elsewhere on Upolu, Samoans with big brown chins and fleshy noses, carrying Bibles, and dressed all in white – white dresses, white shirts – headed for church. In Samoa, as in other Polynesian places, I found myself muttering against missionaries and generally rooting for heathens. Pacific Christians were neither pacific nor Christian, nor were they particularly virtuous as a result of all their Bible-thumping. Religion only made them more sententious and hypocritical, and it seemed the aim of most Samoan preachers to devise new ways for emptying people's pockets.

I had arrived on a Sunday – day of obstacles. It was impossible to rent a car or do much else on a Samoan Sunday – the sabbath had to be kept holy. Somehow, taxis circumvented this restriction, even if buses could not.

I took a taxi and I looked around the island for a place to launch my boat. I was eager to paddle to a smaller island or even a village. I could not blame Apia for being awful. Apia was miserably typical. Except for bright little Port Vila in Vanuatu, no city or town in the whole of Oceania was pleasant. Islanders were not urbanized at all – they became antsy and deracinated in anything larger than a village and, without the means to be self-sufficient, they generally made a mess of their towns. They were habituated to their own fruit trees and to crapping on the beach and flinging their garbage into the shallow lagoon. Disorderly towns were not so surprising. Apart from Meganesia, where immigrant islanders were considered a nuisance and a social problem, no island in Oceania was industrialized and, except for tourist hotels, few buildings on Pacific islands were higher than three storeys.

Pacific islanders of the traditional sort, as Samoans were, seemed to function best in families, and in order to thrive they needed a hut or a bungalow with a little vegetable patch by the sea. Samoan towns were worse than most, and included Carson, a suburb of Los Angeles, where there were more Samoans than in the whole of the Samoan islands and obnoxious posses (there were also branches in New Zealand) of the violent street gang, SOS – the Sons of Samoa. In America, the Samoans' large physical size served them well in football (nearly every professional football team in the NFL had its Samoan tackles), and some had succeeded as sumo wrestlers or musicians – the Boo-Ya Tribe, a quintet of shaven-headed fatties, had made a fortune in Los Angeles imitating black rappers. Samoans were whispered about in the Pacific for being big and bull-like and, though placid by nature, were said to be capable of extreme violence.

Samoan stories are retailed throughout the Pacific – the Samoan who casually snapped someone's arm in two, the Samoan who ripped off a man's ear, the Samoans who sat in front of a house and then mooned the occupants when they were told to push off, the Samoan who bit off an assailant's fingers, the Samoan who went haywire in the disco, crushing a hairdresser's skull ("Because she touched my plastic toy," the Samoan explained in his defense, in court). In the "Samoans Too Big to Fit" category, there are endless tales of airlines having to unbolt seats or remove armrests in order to accommodate Samoans; too big for telephone booths, too big to fit through doorways, too big for bar stools, for bicycles, for toilet seats. A truthful friend of mine traveling on Hawaiian Airways out of Pago Pago witnessed the mounting terror of flight attendants when a Samoan man, urgently wishing to relieve himself, could not fit through the lavatory door. The employees' desperate remedy was to hold up blankets to create a wall of privacy for the Samoan, who stood just outside the lavatory and pissed in a great slashing arc through the door and into the hopper.

The sympathetic Robert Louis Stevenson liked the Samoans for being unpretentious family people, and he managed them by cozying up to the chiefs and patronizing his hired help. The islanders liked being taken seriously by this raffish and yet respectable *palangi*, who said "Some of the whites are degraded beyond description," but it is clear that Stevenson kept his distance.

"He says that the Tahitians are by far finer men than the Samoans," the bumptious New Englander Henry Adams wrote, after he had visited Stevenson in Apia in 1891; "and that he does not regard the Samoans as an especially fine race, or the islands here as specially beautiful."

Yet Stevenson had done more than put Samoa on the map. He was the magician that some writers are – people who, by using a specific location as a setting, lend it enchantment.

A place that is finely described in a novel by such a person is given a power of bewitchment that it never really loses, no matter how much its reality changes. Not only Samoa, but other islands and, in a sense, the whole of the South Pacific, is a clear example of this sort of transformation because it has been used so effectively as a setting by writers as various as Melville, Stevenson, Somerset Maugham, Rupert Brooke, Mark Twain, Jack London, Pierre Loti, Michener, and even Gauguin in his only book, *Noa-Noa*. Fiction has the capacity to make even an ordinary place seem special. The simple mention of the name of a place can make that place become singular, never mind what it looks like.

I sometimes felt as though I was part of that process of improvement or transformation, too – in spite of my natural skepticism – because I felt such relief, such happiness, paddling my boat through a lagoon under sunny skies. And I suspected that when I came to write about having come to the Pacific in such distress, needing the consolation of blue lagoons, my subsequent relief would perhaps transform a buggy drowsing island into a happy isle.

But Robert Louis Stevenson had the whole world to choose from. He had traipsed through Europe and Britain, he had bummed across America, he had sailed throughout the Pacific, from California to Australia and back. The King of Hawaii, Kalakaua, personally urged him to settle on Oahu. Instead, Stevenson chartered a schooner and sailed to scores of islands, seeking the perfect place, which he had depicted long before, as a young man, in a verse he had written in Edinburgh:

> *I should like to rise and go*
> *Where the golden apples grow;*
> *Where below another sky*
> *Parrot islands anchored lie.*

No golden apples in Samoa, and no parrots. There were quarreling islanders and drunken *palangis*. The Stevenson family arrived in the rainy season, when Apia is at its most dismal – hot, clammy, humid, muddy, with gray skies. Yet Stevenson homed in on it, knowing that he had few years left to live (in the event, only four). So what was the attraction of Samoa?

In a word, the postal service. Other islands were prettier – the high islands in the Marquesas overwhelmed Stevenson with their rugged beauty, and the atoll of Fakarava in the Tuomotus was bliss – the Stevenson family rented a cottage on the lagoon. But on those islands it could be many months between mail-boats. In Samoa the mail came regularly, at least once a month, via New Zealand, or else from ships in the Sydney to San Francisco run. Stevenson was a zestful letter-writer and, as a novelist who depended on serializing his books in magazines, he needed a reliable postal service in order to make a living. That settled it, because the mail was his lifeline.

Afterwards, when he became acquainted with the island, he found ways of fitting in and even becoming predominant. The Samoan social structure of clan chiefs and drones and hangers-on and peasants and pot-wallopers was familiar enough to an upper-middle-class Scotsman. Partly through insinuation and partly through recruitment, Stevenson became important in Samoan society. This allowed him to live like a Scottish laird among obsequious chieftains – and that suited him best of all. He was not a snob, though he had the Scottish love of stern affectation and obscure formality, and especially the Highland proclivity for fancy-dress at ceremonials: all the household staff at his house Vailima wore a Royal Stuart tartan *lavalava* – the nearest thing in Oceania to a kilt.

The power and the dignity of lairdship Stevenson found very handy. He made the most of his four years in Samoa – the late 1880s and early 1890s were years of disruption on the islands (Britain and Germany vying with America for control of the archipelago), and Stevenson – who was partisan, on the Samoan side – recorded it all in his *A Footnote to History*. The Samoans were masters of manipulation – they had made a fine art of obligating outsiders as part of the family and then taking them for all they were worth, while at the same time making these suckers feel important. Blending Samoan traits with those of the Scottish Highlands, Stevenson returned the favor and bamboozled them into believing they were part of his big tangled family – his elderly widowed mother had joined them, his wife's two children by her first marriage, his stepdaughter's drunken husband – it was all *fa'a Samoa*. He was Laird of the Manor as well as their historian and *tusitala*, "writer of stories." Stevenson in Samoa is a tremendous success story, a masterful example of forward planning – and everyone profited by his perfect choice of island: his family, his readers, the Samoans, and Stevenson himself. As Byron had done in Greece, he had found a great place to die.

I stopped by Vailima, Stevenson's house, but was sent on my way by an officious sentry who told me it was occupied by a paramount chief and not open to the public.

"You can visit his grave," the man said.

"Gravestones depress me," I said. They were for pilgrims and hagiographers.

I wanted an inkling of his spirit. It was the house he had built, and where he had lived, that I wanted to see – there were always vibrations of past tenants in houses. Why should I want to climb all morning up Mount Vaea to see the little plot which contained his moldering bones?

After a tour of the north coast, the taxi-driver dropped me back on Beach Road, the empty main street of Apia, and demanded extra money.

"Because I waited for you."

He meant he had waited while I had walked fifty feet to a possible launching place on the coast.

I said, "Don't be silly," and gave him only the taxi fare.

"You not paying me," he said, muttering darkly. "I going to the police station."

"What are you going to do at the police station?"

"Tell them. I waited."

"How long did you wait?"

"A long time," he said, and looked away. Finally he said, "Fifteen minutes."

"What is your name?" I asked.

"Simi."

"Is fifteen minutes a long time in Apia, Simi? I would have thought it was a very short time."

Simi said nothing.

"How much more money do you want?"

"Two *tala*."

I handed it over.

The next day, I drove to the ferry landing on the northwest corner of the island, Mulifanua Wharf, but there was no ferry to Savaii that morning and no one knew when it might leave. I went farther west and at a little bay was set upon by five fierce guard dogs – German shepherds, the sort that, spitted and grilled, would be considered the high point of a Tongan feast. A German in an expedition hat appeared and called them off.

His name was Stefan. The company he worked for had been granted a lease on this neck of land by the owner, the head of state for life, Malietoa Tanumafili II, who lived in Stevenson's grand house, Vailima. Stefan was supervising the building of ten traditional huts, called *fales*.

"I saw this beach from the road yesterday," I said, "when everyone was at church. They pray a lot here, eh?"

"If you steal a lot, you pray a lot," Stefan said.

He confirmed my impression that there were very few beaches on Upolu. There were more on Savaii, he said. I told him that it was my intention to paddle there, across the Apolima Strait.

"That's very dangerous," he said.

It seemed to me that people on Pacific islands were inclined to say a thing was dangerous when they knew very little about it, but I intended to ask a local fisherman just the same.

Stefan showed me around the thatched-roof huts at the edge of the lagoon. He said the huts were not finished but that I could stay, for a fee. The sky was gray and the lagoon was dark and muddy, but it was a pleasant enough place to stay – quiet, remote from Apia – and a good spot to launch from.

I moved in and assembled my boat, and that became my base for a time.

My first paddling objective was an island, Manono, across a three-mile channel. There were 1,500 people on Manono, but no dogs, no roads, no vehicles, no electricity. I thought of it as a hundred years offshore.

There was a legend about Manono, how it was not a fixed island at all, but rather a piece of land, a sort of floating fortress owned by Chief Lautala of Fiji. The chief had sailed it to Samoa in the year dot in order to fight and conquer the Samoans. It was a bloody battle, and though he lost it he inflicted so many fatalities on the Samoan side that the numerous dead gave an identity to the floating piece of land – Manono means "numerous."

I drank beer that night in my hut and listened on my short-wave radio to what turned out to be the collapse of Iraqi resistance in Kuwait – an all-out rout of a raggle-taggle, underfed and demoralized army of cowards and persecutors. And after that, when the clouds parted in the sky, I looked at the stars – ignorant star-gazing providing for me one of the most vivid experiences I had, traveling through Oceania. And I was reminded that such stars were the best part of being in a wilderness or an ocean – and could take the curse off even so sorry a place as Apia.

It was windy when I slipped into my boat the next morning, preparing for Manono. Stefan repeated that my real problem was the current in the middle of the channel – because of an incoming tide I might be swept onto the reef to the southeast.

At such times in Oceania, I always reflected on my paddling between Falmouth and Martha's Vineyard in the summer – a greater distance, stronger wind, less predictable current, and much more irascible and inhospitable natives.

With that thought in mind I set off and paddled hard for an hour or so until I was within half a mile of Manono – I had passed through a strong but not obnoxious current. Beyond it I could see the tilted volcano cone which was Apolima Island. In the distance, about nine miles away, was the island of Savaii – another good paddling trip and a place I wished to see.

All that was visible on Manono from my kayak were a profusion of outhouses on stone jetties – some of them hanging over the sea, others poised above the shoreline. They were called by various names – *fale ki'o*, "shit house," or *fale sami*, "sea house," *fale laititi*, "little house," or the more euphemistic *fale uila*, "lightning house."

Closer to the island, the Samoan houses that were visible were traditionally made and as symmetrical as on Upolu, with open sides, but the whole thing had the general shape and contours of a Spanish conquistador's helmet. A breeze wafted through the hut in the day, and at night the rolled-up woven blinds were let down, and served as walls. The huts of Western Samoa were attractive and comfortable structures, and were stronger than any huts I saw elsewhere in the Pacific. It has been said – by Margaret Mead, among others – that the Samoan extended family, the *aiga*, is a closely knit and effectively interdependent household; and I wondered to what extent this well-made hut played a part. Certainly it was able to house many people – and with these open sides it was always possible to see children playing inside, or women weaving, or people talking or napping – an atmosphere of activity or repose, seemingly at times almost idyllic.

I heard roosters crowing and children screeching, but – unusually for a Pacific island – no barking dogs. About eight or ten children met me on the rocky shore as I paddled to the edge and got out, below the village of Faleu. They were chanting *"Palangi! Palangi!"* and they quarrelled among each other as they vied to help me put my boat on the village canoe rack.

*Foreigners walking, cycling or riding motorbikes through* [Samoan] *villages will frequently be considered moving targets by village children, and stones will fly,* a current guidebook to Samoa advised. *They will often surround you mockingly and demand money or sweets and will make great sport of trying to upset you.*

This gratuitous hostility I found to be generally the case, from that day onwards, and throughout my time on whatever island in Samoa. Samoans could be merciless to outsiders. It was bad for a man and worse for women. A stranger was persecuted precisely because he or she was a stranger – alone, unprotected, unfamiliar with the language, uncomprehending, easy to confuse, not part of any family, unconnected, weak, an alien, the perfect victim.

You were mocked if you became angry with your persecutors (who always outnumbered you), and if you attempted to be conciliatory they took this as a sign of weakness and were worse. The conflict – a wicked game – was unwinnable.

These children pestered me from the moment I stepped ashore on Manono, but I thought it was probably better not to warn them about stealing or damaging my boat, because I didn't want to give them any ideas – knowing that I was concerned, I guessed it might be the very thing they would do.

I walked east, counter-clockwise, around the island, ignoring the screeching kids and making a point of talking to older people. The teenage boys I passed were fairly monotonous in their mockery, but I walked on, leaving these Christians behind.

In spite of their ill-nature, the island seemed traditional – and very likely there was something in their ill-nature that was traditional, too. All explorers in the Pacific, from Abel Tasman in 1642 onward, had to confront thievery, silliness, aggression, greed, and rapacity. Perhaps Samoan mockery was nothing new, but it was rather boring to have to endure this and then have to listen to either a travel writer or someone at the Samoan Visitors' Bureau extolling the virtues of Samoan hospitality. Of all the places I had traveled in my life, Samoa was one in which one needed letters of introduction or the names of natives. Otherwise, you were condemned to being alienated.

But alienation was my natural condition. As for their hostility, I kept strolling and watched my back.

"We are traditional here on Manono," a man told me, when I asked him to characterize the island. "We relate the stories of our ancestors."

This sounded fine, but when I asked him to tell me a few, he went blank – I suspected he meant family histories rather than island legends or myths.

Another said, "Manono is a good place, because we have no air pollution."

We were looking in the direction of Upolu. I said, "Is there air pollution on Upolu?"

"No," he said.

The fact was that the nearest air pollution was perhaps five thousand miles away in Los Angeles.

"And we have no buses."

"Is that good or bad?"

"Good. Buses have fumes. They cause dust."

It would have been something of a miracle to find a bus on an island with no roads. The path around the island was at its widest not more than twelve inches.

A man I met on this circumambulation said he was a minister of the church. But his necktie – ties were required among the clergy – was lettered *Malua Theological College*. He admitted that he was still a divinity student and that he had come to Manono to practice his preaching.

While the younger people were almost uniformly mocking (*Palangi! Palangi!*) the older ones were correct – neither friendly nor distant.

There are complex rules governing greetings in Samoa, as well as extensive aspects of etiquette, including many prohibitions. A stranger, unfamiliar with the Samoan way, is therefore a sitting duck. The Samoans had not seen many tourists, and their attitude seemed to be that if you were part of the family you were left alone, and if you were a stranger you were fair game.

I was followed by more kids, and always I heard the word *palangi* in their muttering. I usually turned to face them.

"Yes. I am a *palangi*. Do you have a problem?"

In a shouting, jeering way one would say, "Where are you coming from?"

"I think Japan," one would say.

This they regarded as very funny.

"Do I look Japanese?"

"Yes! He Japanese!"

A woman sidled up to me at the edge of a village and said, "What you religion? You a Cafflick?"

'I said, "Yes, in a way."

"Come with me," she said, and brought me to her house and showed me little shrines and holy pictures tucked into the eaves of her *fale*. She was like an early Christian in the furtive way she revealed these items to me.

"I am the only Cafflick in Salua," she said. "Please stay with me."

This seemed rather awkward, but she said that her husband was on his way back home and that he would be pleased. Her name was Rosa, she was twenty-five, and had five children. Her husband returned soon after, and though I half expected him to be angry over finding me alone with his wife – it is very bad form in most societies – he did not take it amiss. He repeated the invitation to stay.

I said I had other plans, and when he told me he had just been fishing, I asked him whether he ever went to Apolima, the island beyond the reef, two or three miles from Manono.

"We don't fish at Apolima. It is too deep."

They poled their canoes through the shallow reef and never ventured into water deeper than the length of their poles.

Continuing my walk, I was accosted half a dozen times and asked, "You have a wife?" and "What is her name?" and "Where is she?" – questions that always presented difficulties to me.

But I could see that the island had a pleasant side. It was backward-looking, with its coconut palms and its mango trees, its well-tended gardens and its tidy huts set on well-made house platforms, all of black boulders, the sort of stonework that is found in the most traditional parts of Polynesia. The wood carvings in Polynesia did not interest me. The music I found ineffectual – though the drumming could be attractive, when it was strong and syncopated. The cannibalism was just a story of goblins, meant to give you the willies – very few people could vouch for it, and little of it had been documented. But two aspects of Polynesian culture always impressed me – the old navigational skills of the sailors (and canoe-building in general); and the magnificent stonework – altars, dancing platforms, house foundations, plinths for statues, and the statues themselves (though there were no statues in Samoa; there had never been). In Samoa, both of these skills had vanished – there were no more navigators nor any stonemasons. These boulders had survived from an earlier time.

After two hours of circling the island, I sat on a stone near the shore and began scribbling notes, when I was approached by a woman – I took her to be in her twenties. She was friendly. We talked in general about Manono. Then she said her *fale* was nearby and did I wish to see it?

I equivocated until she said, "I want you to see something very important."

"Show me the way," I said.

Her name was Teresa, and although she was twenty-seven, she was not married. The kids fooling around the hut were her brothers and sisters and more distant affines.

Was I hungry? Was I thirsty? Was I tired? Teresa galvanized the household and I was given a cup of tea and, when I said I had liked the *palusami* I had had in Tonga, I was served what I was told was the real Samoan thing – taro leaves mixed with coconut cream, then wrapped and steamed in banana and breadfruit leaves. With this was a disk of hard gray taro.

"In Tonga they put corned beef inside," I said. "But I prefer this."

"Sometimes we make with *pisupo*," Teresa said, using the Samoan word for corned beef, an adaptation of "pea soup," which was also shipped to the islands in cans.

While I was eating, Teresa changed her clothes, from a dress to a T-shirt and shorts. The light was failing, too – it was certainly too late to paddle back to Upolu – and rain was softly falling, whispering against the triangular leaves of the taro plants and making them nod.

So far there had been no further mention of the thing she wished me to see. But after a while Teresa removed it from the pocket of her shorts. It was an American Express traveler's check for a hundred dollars – quite a lot of money in Manono Tai.

"Where did you get this, Teresa?"

"A man gave it to me. But the bank refuses to cash it."

Of course: the check lacked the necessary second signature. As for the first, even holding the check near the bright pressure lamp I could not read the name.

"Who was the man?"

"He was staying here. For a week."

"*Palangi?*"

"Yes. From Germany."

We talked about the check. I explained the niceties of traveler's checks – the need for another signature – and that she would have to send the check back to the man so that it could be cashed.

"He said he wanted to marry me," Teresa said, in a tone of complaint.

"Maybe that's why he gave you the money."

"No. He was here more than a week. He did not give us anything," Teresa said.

"What about this check? You said he gave it to you."

"Yes. But I did not want to marry him," she grumbled.

That was another trait of the Samoans – evasion that expressed itself as tetchiness.

"Why not?"

"He was too old. Born in 1946, something like that."

It was now very dark beyond the reach of the lamp, but in that darkness children were seated with older people, all of them watching me with bright eyes.

"How old is too old?"

Teresa gnawed her lower lip, and then said, "He was too old for games."

"What kind of games?" I asked. Though I knew.

The lantern hissed, leaking light everywhere.

"Night games," she said softly, her voice just a whisper more than the sound of the lantern.

After that, again and again, I remember the way she lowered her head, but still watched me closely, and spoke those words deep in her throat.

I asked her again about the man. His name was Kurt, she said. He was a teacher, and he did his teaching in various countries. (*Cheechah*, she said, and *cheeching*. I was trying to get used to the Samoan accent.) He loved her, she said, but she disliked him.

I said, "He might be too old for some night games but not for others."

This observation interested her greatly.

"Which ones do you mean?"

But at this point her father interrupted me and asked where my boat was.

I told him it was in Faleu.

"The children will destroy it," he said, without much concern.

"Why would they do that?"

"Because you don't have a family."

I heard that explanation many times in Samoa: having a local family gave you status and protection. Samoans quite freely co-opted strangers and made them part of the family – and you didn't need to be dusky, with webbed feet and a big belly – *palangis* qualified, as long as they were endlessly generous; but if you were alone on the islands and did not know anyone you would be victimized.

"And because they are stupid in that village," the father went on.

It was a Samoan trait for them to speak ill of each other, so I was not convinced that my boat was in danger. But it was too dark to go looking for it, in any case. That would have to wait for the morning.

"Everything is so espensive here," Teresa said, apropos of nothing – or perhaps apropos of the check.

She was looking at the lantern.

"The fuel. So espensive."

I said, "There is a Chinese proverb that says, 'It's no use going to bed to save candles. The result will be more children.' Get it?"

Then, seeing the others drifting away, she asked me again about the other games that the man might or might not play.

In the end, the sleeping arrangement was modest, though all night the *fale* purred with the snores of her large family. I slept beside the small boy Sefulu, whose name meant Ten.

In the dark I worked it out. The man, Kurt, had stayed for a week or ten days. He pestered Teresa to marry him, though he had come empty-handed and had not given them any money for his stay. At some stage, Teresa had boosted the traveler's check – extracting it from his rucksack – but it had been in vain: the bank would not cash it without the other signature. She now realized that she needed a signature. Was she asking me to do that?

Yet I was more concerned about my boat than her possible thievery, and so at dawn I hurried back to Faleu to look at it. Children were playing near it, as though waiting to pounce, but the boat was undisturbed.

Over breakfast – more taro, mashed this time – Teresa took out the check and frowned at it.

I said, "Do you want me to sign it?"

"If you don't mind."

There was no date, and the man's own signature was no more than a squiggle.

What to do? They had been kind to me, even if they had had an ulterior motive. And though the money had been thieved, it had in a sense been owed by a tight-fisted *palangi* who had lived with them. Indeed, I had accepted their hospitality too. So perhaps I owed? Forgery seemed a small matter, and yet it interested me. Without the signature, the check was worthless. And there was always the chance that the forgery would be detected, in which case Teresa would be in trouble – and was that my affair?

I could be a totally disinterested forger, a sort of philanthropic felon.

I sat there on the steps of the *fale* practising the squiggly signature in my notebook, and then I placed the check on my lap and, watched by her family and the neighbor kids – I executed the signature on the traveler's check – very well, I felt.

"It's perfect," I said.

"It is close." She squinted critically at it.

Everyone crowded close to have a look.

"Put the date," Teresa said.

I wrote the date, as Kurt might have.

"Will it get stale?"

"Did you say 'stale'?"

She said yes, she had, and so I explained the nature of traveler's checks, how they never went stale, how she could wait a while before cashing it – thinking that I could be safe and out of the way on another island by then.

The fishermen said a strong current ran through the Apolima Strait, which separated Upolu and Savaii, the two largest islands of Western Samoa. If I had not been alone I would have risked the trip – I was almost halfway across when I had been at the far side of Manono: I didn't see a problem. The fishermen did not cross the strait in their canoes, and yet they warned me. Did they know something? I heeded the warning, and with regret took the rusty ferry across to Savaii, with my packed-up boat among my other bags.

"The worst Samoans and the worst *palangis* come to Apia," a schoolteacher named Palola told me. "All the failures. But they never get together."

His description made the place sound more interesting than it was. Its Third World dereliction made it look simply unsightly, neglected, abused, and even the sea was hidden from it. From the harbor's edge, where water lapped feebly at the shore, the reef was a great distance and the lagoon was gray and turbid, the water the ghostly gray color of dead coral.

"It is worse in Pago," Palola said. He was polite and well-spoken, on the ferry to visit his folks in Papalaulelei.

No sooner had I made my mind up that these people were brutes than I met a person who was decent and restrained, dignified and helpful, among the most hospitable I had ever met in my life.

"The main difference is in the attitude of people," he said, trying to answer my question comparing Western Samoa, an independent republic, with American Samoa – a territory belonging to the United States. "Take the attitude towards money. If we get money we spend it on our family, on our house, or food and necessities. In American Samoa they use it to buy a car, or for entertainment. They spend it on themselves. They care less about the family."

"Why is the family so important?" I asked, pressing him.

"Because it helps you – it looks after you. It is your life," Palola said.

"Is the house part of your life?"

"Yes. If you go to Pago and see a fine house you will probably discover that the people in that house came from Western Samoa. We are still following our old ways."

"But why is Apia in such bad repair? And the rest of the island isn't much better."

"It is getting worse. We had a hurricane last February –"

Everyone spoke of this three-day gale which wrecked houses and uprooted palms and destroyed roads with high tides and floods. But that was over a year ago and the wreckage remained.

"– we have not rebuilt it," Palola was saying. "We have no money. And the government is also to blame."

The family looked after itself but was indifferent to the plight of other families, and it was no concern of a family if there were tree trunks and splintered houses up the road. The breakdown of the family in American Samoa (the main island of Tutuila was only forty miles east of here) was said to be the cause of the strife there. Depending on who I was talking to, Samoans either said they were one people, or else as different as they could possibly be. "We have a different language!" one man insisted. "*Sapelu* means bush knife in Western Samoa and shovel in American Samoa. *Ogaumu* means an oven here but it means a pot over there. We have different words for east and west!" Great stress was laid on the fact that money mattered more in American Samoa than here, its poor cousin.

I had a standard island question, which I tried to remember to ask everywhere I went: Why are islands different from the mainland?

Palola said, "Because you are free on an island, and you can control your own affairs."

He went on to say that he had visited his brother in Auckland and that he had been too frightened to drive his brother's car. "Everything was so fast there," he said, meaning the traffic, the marching people on the sidewalk, the way they spoke and did business. He had found it unendurable.

No one was seasick on the ferry – I had assumed that, being Polynesians, they would be puking their guts out, even on this half-hour run. On the other hand, they were none too healthy, and they made their way onto the jetty with a side-to-side duckwalk that was characteristic of these obese people.

They valued fatness, and to make themselves physically emphatic they ate massive amounts of bananas, taro, breadfruit and such snacks as were on the menu of the eateries in Apia. *Toasted spaghetti sandwich*, was one I noted. (The New Zealanders have a lot to answer for.) They ate the cuts of mutton that were whitest with fat. Meat that the Kiwis and Aussies refused to eat, unsaleable parts of dead animals – chicken backs, parson's noses, trotters, withers and whatever – were frozen and exported here. A scrap of meat on a chunk of fat attached to a big bone they found toothsome. The imported canned corned beef they called *pisupo* was up to ninety percent fat. It was not the solid meaty thing that we sliced with a knife in the United states and made into hash; this Pacific corned beef was often like pudding it was so loaded with fat, and it could easily be eaten with a spoon. Not only was beef tallow added to it, but some brands contained hippo fat.

Heart disease was endemic and people died young, but still there were only two doctors on the island of Savaii (population 46,000) – one was Italian, the other Burmese.

I met the Italian doctor, Peter Caffarelli, in a roundabout way. He lived just outside the village of Tuasivi where my younger brother Joseph had been a Peace Corps Volunteer. Tuasivi was a number of *fales* on both sides of the coast road, near a headland occupied by a college, where my brother had taught English. The settlement – a large village – had none of the raddled rundown look of the comparable places on Upolu that I had seen. The *fales* were well made and there was a busy air to the place, people gardening, feeding their chickens, and a profusion of *lava-lavas* flapping on clotheslines. The wreckage of last year's hurricane lay farther down the coast – tipped-over trees, broken culverts, washed-away roads.

Tavita Tuilagi, one of Joe's former colleagues, was building a new *fale*, not only in a traditional style but by a traditional method: none of the men working on the house were paid. They were relatives, part of the extended family, and friends. In theory this was all a labor of love; in practice it could be expensive, since Tavita – Samoan for David – was obliged to supply all the men at all times during the construction with food and drink – and the better the food the harder the men would work. Indeed, if the food and drink ran out, the men might decide to work elsewhere.

"This man Tavita has just been given a title," said the Samoan who had shown me the way to Tuasivi. "He is now *Oloipola*."

"It is not much," Tavita said, sounding suitably modest, and hardly looking titled and chiefly in his LA Lakers T-shirt.

But saying it was nothing was not modesty. It was the truth. This title, which meant "matai chief" – head of the family – had once been a powerful position. But lately such titles had been handed out willy-nilly by chiefs as a way of getting themselves re-elected to positions of power.

"Sio was a good boy," Tavita said, giving Joe his Samoan name. "He was a good teacher too. I want him to come back."

"Why don't you write him a note and say so?" I asked. And I found a blank page in my notebook and gave him a pen. "You could invite him back, and I will make sure he gets it."

"That is a good idea," Tavita said, and began scribbling.

"I doubt whether I'll get a chance to read it," I said, when he had finished. I put the notebook into my pocket and walked up the road.

The note said: *Dear Joe Theroux, I'm so happy to meet your father* [crossed out] *brother. Remembering you for the past years since you were here. I am building a new fale. If you could give me a donation through finance I would like to accept it. May God bless you. Thank you. Tavita Tuilagi.*

On my way back through the village I gave Tavita thirty Samoan *tala*, which he accepted without ceremony.

The Italian doctor, Caffarelli, lived up the road, near the beach in a straggling village beyond Tuasivi. He was skinny, burned dark by the sun, wearing a *lava-lava* patterned in red flowers. I took him to be in his late sixties. His wife was Samoan. Children seemed to be scattered everywhere around his house, and we were outside, strolling around his tussocky grass, among lanky pawpaw trees. The house was badly mildewed stucco in the European style and (so he said) it stood on one of the few plots of freehold land in the whole of Samoa. It had apparently been doled out by a chief on the understanding that as long as the doctor lived on that land he would look after the chief's health.

When I asked the doctor direct questions about himself he became unhelpful and vague – vague even about the number of his children. "Ten," he said in a tone of uncertainty, and then, "Eleven." Answering my questions about Samoan life he spoke with greater confidence.

"The family is very important here, yes," the doctor said. "But when we say 'family' we are talking about a very large number of people. Times have changed and that has made it all more complicated. There are obligations, but that is not so bad when you are in a non-money economy. When someone offers to work, or gives you fruit, you offer food at a later time."

"I noticed. There are always gifts in circulation here," I said.

"But when money comes into the picture" – the doctor made the Italian hand-weighing gesture which signifies tribulation – "it can be expensive. Money for this, money for that. And the rule is that you don't refuse."

"Does that mean you give it every time it's asked for?"

"You look after children," the doctor said. "But how far does your obligation extend if the father of those children is out chasing a bar-girl in Apia? Do you go on pretending that he's just doing his duty and turn a blind eye?"

"Does this happen often?"

"All the time," the doctor said. "And there's a moral dimension. Why should I give money to someone if all he plans to do with it is waste it on prostitutes? The rule is that you give, if someone asks. But it raises moral questions sometimes."

I asked about stealing, since it was mentioned by many other travelers I had met, and all the guidebooks contain warnings. I had not lost anything, but the fact was that so much had been pinched from me in Tonga I had little else of value that could be stolen.

"When this was truly a non-money economy, when cash didn't come into it at all, everything was shared," the doctor said. "So my bush knife was also yours. A person would come and take it. There was no concept of private property. There was perhaps a little pleasure in a person's taking something. Nothing was privately owned, there was no idea of personal property."

He went on to say that money had complicated this traditional arrangement – everyone in Samoa blamed money for their problems: the lack of it, the greed for it, the power that wealthy people had.

"People steal all the time now," the doctor said. "Yes, it is the old habit, but it is stealing. Yet no stigma is attached to it. They even admire trickery."

"What if you steal from them?"

"In theory, that is what you are supposed to do. But they are not always so tolerant, eh? They are communal-minded when it suits them, but there are plenty of instances when a person gets something and never shares it."

I told him that it wasn't the stealing, but the inconsistency and the hypocrisy that caused the problems.

"Yes. I will give you an example," he said. "A man I know had a very big mango tree. He noticed that everyone was stealing his mangoes as soon as they were ripe. By the way, he was an Australian, but he had lived here for some years. He didn't say anything to the people, but he thought, 'Ah, so that is what they do.' Thus he began picking bananas from the trees of these people. And they didn't like it!"

"What did they do about it?"

'There was a hell of a fuss."

"How bad?"

He shrugged and made the Italian fishmouth that signified a paradox was in the air.

"They wanted to kill him."

We talked about the birth-rate. It was very high – but although sixty percent of the births were illegitimate, the children were well looked after and always part of a larger family. Still, the government authorized the use of birth-control remedies – Depoprovera.

"Isn't that a dangerous drug?"

"Yes, it is bad, but who is sentimental here? You might be sterilized for life, you might die – but isn't that the motive of the people who give out contraceptives? They want to bring down the birth-rate, at any cost. They are not sentimental." After a moment he said, "I don't have anything to do with contraceptives."

He walked me to the road, his *lava-lava* flapping, his numerous children frolicking around us.

"You must like it here to have lived here so long." Twenty-five years he had spent in Samoa.

"A doctor here is a despised person," he said, smiling. "The great thing is to be a minister in the church. People give you food and money. You have status. You can be rich. But they regard me as ridiculous, because I am a doctor. When my surgery building blew down and was demolished in the hurricane everyone stood near it and laughed. 'Look at what happened! The doctor's house is down!' The Samoans thought it was very funny."

There are not many wild creatures in Samoa, and most are near the road, so just walking home I saw nearly every one of them – the black rats, the endangered bats, the pigs, the rails, swiftlets, reef herons and crazed limping dogs.

I was staying in a *fale* myself, at Lalomaleva. It often rained in the dark early morning, three or four o'clock, the downpour drumming on the thatch and tin roof – a lovely sound, half roar, half whisper, and it made a tremendous slapping of the big broad leaves just outside the blinds. Then dawn broke, the gray sky lightened, and the rain still fell; finally, when the sun's rim appeared against the palm trees at six or so, the rain pattered to a stop.

I lived among a farrago of aging expatriates and more youthful Samoans. In the near distance there was always the full-throated sound of mocking laughter – always children. This sudden explosive laughter I found unaccountably jarring and demoralizing, but it only seemed to bother me – no one else. The expatriates more or less assumed that they would be buried here eventually, though the Samoans all expressed great homesickness for places like Auckland and San Francisco.

Loimata was typical.

"*Mata* means 'eye' in Malay," I said.

"And also in Samoan," she said. "Loimata means tears."

She had relatives in Hawaii, Los Angeles, San Francisco, New Zealand and Australia. Visiting some of them, she had lingered to work, and for a while lived in the Samoan enclave outside Honolulu, called Wahaiwa. She had been traveling with her mother, who missed Samoa, and so mother and dutiful daughter had returned to Savaii.

"I miss the work," she said.

Her friend twitted her and said, "You don't miss the work. You miss the money."

"Yes, I miss the money."

Warren Jopling, a New Zealander in his mid-sixties, had simply come to Samoa and become so entangled in his newly acquired Samoan family that he had stayed. He said he liked Samoa. And of course the family had adopted him – but two or three Samoans were attached to twenty more, and in the end they took possession of him and moved wholesale into his house in Apia, occupying it so fully that he moved out and came here to Savaii.

I had wanted to see an ancient stone mound, called Pulemelei – a great stepped pyramidal structure, the largest mound of its kind in the whole of Polynesia. I asked a number of Samoans about it. Most knew nothing of its existence. The two that had heard of it had never seen it. I asked Warren whether he knew about it – and of course he, a *palangi* living on the fringes, had visited it many times and knew this obscure ruin in the jungle intimately.

No one has any idea what this enormous ruin was used for – whether it was a tomb, a fortress, or a so-called bird-snaring mound. It is all the more intriguing for that – for its size and its mystery. It lies in the depths of the Samoan jungle behind the village of Vailoa and it is so seldom visited that there are no paths around it. Even Warren Jopling, who knew it well, became a trifle confused on our approach through the bush.

Built against the brow of a hill it was covered in jungle greenery – vines and bushes – and yet its architectonic shape in two great steps was vivid: with the contours of a titanic wedding cake it had the look of a ceremonial mound, but it offered a wonderful prospect of the sea. In its day, before any of the palms had been planted, it must have had the grandeur of the great Mayan pyramid at Chichen Itza, the so-called Castillo, a structure it somewhat resembled in size and complexity. Some archeologists have conjectured that there was a large dwelling on the top of it, which would truly have given it the look of a castle. It was forty feet high, about a hundred and eighty feet wide and over two hundred feet long, with battlements and parapets and flights of stone stairs.

"You know the oddest thing about this place?" Warren said. "This is an island that is rich in legends. They have stories about the blow-holes and the waterfalls and the caves. They have stories about things that don't even exist. Giants, dwarfs, ghosts, spirits. How this volcano appeared, where that island came from. But there are no stories about this, not even fanciful ones. Don't you think that's strange?"

He showed me a number of other rock mounds – graves, house platforms, altars, all covered with jungle, buried in ferns and vines, all unknown, none of them excavated.

"A great civilization lived here," he said. "It must have been here, because there was a great deal of available water – two rivers, the only real year-round rivers on Savaii."

The volcanic nature of the soil helped all water to percolate through very quickly, Warren said – he had spent a career as a geologist. Rain fell and then it disappeared, he said. There were few pools, but no lakes. Yet just here there were springs and rivers.

One of these rivers, the Faleala, ran over a high ledge farther into the jungle and turned into Olemoe Falls. Warren had brought along two Samoan boys in case we should have an emergency – a blow-out, a wreck, whatever. They would come in handy. They were frisky and willing – one named Afasene ("Half a Cent"), the other Siaki (Jack). We sat by the pool and they wove crowns of fern for me and put them on my head, making me feel like the Unbearable Bassington in the Saki novel.

And then they splashed and dived.

"Look at me, Paul!"

"I will get a stone from the bottom!"

"I will jump!"

"Don't look at him – look at me!"

Into the falls, down the sluice, diving backwards, fooling and loving it. They were fourteen and sixteen, but seemed much younger.

So this was what it was all about. You came here and frisked with brown boys, and slept with their sisters, and gave money to their parents, and lived and died. You slept and ate and laughed.

Savaii was a maddening place from the paddling point of view – either surf crashing on rocks and nowhere to launch from, or else a lagoon so shallow that my paddle blade struck bottom with each stroke. The Samoans were not boat people themselves – only the oldest ones could remember ever crossing from island to island paddling in a canoe or sailing an outrigger. This skill of using small craft, by which I tended to judge Pacific islands, had just about vanished in Samoa.

The Taga blow-holes were not far from the mysterious stone mound of Pulemelei. The blowholes, locally know as *pupu*, were volcanic fissures in the cliffs of black lava that made this part of the coast of Savaii so dangerous. The swell crashing into the cliffs traveled through the sea-caves and the hollows and shot into the vertical holes, producing a geyser or waterspout that made a plume of water eighty feet in the air.

We stood by one of the dozen or so blow-holes and chucked coconuts into the hole just as the swell hit the cliff, and within a few seconds the coconut was shot into the air like a cannonball. The kids did the same with palm fronds and watched them flung upward, twisting and turning in the spray.

The whole place was deserted. It was one of the great natural phenomena of the Pacific. We stood under sunny skies and big puffy clouds, by the lovely sea, the boys fooling, the coconuts shooting skyward, and I thought, *My God, this is stupid.*

But it was a feeble protest. By then a lazy sort of boredom had taken possession of my soul, the Oceanic malaise. I never saw anyone reading anything more demanding than a comic book. I never heard any youth express an interest in science or art. No one even talked politics. It was all idleness, and whenever I asked someone a question, no matter how simple, no matter how well the person spoke English, there was always a long pause before I got a reply, and I found these Pacific pauses maddening.

And there was giggling but no humor – no wit. It was just foolery. The *palangis* were no better. Warren got up a picnic with an American named John, who had started his own farm in the Mid-West, and with Friedrich, who told me, "I am studying the smell of roast beef." He meant just that: he roasted a chunk of beef every day in his laboratory in Munich and then distilled its essence and tried breaking the flavor down into its chemical components. "This has many applications," he explained. In our party there were also the usual contingent of Samoan youths, clambering and laughing.

We were sitting under the palms at Asuisui, and when Warren passed out the sandwiches, I said, "I can't eat Spam. Hey, that reminds me. Ever read Descartes – René Descartes?"

Silence from John, silence from Friedrich, silence from Warren, giggles from the Samoans.

"As in 'Don't put Descartes before the horse'?"

In the ensuing silence, Warren cleared his throat. "I've read him," he said, "but it was years ago, and I don't have a retentive memory."

"I was just going to make a joke."

They stared at me.

"Descartes – didn't he say, 'I'm pink, therefore I'm Spam'?"

A look of apprehension settled over them, and only Manu broke the silence.

"What you tink?"

"What do I think about what?"

"Da wedda."

So we discussed the wind and clouds.

Later in his car Manu said, "I got a wife."

We were driving towards Lalomalava. His car was a jalopy which contained an expensive cassette-player, and reggae music was blaring from his stereo speakers, mounted with some stuffed toys on the back shelf.

"Any kids?"

"I got a kid in here," he said, and banged the glove compartment. He was having trouble opening it, until he thumped it very hard. "Kid – in here – somewhere."

Finally he took out a crinkled photograph of a fat brown baby wrapped in a clean blue blanket. The picture had not been snapped in Samoa.

"My son," Manu said proudly.

"What's his name?"

"I dunno."

"Where was this picture taken?"

"Auckland."

"You want to go to Auckland?"

"No," Manu said, and tossed the picture back into the glove compartment and hammered it shut with his fist.

What exactly was the story here?

I traveled to the northwest of Savaii, to Asau Bay, to paddle, and there I met Fat Frank, who had recently arrived from California and was scouting the island. He was an alcoholic, and he had taken up residence at a motel at Vaisala. Apart from Fat Frank there was only one other guest at the place, a Finn from a freighter in Apia, who complained bitterly about Frank. His habit was to rise at eleven, drink a bottle of Vailima Beer for breakfast, follow it with a half-bottle of tequila and then paw Samoan waitresses until he passed out. He was a chain-smoker and his huge pendulous belly hung over his belt. He sat hunched over, breathing hard. I met him in the late afternoon, after his second snooze, when he was wheezing and on whisky.

He grumbled about his feet swelling up. He hated the heat. He said he didn't sleep well. He was one of those fat people who when they are horizontal begin to breathe irregularly and snore in a choking, strangling manner all night, *Aaarrrghh*!

"I'll be here six weeks or so," he said.

"That seems such a long time for such a small island."

"Thing is, I'm thinking of relocating."

"Moving here to Samoa?"

"Yeah. Changing my whole life-style. Why wait until you retire? Why not do it now?"

He was only in his thirties, but had a certain swollen look that made him seem much older, like a fat elderly baby.

"Ever been here before?"

"No, but I think I could fit in. The people here are very friendly – very warm. Not like Pago. That's a dump. I was supposed to stay there a week and I stayed one night. But these people take you into their family."

"I think they expect something in return. I mean, wouldn't you have obligations?"

"We could work something out. I'll look around. Look for a house. Look for a village. Then find the chief and talk it over."

He was looking for a life and he made finding it seem simple. *A Somerset Maugham character*, people say, but in the flesh Somerset Maugham characters could be such slobs and bores.

"And I might do some business."

He had a very furtive way of lighting a cigarette, palming it, turning his lighter on it, sucking it hard, then spitting the smoke out. He was from Mile City, somewhere north of San Francisco.

"Want to know the trouble with business here? You can't make any money in a country where the people have no money."

Delivered of this wisdom he took a long pull on his bottle of hooch.

"But I figure a dive shop might make it. The Japs will come here eventually."

"Why would they come here? They want golf. Beaches. Luxury. Mickey Mouse logo shops. They like to shop. God, you can't even swim here. I'm just managing because I have my own sea kayak."

"I can make out."

"You might be a teeny bit bored."

"Go back" – he wasn't listening to me, he had a slow wheezing way of talking, and this sentence had begun long before – "get my toys. Motorcycle. Hi-fi. Diving equipment. Scuba gear."

Heavy people are often divers. Was it the sense of weightlessness that attracted them – the experience of being light and buoyant, as they chubbily made their way among the coral and the flitting fish?

"What do you do?" he asked me, wiping his mouth.

"I do a little writing."

"That's why you got all the questions!"

He looked around and laughed. He was laughing at the blazing sun, the palms, the wrecked beach – the worst of the hurricane had come here. His laughter showed in the rolls of flesh on his gut.

"I knew I was going to meet a writer here. As soon as I saw this fucked-up place I said to myself, 'I'm going to meet a writer.' And a painter. Where's the painter? There must be a painter here."

So he was thinking of leaving the vastness of northern California, and the friendliness of this small American town, and settle here in a jumbled family, taking up residence in a *fale* in a Samoan village, with all its Christians. I said this to him in so many words.

"It's a trade-off, isn't it?"

He wanted a new life. He wanted the pleasure of retirement now – not when he was arthritic and unhealthy. That in itself was sensible: at this rate he wouldn't last – fat and tanked up and chain-smoking.

"I got the answer. People will buy anything from someone they like."

"Meaning you?"

"Yeah. Like me. A real character," he said. He rested the bottle on his belly. "An interesting guy."

And then I understood, and I saw him in America, on his Harley-Davidson. He was one of those terrifyingly fat fellows in a Nazi crash helmet that are seen roaring down the highway, sitting behind the immensity of his belly, that shoot out in front of sober motorists who say, "Look at him, Doris. Hogging the road!"

"Don't make him mad," Doris says. "Please don't honk the horn."

And you don't.

Fat Frank was looking for an indulgent family, and it was possible that he would find one in Samoa, where you could develop a relationship with a family that had strong ties. I was not worried about Frank taking advantage of them; in the end, they would take him for all he was worth. But it was a paradoxical society. Outside the family there seemed to be no driving force, no loyalties; and the interdependency that was limited strictly to the family made it seem less like a society than like a simple organism, a certain type of jellyfish, perhaps, the hydrozoan that was a little colony of tentacles, some for stinging, some for eating, that sways and bloops along the surface of the sea.

Whenever I attempted to do something in Samoa – buy a ticket, rent a car, obtain information – the Samoan I asked looked a bit surprised and seemed totally unprepared to help. In their own lives, Samoans managed to scrape along with a little farming and a lot of remittances. It was the most cohesive society that I saw in the Pacific, but the least individualistic – perhaps the most traditional in Polynesia. But apart from the immediate needs of the family, nothing was achieved – where were the doctors, the dentists, pilots, engineers, architects and skilled people? Many Samoan teachers fled to better-paying jobs elsewhere, and their positions were filled by Peace Corps volunteers. Even the grubbiest road supervisors and heavy-machinery operators, driving bulldozers and augering holes for power lines – were from New Zealand and Australia.

Or was I taking the whole business too seriously? Perhaps it was all a comedy. But if you weren't in the mood for that sort of low hilarity it was the wrong place to visit.

"I tone like Tonga," a Samoan said to me.

"Why not?"

"Because it is too much sandy."

"Too sandy?"

"Yes. And dey tone like Samoan people."

"What a pity."

"Because a Samoan kai cut off da head of a Tonga kai."

"Is that all?"

"And cut off his leck."

"I see. The Samoan guy cut off his head and his leg."

An ancient quarrel shrouded in myth? No. It happened in Auckland, he explained, just a few months ago.

Some of these wild cannibal-looking youths were very sweet. The surliest-seeming ones, obstinate one minute, could be unexpectedly helpful the next. The policemen were ineffectual but in their white helmets and epaulets they were at least picturesque. Was it because I was in Samoan backwaters? But in Samoa it was all backwaters. And at those moments when I was most exasperated I would look up and see the oddest thing – a man holding a pig in his lap, or a man standing up to his neck in the lagoon, smoking a cigarette – and I would laugh the witless Samoan laugh and think: *Take this seriously and you're dead.*

# 17

## *American Samoa: The Littered Lagoon*

No one in the Pacific has a good word for American Samoa. This alone predisposed me to liking these islands and finding them habitable and bounteous, the sort of carefree archipelago I might want to fling myself into and be happy as an Oceanic clam.

The place was generally hated, but what was the problem? Six little islands and one biggish one, Tutuila; a total population of 37,000 people – American Samoa had only half the population of the town where I was born, Medford, Massachusetts, which I had always thought of as unbearably small. And every year the United States government handed over roughly seventy-five million dollars to American Samoans. You couldn't get much more carefree and bounteous than that, though politically Samoa is perhaps a kleptocracy.

On the face of it, there was no reason why these islands should not be paradise – indeed, they are, in their own pot-bellied way: the islanders are very happy. Life in American Samoa is one long yankee boondoggle, and the people are so hoggishly contented that they cannot stand the idea of ever forming an independent political entity with their brothers and sisters in Western Samoa, just across the water, because that reunion might diminish the money supply. The average per capita income in Western Samoa was $580 a year; in American Samoa it was almost ten times that. But it was all funny money in any case – intravenous, drip-feed cash, as they said in Australia – most of it foreign aid. New Zealand had gone on financing its former territory of Western Samoa, and America still stumped up money for its indigent islands which, politically, had the same status as Puerto Rico.

So much for all the guff about the sacred concept of familyhood in the two Samoas. "Corrupted" is the perfect word, though an American Samoan can revert from being a fat guy in a Bart Simpson T-shirt, with a can of Coke Classic in his hand, watching the Super Bowl; and, at a moment's notice, turn into a big dark fire-breathing islander, confounding you with obscure incantations and unfathomable customs. When

Samoans have their backs to the wall they put on a *lava-lava* and pretend to be islanders. The rest of the time – it seemed to me – they were fat jolly people, with free money, having a wonderful time.

The last sight I had had of real life in Western Samoa was that of some women at dawn on the coast of southern Savaii, washing their clothes and themselves at the edge of the Falealila River – the soap suds vivid as surf against the black rocks. Virtually the first thing I saw in American Samoa were four enormously fat women sitting in Danny's Laundromat in Pago Pago, watching their clothes being tossed in washers and yakking about the high cost of living. They were an extraordinary size, guzzling Cokes and glowing with perspiration, and sitting with their chubby knees apart, Samoan style.

Houses in Western Samoa are true *fales*, shaped as though modeled on the humpy helmet of Hernando DeSoto, and enhanced with mats and blinds and thatch; in American Samoa the so-called *fales* are little boxy bungalows, prefabs made in California – flat roof, single walls – plopped on a slab. Poverty in Western Samoa has forced people to build in a traditional way, because it is cheaper. And the *fales* there are better suited to the climate than the cinderblock bungalows of Tutuila, which are unendurable without a rusty, howling air-conditioner propped in a window. Even the churches are less impressive in American Samoa, because of their dreary modernity.

But in both Samoas dead ancestors are buried in the front garden, or next to the house, in a colorful sarcophagus. Samoans had all sorts of explanations for this burying of the dead beside the hibiscus hedge on the lawn – grief, affection, tradition, ancestor worship, the vulgar love of a good in-ground necropolis, a wish to be near Auntie Ida, and so forth. But the true answer seemed obvious to me. On an island where land tenure was always subject to lengthy deliberation, wasn't it a way of taking possession of the land? You could evict anyone from a house, but how did you go about ridding the place of a dozen dead relatives, sealed in coffins deep in the ground?

*Kind of a crazy place*, Verne in Tonga had told me. *But I'm kind of crazy, so I liked it there.*

The ferry from Apia to Pago Pago had been full ("We sell three hundred and twenty-one tickets, because we have three hundred and twenty-one life jackets," the man in the office explained) so I took the short airplane ride.

"You are overweight," the 350-pound Samoan at the check-in desk said.

It was nothing personal – it was my boat and my gear, but the chunky airline employee said that it was too much trouble to collect the additional charge, and so he waved me through.

Pretty was not the word for Tutuila – it looked fabulous, with green steep-sided mountains that had black peaks – dark splintery antique volcanoes – precipitous valleys plunging down to sea-cliffs and rocky headlands. It was a high vertical island, with a wide lagoon and many fine bays and the deeply indented harbor of Pago Pago – a lovely place, more vertiginous and dramatic, steamier, much lusher than its sister islands to the west. Not pretty at all, but hot, langorous, ravishing, dangerously attractive, like the person you pass on the sidewalk – what is it about these lucky people? – who makes you feel flustered and breathless and forgetful. You could fall in love at first sight with Tutuila.

But on second glance, a moment later, looking closer, you recover and decide not to throw your life away. Pago Harbor is muddy – it doesn't get properly flushed by the tides – and it reeks of the tuna canneries on the eastern side, Starkist and Van Camp. The rubbish on the beaches, flung everywhere and seldom collected, is worse than anywhere else in the Pacific and would make any sort of beach activity in Samoa depressing – but the lagoon is too shallow for swimming, the coral is broken and dead, there is a sensational litter of old soft-drink cans underwater; so there is not much beach activity.

When an American Samoan is finished with a can or a box or a bag, he or she flings it aside. In the past such items were palm fronds and coconut husks and banana peels: biodegradable. These days the trash is beginning to accumulate. The island is noisy, vandalized, and all somehow familiar – it is not the seedy poverty and squalor of Apia, where there is no money and nothing seems to work; it is the fat wasteful American-style conspicuousness epitomized by much too big, much too expensive, rusted cars. Greedy, wasteful, profligate and proprietorial, American Samoans are living on large handouts, forever pushing supermarket shopping carts full of junk food, packages and cans, the Cheez Ball diet of fat-bellied Polynesia – seedy prosperity.

The two Samoas are close together, but while Western Samoa looks to New Zealand and Australia, American Samoa looks to Hawaii and mainland America. New Zealanders have taught Western Samoans the elements of thrift – the roadsides and lagoons are dreary but noticeably tidier in those islands. What America has accomplished in its Samoan islands – and this is instantly visible – is the removal of the cultural props, by creating a cash economy. The worst effect of this has been a kind of competitive selfishness which has fragmented the family. Most people I met in American Samoa spoke with regret about the loosening of these family ties, which has meant a decline in traditional formality and courtesy and a widespread casualness that borders on insult and disrespect.

I tended to evaluate Pacific islanders by the way they related to the ocean around them. Did they swim? Did they fish with nets or spears? Did they build boats, and paddle and sail? Could they go from one island to another on their own in one of those boats? Once, these people had been among the greatest sailors in the world. But what now? I wondered whether they were afraid of the sea – whether they knew anything about it, whether they cared. Did they know which way the wind was blowing, could they forecast weather from the patterns of the clouds and the color of the sky? Did they ever venture beyond the breakers on the reef?

On some islands, it was possible to say that the islanders were still people of the sea. Western Samoans did some fishing and boating in a limited sense, and in a Christianized pig-headed way, they were traditional. In American Samoa some subtle and obscure customs were still practised in their dull bungalows, but the people seemed indifferent to the ocean. No one went sailing. No one paddled. They jumped into the water and splashed – but they hardly swam. Now and then you saw a fat kid on a jet ski. The rest of them hid from the sun. They stayed away from the lagoon. Their fish came out of cans. It had been years since anyone had made an outrigger. It was as though the entire population (and this seemed pretty odd in the Pacific) was possessed by the most virulent form of hydrophobia.

The tradition is that the first Samoans – the first real Polynesians – arrived from Tonga and Fiji in about 600 B.C., at the eastern tip of Tutuila, near the village of Tula. Never mind that it was now an unprepossessing village, of flimsy bungalows and littered roads and stray dogs; it was the ancient landing place of the canoes. I decided to paddle around there and set my sights on the only island I could possibly paddle to, Aunu'u, off the southeast corner.

"You'll never make it," a Samoan told me.

This was a true landlubber's point of view: the island was only a few miles. Even with a rip-roaring current I could have made it, I felt.

Later, I was looking around Alofau, having just come on the coast road. In an equivalent place in Western Samoa the people would have been watchful and circumspect. Here they were talkative and pushy.

Kenny, a big brown man, said to me, "You are new here."

It was not a question, so I asked whether he meant here in Alofau, or on the island.

"On the island," he said. "In Samoa."

"How do you know that?"

"By your face."

"I look new to the island, you mean?"

"We know all the faces. I haven't seen you before," Kenny said. "I think you have arrived very recently."

"That's true. But I'm surprised you know that."

He said, "We can know everything, because we know everyone on the island."

Elsewhere in Oceania, and in Western Samoa in particular, such a conversation would have been essentially friendly, but in American Samoa it seemed intrusive and aroused my suspicions – the man seemed determined to nose around and probe, to find something out. And even the most innocent-seeming remark put me on my guard.

I made my way around the island. I looked at Tula, I scoped out the island of Aunu'u. At night I returned to my hotel in Pago. I came to think of it as a soggy good-hearted town. Like most other visitors I reflected on Maugham's "Rain." Maugham was another writer who had sanctified a place by using it as a setting – he had done the islands a great favor – made them seem exotic and interesting. Camping was out of the question here – all the land was owned, accounted for and heavily protected against any intrusion. A camper seemed like a squatter – indeed, that was how the Samoans themselves sometimes staked their claims – he or she might never go away. And it must be said that not one square foot of land in American Samoa could be owned by a non-Samoan. The Samoans were noted for not being particularly fastidious about other people's rights, but they were fanatics about their own – being selfish and infantile seemed appropriate to their clumsy obesity, like children who are always insisting *It's mine!*

I was assembling my boat on a beach one day – a futile-seeming operation: the lagoon was inches deep and littered with rusty cans, there was no break in the reef, the surf was high and impenetrable. But I soldiered on, just to see what I might find. And, having left one small item in my rented car (the stoppers for my inflatable sponsons), I found I could not finish setting up the boat until I got them. I had been talking to two fellows – any activity at all seemed to interest people here. No one ever offered to help me, nor did anyone refuse when I asked them to lend a hand.

I had parked my car discreetly, so that it couldn't be broken into (the island was rife with break-in stories), and I was in two minds about whether to get the items out of the car. I decided to be oblique.

"I have to buy something at the store," I said.

I went down the street, into the store, bought a drink, went out the back way, tiptoed behind the building and slipped past some thick trees, ducked down, and opened the car door, retrieved the stoppers, crept back to the rear of the building and left through the front door, still sipping the can of Fanta.

"Is that your car?" one of the men said when I got back to the beach.

How had he seen me? And of course the question worried me, because he knew I was just about to set off into the lagoon, where I could be seen. It would have been so easy for them to break into my car.

"Where are you going in that boat?" the other man asked.

"Just paddling."

"How long will you be out there?"

What was this? Again, their nosiness seemed to give them away. In Western Samoa they would simply have watched me. Here, artless and intrusive at the same time, they seemed to reveal their intentions in all their nosy questions.

But in the event, the lagoon was too shallow for paddling, and that was the day I planned my trip out of historic Tula, to make for the offshore island of Aunu'u.

I was continually worried about Samoans stealing my gear. Everyone – even Samoans themselves – spoke of the predilection for theft here in the islands; and everyone had a theory as to why it happened – ranging from *It's-an-old-Samoan-custom* to *They're-natural-kleptomaniacs*. It was always assumed that if you left something sitting idly by it would be instantly pinched, and no one was very subtle about it. If someone stole a shirt from you, he would probably be seen wearing it the next day; if someone stole a hammer or a knife, the thief would be observed using the item very soon after. "And if you say, 'That's mine!' they'll laugh at you." So I was told.

I was careful, but any traveler is vulnerable. In Tonga my hotel room had been plundered while I was out. Yet nothing was stolen from me in Samoa.

I paddled from Tula to the little hamlet of Au'asi, where there was a breakwater, just to verify that there were motor-boats that plied back and forth from Aunu'u Island at a dollar a trip. I thought I would ask one of these motor-boaters about the sea conditions between here and the island.

A boatman was hunkered down on the jetty, so I asked him, "Is there much of a current out there?"

It seemed calm enough, but there were waves breaking on all the reefs and shoals, and there was about a three-foot swell – not bad looking, but the sea is a riddle.

"The sea is move," the man said.

"You mean, the sea is moving – a current?" And I made the appropriate gestures with my hands.

"The sea is move," he said placidly.

I muttered it to myself.

"The sea is smooth?"

"Yeh. Is move."

It was too late that day to paddle out, so I returned the following day and set up my boat. Seven boys – big bulky teenagers, just out of school – sat under the palms at Au'asi, watching me struggle with my boat parts. The scene could have been idyllic – healthy youths under the shade of the coconut palms, by the beach, on a sunny day in Samoa. But the tussocky grass was littered with paper, the fence was broken, the beach was scattered with broken glass and in the shallow water there were bottles and cans and soggy sunken blobs of paper. Dogs barked nearby, overloaded buses wheezed past (because the shoreline in Samoa is a road), and music played – reggae or rap – from each bus.

The boys wore T-shirts with various motifs – one showed a black Bart Simpson making an obscene gesture and was captioned *Fucking Bart*, another showed an angry duck – *I Got An Attitude!*, it said. One said *Hawaii*, another – the most preposterous – *Samoa: People of the Sea*; and still others were simply numbered and colored athletic shirts.

"What's that – a tent?" one said.

I was unfolding the canvas hull. Before I could answer, another said, "Is a pig boat. Is a chip."

I said, "It's a boat."

I was trying to assemble it quickly and get out of there.

"What kind of boat? You can give us a ride?"

"It's for one person," I said.

"He don't want to give you a ride, you stupid shit."

They hovered around me.

"Did you just come from school?" I asked.

"We just come from fucking these guy's girlfriend."

"Shut up, you stupid."

I found their insolence remarkable, because on arriving at Pago Pago Airport I had been given a pamphlet with no less than a dozen admonitions on how to behave in American Samoa. One concerned general behavior: *It is hoped that you will take extra care to ensure that none of your actions is misinterpreted as dissatisfaction with your host*; and the reason was given: *The Samoan people are, by nature and culture, extremely anxious to please their guests.*

"Where you come from, mister?" asked *People of the Sea*.

"I'm from the States. What about you?"

Would they say "American Samoa"? "Samoa"? "Tutuila"? or what?

"I'm from Compton," one said, naming a black area in Los Angeles – the name frequently occurred in the violent songs of a rap group that called itself *NWA* or *Niggers With Attitude*. Needless to say, this group was immensely popular in American Samoa.

I said, "Are you really from Compton?"

"He lying," another said.

"I'm from Waipahu."

"Isn't that in Hawaii?" I asked.

"He never been to Hawaii!"

"Me, I'm from California, man."

"Dis a lie!"

And so they went on, giggling and yakking, and none of them told me where they were really from, the offshore island of Aunu'u.

"I think you're waiting for the boat to Aunu'u," I said. "What do you do out there?"

"We kill people!" the one in the *Fucking Bart* T-shirt said.

"Ya, we do dat!"

*Tedious little bastards*, I thought, but I said, "You are being very rude to me. Do you think it's funny?"

They were silent a moment, and then one jabbed his finger sideways. "He tink so."

It seemed to be one of the oldest Samoan customs to victimize the person without a family, the individual, the outsider, the stranger; because it was a society where, if you had no family, you had no status. Perhaps this was the reason they had achieved so little, either here or on the mainland. They did not want to stand out. They were the most pathetic conformists, and so the greatest bullies, in the Pacific. Who was I but a middle-aged oddball on the beach, trying to assemble a foreign-looking object that they did not recognize as a boat. They mocked me because I was an outsider, and they mocked me because they outnumbered me. None of them would have had the guts to face me alone, unless he had been suffering the Samoan affliction of extreme bad temper, a sort of hideous Black Dog mood called *musu*. A Samoan with *musu* was a man to avoid.

When my collapsible boat was once again set up, one of the youths stood and said in a demanding way, "You give me a ride."

"I don't think so," I said.

"Where are you going?" another asked.

"I think I'll paddle out there."

"You go to the island?"

"Maybe. Do you live there?"

"I live in Hawaii. Hee hee!"

I said, "You're all very funny guys," and turned my back on them.

Some older people, eight or nine of them, were sitting nearby, also waiting for the boat to Aunu'u – fat women, fat men. They heard this bantering, but took no interest in it; they looked hot, and bored, and irritable. They carried parcels of food, and when they walked to the water's edge to look for the boat they crunched old crumpled soft-drink cans.

I vowed that I would not leave the beach until the boys did, because I suspected that such cranky kids might find my car and break into it. The launch came and went. The boys stayed. I wondered what to do. And, waiting, I slapped on some suntan lotion, because of the dazzling sun.

"What dat stuff?"

"So I won't get sunburned," I said. I knew if I ignored their silly questions it would be worse: they would consider it a victory to irritate me.

"Looks like sperm," one said.

"He putting sperm on."

I said, "Is that funny?"

"You got sperm on you face."

I said calmly, as though seeking information, "Why are you saying that to me?"

He laughed at me, but I pursued it, and finally said, "What's your name?"

"M. C. Hammer."

More insolence – another name from the rappers' Parnassus.

This was ridiculous, but it was wrong to think that it could have

happened anywhere else in Oceania. I had traveled enough in the
region to realize that this was a uniquely American Samoan experience.
They were victimizers, they were oafish, and lazy, and defiant and
disrespectful. Would they be different when they grew up? It was impossible to say. Perhaps, like so many others, they were just waiting for a
chance to go to Honolulu or Los Angeles like a hundred thousand other
Samoans whose culture had become degenerate.

Eventually they boarded their motor-boat, and were swept away,
jeering, and the oafs I had met in Western Samoa now seemed to me the
very picture of innocence.

Paddling out to the island of Aunu'u I thought again of the pamphlet
that had been given to me, with the rules that all visitors were urged to
observe.

- *When in a Samoan house, do not talk while standing.*
- *Do not stretch your legs out when seated.*
- *Do not carry an umbrella past a house.*
- *Do not drive through a village when chiefs are gathering.*
- *Do not eat while walking through a village* [it seemed to me that Samoans
  ate no other way, and usually were munching a very large jelly donut].
- *Samoans are deeply religious – pray and sing with them.*
- *Do not wear flowers in church.*
- *When drinking kava, hold the cup in front of you and say "manuia"* ["when
  drinking Coke" would have been more apposite, since that seemed
  firmly part of the culture].
- *Bikinis and shorts are not considered appropriate attire in Samoan villages or town
  areas.*
- *Ask permission before snapping photos or picking flowers.*
- *Be extra quiet on Sundays.*

And there were more. How odd that this joyously piggy society should
be so obsessed with travelers' etiquette, or apparently so easily offended.

*No,* I told myself, *this is a comedy.*

I continued paddling out to this small low crater in the sea. I was
always concerned, in one of these stretches of open water or channels,
whether a current would pick me up and sweep me sideways, into the
blue *moana.* I had left the safety of a shallow lagoon, cut through a break
in the reef, and now I was between a large peaky island and a small
green islet.

It was a lovely day. My consolation on such a day was that if
something went drastically wrong I would still have plenty of time to get
straightened out, either by paddling hard for shore or sending up flares.

But so far it seemed easy paddling to Aunu'u, and as I glided down the back of the swell towards the island, I congratulated myself on having found in this somewhat degenerate and tentative territory a good place to go.

And where would I have been without my boat? At the mercy of mocking and xenophobic islanders, or worse – people who hated boats. An astonishingly large number of people in American Samoa seemed to hate the water, or at the very least were indifferent to it – didn't go near it. How odd for them to be islanders, and to live on a small island at that.

I set my compass for a low white building and when I drew nearer to the island I saw a pair of breakwaters below it. A launch was just leaving this enclosure – so this was the place to go. I was there in twenty more minutes, and paddling into this tight harbor I saw eight or ten boys swimming and diving – jumping from the little stone jetty. Three of them immediately jumped into the water and swam towards me and tried to tip my boat over.

*The Samoan people are, by nature and culture, extremely anxious to please their guests,* the pamphlet had said. This might well have been true of some villages, of the attitude of elders or chiefs. If so, I was not privileged to encounter it in American Samoa. It was all foolery and antagonism for no good reason.

"Go away," I said. "Let go of my boat."

Brown hands were fumbling and snatching at my lines.

"Bugger off!" I said, very loudly.

It worked. They splashed back to the jetty. But I still had a problem. The wharf was too high for me to land. I could tie up, but I would have to climb a ladder and leave my boat to the frenetic attention of these jumping screaming kids and some other lurking adults.

Some coconuts were being unloaded from another boat. I asked a man what they were used for here.

"To make *palusami*," he said.

Sticking to that traditional dish of steamed taro leaves and coconut cream seemed old-fashioned and civilized, and it reassured me. It made me curious and encouraged me to look for a landing place on the island.

I had a good nautical chart of the whole coast of American Samoa, and it showed me the particular jigs and jags of this little island. I paddled out beyond the breakers and then went counter-clockwise, past a shipwreck and another beach and reef. But the beaches were too steep for a landing – they all seemed to be ledges of pale crushed coral bashed by waves. I needed a more sloping beach.

Farther on, and at the eastern shore of the island, was an inlet, Ma'ama'a Cove, where I thought I might land, until at the last moment I saw surf rolling and smashing on rocks. And so I paddled on.

There was a lake of quicksand near the northwest coast, or so I had been told. I continued paddling toward this part of the island, still looking for a landing place. I was now approaching another reef, and more breakers, but I could see how I might squeeze myself in between them, and did so, leaping out at the beach and hurrying out of the path of the waves just before they broke over my boat.

How odd, among all those awful teenagers, and the junk food, and the suspicion, to have been subjected to these tricky sea conditions. But that was the paradox of Samoa: American bad food and popular culture, on a lovely volcanic island that was set in turbulent and reefy seas.

This small island of Aunu'u was a beautiful place, with a good view of Tutuila and its easternmost point, Cape Mata'ula. I also suspected that it might be one of the best places in American Samoa, since there were no cars here, no amusement arcades, no fast food, no laundromat or takeaways. There was one village and in it, one shop. Like other tiny offshore islands I had seen, this too was a quiet preserve, still living partly in the past. Given the state of American Samoa, this was amazing.

I pulled up my kayak and hid it, and then walked to the Pala Lake to look at the quicksand. I found it easily – it was sludgy red sand, covering the whole of the lake's surface, and it shimmered in the sun. But how was I to know that it really was quicksand? I had read that men hunting ducks swam in the quicksand by lying horizontal, keeping themselves perfectly flat. I was alone and decided not to test it by trying this. But these stories about quicksand were the first ones that had ever stirred my imagination when I was ten or so and considering travel to distant places: the idea of being sucked down and smothered by depthless sand the consistency of cold Quaker Oats.

The idea was that a stranger was supposed to ask permission before making camp here – the old fear of people squatting on your land and never leaving. But I decided not to announce myself. I wanted to be on my own, and I knew that if I asked I would either be forced to stay in one of their *fales* with an inquisitive and imprisoning family, or else I would be made conspicuous in my camp site and perhaps robbed.

I walked around looking for a place to pitch my tent, and nearer dusk found a sheltered spot in a grove of trees and set up camp quickly. I did not bother to make tea. I did not light my stove. I ate sardines and bread and listened to the BBC, and did not switch on my flashlight. When it was dark I crawled in and spent a fitful night, wondering whether I would be discovered, or my kayak stolen. And, meanwhile, what about my car on Tutuila? That was the terrible aspect of American Samoa – I could never tell for sure whether I was in America or Samoa.

At dawn I crept out and checked the boat. It was still well hidden, but a woman walking along the beach saw me. She said hello and I greeted her.

"How did you come here?" she asked.

"By boat," I said, trying to be ambiguous, and to change the subject I asked her the meaning of the island's name.

"I dunno," she said, and laughed, and walked on.

That morning, after I had packed and hidden my gear – so that it would not be seen and stolen – I walked along a circular track to a marsh and back to the cove where I had seen the thrashing surf. It looked much worse from here on shore than it had from the backs of the waves.

I killed the day swimming and then walked to the village, hoping not to meet the boys who had been so irritating the day before. The older people were polite, although the kids were still a nuisance, preening themselves and trying to be defiant. It was wonderful to be in a place with no cars, and yet most of these older people and all the schoolkids made a daily trip to Tutuila. And that afternoon, when I paddled back across the channel to Tutuila, I was both uplifted by the mountains and the glorious vistas along the south coast, and also depressed by the seedy modernity of this seemingly spoiled society.

The next day in Leone, the second town of Tutuila – a shopping mall, a school, supermarkets – I met a woman who was visiting her family. She said she lived in Las Vegas. She was half-Samoan and looked very weary but not old. "I love Las Vegas," she said. An islander in the desert. It seemed incredible to me, and I remarked on that. "I miss Las Vegas," she said.

And that same day, getting a haircut, I asked the barber where he was from.

"Western Samoa," he said. "But my wife is from here."

His two children had American passports. He said that they would almost certainly end up in the United States, while he would probably go back to his home village on Savaii. So American Samoa was like a convenient ship which people boarded to get them where they wanted to go.

"I don't want them to stay here," he said. He was very polite – and he did not put into words the other thought that must have been in his mind: that there was nothing for them in Western Samoa.

The traveler's great fear in Samoa is of *musu* – the ferocious mood that turns a Samoan man into a brute. You can see it in their eyes, people say, and if a Samoan behaves like a bear with a sore head he is in the grip of *musu*. My apprehension had made me overly cautious in Samoa, but just before I was about to leave I sat down and examined my Samoan experience, and I realized that most Samoans, on whatever island, had been kind to me – generous, good-humored and helpful. I felt bad about carping, and was it wrong to make so much of their physical size? It was a race of giants, with big flapping feet, and when they walked their thighs rubbed and made a chafing sound that was audible ten feet away. I could only conclude that when Samoans were good they were very very good, and when they were bad they were horrid. But most of the time they were indifferent.

It was when I was in Samoa that American troops flushed the remaining Iraqis from the suburbs and rode in triumph through Kuwait City. This was a news item in the Samoan newspapers, but it was not a topic of conversation, there was no air of celebration, and not even much interest in it. There was no flag-waving, but was that so surprising?

American Samoa wasn't a political entity. It was a social phenomenon – a rescued orphan, a fat feckless child that we had adopted. The arrangement perfectly suited *fa'a Samoa*, the Samoan way and its family ideal in which everyone was looked after. If you didn't have one you found one. I met many foreigners who had attached themselves to Samoan families, and were perfectly happy to support everyone. The Samoans remained hospitable as long as someone else paid their bills. They sat by the littered lagoon, cooling their bellies, and eating.

Samoa had become part of the American family and was content. Samoans were generally unenthusiastic, but similarly they were uncomplaining, and this little-brown-brother relationship would continue as long as America fed them and paid for their pleasures.

# 18

## Tahiti: The Windward Shore of the Island of Love

One day in 1768 a bare-breasted Tahitian girl climbed from her canoe to a French ship under the hot-eyed gaze of 400 French sailors who had not seen any woman at all for over six months. She stepped to the quarterdeck where, pausing at a hatchway, she slipped the flimsy cloth *pareu* from her hips, and stood utterly naked and smiling at the men. Down went the anchor, and in that moment the myth of romantic Tahiti was conceived, a paradise of fruit trees, brown tits and kiddie porn. Like Venus rising from the waves – that was how the naked girl was described by the captain of the ship, Louis Antoine de Bougainville, the first Frenchman in Tahiti, who believed he had discovered heaven on earth ("I thought I was transported into the garden of Eden"), the abode of Venus, the Island of Love.

Now I had a similar experience in Tahiti, involving stark nakedness, the lagoon, the hot-eyed gaze, and an outrigger canoe, but in its suddenness and coloration this incident was more up to date and more representative of Tahiti today. And I was the one in the outrigger canoe.

After a day or so rattling around the streets of Papeete, Tahiti's capital, I rented an outrigger from a Frenchman (he called it his "*petite pirogue*") and paddled for a day to Tahiti-Iki – "Little Tahiti," the volcanic bulge that is attached to the eastern shore of the island. The ancient name of the island of Tahiti is *Tahiti-nui-i-te-vai-uri-rau*, "Great Tahiti of the Many-Colored Waters."

The name is apt. The lagoon beneath Tahiti's dead green volcanoes is a luminous varying blue, not sea-water colored, but with glittering opalescent depths, and elsewhere shallow coral shelves, white and knobbed like bones, rippling with fish. Overall the water is limpid and unexpectedly bright, like those candy-colored liqueurs made from berries, cordials that are so pretty in the squat glass bottles in a bar that just looking at them cools you and takes away your thirst. The surface of Tahiti's lagoon was spangled with stars of sunlight. A mile or so offshore was the reef, being pounded by surf that was so heavy it had the muffled boom of distant cannon fire, and it ringed the entire island with a white flash of foam.

Tahiti has its drawbacks – it is expensive, traffic-choked, noisy, corrupt and Frenchified – but it is impossible to belittle its natural physical beauty, and in spite of the car exhausts there is nearly always in the air the fragrant aroma – the *noanoa* – of flowers, the *tiare* especially, a tiny white gardenia that is Tahiti's national blossom. Visitors are full of complaints, though. Just that morning, on the public vehicle they call *le truck* (a cross between a mammy-wagon and a school bus, and Tahiti's only bargain) I had fallen into conversation with a man from Maryland. His name was Don Kattwinkel – he wore a get-acquainted badge – and he was obviously a sucker for carvings, from the look of his war club and his letter-opener. He was on the three-day tour, just arrived at Faa'a a few days ago – today Tahiti, tomorrow New Zealand. And he tried to sum up Tahiti for me.

"No one smiles here," he said. "And you can't drink the water."

I broke it to him gently that both were half-truths. The locals smiled at each other, even if they didn't smile at us, and they boiled their water before drinking it.

Don made no comment on that. He said, "You sound like you're from Australia."

I wanted to tell him that people have been killed for uttering an uncalled-for libel like that.

"You're sure not from Mass," he went on. "I know that dialect."

I was thinking about this irritating fart while I was paddling my canoe – nothing like meeting a man like that to preoccupy yourself. There was a current campaign put on by the Polynesian Tourist Board called *Put On A Smile!* – encouraging Polynesians to smile at tourists, mostly Japanese, none of whom smiled themselves. Is there a Japanese smile that does not seem like an expression of pain?

By mid-afternoon I had paddled halfway around this part of the island, and was nearing the village of Atimaono. It was not much of a place, but it was the setting of one of Jack London's masterpieces, his story "The Chinago." In the story some Chinese laborers – "Chinagos" – are accused of murder, and though all are innocent of the crime they are found guilty by the French magistrate and one, Ah Chow, is sentenced to hang. Another, Ah Cho, is given twenty years in a prison colony, but one morning he is taken to this village, Atimaono, and told that he is to be beheaded. He protests to the various gendarmes – it is a case of mistaken identity, because the names are so similar – and at last, pleading for his life and proving he is not the condemned man, he is believed. But the French officials confer. They have come a long way from Papeete. The guillotine is ready. Five hundred other laborers have been assembled to watch. A postponement to find the right man would mean being bawled out by the French bureaucrats for inefficiency and time-wasting. Also it is a very hot day and they are impatient.

All this time Ah Cho listens and watches.

At last, but knowing they have the wrong man, one French policeman says, "Then let's go on with it. They can't blame us. Who can tell one Chinago from another? We can say that we merely carried out instructions with the Chinago that was turned over to us . . ."

And, still making excuses, the French strap down the innocent Chinese man and strike off his head.

"The French, with no instinct for colonization," London writes at one point, and that is the subject of the grim story.

An hour past Atimaono was the harbor of Port Phaeton. In a lovely garden by the sea was the Gauguin Museum, but in spite of its name it contained no paintings by Gauguin, only a haunted grimacing tiki. Farther on, the village of Papeari was said to be the first settlement of the seagoing people who originally landed on Tahiti and it lay next to the piece of land, like a pinched waist, where Little Tahiti was attached to Big Tahiti. But it was all so suburban.

One of the curious facts of Tahitian life was that strictly speaking there were few usable beaches on the island – the public ones were dismal and littered, the others were the property of proprietorial Tahitian villages. Looking toward the island from the lagoon, I could see that the coast was an unbroken stretch of bungalows and villas, one enormous attenuated suburb that encircled the whole of Tahiti. Undermined by French aid programs, and besieged by French construction companies, the Polynesians have abandoned their traditional house-building. The houses were extremely unattractive and they were packed cheek by jowl along the coast, surrounded by chain link fences and walls and high hedges. Most Tahitian bungalows had signs saying *Tabu*, which needed no translation, and the French houses had security cameras and signs saying *Attention Chien Méchant!* (Beware of the Fierce Dog!).

Earlier in the day, paddling near Punaauia, I had passed a pair of *fares*, or traditional huts, but there were not many others like them in the whole of French Polynesia. I was so interested in them that I went ashore there and was told that these two at the edge of the beach at Punaauia were owned by the Swede Bengt Danielsson, who had run aground in Polynesia forty-odd years ago on the raft *Kon-Tiki*. In his book recounting the adventure, Thor Heyerdahl wrote, "Bengt was right; this was heaven," and Bengt stayed in Polynesia.

"Monsieur Danielsson is on holiday in Sweden," a Tahitian woman on the lawn told me.

I was sorry to miss him, because Danielsson and his French-born wife Marie-Thérèse have courageously fought a vocal battle against French nuclear testing in the Pacific, and in this small and politically incestuous French colony Danielsson has been threatened, obstructed and shunned. Yet he perseveres in publishing to the world the fact that the French have been continually detonating nuclear devices – 160 so far – in one of the world's most fragile ecosystems, a coral atoll, nuking it to pieces, killing fish and causing cancer.

Perhaps it was just as well that I did not engage Danielsson on the subject of French colonialism, because just a short trip to any French territory in the Pacific is enough to convince even the most casual observer that the French are among the most self-serving, manipulative, trivial-minded, obnoxious, cynical and corrupting nations on the face of the earth.

*Et c'est vous qui parlez!* a French person might reply. *Look who's talking!*

It is true that America has overwhelmed its own territory in Samoa and made it a welfare state, but Samoans have emigrated wholesale to the mainland United States, where they flourish or fail, according to their abilities. There is no profit in Samoa for us. But Polynesia is all profit for the French – they need the land and the distance to capitalize on world air routes for French airlines; and they need Polynesia as a military garrison, and – most profitable of all – they need nuclear testing facilities for their arms industry. As an old-fashioned colony it is a racket. The French effort is devoid of idealism.

Only a minuscule number of Polynesians ever make it to metropolitan France to qualify as doctors or administrators – the French run the entire show. But the patronizing racism inherent in French colonial policy has not had the demoralizing effect that was intended. They planted themselves in the islands and consistently discriminated against Polynesians and refused to learn their language – there was a law passed in French Polynesia in the 1960s forcing Polynesians and Chinese to take

French names so they could be more easily pronounced. In this way, the French turned most of these friendly people into sullen adversaries and some into lapdogs. But though they have lost most of their traditional skills of weaving and house-building and fishing and sailing, the Polynesians have retained their oral culture – and that is a good thing, because no one needs their culture more than colonized people. What else do they have?

The Polynesians paid lip-service to the French and so the French truly believed they had subverted the islanders. But in fact they only made a greater burden for themselves. By encouraging the islanders to be "colorful" they distanced themselves. The French are at their most obvious, their most bourgeois and sentimental when they are dealing with people they regard as savages, but it seems to be a fact that sentimentality is a trait one always finds in bullies and brutes.

The honest thing, in dealing with Tahiti, would be to discuss French Polynesia as a depressing political problem, because it has been a French colony for 150 years. Everything else ought to be irrelevant – that is, whether the beaches are pleasant and the food is tasty, and the hotels are comfortable, and what's the music like? The very fact of politics mattering in the Pacific seems strange – few people in other islands care about politics – yet it is the only place in the Pacific where there is a political situation. It is a characteristic of colonies that unless political life is manipulated or made ineffectual the place won't work.

But it is all so boring. I liked Pacific islanders generally for the way they guffawed at politicians – I admired their sense of family, their practicality, their usual indifference to world events. They were out of the mainstream, on the other side of the world – the brighter, happy side. For those with televisions, "Operation Desert Storm" had been to them not much more than a nightly entertainment video. That attitude seemed informed by a healthy combination of wisdom and vulgarity, and a taste for sensationalism – but most of the world's couch potatoes are much the same.

There was always a mixture of motives among Polynesians: they made you feel at home and then they stole from you. If you complained, they would say that it was nothing personal – and if you couldn't afford it, what were you doing here, so far from home, in the first place? Colonial politics was just another complication. Yes, the French built court-houses and schools, but the French colonialists needed such institutions far more than Tahitians did. I just kept wishing that the French were a bit nicer and more generous, and weren't so keen on nuking everything in sight. They said they had to – for world peace, but that was *merde*. The French arms industry, third largest in the world, and exporter of nuclear technology, now more than ever depended on extensive nuclear testing.

I paddled past Bengt Danielsson's two thatched-roof *fares*.

Buffeted by the trade winds – the wind never ceases to blow in Polynesia – I kept within the reef, glorying in the sight of the lovely island of Moorea, its mountains looming dark and spiky – local myths claimed they were the dorsal fins of giant fish, but the island looked to me like a seagoing dragon, crossing the channel known as the Sea of the Moon.

It was then, squinting into the intense glare of a cloudless oceanic afternoon – the sun slanted into my eyes – that I saw a small raft drifting perilously near the reef. There were some inert specks on it – humans probably – but it was the oddest possible place for a raft to be. If it went on drifting it would be smashed to pieces by surf. It had no mast or sail, nor was anyone paddling it. I had the idea that it had broken free of a ship and that somehow it had floated through a break in the reef. What was beyond question was that it was hardly visible from shore. The only reason I could see the raft was because I was in a seaworthy outrigger canoe and paddling along the margin of the reef.

You sometimes heard stories of the ordeal of the people on such rafts; how their expensive yacht had been sunk by a killer whale, and how the quarreling castaways had clung to the wreckage for days or weeks, praying for deliverance, until, one sunny morning, the battered thing hove into view on a tropical shore, where holiday-minded families frolicked with beach balls, the raft looking as though it had floated straight out of Poe's *Narrative of Arthur Gordon Pym*, and it was immediately, grotesquely clear that the survivors had made it through by using each other with the utmost barbarity – human bones, scraps of flesh and the evidence of cannibalism. "Daddy, what's wrong with those people?" – one of those rafts.

That made me paddle faster, and I could see that there were only two figures on board and that I was gaining on the raft. It excited me to think that I might be the first person to witness the arrival of this desperate craft in Tahiti, and I alone would hear their ordeal – what a piece of luck for someone like me, who intended to write about these islands where in the normal way nothing much happened.

Now I could see that the two figures on the raft were lying flat, as though prostrate from the sun, and there was something melancholy about the solitariness of their situation – within the reef and yet still so far from shore. You could drown, or starve, or die of thirst, or suffocate with heat exhaustion, even in this bewitchingly lovely place.

I had a water bottle and the remains of my lunch in my boat – enough to revive them, I was sure. They were upwind, so they did not hear the thrashing of my canoe, but I was soon close enough to recognize the strangeness of this simple raft. It was not drifting; it was tethered to a mooring. Apart from the two people, there was nothing else on it, not an object of any kind – no flag, no scraps, no bones, no bucket, nothing – nor any clothes.

There were two skinny women on the raft and they were naked. As I drew near – I was only thirty feet away – some warning vibration of my maleness must have charged the air: suddenly each woman sat up straight. Or had they heard my paddling? They were young, in their twenties, rather pretty and, from their demeanor, French. They were browner than any Tahitian I had seen – the gleaming darkness of the most lizard-like sunbather. It was the sort of tanning that made you think of leather. Seeing me, they arranged their bodies compactly, as modestly as they could, folded themselves with ingenious economy, their knees drawn up under their chins, and their feet jammed together, and they hugged themselves, like monkeys squatting in the rain.

To preserve their modesty, I did not go much closer, and yet I was close enough to be able to marvel at their nakedness, at the exoticism of this sight – a pair of nymphs on a bobbing raft in the Tahitian lagoon.

"Hello," I said, trying to be jaunty, so as not to alarm them. But it had a hollow sound – and I realized it was just the sort of thing a rapist or voyeur might say to give false reassurance to his victim.

They narrowed their eyes, their gaze did not meet mine, and their tense posture, with this grim indifference (which I took to be fear and apprehension), was meant to shame me. They wanted me to go away, of course. And now I saw a Tahitian fisherman, trolling from a small motor-boat. He looked up and leered at the crouching sunbathers. They shrank from him, too, and wished him away.

It irritated me that they felt we had no right to go bobbing past them – that, simply because they had taken all their clothes off, they regarded themselves as inviolate, and treated this part of the lagoon (which belonged to everyone) as their private property. For that reason I lingered and then I left, paddling onward towards Papeete. There I was told that this was a fairly common practice – a French thing, women sunbathing nude in order to eliminate bathing-suit silhouettes on their skin. A speed-boat dropped them on the raft and returned two or three hours later to take them back to their hotel.

It was dangerously silly to lie naked under this blistering Oceanic sun, and there was not a single Polynesian who would dare it. Apart from being bad for the skin, and a cause of premature wrinkling, if not cancer, it was blatant immodesty.

Once upon a time the Tahitians had reveled in nakedness and seduced European sailors and tempted them from their stern duties on shipboard. (". . . for when we were sent away, 'Huzza for Otaheite!' was frequently heard among the mutineers," Captain Bligh wrote bitterly, after seeing his ship the *Bounty* headed back to Papeete and the local women.) But these days only the tourists went naked, and the bare tits you saw were always those of visiting sunbathers. The Tahitians were all covered up and decent; history's wheel had taken a complete turn, the fantasies were reversed, and now it was the Christian Tahitians who leered, and the pagan French who were naked.

As soon as the nameless Tahitian girl on Bougainville's ship dropped her flimsy cloth in full view of the impressionable sailors, Tahiti's fate was sealed, and the South Sea Island myth was born. Ogling a woman's private parts is the Frenchman's version of a glimpse of paradise in any case, but to these horny and fanciful sailors this was even better – the woman was a dusky maiden, just the sort of uncorrupted savage living in her natural state that Rousseau had described only fifteen years earlier.

Captain Bougainville was ecstatic. He paid Tahitian women his highest compliment: "for agreeable features [they] are not inferior to most European women; and who on the point of beauty of the body might, with much reason, vie with them all." He wrote that the naked girl on board "appeared to the eyes of all beholders, such as Venus showed herself to the Phrygian shepherd, having indeed, the celestial form of the goddess."

From that moment – and Bougainville encouraged the view – Tahiti was known as the New Cytherea, the abode of Venus. When Venus Aphrodite rose from the sea foam she stepped ashore (according to the poet Hesiod) at Cythera, in Ionia. This naked Tahitian girl was Venus made flesh, a goddess of love and beauty, the physical embodiment of the life force. But there was more. Every detail of Tahiti excited Bougainville, and when he settled down to write about his voyage he described how like the world before the Fall this island seemed, and he used Rousseau's precise expression "the golden age" for this uncorrupted place: Polynesia was one of "those countries where the golden age is still in use." Even the creatures associated with the mythology of Venus could be found in Tahiti. The dolphin, the tortoise and the gentlest birds were sacred to Venus – and there the captain had found them in the very spot where this dusky Venus smiled upon him.

More than that, more rousing than the unashamed nakedness, were the sexual practices – and they were of the most unfamiliar kind. This seemed to be an island of exhibitionists. Officers and sailors invited into the islanders' houses were given food and afterwards the Tahitians "offered them young girls." Neigbours crowded into the house, music was played, the floor was spread with leaves and flowers; and the Europeans were encouraged to strip naked and make love to the girls, there and then, under the approving eyes of the islanders. "Here Venus is the goddess of hospitality, her worship does not permit of any mysteries, and every tribute paid to her is a feast for the whole nation." In short, public copulation, group sex, fruit trees and freedom.

The islands were bountiful and lovely, and what distinguished them from all other happy islands on earth was their dedication to free and joyous and unsentimental sexuality. Captain Cook was shocked by what he saw in Tahiti, and he wrote, "There is a scale of dissolute sensuality which these people have ascended, wholly unknown to every other nation whose manners have been recorded from the beginning of the world to the present hour, and which no imagination could possibly conceive." On one occasion in Tahiti, in a presentation that was organized by the islanders for the amusement of the foreigners, Cook and some of his men watched a naked six-foot Tahitian man copulate with a fourteen-year-old girl, and he noted that neither was embarrassed – indeed, the young girl was skilled in the arts of love.

Bougainville's extremely well-written *Voyage Around the World* (1771) made Tahiti a byword for everything beautiful. The book was quickly translated into English, and it delighted and inspired – and stimulated – its readers. Just a few years after the book appeared, James Boswell got a hankering to go to Tahiti, and he mentioned this to Dr Johnson, who told him not to bother, because "one set of Savages is like another."

"I do not think the people of Otaheite can be reckoned Savages," Boswell said.

"Don't cant in defense of Savages," Johnson replied.

"They have the art of navigation," Boswell said.

"A dog or a cat can swim," Johnson said.

Boswell persisted: "They carve very ingeniously."

"A cat can scratch, and a child with a nail can scratch," Johnson said.

But Boswell was right, and he went on yearning to go to Tahiti, in order to "be satisfied what pure nature can do for man."

The Tahitians were anything but primitive. They were among the greatest navigators the world has ever known. They had been brilliant stone-carvers and masons. At Papara they had raised a large eleven-step pyramid, the Mahaiatea Marae, and there were more temples and altars at Paea and on the island of Moorea. The people whom Wallis, Bougainville and Captain Cook met (these captains visited Tahiti within three years of each other) were skilled in the arts of wars, of boat-building, and navigation. And far from depending on the fruit trees of the island for their food, they practiced complex and organized cultivation – growing yams, sweet potatoes, gourds and sugar cane; they raised pigs and chickens, and dogs – they preferred dog meat to pork. Speaking of the first Europeans in Polynesia, Fernand Braudel wrote (in *The Structures of Everyday Life*), "But were the savages they described really primitive people? Far from it." Yet to nearly everyone, the sophistication of the Tahitians was the least interesting thing about them.

Because of its reputation for innocent sex, for pretty people in a pretty place, Tahiti has been one of the most inspirational pieces of geography in the world. Even writers who never saw it praised it – Lord Byron, who wrote a poem about it ("The Island"), and the philosopher Diderot (cribbing from Bougainville) set a novel there. Melville made his reputation by writing about it in *Typee* and *Omoo*, and Robert Louis Stevenson vastly preferred it to Samoa. Most of the people who subsequently wrote about it described it in much the same terms as Bougainville. Pierre Loti went one better and in the purplest prose imaginable described his marriage to a Tahitian; after reading this book, Paul Gauguin was encouraged to set sail. They were all male writers, of course; it would have been interesting if someone like Edith Wharton or Simone de Beauvoir had gushed in quite this way about Tahiti.

Even the sexually ambiguous Somerset Maugham regarded Papeete as pleasant – but he had reason to feel lucky for having gone there. He had sailed to Tahiti after Samoa (which he hadn't liked much) in order to collect material about Gauguin for his novel *The Moon and Sixpence*. This was in 1917, only thirteen years after Gauguin's death, and so memories were still fresh. Indeed, one old woman remembered that the obnoxious Frenchman had painted the glass panels of a door in a decrepit village house. Maugham went immediately to the house, where the door was still hinged and swinging, and bought it from the innocent owner for 200 francs (he later sold it for $37,400). Years later, Gauguin's son Emil, an overweight buffoon, was a colorful local character. Emil hung around the bars of Papeete, and visitors bought him drinks and badgered him for information about his father (whom he had never known), and for ten francs he let you take his picture.

For literary reasons, Maugham regarded Tahiti as a seductive place (Gauguin certainly didn't, which was why he abandoned it for the Marquesas). It is questionable whether all Tahitians were ever as sexy as Bougainville described – he was only on the island a matter of days, his ship anchored off Hitiaa – but proof of the power of this book is the fact that Tahiti in particular and Polynesian islands in general are still regarded as Cytherean. Yet, manifestly, they are not. Pleasant and feckless, yes; paradise, no.

Bougainville's descriptions stimulated two quite different sorts of people, polar opposites actually – adventurers eager to taste the Cytherean delights of willing women; and missionaries determined to clothe and convert the islanders to Christianity. Over two hundred years later, these people are still contending for the souls of Polynesians. But for every Melville or Gauguin, or Don Kattwinkel on the six-day Polynesian package-tour ("Features include welcome flower *leis*"), or anyone else searching out a seductress, there are many more zealots with fire in their eyes who have made it their life's work to convince these people that they are imbued with Original Sin. No adventurer's book is complete without an attack on missionaries – Melville despised and ridiculed them for their subversion and hypocrisy; no missionary's memoir omits to mention the sinfulness and opportunism of beach-combers and remittance men. Each saw the other as a corrupter.

It is almost axiomatic that as soon as a place gets a reputation for being paradise it goes to hell. Tahiti seemed to me dramatically beautiful, but its population lived entirely on the fringes of its steep and inaccessible slopes; and so it seemed small and crowded. It was full of French soldiers and expatriate bureaucrats cashing in on the fact that overseas salaries were double what they were in France and here there was no income tax. The businessmen wore a perpetual scowl of disappointment, because business was so poor. The hotel-owners and tour-operators complained that tourism was off twenty to thirty percent. Even in its great days Tahiti prospered because of French aid rather than from the receipts of tourism, but if it was ever to become independent it needed to make a show of self-sufficiency. By the 1980s it had become noticeably poorer and more careworn. The bureaucrats were overpaid, but the place itself was undercapitalized, and the locals were penetrated by the aimlessness and vague resentment that characterizes most colonial people. Treat people like children and they become infantile and cranky. The clearest evidence of this was the government's official *Put On A Smile!* campaign.

Another campaign – the Tourist Board was unimaginative but desperate to please – was a contest to find "the most hospitable Tahitian" who would qualify for a *Mauruuru* (Thank You Very Much) Award. Visitors to French Polynesia were encouraged to write letters to the *Tahiti Sun Press* recommending a person who had impressed them. I found the letters laughable but engaging, as they described a particularly helpful bellhop or swimming-pool attendant or taxi-driver. One day, I read a laudatory letter from some visiting Americans (Mr and Mrs Albert Crisp, from Los Angeles) who had spent a week in Moorea:

*Since our stay at the Hotel Bali Hai in Moorea we have enjoyed meeting and getting to know* Helene ("Mimi") Theroux, *a sweet girl who tends bar.*
     Mimi Theroux *is extremely friendly and helpful, and we would like to show our gratitude by nominating her for a* Mauruuru *Award. She works very hard and this is to show our appreciation.*

Seeing your own strange, hard-to-spell name correctly printed on the pages of a Tahitian newspaper can give you a powerful sense of belonging to the islands. And it is a belief in my family that every person with that surname is a relation – a descendant of Peter Theroux (1839–1915) of Yamaska, Quebec, who had nine prolific sons, Henri, Louis, Ovide, Leon, Dorel, Joseph, Peter, Alexandre, and my grandfather, Eugene. I immediately called the Hotel Bali Hai and asked to speak to my cousin.

"Mimi Theroux doesn't work here anymore," the manager told me.

He thought I might find her somewhere in Moorea, but he wasn't sure. He promised to find her address for me.

I planned to paddle around Moorea sometime soon, and I vowed that I would seek out Mademoiselle – or was it Madame? – Theroux, when I got to that island.

Two things kept me in Tahiti for the moment – the arrangements I was making to go to the distant Marquesas on a freighter, and the prospect of watching the Bastille Day parade. I also wondered whether I ought to get a tattoo in this the homeland of tattoos – even the word was Polynesian (*tatu* means "puncture"). The idea of a tattoo on my ankle seemed an inoffensive way of satisfying my curiosity, but the sight of the only tattooist in Papeete, an excitable Belgian in a bloodstained room, made me change my mind.

Papeete is rather an ugly, plundered-looking town. Its buildings are scruffy, and flimsy and ill-assorted, and they clutter the lower slopes of the extinct volcanoes, Aorai and Orohena, that rise six or seven thousand feet behind it. Tahiti's road – there is only one narrow one, inevitably a speedway, that encircles the island – is quite famously bad and dangerous. To complete this unromantic picture, Tahiti I found to be one of the most expensive places I have ever visited – a pack of cigarettes is $5, a liter of petrol $4, the simplest cotton shirt $50, and a meal in a good restaurant almost prohibitive, but as there are few good restaurants this is academic; and yet if you decide to have a pizza instead you will be paying about twice what you would at the Pizza Hut in Boston. There is no income tax in French Polynesia, yet indirect taxation can be just as brutal. You may congratulate yourself that you don't smoke or drink alcohol, yet even the most frugal vegetarian is in for a shock when he sees the Tahitian cabbages (grown in California) priced at $8 in Papeete's central market.

But for the Tahitians themselves the price of cabbage was academic. The islanders, who were always tidy and clean – impressively so, in a place where fresh water was scarce – managed to survive, and even to flourish, by cultivating small vegetable gardens and applying for welfare and using the extended family. They were a chunky breed, and I felt that there was perhaps something assertive in their obesity. They seemed to revel in being a different size and shape from their colonial masters or mistresses – apart from enthusiastic teenagers, who were imitative, there was almost no emulation among Tahitians of French physical types or styles – no joggers, no fashion casualties, no snobs or socialites. Few of them were even smokers.

The Tahitian's most obvious indulgence was a kind of relentless snacking – they were forever munching and manipulating Planter's Cocktail Nuts, potato sticks, Porky Snaks (*Porc Frites*), Rashuns (*frites au bacon*), Kellogg's Corn Pops, Figolu Fig Newtons, Champagne Crispy Sponge Fingers, Cadbury's Crunchies, Pinkys, Moros and Double Fudge Chocolate Biscuits, Toscas, Millefeuilles and Tiki *crousti-legers*, and Cheez Balls at five bucks a five-ounce can. To pay for this they spent their welfare checks or else got jobs catering to the dwindling number of tourists, few of whom were big spenders. But even the poorest, scrounging Tahitian did not solicit tips and regarded tipping as one of the more insulting of foreign habits.

Tahiti was typical of Oceania generally in the frugality of its long-term expatriates — it seemed through a kind of caution, not to say fear, that these people saved their money. Because people were so vulnerable, they made a point of not appearing to be well-off — it was altogether too easy for anyone to be burgled. There were retirees here, but they had gone to ground — they hid in bungalows deep in the valleys of Tahiti and Moorea. There were always yachties in Papeete harbor, but yacht people the world over are notoriously careful with their money — circumstances force them to be self-sufficient.

Elsewhere on the island, the villages were fenced off and seemed contented, and the most conspicuous people in Papeete — apart from Japanese tourists and French soldiers — were the two sorts of folk who had been there since Bougainville described it as paradise: the adventurers and the missionaries; the drunks and the God-botherers. At any time of day in downtown Papeete it was possible to see a sanctimonious clergyman passing a bar where a wrecked-looking Frenchman was sitting glumly over a bottle of Hinano beer. It was still possible to go to pieces here, and any number of Frenchmen had married teenaged Tahitians, given them six kids, and turned them into twenty-year-old hags, thus keeping alive the South Sea Island myth.

I had longed to be in Tahiti for Bastille Day and I made a point of lingering on the island to witness the parade. Rather disingenuously the French authorities on the island had converted Bastille Day into a gala they called *Heiva Tahiti*, the Tahiti Festival — they hadn't the guts to come clean and celebrate their independence day in full view of people who had yet to gain their freedom. I expected it to be a wonderful example of colonial comedy and hypocrisy and it was, "Sponsored by Toyota."

To make matters even more puzzling, the posters anounced in French *The 109th Tahiti Annual July Festival*, and to work this out you had to go to a history book and establish that it was in 1880 that Ariane (Pomare V), the son of the intransigent Queen Pomare (IV), was pressured by the French into abdicating and handed his entire administration over to France, who proclaimed the island a French colony. With an astounding insensitivity the French had conflated the dates, and the Tahitians were being persuaded to celebrate the anniversary of their subjection on the very day the French celebrated their own freedom.

At eight o'clock on Bastille Day morning I joined the crowd of impassive Tahitians and frisky French people on the Boulevard Pomare, wondering what I would see, and fifteen minutes later I heard the first distant syncopation of the parade, a French army band playing the First World War song *Auprès de ma blonde (il fait beau blah-blah . . .)* – strange in almost any circumstances, but especially bizarre on an island of dusky dark-haired people.

There followed a regiment of Marine Fusiliers carrying a French flag lettered *Honneur et Patrie* and about fifty men from the Special Forces holding hi-tech weapons. The "Régiment du Tonkin" band seemed harmless enough, but the oncoming ranks grew increasingly menacing – three units of legionnaires with fixed bayonets, and one with a French flag down the muzzle of his rifle; a black-beret regiment with fierce dogs in personnel carriers and more infantrymen, followed by men from the Foreign Legion, all of them bearded and wearing white leather aprons and white gauntlets, and each man shouldering – because this was the symbol of this unit of sappers – a wicked axe.

The word *Camarone* was inscribed on the flag of these marching men, commemorating a battle in Mexico in 1863 in which a detachment of sixty-five legionnaires with their backs to the wall faced an army of 2,000 Mexicans and, refusing to surrender, were wiped out by the admiring yet remorseless enemy. This was the battle in which the famous Captain Danjou lost not only his life but his wooden hand (it was later retrieved and became a sort of Foreign Legion relic and talisman). "Life – not courage – abandoned these French soldiers," was the official summing-up, and the event entered the language in the form of a colloquialism – "*faire Camarone*" means to fight to the end.

I had the feeling that these parading regiments had been chosen for their ferocity. Anyone watching them pass by would think twice about mounting a revolt or starting an uprising, and so the Bastille Day parade, the so-called Festival of Tahiti – this part of it, at least – was unambiguously intimidating to the Polynesians, who watched in complete silence, even when the wives and children of the French soldiers were applauding.

The French Foreign Legionnaires are very thick on the ground in Polynesia. Their toughness and intransigence are needed in such a sensitive place, and the romantic pose suits their swashbuckling image. I was told that they often take Tahitian mistresses. Owing to an indifferent diet and their love of snacks and sweet drinks, Tahitians frequently have bad teeth. The legionnaires' first – or perhaps second – demonstration of their love is to buy their Tahitian girlfriend a set of false teeth. You can often spot these spoken-for girls on the public trucks, sitting and smiling a lovely white smile.

When the legionnaire goes back to France (and it might well be to revisit the wife and children he left behind) he takes his girlfriend's teeth with him, so as to leave her less attractive to men.

"Sometimes the girl does not want to give her teeth back," a legionnaire told me in Papeete. "Then we turn her upside down and shake them out of her."

The second part of the parade was much friendlier and less deadly-looking. It began with fire trucks and local school bands, and continued with majorettes and kids in cowboy hats, and Miss Tahiti, who was carried in an outrigger canoe by six muscular men.

"Smile, woman," the islander in front of me called out in French to Miss Tahiti.

Twenty-eight women in white *muumuus*, twelve in purple, a gang of drummers, dancers wearing feather head-dresses and coconut-shell brassières, trick cyclists, the fat and wicked-looking men on motorcycles flying a skull-and-crossbones flag reading "Le Club Harley-Davidson du Tahiti," and local kids doing handstands on skateboards – and now the Tahitians cheered, yelling from balconies and clinging to tree branches beside the boulevard, and I kept imagining a painting – full of Oceanic color and tropical light, and packed with chubby islanders and children and large laughing families, and severe and authoritarian-looking French soldiers, called "Bastille Day in Papeete," illustrating the paradoxes of French colonialism.

This happy back half of the parade put me in a better mood and I followed a sniggering group of Tahitians through the side-streets and into the fenced-in garden of the French High Commission, where a garden party was in progress under a huge Polynesian tree. Half of us had clearly crashed the party, and the rest – the VIPs, the beefy-faced *faranis* and *colons* in tight suits and the threadbare old soldiers wearing heroic clusters of medals and battle ribbons, and one conspicuously decorated with the Legion of Honor – were too drunk to notice us. "This *France Libre* was given to me by General de Gaulle," one elderly man told me, and other old soldiers – some were African and some Vietnamese – had seen action in Indo-China in the 1950s. The Tahitians especially were having a grand time: they ignored the waitresses with drinks and made a beeline for the hors-d'œuvres, which they managed with wonderful dexterity, scooping up three or four at a time, squeezing them between two fingers, and cramming them into their mouths.

A French army band set up their music stands in the shade of the tree and perspired and played rousing songs, *Sang et Or*, and *Tenth Festival*, and *Adios Amigos*, and the stirring *Marche des Mousquetaires Noirs*, while the bandleader conducted them without a baton, using only his hands, the slapping gestures of a man making a sandcastle.

For the people watching the parade or in this festival garden, Bastille Day in Tahiti was an excuse for a party, to play games at the funfair in the park, and buy balloons and amuse the kids. But walking back to the wharf along the rue du Général de Gaulle I saw a wall urgently spray-painted with the word *INDEPENDENCE*.

The next day I went to Moorea, in search of Mimi Theroux. The ferry left from a wharf on Papeete harbor — and as it entered the Sea of the Moon I looked back and saw the great greeny-black crags of Tahiti's volcanoes. They weren't rounded and plump and undulant, but like a starved sierra, like the corpses of mountains, with bony protruding ridges and hard sharp hips and shoulders, narrow valleys with hollow sides, knobs and angles on the escarpments and an intense steepness all over them, as though in their ancient years of vulcanism they had hurled out their life and left themselves exhausted.

The peaks and slopes of Tahiti — and of volcanic islands all over Oceania — are so steep and dark and so thoroughly wicked-looking that the coasts by contrast are gentle, and their pale pretty lagoons seem unutterably sweet. There is always a scrap of mist around the peaks, and sometimes a great torn pillow of black cloud hovering. The vertical roughness is visible on these islands, but so is the mildness of their fringes. "Seen from the sea, the prospect is magnificent," Melville wrote of this same view of Tahiti. His words are still true. "Such enchantment, too, breathes over the whole, that it seems a fairy world, all fresh and blooming from the hand of the Creator."

It cost seven dollars each way for the one-hour trip, and no charge for my collapsible boat. Most of the passengers were Polynesian, either full-blooded or else part-French, the people known locally as *demi* or *afa*. There were Chinese, too, and a smattering of *faranis*, the French who have attached themselves to the islands. The Polynesians were of two distinct physical types — either slender and nimble (the children and teenagers), or else (the over-twenties) fat and rather shapeless. Girls and boys were equally winsome, and men and women were precisely the same shape and almost indistinguishable.

It ought to have been possible to paddle my own boat from Papeete

to Moorea, but the wind discouraged me, a strong current ran between
the islands, and apart from the ferry landing at Vaiare there was only
one break in the reef, Avarapa Pass, on the northwest side of the island.
The reefs of these islands were a great disincentive to any sort of casual
boating, and as I intended to sail for the Marquesas within a week I
could not mount the sort of expedition that had gotten me safely around
the archipelago of Vava'u in Tonga. I planned to make camp on
Moorea, to paddle within the reef, and to seek out Mimi Theroux.

There is no town near the ferry landing, there is hardly a village, and after
the trucks had taken the ferry passengers away Vaiare seemed deserted.

"I'm looking for a place on the shore to camp," I said to a Moorean
at the roadside.

"Not possible," he said – and he was sympathetic.

It was a Polynesian problem: all the land was spoken for. I did not
argue. I rented a motorcycle and went in search of a hotel with a beach,
but this was an easy matter. Moorea had many hotels, and business was
so terrible I could take my pick. When I had settled this, I went back to
the rental place for my boat. But I kept my motorcycle.

I rode to the Hotel Bali Hai and found the manager, who seemed to
be American. Yes, he said, Mimi Theroux had worked here not long
ago, but she had left.

"She lives with her mother at Paopao."

That was Cook's Bay, not far off.

"Is she married?"

"I never saw any husband," the man said, and he described her house
so that I could find it.

It was a white building, but it was not a house. Large and square, two
storeys, with verandas above and a restaurant below, and with a flat
roof, it had the geometric look of a commercial structure. But it was in
good condition, freshly painted, gleaming in the sunshine, and facing
directly onto the bay.

I parked my motorcycle and walked around. A Tahitian was tinkering
behind the building, but as it was high noon and very hot there were
few other people in sight.

"Mimi Theroux?" I asked the Tahitian.

He pointed upstairs, to the porch where laundry was hung. I knocked
on the door at the foot of the stairway, but there was no response. I
knocked again, and excited a dog in the next yard. I called out, and a
young woman appeared at the top of the stairs.

This was Mimi. She was Chinese. I told her my name and she invited me up the stairs where, at the top, a small dark child was playing with an older girl.

"This is Moea," Mimi said, hoisting the smaller child.

"Your daughter?"

"Soon she will be." She spoke English with a slight American accent.

We were walking through the cool interior of the upper floor where, at the far end on the front of the building, I could see the blaze of the sea and the glarey sky of Cook's Bay – one of the most beautiful spots in the whole of Oceania, lovely, secluded, dramatic and rather empty. But this was French Polynesia. Because it was secluded it was neglected; the beach was no good, the shore was littered, and if you didn't have a motorcycle how would you get there?

It seemed to me that Mimi had a tincture of Polynesian blood. She said that this might have been so – she vaguely remembered seeing an elderly Tahitian relative, but she was not sure whether this was a blood relation. I rather liked her for not being sure and for not caring much about it.

"I'm sorry to drop in on you like this," I said.

"It's okay. Jim has spoken about you."

She explained that she was married to James Theroux, who was a distant cousin of mine and, as he had spent years sailing back and forth across the Pacific, from Samoa to Fiji and Tonga, to Port Vila and Australia, Jim was well known in Oceania. He was an expert surfer and experienced sailor and navigator. His name had been mentioned to me and sometimes, introducing myself to a yacht-owner, I was mistaken for him. People knew his boat in the way they knew my books: just names that had become familiar.

"He is in Australia, at the moment, in the Whitsundays, taking charters," Mimi said. "I saw him seven months ago. Maybe I will see him again in a few months. He is like you, always traveling."

"Does he look like me?" I asked.

"No. He is more handsome," Mimi said, and went to chase Moea, who was throwing toys at the wall.

Mimi was relaxed, she seemed capable, she was slender and barefoot, wearing a *pareu* on her hips; a loyal and energetic Chinese who did not make a fuss about a seven-month separation. She was small, quick and attractive. After she told me a few details of her life I figured her age to be thirty-four.

She had met Jim when she was twenty-one, at the girls' college in Punaauia, on Tahiti. Her maiden name was Tshan-lo.

"Jim said, 'Come with me,' so I went. Yes, it was romantic," Mimi said. "He had a boat. I had never been on a boat like that before. First we went to Pago, and I was sick, from the sea. Then we went to Fiji, Vava'u, Vila, Australia. We were in Vila for a couple of years, but when independence came there was trouble" – the Jimmy Stevens uprising – "and we left. In Vava'u the Tongans stole our laundry from the lines. But we liked it. Jim fished with the local people in the night."

"Do you still get seasick?"

"No. Now I am a good sailor. I have done it for more than ten years," Mimi said.

Each phase of her life had been difficult, and she was one of those people who seemed to have been strengthened and made confident by the sudden changes. It seemed to me Chinese tenacity, but in this Polynesian setting – in the beauty of Paopao – it had no edge to it. She had traveled from Moorea to Tahiti; she had gone off and married this impulsive American; and they had sailed the seas together. In Australia, Jim sold his boat and then, hearing that Alan Bond's twelve-meter yacht *Southern Cross* was for sale, they flew to Perth and bought it. It was a wonderful boat but it was empty. They rigged it and sailed it across the top of Australia, through the Torres Strait and past Cape York to Cairns. That took a year, because they had spent all their money buying and refitting the boat.

"We stopped in many places – to work and make money. But they were interesting places," Mimi said. "In Darwin we stopped for months. I worked as a waitress and Jim was a gardener. We didn't mind. It was an adventure."

Moea was still running around the room with her little friend. The room was large and breezy, with a few pictures – Jim's yacht was one – and some calendars and plain furniture. It was clean and more pleasant for being mostly bare.

"Moea is very pretty," I said.

"Soon she will be a Theroux," Mimi said.

Seeing the impish face of this little islander and hearing my own name made me glad.

"Her mother is a Marquesan," Mimi said. "My sister knew her mother when she was pregnant, and she knew that I could not have a child myself and that I wanted to adopt one. The woman already had two children and no husband. You know how it is here. Anyway, as soon as she had the baby she gave it to me. She told me the father is

French, but look at her – that baby is Marquesan – very black hair and dark eyes and skin."

Mimi turned to the child with admiration. Moea was a very sweet, very strong and upright two-year-old; and happy, her laughter ringing in the room, as she played.

"The father went afterwards to the woman and asked, 'Where is the baby?'" Mimi went on. "But the woman said, 'You didn't come the whole time I was pregnant. I gave the baby away.'"

"Where had the man been?"

"The man just left her and ran after a young girl when the baby was in the stomach," Mimi said. "That was two years ago. I have been happy. But now I am getting worried. In the past weeks the mother has been calling me. I know that if she sees Moea she will take her. She signed the document for adoption but it does not become final until two months more. I have to hide. The woman does not know where I am, but somehow she knows my telephone number. I would never give Moea away. She was such a lot of work when she was small, but she is so intelligent and she understands everything I say."

We were seated at a table, looking past Paopao to the bay.

"It is so lovely here," I said.

"It is a picture postcard view," Mimi said. "You should have seen the sunset last night. The sky was all pink – no sun, just clouds and sky. I sat here and watched it with Moea."

I was touched by the thought that after seeing twelve and a half thousand sunsets in the Pacific she still marveled at one.

Suddenly she said, "How did you find me?"

"I asked at the Bali Hai. You know you were nominated for a Mauruuru Award?"

"No," she said without much interest. And then she called out to her mother. Was she conveying this news?

Her elderly mother, Madame Madeleine Tshan-lo, was seated silently on the porch, looking off to sea. Mimi did not know the old woman's age – she said it was impolite to ask. Madame Tshan-lo had had nine children, of whom Mimi was the youngest ("I am the runt"). All the rest were married – to French, American, Tahitian, Chinese – and they lived all over, in many countries.

The old woman smiled at me and spoke in Cantonese to her daughter.

"Give that man some food," she said.

Mimi went to the kitchen and brought me a plate of vegetable stew – carrots from New Zealand, potatoes from France, rice from China. You needed a garden in order to live, Mimi said. There was no work, she said, but many people got by on breadfruit and taro and mangoes. Talking about food, Mimi remarked on the high cost of living.

"We have the most expensive electricity in the world," she said. "Every month I can't believe the bill. It costs me fifteen thousand francs a month, for just a TV, a freezer, a fridge and lights."

That was $160.

"They want to give us income tax, but everything is taxed! That is why it costs so much to live here."

The reason there was no income tax was because people were taxed on the things they bought. Tax had been reduced on alcohol in order to encourage tourism, but that had not done the trick.

"Three weeks ago there was a roadblock in Tahiti, because they raised the petrol ten cents and the diesel twenty cents."

This was a few days before I had arrived but people were still talking about it and marveling at the disruption it had caused. The roadblock of bulldozers and trucks had been put up just outside of Papeete, between the town and the airport, so that in order to get to the airport it was necessary to take a ninety-mile (117 kilometer) detour around the island. No one was arrested. There were negotiations, and at last the government reduced the price. What was clear in most people's mind was that if it happened again, if the government passed an unpopular measure, roadblocks were the answer – though in the past (as recently as 1987) the government had used riot police against protesters.

"What about the French?" I asked. "Do you think they'll hang on here?"

"Good question," Mimi said. "Eventually we will be independent, I suppose."

I left Mimi, admiring her strength and her filial piety, and I mounted my motorcycle and went the rest of the way around the island. It was a stormy month – three or four times I was caught in a downpour, either in my boat or on the motorcycle – and so I was not sorry to be denied the chance to live in my tent. The raindrops pelted so hard they stung my skin. And after the rain there was always a lovely aroma of *tiare* and oleander, and enormous complete rainbows, every color in a whole archway.

One day I paddled to Maatea. Melville had lived for a while here in 1842, and he mentions it a number of times in *Omoo* ("Fair dawned, over the hills of Martair, the jocund morning"). It had been a long trip for me, because I had stopped at a little island called Motu Ahi. And when I was caught in the rain on the way back I headed for the shelter of a little beach, where – sheltering with me under a tree – was a cyclist, Dominic Taemu, who was in his twenties and pedalling around the island.

We talked about Bastille Day and the *Heiva Tahiti*. He laughed.

"Bastille Day. That is a French festival. That is historical. It is not our day."

"Do you want Polynesia to be independent?"

"How can we be independent? We have no resources," he said. "The Japanese have taken all our big fish – they come in their big ships and use drift nets. We had lots of fish before, but now they are small and few. The coconuts and the copra are nothing. We have nothing."

"What about other work?"

"There is no work, because there are too few tourists," he said. And he thought awhile. "We know other places are cheaper. For us this is a big problem. We don't know what to do."

It was the fear of destitution; the fear of losing French protection and aid. But it was perhaps like a woman anxious about divorcing, fearing to be alone, without support – even though the husband is an opportunist and an exploiter.

"Independence – yes, certain people want it. It might come. But what will we do then?" And it dramatized the paradox of French Polynesia that Taemu, a native of what has been called the most beautiful place on earth, then said, "We have no means to live."

# 19

## A Voyage to the Marquesas

It was very hard for me to board a ship for the Marquesas Islands, where Paul Gaugin lay buried, and not squint at the passengers and recall the title of the painter's enigmatic picture, *Where do we come from? What are we? Where are we going?*

Perhaps it was premature to size them up, but I couldn't help attempting to spot the smokers, the drinkers, the boasters, the fanatics, the Germans. This looked like a honeymoon couple and surely that one was an escapee and why was that skinny old man – Gandhi to his fingertips – wearing such a skimpy bathing-suit and nothing else? The two butch women looked rather fearsome in their iron pants and their tattoos. The mother and her middle-aged son seemed rather touching, sharing a cigarette by the rail. But those big beefy Australians with the flowers behind their ears were certainly a bit worrying. The more nervous among us reverted: it became an assertion of national characteristics, the French pushing, the Germans snatching, the Australians drinking, the Americans trying to make friends, the Venezuelan couple holding hands.

How wrong I was about most of them. The "honeymoon couple" had been married for three years, the "escapee" was simply a dentist, "Gandhi" was an elderly fresh-air fiend, the butch women were mother and daughter, the "mother and son" were a married couple – Americans; and the fellows from Melbourne lovably challenged me with their tolerance. I would say something critical of a passenger and when I was through they'd disagree, saying, "We think she's *fabulous!*"

But that was later. In the meantime we were settling in for a longish voyage of eighteen days in the Marquesas. True, Herman Melville was in the islands for about ten days longer, but he wrote an entire book about it – his first, and by far his most successful, *Typee*.

Named after a valley on the island of Nuku Hiva where Melville claimed to have lived (the exaggerated subtitle of the book is, "A Four Months' Residence"), *Typee* appeared in 1846 and was an instant hit. It had everything – sex, nakedness, fresh fruit, warfare and cannibalism. It was the ultimate South Sea Island adventure and further confirmation that Polynesia was paradise. Melville, thinly disguised as the narrator Tommo, flees a brutal captain by jumping ship at the Marquesan island of Nuku Hiva. He first travels among the friendly Happar people, but soon finds himself among the cannibalistic Typees, and being pursued. The book combines anthropology, travel and adventure, and even today it is not merely enjoyable but informative. Melville practiced a little cannibalism himself in writing the book, by hacking out and serving raw and still bleeding many passages and incidents from other writers who had published eye-witness accounts of the Marquesas.

The most compelling feature for most of its readers was that it was also a love story, Melville's passion for the dusky, delectable Fayaway. The book was frankly physical, particularly in the unexpurgated first edition – scenes of Tommo swimming and frolicking with island girls, smoking and eating with Fayaway who sometimes wore a piece of bark cloth, but was usually clothed in the "garb of Eden" – starkers. The incident that whipped up the blood of most readers was the one in which Tommo takes Fayaway on an idyllic canoe trip across a lake in the Typee valley. Feeling impish, Fayaway stands erect in the canoe, unknots her tapa cloth robe and unfurls it until it fills with wind and becomes a sail. And there she stands, this "child of nature," her naked body a "little mast," and holding the sail with her arms upraised, making the canoe glide along, and "the long brown tresses of Fayaway streamed in the air."

I did not know much more about the Marquesas than this, and the fact that Gauguin had more or less chosen another island in the group, Hiva Oa, as a place to die.

The Marquesas were far and few: way beyond the Tuomotu chain, three days' sailing from Tahiti, a dozen high islands, six of them populated, and only 7,000 people on them altogether. These details don't make a picture, but I heard better arguments for going there. With greater justification than Tahiti and Moorea, it was said, the Marquesas had the reputation for being the most beautiful islands on the face of the earth. Because of their steep cliffs and poor anchorages and few good harbors, only a handful of yachts called there. The islands were filled with the same so-called "tabu-groves" that Melville had described: they had never been excavated and so the islands were an archeological treasure house. Distant, and difficult to traverse, the Marquesas were seldom visited. That did it. The fact that few people go there is one of the most persuasive reasons for traveling to a place.

The *Aranui* was one of several ships that made the inter-island trip; there were two other cargo ships that carried some passengers, there was a luxury vessel, the *Wind Song* – very chic, very expensive, nice boutiques, no cargo. The *Aranui* had a hold full of cargo, forty-odd passengers amidships in cabins, and an indefinite number – it varied according to the run – sleeping on mats on the stern decks and sharing a rudimentary head. But nothing is cheap in French Polynesia – the fellows from Melbourne were paying almost $1,400 apiece to sleep on the bridge deck and although this included meals their nights were noisy with humming ventilators, winds in the ratlines, the sloshing sea – and one said to me, "Earplugs are a must." I was paying about $2,000 to share a tiny cabin, near the plimsoll line, with Señor Pillitz, a young man from Argentina. On rougher days when the porthole was awash with the sudsy ocean it was like being in a laundromat.

I had so little space in my cabin that I was told that I could not bring my collapsible boat, but it was emphasized that this was a handsome favor to me, because it removed a fatal temptation: if I tried to paddle anywhere around these islands, with their notoriously bad anchorages and rough seas, I would probably drown.

The lights were twinkling on the slopes of Orohena as we left Papeete harbor and headed northeast through Matavai Bay. A few miles farther on, we rounded Point Venus. Captain Cook camped here in 1769 in order to observe the transit of Venus across the sun, and this was also the spot where Captain Bligh collected the breadfruit trees he stowed on the *Bounty*. As soon as we were at sea I went below and raided the ship's library. By this time the South Equatorial Current rose against the hull of the *Aranui*, and the wind picked up, and my stomach rose and fell.

The movement of the ship convinced me to eat sparingly, and after dinner I went back to the library and read *An Angel at My Table*, the second volume of the autobiography of the New Zealand novelist, Janet Frame. The central part of the book concerns her committal to an asylum, and I was held by her story, which was written entirely without bitterness or self-pity. As I read on about her suicide attempt, her treatment, her matter-of-fact madness – she uses the word "loony" to describe her condition – the ship pitched and rolled. Some other passengers discovered the seclusion of the library, and when one of them gulped, went glassy-eyed, and then noisily and messily puked onto the floor, I went on deck for air.

We had sailed straight into a gale, and all night the ship rolled in a figure eight. In the morning there was a certain amount of hopeless hilarity.

"Whoops! There we go again!"

"I spilled my tea."

"I'll be spilling more than that if this keeps up!"

"That woman's laugh is diabolical," I muttered.

"We think she's *fabulous!*"

Bad weather and heavy seas inspire facetiousness and intensify the confinement: passengers stay below and giggle insincerely. That day and most of the next, people kept staggering and falling; and they talked disgustingly about being sick. Most wore – uselessly – seasickness bandages behind their ears. The folk wisdom is probably true: "The only cure for seasickness is to sit on the shady side of an old brick church in the country."

Señor Pillitz said that he had suffered badly in the night, that he had felt desperate, as they said in Argentina, "between the sword and the wall" (*entre la espada y la pared*). He was full of robust wisdom and pithy sayings. Later, at a dismal place in the Tuomotus, he glanced around and said, "All you would ever find here is three crazy cats" (*tres gatos locos*).

I did not feel so wimpy when Señor Pillitz added that he had worked his way on a ship, chopping vegetables, from Buenos Aires to Rotterdam; so he knew a thing or two about sea conditions.

During breakfast, dishes slid to the floor, bottles fell and smashed, Mr Werfel tripped and fell at the feet of Dennis and Bev, from Vancouver. Later in the morning, a man who had been full of complaints ("How do I get my faucet to work?" "Suppose I want to shut off my hot water?" "What's the story with my fan?") fell off his chair in the library and moaned. He lay on his side. He said he could not get up.

"I musta cracked a rib or somesing."

He was Middle European, with American in his Teutonic accent.

"Breathe deeply," I suggested.

He did so, and winced.

"Does it hurt?"

"Sorta."

It was my distinct impression that he was faking, and when people began to ignore him he crept to his feet and went away. He was happier after the captain gave him a tour of the britch and on most days he was the first to examine what he called the vezza shart to see whether we were in for another gale.

That second day, as the sea moderated, a succession of green stripes appeared on the horizon. These were the outer islands of the Tuomotus, a chain of flat coral atolls of which Mururoa is one. Since 1966, the French have been using Mururoa as a testing site for their nuclear devices and they have just about succeeded in making that atoll unsafe for human habitation for generations to come. More than 160 nuclear devices have been detonated, atomic and hydrogen bombs as well as neutron bombs; and there have been atmospheric tests – fastening nuclear devices to French balloons and exploding them over the atolls. Recently the explosions – averaging eight a year – have taken place in the core of the coral reef, or underwater, and the more France has been criticized for the danger and contamination, the less willing the French government has been to allow any sort of inspection to take place. There have been leakages of plutonium and radioactive debris, notably in 1979 and 1981. But the French did not abandon testing at Mururoa when they saw how they had damaged the atoll; they simply detonated fewer bombs there and switched their heavy testing to the neighboring atoll of Fangataufa.

Even the most user-friendly travel guide becomes Francophobic when the question of testing is raised. "French radioactivity will remain in the Tuomotus for thousands of years," David Stanley writes in *The South Pacific Handbook*, with justified indignation; "the unknown future consequences of this program are the most frightening part of it. Each successive blast continues the genocide committed by the Republic of France against the people of the Pacific."

Elsewhere on the Tuomotu archipelago, the many shoals and poor anchorages have given it the reputation of being one of the most notorious ship-swallowers in the Pacific.

Under a cheddar-coloured moon that rose through black shreds of cloud and glimmered in shattered light on a rippling tropic sea, the crew began emptying clattering barrels overboard – waste paper and plastic bottles and crushed tins and vegetable peelings – but it hardly disturbed the sea, because the radiant rubbish was bobbing in the moonglow in this remote and peaceful place, and the junk and detritus had a lively phosphorescence all its own.

I woke to shouts and the sound of cranes the third day. I could see the whaleboat through my porthole, ferrying cargo to the tiny village on the harbor at the croissant-shaped atoll of Takapotou. It was too deep to anchor, and there was no harbor here, and so we were pitching just offshore as the whaleboats came and went. In the whole voyage only once was the ship moored alongside a quay, with a gangway from the deck to dry land. In every other instance we were brought ashore in the whaleboats, which necessitated a delicate (and at times wet) transfer. It should have been hell for the elderly passengers, but it wasn't: the powerful Marquesan crew members lifted the feebler ones bodily into the whaleboats and at the edge of the pounding surf hoisted them again like kids and carried them to shore – little twittering women and men in big tattooed Marquesan arms.

These same crewmen also hauled the cargo – thirteen hours repeatedly going from the ship to the quay and back again, that same quarter-mile – the twenty-foot whaleboats always piled high. The cargo covered all aspects of human activity    loaves of bread, sanitary napkins and toilet rolls by the crate, mineral water, breakfast cereal, a large pea-green three-piece suite, and in a place that teemed with live fish, crates of canned fish. Two whaleboat-loads contained cardboard boxes of Tyson's frozen chicken pieces (from Arkansas). The rest was predictable – building materials, lumber, bricks, pipes, cement; and rice, sugar, flour, gasoline, and bottled gas. (Many of these staple items were heavily subsidized by the French government. The rice, for example, cost twelve dollars for ten kilos, which was not much more than thirty-six cents a pound.) There was crate after clanking crate of soft drinks, Budweiser beer, bottles of Hinano, Arnott's "Cabin" Biscuits in ten-pound tins, and cartons of snacks, including immense quantities of Planter's Cheez Balls.

A cloying odor of decayed copra hung over the quay at Takapotou, where it was stacked in bulging sacks, quietly humming, like a mountain of last week's dessert. Copra has the look of brown rinds and is in fact chunks of dried coconut meat that is later processed into coconut oil. The French heavily subsidize the copra crop (paying $650 a ton), making it profitable for the grower. But the islanders shrug, the harvest is in decline and the shortfall is made up by copra imported from Fiji (where growers are paid $100 a ton).

Forget copra, the locals say – the great business today in Takapotou is black pearls. The seed pearls are slipped between the valves of the giant black-lipped oyster which is happiest in the lagoons around Takapotou and, if the transplant is successful, in about three years a pearl-fisher could become very wealthy.

The Japanese have thrust themselves into the black pearl industry and now – to no one's surprise – almost totally dominate it, from seeding the oysters to stringing the pearls and selling them. Even so, fortunes have been made by Tuomotuans on some atolls that are little more than desert islands – a coral beach, a few palm trees and cringing dogs.

I had hardly been in Takapotou an hour when a woman named

Cécile sidled up to me and asked me in French whether I wanted to buy some black pearls. She said they were from Takaroa, a neighbouring atoll where the best colored pearls are found.

"This is my son," Cécile said.

But he didn't hear anything: he was listening to a rock music cassette on earphones, and it was presumably turned loud – I could hear it – to overwhelm the sound of the pounding sea. And the dogs – we were being followed by nine barking dogs.

Cécile was in no hurry, nor was she interested in bargaining – haggling is not a habit in Polynesia. She slid open a matchbox and showed me the four pearls – a tear drop, a polyp, and two round ones – and she mentioned the price. That same amount would have bought three loud Tahitian shirts or two meals in Papeete.

"Done," I said, and handed over the money. As we walked back to the quay, where the atoll's whole population ("Four hundred – plus children," Cécile said) had gathered, we were still followed by the dogs – about fifteen of them now.

"About those dogs," I began. We were speaking French.

"So many of them," Cécile said, not looking.

I wanted to be delicate. "In the Marquesas the people eat dogs."

"We eat them too!" She seemed to be boasting, as a way of setting me straight.

Now I began to see something canine in Cécile's features, her teeth more dog-like than is usual, her nose looked damp, her jowls a bit loose, her eyes rather soulful.

"What does dogmeat taste like?"

"Like steak."

Most dog-eaters stew it, the meat is so tough, but the French had made steak and chips so popular in their colony this had obviously influenced the manner of serving up woof-woof.

"Entrecôte of dog, dog steak, and what about dog stew?"

She shrugged and said, "Sure."

"Do you eat sea turtles?" I had noticed the shells of this endangered species were hung up to decorate many of the box-like houses on Takapotou.

"We love turtles," Cécile said. "We make them into soup."

It turned out that food was not a problem on an atoll like this, where fish and coconuts were plentiful. There were pigs in the place too. They could have managed without dogs, but as Cécile said, they ate them because they tasted good. The rest of the time they subsisted on fish and rice and coconuts. When the *Aranui* called they had carrots and onions. No one on Takapotou had a garden – the soil was too poor; it was hardly soil at all, but rather crumbled coral, and all that grew were palms and feathery Australian pines.

I met an American named Tim at the landing-stage. He had the look of a surfer. He was from California and was making his way from atoll to atoll, any way he could. He had been here for several months. He liked Takapotou more than any other atoll, so far. I asked him why.

"The sharks are smaller, and there are fewer of them, for one thing," he said. "And the people are really friendly. As soon as you arrive they sit you down and give you food, even if it's the only food they have – even if their children haven't eaten."

"I was thinking that it doesn't look as though there is much food here," I said.

"There's more than you might think," Tim said. "These houses look poor, but in each one there's a TV, a video machine, a gas stove and a freezer. They freeze the fish they catch and sell it to the boats that stop by. The *Aranui* will pick up a lot."

"Is that how they get their income?"

"That's it, mainly. Apart from the child allowance, they don't get handouts from the French. The copra price is subsidized. Otherwise they provide for their own needs."

"I noticed that quite a few cases of whisky were unloaded."

"Drinking is a problem here," he said. "And it really has an effect on them. They get very violent – their whole personality undergoes a change. There were four serious fights last Saturday night."

The cargo, including booze, was still being carried past us by men who were so heavily laden they sank up to their ankles in crushed coral.

Tim said, "They say that if you hand someone a bottle of Jack Daniels you can get anything done – anything."

"What if you had a whole case of the stuff?"

"You'd probably get a handful of black pearls."

Such a strange, recent-looking piece of land, a few feet above sea-level in the middle of the ocean, so flat, so thinly wooded – no grass, few people. If it were not for the pearls it might have been forgotten long ago and left to itself. Seeing the entire population gathered there at the landing in the failing light I thought of people clinging to coral, frail people holding on to the frailest and most crumbly living rock. The whole place was like a small fragile organism.

It was dark when the last of the copra was brought aboard and by then I was sitting with some of the Marquesan passengers: Thérèse, a medical worker; Charles, a powerfully-built former soldier in the French army (he had seen action in Chad and had the scars of bullet wounds to prove it: "The Africans are real savages") – none the less, he had tiny white *tiare* blossoms in his shoulder-length hair; and Jean, who claimed that he was descended from the last king of the Marquesas and was just returning from Tahiti where he had been combing through the birth records and genealogies to establish his royal connection.

They had not known each other before the voyage, but had fallen in together and they agreed on most things – hated Tahitian politics, were against French nuclear testing ("Everyone is against it. It poisons all of nature, the sea, the fish, and it causes sickness," Thérèse said), and they wanted the Marquesas to be independent of the rest of Polynesia.

"We want a free Marquesas," Charles said, and then confusingly added, "It doesn't matter whether the French are there or not. We just don't want Tahiti politics."

He also repeated what many Marquesans said: his islands were a family, a large Catholic family. The rest of French Polynesia was rather despised for having abandoned the faith and gone over to the Mormons and the Jehovah's Witnesses.

Just before I went below I saw Patrick, one of the fellows from Melbourne, looking over the rail.

"Did you see that movie *Cocoon*, where all those people got into the boat and then the boat was beamed up to another planet?" He was smiling. "When I saw these people hobbling on board the first day I thought to myself, 'Oh God, hold on, we're off to outer space!'"

In a way it was true: the Marquesas were a world apart. It was a thirty-six-hour run from Takapotou to the first of these high islands.

In that time I got acquainted with more of the other passengers. Señor Pillitz had once trained as a waiter at the Ritz in London, but one night he spilled an entire tureen of onion soup down a woman's back ("She was wearing a lovely green dress") and that convinced him that he should take up photography. The Germans kept to themselves and hogged the best seats, the most food, and with an instinct for invasion went up and down the ship, claiming the prime areas for themselves. Carmelo and Amelia from Venezuela had been around the world several times. India was their favorite country, "for cultural reasons." Ross and Patrick, on their first foray out of Melbourne, found everything just fabulous. Horace, a neurosurgeon from Sarasota, held me spellbound when he described the process of removing a brain tumor, which was his business. After a person's head was opened (the cut was made behind the ear, at the base of the skull) the tumor was taken out with unbelievable slowness, "like removing sand, one grain at a time, and at the end of the operation, when you are very tired, there's a chance you might slip and cut vital nerves." Philippe, who was also a doctor, was doing his National Service at Papeete Hospital, and had a Tahitian grandmother. Pascale, a young and pretty Frenchwoman, who was usually topless except at mealtimes, worked as a nurse at the Papeete hospital and had helped deliver Cheyenne Brando's little boy. "This Brando is a strange woman    she will not let anyone touch her. You think it is possible to have a baby and not be touched?" A woman from Chicago who called herself Senga (she hated the name Agnes and so spelled it backwards) said she was seventy years old and had come on this trip, "because I want to do everything before I die." There was a sunburned Frenchman we called Pinky who, when he got drunk, which was every evening at eight in the bar on C deck, praised the racist French politician, Jean-Marie Le Pen. Pinky's nemesis was Madame Wittkop, whom we called The Countess; she often said, "I'm outrageous," but so far she had seemed unprepossessing. That was most of them.

Four and a half days after leaving Papeete, we reached the first of the Marquesas, the little island of Ua-Pou.

Several passengers on board said that Ua-Pou did not look anything like a South Seas island. Melville had anticipated that reaction. "Those who for the first time visit the South Seas, generally are surprised at the appearance of the islands when beheld from the sea. From the vague accounts we sometimes have of their beauty, many people are apt to picture to themselves enameled and softly swelling plains, shaded over with delicious groves, and watered by purling brooks," he wrote in *Typee*.

"The reality is very different," he went on, and he was speaking of Nuku Hiva but it might have been Ua-Pou he was depicting: "Bold rockbound coasts, with the surf beating high against the lofty cliffs, and broken here and there into deep inlets, which open to the view thickly wooded valleys, separated by the spurs of mountains clothed with tufted grass, and sweeping down to the sea from an elevated and furrowed interior."

The rock, most of all, and the way it was arrayed in pinnacles – that was the most unexpected feature. It was high and where it was wooded it was dark green. Some of the mountains were shaped like witches' hats and others like steeples and domes – everything eroded and slender and perpendicular, and the cliffs of black rock plunging straight into the sea and foaming surf. Where are the sandy beaches? Where are the translucent lagoons? There are not many in the Marquesas, and they are hard to find. It is almost impossible to overstate the ruggedness of the islands – the almost unclimbable steepness of their heights or their empty valleys. And at the head of every valley was a great gushing waterfall, some of them hundreds of feet high.

We went ashore at Hakehau – a tiny town on a snug harbor – and Señor Pillitz and I, egged on by a Frenchman desperate for customers, went for a two-hour ride to the stony beach at Hohoi, where we saw a brown horse. "And two crazy cats," Señor Pillitz said, snapping a picture. Several minutes later the Frenchman said we must leave. The road was muddy. The Land-Rover got bogged down. I wrenched my spine helping to push the thing. Back in Hakehau he charged each of us twenty dollars and tried to sell us for another twenty dollars framed photographs he had taken of the volcanoes. We were just in time for the dancing – fifteen young men doing "The Pig Dance" – snuffling and oinking and nimbly hurrying on all fours. They finished with a great shout and then we feasted on langouste, and octopus, breadfruit, bananas, and raw tuna marinated in lime juice and coconut milk, the raw fish (*ia ota*) that the French call *poisson cru*.

Strolling back to the ship I found myself walking among flowering bushes which exuded a delicious fragrance, a *noa-noa*, and then I came upon a big family behind a hibiscus hedge hacking a dead cow apart with axes and machetes. They were skinning and butchering it at the same time, while seven dogs fought over the scraps. Just before we set sail I saw these same people running up the gangway, with bulky sacks of the butchered cow slung over their shoulders. They were off to another island with enough meat to last them a month.

In the afternoon, the *Aranui* sailed to the other side of the island, to another village on a bay, Hakehetau, where whaleboats brought bottled gas and provisions ashore. The sky was full of birds – brown noddies, white terns, grayish-yellow finches, and – two or three at a time – the slowly soaring frigate birds. On the high slopes of Ua-Pou there were flocks of wild goats, which had nibbled the mountainsides bare.

Then, in a puddly golden sea, that was calm and mild in the same golden sunset, with the scent of flowers carrying from shore, we sailed to Nuku Hiva, and at night we anchored off Taipivai, where there was a bay – but no mooring, no quay, no landing-stage, nothing but a stinking sandbar at the river mouth.

We went ashore the next day to the village of Taipivai, the whaleboats sputtering up the deep river valley. This was in the southeast of Nuku Hiva. At the sacred site nearby, the passenger I thought of as Gandhi displayed for the first time his uniquely obnoxious habit. At every ancient platform, and at all the stone tikis, he turned his back on the rest of us and yanked his swimsuit down and, sighing with pleasure, relieved himself against the noble ruins. I noticed this first at Taipivai, and thereafter, for reasons that are still obscure to me, Gandhi desecrated every *marae* in every tabu-grove we visited in the Marquesas.

"That man is so disgusting," I would say.

"Isn't he *fabulous*?"

Perhaps he was no worse in his way than the missionaries who had castrated these very statues. There is not a dick that has not been hacked off, nor a statue that has not been tipped over, in the name of God Almighty. "But what matters all this?" Melville remarks sarcastically. "Behold the glorious result! The abominations of Paganism have given way to the pure rites of the Christian worship – the ignorant savage has been supplanted by the refined European!" Some of the people struck back, and even statues were said to be rebellious. All tikis are "live" and they can be vindictive, the Marquesans say. Anger these fat black demons that look like the gods of constipation and you will be cursed with bad luck or death.

It was up this path in Taipivai that Melville had spent most of his month. Here it was that he had got the title for his book: Typee was just another way of writing Taipi, and "vai" or the variation of it means "water" all over Polynesia.

The ruins and the tikis in the *marae* just above the village were only part of the story. There were ruins all over the valley, which was fragrant with wild vanilla, and they were practically invisible until you looked closely into the jungle. Then you could see stone walls, platforms, altar-like structures, carvings and petroglyphs, tangled in the vines, and with trees – very often a banyan, associated with sacredness in the Marquesas – bursting through them.

And this was true of the Marquesas generally. Entire hillsides, covered in jungle, hid enormous ruins made of black boulders. It was in this respect like Belize or Guatemala – full of huge tumbled structures, strange statues and walls. Where the walls were intact the construction was like Mayan stonework. These jungles had once been full of villages and big houses; the population must have been immense – estimates are that it was more than ten times larger (80,000 is one guess) at the time of their initial contact with the outside world. This first emissary was Captain Ingraham of Boston, Massachusetts, though the islands were first sighted by the ubiquitous Spaniard Mendaña and named Las Marquesas after his patron, the Marquis of Mendoza.

What had happened to all those Marquesans? The Pacific historian, Peter Bellwood, has an explanation in his book *The Polynesians*. "The Marquesans, together with their close cousins the Maoris, were by all accounts the hardiest and most robust of the Polynesians, and life was never pervaded with the indolence associated with an island such as Tahiti. Heavily dependent on the breadfruit – a tree which fruits season-ally and not all year round – they were subjected to famines of devastat-ing proportions, and these naturally increased the incidence of warfare. Many early visitors reported that impoverished and defeated Marquesan families would set off in canoes to find land over the horizon."

Now most of the ruins were buried and all of them overgrown; some had been documented, but very few had been excavated. Except for the jungles of Belize and Guatemala, I had never been in a place where the foundations of so many stone structures existed, covered with moss and ferns. All around them were petroglyphs, of birds and fishes, and canoes, and turtles, finely incised in the rock. In the damp shadows of the tall trees, and teeming with mosquitoes, the sites had all the melancholy of lost cities. It was exciting to see them sprawled in the gloom, on those muddy slopes – the immense terraces, the altars, the scowling, castrated tikis. To anyone who believes that all the great ruins of the world have been hackneyed and picked over I would say that the altars and temples of the Marquesas await discovery.

A woman I met in Taipivai, Victorine Tata, had just bought a pick-up truck. She drove, riding the brake like my grandmother, but never mind; what bothered me most was that she had floated a loan from the bank to finance the vehicle on the instalment plan, and it had cost her $35,000. Would she ever pay off her debt? Victorine just laughed.

The *Aranui* sailed to the administrative center of Nuku Hiva, Taiohae, where it would be unloading cargo for a few days, and so I stayed in Taipivai, and asked Victorine, for a fee, to drive me around Taipivai in her new truck. She said she would be delighted. She was a big bulky woman, with a square jaw and heavy legs. She was impassive, but she was honest, and seated in her truck she was so huge and immovable she seemed to give the vehicle enough extra weight to hold it firmly on the precipitous narrow curves of Taipivai's heights.

"Melville lived over there," she said in French, and pointed into

Taipivai, about two miles above the estuary, near a large *marae* on the eastern side of the valley.

We were now driving up a steep muddy path.

"My uncle traveled with him for a while. He showed him tikis and taught him about the flowers and the trees."

"Do you mean he traveled with the real Melville?"

"Yes. The American Melville." She pronounced it Melveel. "My uncle liked him."

Her uncle had given Melville many a helping hand.

"Wasn't this a long time ago?"

"Eighteen twenty-something," Victorine said. "Long ago. My grandfather also knew Melville. He showed him the island – all around."

"How do you know this?"

"My father told me many stories about my relatives and Melville."

It was not clear to me whether there was even a grain of truth in what she said, but she was a good sober person, and she believed it, and that was what mattered.

"The Marquesans were anthropophagists, weren't they?"

"What's that?"

I had hesitated to use the word "cannibal," but I steeled myself and rephrased the question.

"Oh, yes, before – long before. They ate people. But not now."

*The word "Typee" in the Marquesan dialect signifies a lover of human flesh,* Melville had written. True? Victorine said no.

"Now, I understand they eat dogs here," I said after a while.

"No. The Tuomotus – that's where they eat dogs. We eat goats and cows."

The Taipivai hills were empty. In Tonga and the two Samoas, in Fiji and on other islands, I had become used to seeing concentrated populations – crowded towns, and hillsides filled with huts, and every twenty feet of shoreline claimed and occupied. This place was extraordinarily depopulated – there was no one in sight. This was simply a great empty island of dense trees and the deserted magnificence of the black stone ruins.

*We sometimes enjoyed ... recreation in the waters of a miniature lake, into which the central stream of the valley expanded,* Melville had written. *This lovely sheet of water was almost circular in figure, and about three hundred yards across. Its beauty was indescribable.*

That was where the naked Fayaway had mischievously played at being Tommo's mast, and where Tommo had splashed among the dusky bathing beauties.

"What about the lake?" I asked.

"There is no lake," Victorine said, and another illusion was shattered.

Although Victorine's pick-up truck had a radio cassette player, there was no radio station in Nuku Hiva – there was none in the Marquesas – and she had no tapes. But I had replaced the Walkman that had been stolen from me in Tonga, and I still had the Kiri Te Kanawa tape (*Kiri – A Portrait*) that had soothed me in the Solomons. I popped the cassette into Victorine's tape deck as we chugged across the Taipi mountains.

There was a sudden plangent burst of Kiri singing *Dove sono* from *Le Nozze di Figaro*.

"That is a song from an opera."

"Opera, yes. I have heard of opera."

The next aria was *Je dis que rien ne m'épouvante* from Bizet's *Carmen*.

"That's French," she said – we were still speaking French. "But do men sing like that, in that sort of voice?"

She pretended to be a man singing in falsetto.

"Sometimes they do, but they don't sing exactly like that."

*Vissi d'arte* was issuing from the loudspeaker of the muddy truck.

"Do you like that one?"

"I love it," Victorine said.

"I'll tell you something interesting," I said. "That singer is a Polynesian – a Maori, from New Zealand."

"I am happy to know that."

Her face was blissful. I imagined Victorine traversing these roads, from Taipi to Taiohae and back, dropping off eggs, picking up passengers, and on every trip, listening to these arias, and *Rejoice greatly* and *I know that my Redeemer liveth* from the *Messiah*, and the others – perhaps looking forward to listening, and mumbling the words that might become familiar.

And so after a while I said, "You can have the tape. A present."

She was pleased, she started to speak, then thought a moment. Finally, she spoke in English, "Sank you."

Victorine dropped me nine miles above Taiohae, because after the confinement of her little truck, I craved a walk. I hiked across a high ridge and on a switchback road down to the main town of Nuku Hiva, where the *Aranui* was still discharging cargo. Although it was also the main administrative center of the Marquesas, it was a small settlement, a few grocery stores selling expensive canned food and some imported vegetables. In Taiohae I saw nine-dollar cabbages, from California; and that same day there appeared carrots and onions from the *Aranui*.

The ship was headed to a village on the north coast of the island, Hatiheu, and as I could get there myself by road I lingered in Taiohae, enjoying the novelty of walking. I had begun to dislike the sedentary voyage, and all the meaty food. In Taiohae I felt better for missing meals, and although I stayed in a hotel, I occasionally bought a liter of fruit juice (from Australia) and a can of baked beans (from France) and a baguette (from Papeete), and sat under a tree on the seafront and made my own meal.

All canned goods were luxuries in the Marquesas. The people grew breadfruit and mangoes, and they caught fish. If they had spare money they treated themselves to a can of Spam or one of the crunchy snacks they liked so much.

"A girl might work as a waitress simply to be able to buy cigarettes," Rose Corson told me. She ran a small hotel on the western side of Taiohae's pretty harbor. "At five dollars a pack the cigarettes would take most of her salary."

The Marquesans I met were big and ponderous. They were noted for their gloom and their heavy moods, and unlike the Tahitians they were not at all quick to play music and sing. At sundown, fat men in T-shirts gathered at the seafront in Taiohae, near the jingoistic French memorials, and cooled their toes in the breeze and shared Family Size cans of Cheez Balls.

One plaque said, *À la Mémoire des Officiers, Soldats et Marins Français morts aux Marquises 1842–1925*, but no mention of the thousands of Marquesans who had died fighting in vain to keep possession of their homeland. Another, ignoring the fact that the islands had been discovered by brave Polynesian navigators who had probably crossed the ocean from Samoa about eighteen hundred years ago, extolled the spurious claim of a "discoverer" – *Au nom du Roy de France le 23 Juin 1791 Étienne Marchand découvrier du groupe N.O. de Marquises prit possession de l'île Nuku Hiva*. This also took no account of the fact that Captain Ingraham had claimed it two months before.

Nuku Hiva was annexed in 1813 for the United States by Captain David Porter. He put up a fort and renamed Taiohae after James Madison, who was president. But Madisonville was no more than an impulsive gesture, and as Congress never ratified the act it had no force. The French would have fought us for it in any case, battling just as fiercely as they did in 1842 when they slaughtered thousands of islanders in order to gain possession. Melville witnessed the shelling. His Marquesan jaunt coincided with the French adventure, and in his book he mocks the French part in the affair: "Four heavy double-banked frigates and three corvettes to frighten a parcel of naked heathen into subjection! Sixty-eight pounders to demolish huts of coconut boughs, and Congreve rockets to set on fire a few canoe sheds."

After my two days alone in Taiohae, I made my own way across the island to Hatiheu, where the *Aranui* was moored in the pretty bay – there was no dock for the ship: the whaleboats brought the cargo through the surf to a crumbling pier.

Hatiheu was a small exquisite village at the foot of three steep mountains, and in a meadow at the center of the village was a large church, with two steeples and a red tin roof, dedicated to Joan of Arc. Horses cropped grass in the churchyard. And standing under a tree outside Hatiheu's tiny post office, with dogs barking and the waves breaking on the black sand beach, I made a telephone call to Honolulu.

Later, I found Señor Pillitz, and we walked into the woods behind the village, through the palm plantations – and the palms were interspersed with kapok trees, laden with bursting pods; kapok had once been cultivated commercially here. But now all this farming was outdated. Beyond the plantation was a ceremonial area, called a *tohua*, which was about the size of a football field and enclosed stone platforms, and altars and carved statues. Such an area tended to be avoided by the local people, who believed the *tohua* to be haunted and that it had a *mana*, or spirit, that was at odds with their Christianity. There was an enduring fear, if not horror, among locals for these ancient sites. Most of all it was a fear of the spirits of the dead that haunted these glades after dark, the malevolent *tupapau*.

Deeper in the forest there was another site that was larger but much harder to see, because it had all been tumbled apart – the terraces, the altars, the boulders cut with petroglyphs. It was overgrown with banyans, several of them giant trees. In an earlier time, the Marquesans had placed the skulls of their enemies among the exposed tree roots, and there on a higher slope was a round pit, lined with stone, where captives were held in order to be fattened before they were killed and eaten.

"Zey wair cooking zem wiz breadfruit," a Chinese woman told me later. Her name was Marie-Claire Laforet. Her father had dropped his Chinese surname ("The French didn't want foreign words," Marie-

Claire said) in the great Tahitian name-change of 1964. It was an appropriate choice. His Cantonese name, Lim (Lin in Mandarin), is the character for wood or trees.

That same day I went with Philippe and Señor Pillitz across a ridge beside Hatiheu to Anaho Bay. Well enclosed, with extensive ruins, a white sand beach and a coral shelf − one of the few reefs in the Marquesas, the only lagoon − it was the loveliest spot I saw in the Marquesas, combining the color and gentleness of a tropical beach with the ruggedness of surrounding mountains. Robert Louis Stevenson had stopped in this very bay in 1888 in the *Casco* with his wife and his two stepchildren and his elderly mother. It was the sight of Anaho Bay, and his dealing with the tattooed Marquesans, whom Stevenson believed still to be cannibals, that convinced him of the rightness of his decision to spend the rest of his life in the Pacific. Anaho had a profound effect on him − and on his mother, too: for the first time in her life this fastidious Edinburgh matron gave up wearing stockings, "and often shoes as well." Bewitched by Anaho, the whole family went native. Anaho was − and still is − the apotheosis of the South Seas: distant, secluded, empty, pristine − ravishing, in fact.

"Are there sharks here?" I asked two spear-fishermen, wading out to the edge of the reef.

"Many sharks."

"Big ones?"

"Very big ones."

"Do they bother you?"

"No."

They left a machete behind. I knocked some coconuts from a low palm tree and slashed them open. We drank the sweet water and ate the meat. Walking back past the scattering of fishermen's shacks and through the humid forest we were followed by a small so-called *demi*, a Chinese–Marquesan boy, about ten years old.

"I am happy here in Anaho," he said stumblingly in French. "I would not like to go to France. There are no langouste there and no breadfruit. Here we have food. We have fish. We can build a house anywhere in the woods. I can swim, I can fish from my father's pirogue. I would not be happy in France."

In the early evening we sailed to the island of Tahuata, anchoring off the black sand beach of the village of Vaitahu. In the morning we were taken ashore by whaleboats. Vaitahu was typical of most of the larger Marquesan towns in a number of respects: a Catholic church, a canned-food shop, wonderful ruins at the edge of town, steep green valley walls, flowering trees, and fruit trees – avocados and grapefruit trees in the gardens of little wooden bungalows, hairy black pigs, fretting mongrels, a new church, and an insulting plaque on the seafront speaking of all the Frenchmen who had given their lives battling to take possession of the place.

The monument in Vaitahu spoke of the French soldiers and sailors who had "died on the field of honour" in the battle for Tahuata in 1842. Melville had ironized about this very place, and how the French had prided themselves on the good order they had brought to the Marquesas, though it had caused human fatalities; and "to be sure, in one of their efforts at reform they had slaughtered about a hundred and fifty at Whitihoo [Vaitahu]."

I was overheard jeering at the plaque by the woman known on board as The Countess. She was half French, half German and often strolled along, holding a tape recorder to her lips and nagging into it. She said she was somewhat struck by my sarcasm. It so happened (she went on) that she was a travel writer. Thus the tape recorder.

"I am writing a story about this trip for the best and most brilliant newspaper in the world" – and she named a German daily paper. "They respect me so much that in seventeen years they have changed only one sentence of mine."

"What was the sentence?"

"It was very reactionary you will think," the Countess said.

"I'll be the judge of that."

"All right then. 'Three hundred years of colonialism have done less harm to the world than thirty years of tourism.'"

I smiled at her and said, "That's brilliant."

Thereafter whenever she felt the need to unburden herself she sought me out.

"My husband was a genius," she said later. "I myself have written many books about clothing."

"I hate children," she told me another day. "I love doggies."

I told her I had seen some puppies with wire on their necks being taken out of Vaitahu to be used as shark bait by some Marquesans in a canoe.

"They should use babies instead," she said, and laughed like a witch in a pantomime.

Speaking with some youngsters in Vaitahu, one of them asked me, "What are you? What is your country?"

"I am an American. And you?"
"I am a Marquesan."

Dolphins riding our bow wave preceded us the next day as we plowed into Traitors Bay, to enter Atuona Harbor, on Hiva Oa. Tahuata was clearly visible beyond the bay, in a nameless channel, and to the southeast was the tiny Marquesan island of Mohotani.

An old red Citroën was swung out of the hold of the *Aranui* and driven away. Then the crates were unloaded – sacks of farina, cases of beer, gasoline, building blocks, snack food. A Hiva Oa nun picked up a parcel that had been shipped to her and then drove off in her Toyota.

Three Mormons, two of them islanders, watched the unloading, and surveyed the disembarking passengers as though looking for possible candidates for conversion.

I asked them whether they had saved any souls.

"In a year and a half I have not converted too many people," Elder Wright (from Seattle) said. "Two families. But we also help in other ways. We teach games. We play basketball."

"I saw you talking to those Mormons," Ross said, sidling up to me as I was walking into town. "They're supposed to be so holy, but some of them are unbelievable root rats."

"Do you have any scars to prove it?"

"Isn't he fabulous!" Ross called out, but he was soon confiding his proof. "A couple of Mormon chaps came to the door of a gay friend of mine in Melbourne. They had some cold drinks – non-alcoholic – and about ten minutes later they were all in bed together!"

Hiva Oa was Gauguin's last island.

Gauguin is often represented as a bourgeois stockbroker who suddenly upped and left, abandoning his job and his wife and five children and recklessly fleeing to Tahiti, where his artistic genius flowered. But he had always been reckless, and he began painting only a few years after his marriage. And he knew something of the wide world: he had spent part of his childhood in Peru (his mother was half Peruvian Creole); he had gone to sea at the age of seventeen and sailed as an ordinary seaman for six years. His marriage was unhappy, and it was not he who quit the stock market but rather the other way around, for when it went bust he began painting full-time – there was a stock market crash in 1883. By then he was already accepted as an Impressionist.

Rejecting Europe, he tried Martinique, in the West Indies, and when that didn't work for him he went to Tahiti, thinking it to be Cytherean.

It was the opposite: Papeete was bourgeois and westernized, full of puzzling colonial snobberies and irritating bureaucrats, sanctimonious missionaries and corrupt townies; and people were generally as unsympathetic towards him there as anyone might have been, seeing a long-haired Impressionist, in metropolitan France. His hair was long – shoulder length – and he wore a velvet cowboy hat. They loathed him for his repulsive manners and his mode of dress. The Tahitians were more tolerant but still they called him *taata-vahine*, "man-woman," because of his hair. He moved to a seaside village, painted madly and wrote letters home grumbling about the colonials and about life in general. After two years he packed his things and went back to Paris, where the exhibition of his paintings was a critical and financial disaster.

In *Noa-Noa*, he celebrates island life and the beauty of the people, but *Noa-Noa* was written by a man who was eager to convince himself, and others, that he had been resident in paradise. It is vastly at odds with his letters. But the love affair in *Noa-Noa* had a basis in fact, for Gauguin had met his Fayaway in Tahiti. Her name was Tehaamana and she was thirteen ("this was an age Gauguin was greatly drawn to in females," the Pacific historian, Gavan Daws, has observed); and Gauguin painted her over and over until she became the embodiment of his South Seas fantasy.

In his two-year interval in Europe he was miserable. "Literally I can only live on sunshine," he said and returned to Polynesia, and although he intended to head straight for the Marquesas he procrastinated. He still hated the colonial life in Tahiti, the bureaucracy, the tyranny of the Church – hated these aspects of Tahitian life so deeply that they never appear on his canvases. You look in vain in a Gauguin painting for anything resembling details of the colonial life he must have seen most days in Tahiti: no ships, no sailors, no traders, no officials – nor their wives or children; no roads or wagons, or mechanical contraptions; no books or lamps or shoes; no *faranis* at all – and the place was full of white folks, and not only whites but Chinese. The islands had endured sixty years of colonial rule, and yet in Gauguin's paintings – in the fragrant vision he created for himself – Polynesia is inviolate. The only indication we have of foreign influence is the bedstead in several of the paintings. Tahitians slept on mats, not on beds.

"In Gauguin, a need to persuade always went hand in hand with a desire to offend," one of his biographers has written. Living in the bush with yet another Tahitian teenager, Pauura, he quarreled constantly with the authorities (his starting a little newspaper did not endear him to them either), and eventually – still seeking savagery – he set sail for the Marquesas, leaving Pauura and their son, Emil, who was destined to become a tourist attraction.

He arrived in Hiva Oa in 1901 and died less than two years later, having spent ten years altogether in Polynesia – two extended visits, during which he fathered numerous children between painting masterpieces. Here in the little village of Atuona, under the great green Matterhorn of Temetiu he had built a fine two-storey house, which he called The House of Pleasure, and having carved on the wooden frames his favorite maxims, *"Soyez mystérieuses"* ("Be mysterious") was one, and *"Soyez amoureuses et vous serez heureuses"* ("Be in love and you will be happy") was another, he took a fourteen-year-old girl, Vaeloho, as his mistress. He had come to some sort of arrangement with her parents. Gauguin was in his mid-fifties, and Vaeloho was soon pregnant. Their child, who had become an old woman, was still living in the valley in the 1980s.

It is surprising, given the heat, the disorder, the difficulties of living, all his enemies and the simple necessities of stretching and preparing canvases – never mind buying materials – that Gauguin painted at all; yet his output was large, and he was a steady worker, sometimes turning from his painting to wood-carving or pottery. Gauguin was also plagued by bad health – he drank, he took drugs, he had syphilis and stress and a fractured leg. The Church authorities in Atuona hated him, and he had protracted legal problems there, too – a libel action against him. He suffered; and one day a Marquesan neighbor, Tioka, ventured into his house and found the *farani* stretched out and apparently lifeless. Following Marquesan custom, Tioka bit Gauguin's head. The man did not stir.

Gauguin lies buried high on a slope in the cemetery above the village. Near him are the graves of Thérèse Tetua, David Le Cadre, Jean Vohi, Josephine Tauafitiata, Anne Marie Kahao and Elizabeth Mohuho, who were alive at the turn of the century and died in Atuona and must have known the strange wild painter. Gauguin's grave is simple, made of pockmarked volcanic rocks and shaded by a large white-blossomed frangipani. Garlands of flowers were strewn over the grave. The grave marker was his own statue of a wild woman, lettered "Oviri."

Some children were playing nearby. I spoke to them in French, and then asked them, "What does *oviri* mean?"

They said they didn't know. I had to look it up. It is a little ambiguous but appropriate. The word means "savage." Gauguin applied the word to himself in his bronze self-portrait of 1895–6, his face in profile. He wrote in 1903 to Charles Morice (who had collaborated with him on *Noa-Noa*), "You were wrong that day when you said I was wrong to say I was a savage. It's true enough. I am a savage. And civilized people sense the fact ... I am a savage in spite of myself." But the goddess Oviri-moe-aihere is not only a savage; it is she who presides over death and mourning.

As with his paintings, the grave was a colourful mixture of truth, imagination, suggestion and rough brilliance. The faces in the paintings can be encountered all over Tahiti and the Marquesas, but the backgrounds and landscapes are idealized and dream-like. Gauguin needed to believe he was a savage – and perhaps he was, but of a different kind entirely from the gentle islanders he had wished himself upon.

Gavan Daws tells a lovely story about Gauguin in *A Dream of Islands*, his wonderful account of the numerous men who came to Oceania to revisit and verify their fantasies.

"One night at sunset [Daws writes] Gauguin was sitting on a rock outside his house on Hivaoa, naked except for his *pareu*, smoking, thinking about not very much, when out of the gathering darkness came a blind old Marquesan woman, tapping along with a stick, completely naked, tattooed all over, hunched, tottering, dry-skinned, mummy-like. She became aware of Gauguin's presence and felt her way toward him. He sat in inexplicable fear, his breath held in. Without a word the old woman took his hand in hers, dust-dry, cold, reptile-cold. Gauguin felt repulsion. Then in silence she ran her hand over his body, down to the navel, beyond. She pushed aside his *pareu* and reached for his penis. Marquesan men – savages – were all supercised, and the raised scarred flesh was one of their great prides as makers of love. Gauguin had no savage mark on his maleness. He was uncovered for what he was. The blind searching hand withdrew, and the eyeless tattooed mummy figure disappeared into the darkness with a single word, '*Pupa*' she croaked – White man."

The ship was anchored for the night, so I walked with Señor Pillitz over the ridge to the next wide bay, Taaoa, about four miles up and two down, but by the time we came to the archeological dig the day had grown too dark for us to see anything. Walking back in the dust to Atuona we passed two parked cars. There were half a dozen people in them, Tahitians and Marquesans and French, having a wonderful time. Footsore, we asked for a lift.

They said no. It was inconvenient.

"We want to look at the airport," one of them explained.

Señor Pillitz said, "You are visiting Hiva Oa?"

"We are officers with the Department of Tourism," one of the women said.

"What a coincidence. We are tourists," Señor Pillitz said, "and we need a ride back to our ship."

Someone muttered in the back seat. They laughed and drove away.

"He eats it doubled up," Señor Pillitz said. It was an Argentine term of abuse: *Se la comio doblada.*

We saw them later in the bar of the *Aranui.*

"You say you're a writer," one of the Tourism officials said. "What do you write about?"

"Everything I see."

We sailed to the north coast of Hiva Oa, and anchored and went ashore. There at Puamau, at a *marae* at the end of a muddy path in the jungle, was a vast ruin. Finding such a place unmarked in the jungle behind a remote village was one of the singular pleasures of cruising the Marquesas. This one was a jumble of overgrown and scattered stones, and many carvings, some beheaded and castrated by souvenir-hunters or missionaries. Others were fiercely intact, one of which is the largest tiki in Polynesia – a seven-foot monster, grimacing and clutching its belly – and another the strangest and most beautiful frog-faced creature, horizontal on a pedestal. It had a jack-o'-lantern mouth and donut eyes and fat extended legs, and it was apparently flying.

"It is a tiki woman," a Marquesan told me.

*The giants* [tikis] *of the cliff-girt Puamau Valley displayed such a contrast to the lazy people on the beach,* Thor Heyerdahl writes in *Fatu-Hiva, that the question inevitably came to mind: Who put these red stone colossi there, and how?*

His answer, refuted by every archeologist of any reputation, was: People from South America.

Farther west on Hiva Oa the *Aranui* provisioned the village of Hanaiapa, and I hurried up another muddy path in a light mist until heavy rain began to fall – so heavy I had to shelter in a deserted building. It was a rickety wooden church, with vines reaching through the windows and a crude pulpit, and a quotation painted high on one wall: *Betheremu* (Bethlehem) and *Miku 5.5,* a gnomic reference to the text from Micah, in which the prophet mentioned Bethlehem and foretold the coming of the Lord, "For now shall he be great unto the ends of the earth. And this man shall be the peace, when the Assyrian shall come into the land –"

Through the tilted door-jamb I could see coconut palms and breadfruit trees, mangoes, papayas, grapefruit, avocados – and the wet straggling village next to the gurgling stream.

Walking back to the beach (muddy gray water washing muddy gray sand), I passed a house where three young Marquesans were listening to music from a boom box.

"Who is singing?" I asked.

"Prince."

And farther on I met a woman walking hand in hand with a young girl. The woman was attractive, in a green blouse and wearing a flower-patterned *pareu*. She smiled at me and stood with her feet apart, blocking the path.

"Hello. My name is Mau," the woman said in English, and she showed me her name tattooed on her wrist.

"Where did you learn English?"

"From the boats." And she pinched the little girl's cheek. "This is my daughter Miriam."

The woman was wearing a *lei* – a Marquesan one, with mint and other fragrant herbs entwined with flowers.

"That's very pretty."

She immediately took it off and put it around my neck and kissed me on each cheek, more like a French formality than a Marquesan custom.

"Where are you going?"

"Back to the ship."

"Too bad."

She smiled a little ruefully, but the ship would be back, and perhaps next time it would stay a bit longer, and she would meet someone else, someone more willing.

She was as near as I came to finding Fayaway. But she was much like the other people I had met, who seemed decent and hard-working and happy. She was the one who seemed to possess just a flicker of coquettishness, and none were flirts. Most of the people were tough and down to earth, a little gloomy and very religious. Where was the romance? I had no idea. Even the islands, so dramatic at a distance, were quite another story close up – muddy and jungly and priest-ridden, and the beaches teaming with no-see-ums they called *nonos*.

Instead of painting the great rocks, the black cliffs, the crashing waves, the deep Marquesan valleys, the sea-washed crags, the cataracts and mountainsides, the hypocrites and colonials – instead of dealing with this reality, Gauguin decided to test his own theories of color and perspective. He painted pink beaches, yellow fields, Buddhist images, Javanese statues. He created a tropical horse culture in which France did not figure. He invented Polynesia. So people came. They don't find his Polynesia, but what they do find is just as magical, though undoubtedly forbidding, and just as *luxe, calme et volupté*, as Baudelaire wrote in *L'Invitation au voyage*, one of Gauguin's favorite poems.

But some of the islands were anything but voluptuous. Ua Huka was one of these. The harbor at Hane was so narrow, no more than a pair of granite jaws, and the *Aranui* lay tethered between them, on short lines, and bouncing in the swell. The island was bereft of trees, and in the interior wild goats and horses and wild donkeys were desperately foraging. The island, the smallest in the Marquesas, looked nibbled to death. There were only 500 people on Ua Huka. Some were carvers, and they came forward, trying to sell expensive tikis, and war clubs, and bowls that cost $350.

After looking at the ruins – muddy path, boulders, the shattered buttocks of a tiki – I found a place to eat and had a feast: breadfruit, and *miti hue* (river shrimp in fermented coconut milk), *poe* (sweet starchy pudding flavored with papaya), *poisson cru* made with tuna, and sweet potato, *umara*.

I walked until the hard driving wind-blown rain forced me inside. The post office in Hane was a small bare room – about the size of the average bathroom. The postmistress, Marie-Thérèse, a hibiscus flower in her hair, sat at a trestle table with a telephone and a cash box. Here, while Marie-Thérèse read a French magazine, *La Nouvelle Intimité*, I called Honolulu again, collect. The connection was clear, and the only problem was the driving rain and the banging door.

I sat beside Marie-Thérèse, who was reading a section called *Dossier*, which was headed, *Le Plaisir au féminin – Pour une sexualité sans tabous*. What a coincidence, that word that had found its way back to Polynesia in an article about uninhibited women's pleasures. It spoke of orgasms, sexual response, diseases, and sexual variations (*mille et un*), and Marie-Thérèse was so engrossed she hardly noticed when I hung up the phone.

Waiting for the whaleboat to take me back to the ship, I fell into conversation with some youngsters who were seated near the beach for this monthly event, the visit of the *Aranui*.

"Are there any *tupapaus* here?" I asked one of them, Stella, who had been listening to the lambada on her brother's Walkman.

"Not here, but beyond the restaurant."

"At the *marae*?"

"Yes. And in the forest."

"Are you afraid of the *tupapaus*?"

"Yes."

And then the whaleboats came, and the older passengers were carried in the arms of the Marquesans. It was accomplished quickly, but I was struck by these arrivals and departures through the surf: most of them were exactly like rescues, just as wet and urgent and precarious.

There were more stone terraces and house-platforms on pretty Fatu-Hiva (population 500), the smallest, the prettiest and most vertical island in this group. Thor Heyerdahl's account in *Fatu-Hiva: Back to Nature* – how he got away from it all by coming here – resulted in a influx of people to Fatu-Hiva similarly trying to get away from it all. There were so few habitable valleys that these foreigners were concentrated in only a couple of places and produced a rash of thieving and conflict: a period of intense xenophobia among Marquesans, and disappointment among the foreigners. Everyone had been misled. Characteristically, Heyerdahl's book was fanciful and inaccurate and self-promoting, with many narrow escapes and improbable incidents (in one, the ponderous Norwegian buys Gauguin's rifle, and it is obvious to even the most casual reader that he is being bamboozled), and long misleading chapters about cannibalism as well as tendentious detail – Heyerdahl's hobbyhorse – about the peopling of Polynesia by South Americans.

The *Aranui* first stopped at Omoa, and the walkers among us trekked seventeen kilometers over the high ridges among wild horses and wild goats to Hanavave and the Bay of Virgins. The interior of the island was perfectly empty. Walking was something Marquesans seldom did. They sat, they hung out, they rode four-wheel-drive vehicles and sometimes horses; but I never saw any islanders hiking the up-country paths. Some frankly said they were afraid of the *tupapaus* that lurked in the dense upland foliage. That could have been one reason. But Marquesans also seemed a sedentary lot and were never happier than when sitting under the palms on the seafront, near one of the pompous and vainglorious French plaques ("To the French Dead"), holding a big blue can of Cheez Balls between their knees and munching.

The Bay of Virgins was a misnomer, but deliberate. The bay is surmounted by several unmistakably phallic basalt pillars, and was originally called Baie des Verges – Bay of Dicks is a fair translation of that. But outraged missionaries slipped an "i" into the word, making it *vierges*, virgins. If they had been English missionaries they might have slipped an "r" into the word, turning Dicks into Dirks ("because they resemble knives").

At the tight little harbor of Hanavave there were children and dogs running in circles – I counted twenty dogs in one place alone – and big bulky Marquesans waiting for the ship's cargo. They had been without beer for two weeks, they said. They had run out of gasoline. The snacks had been gone for some time. The whaleboats came and went, leaving provisions, taking away fish. A Marquesan woman watched wearing an *AC/DC* T-shirt, a man watched in a baseball hat that read *Shit Happens*. As Gauguin indicated in the androgyny of his portraits, the men and women physically resembled each other, and became almost indistinguishable as they grew older.

The island of Fatu-Hiva was without doubt the most beautiful of the Marquesas, not just for its great vistas, and the wild horses scrambling on the slopes, the sheerest cliffs, the greenest ledges, and the beautiful bay. It was its greenness, its steepness, its emptiness; the way daylight plunged into it only to be overwhelmed by the darkness of its precipitous valleys, and the obvious dangers of its entire shoreline gave it the look of a fortress or a green castle in the sea.

The Marquesans were gloomy and laconic, and they lived quietly, out of the sun, in the depths of their damp valleys. They seemed to be gentle people. They harvested coconuts. They fished. They raised kids. On Sundays they went to church and sang the whole mass. They tattooed themselves and ate breadfruit and fish. They grew fat, and then their children served them. It was not a bad life.

Still, the islands seemed paradoxical to me. The soil was fertile, but the vegetable gardens were small and insufficient. The people were intensely proud of their ancient Marquesan culture, but they were also God-fearing Catholics. They spoke proudly of their ruins and carvings in the jungle, but did nothing to preserve them, letting them fall into greater ruin. They said they disliked the French, but they let the French run all their affairs. It made no difference to them that eighty-five percent of their food was imported as long as the few really important items like rice were subsidized. They loved eating loaves of French bread, but there were only a handful of bakeries in the islands; they let the *Aranui* deliver bread from Tahiti – it was stale and expensive coming by ship, but that seemed preferable to their baking it themselves. They lived hand to mouth, but no matter how hard-pressed they were for money they would not accept a tip. They were eager for tourists, but there was hardly a hotel on the islands that was worth the name. The Ministry of Tourism – no doubt this is a blessing – is almost wholly ineffectual where the Marquesas are concerned.

There are all sorts of little guidebooks to the Marquesas, but the liveliest and the most informative, for all its fiction and inaccuracies, is Herman Melville's *Typee*. Give or take a few roads, and one video store, the little post office and the usual curses of colonialism, not much has changed in Nuku Hiva since Melville fled the cannibal feast almost a hundred and fifty years ago. There is no cannibalism in the Marquesas anymore – none of the traditional kind. But there was the brutality of French colonialism. Gauguin had noticed the peculiar hypocrisy, and Gavan Daws quoted him as hectoring the bourgeoisie of French Polynesia.

"Civilized!" Gauguin cried. "You pride yourself on not eating human flesh, [yet] every day you eat the heart of your fellow man."

Now the islands are emptier, the valleys are silent, the tabu-groves more ghostly, and at the head of most valleys there is an enormous waterfall – and sometimes three or four – coursing hundreds of feet down from the cliffs.

About that water. Seeing those cataracts often made me thirsty. One day in Nuku Hiva I went to a bar and asked for a drink of water. A half-liter of Vittel was opened for me, and I paid – $2·50. It was unthinkable that I should want the vile water from the pipes of Taiohae, and no one questioned the absurdity of buying this little bottle of Vittel from halfway around the world. That it is available at all is something of a miracle; that it might be necessary is a condemnation of this lovely baffling place.

The French praise and romanticize the Marquesas, but in the 1960s they had planned to test nuclear devices on the northern Marquesan island of Eiao, until there was such an outcry they changed their plans and decided to destroy Mururoa instead. It is said that the French are holding Polynesia together, but really it is so expensive to maintain that they do everything as cheaply as possible – and it is self-serving, too. Better to boost domestic French industries by exporting bottled water from France than investing in a fresh water supply for each island. That is what colonialism is all about. You can hear the bureaucrats say, "Let them boil their water." The French have left nothing enduring in the islands except a tradition of hypocrisy and their various fantasies of history and high levels of radioactivity.

So what is this part of Polynesia today except France's flagpole in the Pacific, and a devious way of testing nuclear devices?

"The people are helped, but the help is not handed over – it is bounced to them," Señor Pillitz said – another Argentine expression, *la agaro de rebote*, meaning that something is grudgingly given.

When France has succeeded in destroying a few more atolls, when they have managed to make the islands glow with so much radioactivity that night is turned into day, when they have sold the rest of the fishing rights and depleted them of fish (already in Tahiti the surrounding islands have been over-fished), when it has all been thoroughly plundered, the French will plan a great ceremony and grandly offer these unemployed and deracinated citizens in T-shirts and flip-flops their independence. In the destruction of the islands, the French imperial intention, its *mission civilisatrice* – civilizing mission – will be complete.

# 20

## The Cook Islands: In the Lagoon of Aitutaki

I was paddling in the huge lagoon of Aitutaki, which was green sea ringed by tiny islands and a reef that was like a fortification made of coral and sea foam. An old man fishing from a dugout canoe called out to me.

"Why are you paddling there, listening with those earphones?"

I was listening to Chuck Berry.

"Because I am unhappy," I said.

"Where is your wife?" he yelled.

Then the wind took the rest of his talk away, and it also separated our boats.

I had come to this lagoon in the Cook group from the Marquesas for a reason. The Marquesas were the dispersal point, from about 300 A.D. onward, for people who populated the three corners of the Polynesian triangle. They sailed to the top of it, the Hawaiian Islands; to the Cooks and beyond, to New Zealand; and to Easter Island. No one is certain why the Marquesans embarked on these long and difficult voyages, some of them over two thousand miles. The people were skilled in the arts of warfare, gardening, navigation and boat-building. They had found every island of any size in the eastern Pacific, bringing to it their arts, their gods, their chiefs, their domestic animals and their favorite vegetables. They worked in stone, they made tools, they wove ingenious baskets, but they did not make pots. They civilized these islands with a peculiarly harmonious culture that combined a reverence for flowers, a fondness for music and dancing, and a predilection for cannabalism.

Letting these old discoverers determine my itinerary, I had decided to leave the Marquesas to paddle in the Cook Islands. After that I planned to paddle around Easter Island, and finally Hawaii.

It was a short flight from Papeete to Rarotonga, the main island in the Cook group. I arrived late at night in a cold drizzle and was watched by heavy Maori-looking people with big fleshy faces, large and not very dexterous hands and bulky bodies. They looked like unfinished statues and were handsome in the same sculptural way, with broad open faces and big feet. Every adult, whether man or woman, had a rugby player's physique.

"This is camping equipment?"

"It's a boat." I had checked *"camping equipment"* on my arrival form.

"Is it clean or dirty?"

"Very clean."

"You can go."

Two different New Zealanders, seeing my boat bags and my gear, said sarcastically, "You travel light!" But the Cook Islander heaving them off the baggage cart said, "My woman weighs more than that."

It was like landing at an airstrip in the middle of Africa – one plane, three small buildings, few formalities, only one person around, seeing to everything. It was easy to get information because there was so little to know. It was nearly midnight. I asked the only person there whether I could fly the next day to Aitutaki.

"The first flight's at eight o'clock. I can put you on it."

The speaker was Mr Skew, a New Zealander. He told me about the political system, which seemed simple enough. Then he asked where I was staying. I saw the name of a hotel on the wall, and said, "There." He drove me to the place ("And that's the Cook Islands Parliament House," Mr Skew said, as we passed a very small wooden shed beyond the airport).

Viv, the dour New Zealand clerk at the hotel, at first pretended she wasn't glad to see me, and then said, "We have plenty of rooms. Do you want a sea view?"

"I'm getting up at six." It was now twelve-thirty.

"You should get one of our cheap rooms," Viv said. The room had a Soviet look, chipped paint, plastic chairs, easily-tipped-over lamps and a blocked drain in the sink. And it was barely furnished. I had last stayed in a room like this in Wellington, but this made pretty Polynesia seem chilly and frugal. The Cooks were still informally linked to New Zealand, but the smug and self-denying Calvinism of Kiwi-land was at odds with everything Polynesian, and the Kiwis themselves looked rather out of place here, so beaky and pale, with short pants and knobby knees.

"I'm from Aitutaki myself," a Cook Islander said to me the next morning at the airport. He had a strong New Zealand accent. His name was Michael Rere.

"There's supposed to be a great canoe-maker in Aitutaki," I said.

"Probably my father."

"Is his name Rere?"

"Yes, but they call him 'Blackman,' because he's always out fishing. That makes him black."

Cook Islanders were standing in a light rain, holding garlands and crowns of flowers, watching passengers disembark from a flight that had just arrived from Auckland, watching lots of bundled-up and brightly dressed people hurrying through puddles towards the arrival building. Fat people greeting even fatter arrivals – happy families.

Inter-island planes began to arrive. Besides the high volcanic island of Rarotonga, the most populous (10,000) and developed, there are fourteen other islands in the Cook group, ranging from coral atolls like Suwarrow (with six inhabitants) to Mangaia, which is nearly as large as Raro. Small planes flew to most of these islands. Aitutaki had been recommended to me as a friendly and pretty place, and so I decided to go there with my collapsible boat.

A woman was yapping in Maori, and among her unintelligible mutterings I caught the phrase, *no place like home*.

That same hour I was flying in sunshine over the lagoon at Aitutaki, looking down at its wonderful configuration of reefs and *motus*, and after lunch I was paddling there.

It was then the old man called out to me, "Where is your wife?"

I spent the night at a small seedy house by the shore called Tom's. Camping was forbidden, because all the land was spoken for and constantly being quarreled over, subdivided and renegotiated. Mr and Mrs Tom were islanders; they were out but their daughter had shown me around. The walls of the house were plastered with religious pictures, and copies of *The Book of Mormon* were lying about, bristling rather ominously with bookmarks and dog-eared pages.

"You can cook here," Winnie said, showing me a greasy stove. "You can put your food here." She opened a dusty cabinet. "You can share this bathroom," and she shoved a plastic curtain aside, "with the others."

But what I felt most keenly was the absence of beer. And even if I found some in town, how could I guzzle it in front of this pious family of Mormons?

It was next to the lagoon, so I stayed awhile, and I became friendly with the three fearfully solemn evangelists who could usually be found conferring on the porch, their black ties dangling – a Cook Islander, a Maori from Auckland, and Elder Lambert, from Salt Lake City.

"I'm from Massachusetts," I said on first meeting them, and when they gave me blank looks I added, "which is not far from Vermont."

The big booby face of the islander was in marked contrast to the consternation on the face of Elder Lambert.

"And you know who was born in Sharon, Vermont," I said.

"Who was born there?" the Maori asked.

After an uneasy pause, the Cook Islander laughed. "I doon know eet!"

Elder Lambert said, "Joseph Smith was born in Sharon, Vermont."

They were so transfixed by the fanciful details of their absurd millennialism (Jesus's visit to the Mayans in Guatemala, golden tablets buried in New York, the prophecies of the Angel Moroni, God encouraging polygamy, and so forth) that they had lost sight of the simplest facts, such as where the founder of their Church, their prophet, was born.

I urged them to read *No Man Knows My History: The Life of Joseph Smith*, by Fawn Brodie, and they said I should look into *The Book of Mormon*.

"I will," I said. "I want to read about the Lost Tribes of Israel sailing into the Pacific."

This made Elder Lambert hitch his chair forward and begin pointedly tapping the air with his finger.

"In the first chapter of Nephi, Lehi went east from Jerusalem. His descendants are in the Pacific. And in the last chapter of Alma – sixty-three – Hagoth and many others built ships and sailed into 'the Western Sea.' Those are the very words. The Pacific, in other words. They were Nephites."

"Sailed from where?"

"America. Central America." Tap-tap-tap went his finger." "'A narrow neck of land.'"

"And they made it to Polynesia."

"Yes. The Polynesians are descendants of these people."

The Maori was beaming. His expression said: *Take that!*

"What about the Melanesians?"

"Sons of Ham."

"What about the Micronesians?"

Elder Lambert narrowed his eyes at me. He said, "Corrupt defilers."

After all this disputation I needed air. I thought: You had to admire Joseph Smith for trying to come up with a home-grown faith – it was the most Americanized religion. (Christopher Columbus and the American Revolution made appearances in *The Book of Mormon*.) But Mormonism was like junk food: it was American to the core and it looked all right, but it was our version of food; and it wasn't until after you had swallowed some that you felt strange.

I strolled into Aitutaki's town, Arutanga. It was a very small town — hardly a town at all, more a village, and its small size and its dullness kept it pure. It was the post office, two shops, four churches, a muddy harbor, a school, some houses. The shops sold only canned goods: fish, beans, corned beef, cookies, crackers — the South Pacific standbys.

Poo, the postmaster, was sitting on the post office steps. He told me he disliked Rarotonga for being too busy and stressful.

"Are you busy?"

"Not really," he said.

Eleanor at Big Jay's Take-Away fried a fishburger for me, a chunk of wahoo in a bun, and said she had lived her whole life on the island, but that she was trying to make a go of this business.

"Are you busy?"

"Not really," she said.

It began to rain very hard, and walking back to Tom's I had to take shelter under a big tree. A girl of about twenty, who had been headed out of town on her motorbike, was doing the same thing. The rain crashed through the branches and leaves.

"You mind this rain?"

"Not really," she said.

But it let up after an hour, and the sun came out, and I went paddling again.

On the beach, near Tom's, I met two enormous women, Apii and Emma. They looked elderly, but they were exactly my own age. They referred to me as a *papa'a* – a white man.

"What if I were black – what would you call me?"

"Then you would be a *papa'a kere kere.*"

"What if I were Chinese?"

"You would be *tinito.*"

"What if I were from another island?"

"You would be *manuiri* – a stranger."

I asked them whether there were community activities on the island. They said there were the churches and sometimes there were festivals.

"We used to have a cinema in Aitutaki, but videos are better," Emma said.

"Do you think that videos from America make the young people violent?" I asked.

Emma said, "Maybe. But the young people in Aitutaki are all right. The problem is with these Cook Island kids who come home from the holidays. They live in New Zealand and they learn bad habits. They are troublemakers. We call them 'street kids.' They give a bad example. Cook Islanders go bad in New Zealand."

"I like watching videos," Apii said. "Most people in Aitutaki have a video machine. We have had them for four years. Or maybe three."

"And blue movies," Emma said. "Did you ever see blue movies?"

"I have seen some," I admitted. "What about you?"

"We have," Emma said. "One called *The Tigress* – something like that."

"Naked *papa'as*," I said. They laughed. "Do young people watch them?"

"No. Only adults," Apii said. "Men like them."

"Women find them silly," Emma said.

I asked, "Why do you think men like them?"

"They get ideas. They like to watch. And sometimes" – Emma raised her large hands to her face and giggled behind them – "sometimes they end up."

"What does that mean, 'end up'?"

"They end up doing what they are seeing," Apii said.

"Because the blue movies make them hungry," Emma added.

We were standing under some palm trees. It began to rain again, but still they shifted themselves and said they had to go. Before they left, I gave them some chocolate.

"I would rather have nuts," Emma said, and laughed.

The next day I got tired of the Mormons and the tiny mildewed house, and I moved to a bungalow at a lodge another mile up the road, but also on the lagoon. Not long after I moved in, I switched on my short-wave radio and, searching for world news, I heard a familiar voice.

*I am a little incredulous still, that I am the representative of Her Majesty the Queen in New Zealand –*

It was Dame Cath, whom I had met in Fiji, who had made herself famous in New Zealand by calling one of her political enemies "a fuckwit." She was back in Auckland, and still harping with false modesty about carrying out the Queen's wishes.

*– and that the daughter of poor Scottish migrants should be standing here today, is testimony to –*

I switched the thing off and somewhere in the palms a cockatoo shrieked.

That day I paddled to the edge of the reef, a place marked Nukuroa on my chart, where a father and son were fishing.

Toupe, the father, said, "I can only live here in Aitutaki. It is small. Rarotonga is big. If you have a small place you have few people. But in a big place you get Samoans, Tongans, and all different people. I don't like that."

I pointed to one of the little islands south of us. "Do you call that a *motu?*"

"Yes."

Then I pointed to Aitutaki, which was low and green and glimmering in the sunshine. "Is that a *motu?*"

"No. That is *enua.*"

*Enua* was land. *Fenua* in Tahitian. *Vanua* in Fijian. An island was a little parcel in the sea. It was something you could see the whole of in a glance. But land was something else – it had a sense of home, it had size, it was divided, it contained more than one family. I asked Toupe for a definition.

"*Enua* is not an island. It is a small land," he said, and then he asked, "Are you married?"

"That's a long story," I said.

"But where is your wife?"

"That's what I mean."

"Not with you?" He was very persistent.

"No," I said.

"That is bad." He looked genuinely annoyed. "You will go with girls from bars."

"Not a chance," I said. "I am too old."

"They like older men."

"I am not interested."

Anyway, where were these girls? Where were the bars, for that matter? They were mentioned in Tahiti, too. I never saw them. In Taiohae in Nuku Hiva one night a man said to me, *All the boys have gone to the bar to pick up girls.* I did not see any bar in Taiohae that had a woman in it. Fast women were muttered about in Fiji. What a shame – all the prostitutes, people said. I looked and did not see a single one. Rarotonga was reputed to be a hot place. You could have fooled me. It was jolly, but in a hearty unambiguous way. Bar girls were mentioned in Nuku'alofa, in Tonga. There were two bars; I looked; no one. I never saw anything vicious on the streets or bars of Polynesia, and my only brush with the local libido was in the Trobriands, where I had sometimes been woken with a drunken cry, *Mister Paul, you want a girl?* but I usually assumed it was a clumsy attempt to rob me and always went back to sleep.

Before I left Toupe I asked him about sharks. Yes, he said, there were plenty of them in the lagoon. I showed him the four-foot spear I kept beside the cockpit of my kayak.

"That will do nothing to the sharks we have," he said. "They are bigger than your boat."

That gave me pause. My boat was almost sixteen feet long.

On the other hand, Aitutaki was famous for not having any dogs on it. No one had an explanation for this, but I was glad in any case, because Polynesian dogs were bad-tempered scavengers. It was as though they knew that human beings were not to be trusted: and that the fate of all dogs was to be cooked and eaten.

I went back to my bungalow that day and found six ripe mangoes on my table. Somehow the two fat ladies, Apii and Emma, had found out where I was staying and had brought the fruit to me.

My intention was to paddle to the *motus*. Because it was forbidden by custom for any stranger to stay overnight on them, these involved round trips of anywhere from eight to twenty miles. But I had to be prepared for emergencies: I might get stuck on a *motu* if there was a storm. I bought food at the local shops – beans, sardines, raisins, cucumbers, bread – and set off, launching into the shallow lagoon. There was no local market. The meat in the shops was canned, and one store sold frozen New Zealand lamb and mutton.

"What about chickens? Don't you raise chickens?"

An islander said, "We have wild chickens."

"Do you eat them?"

"Sometimes. But they are too tough."

I loved the expression *wild chickens*.

At low tide great bristling shelves of coral were exposed in the lagoon, and fighting the wind I was sometimes blown onto the spikes. Then I had to get out and disengage my boat and tramp away, pulling it carefully, before getting in. I always wore reef shoes in Aitutaki for this reason. After a few days the rubber bottom of the boat was terribly gouged, but I had no leaks.

The skipping fish seemed to be stirred by low tide, too, and they sometimes surfaced in a silver sheet – hundreds of sardine-sized fish – shimmering seventy-five feet across my bow, dancing on their tails, and into the distance, a lovely sight.

One day, making for a little *motu* called Papau at the edge of the eastern edge of the reef, I realized that I was low on drinking-water. If I happened to become stranded on Papau I would have no water at all, and would have to rely on the coconuts I might knock down (and that was never easy). Spotting a village called Tautu marked on my chart, on the east side of Aitutaki, I paddled there and went ashore.

Two naked boys watched me drag my boat onto the sand.

"What is that?"

"That's my boat," I said.

They laughed. The kayak did not look like any boat they had ever seen.

I walked up a path and over a jungly hill and found some houses. There was no one home at any of them, though the houses looked cared-for and the gardens well tended. On the veranda of one of the empty houses, a washer was going – a wash-tub, which was open and agitating clothes, this way and that, *shlip-shlop, shlip-shlop*, with a laboring motor. It was a sound from my past, my mother's washer going most of the day, it seemed – all that distance to hear that evocative noise and recover a memory of early childhood.

Farther along the road, I saw an islander. I said I needed some water. He pointed to a house.

A white man came out, followed by a small grubby child.

"What is it?" the man asked in what was perhaps a New Zealand accent. He seemed tetchy.

"I wonder if you could give me some drinking-water, please."

Without a word, he took my bottle and went into the house. Then he was back, handing it to me, again in silence.

"I came by kayak," I said. "I saw this village on the map. My boat is on the beach."

He simply stared at me, without any interest.

"Have you lived here long?" I asked.

"Eighteen years."

"You must have seen some dramatic changes," I said.

He pressed his lips together, then said, "No paved roads then."

Yet I had not seen any paved roads even now.

"This was all jungle," he said.

Wasn't it still jungle, except for the odd little bungalow?

"That kind of thing," he said.

I said, "Do the high prices bother you?"

This seemed to irritate him.

"It's all relative, isn't it?" he said defiantly.

"That it costs three dollars for a cucumber?"

"You learn to live with high prices," he said, and now he was cross, though I could not explain why. "Just like you learn to live with low prices. You go to Australia" – perhaps he was an Australian? – "and the prices are low, and you learn to live with them. And you come back and the prices are high and you learn to live with them."

I said, "I suppose if you have a garden you can reduce some of your costs."

"A garden?" he said, sneering in incredulity. "Do you know how much time a garden takes? You could be at it all day, weeding it, watering it. Time – that's the rarest commodity here. Time."

That was news. I would have thought that time was plentiful on this little island – that the one commodity everyone had in abundance was time.

The man had a rising tremor of mania in his voice as he said, "You wake up and you're off and there's never enough time to do everything that needs to be done, and if it's not one thing it's another. Time is scarce here" – and he leaned forward at me: he was barefoot, in a dirty T-shirt, the grubby child nuzzling his legs. "I never have enough time!"

"I'd better be going," I said.

"And another thing," he said. "I'd rather pay three dollars a pound for tomatoes than thirty dollars and all the time it takes to grow them."

"Of course. Well, I'm off – headed out to that island" – Papau, in the distance, was partially misted over.

"It's two miles, you know. Maybe more."

"I've just come six miles from Arutanga. I can manage."

"And the wind's against you," he said.

"True. But it will be an easy paddle back, or to that other island."

"Unless the wind shifts. Then it'll blow you straight out to sea or onto the reef."

Now I saw that he had a stubbly face, and bitten nails, and spit in the corners of his mouth.

"I was under the impression this was the prevailing wind – south-easterly."

"It shifts at times. Not usually at this time of year. But it shifts."

I had a sudden urge to push him over, but I resisted, and turning to go I said, "At least it's not raining."

"It might rain," he said eagerly. "We need rain. I hope it does rain." He grinned horribly at the blazing sky. "And it's four miles to that island, Papau."

"Then I'd better get started," I said.

"The reef's at least three," he said.

"I was told there's an ancient *marae* on the island."

"There's said to be. I haven't been out there."

And he had lived here for eighteen years?

"Haven't had the time," he said, as though reading the query in my mind. "There's never enough time." He looked extremely harassed. He clutched his T-shirt. He said, "Now, I'm sorry, but you're just going to have to excuse me. I haven't got all day for chatting. I've got masses of paperwork to get through. That's what I was doing when you came. You interrupted me. You see? Time. Not enough."

"Thanks for the water."

"It's good water. From an artesian well. It's all drinkable here," he said, as though I was on the point of accusing him of poisoning me.

It took me an hour, paddling into the wind, to get to Papau. There were herons and egrets wading in its shallows. From a distance it looked as though it had a white sand beach. Close up it was broken coral and bleached rock, and it was littered with rubbish and flotsam that had floated from Aitutaki or had been chucked from ships.

As I sat on a log, eating my lunch, the whole beach got up and started walking sideways. Shells, big and small, were bobbling all over the place. This was amazing, like a Disney cartoon, where nature starts to frolic – singing trees, nodding flowers, dancing shells. It was because I had been so still. The hermit crabs I had startled earlier began to move, but I had never seen so many of them on the move.

I tramped around the island, looking for the ancient site, but saw nothing. It was a deserted island, with dense jungle at its center, and the remains of campfires at the edge. I had told myself that I had come here to look at the *marae* but once on the island, faced with thorns and tall grass and spiders, I could not be bothered to look, so I went for a swim instead, and after that knocked down some foul-tasting coconuts.

It occurred to me that I might work my way down this long chain of *motus*, starting here, and then going on to Tavaeraiti and its sister *motu* Tavaerua. The fifth one along was in the far corner of the lagoon, almost out of sight of land. I could get close to it tonight, hit it tomorrow, and then head back.

The idea of trespassing excited me, and there was enough daylight for me to make it to the largest of the *motus*, Tekopua, where I could hide.

The wind helped me by beating against the beam of my kayak and slipping me quickly past Akaiami and Muritapua, and by then Aitutaki was almost lost on the horizon. It was a low island and at this time of day no fishermen came out this far. My only problem might be a fisherman who had came to the same conclusions as me and decided to spend the night – but there was none. I went ashore at the top end of Tekopua, and dragged my boat off the beach. I had everything I needed: water, food, mosquito repellent, and enough canvas to keep the rain off my sleeping-bag.

Darkness was sudden. No sooner had I finished eating than night descended. There were no stars. No lights – not even any on the distant island. The palms rattled and the surf broke on the far side of my *motu*. That sound of surf and thrashing palms woke me throughout the night – there were no real silences on Polynesian nights: at the very least it was wind or waves. But this sound was noisier than city traffic.

I woke very wet, not from rain but from the residue of heavy mist, and after breakfast began to worry about having camped. Now I had used up most of my water and food. If I had a problem, I'd be stuck.

The last *motu* in the chain, Motukitiu, was only an hour away. I started paddling for it before the sun was up, before the wind had begun to rise; and after I had landed and had a quick drink I headed north across the widest part of the lagoon, to catch the rising wind that would take me west to the safety of Te Koutu Point.

There were turtles on the way, and more dancing fish, and spikes of slashing coral. I realized that I had not rested well in the night when, after I had reached the shore of Aitutaki, I lay back and fell asleep. It was not even noon. But after I woke I felt refreshed, and more than that, felt that I had accomplished something in seeing each of the islets on this entire side of the huge lagoon – the desert islands of Aitutaki.

I swam at Te Koutu – this whole part of Aitutaki was empty, except for screeching birds; and then I headed back, with a tailwind to Arutanga.

Although I stayed a mile offshore, because of the jagged coral, I could hear loud singing as I passed the beach below a village that appeared on my chart as Reureu. I could just make out a group of men under a wooden shelter that was next to a large tree. I paddled nearer, avoiding the coral, and was debating whether to go ashore when I heard shouting. The men were waving me towards the beach.

I parked my boat and joined them. There were about fifteen men. Most were drunk and all were singing. One man had a guitar, another a ukelele.

"Please come," one man said. He was wearing a T-shirt that said *Rarotonga*. "Have some kava."

He gestured to a cut-off metal drum that sat in the middle of the group of men. One of the men worked a coconut shell around in it, slopping the brown opaque liquid.

"Is this *yanggona*?"

"No. This is Aitutaki kava. Made from malt, sugar and yeast. This is beer, my friend."

"Bush beer."

"Yes. Have some."

I was handed a black coconut shell brimming with it. The taste was sweetish and alcoholic. I sipped. They urged me to gulp it all. I did so and almost hurled.

"So you're out paddling that little boat?"

"Yes. I was out to the *motus*," I said. And then, to confirm that I had indeed trespassed, I asked, "But what if I wanted to spend the night on one?"

"If no one sees you, what is the harm?" one of the men said.

They all wore filthy T-shirts and were squatting on logs.

"You come from?"

"America. But not in that boat."

They laughed. They were drunk enough to find this hilarious. Then they began to tease one of the men, who appeared to be very shy and possibly mentally disturbed.

"This is Antoine," the man in the Rarotonga T-shirt said. "He comes from Mururoa, where the French test the bombs. He is radioactive. That is why he is so strange."

Antoine lowered his head.

"Antoine speaks French."

I addressed Antoine in French, just saying hello. All the men laughed.

Antoine left the group and mounted his motorbike and then rode away.

I said, "Is this a bush-beer school?"

That was the Aitutaki term for a drinking-party, I had read.

"Yes. He is the teacher."

The man dipping the filthy coconut shell into the metal drum smiled and went on dipping and slopping.

"But it is more like a ship," another man said. "He is the captain. He is the first mate. He is the second mate. He is the engineer —"

"It is a club." This man was standing against the tree. "We call it Arepuka Club. This is a *puka* tree. And this is an *are*." He meant the little wooden shelter.

"He is chairman."

The standing man smiled: the only man sober enough to be able to stand up had to be chairman, I supposed.

"How long has this club been in existence?"

"Three years."

"You come to drink every day?"

"Excuse me. We have meetings every day."

"What do you do at your meetings?"

"We drink beer."

"And then?"

"We sing."

"How long do you stay here each day?"

"Until we are drunk and cannot stand up."

All the men laughed hard as this unsmiling man explained the workings of the club to me.

"And then we go home."

"What songs do you sing?"

"About the island."

"Is it a nice island?" I asked.

"It is like paradise," he said.

"Why do you say that?"

"Because we have everything we want – food, beer, vegetables, fish –"

Suddenly the man next to me snatched my hand and began reading my palm.

"You are thirty-six years old," he said, squeezing my hand. "I can see it here."

Another man said, "It is better here than in New Zealand."

"Have you been there?" I asked.

"Yes. It is too fast there. Too much busy."

"Some Cook Islanders come back to Aitutaki from New Zealand and go to the latrine and say, 'It is dirty. There is no flush. Look at all the cockroaches.' But there is much water in New Zealand for flushing. We have little water."

"After two or three weeks they stop complaining," someone said.

"What do you think of New Zealand people?" a man asked me, handing me another shell of beer.

"They are very careful people," I said. "They obey the law. They eat carefully. They speak carefully. They spend money carefully."

"Because they have no money!" one man cried out, and the others laughed. "They are poor."

"Are you rich?" I asked.

"No."

"Being poor doesn't mean you spend money carefully. Poor people can often be very generous."

"And rich people very mean with money," a man said.

We discussed this and I became so engrossed in this topic I soon realized that I was drunk and that my head hurt. When I shut up for a while they began to sing.

"What was that song about?" I asked when it was over.

"About Ru. Our ancestor. He found Aitutaki. With his four wives and his brothers."

That legend was mentioned in my guidebook, how Ru had voyaged from the island of Tupuaki, in what is now the Society Islands, which had become overcrowded. The first name of Aitutaki was *Ararau Enua O Ru Ki Te Moana*, "Ru in search of land over the sea."

In spite of the missionaries, local legend was alive and well. And the Cook group had been one of the first in the Pacific to be converted by the passionate clergyman John Williams: he had left Aitutaki a Polynesian convert, Papeiha, in 1821, and the Aitutaki Christian church, oldest in the Cooks (1828), had a tablet in the churchyard, one side extolling Williams, the other extolling Papeiha.

I said, "Where did Ru come from?"

"Maybe the Society Islands. Maybe Samoa."

"And before that?"

"Not Asia. I think Asia Minor. Where Adam and Eve came from."

Ah, that was the link between Polynesian legend and Christian tradition. Ru the voyager had sailed his canoe from the Holy Land.

I said, "What do you like best about living on an island?"

"We are free," one said.

"We can do whatever we like," another said.

I said, "But what if other people come? *Papa'a*. Or *tinito*. Or *manuiri*. Or Japanese?"

"We would kick them out."

"This is our island. We have everything."

They sounded fierce, but they were merely tipsy, and they followed me staggering to my boat and urged me to come back the next day. They promised to sing for me.

I could not explain why, but in the waning light of day, the sun going down beyond the lagoon, and paddling past one of the prettiest – and friendliest – islands I had seen, I felt very lonely. I heard that man saying *Where is your wife?* and the fact was that I no longer had one.

Soon I was paddling in night-blackened water, splashing like mad toward the lights on shore.

Being alone was the oddest aspect of my traveling in Oceania, because the island people of Oceania were never alone and could not understand solitude. They always had families – wives, husbands, children, girlfriends, boyfriends. To the average person on a reasonably sized island, nearly everyone was a relative. Wasn't this extended family one of the satisfactions of being an islander? Living on an island meant that you would never be alone.

There was no concept of solitariness among the Pacific islanders I traveled among that did not also imply misery or mental decline. Book-reading as a recreation was not indulged in much on these islands either – for that same reason, because you did it alone. Illiteracy had nothing to do with it, and there were plenty of schools. They knew from experience that a person who cut himself off, who was frequently seen alone – reading books, away from the hut, walking on the beach, on his own – was sunk in deep *musu*, and was contemplating either murder or suicide, probably both. Now and then, people would mention that a place had a much higher suicide rate than I could possibly imagine, and in truth I was usually rather surprised to hear the figures. Then they would describe the method – nearly always taking a dive off the top of a palm tree.

Marriage was seldom stressful, because the rest of the family was usually so supportive – the husband had his male friends, the wife had her female friends, the children were raised by all these uncles and aunties. When a marriage was that complex and seemingly casual, divorce was somewhat irrelevant. (And lots of people stayed married by having absolutely nothing to do with each other – by rarely being in contact.) This big family was circumscribed by the island, and so an island family was like an entire nation.

I met divorced people now and then. In the Trobriands a divorced woman was permanently eligible for marriage and was regarded with horror by single men: "I might have to marry her," they said. The Presbyterian stigma of divorce which had been imposed on the islands by severe missionaries in the nineteenth century was harsher than tradition had ever been, and was like the Mark of the Beast. Often a divorced person simply left the island – he or she had disappointed too many people or made enemies. They were the women who worked in hotels in the capital; they were the men who emigrated. Generally, it was not easy to become become divorced without seeming like a traitor.

All this made my position awkward: being solitary made me seem enigmatic, paddling alone made me seem like a true *palangi* "sky-burster," reading and writing made me look like a crank, and my being wifeless was a riddle. My condition was hard for anyone to relate to and impossible for me to explain. And I seemed to be challenged a lot in the Cooks. *Where's your wife?* Oh, God, let's not go into it. I could only approximate my feelings to them, and it would be like explaining something like Westminster Abbey but using only their references: "This very big *are* has a *marae* inside, and petroglyphs on the walls –"

I sometimes felt like the only person in Oceania who had wrecked his marriage, and I was reminded of that overwhelming sense of remorse I had felt that dark night in New Zealand, when I looked through the front window of the California Fried Chicken Family Restaurant on Papenui Road in Merivale and I saw a happy family and I burst into tears.

My solution was to keep paddling.

One evening, musing in this way, I was dragging my boat up the beach and saw a man strolling among the palms. He was white, probably a tourist, but something about his physique commanded my attention. He was an unusual shape – he was tall, with a full belly, and narrow shoulders, thin arms, rather spindly legs, and a large head; he was as unlike an islander in his general shape as it was possible to be. He looked like an English squire or ship's captain, who never missed a meal but seldom walked anywhere; well fed but under-exercised.

I turned my boat over and parked it under a palm. The man had paused and was looking back at it. He was gray-haired, with thick glasses, rather dainty hands that matched the slenderness of his arms. He was alert, perhaps restless, but he had a ready smile. For all I knew it was the simple good-will and fellow-feeling of one *papa'a* for another, but it was a bit more penetrating than that, not just an acknowledgement but a welcome.

"You look familiar," I said.

"David Lange," he said. "I used to be prime minister of New Zealand."

"How about a beer?"

"Lovely."

Now you are not alone, I told myself.

I had admired David Lange from a distance for helping to make New Zealand anti-nuclear. Here was one of the poorer industrial nations, needing world markets for its butter and lamb and wool, risking the economic retribution of America and Europe by lecturing them on the dangers of nuclear dependency, and going further and not allowing warships carrying nuclear material into New Zealand's harbors. It is usually expensive and lonely to be principled; this seemed like political suicide. But Lange stuck it out and won friends, and more than that he became an example for many world leaders. There were some exceptions. It was well known that the prime minister of Australia hated Lange for taking a stand, but then Bob Hawke – as Lange himself might have put it – had uranium on his breath.

And there was Lange's separation. It had been the current topic when I was in New Zealand – his estranged wife yelling her grievances, his mother denouncing him, and the combined snipers in the Kiwi press doing their best to destroy him. I had felt for him. His turmoil had come at the time of my own separation. I had identified with him, and in a quiet way felt he was an alter ego. We were almost exactly the same age. I read items with headlines like *"David Deceived Me," Says Lange's Wife* and I would cringe for him and for myself.

Yet what a funny old world it was. Here we were under the trees of Aitutaki, by the lagoon, in the failing light of day, the former prime minister and the former writer – which was how I felt – two clapped-out renegades taking refuge on a remote island.

I told him my name.

"Really? The writer?" and he named some of my books. "Are you writing something here?"

"No, just paddling."

But he of all people had to understand how a writer's denial was not very different from a politician's denial.

"I'm glad to hear it," he said, though he didn't seem convinced. "I'd love to write something about Aitutaki. I've been coming here for years. I've thought of writing some kind of book – like one of yours, about this place. Aitutaki is full of wonderful characters."

While we were seated having a beer, he said suddenly – his manner of speaking was rapid, he had a restless impatient intelligence – "You write about trains," and gulped his beer, and said, "Ultimate railway story. I was traveling from Delhi to Bombay in 1967. I was a student. In those days it took thirty-seven hours, but they had a wonderful dining car, with heavy silver and cloth napkins and waiters running to and fro. I had beef curry. The meat tasted strange, but of course it had been heavily spiced. I was violently ill afterwards, and I spent days in bed. I have never been so ill with food poisoning. And I wasn't the only one.

Most of the people who had the beef curry on that train ended up in the hospital."

He chuckled at the memory and then went on, "About a month later I read that one of the waiters on the Delhi to Bombay run had been arrested for supplying dismembered human corpses to the dining car, claiming they were fresh beef. They were hardly recognizable, of course, after they had been turned into curry."

The nature of a politician is to talk; the nature of a writer, to listen. So here we were on this lovely island, the public man and the private man, with plenty of time to practice our peculiar skills.

Lange talked often and well, and was affable. He greeted strangers, he had a good word for everyone, he introduced me around the island. If a small group congregated he took charge, and to simplify matters he would launch into a long humorous monologue as a substitute for a halting conversation. He had a parliamentarian's talent for avoiding all interruptions – rain, falling coconuts, loud music, pestering strangers, awkward questions; and he had the successful politician's gift for being able to repeat himself without being boring. I could vouch for Lange's ability to tell the same complex story (involving accents, mimicry, histori-cal detail and mounting suspense) three times in as many days with the same gusto.

I had gotten a sunburn on my jaunt down the chain of *motus*. I needed to stay under a tree for a while, and so the next three days I spent on and off with David Lange, who knew Aitutaki well, and we discussed (he talked, I listened) the *Rainbow Warrior* affair, the future of New Zealand, ditto of Australia, Ronald Reagan's senility, Saddam Hussein's paranoia, Margaret Thatcher, the Queen, Yoko Ono, Lee Kwan Yew of Singapore, Rajiv Gandhi, Chandra Shekar, the characteristics of various Pacific islanders – Tongans, Samoans, the Cooks, the characteristics of various Christian religions.

The most unsatisfying international gatherings Lange had ever attended, he said, were Commonwealth heads of government meetings. It was not just Margaret Thatcher nannying everyone and swinging her hand-bag, or Bob Hawke of Australia being personally abusive. It was the utter waste of time. The Bahamas meeting of 1985 was notable for its host, the prime minister of the Bahamas, "a remarkable character who came unscratched through an inquiry as to why in the past year he had put in his bank account an amount eighteen times greater than the total of his salary." At a similar meeting in Vancouver, Lange discovered that the Botswana delegation had made $1,300 worth of phone calls and charged them to his total bill. The Ugandans at that same conference, "took advantage of their leader's absence at a retreat to invite a fair number of Vancouver's prostitutes to their hotel. They refused to pay and had the police evict the women. Those were the greatest excitements of the conference."

I liked his frankness, and I found him funny. Lange was on familiar terms with the entire world and with its events. He had spent his working life making the acquaintance of powerful people. Whom had I met? I fished around and mentioned my trip to Fiji. Lange brightened. "Rabuka's a bully, and Kamisese Mara the prime minister is a stooge of the military government."

"I want to ask you about Dame Cath Tizard, your governor- general," I said.

"She won't be doing much governor-generalling," Lange said, talking a mile a minute and never ceasing to smile. "She'll be in court most of next year in a libel suit – she called someone an incompetent, and she's being sued for fourteen million dollars."

I began to explain my impression of her extraordinary table manners, but Lange rumbled on, still smiling.

"Her ex-husband's quite a character – caused an amazing fuss in Japan after the Emperor died and various world leaders were sending their condolences. He said the Emperor of Japan should have been cut into little pieces after the war."

Any conversational lull was my cue for asking a question, and he always gave me a straight answer, and this included questions about the break-up of his marriage and his relationship with his speech-writer, Miss Pope, and his mother's sticking her oar into the whole affair.

"Your mother apparently denounced you."

"Yes!" He was smiling. "She went on television! You should have heard her!"

"Was it one episode that ended your marriage or –?"

"We had been drifting apart," he said. "It happens so subtly you hardly notice. Then one day you look up and your marriage is over."

"But there's a woman in your life now?"

"Oh, yes. Margaret. Lovely person – you must meet her."

"What did your children say about the divorce?"

"Older child's in India, studying. That's my son. My daughter said, 'I suppose I'll have to get used to being spoiled, the way children of divorced parents always are.' She doesn't miss much."

"Did you ever get sad afterwards, thinking of the happy days of your marriage?"

"We had rather a turbulent marriage. Didn't you?"

"No. It was pretty quiet most of the time," I said. "I often find myself looking back and feeling awful."

"You've got to look ahead," he said, sounding decisive.

"Do you think you'll ever go back to your wife?"

"It's much too late for that," he said. "She's not doing too badly. She's just published a book of poems."

"What about you?"

"Here I am at the age of forty-eight and I don't have a bed or a chair. My wife got the lot."

He laughed out loud – not a mirthful laugh, but not a bitter one either. I was inexpressibly grateful to him for not evading my questions. He was not whining or blaming or trying to turn the clock back. I wanted to be as resolute as that, and in a way I wanted to stop paddling and reacquaint myself with the sort of contentment I had known in my early life – loving and being loved.

This divorce conversation produced the only silence that occurred between Lange and me.

And then he was back on world leaders, Oliver Tambo of the African National Congress: "When I met him he tried to justify 'necklacing.'"*

"As prime minister of Britain, Harold Wilson was a tricky man," he said, "but what's the future of the Labour Party of Britain? Bryan Gould? He's a New Zealander. He was my room-mate at college. How could he lead the Labour Party – he's not even British!"

He had just finished a book, *Nuclear Free – the New Zealand Way*, about his anti-nuclear policy in the Pacific and he was full of stories about sinister French plots.

"The French are swine," he said. "The night before the Arbitrator in the *Rainbow Warrior* affair delivered his verdict to the tribunal his house was broken into. Only one item was missing. The word processor which contained his files of the proceedings had been stolen, and a carving knife was left in its place."

In his book he wrote, *The testing at Mururoa still continues. Nothing in French history suggests that it will stop until countries more powerful even than*

---

*Note: A violent mode of aggression between political rivals in South African townships, this involved the placing of a gasoline-soaked rubber tire over an opponent's upper body and setting it and the live person on fire.

*France put a stop to it. I can only look forward to the day when they will want to.*

We talked into the night. The nights were starry on Aitutaki. It was an ideal island; it had one of the largest and most beautiful lagoons I had seen in Oceania. Its people were friendly and gentle, its food was plentiful; it had no telephones, no cars, no dogs.

More than once, after a peroration or an anecdote, Lange leaned over and said, "Are you sure you're not writing about this island?"

Towards the end of that week, I bumped into Lange on the beach again, and he said, "The Queen's Representative is leaving the day after tomorrow. There's a sort of do for him in town. Want to come along as my guest? Might be fun, even if you're not writing about this place."

"What is a Queen's Representative?"

"In this case an anachronism named Sir Tangaroa Tangaroa."

I spent the next day spear-fishing, using my mask and snorkel, and dragging my boat behind me. My idea was that I would make my way along the reef, and when I got sick of fishing I could paddle the remaining distance to the only *motu* I had not visited, Maina ("Little Girl"). There was the hulk of a ship near it that had been wrecked on the reef in the 1930s with a cargo of Model-T Fords.

Beyond the twists of plump black sea-slugs and tiny darting fish were the lovely parrot fish. I swam between the bulging lumps of coral, pursuing fish. *After you have seen the lovely colors of live fish, and how gray they look when they're dead on a slab, how can you eat them?* a vegetarian had once said to me. Soon I lost all interest in spearing fish and just snorkeled, and then – remembering there were sharks around this reef – I got back into my boat, and put on my Walkman and paddled.

On this lovely morning in the lagoon of Aitutaki I was listening to *Carmina Burana*. It was one of those days – I passed many in Oceania – when I forgot all my cares, all my failures, all my anxieties about writing. I was exactly where I wanted to be, doing what I liked most. I was far enough offshore so that the island looked distant and mysterious and palmy, and I moved easily through the greeny-blue lagoon, and I could hear the surf pounding on the reef between the movements of music.

The wind strengthened and I paddled on and saw more wrecked ships. They were strange monuments to the danger of this reef, and seemed fearsome and skeletal. They had a look of frozen violence – so large and rusted black. The oddest aspect of that was that there was no sense of anything happening on shore. It seemed so absurd that a captain should even steer his ship to Aitutaki, much less risk his whole enterprise on this reef. The island seemed to slumber dreaming its green dreams in its green shade. There was no industry, no traffic, no smoke even. It was the simplest quietest society I had seen. I seldom saw anyone cooking or gardening, or doing anything energetic except fishing. The island was almost motionless in the still hot mornings, and only at night after the drumming and dancing started did it come alive. The people were alert and could be talkative. It did not surprise me that life proceeded at the slowest possible pace, but rather that it proceeded at all.

Something about Cook Islanders (there were only 20,000 of them altogether) made them seem special. Even with all the patronage from New Zealand, and their passionate interest in videos, the people remained themselves. They were not greedy. They were not lazy. They were hospitable, generous and friendly. They were not violent, and they often tried to be funny, with little success.

One day early in my visit I had speared a parrot fish. I showed it to a man on shore, when I was beaching my boat.

"What do you think of this?"

"It is a fish," he said, deadpan.

"A good fat fish?"

"A normal fish," he said.

"But it's a good one, don't you think? A big one. Good to eat."

"A normal parrot fish," he said, refusing to smile. "A normal parrot fish."

Meanwhile I was still paddling to Maina. I had asked David Lange about the distinctiveness of the Cooks, and his explanation was that they had retained their character because they were still owned by the islanders. Not one acre had been sold to a foreigner. The land was sometimes leased, but it had not left their hands. This was also the basis of an anxiety – that the Japanese would come and somehow wrest the land away from them, trick them somehow. They hated and feared the Japanese, and I saw no Japanese tourists in the Cooks. "We don't want them!" a man in Aitutaki told me. "We will send them away!"

The wind was roaring in my headphones, blowing waves across my deck and slewing me sideways. I paddled on, feeling happy in this vast green lagoon, among turtles and glimmering coral, and at last reached Maina. Isolated and empty and hardly ever visited, in a distant corner of the lagoon, it was one of the most beautiful islands I walked upon in Oceania.

On the way to the feast for the Queen's Representative, David Lange showed me some new trucks parked in the Ministry of Works depot.

"They can't use them. They've been here for months. But they're using that dangerous old banger" – he indicated a jalopy, dumping logs – "you'll never guess why."

"Someone put a curse on them?"

"Close. They haven't been dedicated. They need a proper ceremony. It might be months before they manage that."

It was a God-fearing archipelago. Mormons, Jehovah's Witnesses, Seventh-day Adventists, Catholics, and the local outfit, Cook Island Christian Church, the CICC. The plaque to the martyr John Williams (eaten by Big Nambas in Erromanga in Vanuatu) should have been a tip-off, but there were churches everywhere, and crosses, mottoes, Bible quotes, grave-markers and monuments. The history of the Cook Islands was the history of missionaries – that, and a small trade in fish and coconuts. But mostly it was people's souls that were sought after, and some of the earliest photographs of Cook Islanders showed the men in long pants and women in Mother Hubbards, the modest all-embracing *muumuu*. The Mormons didn't drink, the Jehovah's Witnesses didn't smoke or vote, the Seventh-day Adventists didn't dance, the CICC didn't fish on the sabbath.

Still, life went on in its passive Polynesian way and somehow people managed still to dance, to drink, to smoke and sing and fish and make love. There was a local woman who had a reputation for simply appearing on the beach, offering herself, welcoming any and all fishermen, who made love to her. As for the dancers, they cleared their consciences by saying a prayer before every dance – then they drummed and twitched their bums and shook their tits; and afterwards they said another prayer.

There were prayers in the garden of the small tin-roofed bungalow that was the residence of the Administrative Officer of Aitutaki. Just a simple hut with a pretty garden. About thirty men and women joined in the prayer, and they all wore colorful shirts and dresses – there was no clothes snobbery at all in the Cook Islands. You wore a T-shirt and shorts, a bathing-suit, a *lava-lava*, and that was it. No socks, no shoes, no ties, no dress code at all.

Another day in Fatland – fat men, fat women. The fattest was the Queen's Representative, an older man – perhaps seventy – in a very tight Hawaiian shirt, a button missing where his belly bulged. This was Sir Tangaroa Tangaroa, QR. In spite of his titles he was a simple soul. But I had heard this word *tangaroa* before, in connection with Polynesian cosmology.

"What does 'tangaroa' mean?" I asked the mayor.

The mayor was the brother of the prime minister. *It's all nepotism here,* Lange had told me.

"His name is the name of god."

"God in Heaven?"

"No. One of our old gods."

"Which one?"

The mayor's own name was Henry and he looked a bit flummoxed.

"God of the sea? I think god of the sea."

This man Henry was very vague altogether. There was a big *marae* in the south of the island. I asked him where it was. He said, "Somewhere in the jungle. You will never find it."

Aitutaki was less than two kilometers wide at its widest point, and it was less than six kilometers long. *Somewhere in the jungle* had no meaning when dealing with a place this small, unless one was an islander and considered this island an entire world.

"Can't you tell me how to get there?"

"No. It is not easy. Someone will have to take you."

That was another thing about islanders: they were almost incapable of giving clear directions, because they had never needed to encapsulate directions by giving the location of a particular place. An island was a place where everyone knew where everything was, and if you didn't you had no business there.

I said, "But this is not a very big island."

"The *marae* is in the jungle."

"Even so, there's not much jungle. Do you ever go there?"

"I am so busy."

But this were merely an expression: no one was busy in Aitutaki.

I then approached the Queen's Representative.

"Have you spoken to Her Majesty?"

"Yes. For hours," he said, and blinked at me. "For many hours."

His English was very limited – in fact this was the whole of our conversation, for he soon lapsed happily into Maori – but he insisted that he had had long talks with Queen Elizabeth.

Lange had heard me quizzing the man. He said, "If you get the Queen alone she's very good – very funny. Loves New Zealand."

He said that he had spent some time with her alone when he'd been awarded the title CH, Companion of Honour, which was more coveted than a knighthood.

After the prayer in the garden the food was uncovered – and men and women stood near it, fanning away the flies, while we filled our plates with octopus in coconut milk, taro, sweet potato, pig meat, marinated raw fish (with skin and bones), banana fritters, fruit salad.

Lemonade was served, and then there was dancing – young men and women in grass skirts. The drummers sweated and smiled and people wandered into the garden from the dirt road to watch, gathering at the hedge or sitting on the grass. Children who had been playing on the grass since before the party began – they had no connection with the party – went on playing. It was all amiable. There were no ructions here.

The Queen's Representative smoothed his shirt-front – it was now splashed with food – and accepted his gifts, a woven mat and a piece of nicely stitched cloth. He spoke briefly but in a formal chiefly way, in his own language, Maori. He was from the little island of Penrhyn, an almost inaccessible atoll in the far north of the Cook group. He had spent six years making the rounds from island to island. Now he was on his final round, collecting gifts. A new QR would soon be sworn in – someone's relative.

Leaving the party, Lange turned to me and asked again, "Are you sure you're not writing about Aitutaki?" And he smiled, but instead of waiting for an answer he began to describe for me his recent experiences in Baghdad.

When I left Aitutaki it was Lange who saw me to the plane and we agreed to meet again. I went to Rarotonga, a pretty island entirely ringed by bungalows and small hotels. You couldn't paddle without paddling in someone's front yard. But there I had a sense of the murmurs of island life.

A New Zealand couple from Aitutaki recognized me on the road in Rarotonga and told me about the woman who wandered the beach and was such a rapacious fornicator with the Aitutaki fishermen.

When I tried to verify this story with an Australian he told me that the gossiping New Zealand couple had been heard quarreling loudly and abusively in their bungalow.

"He's the world's authority on giant clams," someone said of the Australian.

"You could get killed for fooling with fishermen," someone else said.

The gossips were gossiped about, and everyone had a story.

"Never guess who's in Aitutaki," another Australian said to me in a bar in Avarua, Rarotonga. "David Lange. Someone saw him get on the plane. He split up with his wife. He's out of office. He's fucked-up and far from home."

I said, "I have the feeling he's going to be fine."

# 21

# Easter Island: Beyond the Surf Zone of Rapa Nui

It was too dark to see anything, even at seven in the morning when I arrived on Easter Island, but there were the insinuating smells of muddy roads and damp dog fur, wet grass, briny air, and the sounds of barking and cockcrows, the crash of surf, and people speaking in Spanish and Polynesian. The Customs Inspector had been drinking. Someone muttered *"Borachito"* – tipsy.

On winter days on Easter Island the sun rises at eight in the morning and by five-thirty in the afternoon the light has grown so crepuscular there is not enough to read by – not that anyone reads much on this lost island of damaged souls. Long before sundown, the horses are tethered (there are few vehicles); the motor-boats are moored (there are no canoes, and haven't been for a hundred years); and anyone with money for a bottle of *pisco* – hooch – is quietly becoming *borachito*.

The island goes cold and dark, and except for dogs barking and the sound of the wind in the low bushes, there is silence. There are not many trees, there is only one town – a small one, Hanga-Roa – and as for the *moai*, the stone statues, no one goes near them after dark. They are associated with *akuaku* – spirits – and are the repository of the island's secrets. Many, many secrets, you have to conclude, because there are hundreds of stone heads on the island – upright and staring, lying down and eyeless, shattered and broken, some with russet topknots, others noseless or brained – more than 800 altogether. They are also known as *aringa ora*, "living faces."

The rest of the island is yellowing meadows with thick wind-flattened grass, and low hills, and the weedy slopes of volcanoes, but never mind that, or the fleeting thought that its landscape looks in some places like the coast of Wales and in others like Patagonia. It is totally itself, the strangest island I saw in the whole of Oceania – a place penetrated by gloom and anarchy. And a spooky place, too. *Te Pito o Te Henua*, "The Navel of the World," the early inhabitants called their island, and more recently Rapa Nui. Easter Island is smaller than Martha's Vineyard, and probably has fewer stony faces.

I passed through the airport building, which was just a wooden room with signs in Spanish, and went through Chilean customs (Easter Island, Isla de Pascua, is part of a province of Chile).

An attractive woman, obviously Polynesian, approached me.

She said, "May I offer you my residence?"

It takes an hour to fly from Rarotonga to Tahiti, and five and half from Tahiti to Easter Island. But connections in Oceania are seldom neat. I had two days to kill in Rarotonga, and three days in Papeete before I could head to this little island, the easternmost outpost of Polynesia.

My traveling time must be compared with that of the original migrants to Easter Island. They might have sailed from Rapa – now called Rapa-Iti – in the Austral Islands, 2,500 miles away. Or it might have been from Mangareva in the Gambier group. In any case, the journey in double-hulled canoes took them 120 days. This was sometime in the seventh century (though some archeologists have dated it earlier). On the other side of the world the Prophet Mohammed was fleeing to Medina (in the year 622), the start of the Moslem Era. The Dark Ages had taken hold of Europe. The glorious T'ang Dynasty had begun in China. In the Pacific, people were on the move, for this was the most active period of Polynesian expansion, which one Pacific historian has called "the greatest feat of maritime colonization in human history."

Before I left Tahiti I had called on the airline representative. He was Chilean. We conversed in Spanish. He spoke no other tongue.

"The plane is half full, maybe more," he said.

"All those people going to Easter Island!"

"No. Only four passengers are getting off there. The rest are going to Santiago."

"Will the weather be cold on Easter Island?"

"Sometimes. Especially at night." He flapped his hand, equivocating. "You have a sweater? That's good."

"What about rain?"

"It can rain at any time. And wind. You will have some wind. But not too much." He smiled at the ceiling and he blinked for effect as he chanted, "Sun. Cloud. Sun. Cloud."

He was trying to encourage me.

"Now the hotels are interesting," he said. "I know you don't have one. You never have one before you go. But at the airport, the island people will look at you and offer their houses to you. You will see them and talk to them. That way you can find the most economical one."

He then searched for my reservation.

"Your name is not on the passenger list," he said. "But come tomorrow. If you don't have a ticket we will sell you one. There is space. There are always seats to Easter Island."

That was my preparation for the journey – that and a vast tome entitled *The Ethnology of Easter Island*, by Alfred Metraux, and the writings of other archeologists, and much colorful and misleading information by the enthusiastic Thor Heyerdahl, who is regarded by many Pacific historians and archeologists as of minimal consequence to serious archeology. Scientifically, his books have as little value as those of Erich von Danniken, who theorized that the Easter Island *moai* were carved by people from outer space.

I found a place to stay, a guest-house, and agreed on a price – sixty-five dollars a day, which included three meals a day. I planned to camp, too – no one seemed bothered, as they had on other islands, by the threat of my pitching a tent.

Stretching my legs after arriving, I walked to the Easter Island Museum. It was one mute room on a hillside at the edge of town. There are some carvings, and some dusty skulls with drawings scratched on the craniums, and artifacts, but no dates have been assigned to anything in the room. There are old photographs of melancholy islanders and hearty missionaries. There are ill-assorted implements – axes, clubs, knives. One exhibit shows how the *moai* had carefully fitted eyes, most of them goggling – the sclera of the eye made of white coral, the iris of red scoria and the pupil a dish of obsidian, which gave the statues a great staring gaze.

Many of the *moai* had been ritually blinded by the islanders themselves. The archeologist JoAnne Van Tilburg mentions how "specific, probably ritual damage was done to only certain parts of the figures, in particular the heads, eyes, and occasionally the right arms."

That first day, I ran into an island woman who was secretary of the Rapa Nui Corporation for the Preservation of Culture, known locally as *Mata Nui o Hotu Matua o Kahu Kahu o Hera* ("The Ancestral Group of Hotu Matua of the Obscure Land"). She confirmed various stories that I had read about the island.

Hotu Matua was the leader of the first migration to Easter Island. Descended from ancestral gods, this first king had *mana*, great spiritual power, and is credited with the founding of this civilization. Much of the early history is conjecture – there are so-called wooden *rongo-rongo* tablets, with strange figurative script incised on them, but no one has ever been able to decipher them. In spite of this, most of the stories regarding Hotu Matua agree on the salient points. That he sailed from an island (Marae-renga, perhaps Rapa) in the west, commanding two ninety-foot canoes. That he brought with him "hundreds and hundreds" of people. That some of these people were nobles (*ariki*) and others skilled men and women (*maori*) – warriors, planters, carvers – and still others commoners. That the captain of the second canoe was a noble named Tuu-ko-ihu. That on board these canoes they had "the fowl, the cat, the turtle, the dog, the banana plant, the paper mulberry, the hibiscus, the ti, the sandalwood, the gourd, the yam" and five more varieties of banana plant. (Later generations gave Hotu Matua credit for introducing animals which early explorers introduced, such as pigs and chickens).

After sailing for two months in the open sea, the voyagers came upon the island and they sailed completely around it, looking for a place to land. After their tropical home, this windy treeless island must have seemed a forbidding place: then, as now, black cliffs being beaten by surf. They found the island's only bay, its only sandy beach. They went ashore there, and named the bay Anakena, their word for the month of August. It was an island of seabirds and grass. There were no mammals. The craters of the volcanoes were filled with *totora* reeds.

Another happy incident, which occurs in all versions of this first-arrival story, is that shortly after Hotu Matua's canoe reached the shore of the island, one of Hotu Matua's wives, named Vakai, gave birth to a baby boy, Tuu-ma-heke, who became the island's second king. The cutting of the infant's navel cord caused the place to be called *Pito-o-te-henua*, Navel of the Land.

The woman who was telling me these stories said that she was a teacher of the Rapa Nui language. But was there such a language? She claimed there was, but linguists said that the original tongue had been lost, and that the language spoken on Easter Island now was the Tahitian the Christian missionaries had brought – because that was the language of their Bible and hymn book. Because this Tahitian had many similarities to the old Rapa Nui it had displaced it. Easter Islanders were identified as Polynesians when they boarded Cook's ship in 1774. As soon as they spoke, Cook recognized that their language was similar to Tahitian.

Looking for a place to launch my boat I walked down the main road of the town, a dirt track called in the local language Navel of the World Street, past grubby little bungalows – they had the shape and dimensions of sheds: flat roofs, single walls – to Hanga-Roa harbor.

It was not like any harbor I had ever seen, and it explained why if you totalled the time all the early explorers spent ashore on Easter Island, it would amount to very little. Few of the nineteenth-century explorers, Metraux says, "stayed on the island for more than a few minutes." Some of the explorers, having made the 2,500-mile run from Tahiti (and it was nearly as far from South America), were unable to go ashore – too windy, too dangerous, too surfy. In 1808, for example, Captain Amasa Delano of Duxbury, Massachusetts (and of Melville's story "Benito Cereno") arrived at the island and sailed around it, but could not set foot on the island, because of the heavy surf off Hanga-Roa.

Some ships did land, to the sorrow of the islanders. In 1804, the men on an American ship, the *Nancy*, kidnapped twelve men and ten women from the island after a fight – the intention was to use these captives as slave-laborers at a seal colony on Mas Afuera, a rock halfway to Chile. When the islanders were allowed on deck after three days at sea, they jumped off the ship and began swimming in the direction of their island, and all drowned. Whaling ships plying the southern oceans often abducted Easter Island girls, for their sexual pleasure.

"In 1822 the skipper of an American whaling ship paused at Easter Island long enough to kidnap a group of girls who were thrown overboard the following day and obliged to swim back to the island," Metraux writes. "One of the officers, simply for amusement, shot a native with his gun."

After more raids of this sort the islanders became hostile to any foreigners. But the foreigners persisted, either fighting them or employing more devious means to subvert the islanders, using gifts as bait, as in this raid in 1868: "the raiders threw to the ground gifts which they thought most likely to attract the inhabitants and . . . when the islanders were on their knees scrambling for the gifts, they tied their hands behind their backs and carried them off to the waiting ship." The King, Kaimakoi, was kidnapped with his son and most of the island's *maori* (experts). These and later captives were sent to work, digging on guano islands, where they all died.

The history of Easter Island in the nineteenth century is a long sad story of foreign raiding parties (mainly American and Spanish), of slavery and plunder, leading to famine, venereal disease, smallpox outbreaks, and ultimately the ruin of the culture – the place was at last demoralized and depopulated. In 1900 there were only 214 people living on Easter Island, eighty-four of them children. A hundred years of foreign ships had turned Easter Island into a barren rock.

The island had flourished by being cut off, and then it became a victim of its remoteness. Since the earliest times, it had never been easy to land on it, but it was so far from any other port, and in such a rough patch of ocean, that every ship approaching it took advantage of it in some way – looking for water or food, for women, for slaves.

How was it possible for even a small ship to land here? In fact it had never been managed. No more than a scooped-out area, with boulders lining the shore and surf pounding beside the breakwater, the harbor was a horror, and it was difficult even to imagine a ship easily lying at anchor offshore, with a whaleboat plying back and forth with supplies. Problem one was mooring a ship in the wild ocean off Hanga-Roa; problem two was getting the whaleboat through the surf to shore and, since there was nowhere to land, steadying it long enough to unload it.

I saw that I could paddle through the surf zone. But it was usually easier to get out than to paddle in. The danger here was that the surf was breaking on large rocks at the harbor entrance. Even if I surfed in I might be broken to smithereens on the rocks.

The most ominous sight for a potential kayaker was that of Rapa Nui boys surfing into the harbor on big breaking waves. This surfing, locally known as *ngaru*, had been a sport here since the earliest times, and was the only game that had survived all these years. They had abandoned the ancient games of spinning tops, flying kites and going to the top of volcanoes and sliding down "tracks on which they had urinated to make the path more slippery." But surfing had been useful in the early innocent days of foreign ships anchoring off Hanga-Roa in a heavy sea. Surprising the seamen, the islanders swam out to the ship, using "swimming supports" – a plank or a rush mat. Some of the islanders were observed surfing back to shore afterwards, riding the waves and using the planks as surfboards.

In the Rapa Nui language there was a complete set of surfing terminology, which described the board, the surfer's waiting for the wave, allowing the wave to crest, and settling on the wave; what in current surfing jargon would be the banana of the pig-board (or sausage-board), the pick-up and take-off, the cut-back on the hump, hotdogging, hanging ten and walking the plank. In the olden days there had been surfing contests and some men, real Rapa Nui beachies, had gone far from shore to surf a long distance on the large ocean swells.

But the sight of surfers convinced me that this was not a good area to paddle from – and it was the harbor!

A place called Hanga-Piko, a rocky bay farther along, looked slightly more promising, but studying it closely – I walked along the shore and watched the breakers for about twenty minutes – I saw that it would be tricky here, too, because of big rollers – they tumbled in from the deep sea without anything to stop them or modify them.

I walked another mile to Anakai Tangata, an ominously named cave (meaning "The Cave Where Men Are Eaten") with petroglyphs on the walls, and nearby some stone foundations of ancient houses still existed. The stones had holes in them, where poles were inserted, for the tall tent-like structure which was then thatched. Below this place were sea-cliffs, and beyond was the volcano Rano-Kau. In the sky here and all over the island were hawks – the *cara-cara*, which the Chileans had introduced to rid the island of rats. The hawks were numerous, and highly competitive – they flew close to the ground, they perched fear-lessly, they swept down on anything that moved, they were intrepid raptors.

There were groves of thin peeling eucalyptus trees rattling in the wind on the lower slopes of the volcano. These had been planted by the Forestry Commission. I followed the dirt road that wound through them, seeing no one, only hawks. At the top I had a lovely view of the crater, and because this volcano was at the edge of the sea, beyond the crater's rim was the blue ocean. In the depths of the crater was a lake, with totora reeds, papyrus thickets and steep walls, and in the most protected part of the crater – the lower edge, out of the wind – there were banana trees and an orange grove.

Orongo, the site of the Bird-Man cult, was at the lip at the far side of the crater, high above the sea. That was another mile onward, and on the way I ran into a Rapa Nui man, Eran Figueroa Riroroko.

Riroroko was about thirty, a handsome stocky man, who lived in a hut near Orongo and passed the time carving hardwood into animals shapes. In halting Spanish, he explained the Bird-Man cult – how in the ancient times the men gathered on the cliffs here every September (the austral spring). At a given signal they went out to the island, Motu Nui, about two kilometers offshore. It was not far, but the water was notorious for sharks.

"They went in canoes?"

"Swimming." *Nadando.*

Every ship that called at Easter Island in the eighteenth and nineteenth centuries remarked on the brilliant swimming skills of the islanders, but these *hopu*, candidates for the title Bird-Man, had to bring food with them. They scrambled up the ledges of Motu Nui to bivouac and wait for the first sooty tern's egg of the season. When the first egg was laid and seized, the lucky man who held it called out his victory, and then tied it to his head in a little basket and swam to shore. He had no fear of sharks or waves, for the egg contained powerful *mana*. And his capture of the sacred egg meant that for a year he was Bird-Man – he had great authority, he lived in a special house, gifts were brought to him, and with this sudden assumption of power he settled any old scores he had – *I'm the king of the castle, and you're a dirty rascal*, as a schoolchild might put it – for now, with this *mana*, he had warriors on his side, who would do as he bid.

Bird-Man petroglyphs – a beaked creature of grotesque strength – were incised in the boulders and cliff faces all over Orongo, along with portraits of the great god Makemake, who was on Easter Island what Tiki or Atua were elsewhere in Polynesia. Smaller, broken ovals cut into the rock were depictions of vulvas – all over the island, on cliff faces and in caves, there were old carvings of vulvas (*komari*), which were cut by priestly elders when a girl reached puberty. These priests comprised a special class and were given the title *ivi-atua*, "kinsmen of the gods."

The Bird-Man cult, with its eggs, and the vulvas, and the solstice, all suggested that Orongo was associated with sexuality and fertility. On the bluff at Orongo there were also small stone dwellings built into the cliffs, dry-stone burrows and pillboxes with crawl-in openings, in which people had lived when this cult flourished.

"Do you get frightened at night up here by the ghosts?" I used the local word for ghosts – *akuaku*.

Riroroko said, "Yes, there could be *akuaku* here. Devils, I mean."

"Are you a Christian?"

"Yes. Catholic."

"Have you traveled away from the island?"

"I have been to Tahiti. To Santiago. To Venezuela."

"Were you tempted to stay at any of those places?"

"No. Tahiti was unbelievably expensive," he said (*tremenda-menda caro*). "But I was just looking. I just wanted to get to know them. I would never live in those places. Santiago is full of people, traffic, and bad air. I needed to come back here where the air is clean."

"What language did you speak in Tahiti?"

"I spoke Rapa Nui and people understood me. Tahitian is very similar – close enough so that they can understand. I liked the people."

I walked down the volcano, five miles, taking a short cut through the eucalyptus plantation, but on the outskirts of Hanga-Roa I was footsore, and now from every roadside hut a crazy hostile dog ran at me.

A beat-up jeep, with music blaring, shuddered along the road. I stuck out my hand.

"I'm Rene," the driver said. "He's Mou."

They were two grinning wild-haired youths.

"You speak Spanish?"

"Yes. But Rapa Nui is better."

"What's that music?"

"AC-DC." An Australian rock group.

They dropped me on Navel of the World Street and sped away.

When night fell at six or so, the island went black, and apart from wandering boys and homeward-bound drunks, no one stirred. I went to bed early and listened to my short-wave radio in the dark. The news was of floods in south China, which had drowned two thousand people. That was the entire population of Rapa Nui.

The west coast seemed as unpromising for paddling as the south coast. There was a heavy swell, and high surf dumping on black bouldery shores. The islands marked on my chart were not islands at all, but like Motu Nui in the south – slick black rocks, washed by foaming breakers. God help anyone who tried to land a boat on one.

I hiked along a road that narrowed to a path, which degenerated and lost itself among the grass on the high cliffs. But I liked the island's obscurity. It resembled the Marquesas in having no signposts, no information at all. Half a mile from town there was an *ahu* with a line-up of five heads. I knew this was Tahai because of the paddling chart I had with me. Farther on there were more *moai* and some of them had had their eyes reinserted and were staring inland – in fact, all the statues on the island had their backs turned to the sea. They were carved from brownish volcanic stone, they averaged five or six tons apiece, some had topknots or hats carved from red scoria.

Their size would have been overwhelming enough, even if they had been badly carved. But these were brilliantly executed, with long sloping noses and pursued lips and sharp chins. Their ears were elongated, and the hands clasping the body had long fingers, the sort you see on certain elegant Buddhas. Some of the statues had a mass of intricate detail on their back. And although there were similarities among the statues' profiles, each one had a distinctly different face.

When the first Europeans came to this island in 1722 all these "living faces" were upright. The first chronicler (Carl Beherns, who was on Roggeveen's ship) wrote, "In the early morning we looked out and could see from some distance that [the islanders] had prostrated themselves towards the rising sun and had kindled some hundreds of fires, which probably betokened some morning oblation to their gods . . ." And this veneration might also have been related to the fact that the islanders had just had their first look at a Dutch ship and a mass of pale jug-eared sailors.

A little more than fifty years later, Cook recorded that many of the statues had been knocked over. And by 1863, all the statues were flat on the ground and broken – a result of warfare, competition, and an iconoclastic frenzy that periodically possessed the islanders.

Stranger than the towering statues that stood and stared were the enormous fragments of broken heads and faces, tumbled here and there on the cliffs – just lying there among the cowshit and tussocky grass.

Every rock on Rapa Nui looks deliberate, like part of a wall or an altar or a ruin. Many of them are carved or incised – with mystical symbols, with images, with vulvas. Most are black basketball-sized boulders and have the character of building blocks, as though they have been shaped for some structural purpose. I wondered whether it was ignorant of me to imagine this. Hiking alone all day can inspire fanciful thoughts. But at lunchtime, sitting among a mass of boulders, I saw that they led to a cave entrance, and I crawled into one that was walled, big enough to hold three people. (Islanders had hidden in these caves to escape the attention of slavers, the so-called "blackbirders").

I walked along the high cliffs of the west coast, to Motu Tautara and the caves near it in which lepers had once lived, and beyond to where the island's highest volcano, Mount Terevaka, sloped to the sea. There were *moai* on this northwest coast, too – isolated heads, some of them fallen and broken. Heads like these, looking complete and final, were so far from any habitation that they had that hopeless and rather empty gaze of Ozymandias.

You come to a place you have read about your whole life, that is part of the world's mythology of mystery and beauty, and somehow you expect it to be overrun – full of signs and guidebooks and brochures, and other similarly rapt pilgrims and individuals. That very anxiety can forestall any real anticipation, and so you might procrastinate, fearing that it might be another Stratford-upon-Avon with Willy Shakespeare souvenirs, or Great Wall of China packed with tour buses, or Taj Mahal, entrance fee ten rupees. Instead of risking disappointment, isn't it better to stay away?

But Easter Island is still itself, a barren rock in the middle of nowhere, littered with hundreds of masterpieces of stone carving, blown by the wind, covered in grass, and haunted by the lonely cries of seabirds. It is not as you imagine it, but much stranger, darker, more complex, eerier. And for the same reason that it always was strange: because it is so distant and infertile an island.

Late in the afternoon there was a sudden downpour, and as the heavy rain persisted I ran for shelter, taking refuge under a cliff. I crouched there for about twenty minutes before it dawned on me that other people had done exactly what I had done: I was crouching in an ancient shelter, which had been hollowed from the cliff and decorated with petroglyphs, and the sides shored up by bouldery walls. If it hadn't rained I would not have found it.

Walking up this west coast, looking for an ancient canoe ramp or a place to launch my boat, I marveled at the emptiness of the island, and lamented the decline of its ancient culture. It is not as though it was swept away. The material culture was so substantial that now more than twelve hundred years after the first *moai* were carved (Tahai I, just down this coast, was dated and shown to have been in use around A.D. 690) they still exist and still look terrifying, their expressions sneering, *Look on my works, ye Mighty, and despair!*

I didn't find a place on this coast to launch from but I was heartened none the less by the utter emptiness – just me, and the staring heads, and the soaring hawks.

On my way back to Hanga-Roa I took an inland route and first met a man herding cows who said hello in Spanish, and then ran across a younger fellow, a Rapa Nui named Iman, about twenty-five or so, who had recently arrived back from Paris where he had been supervising his grandfather's business. He had agreed to look after his aging parents on the island.

"How do you like Rapa Nui?"

"I hate it."

I asked him why.

"There is nothing here," Iman said. "Nothing to do. Nothing happens."

Near sunset we walked towards town. There were cacti and palms growing near some of the houses, and others had banana trees in their gardens. In spite of these plants the island did not feel tropical. It could be warm in the day, but it was cool at night. Always there was the smell of damp or dusty roads and the stink of dog fur.

We came across the carcass of a horse. The thing had died on the road and it had lain there all day. Children were pitching stones at it, but timidly, as though at any moment they expected the corpse to scramble to its feet and neigh at them.

"Look at that," I said.

"It is a dead horse," Iman said. "It collapsed this morning. It belongs to the man Domingo. I saw it fall over."

"And yet you say that nothing happens here."

I rented a jeep and drove with my tent and collapsible boat to the top of the island, to Anakena, where Hotu Matua and the first canoes had arrived, where the first true Rapa Nui person had been born. It was a lovely protected bay, with a sandy beach, and just above the beach seven *moai*, some with cylindrical topknots, others decapitated.

Camping there I dreamed of the writer Jerzy Kosinski, who had killed himself a few months before, how he laughed when I told him that I liked camping. Perhaps the dream had come to me because I had read an article about him recently. The piece said that he had had no writer friends. But I had known him and regarded him as a friend. He seemed a bit paranoid and insecure, and vain in an unexplainable way. One night in Berlin he had gone back to the hotel and put on a type of male make-up, giving his pale Polish complexion an instant tan. What was that all about? He told me that he was afraid of assassination attempts, of being the object of sinister plots.

But it was the opposite that he feared – not notoriety. He was afraid of being ignored, not taken seriously; he could not stand being regarded as insignificant, or of his gifts being belittled.

"He likes to camp," Jerzy said to his then girlfriend (and, later, wife), Katarina. His Polish-Jewish accent made what he said sound like sarcasm, but I didn't mind. He seemed to find my life negligible. I found his horrifying. Oh, well.

He could not understand my incessant travel. I could not understand his need to be a Yale professor, hurrying up to New Haven to give lectures on the evils of watching television. He needed to be an intellectual. East European writers use that word all the time to describe themselves. I hated the word. He liked power. He wanted to be respectable. When he ceased to be respected – in the end he had actually been mocked for being a lightweight and suspected plagiarist – he killed himself.

I woke up in my tent under the palms at Anakena thinking: A

traveler has no power, no influence, no known identity. That is why a traveler needs optimism and heart, because without confidence travel is misery. Generally, the traveler is anonymous, ignorant, easy to deceive, at the mercy of the people he or she travels among. The traveler might be known as "The American" or "The Foreigner" – the *palangi*; the *popaa*, as they said here in Rapa Nui. But there was no power in that.

A traveler was conspicuous for being a stranger, and consequently was vulnerable. But, traveling, I whistled in the dark and assumed all would be well. I depended on people being civil and on observing a few basic rules. Generally I felt safer in a place like Anakena than I would have in an American city – or American camp site, for that matter (mass murderers were known to lurk around camp sites). I did not expect preferential treatment. I did not care about power or respectability. This was the condition of a liberated soul, of course, but also the condition of a bum.

A small Rapa Nui boy watched me setting up my boat later that day on the beach at Anakena.

I pointed to the seven carvings on the huge *ahu* and asked him in Spanish, "What do you call those?"

"*Moai*," he said.

"Are they men or gods?"

"Gods." *Dios*.

The water at Anakena was no colder than that in Cape Cod Bay in July. Because there was no one here to tell me anything about the hazards – the current, the tides, the submerged rocks, the sharks – I paddled out in stages, to test the current and the wind. There was a light northerly wind blowing onshore, into the bay, and moderate surf. I made it to the opening of the bay and paddled east for a few miles and saw only waves crashing against the black rocks of the island. Once past Ure-Mamore Point (Punta Rosalia on my chart) I could see all the way to the far eastern headland of the island, more high cliffs rising to another of Rapa Nui's four volcanoes; this one was Pukatike on Poike Peninsula. There was a surf break nearer shore, which meant that I had to stay about a quarter-mile from the island to avoid being tipped over and dashed against the rocks. But still I felt pleased having come this far, and justified in having brought my boat.

I had water and food in the boat, but the sea was so rough – the wind bashing my beam – that I could not put my paddle down long enough to eat anything. Instead, I went out farther (it was a safe wind: if I had tipped over I would have been blown back in to shore) and then in a westerly direction, past Anakena again, and onward, blundering toward another headland, Punta San Juan. The wind picked up and the sea was filled with breaking waves and cross-winds, and once again, looking along the whole coast toward another corner of this triangular island – Cabo Norte – I was amazed by what a rocky, inhospitable shore it presented: nowhere to land, nothing but breakers and black boulders.

I was listening on my Walkman to a Charlie Parker tape, "Apex of Bebop" – it suited the surf, the tumbling clouds, the chop, the waves, every soaring bird: *Crazeology* and *Yardbird Suite* and *Out of Nowhere* and *Bird of Paradise*.

Standing in the sunshine on the grassy slope of a volcano, among big-nosed stone heads, sniffing the heather, I had had no real idea of what an intimidating island this could seem. It was cows and meadows and huts, and smashed statuary. It was bleary-eyed and rather grubby Polynesians, and Chileans from the mainland.

From my boat the island seemed truly awful and majestic, a collection of grassy volcanoes, beaten by surf, and surrounded by more than two thousand miles of open water. It was not like any other island I had seen in Oceania. Tanna had been rocky, Guadalcanal had been dense and jungly, the Marquesas had been forbidding – those deep valleys, full of shadows. But Rapa Nui looked terrifying.

The tide was ebbing in the late afternoon when I returned to Anakena – the water had slipped down to reveal protruding rocks. I beached my boat and saw a woman walking along the beach. Her name was Ginny Steadman, and she was a painter, who had come here with her husband, Dave, an archeologist, who was digging near the *ahu* above Anakena.

I talked a while with Ginny – about islands we had visited – but I found it hard to concentrate, because all the while I was thinking of how about six or eight months previously I had had a premonition of this exact moment – the way everything was positioned: how the sunlight hit the water, the slope of the beach, the angle of the boat, Ginny herself, the sight of the bay, even the air temperature and the swooping birds, so vivid a déjà-vu – *I have seen this before*, I thought – that I resisted telling her, afraid the poor woman would be startled.

Dave Steadman was up to his neck in a symmetrically stepped pit. He talked without interrupting his digging and sifting and sorting. He had spent years traveling the Pacific, looking for the bones of extinct birds. Later, I read about him, how he had discovered new species of rails, of gallinules, of parrots, and as one of the world's authorities on the extinction of species he had published many articles – *Extinction of Birds in Eastern Polynesia, Holocene Vertebrate Fossils in the Galapagos*, and others. He told me he was looking for bone fragments, but he said he picked up anything that looked interesting.

"Here's some flakes of various kinds – obsidian – and a drill."

It was a chipped stick of stone, about two inches long.

"That was for drilling wood or bone – or making tools."

He had small plastic bags of sorted bird bones.

"These might be shearwaters or petrels." He pointed to the pit he had dug. "There's lots of extinct birds down there. Not many up here on the surface. What have you got here? No trees. Hardly any birds. The *cara-cara* was introduced. They've got that gray finch. A few terns. Masked booby. Frigate bird. That's about it."

He did not stop digging, and now Ginny was sifting through the sand he shoveled into mesh-bottomed boxes.

"You can always tell what a place was like when you dig," Dave said. "Polynesians got to an island and they started eating. And they didn't stop. Within a hundred years or so they ate everything – all the birds are gone. That's the first level – extinct birds. At the next level you find different bones – dogs, pigs. Then another level and, hey" – he glanced out of the pit, just his head showing – "they start chowing down on each other."

"Was there much cannibalism here?" I asked.

Metraux had said there was, but he had done no digging. He had collected old stories about the *kai-tangata*, "man-eaters," on Easter Island: the way that victorious warriors ate their slain enemies after a battle, though sometimes people were killed to provide a special dish for a feast. Human fingers and toes "were the most palatable bits." On at least one occasion some Peruvian slavers were ambushed and eaten.

"Yes. Human bones have been found here, mixed together with fish bones and bird bones," David said. "There was cannibalism all over Polynesia. In the Cooks, in Tonga, the Marquesas. Everywhere. You see the evidence when you dig. As soon as the population gets to a certain level people start chowing down on their neighbors."

He had returned to his digging, but he was still talking.

"Some guy's taro patch is bigger than yours? You want his *mana*? You kill him and you chow down." After a moment, he added, "Cannibalism was big here in the sixteenth century."

Inevitably, our discussion turned to Thor Heyerdahl.

Dave, who as an archeologist was the straightest talker I had met, as well as the most down-to-earth, said, "Thor Heyerdahl is perhaps the most fanciful adventurer to hit the Pacific."

This made Ginny wince, but then she smiled and nodded agreement.

"Many things he says about Easter Island are incorrect," Dave said. "He dreams something one night, makes a connection, and the next day he puts it into his book. See, he already has his theory. He just looks for ways of proving it. That's not scientific. And he commits the worst sin of an archeologist – he has been known to buy artifacts from the locals as well as carrying out digs. If you dig them up you get provenential information. But when you buy them you know nothing."

He dumped another bucket of sand for Ginny to sift.

"I guess you could say that because of him, Easter Island is on the map," he said. "There's been more archeology done here than on any other single place in the Pacific. But want my opinion of it? It's shitty archeology. It's some of the worst excavation in the Pacific. No one knows anything here. They get a big bag of bones and chips, and they don't know where the stuff comes from. It's all a mystery."

Dave pointed with his trowel at the *ahu* with the seven *moai* on it, their backs turned to us.

"Look at that *ahu*. To rebuild it, they had to move tons of sand – right here, a whole mountain of it. What was in it? Where did it go? Think of all the information that was lost! And you can't criticize the guy who did it, because he's an archeologist."

"What about the reed-boat theory?" I asked. "That was disproved, wasn't it?"

"Yes. By Flenley's pollen studies. He proved that the reeds in the crater are 28,000 years old. How could they have been brought by South Americans? And the thing is, Heyerdahl was here when Flenley read his paper. He just sat there. He didn't say anything. It was ridiculous."

But closely questioned, Dave became less rambunctious and more scientific. He even stopped shoveling to explain.

"See, the lake sediment contains pollen, and the anoxic mud preserves the pollen. So you do a core, for $x$ number of meters, and then you radiocarbon date it. They're good tests. They're real diagnostic."

The Steadmans covered their hole and left, and when they were gone it began to rain. Then the clouds blew past, and I was alone in pink late-afternoon sunshine. And I thought that, even without the *moai*, it would be a lovely island, because of the volcanoes – the craters and hornitos – and the long grassy sweep of their slopes.

The sunset, purple and pink, altered slowly like a distant fire being extinguished, and then cold black night fell for thirteen hours.

Everyone goes home and shuts the door when darkness falls, and at night on Easter Island I had a sense of great suspicion and separation, of distinct households, of a competitive, feuding society, full of old unresolved quarrels, in which there was quite a lot of petty theft, suspicion, envy, evasion, and insincerity. The toughness and self-reliance of the people made these traits even more emphatic.

The next morning I went across the island, into town, to send a fax. It was simple enough. It went through the only phone in town, at the Entel/Chile communications center, where there was a large satellite dish. It was also possible to receive a fax there, for a dollar a page, or to make international phone calls (Easter Island was in the same time zone as Denver). Every day that office received by fax the news pages of the Santiago newspaper, *Las Noticias*, and these pages were tacked to the wall of the office: this wall newspaper was the nearest Easter Island got to having a paper but, in any case people only read it when they were making a long-distance call.

The Steadmans were back at Anakena, digging again the following day, sifting for bird bones and chips, and they seemed to me among the unsung heroes of Pacific archeology. Their fieldwork, like most scientific research, was laborious and undramatic, but it yielded indisputable results. And nearly every shovelful had something of value in it.

Dave picked up a small bone from the screen. He blew the dust from it.

"This is a bone from the inner ear of a porpoise."

"Did it swim here?"

"No. Someone chowed down on it. This is a habitation site," he said, gesturing at the pit he had dug. "It's all food here. And there's enough organic material in that bone to date it."

"Is this what you've done in other places in the Pacific?"

"Pretty much so. We dig, we collect what we can. Most people ignore us. We don't care about that."

Ginny said, "Except for Tonga."

"We got some hostility in Tonga," Dave said. "'Fucking *palangi*' – that stuff. We kind of like the Cooks."

"Women don't get hassled in the Cooks," Ginny said. "They left me alone."

"There's a rain forest in Eua, in Tonga," Dave said. "When we were there in eighty-seven we said, 'Take care of it. Eco-tourism is the big thing now. People will want to come here and experience this rain forest.' They said, 'Yeah. Yeah. Great idea.'"

He was digging again – digging and talking.

"We went back two years later. Now some Japs are planning a hotel and golf course in Eua, right in the rain forest."

It was pleasant to talk with people as widely traveled and knowledge-able as the Steadmans. I proposed that they write a Book of Extinct Birds. They said they had thought of it already, and might just do it. I asked Dave about the megapode birds I had seen in the Solomons. He was full of information, and had seen megapode skeletons – an extinct one as big as a turkey – but never a live bird. I described for him the pleasure of eating a megapode-egg omelette.

He found the Easter Islanders an even greater riddle than their artifacts, but in their own way just as ruined.

"I've seen more hard-core debauchery on this island than anywhere else in the Pacific."

"Like what?"

"You name it."

It was the drinking most of all that alarmed him. A bottle existed to be emptied. Even a full bottle of whisky was gone by the following morning.

"Their attitude is, 'If you've got 'em, smoke 'em.'"

After I had chosen a spot and set up camp, I saw that I was only a half a mile from the famous *moai* quarry at the volcano Rano-Raraku. I walked there and spent the rest of the day wandering among the stone heads. From a distance, the heads look like the stumps of enormous trees, but walking closer you see how distinct they are. Most of them were two or three times my height. I counted thirty of them, then walked a bit farther and counted a dozen more. There are over a hundred of them here, on the slope of the volcano, from which they were carved. They have enigmatic faces, highly stylized, like the characters in old Virgil Partch cartoons, or like attenuated Greeks, or gigantic chess pieces.

On these slopes, they are standing, lying on their faces, on their backs, broken, and seemingly walking down the slope – some have a whole trunk, a thick upper body, attached to them, buried underground. The inside of the crater had a number of them. And outside, some are half-sculpted, lying horizontal in a niche in the side of the volcanic rock. One of these was forty feet long – a head and body, lying like an unfinished mummy. Another was a kneeling figure. Yet another upright *moai* had a three-masted schooner carved on its chest.

There were no other people at the site, which made the experience eerie and pleasant. It was without any doubt one of the strangest places I had ever been. From the heights of the volcano, I could look south and see more figures, twenty or thirty, strung out along the meadows, as though making their way towards Hanga-Roa.

The questions are obvious. Why and how were they carved? Who are they? How were they moved? Why were so many destroyed?

The long Norwegian shadow of Thor Heyerdahl falls across every archeological question on Easter Island. Even the simplest people I met on the island had an opinion about their history, and they all had views on Thor Heyerdahl.

Drunk or sober, nearly all were skeptical about the man. The drunkest was Julio, a fisherman who, because of bad circulation brought on by his continual state of inebriation, was always shivering, and this in spite of wearing a winter coat and wooly hat (with earmuffs). Although the rest of the men went around in shorts or bathing-suits, I never saw drunken Julio take off either the thick hat or the coat.

"You have heard of Thor Heyerdahl?" he demanded. "I worked for him for six months. I don't like him. Listen, he gets publicity all over the world and what did I get for six months' work? *Nada!*"

Anna, a young mother in a torn T-shirt, also had views. She spoke a little English. She had been to Los Angeles in 1982, but hadn't liked it. "Too many Mexican people."

We were near Rano-Raraku, in view of the quarry, and so I asked her about the *moai*. She said she had taken her little daughter to see them and that the little girl had wondered how they had been moved.

"What did you tell her?"

"Thor Heyerdahl says that the statues 'walked' – that the people used ropes and lines to move them, while the statues were upright. But the stone is very soft and Tahai is nineteen kilometers away. So they would never have made it. I think Heyerdhal is wrong. There were palm trees here at one time. They could have used those trunks as sleds. The people must have pulled them that way."

In *Easter Island: The Mystery Solved*, Heyerdahl writes how a man telling him that "the statues walked" made perfect sense. (It was an island legend, this walking by means of the divine power of *mana*: Metraux heard the same tales.) Of course, ropes must have been affixed to upright *moai* and the great things rocked back and forth, one set of ropes yanked, then the other. Heyerdahl experimented, moving one *moai* twelve feet. This is something less than fifteen miles, but the more convincing argument was put in the magazine *Archeology* by Professor van Tilburg, who examined all the statues for "wear patterns" on the bases, necks and upper torsos and found none. If ropes had been attached to this soft stone and the statues joggled for fifteen miles, the stone would have been abraded.

Much more likely is the sledge theory – the figures were dragged "on a frame or a sledge, to which ropes were attached . . . using a crew of approximately 150 individuals, over specially prepared transport roads." Metraux's conclusion is similar, though he says that skids must have been used, Tongan style, as they had when the forty-ton pillars of the trilithon had been moved across Tongatapu. The average weight of the Easter Island heads (because the stone is so porous) is only four or five tons.

Thor Heyerdahl is shrill but mistaken in many of his assumptions. Far from solving the Easter Island mystery, he has succeeded in making the solution more difficult for qualified scientists and made something of a fool of himself in the process. He is an amateur, a popularizer, an impresario, with a zoology degree from the University of Oslo. And his efforts in the Pacific greatly resemble the muddling attentions of, say, the hack writer of detective stories when faced with an actual crime scene – someone who ignores the minutiae of evidence, hair analysis, or electrophoresis (for typing bloodstains) and in blundering around a crime scene, muttering "The butler did it!", makes a complete hash of it for the forensic scientists.

The mention of Heyerdahl's name in academic circles frequently produces embarrassment or anger, and even villagers on Rapa Nui find Heyerdahl ridiculous. The Rapa Nui know they are the descendants of Polynesian voyagers and regard themselves as the creators of the monumental figures, which they claim are representations of various prominent ancestors. The figures are not gods, but men. (Forster, who went with Cook, claimed that the statues were of "deceased chiefs.") Historians back up the Rapa Nui beliefs, even if Heyerdahl sneers at them. In an important article in *Scientific American* in 1983, "The Peopling of the Pacific," P. S. Bellwood writes, "At least one thing is now quite certain: the Polynesians are not of American Indian ancestry, in spite of some evidence for minor contacts with the Pacific coast of South America."

"There is absolutely no hard data known from the cumulative effort of nearly 100 years of investigation," Professor van Tilburg writes, "which would archeologically link the island to the mainland."

This view is supported by other Pacific historians and scientists, by Professor Sinoto of the Bishop Museum in Honolulu, who has carried out excavations throughout French Polynesia and who has studied Easter Island; by P. V. Kirch in *The Evolution of the Polynesian Chiefdoms*, regarded as the best documented study of Polynesian settlement; indeed, the view is supported by almost everyone except Heyerdahl himself, who clings to his absurd theory that Peruvian voyagers carried their culture – their stonework, their gods, their sweet potato – into the Pacific. Polynesians came later, he says, and brought these thriving cultures to an abrupt halt.

What about the totora reeds upon which Heyerdahl places so much emphasis in attempting to prove his reed-boat theory? As David Steadman said, pollen studies such as John Flenley's have proven that the reeds have been growing in the craters for about thirty thousand years. Thor Heyerdahl claims that they were brought from South America about a thousand years ago, and this is one of the cornerstones of his reed-boat theory – that South Americans with reed-boat technology sailed to Easter Island bringing sweet potatoes and creating masterpieces of stonework.

Why, you may ask, does the authoritative *Encyclopaedia Britannica* disagree with the botanists and support the conclusions of Thor Heyerdahl? The *Encyclopaedia Britannica* text supports all of Thor Heyerdahl's assertions: "boggy crater lakes are thickly covered in two imported American species." The answer is that the lengthy entry on "Easter Island" in Volume 6 of the Macropaedia bears the initials "Th.H." and was written by the Norwegian.

Probably the most obnoxious aspect of Heyerdahl is that he appears to display a contemptuous bias against Polynesians. In *Fatu Hiva*, he maintains that the Marquesans are too lazy to have created the ambitious stonework and carvings on Hiva Oa. In *Akuaku*, reflecting on the stonework of Easter Island, he writes, "One thing is certain. This was not the work of a canoeload of Polynesian wood carvers . . ." In *The Mystery Solved*, he rubbishes the Rapa Nui people even more: "No Polynesian fisherman would have been capable of conceiving, much less building, such a wall." Too lazy, too uncreative, too stupid.

This extraordinary prejudice is not only without foundation, but is the opposite of the truth. A review of his last book in the magazine *Archeology* called it "a litany of hypocrisy, superciliousness, and prejudice against Polynesians in general and the inhabitants of Easter Island, the Rapa Nui, in particular." One of Heyerdahl's most offensive theories is that the Rapa Nui were brought to Easter Island, from another island, possibly as slaves, by ancient Peruvian navigators who were cruising and being artistic elsewhere in Oceania.

In a lifetime of nutty theorizing, Heyerdahl's single success was his proof, in *Kon-Tiki*, that six middle-class Scandinavians could successfully crash-land their raft on a coral atoll in the middle of nowhere. That book made him a folk-hero. And it focused attention on the Pacific. I have not read an article or met a scientist that did not regard Heyerdahl as a nuisance, an obstruction and a pest. Heyerdahl's theory has also been disproved by scientists studying human genetics and DNA.

"In the Pacific there are two distinct branches [of the human family]," stated Dr Steve Jones of University College, London, in the BBC Reith Lectures for 1991. "One – the peoples of New Guinea and the Australian Aborigines – is genetically very variable, and differs greatly from place to place. They have been there for a long time. The other – which fills the vast area of the Pacific Islands – is more uniform and is related to east Asians. These people arrived after the origin of agriculture, a few thousand years ago. In spite of Thor Heyerdahl's crossing of the Pacific on a raft, there is no evidence of any genetic connection between Pacific Islanders and Peru. Population genetics has sunk the *Kon-Tiki*."

In the face of this scientific evidence, one could easily reach the conclusion that Heyerdahl, in clinging to his silly theory that Hagoth-like voyagers set sail from South America to civilize Polynesia, is in the pay of the Mormons.

Meanwhile, Easter Island remains a mystery.

# 22

## Easter Island: The Old Canoe Ramp at Tongariki

Lovely Anakena was penetrated by the past. Although it was a remote beach, the whole history of the island revolved around it. But it was whipped by wind, and I craved to paddle a long stretch of coast. So I folded my tent, packed my boat, said farewell to the Steadmans and drove across the eastern peninsula to Hotu-Iti Bay, which was protected – the towering cliffs of the Poike Peninsula were its windbreak. One of the stranger *motus*, Maro-Tiri, lay about two miles from the head of the bay, on the way to Cape Roggeveen.

I wandered around this new bay, in the ruins of a settlement which was called Tongariki, and found a large broken *ahu* with fifteen smashed stone heads. The *moai* were lying every which way, with tumbled red topknots, and I later learned that they had been battered to pieces by a tidal wave that had engulfed the whole of Tongariki about twenty-five years before. There was also an ancient canoe ramp here, which had been in regular use for centuries, though it was last used, according to historians, a hundred years ago. I thought I would put it to use once again.

Where once there had been a village at the edge of the bay, there was now a tin shack, and when I approached it and called out, some people emerged – about six or seven girls and perhaps five older men. Several of the men were drunk. I asked whether I could camp nearby.

One of the girls said, "I'll ask my father."

The man next to her looked up from his fish-heads and sweet potato, and he muttered in Rapa Nui.

"Of course," the girl said.

Later, I heard the others – the girls, the men: laughter – but did not see them, and so I ate alone, boiling some noodles, and eating it with bread and cheese, and a can of fish. Another feast in Oceania. I slept, awoken every so often by the breaking waves and the surge of the sea.

At dawn, the men were mending nets, but they stopped when I began assembling my boat.

"That's not a boat," one of them said to me in Spanish. "That's a canoe."

"What is your word for it? A *waga*?"

"Not *waga*, but *vahka*. How do you know this Rapa Nui word? We don't use this word anymore."

I did not tell him that the word was similar in the Trobriands, on the Queensland coast, in Vanuatu and Tonga – all over. Later in the morning, one of the girls brought me a boiled sweet potato. I amazed her by saying, "You call this a *kumara*?" In the Solomon Islands, seven thousand miles away, the villager, Mapopoza, had said to me, "*Nem bilong dispela kumara –*"

The other men gathered and watched me putting my kayak together.

"What are they saying?" I asked the girl, whose name was Jimene.

"They like your boat," she said. "They want it."

"If I give it to them I won't have a boat."

"They say they will trade you something for it."

"What will they give me?"

The men conferred and muttered to Jimene.

"They will give you a *moai* for it."

"How will I take a *moai* away?"

"Other people have taken them. That one near the road was taken to Japan and then brought back."

It seemed to me that the men were only half joking, and would have slipped me one of the fallen heads from the *ahu* at Tongariki, fifty feet away, if I had provided the means to dispose of it. Their outhouse had been plunked on the sacred *ahu* site. You could sit on their toilet and gaze upon exquisite carvings.

The men were lobstermen. I asked them through Jimene how big their lobsters were, and speaking in Rapa Nui, she asked them the size ("*Nui nuu?*").

"One or two kilos."

From the ancient canoe ramp here, they went out in their twenty-five-foot motor-boat, plowing through the surf, to check their lobster traps. I engaged them in a discussion about sea conditions and with their encouragement I set off that day for Motu Maro-Tiri, a tall rock stack down the coast.

Large waves were beating the base of the peninsula, but there were few waves breaking offshore. There was a moderate swell and a light wind. Inside the bay there was a high surf, but I skirted it, heading out to sea and then turning back when I got past the surf zone. I was now several miles from shore, and heading towards one of the more notable offshore islands of Rapa Nui. Here it was that people cowered from cannibals, having swum from shore, and in the old stories it was described how the cannibals went out in canoes, and captured the people who had fled from them, who were clinging to the heights of Motu Maro-Tiri, how they were hacked to pieces and brought back to shore to be eaten.

I was listening to my Walkman, playing a tape of oboe concertos, and with Vivaldi's Oboe Concerto in C, I paddled under the cliffs of the Poike Peninsula, onwards toward the island, very happy that I had brought my boat, feeling a total freedom of movement. Seabirds flew from cliff to cliff as I made my way to the rock pillar that they called an islet.

It was like a gigantic grain silo, made of granite, with perfectly vertical sides – so steep that there was no way I could get out of my boat and climb it. The sea-facing side was dashed by waves, and behind the stack of rock the swell continually lifted and dropped me. I touched it with my paddle, adding it to the list of forty-something islands I had visted in Oceania.

On the way back to Tongariki, in the failing light, I was startled by a sudden thump against my boat – *dumpf!* I stopped and turned to see whether I had hit a submerged rock, but there was nothing but black water. There was always the possibility of a shark, and sharks were said to be stirred by thrashing paddles – *Here is a panicky creature that is afraid of me*, the shark reasoned instinctively, *I think I will eat it.* So I made an effort to paddle fairly evenly, without any fuss, and when I got to shore I asked Carlos, one of the fishermen, whether he had encountered any sharks in these waters.

"There are lots of sharks," he told me in Spanish. "Big ones, too. Six or seven feet long. They surround us when we catch a fish."

It seemed a little late in the day for me to start worrying about shark attacks, and so I told myself that perhaps a turtle had bumped me.

The patriarch of this fishing camp was a dignified old gent named Andres, who spent most of the day pulling nails out of wooden planks and cutting pieces of driftwood to manageable size. These he lovingly stacked near the tin shed, to be made into articles of furniture – he was planning a table, he told me. Every early traveler had remarked on the absence of trees on Easter Island, and the great value placed on wood by the islanders: "they made their most precious ornaments of wood. Even today the islanders do not despise the least plank."

"This wood would cost a lot," Andres said, and he mentioned the peso equivalent of a dollar fifty for a small piece. "All wood is expensive here because we have no trees. The Chileans prefer to sell their wood to the Japanese, who have more money."

He went on thoughtfully yanking nails with his clawhammer.

"The Japanese are very intelligent people," Andres said.

"Do you really think that?"

"Well, not compared to you or me, but just in general," he said.

I asked him whether he had spent his whole life on the island. He said no, he had gone to the mainland to work.

"I worked on the railway in Valparaiso, and then I came back here. This is a good place, it's a good life. I like the sea, the fish, the lobster. You live near the sea? So you know what I mean."

"Can I leave my boat here?"

"Yes. There are no thieves. Oh, maybe someone drinks something and takes one or two things. But this is not like the continent. You can take off your clothes, leave them there, and when you come back they will be here. There are no real thieves on Rapa Nui."

"Why not?"

"Because we have no money. Nothing to steal. We're not Japanese, eh?"

The girl Jimene stopped by my little camp that evening. She was nineteen, but had visited the United States – she had a relative in Seattle.

She said, "We were out fishing today. We saw you paddling. We started talking about you. We said how nice it is that you came to our camp."

That inspired me to stay longer. I had to tell the owner of the jeep I had rented that I would need it a few more days. I drove into Hanga-Roa and found him. He was not bothered.

"You're at Tongariki," he said.

"How do you know?"

"Someone saw you."

The owner of the jeep was Roderigo. He was a medical doctor and part-time businessman. He wanted to buy my baseball hat. He wanted to buy my Patagonia jacket, my Walkman, my tent.

His assistant was Mou, whom I had met my first day on the island – he had picked me up on the road.

Mou said, "Give me your Walkman and I will get you some real *rongo-rongo* tablets."

I swapped Mou my "Apex of Beebop" tape for Bob Dylan's "Infidels," which I had been meaning to buy. (A few days later, Mou said, "Can you find my father for me? He is somewhere in Colorado. I haven't seen him since I was very young.")

I asked Roderigo about health problems on the island.

"The worst, the principal problem on Easter Island is drinking," he said. "Not from the medical point of view, but psychological. The drinkers have severe psychological problems. People go crazy. Their livers are all right, but it makes them strange and lazy."

"What do you do about them?"

"We are getting a rehabilitation center," he said. "Also, there are respiration problems, from the dampness and the humidity."

I made it back to my camp just as night fell, as it always did, with a thud. I had so little light I ate quickly and crawled into my tent, and I spent the next few hours listening to the BBC, first the news, then a program called "Brain of Britain."

- *Who was the first Christian martyr?*
- *St Stephen.*
- *What is the center of the best cricket ball made of?*
- *Cork.*
- *What was a "louison"?*
- *A guillotine.*
- *What do we call the descendants of "meganura" which had a two-foot wing-span and lived in the Carboniferous age?*
- *Dragonflies.*

And then I was overtaken by sleep.

Some days traveling in an odd place there is nowhere else I would rather be. I had this feeling now and then in Oceania, as you know. I felt it every day on Easter Island. I wondered why. The island seemed haunted. The people were unpredictable and inbred, which made them by turns both giggly and gloomy. It was a difficult and dangerous place to paddle a kayak. Some of this strangeness added to its attraction. But it was also the smallness of the island, and its empty hinterland, the symmetry of the volcanoes, the extravagant beauty of the stone carvings, the warm days and cool nights, the tenacity of the people, and all the island's mystery, still unsolved.

There was also something wonderful about waking up in a tent, on a beautiful morning, with the great masked noddies hovering and swooping overhead, and looking over the bluff at the ancient canoe ramp at Tongariki and five miles up the island to the cape and thinking: *I will paddle there today*.

"What do you call that cape?" I asked Andres, pointing towards Cape Roggeveen.

"Vakaroa."

"Do you know the name Roggeveen?"

"No."

Jacob Roggeveen was the first European to sight the island, on Easter Day, 1722, and it was he who named it.

"What about the cape beyond it to the north?" On my chart it was Cape Cummings.

"We call it Kavakava."

At that point I saw one of the girls returning to the camp with one of the older men, along the grassy path that led down to the caves and inlets at the edge of the bay. They were carrying nothing. They walked in silence. Andres said nothing to them – obviously they were father and daughter.

I saw more of this furtive behavior, and I was so unused to it – on other Oceanic islands it was taboo for a father to isolate himself with his daughter – I watched closely and I asked oblique questions. I knew from Metraux's ethnology that there was a horror of incest on the island. There had always been. But it did not stop close cousins from marrying. I had met some married cousins in Hanga-Roa. I heard of a brother and sister who had not long ago fled the island – eloped was what actually happened, one of the weirder tales I heard about Rapa Nui. The graphic expression for incest on the island was *eating your own blood*.

At this camp, the daughters seemed to serve many functions. They cooked the food and tidied the place. They untangled and spread the nets (but did not mend them: that was man's work). They fetched and carried. They played among themselves, but when they were called they kept their fathers company. The fathers went fishing and lobstering with their daughters. Often there was a group: the brothers, their daughters and nieces. But just as often the father and daughter were alone. There was always activity, always movement – "He's going for a walk with his daughter" – the men always in bathing-suits and torn T-shirts, looking grubby. The girls were mostly fattish adolescents with bad skin. The eldest was nineteen. Her father was thirty-six, but looked much older. She was born when her mother was fifteen. That until recently was about standard childbearing age.

"My father goes to the disco with us on Fridays," she told me.

"What about your mother?"

"She stays home."

"Where is your mother now?"

"In town, selling fish."

"With your aunties?"

"Yes."

Another vivid sight was that of a father putting some sort of lotion on his daughter's back, the father being roughly affectionate, the daughter giggling.

I trusted Andres's instincts. If something was amiss, he would sort it out. He was the most reliable person at the fishing camp, and because he was always sober I brought him a present of a bottle of vodka. I gave the girls a large box of chocolates. But nothing was said about these gifts. They were never referred to. They were squirreled away as soon as they were handed over.

But Andres was always courtly.

"I like being here," I said in Spanish.

"Good to have you."

"It is my pleasure."

"Equally."

In the pleasantest circumstances, like this, I tended to procrastinate. I planned an expedition for the day, but then I would fall into conversation with someone, and find it interesting, and say to myself: *I'll go on my expedition tomorrow*. Normally, I was not a time-waster – being busy kept my mood bright – but here I adjusted my pace, and I realized that I was living as they were. On a given day they would say they were going fishing, and they would sit around, talking and laughing until nightfall, the fishing trip forgotten.

When I was alone with an islander I enlarged my list of Rapa Nui words. On each island in Oceania, I made a list of thirty-odd words, the same in each place: moon, sun, day, fish, food, big, small, sweet potato, woman, man, water, canoe, land, island, and so forth, as well as the numbers from one to ten. I did it mainly for my amusement, to compare the language on one group of islands with another. The results were always revealing. Fiji was technically Melanesia, but the standard Fijian language was full of Polynesian words. And I marveled at how islands as far apart as Hawaii and New Zealand shared a common Polynesian tongue, that was mutually intelligible.

I wondered about Easter Island. The language was said to be corrupt. I had not read anything definitive about the impact Tahitian had had on Rapa Nui. There had been times when the entire island had been removed to Tahiti for economic reasons (there was still an acrimonious land dispute regarding the ownership by Easter Islanders of a portion of Tahiti).

On my days of procrastination I developed my word lists, and I discovered that many words were not Tahitian at all, and may well have been part of the original vocabulary, which had been traced to the Tuomotus. The numbers were different from Tahitian, though they resembled Samoan. Their word for sun, *tera'a*, was unique to the island (it was *la* in Samoan). Their word for man, *tangata*, differed from Tahitian *tane*, but was similar to Tahitian for human being, *taata*, and identical to the word for man in Tongan. Woman in Rapa Nui was *vi'e*, cognate with *vahine* but obviously different. The word for sweet potato, *kumara*, was universal in Oceania and the prevalence of the vegetable had given rise to one of Rapa Nui's more melancholy proverbs for life on the island: "We are born. We eat sweet potatoes. Then we die."

There was no reef around Easter Island, but there was still a concept of *inshore* and *deep sea*. Their word for the deep blue sea was *moana* – the word is known all over Polynesia. But "inshore" water, the Rapa Nui equivalent of inside the reef, was *vaikava*, "where the green water is," Carlos explained.

I would not have paddled in the far *moana* around Easter Island for anything. If something went wrong I would be lost in cold water, in a high wind, with no possibility of rescue or of being swept to any other island. About a mile and a half was as far as I ever got from Rapa Nui, but that was enough – perhaps more than enough, since there was nowhere else to go. The islands, those vertical rock pillars, were less than a mile from shore, though they were never accessible from the nearest point on shore. You set out and had to paddle perhaps four miles along the coast to reach them.

I planned for my last long paddle a trip past Motu Maro-Tiri to the eastern tip of the island, beyond Cape Roggeveen. I brought food and water, my chart and my compass. I told Andres where I was going and that I would be back before evening. As I had been about a third of the way along this coast a few days before, I knew that if something went badly wrong – tipping over and having to swim to shore was about the worst – I could find a cave or a ledge somewhere in the rock wall of the

Poike Peninsula. When I did not return, I assumed someone would look for me in one of the lobster boats.

The Dylan tape, "Infidels," that Mou had swapped me was playing in my Walkman as I paddled out of the bay. I skirted the surf zone, watched for shark fins, and made a mental note of the configuration of cliffs on the peninsula, looking for a funk-hole.

The sea-caves beneath the 300-foot cliffs were lashed by surf which engulfed the cave entrance and then, after a long pause, and squirts from cracks and blow-holes, that same wave was spewed out, foaming. These waves made the front side of Motu Maro-Tiri inaccessible, and it was only there that it was possible to climb to a ledge or a cave. I made a feeble attempt, but gave it up, afraid that I would tip over.

For the next hour and a half I paddled northeast, about a mile or less from the peninsula, sometimes in choppy water, sometimes in high swells. If I paddled too close to the shore I was the victim of reflected waves, which tossed my boat; but farther out I had to contend with a stronger wind and a swell. I found it simpler, but slower, to paddle into the face of waves than in the direction they were traveling, because going downwind there was always the possibility of the boat broaching, turning sideways, or of your losing control because of the speed of your surfing.

I was just confident enough in this water to have a quick bread and cheese sandwich and a swig of water, and in the meantime I was paddling to the beat of Dylan's guitar riffs. Musically, this was a different and less uplifting experience than the baroque oboe concertos of a few days before, but there was no time to change the cassette.

It seemed to me that a mile past Cape Roggeveen was as far as any sensible person would reasonably go on a winter day off Easter Island in a choppy sea. There were light winds behind the peninsula, but around the corner it was blowing twenty-odd knots.

The worst of it was the heavy surf, which resulted in reflected waves and a confused sea just offshore. I tried to find a middle ground to paddle in, between the chop and the deep blue sea. To take my mind off this, I marveled at the big waves breaking against the sea-caves, and spilling down the ledges – with the foam and the spray whitening the air at the base of the cliffs. It was a lovely and dramatic sight, the dumping sea and the whiteness of the waves.

All this to the sound of music.

And then I took the headphones off, and heard the immense roar of waves and the screaming wind, and I became frightened. The music had drowned the sounds of the beating sea, and without music I felt only terror. My boat immediately became unstable. I paddled hard to give myself direction and stability, and I pushed onward, past the cape to the corner of the island – the edge, round which the wind was whistling. Unwillingly I was thrust out, where I got a wonderful view – much better than I wanted – of Kavakava, Cape Cumming, and then I turned and spun my boat over the crest of a wave and began surfing back to the lee of the island, with a big wet following sea.

I stayed beyond the surf zone, which was especially dangerous on Easter Island because the waves broke on a rocky shore, yet I was curious to see some of these *moai* from the sea. I paddled across the mouth of the bay in a southerly direction, to Punta Yama, where there was a smashed *ahu*, and half a mile farther down the coast there were deep sea-caves. Rapa Nui people were fishing near the caves, a family with some horses were camped on the grassy cliff not far away, and there were more fishermen (and more broken statuary) another mile on.

It was odd to be hovering here, between the surf zone and the *moana*, the deadly emptiness of the enormous ocean behind me, the fatal shore in front of me – landing was impossible. But being here, bobbing in a small boat, demonstrated how resourceful these people had been. They had found ways in and out of the surf (swimming, surfing, using reed floats). They had made canoes, ingeniously sewing scraps of driftwood together in much the same way the Inuit had done to make kayaks in the Arctic. They had incorporated every geographical feature of the island – caves, ledges, cliffs, hills – into their cosmology. And they had done much more than merely survive here – they had prevailed over the inhospitable place and shaped it, made altars and temple platforms and houses with its boulders, and carved from its volcanoes some of the greatest, most powerful statues the world has seen, artistic masterpieces as well as engineering marvels.

They were also known as quarrelsome and competitive people, and there is evidence that warring groups on the island smashed each others' *moai* and some also smashed their own, ritually decapitating them, and building better ones. Many of the statues that were standing when Captain Cook visited had been tipped over and broken a few years later.

About five miles away at a bay called Rada Vinapu I saw marked on my chart the abbrevation *Lndg*, but it was impossible tell what that landing might be. I was afraid it might be a jetty – one that a ship could slide against, in spite of the waves that hit it, but impossible for me. I had been almost around the entire island and had found only two places to launch and land from; the rest was surf breaking on rocks.

Still outside the surf zone I paddled back, and when I got nearer to

Tongariki I put in my tape of baroque oboe concertos and watched the island slip past me, and I felt joyous.

Above the bay at Tongariki there was an unusual ditch-shaped land feature that seemed to cut across the peninsula. One of the island's more colorful stories concerned an ancient battle between two distinct groups of islanders, the Long Ears and the Short Ears, in which the Short Ears had been victorious. The violent battle, involving flaming ditches and fierce pursuit, is part of the island's oral tradition. But it seemed no more based on fact than the arrival – also here at Tongariki – of Tangaroa, who took on a useful incarnation (*ata*), the form of a seal, and swam from Mangareva to this very spot, where he revealed himself as the God of the Sea.

When I returned, I asked Carlos, Andres, and Jimene about these particular island legends. The men just smiled. Jimene said, "There are so many stories here, it is really wonderful."

There was a different man sitting there near the tin hut that evening. He was Juan Ito, a Rapa Nui man, who was caretaker of the great *moai* quarry across the long meadow at the volcano Rano-Raraku. Had he heard those old stories?

"Yes. I know those stories and I believe them," Juan said.

He was one of many people who told me that he would never stay anywhere near the *moai* after dark, because of the existence of supernatural beings. But I was impressed by his fear, because he was among the *moai* nearly every day.

He asked me whether I was driving into Hanga-Roa. I was out of food, but I was not sure whether Andres and the others were planning to invite me for a meal – they had large anarchic meals of sweet potatoes and fish just before dark inside and around the tin shed. They did not invite me for a meal that night, or at all. I tasted their food occasionally, and we talked. They were neither hospitable nor hostile. They answered my questions. They tolerated me. But I asked no more than that.

Realizing that I would need some food, I drove Juan and his son, Roberto, the twelve miles into Hanga-Roa. Roberto was about eight. He was a skinny and rather undersized and neglected-looking boy – he had just come from school, he said. His hair was matted, his face was smudged. He looked very hungry, and when I found an apple and a boiled egg from the lunch I had only picked at he wolfed them in the back seat.

"How do you usually go from Hanga-Roa to the volcano?" I asked Juan.

"Walk. Sometimes I get a ride," he said. "There is no bus. I have no car. If I walk the whole way it takes two or three hours."

Juan's Spanish was like mine, clumsy and functional, which encouraged me to converse unselfconsciously.

"What about a bike?"

"No money."

"Have you got any other children?"

"Three boys altogether. Aged five, seven, and eight."

We were driving along the cliffs I had paddled past that afternoon and they looked lovely and rubbly under the pink sky, with the waves breaking at the foot of them.

"But the mother is gone," Juan said. "She went to Santiago."

"To work?"

"I don't know. I never hear from her. She drank — she drank everything, whisky, pisco, beer, wine, anything. Then she just left."

"Do you cook the food?"

"Yes. And I clean the house. I do the laundry, too." He laughed. "At first I didn't know anything about looking after a house. But after a while I learned."

He was a small, rather sad figure, in his early thirties, and I felt sorry for him, for his having been abandoned. He had a badly paid job, and three young children, and a long walk to work. But he was honest and forthright.

We talked about politics. He volunteered that he hated Pinochet, who had come to power in a military coup that of course had been welcomed by the United States — Pinochet being the sort of bullying right-winger the CIA had found easy to work with.

"Why do you hate Pinochet?"

"Because he's bad. Because he's corrupt. Because he was tough on this island," Juan said. "I liked Allende. I hate militarists."

I spent another night and day at Tongariki, still wondering what the real relationships of my neighbors were. Nor could I understand their reserve. They were tolerant but inhospitable, and without any curiosity. Now and then one of them had said, "Come fishing with us some time." I said, "Fine," but the invitation was never more explicit than that. Their indifference forced me to look after myself, which was what I wanted; but I was not sure whether I could ask anything of them.

That was one of the trickier aspects of camping on a Polynesian island. Anyone who is not a member of a family is in an awkward position and somewhat suspect. There are only two categories — Family

Member and Other. "Other" includes guest, and the responsibilities, though they are never apparent, are complex. For one thing, because a guest was an outsider he or she was never totally trusted. This ambiguity alone was like proof that Easter Islanders were Polynesians.

I also left Tongariki because after four nights camping by the sea I needed a bath. My hair was salty, I felt grubby. What did these people do? They did not take many baths. There are no rivers at all on Easter Island, and there is a serious shortage of fresh water.

Carlos said to me, "Come back some time."

After this vague salutation, the whole fishing camp of fathers and daughters went back to their own affairs.

The rest of the time I spent in Hanga-Roa. The wind changed and blowing now from the south, from Antarctica, it was much colder, and I was glad that I had done my paddling in the fairer winds.

I wanted to buy carvings – some were very well done, indeed, so well done that people said they had slipped them to Thor Heyerdahl and fobbed these copies off to him as ancient artifacts. The carvings were expensive. *Two hundred dollars*, a person would say, and when I walked on, *How much will you offer?* I hated haggling, so I kept walking. I wanted a rubbing of the Bird-Man petroglyphs, of the god Makemake or one of the more winsome and presentable vulvas. I wished I had brought the simple materials with me that would have allowed me to make rubbings (and I suggest that anyone who goes to Easter Island, or to the Marquesas, do this). Some of the shops had cloth printed with the Bird-Man motif, and this pattern had originally been a rubbing. I saw the same cloth in four shops (Hanga-Roa had a whole street of curio shops, identical souvenirs, no customers), and prices ranged from $65 to $150 for the same simple item. Each person who offered the cloth claimed that he or she had actually painted it. *I did this with my own hand!*

Nothing had a price. It was all haggling – what the market would bear. This was Chilean influence; in the rest of Oceania haggling was regarded as insulting.

Then I was offered one of those cloths for $45. The woman who was selling it said that she had painted it, but this time the claim was true. Her name was Patrizia Saavedra, she was Chilean, and she had come to the island nineteen years before, "because I am an artist and this is an island of artists."

After nineteen years she had to know the place well.

"It doesn't suit everyone, but it suits me," she said. "The main problem is social conflict. Yet the people are not violent. They might shout at you one day, but the next day they will be kind."

"How do you explain that?" I asked.

"They have a habit of forgetting quarrels. They don't store up their grievances. There is little fighting."

I said that I had an intimation of anarchy and mistrust on the island. Had she felt that?

She thought a moment and then said, "You know, dictatorship is bad in many ways – some that you don't expect. It changes people's minds. It affects their thinking. It affected the people here." She intimated that the people had become rebellious and selfish. Pinochet had put his friends and flunkies into positions of power on Easter Island. The local people resented it, and as a result – yes – they were mistrustful. The young people didn't study.

"Now that democracy has come and the military rule has ended, everyone wants to be king of the island." She smiled a pretty, toothy smile and added, "Yes, that is not a bad thing, but *everyone* wants to run for office." She began pointing. "This man. That man. That woman. Him. Her. Everyone wants to be govenor, or *alcalde* [mayor], or whatever. Elections are coming soon. They will be funny, with everyone's name on the ballot – a big long ballot!"

Some months before, elsewhere in Oceania, I had heard on Radio Australia's reliable program "Pacific News" that there had been a large demonstration on Easter Island. For reasons I could not remember, people had gathered at the airport and, holding an airplane hostage, had prevented it from taking off.

"It was last March," Patrizia said. "The whole island was united, the islanders and the Chileans together. There was a radical group behind it – the Society of the Old Chiefs, *Mata Nui o Hotu Matua*. But everyone supported them, two thousand people, in rotation. They went to the airport after the plane landed – the governor was in Santiago – and they claimed it. They would not let the plane take off. It was not violent – no guns. But the people were very determined."

I asked her why they had done it.

"The cause was a two hundred percent increase in prices – fuel, water, electricity."

"And so the islanders united?"

"Yes. And they won. The increase was dropped. The plane took off."

The important detail was that the core of the rebellion had been a Rapa Nui cultural group. Asserting their Polynesian identity was a way of giving their cause legitimacy. All along, the Chilean government had encouraged the people to be colorful, to dance and sing, to recall their past. The effect of this cultural submersion had been similar to that of Tahitians and Marquesans, who had been urged to dance and sing and who had done so, faced with pervasive Frenchness. The Rapu Nui dance troupe dressed up, the girls in grass skirts, the boys in loincloths. They found that they were welcomed in Tahiti, in Hawaii and New Zealand. They realized that they were part of the great Polynesian diaspora. And dancing and singing was inimitable and became their way of resisting Chilean influence. It had also led to more overt political acts.

For a while in Hanga-Roa I fell in with the drinkers. Their objective each evening was to drink themselves into a state of paralysis, and I was fascinated by their methods. They drank anything alcoholic – beer, wine, whisky. And they combined the drinks.

Martin and Hernando, who were Chilean, made Carlos and his brothers seem positively abstemious by comparison. Martin had been on the island for twelve years, Hernando only four. Both were from farms in the Chilean hinterland, and they had an old leathery and weatherbeaten look, though Martin, the elder of the two, was only forty-one. They drank every day, from the moment they got out of work – they were in the Forestry Department. Given the small number of trees on the island, this did not seem an exacting occupation.

They sat at a table in a small bar overlooking Hanga-Roa harbor. They bought cans of beer and cartons of wine. They drank some beer and then poured some wine from the carton into the beer can, and mixed it, and swigged. They staggered, they shouted, they became absurdly affectionate, then they quarreled and went stiff.

There were two discothèques in Hanga-Roa. Paralysis was the objective in those places too. The Tokoroko was the more notorious of the two. "That is Sodom and Gomorrah," a woman told me. That made me hopeful, but I was disappointed. I visited and saw only youths stumblingly dancing. Their drinking was done with more seriousness. When they were truly rigid, like Martin and Hernando, they went home.

Life in Hanga-Roa made me miss my camp near the canoe ramp at Tongariki, but my time on Easter island was coming to an end. I was headed for another corner of the Polynesian triangle – Hawaii.

"You will have to get up early tomorrow," the owner of my guest-house said the night before I left. "We leave for the airport at six in the morning."

Afraid that I might not get up in time, I hardly slept. I dozed, dreamed of missing the plane, and then woke up in a panic. I was fully awake at five. I was loitering in the driveway at five-thirty. At six, no one appeared. At ten past I began knocking on doors. It was another cold, black, Easter Island morning. I went on waiting. Where was everyone?

I dragged my collapsible boat, my camping gear, and my bag of clothes out to the dirt thoroughfare, the Navel of the World Street, and I prayed to the great god Makemake for assistance.

A small truck trundled down the road, waking the dogs. I flagged him down.

"Are you going to the airport?"

He could only have been, at that hour. He said he was from the post office. This heavy-set Rapa Nui man in his beat-up truck continued down the bumpy dirt road. It struck me that this was the only island in Oceania I had been where people wore lots of clothes, old filthy clothes, and boots, and torn sweaty hats. Their mode of dress gave them a downtrodden, hopeless look. The man asked me where I was going.

"Tahiti, then Honolulu."

"I would like to go there," he said.

# PART FOUR
# PARADISE

# 23

## *Oahu: Open Espionage in Honolulu*

The two most obvious facts of Hawaii are the huge sluttish pleasures of its Nipponized beachfront hotels and, in great contrast, its rugged landscape of craggy volcanoes and its coastal headlands, where lava has been pounded by heavy surf into black spikes. Hawaii is smooth, but it can also be rough. I went intending to sample this fearful beauty. On my first swim in Hawaii, on the north shore of Oahu, off a gorgeous beach, I was yanked by the undertow, carried past the surf zone, and swept into a strong current almost a mile from my towel. I swam hard upstream for an hour and finally struggled ashore on sharp rocks, where I was lacerated and shaken. Was this outing a mistake? I wondered whether I should leave because of that, but people said this happened to newcomers all the time.

Soon after, I was introduced to a dignified old man at a party. He began to tell me about a book he had written, and then he asked me my name and what I did for a living.

"I'm a writer."

"What restaurant do you work in?"

"Excuse me?"

"Where are you working as a waiter?"

He was not hard of hearing, simply logical – there were so many waiters and so few writers. Never mind. As time passed, I felt I might stay there for the rest of my life.

"There's Arthur Murray," someone said, in a restaurant.

It was he, in the flesh, ninety-three years old. Decades ago he had sold the dance-lesson business. He had a collection of French Impressionist paintings and lived in a luxury penthouse overlooking the beach at Waikiki.

"She slipped on a shrimp," I heard an anguished person say at another party. "Hurt her leg real bad. Plus she's real stressed," giving it the slushy Hawaiian pronounciation, *shtressed*. People also said *shtrength*, and *shtreet*.

You expected someone to ask, *What happened to the shrimp?* but no one did.

I procrastinated about paddling my boat, because I wanted to get the hang of this complicated city.

Probably the best view of Honolulu is from the top of the city's mountainous backdrop, Aiea Heights. We have Takeo Yoshikawa's word on that. He was one of the spookiest and most important of history's phantoms and was part of the plot to destroy Hawaii. It was in Aiea, in what were the cane fields (now mostly bungalows), that Yoshikawa, a Japanese spy, watched the movements of ships in Pearl Harbor and, in general, gaped at the life of the friendly city.

No one suspected this man of engaging in open espionage – Honolulu was, and is, a city where Japanese are in the majority. Yoshikawa was twenty-nine. Some days he disguised himself in cane-cutter's clothes. On other days he wore a suit and worked under a false name at the Japanese Consulate – as prettily housed today on the Pali Highway as it was in 1941, looking just as it did when the impostors inside supplied information for Admiral Yamamoto's master plan of bombardment. "If you want the tiger's cubs," the admiral was fond of saying, "you must go into the tiger's lair."

Yoshikawa arrived from Japan in March 1941, and prowling Aiea spied assiduously on the city and harbor for eight months. He was still on the job the day the planes were strafing and the bombs were falling and ships sinking, and the first of the 2,403 people were dying from Japanese bombs.

When he had scoped out the strategic locations, Yoshikawa had noted that the ships were generally moored in Pearl Harbor on the weekends, and the planes were parked at Hickam Field then too. From his tootling around the north shore of the island in a borrowed 1937 Ford, Yoshikawa was pleased to see that North Oahu was very lightly defended – a safe direction for the kamikazes. Admiral Yamamoto had worried about balloons – barrage balloons that would impede attacks by fighter planes. No balloons, Yoshikawa reported, and less than a day before the Sunday morning bombing of Pearl Harbor, Yoshikawa cabled from the Consulate: *There are limits to the balloon defense of Pearl Harbor. I imagine that in all probability there is considerable opportunity left to take advantage for a surprise attack . . .*

Fifty years later, I went to the *Arizona* Memorial in Pearl Harbor to pay my respects. This area of Pearl is a national park. Everyone watches the short documentary beforehand, which describes the events of the morning of 7 December 1941. It is not a flag-waving film and is the more moving for its cruel factuality. After that sobering experience, the visitors are ferried into the harbor to the memorial itself, which is a white shrine-like structure built over the rusty hulk of the sunken battleship in which 1,200 Americans lost their lives when a Japanese bomb scored a direct hit on the *Arizona*'s number two turret. Research is so detailed on the attack that the bombardier's name is known. It was Noboru Kanai, who, like the others in the attack force, wore a white cloth around his head reading *Hissho*, "Certain Victory."

"Do Japanese tourists come here?" I asked the park service guide.

"Not many," he said. "And the ones who do sometimes laugh and snap pictures of each other. I don't think they realize how important this place is to us."

Looking out from the spymaster's vantage point, the heights of Aiea, after arriving in Honolulu from the Western Pacific – from the far corners of the Polynesian triangle, from travel in small simple islands – I was overwhelmed by the city's prosperity and its modern face. It is the most visible city in the Pacific.

You can take in the whole busy panorama of Honolulu by glancing from right to left, beginning at Waianae and Pearl Harbor – the cranes and ships, Hickam's planes painted in green camouflage, Downtown with its banks and skyscrapers, and Chinatown's meaner streets, where the less-motivated prostitutes tend to linger; the scarcity of open space, its heavy traffic, the Bishop Museum, the suburbs on the slopes of its volcanoes, bungalows magnetized to old lava flows and in green drenched valleys; the high-rise hotels like goofy dentures and the surf breaking on the reef at Waikiki, the streets of Korean bars and strip clubs, Punchbowl volcano, and the pretty parks, the green cliffs and peaks that enclose the city, a prospect of the sea, and at last Diamond Head which, a vast and Sphinx-like sentinel, can be seen from almost anywhere in the city. After Diamond Head, your eye is traveling to windward, towards the far side of the island.

Where are the pedestrians? Outside of the seaside honky-tonk of Waikiki (less than a mile long), few people walk. Honolulu, a city of drivers, is dense with private cars, and with two- and three-car families. Even the poorest in Honolulu, the recently arrived Pacific islanders – Samoans, Tongans, people from Christmas Island and Yap – have at least one vehicle, usually a new four-wheel-drive pick-up truck. In fact, the pick-up truck seems part of the personality of these islanders, just as an expensive, usually European car is an aspect of the personality of Honolulu's affluent families. It is a point of pride among Filipinos to buy a truck as soon as the down-payment can be scraped together. The middle class drives Japanese cars, the military buys American. No one walks.

One of the paradoxes of Hawaii, yet one of its most American features, is that it quickly – recently – became a car culture. Why is this a paradox? Because, apart from the beaches and shopping mall, all within a small radius, there is nowhere to drive – no hinterland, no open road. A car is regarded as a necessity not simply because a bus passenger is stigmatized as one of the sadder and more poverty-stricken citizens but, more than that, a car in Honolulu is the badge of one's class. I think the car is the key thing. In such a hot city, where nearly everyone, rich and poor, dresses identically, clothes cannot possibly be a status symbol.

The semiotics of Honolulu, its signs and symbols, are complex and highly colored; the city in particular and Hawaii in general has more class divisions and more subtle aspects of social difference than I have ever seen before. The local idiom is crammed with who's-who designations and signifiers: *malihini* (newcomer), *kama'aina* (old-timer), *pake* (Chinese), *katonk* (mainland Japanese: it is an onomatopoeic word, the sound a Japanese head makes when it is struck by a hard object), *kachink* (mainland Chinese, same definition), *buk-buk* (Filipino; also "Flip" and *monong*), "moke" or *blalah* (young tough), *tita* ("sister," moke's girlfriend), *popolo* (black person – sometimes the word is playfully inverted as *olopop*), and all the gradations of *haole* (Caucasian) – new *haole*, old *haole*, *hapahaole* (half-*haole*). The Portuguese (of whom there are many in Hawaii) are not regarded as *haoles*, but rather are universally known as "Portugees." A Latin or a Jew in this society of fine racial distinctions is not seen as Caucasian. There is no colloquialism for a Hawaiian person, though "part-Hawaiian" or variations of *hapa* are the usual descriptions since so few are full-blooded. There are peasants, and there are aristocrats and royals – that they were overthrown and pensioned-off is a meaningless quibble, for the fact is that Hawaiian ex-royalty, some of it *hapahaole*, are still among the wealthiest people in the islands.

With all these divisions, you would expect trouble, but Honolulu does not have the conflicts usually associated with strict class-ridden societies. Even the ritual "Kill-a-*Haole* Day," popularized at some of Honolulu's public high schools, is merely a macabre (and toothless) prank rather than a piece of racial vindictiveness meant to inspire terror in whites. In the sense that many races work harmoniously together, with only the softest undertones – the murmurs of racial memory, and that the races also habitually intermarry, producing startlingly good-looking offspring – Honolulu may be the most successful multiracial culture in the world. At least, I have not seen another to rival it. One of the proofs of its success is that people in Honolulu are contemptuous rather than envious and resentful about the clubs (the Outrigger Canoe Club, the Pacific Club) which until recently did not admit orientals, or the banks that discriminated against certain races in giving loans.

And oddly, in a city of so many races, there are seldom racial jokes in circulation. The few I heard were almost incomprehensible. They were never about orientals or Hawaiians, or even islanders; nearly always the joke-victim was a Portuguese or Filipino.

> *Q.* How can you tell when a Portugee girl is having her period?
> *A.* She is only wearing one sock.

Filipino jokes are almost entirely concerned with the Filipino reputation for eating dogs.

> *Q.* What did the Flip say when he was shown his first American hot-dog?
> *A.* "That's the one part of the dog we don't eat."

There is a certain slang idiom, loosely based on Hawaiian Pidgin, which conveys a heavy humor and is almost exclusively concerned with eating, drinking beer, being fat, being lazy, being slow-witted, surfing, playing loud music, taunting tourists and owning a four-wheel-drive vehicle. This is purely local and almost untranslatable. It is a manner of speaking, not joking, but joshing, and only mokes engage in it. Like English cockneys, who in temperament and lingo they greatly resemble, mokes are at the bottom of the social ladder, but have such a well-defined place in society that they are proud of it. Some are islanders, some are Hawaiians, some are a complex racial mix, but they are all dark and chubby, and they are ambiguously regarded as both cuddly and lethal. Mokes constitute a fraternity and even greet each other "*Brah*" (brother). They are self-mocking, and they ham it up in their baseball caps and T-shirts, crowding the beaches like the Tons-of-fun, but anyone foolish enough to laugh at them, or even to make sustained eye contact, is quickly in danger.

The so-called mokes, when gainfully employed, work as mechanics or manual laborers, but no matter what the job there is a race in Honolulu which has monopolized it. Tongans are tree-cutters and yard workers, though the more detailed landscaping is done by Filipinos, who are also field workers – accounting for most of the pineapple-pickers. Agriculture was formerly an occupation of rural Japanese. Samoans wash cars. Doctors and lawyers are Chinese and Japanese. A surprising number of *haoles* are engaged in real estate. Yet class distinctions, unlike job descriptions, are not strictly racial but rather economic and, in Honolulu, always geographic.

"We were involved in product transitions," someone told me at a party, explaining why business was bad. "We descoped the high end of our line."

It seemed to me that people in Honolulu talked business most of the time. Business or golf. They rose early – though no matter how early they got up they never managed to beat the freeway traffic, which was dense even at six in the morning; they worked hard, they hustled; they went home and hid – privacy being something that is greatly desired in Honolulu.

Each class has its own turf, from the low-income areas of Kalihi, and Makaha in Waianae, and the middle- and upper-class serenity of Manoa and Nu'uanu, to the super-rich in Waialae-Kahala. All of Hawaii's beaches are public, yet each class sticks pretty much to its own shoreline. Some of the most beautiful beaches in the islands are found on the Waianae stretch of coast, but they tend to be avoided because of the intense territoriality of the locals. *Haoles* are cheerfully tormented and sometimes attacked in Waianae. And each class sticks to its own sports, ranging from surfing to golf, and to its own depravities – the poor using "ice," crystal methamphetamine (*pohaku* in moke slang), the middle-class youth smoking pot (*pakalolo*, "crazy smoke"), the wealthy snorting cocaine. There is no crack and, indeed, no perceived drug problem. Gambling is illegal, and so naturally is very common in a clandestine way, but the preferred games also have class associations – cards for Chinese, cockfights for Filipinos, dice for Japanese, trips to Las Vegas for those who can afford it, and so forth.

This exclusivity is also the case with the military, who exist in their tens of thousands in and around Honolulu, on bases and in married quarters. Soldiers are known to locals as "jar-heads." They constitute a sub-class and they keep to themselves. They don't want trouble. They know they are lucky to have been posted here. They swim at their own beaches, shop at the PX, attend their own churches and schools. Unlike other cities which have bases nearby, there is little casual fighting between soldiers and locals. The military is known only by its violent crimes – a rape, stabbing, a shooting: typically a young jar-head from Schofield Barracks or Fort Shafter committing an offense against a local woman.

Violent crime is always reported in detail in the daily paper, because in this basically humane and gentle society it is still considered extraordinary. Handguns are outlawed on the islands. Not many rifles are privately owned. There is no capital punishment. The population's predominantly oriental cast means that it is not a confrontational society. It is not a horn-honking society, either – anyone leaning on a horn is immediately seen as an ignorant newcomer or a tourist. Drivers are polite. It is essentially Christian, and not a litigious society. In a patient way, scores are settled over the long term. Revenge is a dish best eaten cold, might be a Honolulu motto. The Chinese who were blackballed at the Outrigger Canoe Club started their own golf club, Waialae, and now *haoles* are lining up to join this exclusive club.

Once in a great while there is a meaningful murder or suicide in Honolulu: everyone seems to understand. *Oh, he had gambling debts*, someone will say, or *She was involved in a really hot scandal.* Anyway, these are islands. People are intensely visible and nothing is forgotten. The person you are rude to today might be your golf partner tomorrow. In the absence of satirical magazines or good newspapers or investigative reporting, there is the island standby of gossip, and in Honolulu rumors travel with great rapidity.

Middle-class Honolulu society is law-abiding, churchgoing, and rather sanctimonious – in fact everything but racialistic. A family that has married completely within its own race is the exception, not the rule. Anyway, the Honolulu bourgeoisie is not a racial group but an economic entity, and in spite of its ethnic sentiments, it is Christian and has much in common with the aspirations of mainstream America. There is a strong sense of family, and an even stronger sense of the extended family. Within the bourgeoisie, old Japanese are bumpkins (but friendly), new Japanese are jovially regarded as uptight (and shrewd), Chinese as niggardly (and independent), Koreans as tough (and cruel), Hawaiians as indolent (and mellow), Filipinos as self-serving (but hard-working), Portuguese as excitable (but buffoons). But in Honolulu race is not an indication of class.

The clearest and most concise indicator of your class in Honolulu is your high school, because until very recently this was the highest educational level you were likely to have attained.

"You find out who someone is in Honolulu by asking them where they went to school," a local woman told me.

And it's true. It is the key question in any introduction.

"Never mind college," she went on. "Once you know their high school you know everything. Where they live. How much they make. Their politics. Their outlook, their expectations. If they went to Farrington they're mokes. If they went to St Louis they're bourgeois Catholics. If they went to Radford they're probably military or new *haole*. If they went to Roosevelt, they're mainstream. And at the top is Punahou."

Punahou students are seen as Hawaii's achievers. The school is highly regarded academically and, founded in 1841, was the first high school to be established west of the Mississippi. It produces community leaders, but it also produces obnoxious prep-school pushies, smug and preening and forever gloatingly recalling their schooldays. Like many of Honolulu's institutions, Punahou has its roots in the Protestant missions. There is something pervasively old-world in Honolulu, which Punahou – with its colors of buff and blue and its tribalism and its cultivated silliness – seems to epitomize.

This is undiluted New England anglophilia; Yankee missionaries had a profound influence on the islands – on the class structure, the culture, even the architecture of wooden white frame and shingled houses. In Honolulu, and in Hawaii in general, anglophilia amounts at times to anglomania. The Union Jack boxed-in on the Hawaiian state flag is an ominous sign of this, and at times Hawaii seems more like the Sandwich Islands of yore than the fiftieth state. It is a fact that the upper class – old family, Republican, mainly *haole* – resisted statehood and saw it as a slippery slope. Nearly everyone else agrees that it was statehood that brought racial equality to the islands.

Well-heeled Hawaii, with its garden parties and its snobberies, its cultural affectations, is deeply anglophile (and still resentful of statehood). This ought to make a new *haole* a sure bet for fitting in; but Hawaii's complexities do not insure that. The word *haole* – which means "of another breath [or air]" – carries with it many ambiguous associations and qualities, and because of that it is an enigmatic word, describing an unknown quantity, with a suggestion of someone who is "not one of us." I seldom heard this word without imagining it written as it is spoken, like an angry complainer: *howlie*.

And there are the tourists, but they come and go, and apart from people working in the tourist industry, no one takes much notice of them.

There are six million tourists a year, each one staying on average eight and a half days. Two million are Japanese, and many of those are in the marriage package – room, white limo, nondenominational service, champagne – at $10,000 a pop. Every so often a new bride leaps to her death from an upper floor of a luxury hotel. *These arranged marriages*, local people mutter, as a Shinto priest hurries upstairs to exorcize the ghosts in the room with chants and howls and incense. The room is soon reoccupied. Tourism is the largest industry and the mainstay of the entire state. But tourists, even without realizing it, are also territorial. They keep to Waikiki. Except for the beach, the hotel, the luau, the pineapple tour, they do not stray far afield. They are undemanding, they are generally smiled upon, they are seldom ridiculed, they are hardly ever mentioned, except by people who are paid to look after them. It is acknowledged that they have brought prosperity to the state. A local person who kept away from Waikiki could form the impression that tourists do not exist. In no sense do they enter the life of Honolulu, which is not a city really but a highly complex small town, Main Street running into Polynesia, America-by-the-Sea, the splash of surf at the shore, *Lovely Hula Hands*, the roar and monotony of traffic, and inland the eternal snapping sound of the Weedwacker.

But tourist Honolulu and town Honolulu not only coexist; each makes the other possible – sometimes in unexpected ways.

One night, I went to the "Don Ho & Friends Polynesian Extravaganza" at the Hilton Hawaiian Village – a profusion of leis, *muumuus*, fruity drinks, white shoes and sunburned noses – and Don came on singing *Tiny Bubbles* (*in da wine*) in his bored and growling way.

He was applauded.

Shuffling peevishly, he said, "I am so sick of that song. God, I hate that song. I gotta sing it every night!" Then he sang an encore.

Don Ho is a permanent fixture at the hotel and has been for twenty years. But even his churlishness did not dampen the ardor of the audience. There were dancers, there were more Hawaiian songs, including *Pearly Shells* (*in da ocean*), *The Hawaiian Wedding Song* (the singer accompanied herself using deaf and dumb signs), and a young male singer, a local fellow, joined Don in singing *I'll Remember You* (*long after dis endless summer is gone*).

A week later I went to *Aida*, well staged by the Hawaii Opera Theater, with an imported soprano and tenor. The baritone was Les Cabalas, the man who had sung with Don Ho & Friends. And since the opera is mainly by subscription, no tourists could have known that the colorful

Hawaiian local guy in the ugly shirt with Don Ho was moonlighting, with a powerful voice and a strong presence, as Amneris in a Verdi opera.

Eventually I unpacked my boat and paddled out from Kailua on the windward side of Oahu. Kailua, over the volcanic ridge from Honolulu, is famous for being residential, middle-class and military, mainly *haole*. It is a safe haven of one-storey bungalows, and it is filled with loitering US army kids – brats on bikes. It has one of Hawaii's most pleasant beaches and, in addition, several picturesque islands a few miles offshore, but is part of the great sweep of coast, which takes in three bays and is contained by two magnificent headlands. Even when the tradewinds are strong the surf is tolerable for a small craft, and I happily paddled out from Kailua, past Lanikai, to the Mokuluas ("Two Islands").

They are a pair of rocky peaks standing in the lagoon, near the reef, on a ledge of coral. I saw an endangered green sea turtle as soon as I was half a mile offshore, and of course it was brown – the "green" crept into their name when they were still being eaten, because their fat was green. The windward sides of the Mokuluas were being beaten by surf, but on the lee shore, waves were breaking more gently on a small sandy beach.

I saw other kayakers for the first time in the whole of my trip through Oceania. They were surfing their boats through the waves behind the Mokuluas, they were skidding down the swell between the two islands, they were fighting the chop nearer the reef. I had never felt safer.

I waited for the lull between waves and landed on the small beach of the north island. Signs at the edge of the sand explained that this was a sanctuary for seabirds, ground-nesting shearwaters, and that it was forbidden to venture up the slope of the hill. The reason was obvious – the birds had dug nesting holes all over the slope and were compactly occupying them. Because it was such a small island, visitors and birds coexisted uneasily. There were a few picnickers – one from a kayak, half a dozen from a motor-boat. Every so often a startled shearwater would take off, mutter *ka-kuk*, and fly swiftly away.

This island was a microcosm of Hawaii. It was lovely, it was lush, it was heavily visited, it was threatened, it seemed doomed. Everything had been fine until recently, but then great numbers of people began going to the Mokuluas on weekends. I paddled here half a dozen times, and I noticed that on weekdays there were birds sitting quietly all over the island; on Saturdays and Sundays there were no birds, and there was sometimes litter and the remains of fires – although both were expressly forbidden. Camping is also forbidden. But because the island is so pretty – just like Oahu, you might say – people tend to break the rules.

"Lanikai residents say they frequently see people camping overnight there in tents," the *Honolulu Advertiser* reported recently, "walking beyond the no-trespassing signs and into the bird-nesting areas and climbing to the summit of each island.

"The worst intrusion . . . was two rock concerts . . . held on the small beach," the article went on, and it described the illegal crowds, the loud music, the beer-drinkers on this fragile piece of land. There were strict rules governing the islands, but Hawaii's Department of Land and Natural Resources did not have the manpower to enforce them, and so it seemed – at this rate – that the Mokuluas were doomed, the birds either dead or gone, the beach crammed with pleasure-boats, the hill with campers, the air filled with rock music.

*It's seventy-eight degrees in paradise*, the disc-jockeys say in Honolulu, without a trace of irony.

It often seemed to me that calling the Hawaiian Islands paradise was not an exaggeration, though saying it out loud, advertising it, seemed to be tempting fate. They are the most beautiful, and the most threatened, of any islands in the Pacific. Their volcanic mountains are as picturesque as those in Tahiti, their bays as lovely as the ones in Vava'u; the black cliffs of the Marquesas are no more dramatic than those on Molokai and Kauai. The climate is perfect. And they are highly developed, with great hospitals and schools and social services and stores. But modernity has its price. There is beach erosion. There is pollution. There is a constant threat of water shortage or contamination. The traffic problem seems at times overwhelming. Oahu is overbuilt and so expensive that young people leave, unable to believe that they will ever be able to afford to buy even the simplest house. Maui is overdeveloped – spoiled, some people say – with more hotels than it will ever need. The little island Lanai is losing its pineapple industry. Niihau is an ecological catastrophe, according to environmentalists. The Big Island is wrestling with the issue of development. There is still hope on Kauai, under an enlightened mayor who made campaign promises to limit hotel development and to put islanders' interests first.

The Hawaiian Islands are the most remote – the farthest from any mainland – on earth, and this remoteness made their living things unique. Hawaii's only land mammal was a small bat, and in its waters the monk seal. Both precariously still exist. The islands' birds and plants, which existed nowhere else, have not been so lucky. The impact of humans on Hawaii was catastrophic – Hawaii has lost more indigenous species of birds and plants, driven more creatures into extinction, than any other single place on the planet.

"The tragedy of the oceanic islands lies in their uniqueness, the irre-placeability of the species they have developed by the slow process of the ages," Rachel Carson wrote in *The Sea Around Us*, thirty years ago. "In a reasonable world, men would have treated these islands as precious possessions, as natural museums filled with beautiful and curious works of creation, valuable beyond price, because nowhere in the world are they duplicated."

It would have been difficult even with foresight to preserve these fragile ecosystems, but who could have predicted the destruction that followed? For some of the smaller Hawaiian islands, Doomsday happened quite a while ago – the islands of Lanai and Niihau, for example, do not even physically resemble the islands they once were, having been plowed, planted, over-grazed, and generally blighted, the haunt of immigrant animals and restless humans. The once-pretty uninhabited (and sacred to Hawaiians) island of Kahoolawe, just off Maui, has for fifty years been a target for bombing practice by the US military; although bomb-ing has now ended the island is off limits because of the danger of unexploded bombs lying all over. One end of Johnston Island in the Hawaiian chain is a depot for toxic waste, the other end is radioactive because of a nuclear accident.

Most people go to Waikiki. One in ten of them is a victim of crime, according to a statistic released by the Honolulu Police Department. The sidewalks in Waikiki are heaving with prostitutes and their pimps. In the middle of Waikiki, smack on the beach, is the ugliest and most pointless American army installation imaginable – Fort DeRussy, an eyesore the Defense Department refuses to remove. Much of the sand on Waikiki is trucked in from elsewhere and dumped. Dangerously high bacteria levels exist at the eastern end of Waikiki, near the zoo, because of monkey shit being flushed directly into the sea.

Three of America's billionaires, and numerous millionaires, live in Honolulu, but even the wealthiest people have to contend with Honolulu's plagues – rats and cockroaches. No house is free of them – you hear the rats squeaking and quarreling just below the windows, or sometimes nimbly flashing up the trunk of a tree – and it is one of the realities of Honolulu life that once a month Rat Patrol will visit and set out bait and remove corpses. Pest control is one of Honolulu's growth industries and, because of the fastidious nature of the city's inhabitants, includes exterminating unwanted birds and bees.

Now and then, in the belief that the artist Christo is at work in Hawaii, tourists excitedly point to a large house, or a church or a tall building entirely swaddled in a billowing blue tent – these dwellings under great soft buntings are among the strangest sights on the island. But no, they are not the wrapped-up creations of Christo, it is only the fumigator at work, his last desperate measure, zipping up and tenting the house in order to kill every live thing.

The same fastidiousness extends to the city's attitude towards strip clubs and prostitutes. In the Narcotics and Vice Division of the Honolulu Police Department there is something called Morals Detail. Essentially, this is a posse of undercover policemen, who work at night either in Chinatown or in the streets around Waikiki, the male cops hoping to be propositioned by hookers, the female cops hoping to be importuned by a so-called john. There is no law against loitering, and under the city's new "John Law" a person cannot be arrested unless a deal has been made – but both the man and the woman can be collared.

It all sounded very strict to me until one night I went to Waikiki and examined the matter first-hand. Except for a glimpse I had had of whores braying at passing cars from the sidewalks of King's Cross in Sydney, and *Meestah Boll, you wanna gull?* at night in the Trobriands, this was my first experience of vice in Oceania. Kuhio Avenue was busy in the early evening, but towards midnight there were about equal numbers of tourists, prostitutes and policemen, each category in an unmistakable uniform, whether it was an aloha shirt, a tight skirt and high heels, or a blue suit. And here and there, up and down the avenue, all three were sharing the same slab of sidewalk.

Even without the tight skirts the prostitutes would have been highly visible. There is something in their alertness, the way their gaze travels from man to man, and their over-busy walk.

"They walk like they're not going anywhere," Bill said. "That's what Lieutenant Lum told me."

I had arranged to meet Bill in Waikiki. He was writing an article about prostitution for *Honolulu* magazine and had interviewed a woman who had been arrested for soliciting. He had gone to her trial ($100 for the first offense, $500 for the second). He knew about an older woman, a Baptist preacher they called "The Condom Lady," who had made it her mission to hand out free contraceptives to the streetwalkers. He had made friends with some of the people on Morals Detail.

We watched the prostitutes, who usually seemed to travel in twos, strutting and twitching like herons. They took no notice of us, we were invisible to them, and every now and then they would stiffen and make a beeline for the men behind us – Japanese. On Koa Street, where many girls lurked, a pair of girls pushed past us and pounced on two Japanese, and if you happened to be of a sensitive turn of mind you could find something awfully depressing about the girls ignoring us in favor of two callow sauntering youths in baggy shorts and T-shirts.

After a while, Bill spoke with a girl in a tiny orange skirt, but it was a brief conversation. The girl hurried away from him.

"I told her I was from *Honolulu* magazine and she just took off," he said.

"I don't think these girls want to get their names in your magazine."

"Sometimes saying you're a reporter opens a lot of doors," Bill said.

"Not whorehouse doors."

"I guess not."

Walking past me a skinny girl in a skin-tight dress said, "You want a date?"

"How much?"

"A hundred dollars."

"I'm not Japanese, you know."

The girl laughed – and all her youth was in her laugh; she could hardly have been more than sixteen.

"If you were Japanese I'd charge you double that!"

"So I give you a hundred bucks, and then what happens?"

"We go to my hotel. It's the Holiday Surf, just down there. And you have a great time –"

But the instant she saw me vacillating she walked away. Hustling was the perfect word for this activity.

"There's one wearing a beeper," Bill said. "That's for escort calls, a hotel job. The pimps have beepers, too."

The pimps were much in evidence. The beeper was only one point of identification. Pimps were also stylishly dressed, and they carried leather handbags in which, you gathered, a lot of money was stuffed. Most of the pimps were young black men who walked with a kind of menacing confidence.

"When I started, I wanted this to be a real upbeat American story about free enterprise," Bill said. "But it's depressing. These pimps meet girls in Canada or wherever and say they love them. The typical girl is a runaway. She's been sexually abused as a child. The pimp says he loves her. They come to Honolulu. Then after a week he puts her on the street. It's exploitation, coercion, abuse and disappointment. I'm real unhappy about that."

In the absence of a heavy mob in Honolulu, rackets like gambling and prostitution are a free-for-all. The Japanese mob, the *Yakuza*, are involved in other long-term investments, like real estate and building contracts. This leaves vice somewhat unorganized and even amateurish, and the pimps are very obvious dudes — all *olopops* are, in Honolulu — as though they rather like playing the role of superfly, bobbing between the pair of whores they are currently running.

A pale girl, standing by a lighted doorway, handed us a bilingual (English–Japanese) leaflet reading *Foxy Lady! Girls! Girls! Girls!* and invited us upstairs.

"What have you got for us?" Bill asked.

"Naked girls who love to party."

"Will they sit with us?" Bill asked. He was trying to find out the varieties of sexual experience, for his article. What would they do? How far would they go? What would it cost?

The girl in the doorway began to frown.

"Wanna tip?" she said. "Wanna get laid?"

Bill was smiling through his big beard.

"Crawl up a chicken's ass and wait," the girl said, turning her back on him. "You'll get laid."

"What are you writing?" Bill asked me, but he knew. "My magazine won't print that. I can't put it in my piece. Rats."

"Then I'll put it in mine," I said.

We went to Chinatown, in a corner of Downtown; what had seemed amateurish and depressing in Waikiki looked dirty and dangerous here. "That there's a safe bar," a prostitute called out to us, pointing to a doorway. She accurately saw that we were simply passing through. "The rest of them are bad." There were no cars. Lining the streets were ragged, muttering men and bad-tempered women. The only people smiling were the *mahus*, obvious transvestites, who regard Hotel Street and Mauna Kea Street in Chinatown as their natural habitat. They walk the streets, not going anywhere, waiting for a passing car to pick them up — and they might well be politicians or tycoons living their secret lives. Many scandalous stories originate in Honolulu's Chinatown — and that includes Maugham's story of Sadie Thompson, who began her career here and ended up in Samoa.

"This was going to be a great story," Bill said, surveying the dereliction of Chinatown. "Maybe even funny. But it's not. A whore got stabbed to death in that parking lot last week by a soldier. It's depressing."

On another night, still in search of Honolulu, I went to clubs and I remembered what Bill had said of the hookers – you expect hilarity, you look around, you end up depressed.

There are Japanese clubs, very sedate, where each patron keeps a bottle of Chivas Regal with his name on it behind the bar, the carry-over of a practice common in Japan. At these clubs, which are no more than dimly lit rooms, neatly dressed Japanese hostesses join rowdy Japanese men and smile and act submissive while the men, becoming drunker, grope them. It is all chilly and sexless and overpriced, but the massive number of new Japanese have made it a booming business. So much for the Club Tomo, and Mugen, and the others.

Apart from the Club Mirage, which was empty – perhaps this name was a deliberate joke? – the other clubs were a little livelier. Club Cheri had one naked girl doing kneebends on a table. In Club Top-Gun three overdressed Japanese men screamed songs into a *karaoke* mike in front of a television set, and in Club Hachi Hachi one man was doing that. In the Butterfly Lounge young soldiers heckled a fattish dancer, and in Exotic Nights and Club Turtle naked dusky girls posed on a small stage for sweaty men in baseball hats, who were encouraged to buy beer at five dollars a bottle.

Saigon Passion had a successful theme: the last days of the Vietnam War. It was soldiers from Schofield and Vietnamese hostesses, dressed casually, in jeans and T-shirts, and lots of army memorabilia. It was one of the few clubs that held my attention, because the music and the faces made it seem such an atmospheric time warp. A young girl sat with me – Ruby, from Saigon, lived with her mother in Waipahu, about twenty or so. I began asking her questions until finally she fell silent. Then I prodded her.

"You undercover?"

"No. Of course not. I'm not a policeman."

"I think you undercover."

"Why do you think so?"

"Questions. Questions."

I went to the Carnation Lounge, to the Misty II Lounge, Kita Lounge, Les Girls, Club Rose and Club Femme Nue. There were twenty within a three-block area. Some were run by Vietnamese women, most were run by Korean women – because of this, their generic name in Honolulu was "Korean bars."

At one time they had been famous for the tricks women performed in them – one club was put on the map because a woman in it picked up coins with the skillful manipulation of her vulva, another boasted a woman who inserted a cigar between her labia and puffed it (men crowded near to see the tip of the cigar brighten), and that same woman could play a clarinet in a similar way. There was a club where a woman stood behind a transparent shower curtain while men groped her (introducing another sort of club in Honolulu, the "feelie bar"), and there was one on Keeaumoku (known as "Korea-Moku," because of the nationality of the proprietors) where an agile woman came on stage, leaned back, parted her legs, and expelled ping-pong balls from the depths of her vaginal cavern – and the balls, still warm and damp, were fought over and clutched by grateful men.

This last example of conjuring had been popular at a club called the Stop-Light, but the place had since changed hands, it was now called the Rock-Za, and in its way it was typical: loud music, expensive drinks, naked girls. The bouncer, John – an enormous Samoan from Pago Pago – said it was a gold mine. It was his job to prevent patrons from touching girls.

"They get one warning, and the next time out they go," John said.

But he was ambivalent about the honor of the performers. He said the girls were spoiled and overpaid. Now and then a Japanese tour bus would stop and sixty or eighty tourists would pile into the bar – aged men, old crones, couples, honeymooners – and they would sit, have a few expensive drinks, and would marvel at the big white women displaying themselves stark naked at very close range.

Men – all sorts – sat on low stools, with their elbows on a twenty-foot table. The young women, posturing more than dancing, struck poses and squatted. I sat a while, watching everything. And what seemed at first like a fantasy realized, a centrefold coming to life, turned into a raucous gynecology class, in which proximity was everything. There was a certain amount of comedy in that.

People say, *You have to see this*, and they think you'll see exactly what they do. I went, trying to be open-minded, but my reaction to these clubs (after I had a little time to reflect on it) was quite different. The clubs were so ritualized I came to see them as temples in a pagan rite, in which the women were priestesses, like the women in ancient Babylon who whored in the temple of the goddess Ishtar.

There was something undeniably strange and solemn and even somewhat religious in the fervor of the men who sat like intense votaries waiting for a woman to come near. The man's patience, the woman's confident movements, edging nearer and nearer on the altar-like table, squatting, opening her legs very wide, her thighs enclosing the man's head, and the man staring hard in a frenzy of concentration as though a mystery were being revealed to him that he must memorize. It was public, and yet highly personal – only the chosen man could see clearly. There was as much veneration in this man's goggling at a woman's everted private parts as you would find in most church services. The man slipped a dollar or more into the woman's garter, and she lingered, and the man stared straight on, serious and unsmiling in his own private vision. From this sort of ardent behavior, it was a very short step to the Hindu worship of lingams and yonis, or to the cultism of the *Komari*, the vulvas carved in stone all over Rapa Nui.

Still, it was easy to forget in the flux of Honolulu that I was in Oceania. Sometimes Oahu seemed an offshore island of America, sometimes of Asia. Yet it was the only real crossroads in the Pacific, the junction of every air route, and in many senses the heart of Polynesia. This was noticeable in trivial ways – when Disney World in Florida looked for performers for their "Polynesian Luau Revue" ("One-year contracts with relocation will be offered . . ."), they auditioned in Honolulu; whenever a serious piece of Pacific scholarship was undertaken, it was invariably under the auspices of the Bishop Museum or the University of Hawaii or the East-West Center, or more significantly the Mormon Church, passionate about converting the whole of Polynesia to Mormonism, and which had its Pacific headquarters, as well as its banks, on Oahu.

Whenever I inquired about an archeological ruin in Polynesia I was told that it had been catalogued, or studied, or excavated, or written about by one man, Professor Yosihiko Sinoto, the Senior Anthropologist at the Bishop Museum in Honolulu and one of the world's authorities on the Eastern Pacific cultures. *Ask Sinoto*, was the reply I got to most of my Polynesia questions.

The professor was diminutive but muscular, and from his strong accent and his bearing obviously not local. Clearly an academic, but with the restlessness and vigor of someone used to working outdoors, he inhabited a small, cluttered office at the back of the museum. On the walls of his office were charts and photos of sites, stacks of files and artifacts – bone fish-hooks, stone implements.

I went to see him one afternoon, simply to put my *Ask Sinoto* questions to him. He said he had been to the Marquesas recently and we chatted about the ludicrous necessity of having to drink imported mineral water on these islands of waterfalls and freshwater lakes.

"It is the case all over French Polynesia," Professor Sinoto said. "I was working on a dig in Huahine. While I was there, the mayor of Huahine got a grant of money. He used this money to pave one road, he built a television station, he put street lights in the town. But he did not spend any money at all to provide drinking-water. Can you imagine?"

I asked him about the great number of bouldery ruins I had seen in the Marquesas.

"Every valley in the Marquesas is full of sites," the professor said. "Yet when the first surface-survey was done in 1918–19 they thought there was nothing left – no wooden implements, nothing but stones. They thought that the weather was so hot and the climate so difficult and damp that only stone structures could survive . . . Real excavations were carried out by Robert Suggs in 1956 and '57. I disagreed with his conclusions. I went with Thor Heyerdahl's group in 1963."

"And what did you think of his conclusions?"

"He reached his own conclusions," the professor said, tactfully. "As for me, I am convinced that the Marquesas were the dispersal point for eastern Polynesia. The migration and settlement were very rapid. The canoes seem to have come from the Admiralty Islands" – in northeast New Guinea – "around one thousand B.C., and they found Samoa, Tonga and Fiji. They stayed in those islands, and by staying they developed Polynesian culture."

"That's the point, isn't it? That they became more Polynesian by living on their islands and not venturing farther," I said. "But why didn't they go on navigating and sailing? Is it possible that they lost their nerve, or lost their technology and had to re-invent it?"

"Yes. Possible. They stopped making pottery in 300 to 500 – there was no pottery in Hawaii. We have not found even one shard. They sailed to the Marquesas in about 300, probably from Samoa. From there they dispersed. Heyerdahl said that the South Americans brought the sweet potato to the Pacific, but I disagree. It is much more likely that the Marquesans sailed to South America and brought it back."

"But the canoes would have been sailing very close to the wind – and is that voyage possible?"

Professor Sinoto was hypothesizing a voyage that went in the opposite direction from that of the *Kon-Tiki*.

"Many canoes must have set sail. A lucky canoe reached Easter

Island and later found its way back," the professor said. "I was on Easter Island just a few years ago and met a man who told me a story of how he had sailed away in a small canoe with two boys. They brought a big bunch of bananas and twenty gallons of water. He reached the Tuomotus after three weeks or so, and there he stayed for ten years."

I had heard a similar story on Easter Island, about this same man who had sailed to the Tuomotus.

"Other people might have been put into canoes with some food and deported – the chief ordering them away," the professor said, describing how the voyagers might have been banished.

"What about migrants being refugees from tribal wars?"

"Yes. After about 1500 there were many tribal wars in the Marquesas, one valley against another, or one island against another. The choice was whether to stay in the valley and fight – or else leave. I excavated many fortifications and found many sling stones. The people were very accurate in throwing the sling stones – they could throw them two hundred feet or more. Missionaries have written how the people always had bumps on their head from the fighting."

"So they lived in small groups?"

"They isolated themselves," he said. "I am very interested in fish-hooks. I have found that as the time passed the fish-hooks grew smaller. They were catching smaller and smaller fish. They didn't want to go out so far – perhaps they were afraid of the sea, or else of their enemies. They stayed nearer to the shore."

He showed me a set of fish-hooks, diminishing in size.

"The Little Ice Age was another factor that isolated the people," he said. "And as you say, these cultures always developed after they were isolated. The Little Ice Age was between 1400 and 1500. There was a colder climate and rougher seas, so the people tended to stay on their islands in this period. That produced local culture. All the Marquesan tikis are post-1500, for example."

"I am planning to go paddling along the Na Pali coast of Kauai," I said. "Is it true that the Marquesans sailed there and brought their stonework and techniques of building?"

"Hawaii was settled between 500 and 700, by Marquesans," he said. "You will see in Nualolo Vai – which I excavated, by the way – the people worked with much smaller stones than in the Marquesas, where the stones are very big."

"Why do you suppose they set sail for Hawaii?" I asked. "I mean apart from the tribal wars and the famines that forced them out to sea?"

"It is a good question, considering the distance," he said. "But when I was in the Marquesas some years ago I remember seeing migratory birds arrive – first two or three, then fifteen or twenty. And then many, many birds. I am a scientist, but I am also somewhat romantic, and I began to imagine the people saying, 'Look at those birds! Where do those birds come from? Let's go!'"

"Have you found any evidence of cannibalism in your digging?"

"I once found fifty skulls on a Marquesan site. In some places people say, 'Don't touch the skulls.' But in the Marquesas the people say, 'You want these skulls? Take them.'"

This question of cannibalism animated him. He rose from his chair and began to describe other circumstantial evidence.

"I would sometimes be digging and find – mixed together – dog bones, pig bones and human bones, all thrown in the same garbage pit, as though they had just been eaten. Why else mix human bones with pig bones?" he said. "There was human sacrifice everywhere in Polynesia – for big events, to bring rain because of a drought, or for whatever reason."

"What is the most Polynesian island in the Pacific – the most traditional?"

"Polynesia is gone," he said. "Western Samoa is probably the most traditional place, and perhaps Tonga. The Solomons and the New Hebrides are also traditional. But even so it is spoiled in those places. Fiji and Tonga still have chiefs."

This tallied with my amateur observations: the graceful huts of Savaii, the nobles and commoners of Tonga, the egg fields of Savo, the cross-faced tribes and muddy buttocks of the island of Tanna.

"But I remember Atiu," the professor said, speaking of a small island in the Cook group, not far from Aitutaki, where I had paddled. "I was working there and as recently as 1984 Atiu was totally traditional. Everything was intact. I returned for several years, and then in 1989 the culture was gone. It was finished, just like that. How did it happen so quickly? You know what caused it? The video. I don't know why the government doesn't regulate videos. They are terrible. Rape. War. Violence. Drinking. They give bad ideas to young people, and they destroyed the culture in Atiu which had lasted for over a thousand years."

Then he began to talk about his dig in Huahine, how he had worked on the lovely island for twenty years – the uniqueness of the place, with aquaculture in the lagoon, and farming beyond it, and the chiefs living along the shoreline. He had uncovered thirty-five sites behind the lagoon, one of the richest archeological finds in Polynesia.

"But what do my fellow countrymen do?" Professor Sinoto said. "Some Japanese businessmen want to buy this whole end of Huahine. They want to put up three large hotels and use the lagoon for swimming and water-skiing. They want to put up an airport and have three jumbo jets a week from Tokyo."

It was wonderful to hear a Japanese person becoming indignant over the acquisition and exploitation of Pacific islands. For once, I could shut my mouth and listen to someone echo my sentiments.

"The Japanese are looking for playgrounds in the Pacific," the professor said, barely controling his fury. "What kind of benefit will this bring to the locals? They hire a few people to work in the hotels for the lowest wages. The first big hotel on Huahine was the Hotel Bali Hai. Local people became drunk in the bar. Because of their drinking they needed money. They began to steal money from the bungalows. When I heard that the Japanese were planning to buy this area I hoped they would be turned down. Their application was temporarily denied. After that, I saw someone in the government and said, 'We must preserve this area,' and he helped arrange it. So it might not happen in Huahine, but it has happened in many other places."

He let this sink in. We sat among the artifacts, in front of a great chart with arrows showing the ancient migration routes in Oceania.

Professor Sinoto said, "Everyone is looking for playgrounds in the Pacific."

# 24

## *Kauai: Following the Dolphins on the Na Pali Coast*

There are distinct seasons for everything in the Pacific, though this is not always so obvious to the tourist on dry land. Look at all the people lounging on the beach in Hawaii, remarking on the balmy weather, the wonderful hotels, the funky music, the ya-yas at the local clubs, the great food. They haven't the faintest idea what month it is, because paradise hasn't got a calendar, or seasons. *Aloha*, they say to each other, and after a while they learn to say *Mahalo* (thank you).

They bandy these two words all over the place, and some people laugh at them for it, but why? It is rare – almost unheard of – to find anyone who speaks Hawaiian in complete sentences. This is tragic, because when the Hawaiians lost their language – when it was debased and bowdlerized by missionary literalism – they lost their identity. The movement for reviving the old language, which is melodious and highly metaphorical, is (like the movement for sovereignty) still struggling. What you hear in normal speech is jargon, conversational color, a matter of vocabulary, of knowing twenty or thirty words and scattering them in your English sentences.

The more Hawaiian words you know the more easily you can pull rank. It is exactly what missionaries do in simple societies to ingratiate themselves. In Hawaii this manner of speaking comprises a local idiolect, or lingo, in which every hole is referred to as a *puka*, and all talk as *namu*, and every toilet as a *lua*, and all children as *keikis*, and so forth. Directions are full of Hawaiian jargon – seaward is *makai*, towards the mountains is *mauka*, and west is *ewa*. Like Hawaiian Pidgin, with which it shares many words, it is often used jokingly. Of course, there are words which only native-born Hawaiians know, but they keep them to themselves: why give everything away?

This lingo has a certain charm, though no one forms sentences. No one ever says "Hello, how are you?" in the language, and when I asked some old-timers, who would have called themselves *kamaainas*, they couldn't tell me that the simple greeting was *Aloha kakou. Pehea'oe.* Hawaiian is used simply to gain credibility. In Africa it has an exact counterpart in so-called kitchen Swahili.

Travel writers in Hawaii interlard their prose with this island jargon to give it verisimilitude. Travel writers in Hawaii write about the room service at the hotels, and the efficiency of the valet parking, and whether the hollandaise on the eggs benedict has curdled. Brunch is quite an important subject for the travel writer. So is golf. So is tennis. They are mainly junketers, people on press trips; and they often travel with their spouses – one scribbles, the other snaps pictures – making travel writing one of the last Mom and Pop businesses in America. I thought of such people when I was in my camp site at Vava'u, or paddling in the Trobriands, or squatting on the beach in the Solomons, or sheltering from the driving rain in a ratty cave on the west coast of Rapa Nui.

"I'm a travel writer, too," one named Ted said to me on Kauai. "I'm here covering some hotels. I'm covering some restaurants, too. Pacific Café? It's Pacific Rim cuisine. We're at the Waiohai here. My wife Binky is with me – we always travel together. She's an astrologer. Have you stayed in the bungalows at Mauna Lani? We had three nights there. I'm covering it for a paper back home. We mainly do upscale hotels. Last time I was here I was covering the block party at Waikiki. It was kind of fun."

I asked Binky to tell my fortune.

"I couldn't read your stars unless I had lots of astral information," Binky said. "I do a little writing myself. I like the hotels. But it's funny about Hawaiian hotels. Some of them serve only American wine. And I can only drink French wine. I love Cristal. They made us feel very welcome at the Four Seasons in Maui. They gave me a gold pendant and Ted got a fabulous shirt from the logo shop. They hydrated our faces with Évian atomizers as we lounged by the pool. My real favorite place is St Bart's. Ever been there? I love French food."

I was proud of being a travel writer in Oceania. I stopped seeing it as a horrid preoccupation that I practiced only with my left hand. But when I got to Hawaii I changed my mind. I was not sure what I did for a living or who I was, but I was absolutely sure I was not a travel writer.

As a matter of fact, travel writers seldom wrote about the seas that lap Hawaii. The Pacific was something they squinted at over the rim of the pineapple daiquiri. They gushed about the waves breaking on the reef, but apart from that, water sports are not a frequent subject for travel writers. The proof of this was their love of surf. And yet boat-owners are never so sentimental about surf, which is like a vision of death and destruction.

Boating in Hawaii's waters can be rather uncongenial. Just offshore, prevailing conditions are unpredictable much of the time, and fierce (and of course prettiest) in winter months – frothy seas, stiff winds, and strong currents. The sailor with a problem looks onshore and sees a rocky coast or a reef, heavy surf, or one of the great horrors for anyone in a small boat – surfers having a wonderful time.

"It's not too great when you see surfers," Rick Haviland told me in Kauai. He was a master of understatement. "That's kind of a bad jellyfish," he said one day of a Portuguese man-of-war, and "kind of neat" always meant breathtaking. Rick was in the kayak and bike business, rentals and sales, and as a former surfer he confided to me that the presence of surfers always means high waves and the worst conditions for the rest of us. It was Rick was gave me a crash course on Kauai's sea conditions, and it was Rick whom I successfully bullied into accompanying me on an off-season jaunt down the coast which has the most beautiful cliffs in the Pacific.

If you try to paddle a kayak in the wrong season off the glorious and almost inaccessible Na Pali coast of Kauai you can get into deep trouble – no one does much paddling between October and April, though some of the tour boats run throughout the winter. I was apprehensive, because it was November and I was looking for a window of good weather to make the trip paddling my own little boat. I had a special reason for wanting a closer look at Kauai, because I had traveled in the Marquesas in French Polynesia. There is a great cultural connection between those two places.

Of course there are connections and relationships all over the Pacific – words spoken in Tahiti are also spoken in New Zealand and Samoa, food items and cooking methods are shared in island groups thousands of miles apart, and so are dances and deities. It seems at times – and it is often argued – that this enormous body of water is a single oceanic family of like-minded people with a common culture.

But, as Professor Sinoto had said, one of the closest connections that exists is between the Marquesas and the Hawaiian Islands. In fact, the Hawaiians are the descendants of the Marquesans who sailed to Hawaii and settled there sometime around A.D. 700. But it is generally reckoned that the last place in the Pacific to be settled was here, on the almost inaccessible Na Pali coast. They could not have chosen a more appropriate place. Nuku Hiva in the Marquesas and Kauai in Hawaii might be neighbor islands: they look similar, with volcanic mountains shaped like witches' hats and vegetation as dense and dark green as spinach, the same deep valleys, the same furrows of cold lava flows. Their ancient ruins – patterns of boulders, rock platforms and walls and petroglyphs – are almost identical, and they are just as dangerous to anyone who travels offshore in their peculiarly tricky waters.

"I guess we should kind of angle out here," Rick murmured, looking up at the surf as we set off in our kayaks from Haena Beach Park near where the Na Pali begins. To the right were surfers frolicking in the ten-foot breaking waves of "Tunnels", a well-known surfers' spot; to the left was a reef and more waves nearer shore – another version of sudden death.

I followed him; I liked his mellow mood, the way he relaxed and rode the waves. The happiest campers are imperturbable. So what if the wind was blowing fifteen knots or more? At least it was at our back, helping us along in a big following sea. The outlook was good, but so what if the weather turned foul? We had camping equipment, we had food and water, we had survival gear, we even had a quart of margaritas.

We paddled on, past the first of the cliffs – Na Pali means "The Cliffs" – a corner of the coast, which was the place where Hawaii's best-known deity, Pele (goddess of the volcanos), fell in love with a mortal, the chief Lohiau. It is a hidden and in many respects a spiritual coast, full of *mana*; a place of temples and burial grounds – a holy coast. This coast and much of Kauai is a byword for the exotic. It is the source of many Hawaiian legends, ancient and modern, as well as some of our own sweetest myths: just above us, the Makana Ridge was the location of Bali Hai, in the movie *South Pacific*; a bit further on, Honopu Valley was seen by millions as the home of King Kong; across the mountains the opening of *Raiders of the Lost Ark* was shot; and further along the coast Elvis Presley fooled with Ann Margret in *Blue Hawaii*. Talk about legends!

An eight-foot swell with a strong push to it ("Kind of a surge – feel it?") was dragging us sideways towards the first of the deep Na Pali valleys. This one was Hanakapiai, with a small but lovely beach which is swept away each year by the powerful winter seas and then is piled up again in the spring and summer. The footpath passes here and then continues on to about a third of the length of this coast, the eleven-mile

Kalalau Trail. It is only for the strongest hikers, but is well known among outdoor people as one of the most scenic in the world.

The rocky cliff-face a bit farther along was being battered by waves, and these reflected waves smashing against oncoming ones created a choppy sea and a phenomenon called clapotis – vertical standing waves – which were making me seasick. I had never felt pukesome in a kayak before but, bobbing like cork in this chaotic chop, I felt distinctly nauseous.

Coincidentally it was lunchtime, but paddling out a mile in the wind and streaming sea I was able to settle my stomach. Rick and I divided up our lunch and, eating it – a sandwich, an apple, a bottle of water – we drifted apart, and there we stayed, for an hour or two.

There is a mystical element in paddling a kayak which might be described as the trance induced by the rhythm of paddling, lifting and stroking continuously and gliding along. The paddler concentrates, and falls silent, and without fanfare but with a relentless steadiness goes forward, rising and falling in the waves. It is an effort, of course, but because of this trance the effort is almost unnoticeable. I suppose hikers and joggers must enter that same state of mind, because it becomes a very peaceful and healthful way of breathing, and here it was intensified by the beauty of Na Pali with long narrow fluted valleys, and cliff rims rising to 4,000 feet.

This spell is hard but not impossible to break. In my case it was shattered by the bite of a poisonous jellyfish. In my paddling trance I had spooned up the tentacles of a floating Portuguese man-of-war, and one tentacle – a long gelatinous noodle – slipped down the shaft of my paddle and was flipping around my forearm. The pain was almost immediate: the poison is a neurotoxin, attacking the nerves the way the jellyfish immobilizes its prey. My arm was fiercely stung as I plucked off the tentacle, and then I summoned Rick.

He reminded me gently that the folk remedy is urine. I had tried that without any success in Vanuatu. Papaya leaves or meat tenderizer would have been more effective, and would have spared me three hours of numbing agony.

But the spectacular landscape eased the pain – it had that capacity to bewitch. They were not simple ledges, but rather a multitude of sharp green pinnacles all over the face of the cliff. The whole mountainside had the look of a gothic church in a fantasy – hundreds of steeples and cupolas. Even with my stinging arm in this choppy sea, I would rather be here among the cathedral-like contours of the cliffs on this high island than seeing its architectural equivalent in Europe – and I knew that the next time I saw Westminster Abbey or Notre-Dame I would be instantly reminded of the soaring Na Pali coast and miss it terribly.

The ancient Hawaiians must have known how strange and magical these pinnacles seemed, for – down to the last green cone – they called the whole lot of them *keiki o ka 'aina*, "children of the land," and gave each one a different name.

We passed "a flower-throttled gorge, with beetling cliffs and crags, from which floated the blattings of wild goats. On three sides the grim walls rose, festooned in fantastic draperies of tropic vegetation and pierced by cave entrances." This is Jack London's description of the Kalalau Valley and beach, which is the setting for his powerful story, "Koolau the Leper" (and it is true in most of its details). This valley is as far as anyone can get on foot. The rest of the coast is reachable only by the various tour boats, big and small, which trundle back and forth. And there are helicopters buzzing on high – dipping into the valleys, hovering over the cliffs. Two today were passing the lovely stone arch at the mouth of Honopu Valley, the so-called "Valley of the Lost Tribe," where a pre-Hawaiian people (their origin is the subject of archeological dispute) flourished.

Opinion is divided on the choppers of Kauai. Except for the operators themselves, most people on Kauai would like to see them vanish into the sunset. But there is no question that the chopper, the most versatile of aircraft, offers an unusual way of seeing the Na Pali coast. They are numerous and intrusive and noisy, but their worst fault is not the noise pollution to others but the way they deafen their own passengers – the sound of the rotors drowns out the wind whistling through the valleys, the water music of mountain cataracts, the crashing of the waves against the sea-cliffs; and it gives the false impression that this hidden coast is easily accessible.

"They're kind of a pain," Rick said. This was as close as he ever came to stating his anger, but modest as these words seemed they represented for him blind fury. "I don't want to think about them."

On some days, Zodiacs – huge rubber dinghies – took tourists along the coast, splashing back and forth, mercilessly wetting the passengers and giving them the impression they were on a do-or-die expedition. But the Zodiacs, though noisy and just as intrusive as the choppers, are very safe. If you listen carefully to one boatman talking to another you might hear the following exchange.

"How many burgers you had today?"

"Twenty-three burgers this morning, eighteen this afternoon."

"Lenn had thirty-some-odd burgers all week."

It was their way of referring to boat passengers, and although it was utterly dismissive, there was something horribly appropriate in calling a big sunburned tourist a "burger."

We passed Awaawapuhi Valley, the narrowest and most dramatic of the valleys, where on the tight strip of the valley floor there had been an extensive old Hawaiian settlement.

There was also once a large settlement of Hawaiians living in a traditional way at the next valley, Nualolo Aina. In fact, so hidden was this valley that the people remained as they had been for centuries, living undisturbed into the early twentieth century. They were *alii* or nobles in the valley, and just outside it a shoreside village called Nualolo Kai was inhabited by commoners. The foundations of the dancing pavilions, the houses and temples, garden walls and many other structures – excavated and catalogued by Sinoto – still remain, inside and outside the valley. We returned to them the following day and I was astonished by how closely they resembled the ones I had seen 2,000 miles away in the Marquesas.

Under the cliffs, which were like black turrets, we made for the valley of Miloli'i. Off in the distance the sun was setting behind the privately owned island of Niihau and its neighbor, the little lumpy volcano of Lehua. We were paddling in a headwind. I hate headwinds. I had thought that everyone hated headwinds.

Rick said, "It kind of cools you," and paddled uncomplainingly onward.

That night we camped on the sand of Miloli'i – baked potatoes and grilled fish over an open fire. Afterwards we talked for a while, and then Rick crept down the beach.

I sat by the fire, stirring the coals, and feeling drowsy. I had had some happy times paddling through the Pacific, but their origin had been sights and sounds. I had not experienced much comfort. The hardship had been necessary to the discoveries I'd made. But this was different, this was one of the most pleasant interludes in my trip. It was luxury – the meal, the fire, the night air, and most of all my fatigue, which was like the voluptuous effect of an expensive drug. I loved being numb, utterly senseless, and sitting there dead tired on the soft sand, and then simply easing myself down onto my sleeping-bag, and subsiding.

It was magic, memorable slumber. I slept under a full moon that was as bright as an arc light. All night the surf dumped and slid on the steeply shelving sand. In the early hours of the morning I was wakened by something tickling my nose – a fat and over-ambitious ghost crab perplexed by the task of eating my face, or perhaps wondering how to drag me into its hole in the sand. I slapped the thing away and went back to sleep.

I had thought that nothing could equal the thrill of those cliffs seen from a kayak. I was wrong, for the next day, headed back to Nualolo Kai to look at ruins, we saw some splashing out at sea – probably dolphins – and we headed in that direction. I was totally unprepared for what we were about to see – dolphins, in every direction, dolphins. There were sixty or seventy of them, a variety called spinners, four or five feet long, and some babies. They were jumping clear of the water, swimming upside down, frolicking in groups, and swimming in a vast irregular circle about a quarter of a mile in diameter. And they were gasping. I had always seen dolphins from a bigger noisier craft, so I had not known anything about the sounds they make – how they breathe and sigh and blow. Every time they break the surface they gasp, like a swimmer sucking air, and hearing this laboring breath, which is the most affecting and lovable human noise, I was struck by how much we miss when we can't hear the creature we are looking at.

"Kind of neat," Rick said.

Even the experienced guide was amazed. He had been down this coast hundreds of times and he had never seen anything like it, he said. For the next hour and a half we played with them, paddling among them, and they performed for us. We made no sound, we posed no threat, we merely watched appreciatively – and they seemed to realize that.

After this, who wouldn't paddle into Nualolo Kai, and put ashore, and walk to the great *heiau*, or temple, against the cliff face and leave an offering? We wrapped round stones in freshly plucked *ti* leaves, and placed them on the wall with a wish that we would have a safe trip and would return.

At the end of the trip, riding the surf into Polihale I was very happy, with the pure joy that comes to the traveler whose efforts are rewarded – in my case handsomely, with the sight of those cliffs and ruins, and the antics of those dolphins. Our little boats had given us the greatest freedom. The Hawaiians had always known that simple fact. And it was as true of the dead as it was of the living. In the cliffs above the broad white sand of Polihale hundreds, perhaps thousands, of corpses had been found, and the luckiest – the most noble – had been buried in their canoes, like the greatest Vikings in the bogs and burial places of England.

# 25

## *Niihau and Lanai: Some Men are Islands*

"What you see ahead is Niihau, the Forbidden Island," the chopper pilot said, as his flying-machine went *quack-quack-quack* across the seventeen miles of channel that separated this small arid place from the friendly green island of Kauai.

"We'll be landing pretty soon," he went on, "but I just want you to know that I can't show you any of the people, we can't enter the village – you won't even be able to see it, I'm afraid. In fact, most of the island is off limits, and it has been for over a hundred years."

And then he steered us south, through the clear Hawaiian air, into the nineteenth century.

Hawaii is full of marvels, but one of the strangest aspects of this chain of eighteen islands is that two of them are private property, and neither of them is owned by an ethnic Hawaiian. Some characters in literature also have private islands: they take possession of islands in much the same spirit that they head into exile – in Shakepeare's *The Tempest* Prospero does both. Usually, a person seeking an island craves simplicity and glories in a world that is still incomplete, and therefore full of possibilities. Anything can happen on an island – guilt can be expiated (*Robinson Crusoe*), the forces of good and evil can emerge in the breasts of castaways (*Lord of the Flies*), love can be discovered (*The Blue Lagoon*), so can a great fortune (*Treasure Island*) or a true paradise (*Typee*), or a kind of hell (Conrad's *Victory*); it can be the setting for a great departure (the Nantucket of *Moby-Dick*), or for the oddest landfalls on earth (*Gulliver's Travels*). It is impossible to imagine these island episodes unfolding on the mainland.

The common denominator is not the landscape of the island, or its location on the globe, but rather the fact of a place being surrounded by water – the character of the water itself is the magic element, offering the islander transformation. The water, seemingly nothing, is everything – a moat, a barrier, a wilderness, the source of food and hope, the way out. The ocean – as any true seagoing person will testify – is not one place but many. The sea has specific moods and locations, as any landscape of hills and valleys does. It even has thoroughfares. Oceania is full of ancient named waterways – the paths to other islands or archipelagos. A piece of water off the Big Island is known as Kealakahiki, "The Way to Tahiti" (2,500 miles away), one of the great canoe routes.

A person who emigrates to an island is obviously different from a native islander. There is something rather suspect about a person who seeks to recapture island innocence. But in any case it is a futile search, because no one really can take possession of an island. Being the monarch of all you survey is in reality a mainland conceit; on an island it is you who are possessed. Islands have a unique capacity to take hold of their inhabitants, whether they be natives or castaways or potential colonizers, and that is perhaps why islands are so rich in myths and legends.

An island ought to seem fragile and isolated, and yet I visited fifty-one islands in Oceania and every one of them seemed like a thing complete in itself, self-contained and self-sufficient, because of the surrounding water. Whether that was an illusion or not I don't know, but this sense of mystery and power must communicate itself both to those who are native to the islands and those who seek them. There is something princely in the very situation of someone who builds a house on an island and lives in it. But an island is much more than a principate. It is the ultimate refuge – a magic and unsinkable world.

Owning an island is something like having this entire world to yourself, where you can do as you like – making your own rules, fulfilling a vision or a fantasy. The two private islands of Niihau and Lanai are dramatic examples of that, but they are moving in totally different directions.

Niihau is quite small and so obscure and so seldom visited it is called "The Forbidden Island." Hawaii's second private island, Lanai, is fairly large and has not been much on the tourist map and is hardly known, except as a Dole plantation. Its nickname is "The Pineapple Island." Each place is extraordinary in its own way. The owner of Lanai is just now ending its seventy-year tradition of pineapple-growing and has invested heavily, with two luxury hotels, in the tourist industry. In great contrast to this, the owner of Niihau long ago decreed that nothing would change on his island and his descendants have kept to that promise – forbidding any outsider from entering the community of Hawaiian-speaking people, or looking closely at the land or its inhabitants.

"If any island is inviolate, it is Niihau," Hawaii's historian Gavan Daws wrote almost thirty years ago; "if any man is an island, it is Niihau's patriarch."

One of the pleasures of the Hawaiian island derives from the fact that no beach is private. A tycoon might have a mansion jammed squarely against the sand, but the law allows you to use that same beach, sunning yourself and swimming in the surf. The beaches belong to everyone. And even on the most remote or exclusive beaches there is public access.

The single exception to this is Niihau. I wanted to take my collapsible kayak there. I was told that this was out of the question, that the sand and even the water around the island – to ten fathoms – was private.

Because of its isolation, Niihau has acquired an extensive mythology – the unknown always passes for something particularly wonderful. The very idea of Niihau fascinates people in Hawaii, and to nearly everyone it suggests Shangri-la. Tell someone you've been to Niihau and their face becomes brilliant with curiosity.

"What was it like?" they say. "I'll bet it was fantastic."

A *No Trespassing* sign is like catnip to a travel writer. I was determined to find out about the island, and to visit it if possible. I discovered that there were occasional helicopter tours, but – to maintain Niihau's low profile – the service was never advertised. In the end, interviewing informants, and finding the chopper, and making the trip, turned out to be a bit like mounting an assault on Alcatraz, another Pacific island that Niihau physically resembles.

Niihau was sold for $10,000 to a family of wealthy wandering Scots by the Hawaiian king (Kamehameha V) in 1864. The family successfully transformed this Polynesian volcano into a Scottish estate, turning the islanders into tenants and themselves into lairds. They were muscular Christians. They decreed that everyone on the island would attend church. They discouraged smoking. They forbade the drinking of alcohol. They fortified the church and distributed Bibles, in the Hawaiian language. Even today, in an island on which the main language is Hawaiian, the only reading material in that language is the Bible and the hymn book, and the same prohibitions persist. Little wonder that (as a former resident wrote in 1989), "A favorite pastime of the children is trying to stump each other by reciting phrases from the Bible" – guessing chapter and verse. Fishing, manual work and games are forbidden on the sabbath.

In theory it is a sober and pious island of twelve Hawaiian families (inevitably related). Ask anyone in Hawaii and they will tell you that it is a unique preserve of native culture, of people living in the old way, fishing and farming, preserving the island traditions.

This is of course ridiculous. At best the island is a throwback to the days of soul-saving missionary paternalism in which the hula was banned and singing generally disapproved of, and islanders seeking work were allowed to look after the owner's livestock. It is an insular ghost from the age when Polynesia was condemned as lazy and needing to atone for its Original Sin. Oddly enough, the island and the stubborn, backward-looking Robinson family which owns it have more defenders than attackers, because casual onlookers enjoy the fantasy that an island has been trapped in time – indeed, that traditions have been preserved. Although last year the islanders voted Democratic (for the popular and progressive mayor of Kauai, JoAnn Yukimura), the Niihauans have usually been as staunchly conservative as the Robinson family – they voted against statehood in 1959, the only precinct in the islands to reject joining the United States. Yet it is not possible to stop the clock, even on an offshore island.

So what is Niihau tradition now? It is the language – perhaps the only community in the entire state whose daily conversation is Hawaiian. It is the preservation of family units – and extended families – which are said to live in harmony. It is the practice of fishing – but only by the men and boys; the women are home-makers, and many of them search the island's beaches for the tiny Niihau shells, which they pierce and fashion into precious and exquisite necklaces – much coveted by people the world over who appreciate their rarity. And it is churchgoing.

Apart from all that piety, Niihau tradition is now also welfare checks, food stamps, soda pop and canned food. In the houses with electrical generators, it is video machines. The windward side of Niihau is so horrendously littered with plastic rubbish that has floated from the other island that it was pictured as a sort of spoiled Eden in a recent *Time* magazine. There is no hula, there are no canoes. And their racial purity is another myth, for there is a strain of Japanese blood on the islands.

"They don't live as Hawaiians," cultural historian Sol Kahoohalahala told me. "They have a poor diet and as a result they have severe health problems."

If the culture had been intact and the people had retained their old island skills and pleasures, the experiment of isolating these Hawaiians might have succeeded. But it has been a failure. What remains is the language, and the Robinson family prevents any outsider from studying it there. It is possible that, with such a small number of people speaking Hawaiian in Niihau, the language will degenerate as the people have and become extinct.

It was once the rule that when a Niihauan left the island he was regarded as tainted and was forbidden to return. This is no longer the case. Niihauans regularly cross the channel in a Vietnam war surplus landing-craft to Kauai to work on the Robinson estates, to collect their welfare checks, to buy food and visit relatives (there are large communities of Niihau families on Kauai), or to attend parties – where drinking and smoking are cheerfully tolerated.

On my furtive flying visit to the island I traveled in a helicopter which was the property of the Robinson family – at $200 per person a trip this is obviously a way of paying the upkeep of the chopper, which is also used for medical emergencies (there is no hospital on Niihau).

We banked past the cliffs that rose to 1,000 feet and we landed on the deserted southern end of the island, where some of Captain Cook's sailors (including his first mate William Bligh) spent one night in 1778. They were the first white men to step ashore in the Hawaiian Islands. Cook had unexpectedly discovered the Hawaiian Islands – and this unexpectedness was strange for him, because Cook had a genius for anticipating islands. Like the Polynesian navigators he could read the pattern of the sea, the configuration of waves, the movements of seabirds, the sight of turtles, the quality of light. But Hawaii – his first sight of Oahu – loomed up out of the ocean, without any warning. And he had not expected to see high islands in the North Pacific. He then spotted the islands of Kauai and Niihau, and while he was still reflecting on whether they could be inhabited, he saw canoes, three and four men in each one.

The islanders spoke, "and we were agreeably surprised to find them of the same nation as the people of Otaheite [Tahiti] and the other islands we had lately visited." Cook's meticulous collection of word lists came in handy, and even the crew knew enough of this Tahitian-like language to ask for food – hogs, breadfruit, yams, water. The words were the same.

"How shall we account for this nation spreading itself as far over the vast ocean?" Cook wrote, deeply impressed. But he was aware of the fragility of the culture he had encountered, and knowing that his men were carrying venereal disease he had made a rule that his men were not to fraternize with island women. Offending men were ordered by Cook to be flogged.

The encounter could not have been stranger if Cook had come from outer space, and more than anything it resembled the meeting of Martians and Earthlings – indeed, Cook was seen as possibly supernatural, the embodiment of the God Lono (Orongo in Rapa Nui), whom they believed would appear to them on a floating island, which was exactly what the *Resolution* looked like. There was iron all over the ship, and the metal was like treasure to the islanders. Reckless greed and impatience overcame the islanders' fears – and besides, such creatures, being foreigners, were outside the *kapu* (taboo) restrictions, which were severe in Hawaii. Pilferage was immediate, anything made of metal was stolen; this led to quarrels, one of them fatal, when one of Cook's lieutenants shot an islander.

Two days after sighting the islands, and in spite of Cook's strict precautions, a few of his men got ashore on Kauai and infected some island women. This also happened on Niihau, and there was soon an epidemic of syphilis and gonorrhea on the islands which vastly reduced the population. Ironically, many of the men had picked up the disease in 1777 from women in Tahiti, who had caught it from the French sailors.

The Niihauans who visited Cook's ship asked the captain whether they could leave a token behind. Cook agreed and the islanders cut locks of their hair and left them on the ship, as an act of faith, for having something so personal as hair (or nail parings) empowered the owner to cast deadly spells. Cook took on drinking water from the springs of Niihau and set off to look for the Northwest Passage.

I walked down an ancient lava flow to lean over the steep rock walls and listen to the crashing of surf and the cries of seabirds in Keanahaki Bay.

In the distance I could see the simple wooden structures of the island's only village, Puuwai, as we made the hop to the rocky plain at the northern end. Niihau is very arid – the island recently suffered a seven-year drought – but if there is rainfall it descends on Puuwai, where it is collected in cisterns. Beneath the chopper I could see what is actually a devastated ecosystem – the effects, many of them visible, of hungry cattle and sheep, wild pigs and herds of wild horses. The browsing animals had started the damage, wind-erosion had done the rest. The whole place has the rather tragic look of a Utopia gone wrong, and it has the curiously dusty and deprived atmosphere of a penal colony.

Even in 1863 the Hawaiian staple food, taro, would not grow on the island because of poor soil, and good trees were so scarce they had to be shipped from Kauai. The situation is much worse now. There has been no apparent re-afforestation. It is an island without any visible topsoil. The vegetation that exists is kiawe tree, a thorny bush akin to mesquite. Charcoal made from this wood by the islanders is greatly in demand elsewhere in Hawaii, and the kiawe flower results in delicious honey that is collected by Niihau's beekeepers. But these remain cottage industries.

The protected anchorage at this northern end of the island, just inside Puukole Point, is where the landing-craft – with its food and its passengers – creeps from the sea to the sand. The great black volcano just offshore is Lehua Island, a state seabird sanctuary, on which Hawaiian structures and caves and freshwater springs have been studied.

Walking the beach at the northern end of Niihau I kept wondering what I would do with this island, if I owned it. I knew that I would not want to see it nibbled to death by wild animals or blown, grain by grain, into the ocean. It was admirable that its people still spoke their mother tongue; Niihau Hawaiian is regarded by some linguists as the purest form of the language. But it was a pity that they could not share it, nor did they know the history of their people before the traders and cattle farmers, and the vengeful God of the Old Testament, and the missionaries who convinced them that they were sinners.

Isolation had not worked. There is something fundamentally subversive about the master–servant relationship, and a *haole* family lording it over dusky islanders is hardly likely to be a blueprint for Utopia. Even if that had worked, corruption had set in with the first video machine, if not with the first transistor radio. The intention was that the island would not change, but of course it has, inexorably. Just as mice can nibble a mansion and turn it into a ruin, the animals and alien plants have caused the ecology to degenerate; the people's diet has altered; and perhaps their outlook has adjusted, too, as their trips across the channel have become more frequent.

An island can be owned; but people cannot be owned, nor can they be managed as though they were cattle or, worse, as though they were vaguely animate and supine museum exhibits. So the answer is obviously that the Niihauans themselves would have to be consulted about the future. They are notoriously wary of strangers' questions, as I discovered – even on Niihau they regarded my questions as *niele* – nosy. They are said to be intensely proud of their difference, their separateness.

Ideally, the islanders would choose not be invaded by tourists, but to be put in touch with other Hawaiians – poets, dancers, ethnographers, linguists, farmers – in the hope that their community might be rejuvenated, and gain a measure of self-sufficiency. That could eventually lead to revitalizing the Hawaiian language in the rest of the islands.

The island of Lanai is a different experiment altogether. No one objected to my collapsible kayak – the little airline that flies in from Honolulu is used to dealing with kayaks, surfboards, scuba gear and high-powered rifles (there is hunting on Lanai), as well as Louis Vuitton golf-bags and Chanel hat-boxes: Lanai has some of the simplest as well as the most sumptuous accommodations in Hawaii, and the island is unique in welcoming the backpacker as well as the billionaire.

Like Niihau, Lanai passed from the control of the Hawaiian monarchy into private hands – in fact, it was once owned by the same family that now owns Niihau. After several incarnations – as a ranch, as a promised land (the Mormons owned it for a while), as a glorified botanical garden and game park – James Dole bought it in 1922 and planted 15,000 acres of pineapples. The company town, a cluster of simple houses on a grid of narrow roads, rejoices in the name Lanai City and for seventy years nearly all its 2,200 inhabitants – largely of Filipino or Japanese ancestry – worked for Dole, in the labor-intensive business of pineapple-growing.

Because of high labor costs, pineapple is ceasing to be a commercially viable crop in Hawaii – such enterprises are cheaper and simpler in the Philippines and in Central America. But there was no serious suggestion that the Dole plantations would close until five years ago, when the swashbuckling investor David Murdock took control of Castle & Cooke (which had owned Dole, and the island of Lanai, since the 1950s). Realizing that the pineapple plantation had no future, Murdock sized up Lanai and concocted a scheme on a grand scale for the entire island. He was uniquely privileged to do this; after all, he owned the island. The island had one hotel – a modest and charming old building with ten rooms, at the top end of Lanai City, called inevitably the Lanai Hotel.

Taking advantage of the island's vistas and two distinct climate-zones, Murdock specified that his first luxury hotel would be built in the cool hills above Lanai City, amid the mists and the Norfolk pines. This, the Lodge at Koele, has turned out to be, in style, a sort of turn-of-the-century Anglo-colonial hunting lodge, with verandas and vast fireplaces, that would not look out of place in the highlands of Kenya. The second hotel, Manele Bay, Murdock placed fifteen miles distant, on a spectacular sweep of bay, above a sandy beach, and it has the look of a grand Mediterranean villa – stucco, tile roofs, elaborate gardens.

In the beginning, the sudden change bewildered the people of Lanai City, who had known only the pineapple business and the company routine. There was an *over-our-dead-body* faction, advocating the status quo – this group has diminished in size but is still vocal, because the nearest island to Lanai – Maui – has seriously and seedily degenerated into a destination that in large part looks like a suburb of San Diego. There was a *we-don't-want-rich-people* faction which wondered aloud about the implications of luxury hotels on the island. There is a more moderate *Lanaians-for-sensible-growth* faction, which wishes to have a say in determining the island's future. Mr Murdock has listened to all the contending points of view, sometimes with patience and forbearance, sometimes with the blustering megalomania and single-mindedness one associates with General Bullmoose. There is a strong feeling that Mr Murdock has everything to gain if the islanders are happy and prosperous, even if it means change. And there is an undercurrent of anxiety – terror is perhaps a truer word – that Mr Murdock might get sick of spending his money and sell the whole operation to the Japanese, who would ruthlessly Nipponize it, subdivide it and turn it into a golf paradise and labor camp, a combination that has worked well for them elsewhere.

But in all this turbulence an unexpectedly serene thing has happened. The children of these pineapple-pickers, who had fled the island for more congenial and better-paying jobs on other islands or on the mainland – most of them young people – began to return home, to work in the hotels, literally rejuvenating an island of aging plantation workers. The manager of Koele, Kurt Matsumoto, is a native of Lanai and so are nearly all his staff.

"I would never have come back here to pick pineapples," Darek, a van-driver, told me at Manele. "But this is different. This is a job I like."

"My parents wanted me to come back to Lanai," Linda told me. "But I didn't want to. There was just the plantation and working in the fields for five dollars an hour." And she laughed, thinking about it. But as soon as Linda, who had been working as a waitress in San Diego, heard about the hotels, she returned to her island home and her parents and a job in the dining-room at Manele.

I heard that same story over and over. Some people like Perlita had been working in the pineapple fields for ten or fifteen years and were now on the hotel staff.

"My father worked in the fields for forty-five years," a Lanai teacher, Dick Trujillo, told me – we were in the S & T, having fishburgers, in one of Lanai City's plate-lunch establishments. "He was against the changes. But there was a plantation-mentality on Lanai – the sense that you can't better yourself, that there are managers and field workers – two classes – and if you are the child of a field worker you have no right to go to college or better yourself."

After graduating from the University of Hawaii he had worked for a while in Honolulu, but the traffic, the high cost of living, and the stress of city life had caused him to gravitate back to Lanai, with its quiet pace, a luxuriant garden in the yard of each tidy bungalow.

"We are a throwback, about twenty-five years behind the times," Henry Yamamoto said up at the Ranger's Office of the Lanai Company where he supervises the hunting on Lanai – particularly the monthly Damage Control Hunt. He said that they were trying to keep the deer to a controllable level, about four thousand. As for the ending of pineapples and the beginning of the hotels, "We were due for a change."

Nearly every person I spoke to on Lanai mentioned the strong sense of community on the island. That neighborly spirit is not a myth. The friendliness is evident in the casual good humor of the people and their candor with strangers.

"I want to return to Lanai when I finish college," Roderick told me. His major was recreational leadership, but his summer job was waiting on tables at Koele. "I'd like to give something back to the community." That expression of loyalty and gratitude is not a sentiment that is voiced much these days on other islands, and I felt sure that it was inspired by the good feeling of Lanai.

The ethnic Hawaiians on Lanai are actively interested in their history and culture, studying traditional music and dance, as well as art. Under a supervised program set up by Castle & Cooke, the skilled people of the town did nearly all the artwork – the murals, the decorations, the painted flowers on the new hotels.

Hawaiians date their history on Lanai from about the fifteenth century, and the island is rich in old Hawaiian sites – temples, house-platforms and petroglyphs carved into rock. No extensive archeological digging has been carried out, and so whenever I walked through the tall grass or across a wind-blown hillside to one of these bouldery ruins I felt a sense of excitement. Though any number of guidebooks, or the directions of islanders, can lead you to these sites, the places themselves are unimproved and look undisturbed – there are as yet no signs, no arrows, no plaques. The silence and the look of abandonment gave me the illusion of being a solitary discoverer.

After experiencing the gourmet cooking and the sybaritic life at the hotels at Koele and Manele Bay, I set up camp near Shipwreck Beach, on the northern shore of the island. I pitched my tent in a grove of kiawe trees, out of the wind, at Halulu. This windward side was very surfy but absolutely deserted and wonderful for snorkeling and hiking.

In the night the branches of the kiawe trees rubbed and muttered, sounding like live creatures. To the east I could see the bright lights of Maui, and across the moon-whitened surf of the channel the towering dark shape of Molokai.

In the mornings, before the wind intensified, I paddled along the reef. About two miles up the coast there was a rusted hulk of a Liberty Ship that ran onto the reef. I paddled to it and closer I saw that the remains of many other ships were evident – the wooden decks of smashed ships lay on the beach, twisted in frayed fishing-nets, and farther on were the beached and dented containers that had been flung from the deck of more recent wrecks. This is said to be the best area of the island for beachcombing – for glass floats and shells and messages in bottles. There were deer tracks all over these beaches, though I did not see any of the cautious creatures, and for a day and a half I did not see a single human being.

Beaching my kayak and wandering across the dry cliffs that were blasted by the wind – this side of Lanai has the look and feel of a Scottish moor – I came across petroglyphs and stone terraces that could have dated from the reign of Kamehameha I, the king who suceeded in unifying the Hawaiian islands in 1795. It is said that he spent his summers on the opposite side of Lanai – and it is a historical fact that he lived from time to time on Lanai. He is strongly associated with Kaunolu – an eerie and extensive site on the southern side of the island – but as a Hawaiian historian told me on Lanai, "That could be just a case of 'George Washington slept here.'"

I loaded my kayak on my jeep and traveled down dirt roads to other beaches, to paddle; and then across the island to look at the strange rocky plateau in the northeastern part of the island called the Garden of the Gods, a place where the wind moaned through the long needles of drooping pines and the great boulders that had been exposed by erosion had the look of altars and temple ruins. Crossing the Munroe Trail at an altitude of 2,000 feet I needed to put on a sweater against the cold drizzly air.

The stereotype of a Hawaiian island is sunny beaches and funny shirts, palm trees and surfers. Lanai has those, but Lanai has much else. Passing the pineapple fields and heading down Fraser Avenue, past the numbered streets into Lanai City – the simple houses, the grocery stores, the lunch rooms, the bakery, the laundromat: all wooden buildings – it is difficult to rid yourself of the impression that you are in some ingenious theme park of the Hawaiian past.

But the old-fangled appearance of the town is not an illusion, and not a fake. With the simple sepia look of an old photograph, it is a living breathing remnant of old Hawaii – a plantation town of the sort that flourished all over the islands before the Second World War, and before mass tourism. Almost every building in Lanai City looks as though it could be dated 1935. Remaining true to their past, conservative by nature, the Lanaians never saw much point in modernizing, and anyway the company owned most of the houses. Lanaians with money bought expensive, sturdy vehicles – the only conspicuous sign of material wealth is a person's pick-up, and the island is a four-wheeler's dream.

The $300 million that Castle & Cooke has invested in the island is not immediately obvious. The excellent high school is at one side of town, the new housing at the other side. In Lanaian terms the luxury hotels and the golf courses are remote and hidden – as they should be. It would be a shame if the pleasant homely character of the place changed, and Eighth Street was turned into a shopping mall. It could still happen – nothing is more expensive than preserving the past – but so far it looks as though the owner has found a way of rejuvenating the island without spoiling it.

# 26

## *The Big Island: Paddling in the State of Grace*

I was nervous about asking how much Orchid Bungalow, my luxury dwelling by the sea, was going to cost me – it was said to be the most expensive, the most sumptuous in Hawaii, and that was saying a great deal, because already I had felt Hawaii to be the most orchidaceous place on earth.

Still, I risked the question when I saw Ms L'Eplattenier, the bungalow manager.

"It's two thousand five hundred dollars a day," she said, flinging back the drapes to show me my swimming-pool.

I must have winced, because she turned back to me and smiled.

"That includes continental breakfast," she added.

This was the Kohala Coast, just north of Kealakekua Bay, where Captain Cook was clubbed to death in February 1779. It is impossible to travel in the Pacific, even for a short time, and not develop an admiration for this hero of navigation and discovery, who was – amazingly, for a great captain – a thoroughly good man.

Having sailed from Niihau some nine months before to look for the Northwest Passage – a sea-route to the Atlantic – Cook had been resting in Hawaiian waters after finding only dangerous ice and mountainous shores. His two ships had returned to Hawaii, but this time to Maui, and Cook bitterly logged the fact that the pox they had left in Kauai and Niihau had reached this island. They sailed on to the island of Hawaii and made contact. The islanders were harder to read than any Cook had met before – their behavior threw him. The Hawaiians still seriously wondered whether this was the god Lono, on his floating island.

What followed was a chaotic interaction, a clash of cultures, with blundering on both sides which made violence almost inevitable. Was this *haole* really Lono? Were these sailors dangerous? Cook met the aged King Kalaniopu'u, who treated him as an equal. Meanwhile William Bligh and others were making charts, collecting artifacts, sketching pictures of landscapes and ceremonies. But the pilferage by islanders – their passion for pieces of iron undiminished – was unceasing. There were random desecrations and casual cruelty by Cook's men. The ships were besieged for iron, and the islanders even devised ways for winkling nails out of the ships' timbers.

This situation continued for just under four months and then at last, with the theft of his best cutter – an important boat to the expedition – Cook was so exasperated he went ashore to take the King hostage until the vessel was returned. The King was at first friendly. There was a conversation. But a misunderstanding arose, and soon panic. The islanders became menacing – Cook's frightened men fired their muskets. A thousand islanders had gathered on the beach. Many of them began to throw stones. Cook was struck by stones, and then clubbed and held under water, and stabbed, and drowned.

"Justifiable homicide," Mark Twain snarls in the Big Island chapter of *Roughing It* – he felt that Cook that been ungrateful and belligerent, that he had asked for it by pretending to be Lono. But poor Cook had died in an almost meaningless scuffle, an incoherent event, an accident of panic and riot. It was an unacceptable way for a hero to go, and yet human and horrible, a bit of bad timing, just the sort of end you predict for yourself. And though the conflict was later patched up, the next day some islanders dressed themselves in the breeches and shirts of the men they had killed and went to the beach and showed their buttocks to the seamen, mooning being a traditional Polynesian way of taunting an enemy.

The beach at Kealakekua Bay is still strewn with stones, the right size and shape to use as weapons.

Beyond the bay, and above it, is a lava field – great browny-black cinders and clinkers the size of boulders, called *a'a* – as far as the eye can see, interrupted by the occasional grove of palms or stretch of meadow. Because of that landscape there has not been much building here. There are three large resort developments, but they are self-contained, like small green islands, isolated on the coast at the end of the lava flows. On this leeward side, it hardly rains (ten inches of rain a year) – it is a great sloping desert of black volcanic rock, the Kaniku Lava Flow on the west coast of the Big Island.

Orchid Bungalow was one of four luxury bungalows at the Mauna Lani Resort, and because a golf tournament was in progress, my neighbors were Arnold Palmer (in Plumeria), Lee Trevino (in Hibiscus) and Gary Player (in Bird of Paradise). Jack Nicklaus had just moved out of Orchid. Golfers were the only people swinging clubs on this coast these days.

"A strange things happen to our guests in the bungalows," the resident manager of Mauna Lani told me. "They get what we call 'bungalow fever' – they check in and eat all their meals in them. They use their twenty-four-hour butler service. They give parties, they have cookouts. They don't leave. And when it comes time to check out they don't really want to go."

The current record for staying in one of these $2,500-a-night bungalows is held by the actor Dustin Hoffman, who checked in and did not emerge until twenty-eight days later.

The sun was shining on the snow-capped crater of Mauna Loa the day I checked into Orchid Bungalow, and almost the first thing I saw from the veranda (or *lanai*) was an enormous humpback whale, which breached and slapped its tail throughout the afternoon.

That night I was invited to a party at the hotel – something to do with the golf tournament. The moonlit Pacific lay just beyond the rawbar, where Bryant Gumbel stood, beaming expansively. The president of Rolex, lifting a grilled prawn to his lips, displayed his wristwatch, a Rolex El Presidente – he had handed out at least one that day to a successful golfer. I was in conversation with a man wearing an ugly shirt.

"I've got a twin-engine jet with a Harley Davidson on board. I can go anywhere in the world. Where should I go? Don't say Yerp. I hate Yerp."

"Know where his money comes from?" someone said to me later. "He's a multimillionaire. His father invented the supermarket shopping cart."

"It's like inventing the spoon," I said. "Or the can-opener."

"Charo and Sylvester Stallone have houses in Kauai," someone else was saying. "She was married to Xavier Cugat. We used to see Willie Nelson jogging on Oahu."

"If you understand Japanese banks you understand Japanese investment in Honolulu. People just off the plane were getting mortgages of between two and five percent, and they could borrow up to 120 per cent of the purchase price."

"The Japanese love Disney memorabilia – Mickey Mouse, especially. But they're also into quality. Hermès opened a store in Honolulu strictly for the Japanese market. We're talking silk shirts at thirteen hundred dollars a pop."

"They used to pee in the sink," a hotelier was reminiscing, smiling at the memory. "This was only ten or fifteen years ago, in a good hotel – well-to-do guests. They stood on the toilet seat to do a number two. I guess they were used to poor sanitation in their country. They stretched out on the lobby seats and had naps. They walked in the public rooms in their pajamas – kimonos, whatever. We had to print notices. 'Please do not pee in the sink.'"

Across the lawn, Japanese tycoons looking deceptively child-like were clustered around Arnold Palmer – his name was impossibly difficult for them to pronounce. They had flown in from Tokyo for the tournament, and here they were proferring their caps and visors for him to sign, which he did without a protest.

One of those Japanese gentlemen moved into Plumeria Bungalow after Arnold Palmer had moved out. Each day a stretch limousine drew up to the front door and the family – father, mother, four children – disappeared inside and, hidden by its black windows, were whisked away. But they were soon back in the bungalow garden, sniffing flowers and thrashing in the pool.

A sort of bungalow fever afflicted the golfers. Gary Player wanted to bring the butler with him to South Africa, and he was so taken by the bungalow's design that he asked the management for a copy of the architect's plans. One of the other golfers – Nicklaus, I was told – also insisted on a copy of the floor plan. And all of them said they would be back, as soon as possible: the luxury had not been exaggerated, nor had the daily rate put them off. Or did they get it free? Some of them were walking billboards. Lee Trevino had a contract to wear a hat advertising a Japanese make of car – and he never took the hat off. A prominent golfer like Trevino could get half a million dollars to wear one of those hats. They wore patches on their shirts. They had big visible logos on their golf-bags. They would have called themselves sportsmen, but some of them were merely glorified sandwich boards.

Gillian, the woman who had told me the price of the bungalows and added memorably, *That includes continental breakfast*, stopped in at Orchid Bungalow to make sure I was comfortable.

"I am very comfortable," I said.

The bungalow had two enormous bedrooms, each with its own spa area – steam bath, whirlpool bath, orchid garden; a central lounge area was about half the size of a basketball court, with a cathedral ceiling, and the entertainment center in the southwest corner of the lounge was supplied with a television, VCR, tape deck and CD player.

I could have added, *I often sleep in a tent*.

This bungalow had recently figured in an episode of the popular television show, "Lifestyles of the Rich and Famous," she said. She pointed out how the tables and some of the furniture had been cut from solid blocks of Italian marble, that the carpets had been loomed in England using the designer's marble-matching pattern of burgundy and gray. Had I noticed the bar – seventeen full bottles of liquor? She wondered whether I had any questions about the pool, which was exclusively mine, as was the outdoor jacuzzi nearby.

"We put out some CDs we thought you might like," she said.

Kenny Rogers, Fleetwood Mac, Eric Clapton, Cher. Never mind. I had a whole catalogue to choose from.

"The chef will be over shortly to take your instructions for lunch and dinner," she said, and she vanished.

That was something I was to take for granted – the sudden apparition of a butler or a maid, setting out fruit juice or caviar, skimming the pool, bearing flowers or fruit. It was all accomplished without a sound, as though these people trembled a few inches above the floor. Any request I made was carried out instantly, gracefully and without any pomposity – no Jeeves nonsense, but rather speed and a smile, from Richard, my personal pool attendant, to Orrin my butler, who served the meals and opened the champagne.

Each morning before I did anything else I strolled from the bedroom to the lounge and opened the sliders to the *lanai*, walked around the pool to the edge of my domain, where a fishpond, my own fishpond, with appropriately big fish circulating in it, separated me from the beach. There were coconut palms leaning over the sand, and the lagoon at the edge of the bay was greener than the sea. The beach was mine, the whole Pacific was mine, all the happy isles of Oceania; and so was this luxury bungalow. But wasn't my chef a trifle overdue? When I saw a human being on the beach I became slightly miffed and pouted in my luxury bungalow, wondering whether I should summon my security guard, until I remembered that in Hawaii the beaches are for everyone.

The momentary sense of violation at seeing another person on the beach, the glimpse of Friday's footprint, in a manner of speaking, helped me to understand how quickly I became habituated to this billionaire's life. *Hey, I could get used to this!* people say, when something unexpectedly pleasant comes their way. They are telling the truth. To rephrase Tolstoy, All luxury is the same, but misery for each person is miserable in its own way. And it is the easiest thing in the world to become corrupted by the good life. Once you have flown first-class in an airline an economy seat is intolerable: after you have tasted luxury you are changed, and there is no cure for it. Pain does not create a long-lasting memory, but the memory of luxury exerts itself for ever. That is wonderful, the memory of happiness being so strong, but I can imagine circumstances when it might become a curse. It could be a crueller punishment than torture – giving a person a taste of heaven, creating a habit, and then whisking the victim away to suffer without it.

The hitch at Orchid Bungalow was that the day was not long enough. I wanted to read, lie in the sun, exercise, swim, sit in the jacuzzi, eat lengthy sumptuous meals, drink champagne and listen to music all at once. I discovered that some of these activities could be combined. Now I understood why many multimillionaires – Axel Springer and Somerset Maugham were but two – received annual injections of longevity potions. The science of life-extension is funded by a large number of very wealthy individuals, who have the most selfish motives. There is something about the pure effortless pleasure of being hoggishly, sluttishly rich that must make you want to live longer.

The fact that the sun was shining on me out of a cloudless sky in what was by any reckoning one of the most beautiful places in the world only enhanced what was already wonderful. It is hard to improve on bliss, but Orchid Bungalow proved that it was possible. The only way I could imagine myself happier, more comfortable or contented, was to have someone else to share that bliss with.

"What if I wanted to have a dinner party?" I asked the chef, Piet Wigmans, when he came to take my order one day. "Say six people."

"Anything you like," he said. He suggested the food we might have – the various local fish, tuna and opakapaka (snapper), shrimp from Oahu, crabs and so forth. There were also Maine lobsters, New Zealand mussels, Chilean asparagus, fresh avocados and passion fruit – and he was a master chef; he had run great kitchens in San Francisco and Dorado Beach. ("How did you make out in Puerto Rico?" I asked. He replied, "Fine. I have a whip.")

I chose spicy Dungeness crab soup, followed by spinach salad with avocados. The main course would be sautéed opakapaka with citrus sauce and stir-fried baby asparagus and snowpears and garlic potatoes. For dessert, chocolate Grand Marnier soufflé. As soon as any chief mentions baby vegetables you know you're into three figures.

"And now shall we discuss the wines?" Chef Piet asked.

We settled on the wines – four altogether – and then feeling slightly weary from all these decisions I reinvigorated myself with a swim and a little nap on my sunny *lanai*.

The guests, my new Hawaiian friends, were delightful – intelligent and shining with health and accomplishment, all of them residents of this little paradise and suitably impressed with my bungaloid version of Xanadu.

One of the guests was the distinguished trial lawyer George Davis, still brilliant and active at the age of eight-three, looking a bit like Robert Frost. At one stage in the dinner he recalled the last night he spent with his doomed client Caryl Chessman, which was Chessman's last night on earth, in 1960. Chessman had not killed anyone. He had been convicted of being involved in a bungled kidnapping – he had protested his innocence in a famous and eloquent book, which had been utterly convincing. The crime was not serious by today's standards, and even if he had committed the crime today he would not have been executed for it – it was no longer a capital offense.

That night Chessman said goodbye to his attorney. His parting words were, "George, you're shaking hands with a dead man." A few hours later he was electrocuted.

After dinner, when I was alone, I walked outside. The pool was glowing, the palms rattling, the moonlight lay liquefied on the Pacific. I sat under a jeweled sky having difficulty imagining what Death Row must be like. I took out my pocket calculator and began tapping away – peep, peep, peep. Ah, yes. At $2,500 a day, it would cost me $32 million to live in Orchid Bungalow until the year 2015, when I would be eighty-three years old.

It had only taken two days for this luxury to affect me, but it did so profoundly. It was a shock to my system that in a very short time transformed me, as luxury will – like a drug. It was wonderful being supine and semi-comatose in the sunshine, but it was also a bit like being a zoo animal – wallowing in the sort of captivating comfort that I felt would numb me and then make me fat and crazy. On the other hand, I wasn't terribly worried: at these prices there wasn't an earthly chance of this luxury lasting much longer.

I resisted it a little. I became reclusive and abstemious. I began living in a corner of the bungalow and working hard to break the day into three distinct parts – morning (tea and writing), afternoon (light lunch, swimming, then poaching myself into exhaustion in the hot tub), and evening which was built around one of Chef Piet's dinners, an elaborately choreographed event, no matter what was on the menu – usually a hundred dollars' worth of sealife so deliciously prepared that I stopped asking the butler for the Tabasco sauce.

The sun shone unceasingly upon the sea, and the humpback – my daily whale – bucked and slapped just offshore. I was living in all this Hawaiian splendor, and yet I was also a spectator to it, enclosed by a bungalow so protective it was like a complicated organism, feeding me, cooling me, lulling me to sleep with maternal caresses. It was an existence just about summed up in the expression "splendid isolation."

What was strictly Hawaiian about this? I kept asking myself whether I could have mistaken this place for another sunny paradise in the Caribbean, or the Mediterranean, or the coast of Africa. But no – the flowers and the fragrance were Hawaiian, the great rolling waves could only have been breaking and dumping on a Pacific reef, the high clouds, the coral, the vast dark landscape of lava, some of it gigantic *a'a* cinders and some of it the buckled *pahoehoe* that looks like a melted parking lot; the hospitality, the smiles, the sense of abundance – it was all Hawaiian in its very essence.

The nagging reality of it was the price, $2,500 a day. I began seriously to wonder what the opposite of this might be. What would life be like if I were living as cheaply as possible in paradise? Indeed, how much fun would you have here in Hawaii on one-thousandth of that, say about $2.50 a day?

I still have my Oceanic camping gear: tent, sleeping-bag, cooking kit, water bag and Swiss army knife. I had left my collapsible boat in Honolulu, but I had had the good fortune to meet one of Hawaii's best-known kayakers, who had loaned me an inflatable kayak and a paddle. My idea was to check out of the luxury bungalow at Mauna Lani before my bungalow fever became incurable, and paddle down the coast – find a sheltered cove, go beachcombing and live on next to nothing.

I averaged the cost of the noodles, couscous, fruit and vegetables I packed into the kayak and it came out to $2.18 a day. So I had thirty-two cents a day to play with, but that was purely theoretical – the nearest shops were in Kona, thirty miles away.

My original plan had been to go to the north shore of the island and paddle from one coastal valley to the other – from Waipio to Waimanu, where the steep valley walls allow only helicopters or the sturdiest hikers to enter. But of course a kayaker could enter from the sea, paddling around the headlands. But the seas were bad – everyone warned me against them.

Nainoa Thompson was one of the leaders, and the navigator, of the *Hokulea* expedition – helping to sail successfully a double-hulled canoe from Hawaii to Tahiti and New Zealand in 1986. He took me aside, and said, "I was out in that channel in a sea like this and the glass on the steering house was smashed by a wave – that thing is fifteen feet up, and it's very strong. Don't paddle there now."

Some other time, I thought. I was patient in Hawaii. I would be here a long time, I felt. There would be time for everything.

Instead of staying at Waipio, I paddled about seven miles south of Orchid Bungalow and camped among the palms at the edge of Keawaiki Bay. An estate nearby comprised a dozen rambling stone buildings, and had been built in the 1920s by Francis I'i Brown, champion golfer, bon-vivant, millionaire and direct descendant of one of King Kamehameha's advisers – in other words, in one of the smallest and most select classes in Hawaiian society, an *alii*, a nobleman. The family had once owned a very large slice of Oahu, including Pearl Harbor.

One day at Keawaiki I pressed my nose against the window of one of these stone buildings and looked at the framed photographs on the near wall. One was a picture of Francis Brown standing with Babe Ruth, both of them in golfers' duds, knickers and long socks and cloth caps. In another he posed with a young man still recognizable as Bob Hope. Stories were told in Honolulu and the Big Island of Brown's eccentricities and friendships, and how this strange little seaside estate – accessible only by water – had been visited by celebrities. "Wild parties," people said. In the center of one of Keawaiki's brackish fishponds was a semi-ruined dwelling, which had been a little pavilion once upon a time, where Francis Brown – who had never married – kept the girl of his dreams, known as one of the most beautiful hula dancers of her time, named Winona Love.

The buildings were empty and locked, and had the sunfaded moribund look of neglected houses by the sea. But I had no need of them. I cooked my dollar's worth of dinner – couscous and lentils, fruit and tea – and sat at the edge of the cindery dune above the black lava beach under that same crescent moon that had bewitched me at Orchid Bungalow. I had had air-conditioning there and a pool; here I had a soft breeze and the sea, and for a bath a brackish pool that had been scooped out of the lava, fed by a spring. It is not hyperbole to say that I felt a greater sense of wealth, greater happiness and a more powerful sense of well-being camping here than I had had living in the luxury bungalow. It was the same sense of liberation I had felt on the desert islands of Vav'au and in my little camp at Tongariki, beneath the crumbled *ahu*, at the edge of Easter Island.

I was not only safe and very comfortable, but most of all nothing interruptive like a wall or a carpet or a pane of glass stood between me and this natural beauty. There was nothing to fear – in fact, I felt supported and protected by the palms and the dunes, and that encouraged me and raised my morale. At the bungalow I had only wanted to mooch around the pool – I had become fairly dopey and unambitious. But here, living outdoors, I was filled with a desire to get into the kayak and paddle beyond the bay.

I paddled north into the next bay and around Weliweli Point, where waves were smashing onto the black heap of lava. I paddled a few more miles to Anaehoomalu Bay, where there were two luxury hotels and no one swimming in the sea, much less boating. I found a secluded beach at the south end of the bay, had lunch and headed back. The wind had picked up and the waves had heightened, but this inflatable kayak bobbed along, twisting and sliding.

The humpback whale appeared early the following morning, just offshore, near enough for me to see the blast from his blow-hole. He surfaced and slapped his tail and turned, plowing the sea like a dithering submarine. I paddled out in his direction, and I saw him dive one last time: he did not breach again that day. So I turned south, where a lava flow a mile wide formed the coastline. Just beyond Ohiki Bay was Luahinewai, vividly illustrating the Hawaiian conundrum that most beauty spots on the islands are haunted with grisly memories – this particular area of outstanding natural beauty was associated with the slaughter of Chief Keoua and twenty-four of his retainers by King Kamchamcha in 1790.

My bay, Keawaiki, was particularly rich in fish, which were gold and emerald and silver, surgeon fish and parrot fish and the small, colorfully striped state fish (*humuhumunukunukuapua'a*). They twinkled like jewels among the coral. Because of its protection and its steep beach I could dive in from the shore and go snorkeling and float on the fringes of the tide rip to the edge of the bay, weightless and warm. Here in my little camp exercise required more initiative than at Mauna Lani – no health club, no golf course – but because of that was more rewarding. I swam, I walked.

One of the strangest trails I have ever hiked lay just inland from the palms, a hot narrow path through the lava flow, called the King's Trail, and cut centuries ago by Hawaiians long before *haoles* like Cook ventured ashore. The path is a groove three feet deep, like a single wheeltrack that runs for miles down the side of the island. Like the Inca Trail and Watling Street it is one of the great thoroughfares of the ancient world. I hacked at coconuts, I searched for petroglyphs – the rock carvings that are numerous on the Big Island.

One day I went north to one of the most sacred places in Hawaii, and one of its oldest sites, the Mookini Luakini Heiau. Built on a high point overlooking the sea, the temple is a vast rectangle of cannonball-sized stones. It looks like a crumbled monastery, the Hawaiian version of Tintern Abbey, just as ghostly, with altars and fallen walls, and a nobility that is lent an even greater magnificence by the sight of the waves breaking on the point just beneath it. It was similar in its position and its shape to structures I had seen in Samoa and the Marquesas, but to think that these other ruins were thousands of miles away, across the dangerous *moana*, that made it even more fascinating. Wind and trees, the flattened grass and black rocky shore gave this part of the Big Island an uncanny resemblance to Easter Island – even to its colors and grassy odors.

A ten-minute walk across the meadow was the birth site of King Kamehameha. A signboard nearby read in part, "His prowess as a warrior-statesman destined him to unite the Hawaiian Islands and bring peace and prosperity to his people ... He was true to his own religious beliefs." And there was a regal quotation from the controversial eighteenth-century king who was known as "The Lonely One": *E oni wale no oukou i ku'u pono 'a'ole pau* – "Endless is the good that I have given you to enjoy."

My days were sunny and pleasant. My nights were luminous with stars. I slept as I had on Kauai, pleasurably drugged with fatigue. In the morning I was woken by the mewing and screeching and the ratchet-like scrapings of birds in the palms above me. The exercise and the simple food and the frugality of this enterprise made me feel smugger than when I had been living like a millionaire, and in that gloating mood I slept like a log in my tent, at the edge of the lagoon.

Time passed – months. I was still in Hawaii, I had not left Oceania. I was paddling my collapsible boat, marveling at the way its canvas hull had faded in the punishing sun. Some days I paddled rented outriggers off Honolulu, and open hardshells off windward Oahu. The places I had paddled to write about I was still paddling for pleasure. There were more sea coasts I wanted to paddle – off Maui to the bombsite of

Kahoolawe, and along the north coast of Molokai to Father Damien's old leper settlement of Kalaupapa; and eventually – in good weather – from one island to another. Paddling had taken the place of writing. I thought about my book and then muttered, *Oh never mind.*

Normally, at this point in the trip – in this chapter, say – the traveler is heading home. Or the traveler is already home, reflecting on the extraordinary trip, looking at slides, sorting notes, perhaps wishing the trip had not ended, or at least saying so. But that nostalgia can sound so insincere. You read it and think: *No, you're delighted to be home, dining out on your stories of megapode birds and muddy buttocks and what the King of Tonga told you!*

Isn't one of the greatest of rewards of travel the return home – the reassurance of family and old friends, familiar sights and homely comforts?

I used to go back home and be welcomed, and find months of mail stacked on my desk and spilling to the floor, and after I opened it all, I would answer some and pay bills and burn the letters and envelopes. It could take half a day at the incinerator in the garden, as I stirred the ashes of all the mail I had received. And when I was done and caught up, the routine of home would reassert itself. I would begin writing, spending the day at my desk reliving my trip, and when the pubs opened at five-thirty I would buy an evening newspaper and sit reading it with my elbows on the bar, drinking a pint of stout, thinking: *A month ago I was in a tent by a riverbank, swatting flies.*

Sitting there under the timbers of the cool musty pub, I would have a clear recollection of someone like Tony the beachcomber on the Aboriginal coast of north Queensland – Tony saying, *I found some 'roo meat under a box once. Forgot I had it. Two years old, it was. I ate it. Wonderful in soups, y'know.* And, feeling blessed, I would give thanks that I had returned, that I had a home, that I was safe, that I had been missed, that I was loved.

A trip like that had a beginning and an end; it was an experience in parentheses, enclosed by my life. But this trip, paddling through Oceania, had turned into my life. Now I was in Hawaii, living in a valley full of Honolulu rainbows, writing about the Trobriands and the Solomons and Australia, writing about Tony the beachcomber. I thought of the solemn Aboriginal Gladys as her grandson searched her hair for nits. The Kaisiga children singing *Weespa a frayer* in the darkness. The old man on Savo holding a big old radio to his ear, listening for news of the Gulf War. Mimi in Moorea saying of her Marquesan child, "Some day she will be a Theroux." There were good people in the waterworld of Oceania. I thought often of Easter Island, the haunting stone faces, the lonely wind, and because I had seen so little hunger in Oceania, I thought of the hunger of little Roberto, muttering his thanks in Rapa Nui, as he clawed the shell from the hard-boiled egg I had not wanted, and wolfed it, his eyes bulging.

I spent a great deal of time wandering the beaches of Hawaii. I kept paddling too. One morning, paddling off Kauai, I saw two humpback whales, and I slipped into the water and spent an hour or more with my ears submerged, listening to this happy couple sing and grunt. I was still going, like the man who steps out for a paper and never comes back. I was that man. I had vanished. And there was no reason to go back now. No one missed me. Half my life had been eclipsed.

And then all of it was eclipsed. One morning in July, the Path of Totality lay over the Big Island. I woke at 5am and foraged around for my welder's mask. It had a density factor of fourteen – the most opaque obtainable. I put it on and was in darkness. If I stared at the sun (so I was told) I would see the same darkness, and a dim wafer.

The last total eclipse in Hawaii had been in 1850, and at the time the Hawaiians had felt that their chiefs had abandoned them, that the gods were angry, and that the sun – the great *La* which they worshipped – had lost its *mana*. The stars appeared in daytime, the temperature dropped, flower blossoms closed, birds stopped singing.

People flocked to Hawaii to experience this total eclipse of 1991. There would not be another one like this for 142 years. Fifteen hundred Japanese crouched on the first fairway of the Hyatt Waikoloa, clutching "sun peeps" which would prevent them from being blinded.

The astronomer Edward Krupp said, "Eclipses are the most awe-inspiring event on earth. No one should go through life without witnessing one."

It was also a marketing opportunity. The hotels were serving a special omelette called an "egg-clipse." There were eclipse towels and mugs, eclipse mugs and jewelry, T-shirts saying *Eclipsomania!* and *Totally Umbra!* and *I was there!* A young man named Miles Okirmura of Honolulu sold specially sealed commemorative cans of tinned darkness. The *Honolulu Advertiser* pointed out that "the darkness had been canned before the eclipse."

Walking groggily to the roof of my hotel in the early morning darkness I bumped into a man with a flashlight, who was unmistakably Portuguese.

"It's cloudy," he said, sounding vindictive.

Louis Schwartzberg, time-lapse photographer, had been on the roof since four, assembling two 35mm cameras. He had brought fourteen large crates of equipment.

"I usually bring thirty," he said. "But I'm alone."

We ate grapes. Louis looked anxiously at the cloudy skies over Mauna Kea.

"You're not going to need that," he said, indicating my welder's mask.

"What time will sunrise be?"

"It happened twenty minutes ago," he said.

A cloudless day had been forecast. Most days were cloudless here. This freaky haze was connected with the volcanic ash from the eruption of Mount Pinatubo in the Philippines. Louis fell silent. I walked to the edge of the roof and saw people assembling on the driving range half a mile away.

"What can we do?"

Louis said, "Pray." I thought he was going to scream; his jaw tensed. Screaming is uncool. Louis (from Los Angeles) said, "I accept the clouds. I won't get a good shot. I accept that. At least the eclipse brought all these nice people together."

I hurried to the driving range where little family groups squatted on the grass, peering at the bright clouds, aiming cameras. Bryan Brewer, a tall pale man from Seattle wearing an *Eclipsomania* T-shirt, paced the grass. He was the author of a book about eclipses, called *Totality*. He had seen his first eclipse in 1979 and was hooked. He traveled the world, observing eclipses. This, he had predicted, would be one of the greatest. I greeted him, I asked him how he was.

"Nervous," he said.

It was as though he was personally taking the blame for this act of God.

"We won't see this cloud cover for another hundred and forty-two years," a photographer said.

No one laughed, though I found this very funny.

A woman named Charlene had come to Hawaii to give lectures on cosmic consciousness and solar vibrations linked to the eclipse – *mana* in fact, emanating from the shadow of the sun. Charlene had long hair and a gown-like dress, and she had attached herself to a group of chatty photographers. She had a sense of urgency, and she walked among the group of men and women saying, "Listen guys," or "I've got an idea, guys."

The sky was filled with pearly gray clouds and on the ground the gloom was palpable.

"Guys, there's an answer," Charlene said. "When the Dalai Lama escaped from Tibet he needed cloud cover. He and his followers linked their arms together and chanted '*Om*' over and over."

Having nothing to lose we tried this, and the clouds seemed to thicken. Wasn't that what happened in Tibet? No one said so, but nearly everyone had spent thousands of dollars to come here. Besides the Japanese there were French and Germans, there were people from Brazil, from California, from Canada.

A photographer said, "Mike's in Baja. That's on the Path of Totality. There are never any clouds in Baja —"

Another photographer said, "We should go back to the hotel and watch this on CNN."

On the roof, Louis Schwartzberg was saying, "I accept this."

"So what happened to the eclipse?" a man asked Bryan Brewer.

"I don't know," Mr Brewer said, guiltily. "I'm still hoping."

"Did you see the sign in Kona?" a woman asked. "The eclipse has been canceled due to unforeseen difficulties."

"The eclipse has been eclipsed."

Tedious early morning jollity had begun.

Someone said breathlessly, "The cloud's moving."

People were willing the clouds to shift. And some of the clouds were shifting — sludgy layers of them jostled, allowing sunlight to burst from their seams. It was ten minutes to seven.

Hopefully I put on my welder's mask and was in total darkness. I took it off and saw that clouds were passing across the sun, raveling like great hanks of skeins of wool.

No one spoke, there was scattered applause and intense concentration as the sun burned through the fragmenting cloud, illuminating the wooly shreds. And when it emerged, still in haze but visible, it was not a perfect disk. There was a smooth measured bit out of the top of the sun. And while we watched the bite grew, until the sun looked like a moon crescent, a fat one, glimmering in daylight.

"What's your setting?"

"One twenty-fifth at F-eight, a hundred ASA."

It was like a command to fire, for as soon as the words were spoken there was a sucking sound of shutters and winders, a shooting that was like bolts being shot from crossbows in furious gulps.

"Check the focus."

"Look at that shadow."

"Anybody got an exposure?"

I was putting on and taking off my welder's mask. With it, I saw a dim crescent. Without it, the glare dazzled and almost blinded me. I scrunched my eyes and glanced and then looked away, as though peering at a forbidden thing. The time was 7:24 and the sun was a golden banana, and two minutes later, the air had already begun to grow cool, and the banana had narrowed to a bright horn that kept thinning and was soon a brilliant splinter, and finally a sliver of intense whiteness. The rest was a dark disc, with specks of light glimmering at its edges, a phenomenon known as Bailey's Beads.

At last the sun was in total darkness as though a dinner plate had been slid across it – the hand of God, someone had predicted, and that was how it seemed, supernatural. There was brief, hesitant applause, some worried whooping, and then silence, as a chilly shadow settled over us. In Hawaiian Pidgin the expression for goose pimples is "chicken skin," and I could hear this word being muttered: *cheecken skeen*.

By 7:29 the world had been turned upside down. Again the stars appeared in daytime, the temperature dropped, flower blossoms closed, birds stopped singing, and we sat transfixed on our cooling planet, watching light drain from the world.

We stared blindly at the black sun until there was a sudden explosion at its top edge that showed a flare of red light.

Our amazement was not pleasurable – not fascination, it was compounded of fear and uncertainty, a feeling of utter strangeness. It was like the onset of blindness. I looked around. There was just enough light to scribble by if I held my little notebook near my face. It was not pitch darkness, but the eeriest glow around the entire horizon, a 360-degree twilight. The silence continued, and in the large crowd, all looking upward, the mood was sombre, though the morning air was unexpectedly perfumed by night-blooming jasmine.

It was a world of intimidating magic in which anything could happen.

Before the sun emerged again from its shadow, making the earth seem immeasurably grander than it ever had before, I kissed the woman next to me, glad to be with her. Being happy was like being home.

HAWAIIAN ISLANDS

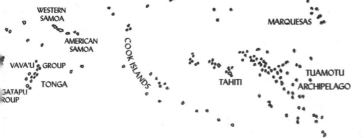

THE HAPPY ISLES OF OCEANIA

WESTERN
SAMOA

AMERICAN
SAMOA

COOK ISLANDS

VAVA'U GROUP

TONGA

GATAPU
ROUP

MARQUESAS

TAHITI

TUAMOTU
ARCHIPELAGO

LAND

EASTER ISLAND

0        500        1000   Statute miles

Solomon Sea

Tuma Island

Kaileuna
Kiriwina
Omarakhana

Munawata
Losuia

Kaisiga Village
Sinaketa
Kitava

# TROBRIAND ISLANDS

0    Statute miles    30

Bougainville
(PNG)
Panguna

Santa Isabel

Tulaghi
Savo    Nggela
Malaita

Cape Esperance
Honiara

Guadalcanal

# SOLOMON ISLANDS

0    Statute miles    125

Nuku'alofa

Eua

# TONGATAPU GROUP

0    Statute miles    15

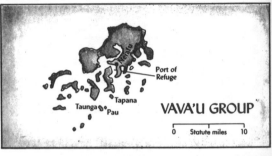

Neiafu
Port of Refuge

Tapana
Taunga
Pau

# VAVA'U GROUP

0    Statute miles    10

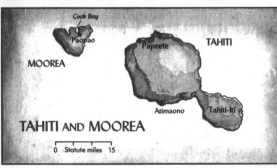

Cook Bay
Paopao

Papeete
TAHITI

MOOREA

Atimaono
Tahiti-Iti

# TAHITI AND MOOREA

0    Statute miles    15

Nuku Hiva    Ua Huka
Taiohae    Taipivai

Ua-Pou    Hakehau

Hiva Oa    Puamau
Vaitahu    Atuona

Hanavave

# MARQUESAS

Fatu Hiva

0    Statute miles    50

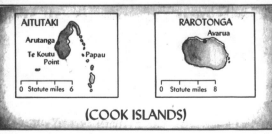

# AITUTAKI
Arutanga
Te Koutu Point
Papau

# RAROTONGA
Avarua

0    Statute miles    6

0    Statute miles    8

# (COOK ISLANDS)

Cabo Norte
Anakena
Poike Peninsula
Cape Cumming
Rano Raraku
Cape Roggeveen
Rada Vinapu
Motu Maro-Tiri
Tongariki
Hanga Roa
Hanga Piko
Rano Kau
Orongo

# EASTER ISLAND

0    Statute miles    8

## VANUATU

Efate

Port Vila

Erromango

White Grass
Tanna

Futuna

Green
Point

0  Statute miles  80

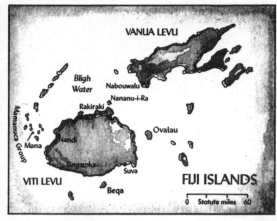

VANUA LEVU

Bligh
Water

Nabouwalu

Nananu-i-Ra

Rakiraki

Mamanuca Group

Mana

Nandi

Ovalau

Singatoka

Suva

VITI LEVU

Beqa

## FIJI ISLANDS

0  Statute miles  60

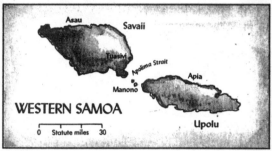

Asau

Savaii

Tuasivi

Apolima Strait

Apia

Manono

## WESTERN SAMOA

Upolu

0  Statute miles  30

Tutuila

Tula

Aunu'u

Pago Pago

Leone

Manua

## AMERICAN SAMOA

0  Statute miles  30

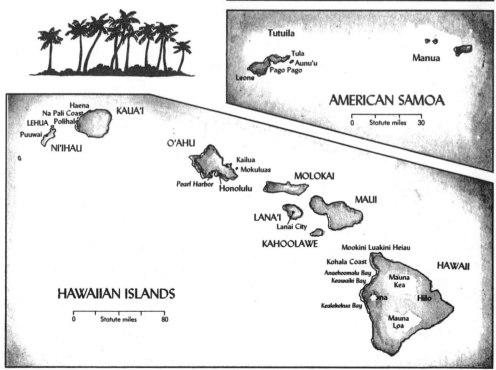

Haena

Na Pali Coast

KAUA'I

LEHUA  Polihale

Puuwai

NI'IHAU

O'AHU

Kailua

Mokuluas

MOLOKAI

Pearl Harbor  Honolulu

MAUI

LANA'I

Lanai City

KAHOOLAWE

Mookini Luakini Heiau

Kohala Coast

HAWAII

Anaehoomalu Bay

Keauwaiki Bay

Mauna
Kea

ona

Hilo

Kealakekua Bay

Mauna
Loa

## HAWAIIAN ISLANDS

0  Statute miles  80